Towards a
Just
World Peace

Committee for a Just World Peace

Bibi Andersson
Actress, Sweden

Professor Emerita Elise Boulding
Dartmouth College, USA

Honorable Jose Diokno
PCHR, Philippines

Honorable Erhard Eppler
SPD, West Germany

Adolfo Perez Esquivel
Nobel Peace Laureate, Argentina

Professor Richard A. Falk
Princeton University, USA

Professor Herbert Feith
Monash University, Australia

Professor Mary Kaldor
University of Sussex, UK

Gyorgy Konrad
Novelist, Hungary

Professor Rajni Kothari
CSDS, India

Professor Saul Mendlovitz
Rutgers University, USA
CJWP Executive Secretary

Marc Nerfin
IFDA, Switzerland

Governor Kazuji Nagasu
Kanagawa Prefecture, Japan

Radmila Nakarada
Economic Institute, Yugoslavia

Honorable Maria de Lourdes
Pintasilgo, Portugal

Professor Yoshikazu Sakamoto
University of Tokyo, Japan
CJWP Research Director

Ousman Sembene
Cinematographer, Senegal

Vandana Shiva
RFSTNRP, India

Mohamed Sid-Ahmed
Journalist, Egypt

Honorable Juan Somavia
ILET, Chile

Archbishop Desmond Tutu
Nobel Peace Laureate, South Africa

Professor R. B. J. Walker
University of Victoria, Canada
CJWP Rapporteur

Towards a Just World Peace

Perspectives from Social Movements

Editors

Saul H. Mendlovitz
Committee for a Just World Peace
World Policy Institute, New York

R. B. J. Walker
Department of Political Science
University of Victoria, British Columbia, Canada

Butterworths

London Boston Durban Singapore Sydney Toronto Wellington

First published 1987

© Committee for a Just World Peace, 1987

British Library Cataloguing in Publication Data

Towards a just world peace: perspective from
  social movement.
  1. International organisation.
  I. Mendlovitz, Saul. H.
  II. Walker, R. B. J.
  341.2   JX1954

  ISBN: 0-408-24400-3

Library of Congress Cataloging in Publication Data

Towards a just world peace
  Bibliography: p.
  1. Peace—Societies, etc. I. Mendlovitz, Saul H.
II. Walker, R. B. J.
JX1952.T66   1987   327.1′72′06   87-10335
ISBN 0-408-24400-3

Photoset by Butterworths Litho Preparation Department
Printed and bound in Great Britain by Biddles Ltd, Guildford and King's Lynn

Foreword

The facts of modern life are profoundly discouraging. The nuclear arsenals accumulated by the two superpowers are enough to exterminate the entire human race more than ten times over. The uneven development of the world economy has been aggravated to such an extent that one out of every ten people is suffering from hunger and undernourishment while 70% of the world's wealth is in the hands of 20% of its population. Deforestation, desertification and depletion of the ozone layer attest to the critical state of environmental degradation. Meanwhile, those who resist these trends, this mal-development that threatens the peace of humankind and infringes on equity and justice everywhere, are often treated as 'subversives' and 'criminals', subject to contempt and even torture.

It is in this context that the Committee for a Just World Peace was established in 1985. It is motivated by the conviction that while this is a time of great danger, it is also a time of transformative opportunities. The Committee is interested in identifying and encouraging the creative energies that offer constructive ways forward. It hopes to contribute to dialogue and solidarity among people who struggle to resist the intolerable and who seek empowering visions of what is possible. It is particularly interested in understanding the relationship between the global structures and processes that affect people everywhere and the social movements that arise in highly specific situations in response to seemingly highly specific problems.

Although many of the major structures that determine how we live are now world-wide in their scale and consequences, most of our political allegiances and capacities remain rooted in particular states. It is in fact instructive to think about the discouraging facts of life for humanity as a whole as if they applied to one state in particular.

Suppose, for example, that a national military and police force seeks to maintain 'law and order' by holding the populace as hostages exposed to the threat of annihilation many times over. Suppose 10% of the citizenry is starving, 50% is more or less on the poverty line, while 20% of the population owns most of the wealth and resources. Suppose those who resist are suppressed as 'subversives' and 'criminals'. Surely, this would be interpreted as a recipe for revolution?

Yet the world is not on the verge of global revolution. The misery and injustice that would not be tolerated if it occurred within a state is tolerated or ignored by a large number of people as long as it is outside their own societies. The fact that many people do not consider the insanity and inhumanity of the modern world to be insane and inhumane is itself a manifestation of this insanity and inhumanity.

This double standard reflects a stark contrast between the global scale of the processes that affect us and the values, communities and institutions that have developed historically within the territorial state. This contrast suggests that movements struggling to resist the intolerable and to seek empowering visions of what is possible must be concerned with reconstructing values, communities and political participation in a way that responds to global forces. They must refuse a double standard.

The idea that world peace is possible by reforming the state-system is not new. Almost from the beginning of the states-system in Europe, proposals for creating international organizations have been put forward by many thinkers. Many prevailing conceptions of peace depend on images of the world as a state writ large. The relevance of such images is now put into question by two groups of problems.

First, they incorporate an elitist conception of political life. The classic proposals for peace since the days of Crucé and Saint Pierre have been addressed to privileged governing elites. Yet we live in an age in which political life is driven by demands for greater democracy. Since existing elitist political frameworks have proved incapable of responding adequately to major global problems, it is increasingly important to create political space for properly democratic processes. Creative responses to the problems of our time must come from people, not from elites. This is why the Committee is concerned less with extending a tradition of peace proposals that depends on creating global institutions on the model of the state than with exploring the way in which social movements are able to enhance democratization in a world of global structures and connections.

Second, although modern history has been characterized by a number of popular struggles for transforming the existing social order—struggles inspired by Rousseau, Marx and other revolutionary thinkers—most of them have centred on the seizure of state power, on the ability to capture the legitimate monopoly of power in a particular territory. This has been true of socialist movements, nationalist movements, and movements for democratic revolution. Further, these movements have tended to resort to violence as a means of taking state power. But we have now seen many, many instances in history where violence as a means has betrayed the goals of revolution. Thus more and more people have become engaged in movements for social change which try to put an end to the violence of the existing order without resorting to violence themselves. More and more social movements act as if they are reinterpreting what it now means to engage in social transformation and revolutionary politics. Again, the Committee is especially interested in the way that some kinds of social movements are able to combine the struggle for greater democratization in a world of global structures with a capacity to rethink the possibilities of non-violent social and political change.

The Committee for a Just World Peace is encouraged by the upsurge of popular social movements in many parts of the world and in seemingly diverse circumstances. It gives special importance to the manner in which so many movements, visible and invisible, have emerged in response to the processes of militarization and ecological degradation that are under way on a global scale, and to oppose war, hunger, poverty, repressive regimes, violation of human rights, and all kinds of discrimination now prevalent in so many places. The Committee is also keenly aware that these movements are still mutually isolated. It is therefore concerned to contribute to the dialogue between such movements and to identify ways in which the potential inherent in the practices and aspirations of such movements can be more effectively realized.

While continuing to prepare its own Report, the Committee has decided to publish some of the studies that have formed the basis for the Committee's attempt to make sense of the relationship between global processes and the practices of social movements. Although the views expressed in these essays are those of the individual authors, the Committee hopes that their publication will serve to stimulate dialogue among concerned citizens of the world and help to extend the horizons of our political imagination.

March 1987

Yoshikazu Sakamoto
Professor of International Politics
Faculty of Law
University of Tokyo
CJWP Research Director

Contributors

Chadwick F. Alger Mershon Professor of Political Science and Public Policy, The Ohio State University, Columbus, Ohio, USA

Elise Boulding Professor of Sociology (Emerita), Dartmouth College, Hanover, New Hampshire, USA; Member, CJWP

Manuel Castells Professor of Planning, Department of City and Regional Planning, University of California, Berkeley, California, USA

Gustavo Esteva Comite Promotor de Investigaciones Para El Desarrollo Rural, Comision del Centro de Informacion Rural, Mexico City, Mexico

Richard A. Falk Albert G. Milbank Professor of International Law and Practice, Princeton University, Princeton, New Jersey, USA; Member, CJWP

Zsuzsa Hegedus Sociologist, Centre D'Analyse et D'Intervention Sociologique, Ecole des Hautes Etudes en Sciences Sociales, CADIS-CNRS-EHESS, Paris, France

Mary Kaldor Professor, Science Policy Research Unit, University of Sussex, UK; Member, CJWP

Rajni Kothari Director, Peace and Global Transformation Programme, United Nations University; Consulting Editor, *Alternatives: A Journal for Social Transformation and Humane Governance*, New Delhi, India; Member, CJWP

Saul H. Mendlovitz Professor of Law, Rutgers University School of Law, Newark, New Jersey; Ira D. Wallach Professor of World Order Studies, Columbia University, New York, USA; Editor, *Alternatives: A Journal for Social Transformation and Humane Governance*; Executive Secretary, CJWP

Lester Edwin J. Ruiz Director for Publications, World Order Models Project, New York; Co-Director, Center for Research and Education, Princeton, New Jersey; Adjunct Professor of Ethics, New York Theological Seminary, New York, USA

D. L. Sheth Director, Centre for the Study of Developing Societies, New Delhi; Editor, *Alternatives: A Journal for Social Transformation and Humane Governance*, New Delhi, India

Vandana Shiva Coordinator, Research Foundation for Science, Technology and Natural Resource Policy, Dehradun, India; Member, CJWP

R. B. J. Walker Associate Professor, Department of Political Science, University of Victoria, British Columbia, Canada; Rapporteur, CJWP

Nigel Young Cooley Professor of Peace Studies, Peace Studies Program, Colgate University, Hamilton, New York, USA

Acknowledgements

The editors are grateful to a number of individuals and foundations whose support for the Committee for a Just World Peace (CJWP) has made this book possible. Grants from the North American Section of the United Nations University Project on Peace and Global Transformation, the United Nations Educational, Scientific and Cultural Organization (UNESCO), the Miriam and Ira D. Wallach Foundation, the World Order Models Project, and the World Policy Institute, have supported the Committee's ongoing work, including this volume.

The editors also wish to thank the contributors, who were generous and patient in meeting the demands that we placed on them. The various participants in the Committee's meetings in Lisbon, Portugal, and Royaumont, France, provided insightful comments on the papers that are included in this book. Our colleagues on the staff of the World Order Models Project, including Ronald Slye and Lester Edwin J. Ruiz, provided editorial assistance as the book was being prepared. Finally, we wish to thank our families for the personal sacrifices which they made so that we could work on the book.

March 1987   Saul H. Mendlovitz
                                                                                         R. B. J. Walker

Contents

Introduction

Peace, Politics and Contemporary Social Movements

R. B. J. WALKER AND SAUL H. MENDLOVITZ

Peace and political practice

Much has been written about peace and war in the past few decades. Calls for peace appear in the languages of social science and theology, in the technical jargon of throw-weights and acronyms and in the emotional chants of mass demonstrations. Specialized academic disciplines have appeared under labels like peace research, world order studies, strategic studies or conflict resolution. The production of books on nuclear weapons and military technology has become a minor industry.

Still, peace remains disturbingly elusive. The drift towards a more violent world is now rapid enough to warrant annual statistical reports. They sound a familiar refrain:

> The arms build-up has continued, at painful cost to the world community . . . Violence is on the rise. There are more wars and more people killed in them. Four times as many deaths have occurred in the 40 years since World War II as in the 40 years preceding it. Increasingly the geopolitical designs of the major military powers are being worked out on the soil of other countries and with other people's lives . . . In a world spending $800 billion a year for military programs, one adult in three cannot read and write, one person in four is hungry.[1]

Yet it is not only peace that is elusive. Even the meaning of peace has become increasingly difficult to define. To link the dynamics of military spending with poverty and illiteracy is to go far beyond the equation of peace with the mere absence of war. For some scholars, this has meant thinking about peace in the context of "structural violence." They argue that peace must involve a sharp reduction not only in physical conflict between military forces, but also in the less obvious though no less deadly violence inherent in many social, political, economic and cultural processes. For others, it has meant a refusal to separate the pursuit of peace from the pursuit of justice. They have criticized the equation of peace with the achievement of some semblance of order, and concerned themselves with the quality of social behavior that might bring about some degree of positive community.

Others have suggested that while the simple conceptual opposition between war and peace may have been appropriate in the past, both the character of modern military conflict and the complexities of contemporary international affairs have now made it obsolete. This is partly a consequence of the way that nuclear weapons have undermined conventional calculations of the relations between ends and means in warfare. It is also partly a consequence of the increasing complexity of the forces giving rise to modern political conflicts.

Now, more than ever before, the accumulation of weapons has to be explained not only in terms of military and strategic interests, but also in terms of much broader economic, social and even cultural processes of militarization. It is increasingly difficult to think of states entering into conditions of war or peace just on the basis of their autonomous sovereign self-interest. States are caught in complex patterns of dominance, dependence and interdependence. Weapons have become vital components of economic policy and international trade. The mechanisms that induce violence seem to be increasingly integrated. In this context, any concept of peace as a mere absence of war can have little more than rhetorical value. It is obviously vital that something be done about "the bomb;" but introducing some sort of sanity into the deployment of nuclear weapons is a necessary but insufficient condition for a more peaceful world.

All of this is now commonplace among those who have thought seriously about the possibilities of peace. Part of the achievement of the outpouring of literature on war and peace over the past few decades has been to show that far from being a marginal activity pursued by pacifists and utopians, thinking about peace must now engage with the most fundamental questions about how people ought to live together. As soon as the simple distinction between war and peace is abandoned, thinking about peace necessarily becomes integrated into much broader currents of political thought and practice. Indeed, it hardly seems possible to think seriously about political life in the modern world without some understanding of the way the characteristic forms of contemporary violence challenge so many of our inherited assumptions about what it means to be human, and how we ought to act towards each other. Peace is neither a technical policy problem, nor an easy utopian aspiration. It is a challenge both to prevailing structures of power and to our understanding of what it now means to engage in political life.

Contemporary thinking about peace, as about political life in general, is still dominated by the existence of the state as the primary political reality. Whether in terms of security, of cultural identity, or of the organization of economic activity, the territorially bounded state has successfully claimed not only a monopoly on the legitimate use of violence, but also a monopoly on how and where political activity occurs.

The emergence of the state as the primary political formation is a complicated historical episode. It is important to recognize that it is an historical not a natural occurrence. Moreover, the character of states has changed considerably over time, and states vary enormously in character in different parts of the world. Variations among states are as important as the fact that states as such have become the primary political formation everywhere. The emergence of the modern system of states can be explained as the consequence of many concrete processes. Different intellectual traditions give varying emphases to economic, technological and social forces. But whether in terms of the transition from feudalism to capitalism in Europe, or of the expansion of European power across the world, the modern state and states-system has to be understood in the context of processes of fundamental historical change. These processes prompted new ideas about what it means to act politically.

Although transformed, such processes have not stopped. Indeed, it has become a cliché that the fundamental conditions of human existence are changing faster than ever before. The state may remain the primary locus of political activity, but all states are now caught up in processes of economic, technological, social, cultural, and political transformation. It is unlikely that these processes will leave states as they are. It is more likely that they will provide both the need and the opportunity for new forms of political practice.

Thus, not only is it necessary to treat peace as more than just the absence of war, and to refuse to separate peace from justice, it is also necessary to understand the pursuit of peace as part of a widespread if often inchoate attempt to generate new forms of political practice in the face of fundamental historical change.

It is true that peace as a value is particularly important now because so many changes in the modern world are felt as threatening—we all live under the sign of the mushroom cloud. Our physical environment has begun to show signs of its serious vulnerability to systematic abuse. Millions starve or live in atrocious conditions even though enough is produced to allow everyone on Earth to live quite comfortably. People are tortured and denied fundamental rights, social domination is perpetuated on the basis of class, race and gender. All these things are altered, and in many situations intensified by the pressures and demands of emerging processes and structures whose outlines are only now becoming apparent. Nevertheless, the pursuit of peace cannot be separated from the attempt to come to terms with the broad dynamics of change in the modern world—dynamics that bring both great dangers and new opportunities.

The essays in this book explore what it now means to struggle not only for a more peaceful world, but also for more powerful understandings of what a more peaceful world might look like. It is recognized that peace is not something that can be simply articulated abstractly, but must be achieved on the basis of ongoing social and political practices. The essays emphasize the rapidly changing context in which the possibilities of peace have to be grasped. On the one hand, they try to articulate a clearer understanding of the practical limits of existing structures, institutions and ideologies in the face of new forms of violence and increasingly complicated international processes. On the other hand, they are concerned with emerging, though still often marginal forms of political action.

These essays suggest that whatever else is going on in the modern world, the most pressing problems on the political agenda arise from or are intensified by the increasingly global scale of the processes that now shape human activity everywhere. They all also agree that whatever else is going on at the level of the state or even among international institutions, some of the most interesting and hopeful political processes are to be found among the numerous recently formed social movements.

While states and the states-system may still dominate political life, these essays suggest that many of the most significant sources of historical change are now to be found in both large-scale structural transformations and small-scale social movements that occur both "above" and "below" the level of the state. They do not suggest that the state is on its way out as a political force. Rather they explore the connections that seem to be occurring between large-scale global processes and local social movements which remain more or less invisible to those who examine political life at the level of the state alone. Moreover, these essays suggest that the character of political life even at the level of the state, will be significantly transformed as a consequence of these processes and struggles. They argue that new understandings of what peace might mean and how it might be pursued, have to arise out of an assessment of these processes and struggles.

Three challenges

Analyses of the most pressing problems on the modern political agenda invariably emphasize three major themes: a crisis of manageability; the emergence of new forces and the radical transformation of old ones; and the bankruptcy of prevailing ideas about what is to be done.

Few people now doubt that it is increasingly difficult to manage the complexities of contemporary political life. Doubts are expressed from many quarters about the capacity of existing authorities and institutions to cope with the stresses and strains now visible in the major structures that have shaped the modern world. It is precisely the apparent lack of control on matters of national security and the escalation of arms deployments that has prompted so many people to protest. In economic life too, even powerful states have found it difficult to exercise control over their own economies given the changing configuration of the world market and the international division of labor, and especially given the present scale and mobility of transnational enterprises. Even in cultural affairs, it is no longer clear that the convergence of nationalist aspirations with the territorial instrumentalities of the state is an adequate way to express the great variety of cultural identities—religious, ethnic, local, and regional—now struggling for expression.

Such problems have led some analysts to speak of an emerging crisis in the legitimacy of the state.[2] They examine the way that so many governments are caught between the extravagance of the claims necessary to maintain legitimacy and the limited options available for their realization. Others observe that states are extremely reluctant to do much about environmental degradation or mass poverty beyond—and often within—their borders. Still others point to the way states claim to be able to ensure security for their citizens while becoming ever more deeply entrenched in worldwide patterns of militarization that induce greater and greater insecurity for everyone.

The outcome of debate on this theme is mixed. Most conventional analysts still expect the state to adapt fairly well to new conditions. They engage in a search for better forms of accommodation and agreement. They advocate more effective arms control procedures, and the non-proliferation of nuclear weapons. They push for new trade agreements, attempt to prevent the collapse of international financial institutions, look for a more effective niche for their own state within the new international division of labor, and promote ways of exercising some control over the worldwide flows of capital. There are also some indications that states have become stronger, more forceful in asserting their sovereignty, often more forthright in exercising the monopoly over the legitimate use of violence. Even so, the resort to force is often an indication of weakness rather than of strength. And it is not always true that where there is a will there is a way.

There is even greater skepticism about the capacity of existing authorities, especially at the level of the state, to manage human affairs effectively in the context of the second perennial theme of modern political life. This emphasizes the emergence of new forces that seem to be remaking the world in unforseen ways. New technologies are often invoked here—whether as weapons or as communications satellites and microchips, new technologies have the capacity to fundamentally alter the nature of human interaction. With the increasingly capital-intensive nature of modern production processes and the global flexibility of capital flows, economic life is being transformed more rapidly than most economists, let alone ordinary citizens, can properly comprehend. With the manipulation of genetic codes, people have the capacity to intervene in their own biological evolution. With new weapons—nuclear, biological and chemical—as well as more effective means of delivery, people have the capacity to put an end to evolution once and for all.

The key issue here is not so much the capacity of existing authorities to manage these things, but that they can occur as global rather than territorial phenomena. If there is little doubt that the state will continue to be the primary political formation for a long time to come, there is also little doubt that some of the most important forces in the modern world occur on a global scale. Not only do these processes create problems of manageability—it is far from clear how such processes can engage with political life as it has come to be known at all. Most political categories remain focused on the state, to the extent that people engage in political life almost exclusively at state level. In a world in which political life is monopolized by the state yet many of the most important forces that affect people's lives are effectively beyond state control, it is reasonable to expect a search for new categories of political analysis, new forms of social community, new forms of group identity. This is the third major theme of modern political debate.

One indication of what is at stake is the extraordinary appeal to fundamentalisms of one kind or another. Change brings uncertainty, and uncertainty invites a leap into the known, or at least, what is assumed to be known—a religious text, a romanticized dream of an earlier and simpler age, a source of authority that can justify the assertion of order, not to mention the iron fist. But more significant than this is the widespread skepticism about the great ideologies that arose in 19th-century Europe and which have subsequently informed political life almost everywhere.

It is not so much that liberalism, socialism or nationalism fail to express values and aspirations that remain potent. It is more that both the ambivalence of the historical record and serious doubts about the way these ideologies remain trapped in the intellectual prejudices of an earlier age, combine to deprive them of popular conviction. There is instead a widespread sense that the aspirations they express require reformulation and revitalization.

Much the same is true of more visionary or utopian impulses. There has been an increasing recognition that utopian schemes for the future have usually involved an artificial separation of theory from practice, and that the future has to be made rather than merely thought into being. There has been an increasing awareness that the best known utopian schemes have involved the ethnocentric projection of Eurocentric concepts which do not translate very well into other cultural or socioeconomic contexts. There has even been an emerging sense, that attempts to bring grand designs down to Earth in this century, have often involved the kind of violence that makes the creation of the envisaged world simply impossible.

All three of these grand themes converge to create an atmosphere of great uncertainty and danger. There is obviously no shortage of people who, following their fundamentalist convictions or assuming that what has worked before will work again, know exactly where they are going, and are too likely to insist that everyone follow them. For those who remain skeptical about the magic of the market, the reliability of space-based defense systems, or the blueprints for "development" imposed by international financial institutions, the contemporary human predicament appears increasingly precarious. Insecurity and survival have become pressing issues even in societies that have become used to material comfort and political stability. The extent to which poverty and abuse continue in a world of plenty, and particularly in a world that prides itself on advanced civilizational values, is a moral scandal of the very highest order. Fundamentalists aside, few people are clear about what is to be done.

It is in this setting that the search for peace leads to the search for new understandings of political life and new forms of political action.

The promise of contemporary social movements

Large-scale transformations always bring forth new political actors and new forms of political action. Social movements are particularly significant in this respect. They have always formed to express opposition to dominant power structures as well as to respond to structural dislocation. This is why they provide such a good indicator of the character of social change, both historically and at the present time. The essays in this book suggest that contemporary social movements provide one of the most invigorating features of modern life. They provide some of the most creative responses to the challenges of the age.

Although there have always been social movements, they have usually been fragmented and scattered, responding to specific injustices in particular places, and with little continuity over time or connection from region to region. Their histories often remain unwritten. The major exceptions to this occurred in 19th century Europe. Even early in that century, the challenge to the old feudal and aristocratic order in the name of democracy was associated with the barely organized masses. But the barricades of the great revolutionary years of 1789 and 1848, contrast with the more systematic activities developed after 1860. The increasing integration of the world economy was accompanied by the integration of movements struggling in response to new economic, social and political conditions. These struggles gradually coalesced around two very broad movements; one concerned primarily with changing the relationship between employers and workers, and the other, with the assertion of identity between competing ethno-national groups. Much of the history of Europe—and indeed much of the rest of the world—over the past century is written in terms of these increasingly integrated nationalist and socialist movements. Indeed, much of that history concerns the deep tensions between them. Yet whatever their differences, social movements in 19th-century Europe were characterized by the development of systematic organizational structures and institutions. These movements still inform our dominant ideas about how social movements organize and participate in political life.

Perhaps the single most important feature of the development of both socialism and nationalism was their identification of the state as the primary locus of political power. Both movements organized themselves in relation to state institutions and associated the possibility of political change with gaining state power. Many states in fact became nation-states, and many others have attempted to do so. And in spite of the internationalism of socialist ideology, and even of many strong anti-statist socialist traditions, socialist organizations quickly became national in structure and sought to attain power within particular states. There were in both cases, important debates about how state power was to be attained—through persuasion and reform or through force and revolution. But the crucial connection was firmly established between these increasingly integrated movements and state power.

In contrast with most of the sporadic and fragmented movements that came before, socialist and nationalist movements have been remarkably successful. They have moulded the character of modern states, whether they be social-democratic, communist or nationalist. They have become part of the primary political structures of the modern world.

Over the past two decades, political life has been marked by a renewed resurgence of social movements. There are peace movements, human-rights movements, environmental movements, urban movements, movements of indigenous peoples and movements for alternative forms of economic life. Massive popular movements have challenged authoritarian regimes and demonstrated opposition to specific policies. Grass-roots movements have sprung up everywhere, they are visible even in societies in which popular mobilizations have been most powerfully expressed in relation to post-colonial nationalisms. While it is possible to interpret their character and significance in different ways, it is not possible to ignore them—no analysis of modern political life can leave them out.

Some observers are content to portray them within traditional analytical categories. They can be seen as a simple continuation of age-old forms of disconnected protest, or as yet another periodic upsurge of populism. They can also be seen as attempts to effect changes within the structures established by earlier socialist and nationalist movements. In the context of affluent Western societies, for example, attempts are made to locate such movements within the primary struggle between capital and labor or to treat them as mere interest groups competing to put pressure on the state to attain specific goals.

Much can be explained in these terms. Yet there is an emerging sense on the part of both the participants in these movements and of a wide range of academic analysts that something new is going on. They are neither entirely fragmented and sporadic in the traditional manner, nor do they resemble the organized movements that arose in the 19th century Europe. They have a sense of vibrancy and a willingness to articulate alternative ways of knowing and acting that puts the claim to politics as usual into serious question.

The crucial point is that, despite their great diversity, contemporary social movements are all responding to a future that is seen as threatening. As Claus Offe has observed even of movements in the more privileged societies, all the major concerns of the new social movements

> converge on the idea that life itself—and the minimal standards of 'good life' as defined and sanctioned by modern values—is threatened by the bland dynamics of military, economic, technological and political rationalization; and that there are no sufficient and sufficiently reliable barriers within dominant political and economic institutions that could prevent them from passing the threshold to disaster.[3]

This is certainly not to suggest that social movements are, or are about to become, the main political force in the modern world. A spectre of popular social movements may or may not be haunting the globe. Neither the world economy nor the states-system are likely to succumb to them. For those who believe that these large systems are co-extensive with social and political reality, movements are likely to remain invisible, or at least minor disturbances at the margins of vision. And although it is possible to show that they are a novel and significant presence in modern political life, social movements obviously face severe problems. Whether they will grow in vitality and significance cannot be predicted. As forms of political practice, their future has to be achieved.

Nor is it to suggest that social movements are the only political forces that are relevant to the pursuit of peace. On the contrary, one of the main challenges facing contemporary social movements is to generate creative connections with other progressive actors, whether they be people working within state structures, international organizations, or even states themselves.

Nevertheless, historical experience suggests that some of the most creative energies for social change do come from social movements. They present a sober assessment of specific challenges that have to be met. They offer some idea of how the grand visions and aspirations of the past need to be reworked to respond more coherently to the conditions of the present. They raise crucial question about the nature of political life in a world of rapid change, both in terms of where political action ought to take place and in what form it ought to occur.

The essays

The essays in this book have all been written by people who have been concerned both with what it now means to talk about peace and with the character and potentialities of contemporary social movements. They all take it for granted that peace must be understood as more than just the absence of war. Hence the juxtaposition of peace with justice. They all take it for granted that peace is threatened by processes that are global in scope. Hence the phrase "just world peace" in which each of these three words is taken equally seriously.

To begin with, Richard Falk, Mary Kaldor and Manuel Castells examine some of the most important global structures and processes to which social movements now respond—specifically the modern system of states, the world economy and advanced technologies. In each case the analysis leads to a concern with the opportunities and spaces for creative action that now seem to be available.

The next section focuses more explicitly on the contemporary meaning of peace. Nigel Young reflects on the experience of peace movements; Rob Walker explores some of the cultural and discursive horizons within which contemporary thinking about peace has become caught; and Zsuzsa Hegedus underscores the civilian emancipatory character of the Western peace movements which have inaugurated a new ethic of responsibility and transnational solidarity.

The essays in the next section suggest that it is not enough to re-articulate the concept of peace unless this also involves a re-articulation of the concept of development. Only in this way does it become possible to speak of a just peace. Elise Boulding looks at the historical experience of utopia building; D. L. Sheth looks more directly at the promises and betrayals of the concept of development; Vandana Shiva examines the meaning of development from the perspective of ecology movements in India and Gustavo Esteva explores its meaning from the perspective of local development movements in Mexico. Then, Lester Ruiz analyses the connections between new concepts of development and emerging forms of political action in the Philippines.

Most social movements act in very specific locations. They struggle locally while the processes against which they struggle are powerful and often global. This raises the problem of how movements can relate to each other more effectively. This is the challenge that is taken up in the final section. Chad Alger and Saul Mendlovitz investigate the challenge of linking grass-roots movements and initiatives in the United States to global transformation. Richard Falk asks how it is now possible to act as if one is a citizen of the world as well as a citizen of a particular state. Finally, Rajni Kothari reviews the relationship between movements, classes and the state in a world of profound transformation. Kothari looks forward to the achievement of minimum conditions for civilized living *for all beings*, in which exploitation does not disappear but is contained, where civil strife is waged within recognizable and predictable limits . . . to a society in which expansionist drives in both men and women and the social-political apparatus are controlled, and where pluralism, including complementarity between genders and generations, is cherished and a society which, above all, allows individual creativity to flower and thereby to contribute to the creativity of the collective.

This aspiration informs all the essays in the book.

Notes and references

1. Ruth Leger Sivard, *World Military and Social Expenditures, 1985* (Washington, DC: World Priorities, 1985):5.
2. For a collection of classic discussions of this theme see William Connolly (editor) *Legitimacy and the State* (Oxford: Basil Blackwell, 1984).
3. Claus Offe, "New Social Movements: Challenging the Boundaries of Institutional Politics," *Social Research*, vol 52, no 4, Winter 1985, p. 853. See also Giovanni Arrighi, T. K. Hopkins and I. Wallerstein, "Dilemmas of Antisystemic Movements," *Social Research*, vol 53, no 1, Spring 1986, pp. 185–205; Ernesto Laclau and Chantal Mouffe, *Hegemony and Socialist Strategy: Towards a Radical Democratic Politics* (London: Verso, 1985); and Raymond Williams, *The Year 2000* (New York: Pantheon Books, 1983).

Confronting Social Structures

The State System and Contemporary Social Movements

RICHARD A. FALK

As long as there has been serious political speculation, thinkers and prophets have put forth images and ideas about a world based on harmony, unity, and happiness for all. Yet the history of organized political life is dominated by narratives of war, fragmentation, and misery for most inhabitants of the planet. This tension between possibility and actuality has become almost unbearable in contemporary circumstances where the dangers of our species' self-annihilation have become persistent themes of popular culture and dreamlife.

The political order of the world is premised upon the interplay of sovereign states, more or less coordinated by diplomacy. These states are of diverse size, endowment, geographic circumstance, developmental stage, cultural heritage, ideological outlook, and governing style. The dominant states set the tone of the international system, raising or moderating tensions, stabilizing or destabilizing economic relations, and establishing, or not, acceptable kinds of leadership for the world as a whole. Since 1945, this hierarchy has informed the most significant issues in bipolar terms: the administration of the war system beneath the shadow cast by nuclear weapons, and the ideological rivalry for the hearts and minds of non-Western peoples liberating themselves from the oppressiveness of colonialism. Yet in both these cases, the superpowers have failed the tests of leadership. A nuclear arms race threatens human survival, diverts vast quantities of resources, and undermines the sovereign rights of all political communities; and superpower diplomacy in the Third World has been neither benign nor effective, producing a continuous flow of interventions and promoting models of development that do not solve the problems of poverty, nor encourage democratic forms of popular participation in political life. These failures of leadership have generated a movement toward non-alignment in the Third World, an effort to insulate sovereignty from the dangers and costs of superpower hegemony. Of course, these failures of superpower diplomacy have also threatened the developed states of the North. As an autonomous unit legitimated by upholding security and by some form of democratic participation, the state

Commissioned by the Committee for a Just World Peace for presentation at its Lisbon Conference, March 1985. First published in a revised form in *Alternatives* XI:1.

here has become virtually a mirage. Because of the bloc system, these states have lost control of their destiny on issues of war and peace. And in the nuclear age this loss of control reduces the citizens of bloc countries to the status of hostages, a situation well captured by the slogan of the European peace movement: "No annihilation without representation."

Still, matters could be worse. World War III has been avoided. Enough political space was cleared, partly as a result of bipolar rivalry, to enable decolonization; both superpowers, despite their opportunism in practice, at least acted out of anti-colonial traditions. United States control over international economic policy was generally enlightened and intelligent, exhibiting some postwar generosity, providing a stable currency, building up trading partners and markets, and enabling sustained growth for all sectors of the world. Similarly, United States influence also lent prestige to institutional efforts at global and regional levels to strengthen the cooperative aspects of international life. These positive features of US leadership have more recently been diminished, if not altogether lost, and this accounts for the current mood of despair about future prospects.

Crises of a geopolitical and economic character have occurred throughout this period of recent history, disclosing in a variety of settings the fragility of the world system, as well as conveying a sense that the situation could collapse altogether. Beginning in the 1970s, a new kind of ecological anxiety emerged from the mix of population growth, pollution, and resource depletion. Compounding this phenomenon is the increasing use of sophisticated computer models which lend an objective imprimatur to more prophetic warnings that industrial civilization on a global scale was running out of growing space.

These concerns amid the complexity of international life have engendered a global awareness of "one world" in key respects. Thus, Bhopal is not just a city in India, it is a city that was the scene of an unprecedented disaster in a world of integrated consciousness. Its victims evoke reactions of sympathy everywhere, and their efforts to receive some form of compensation raise key issues of transnational responsibility for the multinational corporation, an actor that is a curious blend of territorial and non-territorial, and if for this reason alone, hard to pin down.

As the stresses and strains on the state system have cumulatively intensified in the last four decades or so, so too have the responses by way of militarization. Contradictory reactions of a creative sort are also becoming more prominent. A struggle is shaping up to determine the future of specific peoples and civilizations, and of the species and its habitat. This struggle goes unreported in the daily media, although episodes may hit the surface from time to time, usually in the form of some type of turbulence, whether it be a mass demonstration, a campaign of resistance, a world leader who questions the logic of nuclearism or militarism by a concrete act, or a declaration of intent by some movement for societal renewal. Since our perceptual lenses are focused on struggles between alliances and states, between forces from the "left" and "right", or at best, between "top" and "bottom", the struggle to remake our world calls for new categories, new frameworks, and a new political language. And the tools are emerging, especially as a result of the activities of social movements addressing some facet of oppression or arising to deal with immediate problems by relying on grass-roots and local resources. What is plain is that these new forms represent what the Green Party co-founder, Petra Kelly, calls "gentle subversion".[1] The word gentle is, at least, as important as the word subversion.

The resilience of the state system in the face of all these subversive happenings is striking. There is no doubt that the state system has been challenged by modernity, but it has also evolved and responded, and if anything, strengthened its hold. The essence of a state is a function of two quite distinct elements: its capacities to provide coordination and exert control, as well as its legitimacy as a guarantor of nationalist sentiments. According to Ernest Gellner, the former has been important for the evolution of post-agrarian or industrial societies, as the capacities were continuously modernized and reflect the increasing mobilization of science and technology as instruments of state power. And the latter has benefited from the intensity of nationalist sentiments—a faith to die for. Paradoxically, it should be noted, states oppress and destroy hostile or subordinate nationalisms within their boundaries. Gellner estimates that there are 200 states and at least 800 movements of effective nationalism (as well as 7,000 more potential nationalisms, if ethnic identity is taken as the premise).[2] That there is a disparity explains why the state is necessarily both a vehicle for dominant nationalisms and a coercive instrumentality toward subordinate nationalisms. In fact, from the point of view of global reform, statism overwhelms whatever stirrings of globalism that can be identified. This is because the emergence of militant subordinated nationalisms threatens the viability of the state from within, as well as producing a certain globalist solidarity among these struggling movements.

This paper explores the terrain of gentle subversion in relation to state power. In Section I, some observations are made about why the outcome of World War II created a surprisingly unfavorable context for global reform of an anti-statist character, as compared to World War I. Such observations challenge the conventional view that there has been a linear growth of internationalism over the last century or so. Rather, my contention is that the main energy for global reform in the postwar world was statist in character, namely, the anti-colonial movement. There was also the United States effort to administer a global economy of mutual benefit that would avoid the kind of destructive economic nationalism that was widely regarded as a major cause for the breakdown of international order in the 1930s and the slide toward world war.

The second section examines the contradictory side of the ledger of political struggle. It discusses denuclearizing and demilitarizing initiatives that are evident at this time, as well as defensive moves designed to uphold the existing situation against threatened deteriorations. The more radical type of reformist thinking has a blind side: the neglect of tactics and struggles to prevent these further deteriorations (as distinct from the pursuit of enhancements). However, the assumption is made that there exists positive political space to occupy, as well as space to defend against encroachment, within existing structures of world order.

The third and final section reaches out to consider the search for the promised land. Here, the central core is the invention of a new politics that is compassionate, globalist, localist, and spiritual at its core, that centers neither the person nor the group on militarist prowess and its capacity to administer the apparatus of state power. A first act of allegiance would be to declare ourselves citizens of this invisible political community that is to be our promised land. Citizenship in this sense would imply pilgrimage more than membership, but it would dramatize the importance of resisting illegitimate claims of established political orders and symbolize the exercise of a new form of freedom animated by the quest for a peaceful and just world.

I. The illusions of immobilism

If we analyze prospects for global reform by traditional means, there is no ground for hope. The scale of reforms required to realize a world of peace and justice seems decisively blocked by the orientation and dominance of sovereign states. What is worse, the faint glimmer of hope associated only a generation ago with incremental reforms fashioned by the states acting together on behalf of shared interests and of their peoples has been virtually extinguished by the cumulative drift of more recent developments.

Further, it is not widely appreciated that the period of maximum anti-war sentiment was not after World War II, but rather after World War I when substantial sectors of democratic societies were deeply disillusioned by military approaches to security. It was in this inter-war period that the most dramatic efforts to achieve disarmament were pursued, as were also efforts to find peaceful settlement procedures as diplomatic alternatives to war.[3]

The failure to avert World War II has been widely attributed to this drift toward "peace", leading to a popular reaction abhorring "appeasement" as epitomized by the concessions of the liberal democracies to Hitler at Munich in 1938. But other elements have also helped increase the war-proneness of the state system. First, the unacknowledged realization that only the war pulled world capitalism out of the Depression, and that Keynesianism to work in "peace" must operate in the *as if* atmosphere of a war economy, requiring a heightened sense of danger justifying high levels of expenditures. Second, the recognition that the new military technology requires permanent mobilization of opinion and resources, an adjustment dramatized by the (supposedly) surprise attack launched by the Japanese on the isolationist and slumbering United States at Pearl Harbor and by the obvious capabilities of long-range bombers and missile-firing submarines even without the added spur of avoiding a knockout blow from nuclear weapons. Third, there is the ideological notion that preparing for war is a better assurance of "peace" than disarmament, especially given the view of an irreconcilable East–West tension, with leaders of each side demonizing the other. To this extent, theorizing about deterrence is really the crystallization of a deeper reorientation toward security. Fourth, there is the moralizing view that a willingness to fight was necessary and worthwhile, no matter what the costs of war, an outlook captured by the chilling phrase "better dead than Red". And fifth, there is the view that it is better to engage the enemy in peripheral space such as the Third World to avoid the destruction of one's homeland, and as a means to sustain the war system without inviting the mutual catastrophe of yet another world war, this one fought with nuclear weapons.

The point here is that the state system survived the challenge of the 1920s and 1930s, and emerged stronger after the experience of the 1940s, however destructive it was and seems to us in retrospect. Of course, peace in 1945 brought a temporary surge of war-avoidance: the horrors of the just-concluded war were still raw memories, the anxiety about atomic warfare surfaced, the United Nations was founded, a degree of military demobilization occurred, and disarmament proposals were put forward. But memoirs and historical studies, especially on the Western side, have shown that these efforts at global reform were cosmetic, meant half-heartedly as public relations gestures.[4] The real levers of power within the most powerful states, East and West, were held by "realists" convinced that a balance of power built around the logic of containment could keep "the peace". That is, war became the means to achieve peace, or more fairly, lesser war was the price to be paid to avoid greater war. We now have prominent writers of security matters who are quite convinced that "deterrence", even with nuclear weapons, is the best "peace system" a world of states can ever achieve, and a great improvement over the pre-nuclear world of "rational" war-making. Underlying this view is the assumption that the state system is ultra-stable or so highly resilient that it is naïve (and irrelevant) to consider alternative world orders as anything other than an exercise in literary fancy.

The initial focus on war here is not meant to imply that this concern overshadows problems of poverty, repression, or ecological balance. As discussed elsewhere, these normative concerns are fused in such a way that reordering responses can only hope to succeed if they deal with the felt grievances of the various peoples of the world.[5] Rather, the emphasis on war at the outset is a reflection of the narrative history of global reformist thought and action. As well, the distribution of war-making capabilities at the state level is what ultimately stabilizes the existing world order system of bounded territorial units claiming sovereign status (defended space). What will destabilize this system, without generating a collapse into general war, is the grand puzzle that needs to be worked on by world order activists. What forms of political and cultural destabilization are likely to lead in the direction of demilitarization? Developing star wars "defense systems", for example, is a variant of political and economic destabilization that is not desired, as it contributes to further militarization. Similarly, terrorist tactics designed to shock the public, penalize representatives of state power, and create an atmosphere of chaos and uncertainty involve another type of comprehensive destabilization that intensifies and even legitimizes militarization, especially as directed toward behavior within civil society.

The disappointing record of superpower geopolitics toward meeting such concerns establishes the current mood in international political life. The original expectation held by Franklin Delano Roosevelt, among others, envisioned virtually a Concert of the World ("The Four Policemen") administered for the sake of international stability by the most important victors in World War II. This idea has been revived in various forms, including the idea of "a five power world" toward the end of the 1960s: the USA, USSR, Europe, China, and Japan. Such a conception of the leading centers of state power acting on behalf of world interests has not materialized to any degree whatsoever. The closest approximation, actually expressions of geopolitical fracture, are periodic summit meetings of a collective nature held by both blocs and by the non-aligned groups on security and economic policy concerns. Even within these zones of ideological affinity, there is very little disposition to engage in meaningful forms of cooperation, at least outside the scope of alliance politics, and even here, the cooperative aspects seem to reflect mainly the dominance of the respective alliance leaders. More revealing for our purposes is the exclusively managerial outlook that these leaders entertain. Except for sheer propaganda purposes, as at annual speeches in the United Nations, the serious preoccupations of power-wielders are meeting challenges and threats posed by "enemies" and smoothing over the differences and tensions that emerge among "friends". There seems to be no conception of a potential community embracing friends and enemies that is capable of dealing with collective needs and aspirations in a more creative manner than at present. The impoverishment of political imagination during this time of great human danger is tragically notable.

Another line of positive expectation is associated with the promises made on behalf of competing ideological conceptions of development. Even if the international system could not be unified, or modified, at least it seemed possible that the processes of decolonization would produce a series of encouraging models in state-building at the societal level. Of course, controversy and variation abounds as to the results achieved, but what seems evident is that neither socialist nor capitalist models have yet worked successfully, if the assessment includes perspectives associated with world order values. Socialist societies, with their commitment to basic needs and to societal fairness, have encountered a variety of difficulties: most seriously, the emergent state has tended to be repressive and to find itself tied to a circumstance of Soviet dependency. The alternative breakaway experience, either China or Yugoslavia, illustrates the difficulty facing a socialist society within the predominantly capitalist world economy. Even those socialist states that have managed an independent path in foreign policy seem saddled with a governmental apparatus that distrusts, and hence stifles, the creative energies of its own people.

The experience of the capitalist-oriented post-colonial state is no better. Although some of these states have managed impressive records of growth, they have done so by burdening their poorest citizens and by imposing "discipline" in the form of repression. As well, these states have been linked into the wider patterns of militarization in international life. Others, less successful in the economic sphere, have experienced militarization (within and without), and find their economies deeply mortgaged to international creditors and their polities beset by enemies. To survive as viable economic entities, these states accept a variety of "conditions" imposed by the IMF with an eye toward credit-worthiness, thereby further increasing the privations of the poor and augmenting the repressive capabilities of government so as to contain resistance from the opposition.

The Third World has also not produced models of its own, although several notable attempts can be observed. Gandhi's great achievement in mobilizing India around the tactics and principles of non-violence continues to serve inspirational purposes, although its promise was deeply compromised at the moment of independence by the outbreak of massive Hindu/Moslem collective violence and by the emergence in India of a militarized state that has behaved in its region like a traditional great power. Nevertheless, there is a resonance from the Gandhi period that remains genuine, and sets India apart, giving it some disposition to call for a halt to the most destructive patterns of superpower conduct. There are also a variety of Third World experiments in self-reliance, seeking to extend non-alignment to the economic sphere, and thereby invent the meaning of "development" rather than have it derive from either capitalist or socialist antecedents in the North, West or East. Such a path seems difficult, especially given the strength of materialist conceptions of progress, and the pressure to link and adapt to existing models is intense. China's evolution since 1949 is a microcosmic expression of the impulse to forge its own path toward socialism, followed by a tight embrace, at least for now, of the capitalist ethos. Emblematic, perhaps, are recent reports that these latest shifts in China's approach toward its own future have for the first time attracted a heavy inflow of Japanese investment capital.

These tendencies are not linear, nor invariant. Severe militarization in South America during the 1960s and early 1970s, for example, encountered a variety of problems associated with making the economy work. As a result, promising if fragile programs of democratization are underway in several critical countries. In others, repression has engendered a growing tide of opposition. The combined learning experience of failed militarization (along with the dark consequences of fundamentalist revolution in Iran) has induced the search for moderating alternatives that sustain the prevalent structures but ease up on their most repressive features. Whether the search for "a shaky center" of moderation in these polities is an exercise in self-delusion remains to be seen.

The main features of the global setting do not give rise to an encouraging assessment. On a geopolitical level, the arms race seems likely to continue, entering dangerous new domains such as space and non-nuclear weapons of mass destruction (BW, CW, and "the revolution" in conventional weaponry), and neither popular protest nor the powerful symbolic warnings implicit in "the nuclear winter" findings, are able to reverse the destructive momentum. In fact, the mind-set of leaders twists warnings into rationalizations for yet further militarizing initiatives. Hence, alleged moral reservations about deterrence and evident political concern about public protest, stimulated the endorsement of star wars technology (Strategic Defense Initiative). At a time when not a public dollar is being invested in disarming initiatives, a deficit-conscious superpower enthusiastically proposes a minimum of $24 billion to proceed with a new military technology that can only add to current forms of instability, as well as plunder still further the resources available for the alleviation of misery at home and abroad. This misallocation of global resources and the dangers of global-scale catastrophe worsen too, of course, the life prospects of future generations.

The world economy is likely to be bound still tighter into a highly stratified structure reflecting a hierarchy of technologies. On the capitalist side, a restored confidence in market mechanisms, combined with antagonism toward governmental programs associated with social issues, has greatly weakened earlier welfare tendencies. Domestic and international adjustments by way of concession, compromise, or compassion are less likely to occur in the period ahead, except possibly to soften the effects of outright disaster, as has been the case in the famines throughout Ethiopia and sub-Saharan Africa. This renewed posture of indifference is certainly facilitated by the passivity and disarray among the constituencies of victims.

There is, as well, no evident disposition to reverse the deteriorating maelstrom in which the United Nations finds itself. The failure of the law of the sea negotiations to produce a ratified treaty, quite explicitly as a result of the more statist outlooks adopted by several of the richer countries, seems to doom functional internationalism for the next decade or so. Of course, this dark mood could be changed rapidly by an about-face on the part of a leading government or by one notable internationalist success. But, at present, there is very little positive energy being invested anywhere in this traditional type of reform. What is more, the institutions and procedures that exist are being demoralized and weakened through neglect and, in some instances, outright hostility. In this regard, the recent United States' repudiation of the International Court of Justice in the course of its dispute with Nicaragua represented both a refusal to allow its interventionary statecraft to be constrained by international law and an expression of revived unilateralism on the part of the state that had earlier done the most to shape postwar expectations about the desirability of law-oriented statecraft. A similar blow had been struck by the American withdrawal from Unesco earlier, the international agency, which for all of its failings, remains the most closely attuned to Third World priorities.

At the state level, despite some interesting innovations in both socialist and capitalist states, there is no foundation for optimism about prospects for human governance. For one thing, the problems confronting most governments are just too overwhelming given the instruments at hand. In this regard, the burdens of population growth are especially significant. The dynamics of population growth are many-dimensional: the drift to the cities from overcrowded rural areas is one expression; pressure to embark upon illegal and hazardous immigration is another; and hiring oneself out on some indentured basis as "a guest worker" is still another. But clearly in all these instances, the quality of life is diminished by the direct and indirect effects of "surplus" population.

At the same time, all states are caught up in the lethal drift of nuclearism and militarism, as well as in the less spectacular, but not necessarily less serious, hazards of ecological deterioration. Governments are the expressions of the state mechanism, which is caught up within a web of special interests (within and without the bureaucracy) and which subscribes to an obsolete canon of "realist" precepts that place regime-security on a pedestal of such great height that the well-being, and even the survival, of domestic society is mindlessly jeopardized. Nothing takes precedence over the survival of the regime, even in its most bizarre expression of a remnant of the ruling group locked away in some remote underground vault. The societal substance of the human experience is offered as "a sacrifice" to the avenging gods of technological prowess. The earlier republican notion of government as a conditional and limited delegation of societal powers has been completely submerged by these modern security arrangements. Besides, for most states, really for all except the superpowers, there is no way to opt out of the larger orbit of geopolitical disaster, and the actuality of sovereign rights depends on overlooking their subordination to the whim and wisdom of whoever is presiding in Moscow and Washington, and to a degree, in other states possessing nuclear weapons. The two giants are themselves locked in a perpetual death embrace. They lack any prospect of defending their territories against annihilation, and no amount of investment in "defensive" military technologies can alter this stark reality. At most, it reshuffles the tactics of the offensive use of nuclear weapons.

Therefore, it would seem likely that direct efforts to achieve global reform will not be forthcoming in the years ahead from state leaders, and if attempted, will be trivial and unrelated to the real challenges of international life. Further, that the state as now constituted is very unlikely to achieve great normative gains for very many of the peoples of the world, although there will be a diversity of balance sheets enumerating gains and losses. The relevant point here is that we cannot, at present, view the reigning ideologies as capable of either governing effectively and humanely or as providing a liberating challenge to the established authority structure. Indeed, as has been argued, the political competition now taking place in most countries, does not include a serious option of liberation, even if the rhetoric of liberation is relied upon. The most likely result of successful revolution is a reproduction, on occasion even in a less restrained form, of the failures associated with the old regime, especially in the broad domain of human rights. The torments of the new political prisoners in Iran is emblematic: "One day in Khomeini's jails is like ten years in the jails of the Shah!"

To maintain the quest for liberation, then, requires looking elsewhere. It is not "realistic" or "sufficient" to invest our energies in the outworn hopes of earlier decades. We must learn from mistaken expectations. The essence of a political agenda at this historical time is the transformation of the state by non-violent means in the direction of peace and justice: demilitarization as method, as process, as goal, and as the keystone of political ethics. Any *principled* reliance on violence, as in the Marxist tradition, has a reproductive logic and is unacceptable. Yet, even here, creative revisions are possible, as in liberation theology. The Sandinista efforts to commingle Sandino's nationalism with Ortega's Marxism and Cardenal's liberation theology are definitely worth nurturing, even if their expression is distorted by the cruelty of the United States response. It is important also to note that *situational* violence, as in the anti-apartheid struggle, may be justifiable in a context where the only political choice is between liberating or oppressing violence and where recourse to liberating violence appears to have some reasonable prospect of success at an acceptable level of human cost.

The other foundation to build upon is the ongoing struggles of the oppressed, widening our understanding of oppression and establishing solidarity with diminishing respect for boundaries. Such struggles may create tension with the orientation toward non-violence, but a purist stance does not seem warranted. The anti-apartheid struggle, which has so often sought to proceed non-violently, warrants support even if its methods include armed struggle. Perhaps outsiders can diminish the role of violence and ensure that it will spare "the innocent" by finding ways to hasten the success of the movement.

A third element is the identification of social forces that can act on behalf of the oppressed. These social forces may involve reinventing culture, or rather, recovering and strengthening those dimensions of culture supportive of new forms of order, authority, security, and fulfillment. It also requires the extension of the notion of "the oppressed" to embrace the world of living spirits, human and animal. The entrapment of all peoples in ordeals threatening the various dimensions of survival is a potential foundation for unity. This peril extends to nature, and establishes the basis for an ecological partnership between human society and other living beings. An ecological outlook also reinforces a wider planetary ethos of strength-through-diversity. In addition, such an outlook will provide a self-concerned basis for the protection of marginal peoples and cultures. This is vital because universalization of communications, trade, and knowledge flows should not be allowed to become a recipe for the homogenization of world culture.

Finally, the encounter between the state and civil society in all its multiple forms needs to become and remain a central normative focus. Such an encounter will take on the character supplied by each distinctive setting. The normative stakes will vary greatly as well. There is no room for dogmatism, though the state can, on occasion, intervene to protect the victims of communal forms of oppression and defend a social contract that assures decency to all elements of society. The issue of policy and appraisal, then, is one of situation and context. Structural relations do not by themselves sort out normative priorities, and therefore even the connections between state and civil society cannot be specified as if invariably oppressive. Our focus here, however, is upon those situations where the state is the object of concern.

In some settings, the target of societal action is a change of policy and personnel to assure the end to patterns of gross abuse of human rights, individual or collective. In others, the target is a more comprehensive concern with the public good, a challenge directed at the kind of security or resources policy being pursued. Or, the encounter will be about the nature of the state itself, its leadership, bureaucratic scale and balance, and worldview. Among the tactics of encounter will be the disposition to seek non-statal solutions for societal problems such as employment, clean environment; in other words, relying upon grass-roots, local, and regional frameworks to obtain capital, know-how, and legitimacy in effect, to reshape the state by discovering that societal problems can be solved without it. More radical than the withdrawal of dependence is resistance in various forms, ranging from refusal to participate as a soldier or military technologist to engaging in some form of tax refusal. What joins these various postures is a general dissatisfaction with the state as a vehicle for the realization of human values, even if such realization is restricted geographically to the peoples living within the boundaries of a given state. The main thrust here is the internal dynamic of state and society, but given the interlocked character of the modern world, the external dynamic of state-to-state relations is also at issue, especially in the war/peace area, but also with regard to food prices for the poor and the availability of basic services, as well as jobs and credit. There is simply no successful way to seal off the world from the formation of national policy on most matters of critical policy.

At this stage of international history, then, direct paths to global reform seem blocked. As well, more of an adjustment in strategic outlook is called for than shifting from efforts to convince global leaders (top down) to an emphasis upon mobilizing "the people" (bottom up). True, the global leadership reflects entrenched interests, and overwhelmingly adheres to a worldview arising out of several centuries of experience within the state system; at present, despite some notable defections, the leadership of states is not expected, nor does it have the capacity, to handle the world order agenda or to promote humane values on a planetary scale.

Similarly, "the people", as a whole, carry no such vision at the center of their experience. Their preoccupations tend to be immediate, although not necessarily secular or materialistic. Their larger concerns are associated with nationalist or sectarian religious fervor, two forces that intensify the fracturing of the human community, although possibly playing out positive historical roles in specific situations, as in anti-imperial and human rights settings. There are many intense conflicts in the world between a dominant nationalism that controls the apparatus of state power and peoples without states that seek to establish conditions for the realization of their nationhood. In the developed countries, concerns with global reform are often very ephemeral, associated with surges of anxiety about war and/or economic collapse and of fear directed at enemies. And as national revolutions in a variety of settings have exhibited, the oppressed can quickly adopt the role and even the literal trappings of the oppressor. Indeed, recent empirical studies suggest that mass opinion is generally favorable to hierarchy and violence in political life, not very committed to democracy and human rights, especially for others.[6] The simplistic politics of "power to the people" provides no normative assurance that a better civic order or more enlightened view of international relations would emerge.

At the same time, those mass movements animated by purely normative concerns such as the various peace movements of recent decades have quickly fizzled out, and appear to lack either the tactics of sustained struggle or a sufficiency of commitment. If we examine successful social movements that transformed unfavorable power balances, we find they possessed certain common features: a vision of a promised land; a leadership dedicated unto death; a set of tactics that produced illuminating encounters with the established order and resulted in some kind of blood sacrifice; a widely endorsed moral passion; and developments that weakened the old order in decisive respects and made its maintenance appear impractical or illegitimate to an expanding constituency of its former upholders. Movements against slavery, royalism, and colonialism are illustrative of this pattern, as are such struggles as culminated in the Russian (October) Revolution and the establishment of the state of Israel. The anti-apartheid movement is currently proceeding along the path to success. By and large, peace movements, or movements avowedly dedicated to global reform, have been led out of a conviction that a better system is possible, desirable, and necessary. Such concerns have been largely abstract and have not elicited blood sacrifices or even a willingness to take personal risks from followers, at least until very recently. World federalism is a typical instance of a failed social movement.

There are two constructive forms of political activity that are rooted in the same transformative consciousness, but represent different time frames and, often, distinct political sensibilities. The first is concerned with testing the political space *within* and *among* states by imaginative challenges designed to defend against encroachment, roll back existing encroachments, or discover liberated space. Characteristically, this emphasis regards the existing arrangement of states as a framework within which politics as the art of the possible must be practiced. A more transformative perspective is, however, not precluded from acting in the here and now, either to avoid catastrophe or to see the future in the present. Also, some who direct their energies at existing arrangements subscribe to a theory of gradualism believing that shifts in quality are best promoted by a series of shifts in quantity.

The second type of activity is concerned with creating a new setting for politics based on the predicates of a citizenship of pilgrimage. The basic claim here is that a civilizational sea change can occur and is occurring at the level of behavior and culture, thereby providing a new ground for political arrangements.[7] "Freedom" is historically exemplified by renouncing the *constraints* of membership in a state, not membership itself, and acting as if one already enjoyed the rights and duties of a citizen of "the promised land".

	Normative Space in the State System	Predicates of a Citizenship of Pilgrimage
Resisting Encroachment	√ √ √	√ √
Rolling Back Encroachment	√ √	√
Enhancement	√	√ √ √
Revitalization of Democracy	√	√ √ √ √
Revitalization of Religion and Culture	√ √	√ √ √ √ √
Imaging the Future	√ √ √	√ √ √ √ √ √

√ = unit of emphasis

FIGURE 1. Fields for action

Figure 1 summarizes and schematizes these thoughts in a crude and preliminary fashion. There is an effort to draw a line between working within the existing framework and acting within a new one appropriate for a pluralist, yet global, civilization. Yet it is clear acting on either side of the line implies the other. To act effectively against militarization in the current context implies a commitment to the possibility of eventual peace and harmony; whereas the commitment to the future will be empty unless it produces concrete deeds, even if only of the imagination, in the present ferment of contradictory forces. It should be emphasized that this "field of action" is conceived of in this paper only with respect to the vital political encounter between the state and an array of social movements, and then only in an illustrative manner.

II. Social movements and the behavior of states

Aside from studies of the international implications of national revolutions, there has been little serious attention devoted to the interplay between social movements and the overall behavior of states. There has, of course, been work done on a sectoral basis, either through the study of a particular organizational vehicle for a social movement (e.g. Amnesty International in the area of human rights) or of the impact of a social movement on some given international problem (e.g. the effect of the environmental movement on the use of pesticides or on the establishment of ocean standards to regulate the discharge of oil on the high seas). But none of these inquiries has been conducted in relation to a wider concern with global reform, either its process or substance. Some of the neo-functionalist writing does set forth a conception of global reform, but not in the setting of social movements. Marxist theorizing about conflict and change is also relevant as background, but it does not include any systematic effort to link social forces with world order.

In this section, some preliminary ideas are set forth on countervailing societal tendencies that are challenging the state and the state system on a variety of terrains. These normative challenges that can be categorized either by reference to world order values (peace, economic well-being, social and political justice, ecological balance, and humane governance) or by reference to "D^5" (denuclearization, demilitarization, dealignment and depolarization, democratization, and development).

The term social movements is used in a non-rigorous way to cover the range of normative pressure mounted against the state from within civil society, whether or not it attains the organizational persistence and identity associated with a social movement in a rigorous sociological sense. The emphasis is what I have elsewhere identified as normative initiatives originating in the "Third System".[8]

Alternative exploratory perspectives are relied upon. The principal perspective is one of enlightened citizenship in a particular territorial polity. Here the question posed is what can be done within the state system, as it has evolved, to moderate its dangers and injustices. In a fundamental sense, this perspective is "another realism" to that relied upon by entrenched power-wielders, adopting a different calculus to assess short-term and long-term "national interests". This perspective is to be contrasted with that of the pilgrim/citizen who acts here and now on behalf of an invisible community/polity that lacks spatial boundaries, is not yet, and may never be.

The citizen/pilgrim perspective can operate as the foundation for very concrete action, but its commitment is essentially religious in character, not depending on any validation by the prospect of immediate results. The interplay, and tension, between these two perspectives express a dynamic that is experienced by each of us to some degree between the logic of thought and action in the state system with its short time horizon and bounded territory and the logic of thought and action in an emergent, but still inchoate, global civilization generally lacking in institutional embodiment.

The reference to a distinction between social movements above the line and those below the line is intended to express both a difference in emphasis and a potential complementarity in undertaking. Because the terrain is so vast, discussion in each category will be intended only in a heuristic spirit. More careful systematic work will be needed to follow up on all of these issues. Figure 2 summarizes the overall terrain as far as it relates to activities by those whose primary political identity remains rooted in the territorial state. Positive initiatives often cannot be restricted to a particular value zone. And there are occasionally value tradeoffs, as when arms control negotiations or *détente* are promoted at the expense of self-determination and human rights.

Social movements and societal initiatives act directly and indirectly. Their indirect effects may be to constrain or shape government policy. The Australian peace movement seems to have induced Prime Minister Bob Hawke, against his preference, to withdraw in 1985 his earlier willingness to allow the United States to monitor MX flight tests from a site located on Australian territory. Pressures can operate in adverse directions as well. Felipe Gonzales campaigned in Spain beneath the banner of non-alignment, yet as a socialist leader, reflecting external economic pressures, Gonzales has swung over to support for Spanish membership in NATO.

Resistances. Governments have political space to resist encroachments of various kinds. A dramatic recent instance was the refusal by New Zealand to permit the United States to use ports for naval vessels powered by nuclear energy or carrying nuclear weapons. This refusal reflected the influence of the New Zealand peace movement on the Labour Party and its leadership. David Lange, the Prime Minister and an anti-nuclear activist, has so far resisted United States pressure exerted on behalf of the coherence of the ANZUS alliance. Legislation pending in the US Congress threatens trade sanctions in retaliation, and American plans to terminate ANZUS are under consideration.

The United Nations, on the other hand, seems remarkably insulated from the pressures brought to bear by social movements to any appreciable degree. Its undertakings are severely restricted by the most militarized sectors of international society. True, the General Assembly has "resisted" by rhetoric such encroachments as those associated with the extension of Israeli sovereignty over the occupied territories, the latest excess emerging out of South African racial oppression, or such international outrages as the Soviet invasion of Afghanistan. Even this activity, manifesting the ethical consciousness of the world, has caused a backlash, including severe accusations of partisanship from its most powerful members, as well as withdrawals of support.

Direct resistance activities by civil society are of greatest interest for our purposes. The conventional expressions of resistance are those undertaken within the framework of legal action, and amount to appeals to the authorities. In the United States, lobbying Congress or an authorized demonstration are illustrative. More interesting and significant are those initiatives that pose the challenge in more serious terms, defy the authority of the state to varying degrees, and act out of the reoriented consciousness of the citizen/pilgrim. Resistance here is thus a symbolic surrogate in a time of danger for the real commitment to a transformed societal order. The occupation by English women of the area around the cruise missile base at Greenham Common is an excellent illustration. Their resistance activity was also an expression of radical feminism, exemplified by the way decisions were taken within the group and their commitment, seen in the daily round of their encampment, to an entirely different conception of authority and power.

A similar resistance consciousness has been mobilized by the small community in Bangor, Washington State, that calls itself Ground Zero. Their particular project is to blockade a naval base on the Pacific coast and to obstruct the train tracks that carry nuclear warheads as a way of opposing the Trident submarine, which the group castigates as a first-strike weapon. These activists have gone to jail repeatedly and have altered the outlook of important symbolic figures, such as the Archbishop of Seattle, a county prosecutor, and several workers at the base. Their outlook is a kind of amalgam of early Christianity and Gandhism. As with the Greenham women, these militants are citizen/pilgrims at work in their lives and activities in building the normative foundation for what amounts to a new civilization. Their specific acts of resistance are directed against particularly objectionable encroachments upon civil society by the militarized state, but their concern is to reinvent politics. They lack any confidence in representative democracy, political parties, and elections. Their initiatives are assertions of freedom at the grass-roots level, and center upon using the tactics of non-violent defiance and love to expose the illegitimacy of the violent state. The Ground Zero ethos seeks, above all, to enact in political settings the transforming power of love.

There are other substantive settings, of course, where normative initiatives are being undertaken. An initiative of particular interest in the United States is the so-called "sanctuary movement" organized by a series of churches in the southwest to provide sanctuary for "illegal" aliens, especially from El Salvador, who would face persecution and often execution if returned to their country. Here, the religious concern with protection of the weak has led these churches to defy the state and its cruel policies by offering individuals an alternative haven secure against deportation.

A final resistance context is one that exists in many states—movements for the protection of indigenous peoples against the seizure of their lands and resources, and the destruction of their cultural identity. The weakness and helplessness of these peoples has led to increasing efforts to build networks of solidarity across state boundaries. The organized international community, especially Unesco and the Commission on Human Rights, by way of a subcommission, has helped create an expanding societal awareness of the extent of grievance and of the urgency of organizing rapidly some kind of

Value \ Initiative	Peace	Economic Well-being	Social and Political Justice	Ecological Balance	Humane Governance
Resistances —governments at state level	Dutch referral of Cruise Missile deployments	Ethiopian disaster relief	Anti-apartheid campaign		International support for Nicaraguan Government
—organized international community (UN)		←——— Non-Aligned Movement ———→			
—social movements; individual and group initiative	Greenham Common / Ground Zero		Sanctuary Movement for Latin American refugees / Amnesty International Campaign Against Torture	toxic dumps / nuclear power plant sitings	Cultural Survival for Indigenous Peoples
Reversals —governments at state level	5 Continent AC Initiative / NZ refusal of nuclear docking privileges		←——— Family Planning Program (China) ———→		

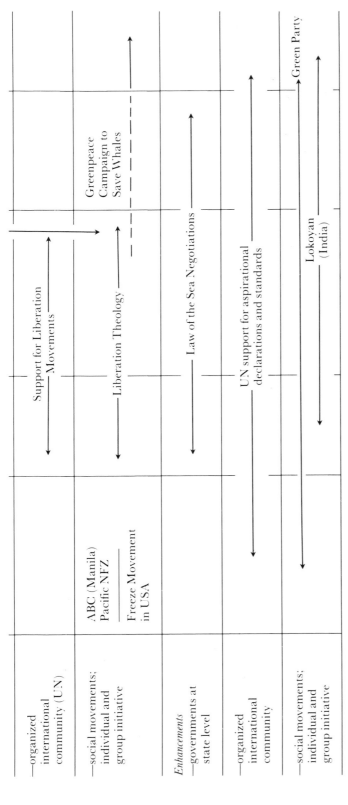

FIGURE 2. Fields of action

effective resistance. As with nuclearism, the issue here is one of survival. Also, the cultural orientation of many indigenous peoples is quite antagonistic to that of the state system. And even if the avowed goal is the recovery of tradition, an additional objective is to provide other models and images of humane governance. In this critical regard, indigenous peoples are prime victims of the existing order and living witnesses to the actuality of alternative orders.

Reversals. The distinction between resistances and reversals is not a sharp one. Particular initiatives often have both features, or can be understood from different angles. The usage is intended to differentiate between resistance to concrete extensions of negative processes and undertakings designed to reverse the process itself. Resistances refer then to "incidents", reversals to "process".

In this regard, the nuclear freeze movement is a clear instance of reversal. Its main political message to the state is "Stop!" referring, of course, to the nuclear arms race. The freeze does not devote its energies to specific destabilizing weapons systems being added to the weapons arsenal. Its tactics, although encompassing grass-roots organizing, have been mild, almost ineffectual, as if the state and the procedures and institutions of representative democracy are responsive to swings in public sentiment on basic national security issues. By challenging the modern state through formal mechanisms for achieving change, the message of the freeze is filtered and diluted, and hence less compelling—the final proposal calling for a mutually negotiable freeze. Leaving aside the merits of emphasizing the momentum of an arms buildup, rather than its most destabilizing elements, the pursuit of a negotiated freeze calls for a bargaining process of unprecedented complexity, one subject to all sorts of bureaucratic ambush in domestic politics by militarist critics of peace initiatives. The deeper point here is that reversals, as distinct from resistances (not building the ABM, cancelling given weapons systems) are very difficult to realize at this time.

Similarly, statist influences at the United Nations make it difficult for this leading set of international institutions to break free of the logic of highly conflictual and egocentric politics. The cynical evasion of "the common heritage" principle during the law of the sea negotiations, a result registered long before the appearance on the negotiating scene of the Reaganites, suggests how difficult it is to promote the common good, or even an enlightened view of longer range state interests, within the auspices of the United Nations.

To some extent, the anti-apartheid movement seems to suggest some normative capacity on the part of the United Nations to promote an initiative that would qualify as "a reversal". And, certainly societal pressures and a variety of anti-apartheid voluntary associations, have helped establish a political climate in which governments opposed to apartheid can occupy virtually all the moral space on the issue within the United Nations. However, the political and economic space is much more difficult to penetrate, much less occupy. South Africa's ideological alignment with the West, its strategic role in relation to sea lanes and vital minerals, and its participation in the world economy by way of providing trade and investment havens have inhibited up to now steps beyond censure on this one issue of agreed normative significance. The resulting gap between a rhetoric of denunciation and an operational code of acquiescence, even accommodation, helps discredit the United Nations on all sides. For conservatives, it provides evidence of "politicizing" the Organization, both because apartheid is emphasized while the allegedly worse practices of totalitarian states of the left are ignored, and also the whole history of producing a stream of resolutions is indicative of the UN's hypocritical role as a center for the dissemination of Third World propaganda. On the other side, liberals and progressives grow equally disillusioned because the main members of the Organization with leverage to act do nothing to make the moral repudiation of apartheid effective in political and economic spheres; on the contrary, they obstruct efforts to close the rhetoric/reality gap.

Social movements and individual and group initiatives are also thwarted when it comes to lending support to *reversals*. The more activist elements in society, being skeptical about traditional procedures for reform, concentrate on resistance against concrete threats at the local level; for instance, by protesting the presence of nuclear weapons or nuclear-powered ships at a local base. An explicit concern about global reform is restricted to matters of war/peace, human rights, and environmental policy. To the extent the broader agendas of reversal are promoted, the initiatives do not take off, as they lack an appropriate political perspective, and are entrusted to voluntary associations with limited resources and no capacity or disposition to mobilize personal forces in opposition to state policy.

The more radical expressions of resistance are often also motivated by deeper and more comprehensive visions. In these settings, as when individuals risk their lives to stop "the white train" carrying Trident missiles or to block entry into port of a Trident submarine, the animating political consciousness is strongly conditioned by the outlook of the citizen/pilgrim, even if not articulated in these terms. More explicitly, this sort of symbolic act of defiance, often at considerable personal risk and cost, is serious politics even if it has no prospects of overturning state policy. Its "success" is measured by the religious element of witness to the choice between good and evil and to the political element of delegitimizing statist approaches to the pursuit of national security. Its operating premise is a shared humanity and its hope depends on the eventual establishment of a political community that shares a vision of peace and justice *in time*.

Recent societal initiatives that seek *reversals* are multi-national blue-ribbon commissions on central problems of international life. Among the most prominent of such initiatives are those associated with the names Willy Brandt (on North–South economic relations) and Olaf Palme (on East–West security relations). A characteristic of these commissions is to make a radical statement of the normative problem, but then to formulate an action program that consists of a very modest series of steps. This latter tendency to tone down reflects the practical view of such commission members that there is no point in losing credibility with the main power-wielders, and that there is no way to achieve even modest ends except through the voluntary actions of leading governments. Unhappily, the results have been disappointing to all constituencies, mass movements tending to find the action programs technical and marginal, and the established leaders tending to find these programs to be less satisfactory than the status quo.

For instance, if we look at the "Principles for Action" of the Palme Commission we find general support for radical ideas of reversal, and even enhancement: replacing deterrence through armaments by a doctrine of common survival premised on a commitment to joint survival; support for general and complete disarmament. When it comes to concrete recommendations, their proposals are framed, in their own words, in pursuit of "realistic and attainable objectives" (code for achievable by way of leading governments in accordance with current outlooks).[9] These objectives are divided into short-term and medium-term measures. Under short-term are such measures as ratifying the SALT II Treaty, preserving the Anti-Ballistic Missile Treaty, non-deployment of mini-nukes and neutron bombs in central Europe, and so forth. These short-term measures are important, but restricted, types of resistances. For medium-term measures, proposals include substantial reductions in strategic forces of the superpowers (deepening the SALT process), establishing ceilings at reduced levels of parity for NATO and Warsaw Pact forces, agreement on substantial reduction of battlefield nuclear weapons in Europe, and so forth.[10] The intention is not to belittle these proposals, but to contend that they are too sweeping for statists and too marginal for transformers. As well, since these commissions are dominated by enlightened statists they have a natural preoccupation with appearing "realistic" and eschewing confrontational tactics. As a result, their contributions are to help shape public discussion, but not to restructure governmental policy. Both in composition, outlook, and working procedure (witnesses, staff) these commissions are hostile to revisionings of the future that form the core attitudes and political style of citizen/pilgrims. No consideration is given to civil disobedience or to the implementation of the Nuremberg Principles in the setting of reshaping national security policy.

Enhancements. As with the other categories, enhancements are somewhat arbitrarily identified. The intention is to consider those social movements, goals, and projects that are intended to make a positive contribution to the improvement of the quality of international life.

Because reversals seek to shift the energy of negative processes and enhancements seek to introduce new positive elements, important and extensive overlaps exist. Thus, whether the various global efforts to establish the unconditional immorality and illegality of nuclear weapons should be regarded as a reversal or an enhancement is largely a matter of judgment. Is the importance of such efforts by religious and professional lawyers' groups mainly a matter of negating the existing role in national security planning of the nuclear powers, or is it the positive establishment and implementation of the norms of prohibition? To conceive of a prohibition as an enhancement means that it is part of the process of establishing a "post"-nuclear world order.

Part of the reason to discuss "enhancements" is to emphasize the constraining character of the state system and its corresponding range of appropriate political identities. As long as one works through the formal, legalist framework of the state, even in a country that nurtures ideological diversity and political democracy, the inhibitions on normative innovation are powerful. For one thing, there is a general acceptance of the view that the militarized status quo is so powerfully entrenched that it can only be challenged symbolically and at the margins. For another, so many countries are linked to the world economy by ties of debt, aid, and trade that their sense of freedom of maneuver seems tightly restricted. In fact, the pursuit of enhancement almost presupposes a different calculus of action, one that proceeds from the worldview identified here as that of the citizen/pilgrim, that is, with an overriding commitment to the possibility and necessity of building a future political community that serves the well-being of all peoples. Citizen/pilgrims are loyal *now* to that future possibility.

For example, the commitment to general and complete disarmament (that is, radical disarmament) or to the establishment of international regimes for the implementation of the right to food are illustrative of substantive goals that are "impractical", given the character of the state system, but essential elements of an invisible global community organized to realize principles of peace and justice regardless of territorial identities. To the extent these goals are pursued by "conventional" political sensibilities and through orthodox tactics, frustration ensues, along with either disillusionment or self-deception. It is the sharp split between ends and means that creates the Sunday school impression that such societal initiatives for enhancement are not serious, lack any appropriate politics, and, finally, foster the view of most experts that only tinkering with the present order by fulfilling its most enlightened potentialities is worthwhile.

In contrast, citizen/pilgrims embodying their future vision in their lives and politics tend to be joyful and hopeful, despite their acute awareness of the militarized power of the state and the menace posed. Their means are adjusted to their ends both in terms of tactics and consciousness. Such an adjustment does not assure success, nor does it rest on an overly optimistic interpretation of social forces. Their strength and vitality arises from the spiritual character of the commitment and from the realization that normative politics cannot be practiced through the procedures of representative institutions. In that regard, there is a natural spillover between the pursuit of enhancements and the revitalization of democracy. Indeed, the revitalization of democracy is itself an enhancement, as well as an indispensable instrument for the transformation of the state and the state system. The adoption of core Nuremberg Principles as the basis for seeking redress from the state has an increasing appeal to those militants who qualify as citizen/pilgrims.

An interesting illustrative instance, here, are efforts to make political parties vehicles of state transformation. In Great Britain, there is a group of intellectuals within the Labour Party now trying to reformulate socialism in more communitarian terms so as to give the party leadership a new basis upon which to appeal to its electorate. Of course, opposition parties are forever seeking reformulations of their political appeal, but what is of immense cultural importance is the extent to which this enterprise of reformulation centers on altering the role of the state by way of strengthening the capacities of civil society to shape political destiny. Similarly, it is also significant that conservatives and neo-conservatives are often concerned with the same agenda, although their prescriptions tend to augment the state's military role and diminish still further its welfare role, whereas progressive critics call for precisely the opposite. Culturally, then, the state are at the center of politics of renewal at this stage, whether the perspective is left or right, and ideological debate is about the aptness of demilitarization as a focus for political renewal.

Enhancement can take other forms. In a more modest sense, institution-building at the regional and global level is illustrative. The creation of the United Nations Environmental Program as an aftermath to the UN Conference on the Human Environment at Stockholm in 1972 is an example of adding something new to world order on a problem of normative significance to the operations of the state system. In our judgment it is a very minor enhancement, not without some negative side-effects by way of pacification, that does not begin to give the world the kind of capacity that is needed to protect the environment against dangerous activities and practices. UNEP, with a restricted budget and the handicaps of operating within the UN system, can do little more than disseminate useful information on environment threats and protection, and even this role must be performed gingerly to avoid antagonizing the very powerful statist and financial interests that pose the most severe dangers to the environment.

Arms control arrangements and human rights treaties can also, on occasion, be looked upon as enhancements. For instance, the Biological Weapons Convention did spell out a comprehensive and unconditional regime of prohibition that has been accepted by leading governments. This enhancement has probably inhibited a biological weapons arms race to a certain extent. Whether it can succeed in preventing such an arms race, without other adjustments in international life, is increasingly being drawn into doubt. Similarly, the Genocide Convention in the human rights area helped focus world public opinion on this particularly outrageous form of statist behavior. Again, the legal arrangement does little more than register outrage, and provide some legitimated foundation for mounting a political campaign against a violator.

In sum, the subject matter of enhancement is preoccupied with the internal and international practices of states. Results are meager because the establishment procedures are themselves controlled, and virtually nullified, by states. In part, this reflects the absence of democratic participation in internal and international settings. And in part, it reflects the militarization of statist outlooks at a time when the overriding enhancement mandate is demilitarization. As a result, on the left of the line in Figure 2, there is not much political space for enhancement, while on the right of the line, there is insufficient power under present conditions to do more than mount symbolic, educational challenges. For these reasons, staying above the line induces pessimism if one is fully aware of the severity of the problems associated with the operation of states in the present world setting.

III. Transforming the state and the states system

Acting below the line shifts the emphasis to the citizen/pilgrim on a political journey of exodus and liberation in search of a promised land of renewal. The foundation of politics here is hopeful, as embarking on the journey itself, not reaching its destination, assures self-esteem and transcendence. By this reliance on the political imagination, entrapment within the confines of territory and violence associated with statism is overcome. The implication in territorial time/space of such a posture for the individual is militant, demilitarizing struggle, that is, active participation to achieve change by taking stands in tangible local settings. Though this is in severe contrast to the passive consequences of the militarized state for conventionalized politics where the functions of citizenship even in formal democracies are often reduced to empty rituals of voting, demonstrating, and petitioning, these rituals are not without substance for many states, ranging from Greece to Argentina, which have eliminated or restored the forms of representative democracy in recent years. That is, there is a wide range of disparity of political situations that is normatively important with respect to the extent of internal militarization within the territorial grid of the state system.

The degree to which a particular governmental apparatus adopts a militarized stance toward its own citizenry causes enormous differences in the quality of everyday life for various elements of the citizenry. As indicated earlier, no matter how vigorous societal democracy appears to be, the global dynamics of nuclearism (as well as of environmental decay and economic waste and exploitation) introduce unacceptable limitations on the capacity of civil society to exert its will. In powerful states, the doctrine and mechanisms of "national security" override the democratic ethos, while in weaker states, either by way of delegation (for alliance members) or by way of vulnerability (for non-aligned states), there is no democratic potential with respect to overriding issues of well-being. A similar dynamic exists, via the world capitalist setting, with respect to human survival and basic needs. The availability of food surpluses, beyond distribution on the basis of an ability to pay or purchasing power, is a matter of charity or geopolitics for the granary states. The various dimensions of environmental decay are also occurring as a result of an interplay of elements that are rarely correlated with the reach of the police powers of a given state.[11]

The entire flow of analysis suggests that below the line, states and the organized international community are resistant or immobilized with respect to our normative agenda, whether expressed by reference to values or processes. In this regard, the field of meaningful action is dominated by social groups acting out of the consciousness called here that of the citizen/pilgrim. This consciousness is also associated with such slogans as "think globally, act locally", a dialectical call for a non-territorial orientation and a grass-roots embodiment. The perspective of the citizen/pilgrim also draws upon ideas of the ecological ethos, the primacy of species or spiritual identity, and the internalization of holistic-thinking in science and culture. Implicitly, these developments produce an acute tension in the form of a direct challenge to the overriding notion of the exclusivity of the juridical concept of territorial citizenship—"think and act by way of the state". The citizen/pilgrim is less a *member* with rights and duties than a *voyager* with goals and aspirations.

Given the range of actual circumstances throughout the world, the specific form of embodiment of this deterritorializing of political energy will vary greatly from setting to setting. There is a natural disposition in the North to focus on nuclearism and the war/peace agenda, and in the South to concentrate upon the daily ordeals of poverty, indignity, and repression. Yet, there are important unifying strands: the various struggles are oriented around survival, but not only physical and material, as surges of fundamentalist passions make clear; the search for solutions involves recreating or circumventing the state; the attainment of power is not connected with the acquisition of military prowess, yet it is deeply associated with mobilizing for militant struggle. When South African militants carry spears and clubs into encounters with South African officialdom, there is manifested both vulnerability to firepower and a will to prevail at any cost.

Whether the participants in these survival struggles are implicitly part of an emergent social movement for global reform is a question of judgment and interpretation. The position taken here is that the most helpful interpretation is one that acknowledges what exists, but does not overstate the case. In this regard, the designation "emergent social movement" expresses the actuality of what is occurring without claiming that the state or the states system is currently being challenged in a manner comparable to the ways in which the South African or Polish regimes are currently being drawn into combat with hostile societal forces organized for coherent action. The organizational vehicles of citizen/pilgrims are generally not yet connected, in visible and familiar patterns, except by way of convergent lines of macro-historical interpretation. The connections across time/space do not even exist yet on the level of awareness. It is quite striking, for instance, that communities of nuclear resisters that have taken shape in the main cities of the United States during the last decade are often out of contact with one another despite their shared agendas and similar tactics. Most of these communities produce their own newsletter distributed to widening circles of sympathizers and devotees who are heavily clustered around the particular locale. There is, as yet, very little effort to form even a national network, although some leading personalities (Daniel and Philip Berrigan; James Douglass) have wide, significant followings. Revealingly, also, the national media virtually ignores this activity even though it is widespread, producing more criminal trials and far longer imprisonments than occurred during the Vietnam years.

At the same time, there is a growth of awareness that is non-territorial (or at least non-statal). The European peace movement, although clearly differentiated on a state-by-state basis, has evolved strong mechanisms for transnational solidarity and identity, especially on a regional scale, perhaps most significantly within the framework of European Nuclear Disarmament (END). END is gradually also seeking to expand its own identity to incorporate the superpowers and the Third World. More significantly, the fulcrum of concern has shifted from resistance struggles (above the line) to revitalization of democracy (below the line), and has extended to solidarity with democratizing tendencies in the Soviet orbit as well as to the promotion of demilitarizing and democratizing struggles in Western Europe. This expansion of concern is also important from the perspective of conflict resolution. The statist mode, whether left, right, or center, is either to blame "the self" or "the other" for the perpetuation of conflict, risks of war, reliance on violence. The new radicalism, neither strictly left nor right, emphasizes the anachronism of statist structures and militarist outlooks, with their tendency to indict and negate a particular actor, thereby polarizing the field of action.

In contrast, the mainstream American peace movement remains overwhelmingly above the line in spirit and inclination, restricting its agenda in a literal sense, and hence easily disillusioned by the unfavorable relation of entrenched forces operating within the formal arenas of representative democracy. This "backwardness" reflects, in part, the one-party character of American politics, especially when it comes to fundamentals, as well as the related sterility of political discourse in a culture that rarely addresses matters of choice except in pragmatic terms of exerting short-run influence on the government.

The remainder of this section will discuss characteristic developments in relation to the three categories of transformational politics: revitalization of democracy; revitalization of culture and religion; imaging the future.

Revitalization of Democracy. For our purposes, the revitalization of democracy is not concerned primarily with the reform of representative institutions. Earlier we acknowledged that restoring some role for elections and parliamentary activity, as well as establishing a climate supportive of political parties and oppositional freedoms, can grant significant degrees of relief from the most oppressive instances of state structure. Our argument, however, rests on the wider perception that given the character of geopolitics, the nature of modern warfare, the distribution of resources and needs, the hegemonic patterns of economic penetration and interaction, and the deteriorating ecological setting there is only a limited distance that most governments can go, even if their disposition is positive. Interdependence is a powerful network of interlocking constraints that binds the spirit and will of political leaders, especially within the familiar pathways of political imagination.

Our sense of "revitalization of democracy", then, emphasizes an agenda that arises out of the realization that the state and the states system must be transformed so as to constitute a new problem-solving framework for international life. Manifesting this realization, by creating alternative problem-solving, or even more modestly, problem-stating frameworks, is the essence of this more esoteric type of revitalization. When Worldwatch Institute issues its State of the Globe Report, summarizing the dangers of current trends in food production, environmental decay, population growth, and resource depletion it is filling a knowledge vacuum created by the refusal of governments and international institutions to face the explosive consequences of their own far vaster collections of data. In this so-called information age, it is necessarily those actors with the best computers and data sets that are politically disabled from effective use of information, because they are confined by the problem-solving frameworks and interest patterns of statist structures. Understanding this need for access to information as a precondition for democratic participation gives the issues of secrecy, disinformation, and propaganda so much importance in our world. Actually, espionage, a preoccupation of the mainstream, is the most trivial dimension, amounting to little more than reciprocal patterns of information exchange among statist rivals, a process that is generally stabilizing, and as with most sources of stability is treated as "illegitimate", even criminal.

The notion of spies employed by civil society or humanity is implicit in Johan Galtung's speculations on these matters. Daniel Ellsberg's release of the Pentagon Papers, and subsequent documents on nuclear strategy, is symbolic and expressive of this need to violate state secrecy laws to enable civil society to know what is *real*. Incidentally, Ellsberg's initial impulse was to revitalize representative institutions and procedures by releasing materials to important, sympathetic members of Congress, but they turned out to be so co-opted or intimidated by the national security consensus that they demurred. Hence, to persist it was necessary to go further, to induce the main newspapers to take on the role, a task they undertook with great reluctance despite its eminent newsworthiness. And recently, in England, Clive Ponting won an extraordinary legal victory when a British court endorsed his claim that sharing information about the sinking of the Argentinian cruiser, *Belgrano*, with a Member of Parliament, was not a violation of the Official Secrets Act.[12] Like the incensed reaction of Nixon/Kissinger to Ellsberg's initiative, Margaret Thatcher has treated the whole affair as an outrageous betrayal—"I have never seen the Prime Minister in such a fury (one of her closest advisers said last week). Like a woman possessed, she could talk of nothing else and think of nothing else." Ponting, like Ellsberg, has resigned from government service, having been stripped of his security clearance. That the people have no constitutional right to know the truth in these modern interpretations of national security policy is an assumed premise, no matter how democratic the formal trappings of government.

It is by challenging these denials of knowledge and information that revitalization is stimulated. For this reason, the various sets of disclosures by former CIA, and now former KGB, operatives are so important. It is not only that they bring insight into the workings of the modern state, especially those located in the two superpowers, but they also dramatize the ineffectual procedures of representative democracy to assess controversial policy. Participation in democratic control cannot occur without transforming the internal bureaucratic power bases of states. In the meantime, at least it makes sense not to have illusions.

It is not only a matter of defiance. There are also creative possibilities to convert law into a societal instrument in the struggle to reassert democratic control over statism. Two quite distinct settings can be mentioned briefly. In one, citizens drawn from many statist backgrounds, come together on the basis of a normative tribunal, to establish a "Permanent People's Tribunal", operating within a framework of law contained in a "Declaration of the Rights of Peoples". This PPT has now organized 13 sessions on such diverse matters as Indonesian aggression against East Timor, repression under Marcos in the

Philippines, Turkish genocide against the Armenian people in 1915, Soviet aggression against Afghanistan, and US aggression in Central America. Governments accused are invited to participate, but they invariably refuse; nevertheless, their arguments are put forward as competently as possible by skilled advocates and by documentary evidence. A tribunal of jurors, numbering anywhere from seven to twelve, listen to the evidence and produce a reasoned judgment, usually supplemented in time by a volume containing the documentary evidence. The publicity attending the event, as well as the political education associated with the written materials, gives a certain prominence to an array of abuses that the state system perpetrates and ignores. The authority of the tribunal is derived from civil society (the people), not the state; its weakness (and strength) is that its judgments cannot invoke any coercive apparatus of the state system, not even that of the United Nations. The tribunal form has been emulated in other settings by the Green Party at Nuremberg a few years ago, and in early 1985, very effectively, in England in the form of a Nuclear War Tribunal. These various activities express, among other things, a loss of confidence in the existing machinery of government to address the normative failures of statism, as well as the legitimacy of spontaneous additions to "government" by societal initiative. In effect, the state is losing its monopoly over law-making, both to expressions of conscience (moral domain) and to counter-state lawmaking (political domain). It is an aspect of revitalization.

Another is an effort to activate formal institutions to take on excesses of the state. Here, the terrain is difficult as the state exerts considerable control over its component parts, even those that enjoy "independence" and whose fidelity is supposed to be directed toward norms and the well-being of society. There is an ideology of subordination that is one expression of militarism, taking the form of some kind of primacy for what bureaucrats call "national security". As with any other strong tendency, some countervailing pressures emerge. A variety of efforts are underway in different settings to induce more judicial and parliamentary activism, whether it be to keep foreign policy within the confines of domestic and international law or to establish some kind of oversight over secret or covert activities of government. A case in Vermont not long ago involved a group of protesters disturbed by US policies in Central America. They had been charged with criminal trespass against the office of their Senator and defended their actions, in part, as *necessary* to induce their representative to take steps to end a course of foreign policy they believed to be illegal. Invoking the Nuremberg Obligation as a justification, the judge charged the jury that if they believed the defendants acted out of a sincere conviction that what they were doing was necessary to end violations of international law, then they could be acquitted. They were acquitted, and the outcome celebrated even by the leading conservative newspaper of the state as a kind of victory by Vermont over Washington. These are admittedly small sparks, but they express a weakening capacity on the part of the state to obtain the services and resources of the citizenry to carry out its dirty work.

Revitalization also depends on new forms of self-reliance, at all levels of society and in most sectors. Such a generalization does not suggest that in some settings intervention by the state may reduce or even overcome local forms of oppression, especially restricting certain extremist behavior that may enjoy pockets of local strength (for instance, the emergence of neo-Nazism in West Germany). Yet, from matters of environmental policy to those of human rights, revitalization depends on initiative at or beyond the boundary of the law. When Kim Dae Jung returned to his native South Korea last month, an accompanying delegation of prominent Americans acted both to deter abuse against Mr Kim, but also to disclose, beyond any ambiguity, the crude character of Chun Doo Hwan's regime in Seoul, despite elaborate public relations efforts to sell it as engaged in a liberalizing process.

When individuals or groups break the law to oppose dangerous weapons deployments they are doing more than resisting. They are exploring new forms of citizen participation under conditions of altered oppression. Also, they are turning their back, for these purposes at least, on the forms of participation that are available, and expressing the societal need for effective modes of redress.

At this stage, ending deference to unconditional state authority is itself of great importance. It is the beginning of freedom and responsibility. Freedom emerges because it becomes evident that creative initiatives for confronting and dealing with the worst of problems exists, and because freedom is discovered, responsibility follows. To the extent this orientation spreads, the climate for a movement of democratic opposition will take shape. It is now in that stage of waiting to be born.

Cultural and Religious Revitalization. The deeper foundations of governance are established by cultural and religious forces, and if these forces shift their ground, the political (and economic) foundations can be decisively shaken, shattering structures of apparent power and authority. The illusion of dominance associated with the Shah's Iran is an important illustration of this dynamic of change. It seemed hardly plausible that the unarmed tattered followers of Shi'ism, demonstrating beneath the image of a then obscure ayatollah living in exile for years in a remote village in Iraq, could challenge the modernized and extensive apparatus of military and political power developed by the Shah's regime to keep all elements of opposition weak, divided, intimated. Of course, if this challenge is mounted by a violence-prone fundamentalism that seeks to invert, and even intensify, the relation of state and society, then the outcome is not an occasion for celebration.

At present, I think, in all major civilizations there are social movements of varying strengths and perspectives that are raising basic doubts about the adequacy of the normative groundings of statism. A broad dedication to an expanded view of human rights is central to many of these more specific agendas of particular constituencies of victims. Four such agendas are especially important because their specific agendas call for the general reconstruction of state/society relations in a positive direction: those of women, of indigenous peoples, of those seeking racial liberation, of those dedicated to ecological balance.

Women. Women, to grasp their oppression, are led to reconsider, and then to recreate the basic myth structures of the civilization. To the extent that sexism arises from a profound hegemony woven into civilization at all levels, it justifies the critique of patriarchy as underlying diverse forms of exploitation, as well as a hierarchical manner of coercing and establishing authority. In this regard, the cultural demands of feminism extend, then, beyond reformist steps to achieve equality within the existing order, to the most basic forms of violence and abuse, especially as embodied in "the war game". The prominence of women in recent stages of the peace movement, as well as the expressions of feminine creativity, suggest that the most radical women are moving beyond strictly gender issues to provide an alternative vision of order, security, and conflict resolution to that contained in realist dogma now providing ideological sustenance for the state system. The tactics and social forms evolved at Greenham Common reveal this drive to include a broad cultural revisioning as the core identity of the women's movement. Of course, sectarian, and even fundamentalist, energies are also at work, making it uncertain as to whether this source of cultural creativity will be sustained by women.

There are also efforts, removed from activism and militancy, to explore the implications of the women's awakening in works of the imagination. There has been a burgeoning of such literature from many, diverse viewpoints. One challenging exploration is Ursula LeGuin's *The Dispossessed*.[13] It bears the subtitle "an ambiguous utopia", and compares the patriarchal earth with a matriarchally conceived alternative society set in a harsh geography where resources are limited, but political violence has been eliminated from societal experience. The utopic elements are not overdrawn. New, painful encroachments on human freedom emerge, but in the end the normative choice is clearly made in favor of the new civilization borne of feminine imagination.

These literary gropings towards a new order both reflect and influence the shape of social activism among women. There are many varieties of citizen/pilgrim, although each is bound to a quest for a promised land organized around principles other than that of the state system, an invisible community beyond time/space calculations. As a result, each withdraws energy from territorial modes of identity and loyalty, thereby weakening the claims of the state in general, disclosing that other constellations of power, authority, and community might be brought into being and deserve our loyalty.

Indigenous Peoples. As with women, the deeper quest of indigenous peoples is only beginning to be understood. So far, the issues here have been treated mainly as ones of social policy and human rights, not fundamental cultural revisionings. And yet, as indigenous peoples form their own networks of social action they have gradually taken shape as a social movement with far reaching goals that run counter to the logic of statism. Here, too, the movement is very segmented, divided between short-term goals of resistance and longer-term goals of self-determination.

Throughout the history of the state system, indigenous peoples have been a principal victim. Their lands have been seized, their peoples killed or assimilated, their cultural patterns derided and challenged, and their overall normative status deprecated as "inferior" or even "barbaric". The life style of indigenous peoples has been understood as a natural casualty of "progress" by dominant social forces operating through the coercive body of the state.

In this regard, indigenous peoples have been victims, but they also provide us with images of alternative civilization that are definitely more nurturing toward nature and perhaps more consonant with species survival in the post-industrial epoch. The worldview of indigenous peoples is less materialistic and possessive than what has evolved in industrial civilization. Preserving indigenous peoples is also part of a broader commitment to cultural pluralism.

These goals are antagonistic to criteria of efficiency and development that shape the outlook of most government officials. The struggle over land use and ownership is severe in many parts of the world. In most settings, behind the specific demands of indigenous peoples, is an assurance that their civilizations (way of life) will be protected against further encroachment. This protection seems secure only if it includes the authority to administer their own community without any interference from states or corporations. To the extent these positions win acceptance, political communities other than territorial sovereign states might begin to have an independent status in the world, augmenting trends toward the assertion of kindred forms of local autonomy (e.g. nuclear-free cities and zones; foreign policies for cities and local communities).

Race. As has often been noted, the structures of hegemony associated with the state system correlate closely with racial variation: within rich countries, whites tend to dominate non-whites; among rich and poor countries, the rich are mainly controlled by whites (Japan is treated as and acts as if "honorary white"), the poor by non-whites. Also, the nuclear deadlock has increasingly shifted the geopolitical conflicts of whites onto non-white battlefields, resulting in the concentration of warfare in non-white settings. Of course, the turbulence of decolonization has generated conflicts on its own, but interventions, and arms sales especially by the superpowers, has often increased dispositions toward war, as well as the magnitude and duration of political violence, if it erupts.

Whether the drive toward radical equality and liberation carries with it wider normative implications is difficult to say. Mere access to existing power/wealth systems by non-white leaders has not yielded encouraging results, possibly because cultural liberation has not been achieved. To the extent that non-Western cultural attitudes toward technology and human relations gain prominence, there might emerge a greater sense of choice with respect to the organization of the future.

Ecological balance. The spreading realization that modern society cannot take nature for granted has called attention to the normative and functional limits of the state as a problem-solving and policy-making framework. As famine spreads across Africa there is growing evidence that a downward environmental cycle of population growth, soil depletion and deforestation, drought, and food shortage has been responsible for an underlying prospect of deterioration. Comparable dynamics are evident elsewhere. Macro-environmental dislocations are also arising as a result of acid rain and air pollution carrying far from the original sources of activity to produce great damage to water supplies and fish.

The state, as such, is helpless to protect its territory and resources from many of these adverse environmental effects. The states system does seem able to produce collective mechanisms of environmental protection. Activist groups, operating with small budgets, are often able to raise awareness and alter behavior more effectively than can governments. The effectiveness of Greenpeace in protecting certain endangered species of whales from extinction is suggestive of what can be achieved by dedicated activists relying upon imaginative and militant tactics.

On a crowded earth, faced by problems of conservation of water and land resources, confronted by an array of global pollution problems, and beset by uncertain risks to global climate arising out of a variety of human activities, the case for some sort of global mechanism to identify and uphold the global/species interest seems powerful. To defer this adjustment until the demonstration is uncontrovertible is likely to mean waiting until environmental catastrophe occurs, and the underlying situation is beyond remedial action.

The main relevance of these concerns here is to underscore the inadequacy of the statist worldview to uphold human interests. It is partly a matter of establishing the inadequacy of the state and partly a matter of emphasizing the possibility of greater coordination across state boundaries. A global mechanism might be able to take advantage of computerized technology to shape policy through interaction among unofficial environmental groups spread around the world.

The relevance of religious revitalization to global reform is largely unexplored. At the same time, the perspective seems fundamentally important. The state, in part, appropriated to itself many of the attitudes and roles previously associated with the religious sensibility. Without overstating, the "worship" of technology and the unconditional claims to destroy on behalf of the survival of governmental regimes appears to represent a displacement of attitudes of reverence and commitment more properly expressed by way of a religious disposition. The passive acquiescence of ecclesiastical authorities to this series of developments contributed to the dominance of civil society by statist outlooks, especially in an atmosphere of political liberalism. In political settings controlled by Marxist/Leninist perspectives, ecclesiastic authorities were severely constrained, if not repressed, and religious activities discouraged, and sometimes punished.

Challenging the militarized state requires, in many settings, a kind of conviction and organization that can only be provided by religious organizations. The importance of religion as a mobilizing social force in Eastern Europe, especially Poland, in Latin America (in the diverse forms of "liberation theology"), and in the Islamic world is beyond serious doubt. In liberal societies, as well, there are signs that ecclesiastical leaders are prepared to confront the state on basic issues of societal policy: reliance on nuclear weaponry; responsibility for poverty; attitudes toward "life" and "death". The programmatic content and ideological lineage of these encounters varies, but there is a shared realization that the quality of life in civil society depends on challenging and transforming the state on the basis of some avowed normative goals. Whether the challenge is more a matter of imposing a fundamentalist creed upon a pluralist civilization or a matter of demilitarizing liberation varies from case to case.

Amid this ferment may be the elements of new religious formations more responsive to the visions of justice associated with the cultural revisionings discussed earlier in this section. More explicitly, we may be witnessing the preliminary stages in the formation of a religion that is centered upon feminine symbolism, resting upon a humanist and ecological tablet of commandments. It may be that the various citizen/pilgrims will begin to formulate the outlines of their sense of a promised land and begin to plan an exodus from the oppressive structures of statism. As we have suggested, this journey may not require traveling through space, but only acting upon the mandate to reconstitute political community for the sake of "the small" and "the large", reconciling individualism, pluralism, and universalism.

Imaging the Future. Marx regarded the attempt to describe the promised land as an indulgence, a species of moralizing. The real work of revolutionary thought was to mobilize social forces against the existing order. True, mere Utopian musing, as associated in his day with "Utopian socialists", were not clear about the need to transform power structures of the old order by means of struggle. Without struggle nothing happens, except provisionally, so that in isolated pockets of civil society harmless social experiments may be allowed to flourish.

But this Marxist bias against normative futurism has harmed the project for societal reconstruction. By its insistence on negation of the dominant class and its uncritical confidence that the oppressed class can provide a vehicle of liberation, the dismal destiny of radical politics in our times has been established. Orthodox Marxist orientations have tended to reproduce, if not accentuate, the patterns of oppression they earlier struggled against. The state as a cynosure of liberated energies is vested with unconditional authority and unlimited power to interpret, defend, and extend revolutionary gains. In the process, most forms of societal friction are extinguished as counter-revolutionary, including those intermediate associations arising from economic activity and religious belief. Nowhere are workers' associations weaker than in Communist states. When the state is presumed to be the vehicle of value realization, all forms of opposition become "criminal", by ideological definition. In Eastern Europe, those who work against the nuclear arms race or the bloc system through independent groups are treated in official circles as outcasts, as enemies of the people. Party bureaucrats insist that there is no need for independent peace activities since a state constituted on behalf of the masses is itself necessarily a peace movement.

We have learned, I think, that mere imaging of the future makes nothing happen, but similarly, that dedication to the acquisition of power may make too much happen. At this stage, following upon despair with existing arrangements and disillusionment with radical traditions, a particularly important challenge exists—to depict the emerging struggle, and yet to restore confidence that it is possible to improve upon current realities in dramatic ways.

As might be expected, the imaging of the future by those oriented toward the persistence of statism is unimaginative and unrealistic. It rests largely on releasing the positive potential of the existing instruments of change, especially technology. It is a future replete with artificial organ implants, star wars protective screens, computerized substitutions for labor and thought, new agricultures of synthetic foods, and even space colonies. It is a dehumanized landscape of automation, manipulation, and pleasureless leisure. Many technocratic futurists are infatuated with this kind of imaging of the future, taking for granted the persistence of political forms or structures, at least short of collapse through catastrophe.

In contrast, those whose consciousness is to some degree drawn toward the outlooks of the citizen/pilgrim are engaged, wittingly or not, in the work of non-technocratic imaging. Explicit undertakings along these lines have not been sustained for a very long time, nor have they been able to touch the direct experiences of those victimized by the existing order. Such undertakings, for instance the World Order Models Project, are gropings by way of intellectual effort in traditions of thought associated with rational and humanistic analysis. If one considers the antecedents of WOMP (world federalism) and its legacy, an emphasis on societal struggle, social movements, the interplay of local concerns and global aspirations, there is evidence of an unfolding theory that helps orient its adherents, as well as provides a tool for educating the young to be citizen/pilgrims. Its discourse remains inadequately adept at considering either the foundations of human action in civilizational and anthropological forms, or the dynamics by which unlikely, but desirable, social movements grow potent.

This type of intellectual activity, seen as a correlate to social action, can make important contributions, both by interpreting countervailing tendencies and by animating society with a hopeful vision of the future that is rooted in normative potential, rather than technological prowess (although no rejection of technology is implicit).

Imaging the future has to do with working out the implications of demilitarization (internal and international) at different stages, in different settings. Understanding the contradictory forces at work suggests a dialectical view of history. When the leaders of New Zealand, or Greece challenge the militarist policies of the superpowers, they both generate wide societal support and unleash a statist backlash by way of diplomatic and economic pressures.

One of the most illuminating forms of imaging of the future, is to study the lives of exemplary citizen/pilgrims who are at work among us. Their lives embody a refusal to be found by either deference or acquiescence to statism, nor do they wage struggle by reliance on violence, or even coercion. Fulfillment is related to the joy of community, not materialist acquisition. Their voices are often filled with prophetic warnings and anger, their call is really one for religious renewal, and a spiritual quest. Among those whose lives express such orientations we might cite Archbishop Desmond Tutu, Paolo Friere, Mother Teresa, Lech Walesa, Kim Dae Jung, and Petra Kelly.

IV. A final note

This paper has explored some aspects of the interplay between social movements and statism in our epoch. This interplay is obscure and very context dependent, varying through time and space. Despite this lack of specificity, some more general trends and possibilities are discernible. A broad framework has been tentatively set forth. The essence of what seems to be happening is an array of quests to overcome the oppressions associated with the exercise of state power. The torments and energies of an awakening civil society are pushing individuals toward the extremes of terrorism and spiritualism. Given the normative identity of this undertaking our emphasis is upon the political potential of spiritualism.

The present situation is confusing. The state and the state system possess a declining functional capacity and legitimacy, while obscuring this decline behind an intensifying reliance on internal violence and international war-making. Looked at in one way, statism is on the way out, in another, it is stronger than ever. More and more various civil societies are experiencing disillusionment with facets of the old ways, but have yet to comprehend the feasibility of full-fledged alternatives. Our task is to join in the work of converting this societal disillusionment into creative social action to overcome the menace and begin to fulfill the promise contained in our situation. Never has the dual reality of danger and opportunity been more deeply grounded in the historical situation than it is at present.

Notes and references

1. Petra Kelly, *Fighting for Hope* (Boston: South End Press, 1984).
2. Ernest Gellner, *Nations and Nationalism* (Ithaca: Cornell University Press, 1983), pp. 44-45.
3. See, for example, Lawrence Wittner, *Rebels Against War* (Philadelphia: Temple University Press, 1984).
4. See Dean Acheson, *Present at the Creation: My Years in the State Department* (New York: Norton, 1969) and George Kennan, *Memoirs 1925-50* and *Memoirs 1950-63* (Boston: Little, Brown, 1967 and 1972).
5. The work of the World Order Models Project is especially relevant in this regard. See Saul H. Mendlovitz, *The Struggle for a Just World Order: An Agenda of Inquiry and Praxis for the 1980's* WOMP Working Paper No. 20 (New York: Institute for World Order, 1982); and Richard A. Falk and Samuel S. Kim, *An Approach to World Order Studies and the World System* WOMP Working Paper No. 22 (New York: Institute for World Order, 1982).
6. A recent study is Harry Eckstein, "Civic Inclusion and its Discontents," *Daedalus*, Fall 1984.
7. One popularization of this view is Marilyn Ferguson, *The Aquarian Conspiracy: Personal and Social Transformation in the 1980s* (Los Angeles: P. Tarcher, 1981).
8. Richard A. Falk, *Normative Initiatives and Demilitarization: A Third System Approach* WOMP Working Paper No. 13 (New York: Institute for World Order, 1982).
9. Independent Commission on Disarmament and Security Issues, *Common Security: A Blueprint for Survival* (New York: Simon and Schuster, 1982), p.178.
10. Ibid., pp.178-181. In all, there were 20 short-term, 16 medium-term, and a few proposals for strengthening the UN Security Council and regional security mechanisms.
11. See Lester Brown et al., *State of the World 1985: A Worldwatch Institute Report on Progress Toward a Sustainable Society* (New York: Norton, 1985).
12. *New York Times*, 18 February 1985, p.A3.
13. Ursula LeGuin, *The Dispossessed: An Ambiguous Utopia* (New York: Avon, 1975).

The World Economy and Militarization

MARY KALDOR

Introduction

The world is said to be facing an economic crisis. What people usually mean by this is a process of economic and environmental degradation that became evident during the 1980s. Its main characteristics are well known.

Advanced capitalist countries experienced a retreat from the "Golden Age" of the 1950s and 1960s. During the Golden Age, it was believed that modern capitalism had found the secret of perpetual growth and full employment and that poor countries, by adopting similar policies, would soon be able to share the benefits of capital accumulation. However, from the early 1970s economic growth began to slow down and, by the 1980s, mass unemployment had reappeared. In 1985, OECD estimated that 31 million people were unemployed in advanced capitalist countries; in Western Europe alone, nearly one person in five is unemployed, many over a period exceeding their unemployment insurance cover. Moreover, poor housing, declining standards of health care, urban pollution, dying forests, dangers of low-level radiation from the growing number of nuclear reactors among many other factors contributed to a sense of angst about the future of the urban and rural environment.

Centrally planned economies also experienced a slow-down in the rate of growth. Imports of Western technology resulted in a growing indebtedness, most dramatically manifested in Poland. East Europeans began to experience rising prices, especially rising food prices, for the first time since the end of the Second World War, combined with stagnant standards of living. Similar environmental problems also became apparent.

Degradation for rich countries was catastrophe for poor countries. During the post-war period, growth rates which barely surpassed population growth were achieved on the basis of gross inequalities, massive social and cultural dislocation, and the erosion of the natural resource base of many communities, causing untold suffering and misery. Some poor countries, the

Commissioned by the Committee for a Just World Peace for discussion at their first meeting in Lisbon, March 1985. First published in a revised form in *Alternatives* XI: 4. This essay is based on research undertaken for the United Nations Subprogramme on Peace and Global Transformation.

newly industrializing countries (such as South Korea, Taiwan, India, Argentina and Brazil) as well as oil exporters, experienced more rapid rates of growth during the 1970s. But, in the 1980s, the recession in rich countries precipitated what is known as the debt crisis. This was an impossible burden of debt repayments affecting most Third World countries which began in the 1970s with the rise in the cost of importing food, oil and arms, and the availability of Eurocurrency loans, and accelerated during the 1980s with falling commodity prices, high interest rates, and declining markets for manufactures. Reschedulings rose from 13 in 1981 to 31 (involving 21 countries) in 1983 and a similar number in 1984. Each rescheduling involved the imposition of an austerity programme. In Mexico, for example, the IMF-imposed austerity programme of 1982 resulted in a real decline of GDP by 4.7 per cent, a decline in real wages by 16 per cent, and a substantial increase in unemployment and under-employment. As of 1985, the ILO estimates that some 500 million people in the Third World are unemployed or under-employed. A sample of 21 countries indicates that the number of unemployed has more than doubled in one decade.

Along with the debt crisis has gone the food crisis. It is estimated that some one billion people in the Third World are chronically undernourished. Third World dependence on food imports has increased. Soil erosion, deforestation, and production of cash crops for export, have also contributed to the vulnerability of large sections of Third World populations to natural disasters—bad weather, flooding, volcanic eruptions, earthquakes. In sub-Saharan Africa, food production actually declined during the 1980s. The famines in Ethiopia and the Sudan have finally intruded on world consciousness. In Africa in 1984, 5 million children died from hunger-related causes.

These characteristics of the current world economic situation amount to a reversal of what, up to the 1970s, was assumed, at least in affluent countries, to be an inexorable march of civilizational progress. This process has been accompanied by a growing militarization of the global inter-state system, characterized by increasing levels of military spending, an acceleration of military-technological change epitomized in the new Star Wars project, the growing influence of the military in politics, the increased intensity of the East–West conflict, and the increased number and lethality of wars in the Third World. Miroslav Pecujlic has talked about the concept of social exterminism, by which he means that the danger of the arms race lies not merely in exterminism, that is, nuclear war, but in the reversal of civilizational progress, what he calls "social involution".[1] If the process continues, millions of people will die by the end of the century, even if not a single nuclear missile is fired.

In this paper, I argue that whether we can overcome what is called the economic crisis, and whether we can ensure global survival and bring about more harmonious relationships both among humans and between humans and nature, depend on political transformation. Furthermore, dismantling the structures of the Cold War and militarism is a necessary precondition or component of such political transformation. This means that the responsibility of peace and human rights movements who struggle against the nuclearization and militarization of their own societies goes far beyond these immediate goals. It is a responsibility to the hungry, the diseased, the displaced and homeless, the casualties of war and natural disasters all over the world.

Capitalism and the inter-state system

The emergence of a global political economy can be traced to two interlinked features of what social scientists call modern society—the rise of capitalism and the emergence of the inter-state system. By capitalism, I mean the system of social relationships that displaced feudalism in Europe and allowed for the rapid accumulation of capital—a major increase in the size of the labour force employed by the owners of capital, in the amount of fixed capital stock (plant, machinery, equipment, etc.) per worker, and in technical progress embodied both in new skills and new "vintages" of capital stock. Capitalism was never territorially bounded. Indeed, the sixteenth, seventeenth and eighteenth centuries are generally known as the era of "merchant capitalism" or mercantilism, since capital accumulation was largely achieved through international trade. European countries made use of superior technology in navigation, shipbuilding and armaments to develop international trade through monopolistic trading companies. Nevertheless, some domestic capital accumulation also took place especially in England, France and Holland. Economic growth was achieved through specialization, by adjusting the division of labour to comparative trading advantages, as described by Adam Smith and David Ricardo. Technical progress also took place. This was particularly important in Holland, the economic leader during the seventeenth century. Holland had a well developed textile industry, making use of low cost peat and cheap canal transportation. By 1700, Dutch income per head was around 50 per cent higher than in its nearest rival, the UK, and only 40 per cent of the Dutch labour force was in agriculture compared with 60 per cent in the UK. Indeed UK levels of income per head only surpassed seventeenth century Dutch levels in the nineteenth century.[2]

In contrast, the modern state was territorially bounded. Nevertheless it was part of an inter-state system. States were defined in relation to other states. Territorial definition was possible because it was recognized by other states. Relations between states were based on an accepted system of norms and rules of behaviour which, along with the growing interdependence of the world economy, have become more elaborate. It was the development of an inter-state system that made international economic relations, especially trade, possible.

These norms and rules of behaviour were generally shaped by a dominant world power. The history of capitalism is also the story of a series of hegemonies—Holland in the seventeenth century, Britain in the eighteenth and nineteenth centuries, America in the twentieth. In contrast to the great empires of antiquity, however, the passing away of any one hegemony did not mean the collapse of the economic system. Hence the inter-state system was much more flexible than any previous international political system. Many writers, both liberal and radical, have emphasized this characteristic of the modern epoch. Christopher Chase-Dunn, for example, contrasts the inter-state system with the Roman Empire. He points out that, in Rome, "the necessity of integrating organisational forms within a single-state apparatus slowed the rate of organisational innovation and discouraged experimentation. Over time, the weight of the political superstructure became greater than the underlying economy could bear. Because the Roman system was so centralised, the demise of Rome also meant the demise of the system. It was not possible for a new centre to emerge to revitalise the mode of production and to allow it to restart its expansion on a new scale."[3]

The inter-state system was made possible because economic expansion was no longer tied to territorial annexation. Under previous modes of production, technical progress was extremely slow and economic expansison was brought about through the acquisition of land and slaves or other types of dependent labour, which were generally tied to land. Under capitalism, land was no longer so important. What was important was the availability of "free" labour (achieved through the decline in infant mortality and expulsion from the land) based on the wage relationship, the growth of markets at home and abroad, access to natural resources used in industrial production such as coal, cotton or iron, and rapid technical progress. Indeed, territorial annexation came to be seen as a regressive form of political expansion. Writing in 1833, Thomas Macaulay argued:

> It would be, on the most selfish view of the case, far better for us that the people of India were well-governed and independent of us, than ill-governed and subject to us; that they were ruled by their own kings, but wearing our broadcloth, and eating with our cutlery, than that they were performing their salaams to English collectors and English magistrates, but were too ignorant to value, or too poor to buy, English manufactures. To trade with civilised men is infinitely more profitable than to govern savages.[4]

In the late nineteenth century, the European states did, of course, revert to territorial annexation. But the "scramble for colonies" was a temporary phenomenon. Decolonization after 1945 was viewed as a way of integrating the Third World into the global political economy. Most international relations theorists, like George Modelski, regard territoriality as a "defensive response to the challenge of oligopolistic rivalry" which "consumes disproportionate resources and drains vitality from the global network".[5]

The global political economy, characterized by the spread of capitalism and the inter-state system, is inherently expansionist and exclusivist. Today, the entire world is parcelled off into separate nation-states and although many rural communities still cultivate their land on the basis of pre-capitalist social relations, and large parts of the industrial economy are organized on the basis of statist social relations, that is, state ownership and central planning, it is difficult to identify any part of the global economy that is not profoundly influenced by the dominance of capitalism as a way of organizing production. The spread of capitalism has given rise to extremes of wealth and poverty. Poles of capitalist accumulation, especially in the industrialized north, have extracted labour and resources from the global countryside, resulting in huge disparities between North and South, town and country, region and region.

The impulsive dictates of intensive capitalist methods of production both in urban and rural areas have ignored the balance of nature and the relationship between humans and their environment, sacrificing the needs of the future to the present.

This unequal process has been "managed", for better or worse, by the interstate system, which is similarly unequal. The modern nation-state is supposed to be a sovereign political entity in international affairs but its sovereignty is limited by the formal and informal rules and regulations that govern its relations with other states. Self-determination, as distinct from sovereignty, is only possible to the extent that an individual nation has a role in shaping those rules and regulations, and whether it has the right to dissent or withdraw from a particular inter-state framework on the basis of popular choice. Since, by and large, such inter-state frameworks are dominated by one or more core states, "sovereignty" or "independence" may merely represent a different, more flexible, mechanism for integrating the global system. In today's world, Nicaragua and Poland are but two examples of the way in which self-determination is constrained by the functioning of the inter-state system.

Capitalism and the inter-states system are mutually *distinct* but mutually *dependent*. In any system of production, in which producers and consumers are separated and in which production or consumption is collective, some form of relationship has to be established between producer and consumer and among producers and consumers in order to reconcile needs and resources, or demand and supply, to decide how much to produce, and by what method. In other words, production and consumption have to be organized in order to produce appropriate quantities for consumption. I will call this relationship *commensuration*. For Marx, the form of commensuration, based as it was on a particular set of property rights, defined the mode of production. But Marx confined this historic insight to the production of material goods, what we tend to mean by the economy. This may have been because it is only under capitalism that the production of what one might describe as state goods, or more accurately services—such as warfare, the legal system, and later welfare—is based on a set of relationships that are quite distinct and separate from the social relationships that characterize the production of material goods. Under feudalism, by contrast, serfs owed military service to their lords, in much the same way as they owed agricultural service.

Under capitalism, the form of commensuration for material goods is *economic*. It is based on the exchange of equal values represented by prices and wages. The existence of markets for labour and for material goods means that a process of social bargaining can allocate a price, representing, in the case of goods, the resources required to produce the goods efficiently and, in the case of wages, the resources required to produce efficiently the goods needed for the workers' subsistence. The worker becomes "free" in the sense that he owns his own labour. But since he owns no capital to buy land or tools or machines, he is forced to sell his labour. Thus capitalist commensuration can be described as a form of economic coercion. Changes in profit rates, reflecting changes in prices and wages, are signals for rapid adjustment in methods of production, quantities and types of output. In other words, the decision about what to produce and by what method is taken by the individual capitalist, who is constrained by his relationship with labour and with other capitalists, and this is reflected in the movement of prices and wages.

In contrast, the production of state services under capitalism is non-economic. State labour may be bought in the market, as in the case of the military sector, or it may be conscripted. State services are exchanged for taxes on the basis of various relationships ranging from consent to various forms of coercion, both ideological and physical. In contrast to the economic sphere, resources and requirements cannot be assessed with numerical precision. Adjustments or changes in the pattern of state production may be brought about democratically, through voting behaviour or political parties or opinion polls, or violently, through war and revolution.

While the social relationships that constitute the production of material and politico-military-legal goods are mutually distinct, they are also mutually *dependent*. The capitalist economy requires the state to guarantee capitalist property rights, to ensure free markets for labour and material goods, and to provide what might be described as a techno-material infrastructure— facilitating internal and international transportation and communication, access to raw materials, and so on. The state requires the economy to provide resources, taxes, loans, and labour, and as a source of legitimacy.

Because the social relationships that constitute the state and the economy are distinct, they evolve at different rates. Because they are mutually dependent, these differing rates of evolution cause major perturbations, such as economic crises or war. The problems caused by these differing rates of evolution are my major concern in the remainder of this essay. Of course, the state and the economy do not encompass the entire society, although my emphasis is on these two sectors. It is also possible to identify non-state, non-material forms of production, such as the production of domestic services or political protest. The social relationships that constitute households or social movements or cultural activities should also be taken into account.

This definition of the state in terms of the social relationships which characterize state production has two corollaries. First of all, it no longer follows that a society can be defined in terms of *either* its mode of material production *or* its form of government. The state is neither an instrument of the mode of production, as, vulgarly speaking, some Marxists tend to assume, nor is it independent of the mode of production as "realist" political scientists would have it. Rather, society has to be defined in terms of the interaction of these two types of relationship.

Secondly, this definition is useful in clarifying the nature of what are called socialist societies. These are societies in which material production has been taken over by the state. The state decides how much to produce and by what method. Insofar as the social relationships that characterize the state are more "advanced" than those that characterize the capitalist production, then socialism can be said to be an "advance" on capitalism. Capitalism was viewed as a progressive development because economic coercion replaced physical coercion in the sphere of material production. If state production is based on democratic consent, then this could be said to be an advance on economic coercion. If it is based on physical coercion, then socialism may represent a regression or, in the case where socialism replaced pre-capitalist social formations, at any rate, no advance. (Of course, this is a very limited definition of what constitutes an "advance".)

The global political economy has developed unevenly, in fits and starts. Recently, there has been a spate of literature and a rediscovery of earlier literature which attempts to describe and define these fits and starts as cycles in economic and political history, recurrent patterns of growth and decline.[6] Some writers have preferred to refer to stages, since this implies some sort of progress and some novel features in each successive cycle. Angus Maddison refers to "phases" in economic growth, periods which may not necessarily recur but which are definable through a set of identifiable economic system characteristics.

Whatever the appropriate term and whether or not these stages, phases, cycles or even waves can be measured or precisely dated, their existence can be treated as a stylized fact which is extremely useful for analysing changes in the state and economy. The study of long waves or cycles has resulted in some important insights into the causes of booms and depressions, and international stability and instability. Whereas the study of short and medium economic cycles has tended to focus on measurable economic indicators—movements of prices and wages, incomes and expenditures, etc, many of which are based on *ceteris paribus* assumptions—the study of long cycles has necessarily drawn attention to less easily quantifiable phenomena—new product mixes, changing production processes, the changing distribution of investment, etc. Similarly, the study of long political cycles has challenged many of the status quo assumptions of international relations analysts.

A comparison of different historical periods helps us to identify those characteristics of the global political economy which operate together; it is a way of defining the boundaries or the constraints on economic and political behaviour in a given period. With hindsight, it is possible to locate the phenomena that challenged the norms of the period and gave rise to radical breaks with the past. This categorization also helps us to identify the significant trends in the present that might not otherwise be immediately visible. Maddison describes a phase as "an orbit within which the countries are constrained to move. This does not prevent them from following different trajectories, but it means that their options are different from those they had in earlier orbits. Each phase has a momentum, which it is difficult to break except by some collective happening."[7] The crucial question is about what it is that determines the breaks in momentum, the shift from one phase to another.

In Table 1, I have used the term "era" and have roughly divided the nineteenth and twentieth centuries into three eras: the textile era, the railway era, and the automobile era.[8] I have defined six characteristics of each era, three demand characteristics and three supply characteristics. The first characteristic is technology, or perhaps more accurately, the material basis for production (on the supply side) and consumption (on the demand side). Each era is characterized on the supply side, by a specific mix of inputs, the intensive use of certain key factors of production, a specific labour process, and, on the demand side, a specific set of skills, and, by a specific mix of products, form of distribution, and process of consumption. The second characteristic is economic. It expresses the material basis in value terms—the price of inputs, the distribution of wages, salaries and profits, the pattern of expenditure as between private and public consumption, investment and trade, and so on. The third characteristic is socio-institutional. It describes typical forms of organization such as firms and trade unions, on the supply side, and households and states on the demand side.

In the literature on economic cycles, some of the most interesting theories focus on the notion of technological paradigms. A paradigm is selective and exclusive. Giovanni Dosi defines a technological paradigm as a "model and a pattern of solution of *selected* technological problems, based on *selected* principles derived from natural sciences and on *selected* material principles." Paradigms "have a powerful *exclusion effect:* the efforts and technological imagination of engineers and the organisations in which they work are focused in rather precise directions while they are, so to speak, 'blind' with respect to other technological possibilities." Dosi also uses the term "technological trajectory" to describe "the pattern of 'normal' problem-solving activity (i.e., of progress) on the grounds of a technological paradigm" or "a cluster of possible technological directions whose outer boundaries are defined by the nature of the paradigm itself."[9] Carlotta Perez-Perez emphasizes the importance of a key factor of production which characterizes each successive paradigm: cheap labour with the introduction of the factory system gave way to coal and steam, followed by low-cost steel, then cheap oil, and now the micro-chip. Associated with the introduction or diffusion of a new key factor are new "best practice" forms of work organization, lower levels of labour inputs per unit of output and the displacement of old skills by new skills, a new mix of products, new trends in both basic and incremental innovations, new patterns of geographical concentration and dispersion, and changes in the distribution of firms and branches of industry.[10]

Technological trajectories typically display an S-shaped curve with increasing returns to investment in the early stages of the trajectory and diminishing returns in the later stages. This need not necessarily be reflected in the movement of the economy as a whole, however, for this depends on the rate at which new technological paradigms replace old ones. In theory, capitalist production, via profit signals, adjusts continuously. But, in practice, the realm of capitalist production is confined by social relationships that constitute the non-economic sectors of society: households, social movements, national and international state forms. Capitalist production depends on these social relationships, particularly the state, to manage the social consequences of technical change, involving as it does sweeping shifts in geographical location, in deskilling and reskilling, in tastes and so on. It also depends on the state in particular to guarantee free markets, to free movements of resources, products and investments, to provide infrastructure such as roads and communications, and to provide a legal framework for companies and trade unions.

Technological paradigms are associated with what one might call

TABLE 1.

	The Past			The Future—The Micro-Chip Era		
	Textile era mid-19C.	Railway era late 19C. early 20C.	Automobile era mid-20C.	"Star Wars" scenario	"Eureka" scenario	"Dealignment" scenario
Supply						
1. Technology; mix of inputs, principles of production, key factors, materials, skills.	Cheap labour, factory system, use of steam.	Cheap steel and coal, craft skills, machinery.	Cheap oil, Fordism.	Micro-chip Neo-Fordism, deskilling, new white collar–blue collar divide	Same as US model.	Micro-chip, reskilling, individualistic programming.
2. Economy; value of inputs, distribution of income.	Low wages, labour-intensive.	Capital-intensive.	Energy-intensive.	Information intensive plus energy and capital intensive.	Same as US model.	Information-intensive, energy and material savings.
3. Socio-institutional; union structure, education, financial system, etc.	Individual entrepreneur, no unions, limited education.	Public companies, stock market and investment banks, craft unions, technical education.	Growth of multinational companies, big state companies, industry unions, higher education.	Same as automobiles, deunionization, use of women and ethnic minorities.	More emphasis on state enterprise.	Pluralistic forms of enterprise, municipal enterprise, workers' co-operatives, economic democracy.
Demand						
1. Technology; mix of products, pattern of use, values, principles of use.	Textiles, canal transportation.	Railways, capital goods.	Automobiles, aircraft, consumer durables.	Video games, office and retail automation, factory robots.	Same as US model.	Collective goods, environmental and welfare services and welfare, e.g., cleaning up rivers and seas, recycling, reforestation, healthcare, more leisure.
2. Economy; distribution of expenditure.	Cheap necessities, growth of commodity trade.	Capital spending, growth of investment abroad.	Private consumption and military spending; economic interdependence.	Same as automobiles.	More emphasis on welfare spending, greater protectionism.	Welfare and environmental spending.
3. Socio-institutional; household structures, national and international state forms.	Urban culture, break-up of extended family, liberal democracy with limited suffrage, free trade imperialism.	Growth of statism (especially Prussian and French models) scramble for colonies, Anglo-German naval arms race.	Break-up of nuclear family, suburban culture. Warfare and welfare states, Cold War, deterrence, US–Soviet arms race.	Individual alienation, inner city anomie, renewal of warfare state, US domination, Star Wars.	Welfare and warfare state, multipolarity with changing allies and competitors, multipolar arms race.	Family choice; accountable state with greater decentralization, international pluralism and co-operation, "Dealignment".

socio-institutional paradigms, specific types of firms of trade unions (on the supply side) specific household and state organizational forms (on the demand side). In the structure of these organizational forms are embedded biases in favour of particular paradigms. Patterns of demand are based on what Immanuel Wallerstein calls "pre-existing political compromises."[11] The mix between public and private consumption, particular combinations of products and so on reflects the structural bias of the state. Likewise, state support for infrastructural projects or for company and union legislation may influence the organizational forms on the supply side. James Kurth has described the "elective affinity" between the textile industry, on the one hand, and the family firm and liberal democracy, based on property suffrage, on the other hand. The railway era was associated with more centralized, interventionist and authoritarian state forms, especially in Germany, France and later the Soviet Union.[12]

These socio-institutional forms, in turn, cannot be disentangled from the inter-state system. The economic leader in each era also enjoyed political hegemony. The internal bias of the state was translated into an international bias via the hegemonic influence over the rules and regulations of the inter-state system. The free trade imperialism guaranteed by Britain during the textile era gave way to the imperial rivalry of the late nineteenth century which provided a protectionist framework within which heavy industry was developed, especially on the continent of Europe. Two world wars established American hegemony, the doctrine of deterrence, and the spread of the automobile era.

International systems do not adjust as easily as capitalist production. Indeed, some international relations theorists argue that the only mechanism for change in the inter-state system is war. Disequilibria develop because war is, by its nature, discontinuous. In the absence of war, the inter-state system is resistant to change. The socio-institutional changes required for a changeover of technological paradigms come up against the inflexibility of the state and the inter-state system. Even if individual states can and do adjust, they are constrained by the overall rules of the international political system.

In this interpretation, the crises that emerge in periods of change-over from one paradigm to another, as in the 1880s, 1930s or 1980s, are the consequence of the failure of states to adjust to changing economic requirements. Depressions can then be described as periods of disharmony between state and economy, booms as periods of harmony. This is not, however, to argue that states automatically adjust, that economic crises produce violent political crises, or that the kind of adjustment is predetermined by a particular technological paradigm. On the contrary, whether and how some new technological invention is applied and diffused and how future technological invention is shaped is the outcome of political struggles, which may or may not take the form of a major war.

The current economic crisis can be explained in terms of the change-over from the automobile era to the microchip era, and the disharmony between American political hegemony and possible alternative systems more suited to a new technological trajectory. What kind of adjustments to the inter-state system can we envisage?

The Cold War and the Fordist paradigm

The United States emerged from two world wars as the global economic leader, far richer and technologically more advanced than any other single nation. It was, as Noam Chomsky said recently, "a dominance with few historical parallels."[13] The Cold War sustained and reproduced American political hegemony and allowed the United States to create an international economic framework that favoured rapid capitalist accumulation based on a technological paradigm, which combined Fordist mass production techniques, the intensive use of oil, and a product mix of automobiles, aircraft and consumer durables. For convenience, we call this the Fordist paradigm. In other words, the Cold War and the Fordist paradigm were the defining characteristics of the automobile era or, as Maddison calls it, the "Golden Age" which he dates from 1950–73.

To say that the Cold War is linked to the Fordist paradigm or to argue that it provided a framework for the diffusion of Fordism is not at all the same as saying that the Cold War happened because of the need to establish an international political framework for the new paradigm. It is not an explanation for the Cold War. It is not my intention, in this paper, to enter the debate about the origins of the Cold War or about which side was most responsible. The Cold War has to be understood as the outcome of political struggles that were occurring in the late 1940s, to which, undoubtedly, organized economic interests contributed. My point is that, whatever the causes, the Cold War did, in the event, provide an appropriate political framework for Fordism. Nor is this to say that there could not have been other frameworks. There were other visions of the post-war political order, for example visions of a united socialist Europe, and, had these been put into practice, the technological innovations made in the United States in the pre-World War II period might have adapted to European and Third World political requirements in very different, and possibly more harmonious, ways.

This approach to understanding the Cold War derives from the definition of the State put forward earlier. The orthodox Western version of the Cold War presupposes that states can be analysed independently of the economic system. The notion of the Cold War as the struggle between freedom and totalitarianism is a notion of conflict between forms of government. The orthodox Soviet version, on the other hand, treats the state as a mere instrument of the mode of material production. The struggle between capitalism and socialism is thus a conflict of economic systems.

The alternative description of the Cold War as a mechanism for sustaining and reproducing American political hegemony encompasses forms of governments in relation to types of economic systems. The political and military dominance of the United States was established in the Second World War. By exploiting the fears of another war in Europe, and by identifying the left with the socialist world, it was possible to use the threat of totalitarianism to ensure Western cohesion around American leadership. The concept of deterrence, in particular, was, at once, supposed to prevent a future war and, at the same time, to serve as a permanent reminder of the last war. The militarization of Europe and the Pacific, the military exercises, the propaganda, and so on represented an imaginary global war in which Europeans and others were dependent on American support. It was a way of upholding America's military credibility in the absence of the actual test of war.

The role played by the Cold War in reducing domestic social tension and in subordinating "economic conflict to . . . common security interests"[14] has been widely observed. Kurth notes the way in which cold war ideology served to keep wages low in Europe:

> The low expectations of union membership, deriving from the privations of World War II, and the political divisions in union organisation, deriving from the anti-communism of the Cold War, were for many years the functional equivalent of wage-repression. The role performed in some Latin American countries by their own armies through authoritarian rule . . . was performed in Europe by the ghost of the German army and the spectre of the Russian Army.[15]

In contrast to radical American interpretations of the Cold War, especially Chomsky, I would maintain that the Cold War was directed, in the first instance, at ensuring the cohesion of the advanced industrialized world, rather than controlling the Third World. This is not to say that controlling the Third World was not important. Rather, Western Europe and Japan were potential competitors for control of the Third World. American liberals were concerned about the resurgence of economic nationalism; their vision of a united capitalist world was, perhaps, akin to Bukharin's concept of Super Imperialism in which the capitalist countries co-ordinate their dominance over the rest of the world.

There were two specific respects in which the Cold War provided a framework for the diffusion of Fordism. First of all, it sustained the prevailing political hegemony and enabled the United States to shape the international economic institutions that were established after the war and were based on the consent of the other advanced industrial countries: IMF, GATT, OECD, the World Bank, etc. These institutions established what might be described as a free trade regime guaranteeing the free movement of goods and of capital. Western Europe and Japan did adopt protectionist policies after the war but, especially in Western Europe, these were gradually dismantled during the "Golden Age".

The free trade regime applied primarily to the products of Fordist technology. Advanced industrial countries continued to maintain protectionist policies against agricultural products, minerals, tropical food stuffs, as well as non-tariff barriers against semi-processed products which were the main exports of Third World countries. In addition, protectionism on older manufactures—iron and steel, textiles and clothing—tended to be higher than the norm. Again these were the manufactures most likely to be exported by Third World countries. Nor did the free trade regime apply to the newer industries that emerged in the 1960s and 1970s and now seem likely to challenge the prevalence of Fordist products and industries. Information technologies, such as semiconductors, computers or telecommunications, are subject to a variety of non-tariff barriers, including patent and copyright restraints as well as "national security" legislation. Similarly, services, which represent a growing share of the national output and make extensive use of the new information technologies, are also subject to barriers and are not covered by GATT.

The free trade framework did allow for an enormous acceleration in what is described as economic interdependence among developed market economies and this, undoubtedly, contributed to rapid economic growth. Trade grew much faster than output as a whole. Between 1963 and 1973, trade among advanced capitalist countries quadrupled and these countries' share of world trade rose from 48 per cent to 62 per cent of the total. Foreign investment also rose rapidly and the global spread of multinational corporations was the most important form of technology transfer.

The second respect in which the Cold War contributed to the spread of Fordism was more concrete. Through the system of military alliances, through the determination of "security requirements", the United States influenced the internal biases of other states. A preference for capital-intensive military spending (rather than welfare), for oil and nuclear energy (rather than energy conservation or other energy sources), for roads and airfields (rather than railways) was built into the structure of the alliance systems. Through NATO, the bilateral treaty with Japan, ANZUS, NORAD, and the various arrangements with Third World countries, the United States contributed to the construction of a techno-material infrastructure that was required for military purposes but which facilitated the spread of Fordist technologies.

The Cold War would not have been possible without a parallel process in the East. The Soviet political and military hegemony in Eastern Europe established in World War II was sustained by the Cold War. The Soviet role in Eastern Europe was far more brutal and oppressive than the American role in Western Europe (although the American role in Southern Europe was more similar). This was probably because the Soviet Union lacked the ideological and economic strength of the United States. Continued oppression in Eastern Europe helped to substantiate the Western notion of the Cold War as a struggle for freedom.

For the Soviet Union, it is probably true to say that Western democracy and Western technology did pose a threat to the survival of the forms of social relationships that constituted the Soviet state and economy. The Soviet Union did need Eastern Europe as a "buffer" or a "security belt" but it was a buffer against Western ideas and Western products as much as Western armies.

The Soviet system is one in which the production of material goods is taken over by the state. The state guarantees full employment and wage levels, and determines prices. Consumers can express their satisfaction or dissatisfaction through shortages or unsold goods but these signals are not necessarily heeded by the central planners. Since there are few political channels through which consumer preferences can be expressed, the inertial tendencies which are to be found in all bureaucracies tend to prevail, except in violent circumstances such as revolution or war. The only sectors in which consumer preferences are heeded are those in which the state itself is a consumer, most importantly the armament sector.

The Soviet system is very effective in bringing about rapid capital accumulation within a centrally determined set of directions or trajectory. These directions were more or less established during the 1930s and 1940s. Rapid industrialization was achieved, based on technology imported from the West, with the aim, in Stalin's words "to create in the country all the necessary technical and economic pre-requisites for increasing to the utmost the power of defence in this country."[16] There was a considerable emphasis on heavy industry—iron and steel, and machinery—the product mix of the railway era. Fordist production techniques were also widely adopted, especially after the wartime experience of mass production of tanks and aircraft.

However, the Soviet system is much less effective in changing trajectory. It is, so to speak, "blind" in relation to other possible technological directions. Many writers testify to the absence of indigenous innovation in the Soviet system. Since decisions are taken at the top, technological creativity which can only emerge from concrete experience, is stifled. Indeed, local enterprises tend to be fearful of innovation, since it disrupts established supply lines and, temporarily perhaps, reduces quantitative output, on which planning indicators are generally based. In the West, unemployment and bankruptcy ruthlessly propel experimentation. In the Soviet system, enterprises do not go bankrupt but nor do they experiment. Innovation, if it occurs, is the consequence of high-level decisions. (This also means that innovation is more likely to be mistake prone.) However, because the internal administrative balance of the state tends to reflect the overall industrial structure, decision-makers tend to be conservative. Economic growth is achieved through incremental additions to existing sectors, through massive capital investment, rather than through the introduction of new sectors or new methods of production. Or to put it another way, the socio-institutional paradigm necessarily corresponds to the technological paradigm. There is no disharmony between state and economy but nor is there economic pressure for change.

In a sense, it could be argued that WWII did for the Soviet state what economic crises do for the capitalist economy. It provided a challenge for survival to which Soviet planners had to respond. The momentum of that period was built into the very structures of the state. Afterwards, the Cold War served to reproduce those structures. To some extent, planners have had to take into account American military innovation. And the examples of the atomic bomb and the ballistic missiles and other new military technologies testify to the possibilities for change in the armament sector. But, even in the military sector, innovation was confined within organizational forms shaped by the experience of war. The Cold War justified the persistence of these organizational forms and, at the same time, was supposed to avoid an actual conflict which might have posed a real challenge to the Soviet state.

Both the United States and the Soviet Union shared a common interest in strictly segregating the two spheres of the global economy. Stalin believed that the creation of a socialist world market was one of the most important consequences of the Second World War. The East European countries, notably Czechoslovakia and the GDR, provided an alternative source for Western technology, relieving the Soviet Union, at least for a few years, of the necessity of trading with the West. As the Soviet system was imposed on Eastern Europe in the late 1940s, so the Soviet Union and other East European countries withdrew or refused to participate in the American-dominated international economic institutions such as the IMF and GATT. The refusal by the Soviet Union to accept Marshall Aid or to allow Czechoslovakia and Poland to receive Marshall Aid has been interpreted both as a response to impossible conditions attached by the United States and as a desire to insulate economically the socialist countries. For its part, the United States, in the late 1940s, enacted legislation which restricted trade with communist countries and tried to impose its strategic embargo on other countries. The Coordinating Committee's (Co Com) international list of embargoed items is still, today, a cause of considerable contention between the United States and its Western allies.

A remarkable shift in trading patterns was achieved by the Cold War. In 1938, 10 per cent of the exports of East European countries including the Soviet Union went to other East European countries and 68.4 per cent went to Western Europe. By 1953, this ratio had been almost exactly reversed. Sixty-four per cent of East European exports, including the Soviet Union, went to other East European countries, and only 14.4 per cent of their exports went to Western Europe.

The Soviet Union and the East European countries achieved very rapid rates of economic growth although growth began to slow down from the late 1950s. It became harder and harder to achieve what was known as extensive accumulation, that is, economic growth based on incremental additions of labour and raw materials to existing sectors. What was required was "intensive accumulation", economic growth achieved through the introduction of new sectors, particularly automobiles and consumer durables, and new methods of production. This was a major impetus behind the renewed Soviet interest in *détente* and in trade with the West. This interest was tempered by the need to maintain control in Eastern Europe.

The segregation of the two spheres of the global economy was, paradoxically, a means of integrating the global political order. The existence of a separate Soviet system did not represent a challenge to the Western system, an alternative example to which social movements could aspire. On the contrary, it provided a legitimation of the Western system, a warning that could be used to divide and subdue social movements. And the opposite was more or less true for the Soviet Union. The existence of the West was used to legitimize the Soviet presence in Eastern Europe, the continued technological emphasis on heavy industry and armaments, and to explain the lack of political participation and the need to work hard.

During the post-war period, the Third World was brought into the inter-state system. Decolonization had allowed for a shift of hegemony from the European states to the United States. The Cold War provided a tool for maintaining American hegemony. Under the rubric of the Cold War, military and economic assistance was provided in large quantities to Third World countries. The Marshall Aid Plan was viewed as a successful example of countering internal subversive threats. The Mutual Security Assistance Act of 1951 was supposed to extend this policy to the Third World: in introducing the Act, Dean Acheson, then Secretary of State, said:

> Military assistance, from a dollar standpoint, is the largest single item of the Mutual Security Program. It is not necessarily and in every instance the most important part. We have seen how political and economic deterioration rot the fibres of military strength. And we have seen how political and economic recovery can contribute to an increase in military power . . . Security is more than a military matter. It requires action against all those forces which undermine the free world.[17]

In effect, military and economic assistance partially reproduced the US socio-institutional structure in Third World countries. Not entirely, of course. Some of these structures—the civil service, the armed forces, the education system—had been established in the colonial period. Moreover, the United States was more concerned with the structures of military and paramilitary forces and development agencies than with, say, parliamentary forms. It would be more accurate to say that military and economic assistance shaped the socio-institutional structures of Third World countries so that their internal biases or partialities were those of the United States.

This was particularly true in the case of the armed forces, which, in many cases, dominated the machinery of government. Indeed, by the late 1950s, the notion that the military were the spearhead of "modernization" or "westernization" had almost become a doctrine of US economic and military assistance. The Draper Report of 1959 argued that "the military in many underdeveloped countries are closely related to domestic affairs at all levels, from the man in the ranks who brings a scarce skill learned in the military forces back to the village to responsible leaders who may be an important element in successful opposition to communist subversion."[18] Military and economic assistance was used to incorporate the Third World into the political structures of the Cold War. This was not simply because it created pro-West or pro-East regimes. Rather, it was because ideas about political power, based on the East–West conflict, were transferred to the Third World.

Other advanced industrial states, including the socialist countries, shared these ideas of political power because of their common participation in the Cold War. It did not matter if economic and military assistance was provided by Western Europe or the Soviet Union. In the 1950s and 1960s, the Cold War imposed a cohesion on advanced capitalist countries so that the prospects for breaking the rules of the global political economy by playing off international rivals was very limited. The Soviet capacity for economic assistance was at this time small. During this period the United States was able to implement its own conditions through such devices as the Hickenlooper amendment, which enabled, and still enables, the United States to cut off aid to any country nationalizing US investments without compensation. Precisely because the United States dominated both the global military and economic order, however, specific conditions were not, in fact, so important. Aid did not have to be tied to US economic or financial interests. What mattered was whether Third World countries joined the global order.

Through military equipment, advice and training, Third World armies were structured to participate in the imaginary global war—the war that was supposed to take place in Europe or the Pacific and that bore a marked similarity to the Second World War; the war that reminded people, in case they should forget, who it was that had won the Second World War. Weapons like the F-16, the Mirage or the Type 42 destroyer are designed for war in Europe. Because they are considered important in Europe, they came to be viewed as necessary attributes of military power, regardless of the actual situation on the ground. In practice, these sophisticated weapons are not useful for internal repression. Nor are they necessarily appropriate for external wars in the Third World. But the process of arms acquisition and the institutions created to operate and maintain them, established a set of criteria for military power that was almost impervious to actual military experience. In other words, the spread of arms, alliances, treaties, assistance, etc. created a world military order with the superpowers at the top. Perceptions of political power were based on how well an individual country would fare in this imaginary global war. Since the war was imagined by the United States and the Soviet Union, it was clear who would win. By accepting the superpower version, Third World countries accepted a subordinate position in the political hierarchy.

The socio-institutional bias in favour of particular models of development underlying the Cold War was also important in the context. The military, in particular, as well as other Third World élites shared a commitment to rapid industrialization which aspired to the Fordist paradigm. The acquisition of sophisticated weapon systems created a chain of supplementary demands for airfields, roads, telephones, radar systems, repair shops, special skills, spare parts, and special types of steel and petroleum products. Similarly, luxury imports of automobiles or consumer durables created a pattern of tastes that influenced decisions about the style of industrialization. Rapid industrial growth was achieved in many Third World countries, but it was heavily dependent on imported technology, especially capital goods. Large multinational corporations played a key role in spreading the Fordist paradigm either through direct investment or through a variety of technology transfer agreements.

To pay for this type of industrialization, Third World countries had to obtain foreign assistance through grants or loans, or increase their exports of primary commodities. The consequent impoverishment of the countryside is well known. Rural producers were drawn into the money economy (resulting in a fictitious statistical increase in agricultural income) as more and more commodities were produced for urban and world markets instead of for domestic subsistence. Millions of people were pushed into the town as poor farmers were squeezed out by the introduction of more efficient methods of production, by worsening terms of trade between manufactured and primary commodities, by imports of cheap food from industrialized countries, and by the destruction of the natural resource base on which their livelihood depended caused by irresponsible dam and irrigation schemes, the use of untested chemical fertilisers the introduction of new strains of grain, or deforestation. Yet jobs and homes are scarce in towns where industrialization is capital-intensive and where big multinationals or state companies squeeze out more labour-intensive local enterprises. Criminalization, the persecution of ethnic minorities, and urban and communal violence are all aspects of this marginalization of human beings.

In effect, the North–South divide was reproduced *within* Third World countries. The absorption of often newly created Third World states into the rules and regulations, the etiquette, of the global political system was linked to the creation of Fordist enclaves which excluded the vast mass of rural producers; the global countryside was ignored and battered, treated as though it did not or should not exist. The modern version of MaCauley's vision of a "civilized" Third World in which third worlders wear our clothes, drive our cars or use our telephones, had another side to it.

The crisis of Fordism

From the 1950s onwards, US economic growth lagged behind that of other advanced industrial countries. In particular, productivity growth was lower than for any other OECD country. During the years 1950–73, US annual productivity growth averaged 2.6 per cent. This was very high by historical standards but it compared with an average of 4 to 6 per cent annual productivity growth for OECD countries as a whole and a startling 8 per cent for Japan. This relatively slow rate of productivity growth was reflected in the declining competitiveness of US manufactures. During the 1950s and 1960s, it was believed that the US could afford an overseas network of military bases and large amounts of military and economic assistance because outflows of dollars returned to the United States in the form of purchases of US goods. As the competitiveness of American manufactures declined, overseas dollars were increasingly spent on West European and Japanese goods. In the 1950s US foreign exchange reserves amounted to $24.3 billion, while the combined reserves of Germany, Italy and Japan were $1.4 billion. By 1970, US reserves had fallen to $14.5 billion, while the reserves of Germany, Italy and Japan had risen to $23.8 billion. In 1971, the United States experienced its first trade deficit since 1936.

The slow American performance was dictated in part by its position as the lead country. The diffusion of the Fordist paradigm simply meant that other countries were following the American example. It is much easier to catch up than to initiate. US enterprises were operating at what is known as the "best practice" frontier. Indeed, Maddison argues that US productivity growth is a rough measure of the rate of advance of best practice productivity. "The productivity acceleration in most countries in the post war period has . . . brought them much closer to the frontier."[19]

However, from the 1960s, US productivity growth began to decline. This is, I believe, most easily explained by looking at the stage reached in the technological trajectory of the Fordist paradigm. Markets for Fordist products were not growing as fast as formerly; improvements to production techniques were increasingly hard to achieve; and the key factor, oil, was becoming more expensive. There was, as it were, a new potential paradigm waiting in the wings, which would be based on new developments in information technologies. During the 1970s, the most rapidly growing sectors were consumer electronics (TVs, videos, home computers) and industrial electronics (numerically controlled machine tools, robotics, CAD/CAM). Initially, the United States took the lead in electronic developments, especially components. But the Japanese have made major inroads into both the components market and consumer electronics, while the Europeans have played a leading role in industrial applications of information technologies.

The emergence of a new paradigm was fettered by the inbuilt bias and prejudices of the American socio-institutional structure. American industry continued to be dominated by the giants of the Fordist era—the automobile companies, the oil multinationals, the aerospace companies—all of whom had privileged access to government. Government fiscal policy (military spending and tax cuts that allowed private consumption) continued to encourage the purchase of Fordist products. The dominance of the AFL-CIO and the pattern of skills and energy-use were all shaped around Fordist methods of production. Insofar as new technologies, especially electronics, were introduced, they were adapted to or grafted on to the existing socio-institutional structure.

Particularly important, in this respect, is the militarization of the American state. The growth of the military sector means that a growing segment of the social relationships that constitute state power is increasingly resistant to the democratic process. This is not just because of the vested interests or because "national security" is used as an excuse for secrecy and lack of openness in Government. It is also because the argument that funds are necessary for national security can never be tested except in the event of war, and the "experts" on what is required to prevent a war are themselves representatives of the military–industrial nexus. In effect, the growing militarization of the American state means growing rigidity and inflexibility.

The military sector is structured to win an imaginary global war. Because the imagination tends to be shaped by past experience and current organizational interests, this war is one which largely leaves the organization of the US military sector intact, much as it was at the end of World War II, in the heyday of the Fordist era. Military technology is often said to be the epitome of advanced technology, the impetus behind America's technological success. It is certainly true that the military sector has made use of radical innovations in hardware but these innovations had to be applied to missions established over forty years ago. Even the missions associated with the use of intercontinental missiles can be seen as extensions of the wartime strategic bombing role. Star Wars, the defence against offensive missiles, reproduces the thinking (and helps to create the mentality) of the Battle of Britain in an American context.

The consequences of this failure to adapt to the new technological paradigm are complex and expensive. The kind of applications suitable for the military sector are inappropriate in other sectors. Electronics enterprises complain that military work absorbs scarce engineering talent and distorts methods and styles of design. Star Wars, for example, makes use of super fast giant computers. The huge Pentagon program for Very High Speed

Integrated Circuits is considered to have handicapped American electronics firms in the competition with the Japanese for the very large scale integrated circuits required for the fifth generation of civilian computers.

Military technology has a special analytical interest because it stands at the interstices of state and economy. The demand for military technology is shaped by the social relationships that constitute the military sector, in which the main form of commensuration is war. But the suppliers of military technology are part of the capitalist economy, they respond to the relationship between profits and wages. They have to innovate to survive, like any other capitalist enterprise. But they do not have to reduce prices because of the nature of the market. Rather, their form of innovation is the perpetual improvement to products, judged by the standards of imaginary war. There is, moreover, no limit to their improvements because there is no limit to the imagination. This proposition reaches its apotheosis in the Star Wars Fantasy, which, quite literally, draws on imaginary film epics. It doesn't matter whether or not Star Wars works. "The Force is with us" says President Reagan.[20] Star Wars can be seen as a bid to confine the new technological paradigm within the institutions of Pax Americana.

If we are to understand the roots of the present economic ills, therefore, we must look at the American institutional bid for the survival of the Fordist paradigm. The new technologies, on this reckoning, do not displace but are merely added to the existing paradigm.

In August 1971, President Nixon announced the end of dollar convertibility into gold and a 10 per cent surcharge on dutiable goods. It marked the beginning of the end of the Bretton Woods system and a new form of protectionism. By March 1973 all the major currencies had abandoned fixed exchange rates. The United States took the opportunity of the 1971 decision to "go on the attack", in the words of Joan Edelman Spero, "demanding major unilateral concessions from Europe and Japan: revisions of CAP [the Common Agricultural Policy which discriminated against US products], revisions of the EEC preference system [which discriminated in a limited way in favour of the products of former European colonies], a halt in the expansion of EEC preferential agreements and a lifting of Japanese restrictions. As part of the monetary negotiations, the United States demanded a permanent guaranteed trade surplus. The unilateral US policy and the aggressive demands and threats led to conflict and confusion and threatened to provoke a destructive retaliatory response."[21]

During the 1970s, there was an increase in non-tariff barriers, in Voluntary Export restrictions on steel, textiles and even automobiles, and in anti-dumping measures and countervailing duties. "Managed" trade, that is to say trade allowed by agreements between states, rose from 13 per cent of world trade in 1974 to 30 per cent in 1982. Other measures that challenged the postwar inter-state system included the cuts in economic assistance that consequently increased the growing dependence of Third World countries on commercial bank loans; the shift from military assistance to commercial sales of military equipment; the end of food aid and the dismantling of US grain reserves which led to a rapid rise in food prices; and, of course, the oil "shocks" of 1973 and 1979.

The new forms of interference in the global economy coincided with the start of *détente*; 1971 was the year that Nixon announced trips to Peking and Moscow. Undoubtedly, this was a response to the political and economic costs of the Vietnam war. *Détente*, in the Kissinger view was another way of managing the two spheres of influence, a kind of guarantee of mutual non-interference. It was, so it seemed, a cheaper way of organizing world affairs. The new aggressive trade policy also included an increased interest in the markets of Eastern Europe and the Soviet Union.

However, *détente*, was contradictory. The 1970s witnessed a new-found independence in the foreign and economic policy of Western Europe and Japan, as well as a series of revolutions in Indo-China, Southern Africa, Central America and Brzezinski's so-called "arc of crisis". No doubt these developments had deep-rooted structural causes, stemming both from the new-found competitiveness of America's allies and the uneven nature of under-development. But the United States, having abandoned some of the economic and military tools of hegemony, was less able to manage these events. In an era of *détente*, when the memory of World War II was replaced by the memory of Vietnam, the imaginary war was a little less convincing.

It is in this combination of circumstances that the origins of the New Cold War, which began in the last days of the Carter administration, must be sought. The New Cold War was a way of redisciplining the capitalist world while maintaining an aggressive unilateralist economic policy. In the 1950s and 1960s, the United States could afford to be generous and create an international economic system to which the élites of other advanced industrial countries could consent. In the 1970s, the United States needed to adopt a more coercive approach. The New Cold War with its emphasis on nuclear and conventional warfighting, was a way of reinvigorating the imaginary global war. Reaganite economic policy, combining huge budget deficits with monetary targets, together with the export of monetarist philosophies, was a way of bringing about American recovery at the expense of unemployment and/or indebtedness elsewhere.

Put in this way, the New Cold War seems like a conscious attack on the rest of the world. It would be wrong, however, to treat it as a thoroughly thought out policy. Rather, it was a coming together of special interests, hit by the decline of the Fordist paradigm, and a vaguer angst about America's inability to cope with global upheaval as it had done in the past. The frustration that arose from the Iranian hostage crisis led the United States to look for all-embracing solutions. Military strength was easy and obvious. Blaming the "evil empire" had similar attractions. Star Wars is the latest offspring of this thinking. It insulates the United States from global troubles by making America invulnerable in the imagination. It takes us back to the 1950s, said Caspar Weinberger, when the United States was the only nuclear power.

The crisis in the rest of the world has to be related to these developments. Unemployment and economic slow-down in Europe can be viewed as a direct consequence of the new protectionism and, later, austerity policies. While the oil shocks did, for a while, provide a heady sense of commodity power, at least for a few Third World countries, which helped to propel the proposals for a New International Economic Order, the reality of arms sales, high food prices, high oil prices and, later in the 1980s, catastrophically high interest rates, undermined whatever precarious benefits had been achieved from the process of industrialization in Third World countries. The socialist countries which had optimistically entered the *détente* period in the hopes that Western technology would shift the trajectory of economic growth, found themselves heavily in debt by the early 1980s. Trade increased substantially between Western and Eastern Europe. But the difficulties of absorbing the new technologies proved greater than expected, especially when large ambitious projects were imposed from above. The recession in the West increased the problems of developing suitable export markets to pay for Western technology. Most East European countries found it necessary to increase prices as a way of reducing consumption to pay for these technological mistakes. The failure to fulfil economic expectations in societies that had been led to abandon political hope, created undercurrents of tension most dramatically exposed in Poland. These tensions may have provided reasons for reciprocating the American Cold War mood.

The economic crisis can be understood, therefore, as a disharmony between state and economy, between the inter-state system as it was established in the late 1940s and the changing requirements of the global economy. The New Cold War is a bid to reinstate the rigid bipolarity of the postwar years in a global economy of growing multipolarity and even pluralism.

But the directions in which the global economy is moving are by no means clear. They depend on political struggles now taking place, of which the Cold War is one. The second half of Table 1 outlines three possible scenarios for the inter-state system and the implications of each for the economy. These scenarios are what one might describe as ideal or pure types. Reality is likely to be a complex compromise between political forces, representing elements of each.

The first is the Star Wars scenario. According to this scenario, Western Europe and Japan participate in Star Wars research. Separate programmes for defending Western Europe and even Japan from tactical missiles and aircraft make use of Star Wars type technology. Hence, research and development in Japan and Western Europe is also geared to military applications. Thus more is spent on technological directions in which the United States has a comparative advantage and less on those in which Western Europe and Japan are more competitive. The United States uses its position as technological leader to limit East–West economic exchanges. Some American recovery is achieved, and hence there is more space for a renewal of global economic growth. Nevertheless, the Star Wars model remains capital-intensive and energy-intensive. It is incapable of recreating jobs or of taking into account environmental considerations. The Star Wars model does not command a political consensus except in the United States. It would be achieved by coercive methods: the ideological coercion of the Cold War which exploits continuing anxieties about nuclear war; the neglect of democracy in its fullest sense among the Western allies; and increasing authoritarianism and repression in the Third World.

The second scenario might be described as the Eureka scenario, after President Mitterrand's so-called civilian alternative to Star Wars. Mitterrand has rejected Star Wars and has proposed to develop similar technologies within the framework of a civilian European programme, although the technologies which interest him are those suitable for Star Wars. Indeed, he has proposed a European version of Star Wars. The Eureka scenario is a model of international rivalry, perhaps closest to the railroad era, leading up to World War I. Hegemony passes from the United States but is exercised by several powers in competition. Western Europe, Japan and the Soviet Union and perhaps even China participate in a multipolar arms race. This scenario would place greater emphasis on welfare and state intervention; perhaps it is possible to envisage the development of a social–industrial complex with growing capital-intensity in health care and education. The Third World would be victim rather than beneficiary of intensified power competition. One possibility is more clearly demarcated spheres of influence. Another is the abdication of responsibility. The Iran–Iraq war may represent a foretaste of the way in which self-interested states can learn to accustom themselves to holocaust.

The "dealignment" scenario, in contrast, starts from the reduction of the military element in relations between states. It moves away from the notion of war as the main mechanism for international change, even if only in the imagination. It envisages the revival and democratization of international institutions and, by implication, it allows for greater democracy within nation-states. It is a more flexible, less rigid system because it is less militarized.

All three scenarios assume that the microchip is here to stay and, in that sense, this approach might be considered technologically deterministic. But to assume that information technologies are going to be important is not to say that there exists a pre-determined linear direction for technology. It is true that we are bound by history, by the directions technology has taken up to now, and we cannot reverse that history. But we can shape the future direction of technology and subordinate technology to broader social objectives. There is no single way in which information technologies are going to be applied. They need not be applied at all, if a political victory is achieved by those who see no use for them.

It is in this respect that the "dealignment" scenario differs from the Star Wars and Eureka scenarios. Both Reagan and Mitterrand, in their different ways, believe in technology, in an abstract sense. Star Wars will give the United States the technological impetus it requires to revive the American economy—the difference between military and commercial or even socially useful technology is simply not recognized. Mitterrand believes Europe only has to develop the same technologies to prevent a technology gap from emerging, and Europe's greatness will somehow be reestablished. Neither scenario can bring back the "Golden Age". The increased degree of state intervention and the increased militarization required to sustain hegemony inevitably limits creativity. Economic growth may limp along on paper but, because it is confined to particular directions, the myopia with respect to resource depletion, unemployment, urban anomie, and polluted rivers and seas cannot be corrected. The "dealignment" model, in contrast, offers space in which social objectives can be identified.

Towards an alternative political economy

Both the Star Wars and Eureka models assume that long waves are inevitable, that we have to experience crisis and upheaval to get to the good times. Even if we suppose that US hegemony can be reinvigorated, or that the tasks of hegemony can be passed on to a collectivity of competing powers without global war, what happens in fifty years time? Even if a renewed bout of economic growth within a Statist framework, on much the same terms as the 1960s, is possible, at least in the rich countries and industrial enclaves of the Third World, what happens to the global poor, the alienated, and the earth itself? And even if the consequences of economic growth can be "managed" or tolerated or ignored, what happens when economic growth begins to slow down again and the rivalry between the core states intensifies?

An alternative political economy must attempt to break the cycle of manic capitalist accumulation followed by depressive phases in which the bits and pieces of society destroyed in the manic period are readjusted, pulverized, or put together again in ways that will hold for the next manic period. An alternative political economy must respect the fragility of human relationships and their relation to nature. It must attempt to establish more harmonious ways of achieving the social and economic changes necessary for survival.

At present, I have argued, the problem lies in the mutual distinctness and mutual dependence of state and economy. The social relationships that constitute the state, on which the production of state services are organized, are rather rigid and inflexible. The more militarized the state, the more this is so because a growing segment of the social relationships that constitute the state are not subject to any form of commensuration except for war, which is to be avoided. Moreover, a trend to militarization is apparent as democratic consensus becomes harder to achieve.

On the other hand, the social relationships on which material production is organized, are profoundly innovative. Propelled forward by the laws of economic survival, the capitalist enterprise overwhelms society in its waves of Schumpeterian "creative destruction". People, regions, families, forests and seas are ruthlessly pushed aside in the quest for ever faster accumulation.

The clash of inertia and change, the inability of a state to respond to the catastrophic combinations of passion and apathy aroused by "creative destruction", the immensity of the inter-state system in relation to the particularities of human problems, are both the cause of current economic ills and the presage of future disaster.

An alternative political economy must establish an alternative set of social relationships on which to organize the production both of state services and of material production. These social relationships have to be compassionate towards humanity and nature. They have to involve participation, co-operation, negotiation and compromise. Individuals have to have a stake in determining and controlling their lives but as part of a society which respects and cares for others. This is why there have to be state services, but it is also why state services have to be organized democratically. The state cannot "take over" the economy in a society in which state services are accountable to those who consume them, who may themselves be producers of material goods or household labour. And the same is true the other way round. Rather, an alternative political economy would be one in which there is no distinction in terms of social relationships between these different types of production and in which the relationships resemble neither those of the militarized state nor those of the capitalist economy. The term democracy can be used to describe this relationship but it means much more than parliamentary democracy. It means forms of co-operation at all levels of society, whether we are talking about healthcare, automobile factories, television programmes, legal services, or the balance between these types of production, in which producers and consumers co-operate to decide how much to produce and by what methods. The aim is to allow for change without dislocation, to solve problems without making bigger ones. How to bring this about, how to establish new democratic relationships domestically and internationally is the central problem of our time.

The essential precondition for an alternative political economy is, I believe, demilitarization. It is militarization that upholds the global inter-state system in its current form, not only through direct and indirect intervention as in Nicaragua or Poland, Afghanistan or South Africa, but also through ties of military dependence and through the discipline of the fear of war. It is the growing military component of state structures that allows resistance to popular demands, that can afford to ignore strong public expressions of opinion. And it is the militarization of the economy that sticks to particular technological trajectories that are "blind" with respect to technological alternatives.

To demand the demilitarization of international relations, to demand the "dealignment" of individual states, is not as Utopian as it may seem at first. Deterrence was, after all a public commitment to avoid war. The notion of collective security to avoid war did in theory represent a radical departure from the past. Deterrence was also a world order concept, that is, a concept for ordering and arranging the hierarchy of nations. But previous world order concepts say the balance of power, did not contain the notion of security as war avoidance.

President Reagan, in announcing his Star Wars programme, announced the end of deterrence. To innocent listeners, this may have seemed as though he was promising the end of a frightening imaginary war. In fact, he was announcing the end of war avoidance (by making the imaginary war less frightening) and this is what so alarmed European establishments. Star Wars has provoked a political crisis in the true sense of the word. Reagan has offered an opportunity to rescue war-avoidance from its link with the imaginary war, to propose new forms of war avoidance based on political co-operation instead of fear. But his plan also poses a risk that he will try to prove the credibility of the imaginary war.

Linked to the notion of collective security was a notion of democracy in international relations, even if this did not mean much in practice. The creation of international political and economic institutions did represent a truly progressive feature of the postwar period. Even if international economic institutions, like the IMF or GATT, are dominated by the United States and exclude Third World countries, the fact that they replaced national earlier institutions like the Bank of England and the Amsterdam Bourse, was, in itself, a promise for the future. Even military alliances can be seen, paradoxically, as a mechanism for governing on the basis of consent rather than direct rule. The establishment of the Warsaw Pact, for example, can be interpreted as a less brutal (possibly more efficient) mechanism for managing Soviet–East European relations in place of the more directly physical bilateral methods of the Stalinist period. The independence of Third World countries replaced direct imperial rule with membership in the inter-state system. Even though a variety of military and economic transactions insured the subordination of Third World nations, at least they were called "independent" and "sovereign". These fig leaves of democracy are not without significance. The problem is that individual states are internally structured to accept the global political hierarchy. Domestic transformation of states could potentially expose the fig leaf and make use of the theoretical possibilities for international democracy which themselves reflect a measure of internal democracy.

The third respect in which the postwar system lends itself to proposals for demilitarization is the rise of welfare states, that is to say, the rise of a significant non-military component of state social relationships in which the state, of necessity, comes into everyday contact with the consumers of state services. The existence of the welfare states has broken the connection between state interventionism and militarism. This is especially true in Western Europe where militarization has been internationalized through the alliance system, and where the relations between West European states have been demilitarized. Today, the advocates of state intervention in the economy and of greater welfare provision are also the proponents of *détente* and arms control. Those committed to the sway of the market in domestic and international affairs, the so-called monetarists, are also the Cold Warriors who have used military spending to attack the welfare state. Of course, within the framework of limited sovereignty resulting from the military alliances and other ties of military dependence, the accountability of the welfare state to democratic processes has also been limited. Forms of commensuration through voting behaviour and political parties are slow and cumbersome; they have allowed for overbureaucratization, hierarchy and inequity, for the use of the welfare state as a form of oppression rather than liberation. But in those countries where militarization and ties of military dependence have been less, the welfare state does seem to have expressed more democratic, flexible state relationships. Finland and Sweden are two examples which suggest possibilities for greater responsiveness to public protest and criticism. The degree to which these countries have insulated themselves from the economic crisis may well be explained by the relatively greater willingness of the state to respond to new demands, like energy care or the environment, and to encourage local and individual initiative.

The new social movements that emerged during the 1970s and 1980s can be viewed as movements aiming to transform the social relationships that constitute the socio-institutional structure, including households (women), the state (human rights), the inter-state system (peace), as well as the relationship between humans and nature (Greens). Whereas labour and peasant movements had been primarily concerned with transforming the relationships that governed the production of material goods, the new social movements are concerned with the relationships that govern the production of state services and human reproduction. The struggles of labour movements succeeded in questioning the notion of production for private profit and obtaining state commitments to full employment and welfare in advanced industrial countries, and to "development" in the Third World. But state structures were hardly questioned. It was assumed that state power could be wielded on behalf of the oppressed classes provided representatives of those classes won power, through elections or through revolution. In practice, the space for manoeuvre, especially at the height of the Cold War, was limited by international and internal institutional biases.

The new movements, especially in advanced industrial countries, are drawn from what might be described as the expanding technocracy which results, on the one hand, from the growing state sector and, on the other hand, the growing science-intensity of the economy. In Western Europe, in particular, peace activists are drawn from what is known as the "caring professions" which have expanded with the growth of the welfare state. Many activists owe their livelihood to the state and recognize the role the state has to play in modern society. But, by the same token, they despair at their powerlessness—the inaccessibility of the state, its imperviousness to poverty, social violence and the pollution and depletion of nature. They recognize the need for social regulation but desire self-regulation.

The new movements do not displace but augment more traditional labour and peasant movements. They are drawn from a narrow but articulate stratum of society, combining demands about the state and about technologies. But they cannot bring about the implementation of their demands without allies, allies with equally insistent demands about their livelihoods—their jobs, their communities, their water, soil, and trees. In Britain, the long-running miners' strike represented a remarkable example of the way in which a community struggle drew in new allies like the women's movement and the green and peace movements (because of nuclear energy). The strike was clothed in traditional labour movement language but it was not a traditional economic struggle. It was about the right to decide the future, a demand which is widely shared with the new social movements. In India the way in which support for local struggles concerning resources, the rights of ethnic minorities, or campaigns against bride burnings and communal rape have been linked through organizations like Lokayan, represent similar examples of such alliances.

The analysis of this paper suggests certain central demands which these alliances need to address if they are to move us towards an alternative global political economy. The point is not so much to specify the demands, which are already made by existing social movements, but to show how seemingly isolated demands are part of broader agenda for economic and ecological survival as well as survival from nuclear war.

First and foremost is the challenge to the structures of the Cold War and deterrence. This is necessary not only because these structures contribute to the dangers of nuclear war, but also because they uphold global power structures that limit the independence of any one state to pursue alternative development policies which, in turn, limits the space for self-determination and democracy. Dissenting from global power structures is, in the nuclear world, ideological. It is a refusal to believe in the imaginary war. It is dangerous because it provokes attempts to prove the reality of the imaginary war. It rests on an appeal to the commitment to avoid war. It cannot be overstressed that this psychological commitment, buttressed by popular sentiment, is the only guarantee against war. The problem for dissenters is that while continuing to imagine war weakens the psychological commitment to avoid war, as with Star Wars, the refusal to imagine war is highly provocative. This implies a massive change in human consciousness. "Dealignment" is a refusal to accept the ideological discipline of imagined war. Its only alternative is the democratic impulse.

The proposed alternative political economy is called the "dealignment" scenario, because it is only through the possibility of dissenting from the global power structure that we can adopt alternatives that depart from the rules and regulations of the inter-state system.

"Dealignment" comprises demilitarization and democratization. It is not just a matter of diminishing the military element in relations between states. It is also a matter of reducing the military component of administration and identifying new ways in which the state can respond and empower. Already, the new social movements have brought about political transformations—the reinvigoration of municipal government, the enhanced political role of women, the insistence on open debates about security matters, the creation of a transnational political culture which can potentially inform international institutions. I believe that we have to start thinking about democracy ambitiously: how to spread layers of power throughout society so that the nation-state is but one layer, one form of access, along with municipal, regional and global layers of power; how to increase participation in segments of power so that patients contribute to the running of hospitals, parents to the running of schools, unemployed to the social security system, tenants to housing programmes, to give but a few examples; how to ensure the balance of layers and segments reflects a balance of special interests, aspirations, and needs, in society as a whole; and, finally, how to ensure the space in civil society for a degree of autonomy to households, social movements, and cultural life.

These socio-institutional changes on the demand side correspond to socio-institutional changes on the supply side. If the organization of the state is to become more flexible and responsive, the organization of the economy has to become more stable and responsible. What is required is a set of democratic relationships that are organizationally distinct but analytically similar to the relationships involved in state production. New types of enterprise need to be conceived that guarantee employment, like state enterprises, but which are responsive to consumer signals. Schools and public radio stations, which now enjoy a fair degree of autonomy, are conceivable models. We can conceive of municipal enterprises or workers' co-operatives in which local citizens or specialized consumers share in management with workers. Decentralization and flexibility is made possible by the new information technologies. These new social relationships will then determine the shape of the labour process and the mix of products required.

Debates about economic policy tend to be debates about monetary phenomena, about the minutiae of taxation, types of spending, forms of tariffs, the level of interest rates, the price of foreign exchange, and so on. These debates are not unimportant. But unless they take into account the material and socio-institutional characteristics of the economy, their utility is limited. In the debates between monetarists and Keynesians, or between free traders and fair traders, I stand squarely on the side of the Keynesians and fair traders. But these are inadequate answers without fundamental changes in material and socio-institutional structures, as the experience of socialist governments in the postwar period has demonstrated. Keynesianism worked in the 1950s and 1960s because it allowed for an expansion in the demand for Fordist products. Today, military Keynesianism can work for the United States in the sense that it can produce short term recovery, and because US trade deficits do not matter as long as the dollar is acceptable. But for other countries, and in the long run, Keynesianism can only work if it shifts domestic priorities and is linked to international co-operation in coping fairly with imbalances of payments. In domestic terms, patterns of state spending have to be shifted away from military spending and private consumption towards welfare and environmental services. Indeed, rapid emergency programmes have to be put into effect to mitigate the immediate effects of famine, to counter disease, to build homes, to conserve resources, to purify water—rivers and seas and lakes—to replant forests and hedges and enrich soil, and so on. These programmes could make use of new information technologies. But they are likely to be more labour intensive and less energy- and capital-intensive than prevailing forms of current production. In international terms, these domestic programmes have to be linked co-operatively and associated with attempts to co-ordinate and plan flows of funds on a regional or global scale.

None of this is possible without a sustained popular mobilization over the whole range of demands. But precisely because these demands are inter-connected, they do not need to be achieved simultaneously. Dissent from the inter-state system, the transformation of state structures, changes in economic priorities, new forms of productive enterprises and indeed transformation of other aspects of social life—families, music, art, film, political culture—all feed upon one another and potentially counter the opposing nexus of the Star Wars/Eureka scenarios. What is important is that those who struggle to have their voices heard are also helping the struggles of those who seek life and livelihood.

Notes and references

1. Miroslav Pecujlic, "The Other Europe," paper prepared for UNU/TNI conference on *Europe and East-West Relations*, 12-13 October 1985.
2. See Angus Maddison, *Phases of Capitalist Development* (Oxford: Oxford University Press, 1982).

3. Christopher Chase-Dunn, "International Economic Policy in a Declining Core State," in: William P Avery and David P Rapkin (editors), *America in a Changing World Political Economy* (New York & London: Longman, 1982), p.78.

4. Quoted by James Kurth, "The Political Consequences of the Product Cycle: Industrial History and Political Outcomes," *International Organization*, Winter 1979, p.10.

5. George Modelski, "The Long Cycle of Global Politics and the Nation-State," *Comparative Studies in Society and History*, vol 20, no 2, April 1978, p.230.

6. See e.g., Robert Gilpin, *War and Change* (Cambridge: Cambridge University Press, 1981).

7. Maddison (Note 2), p.94.

8. Long cycle theories divide the period into four 50-year cycles with an additional cycle between what I have described as the textile era and the railway era, i.e. between c.1830 and c.1880. Also, my dating, which is rough, is somewhat later than other sources. This is because I have focused on the diffusion of a technological paradigm; its dominance in the world economy. In general, a technological paradigm develops in the lead country at an earlier stage. Hence railway building was concentrated in Britain in the mid-nineteenth century. In the United States, the great period of automobile growth was the 1900s and 1920s. See e.g., the dating offered by Ernest Mandel, *Late Capitalism* (London: New Left Books, 1972).

9. Giovanni Dosi, "Technological Paradigms and Technological Trajectories. The Determinants and Directions of Technical Change and the Transformation of the Economy," in: Christopher Freeman (editor), *Long Waves in the World Economy* (London: Frances Pinter, 1984), pp.83-84.

10. Carlotta Perez-Perez, "Micro-electronics, Long Waves and World Structural Change," *World Development*, vol 13, no 3, March 1985.

11. See *The Politics of the World-Economy: The States, The Movements and The Civilizations* (Cambridge: Cambridge University Press, 1984), chapter 10.

12. Kurth (Note 4).

13. Noam Chomsky, "The Evil Empire," *New Socialist*, January 1986, p.11.

14. Joan Edelman Spero, *The Politics of International Economic Relations* (London: George, Allen & Unwin, Third Edition, 1985), p.27.

15. Kurth (Note 4), p.28.

16. Quoted in Clive Trebilcock, *The Defence Sector and Technological Progress, 1890-1945: An Historical Model*, paper presented to the Royal Economic Society's Conference on Government and Innovation, Pembroke College, July 14-17, 1975.

17. *Mutual Security Act of 1951*, Hearings before the Committee on Foreign Relations and the Committee on Armed Services, 82nd Congress First Session, 26 July 1951, vol 65.

18. *Composite Report of the President's Committee to Study the United States Military Assistance Program*, (the Draper Report) Washington, August 1959, p.167.

19. Maddison (Note 2), p.103.

20. See E.P. Thompson (editor), *Star Wars* (London: Penguin Books, 1985).

21. Spero (Note 14), p.110.

High Technology, World Development, and Structural Transformation

MANUEL CASTELLS

I. Introduction

We have the privilege and the responsibility of living through one of the greatest technological revolutions in the history of humankind. It is taking place in the midst of a world-wide process of economic restructuring, and on the edge of a dangerous realignment of macropolitical strategies. Two major features characterize this technological revolution: it is aimed at generating and processing information; its outcome is process-oriented and, therefore, its effects are pervasive, cutting across the entire realm of human activity.

As in all historical breaking points of scientific advancement, there is a whole constellation of discoveries taking place simultaneously, according to an interconnected, self-reinforcing pattern. Some of these discoveries concern new products, such as special materials; others, the technical application of existing technologies, such as space navigation and operation. Yet, the core of the current technological revolution resides in the ability to generate and process information, and to introduce such a capacity into the actions and functions through which we work, produce, consume, manage, enjoy ourselves, live and die. Microelectronics process information in increasingly powerful, yet decreasingly costly, miniaturized circuits. Computers use microelectronics to process, and eventually generate, information at an even greater speed and accuracy. This increases memory capacity and broadens the range of accessibility from non-expert knowledge to the computing system, thus decentralizing and diversifying the information power. Telecommunications transmit and interconnect information, bringing together, at a decreasing cost, and with increasing carrying capacity, all information-processing machines (including human beings), regardless of distance and (almost) of time. Automation introduces pre-informed, flexible

Commissioned by the Committee for a Just World Peace for presentation at its Royaumont Conference, December 1985. First published in an abridged form in *Alternatives* XI:3. The author wishes to acknowledge assistance received for the elaboration of this essay from the Berkeley Roundtable on the International Economy, and then from the Institute of Urban and Regional Development, University of California, Berkeley. Research for this essay was supported by the North American program of the Peace and Global Transformation Project of the United Nations University.

devices into all activities. The new media (potentially) disseminate audio and visual from everywhere to everywhere, with the possibility of differentiating along a time sequence the elements of the message. They also have the potential to create interactive systems. And (possibly the most relevant technology for the future) genetic engineering decodes the information system of living matter in order to reprogram it.

Technology has never been and will never be an independent variable operating in a social vacuum. Scientific revolutions take place in a given social context, being affected by it, and, in return, deeply contributing to its organization and evolution. And yet it is of fundamental importance to understand that new information technologies are completely transforming our societies from their very roots. Such transformation does not come *only* from the characteristics of the new technolgies, but from the interplay between current scientific discoveries and the socio-economic context in which such discoveries are generated and utilized. This analytical perspective is not of mere academic value, since it implies that, by and large, the technological revolution under way is socially undetermined: its effects might be completely different, and even opposed, according to the socio-political management of the process of technological innovation. Furthermore, given the tremendous capacity of information-processing, and given that it is precisely this informational capacity that differentiates the human species from others, the uses of new technologies will amplify and accelerate whatever trends are dominant in our societies. If one wishes to understand the new world and to transform it into a truly humane society, the technological question is perhaps one of the most important we will have to face. It is, in fact, a matter of life and death. This is because we are entering an historical period in which humankind is at once penetrating the secrets of life and the sources of intelligence, while risking the unleashing, at any moment, of the disintegration of matter, or the lethal mutation of life.

This report addresses these questions by examining the specific effects of new technologies in some fundamental dimensions of our socioeconomic structure: the new international economy and the fate of Third World countries in such new conditions; the changing patterns of work and employment; the technological environment in which our everyday life will be taking place; and the implications of this scientific revolution for the fundamental issue of war and peace. To be sure, other aspects and dimensions of the social implications of the new technologies ought to be considered to be able to assess their impact. But the analysis presented here is geared to a more specific purpose: to define the conditions for social uses of new technologies that would be an alternative to the prevailing patterns of exploitation, oppression, and war.

II. High technology and economic restructuring in the aftermath of the crisis

Technological revolution does not take place in a social vacuum. It develops in a very specific socio-economic, historical context, whose characteristics deeply affect the form and goals of the uses of technology, and ultimately, of technology itself (Rosenberg, 1982; Blackburn, Coombs and Green, 1985). This is not to say that technological discoveries happen necessarily as responses to the needs of "the system." Science and research have their own pace of development, with moments of qualitative breakthroughs and acceleration of discovery produced by the interplay between scientific research, the institutional framework where it takes place, and the social demand for technological applications.

The current technological revolution gained its innovation during the 1970s at a time when the world economy was undergoing a major structural crisis whose causes and characteristics I have examined elsewhere (Castells, 1980). In the mid-1980s, the key centers of the world economy have restructured some fundamental mechanisms so that the processes of capital accumulation and social order, on which the system relies, are adequately performed (Camus, Delattre, Dutailly, Eymard-Duvernay, Vassille, 1981; O'Connor, 1984; Bowles, Gordon, and Weisskopf, 1983; Carnoy, Shearer and Rumberger, 1983).

Capitalism has reformed itself through a process of social struggles and victorious political battles. It has recovered some of its dynamism and much of its social control by shrinking the number of people benefiting from the system and reaching out to almost the entire planet to connect all segments of potential beneficiaries of this leaner, more aggressive, more determined type of capitalism. In recent years (around the 1970–80 period), a new model of economic growth has emerged representing a departure from Keynesianism and welfare-state capitalism. Because high technology has played a major role (as a tool, not as a cause) in this dramatic process of economic restructuring, it is necessary to outline, very schematically, the characteristics of the new model of economic policy, and to pinpoint the specific role of new technologies in relationship to each of the major economic axes (Carnoy and Castells, 1985). This model is not necessarily linked to a particular political party or administration, or even to a country, although the Reagan and Thatcher governments seem to be clear examples. Very similar policies have developed in most West European countries, in those governed by Christian Democrats and Liberals, as well as in those governed by Socialists, and even in Communist-led regions (Italy) or Communist-participating governments (France, for a certain period). At the same time, in most Third World countries, austerity policies, inspired or dictated by the International Monetary Fund and world financial institutions, have also developed along the same lines, establishing not without contradictions and conflicts (Walton, 1985) a new economic logic that is not only capitalist but a very specific kind of capitalism that we will try to describe briefly (Carnoy and Castells, 1985). Obviously, the generalization of such a model of economic policy (which is not historically irreversible) does not imply that all governments are alike or that politics does not matter. When a system reaches a historical limit, and the socio-political process is unable to transform it, the only way to prevent social disintegration is to consolidate, reinforce, and make more dynamic the already institutionalized structural logic. Because the economy (under capitalism) structures society, and because the economy is highly interdependent at an international level, individual governments in individual countries find themselves faced with the dilemma of adjusting to the dominant logic in the most advantageous manner, or having to undertake an uphill battle that is unlikely to succeed as an isolated enterprise. Thus, most countries are embarking on a new model of economic policy that is organized around a major series of measures, coming at the same time from governments and private business. These include:

1. Control of inflation through fiscal austerity and monetary restriction, aimed at the partial dismantling of the welfare state (Taylor, 1983).

2. Reduction of wages, working conditions, social benefits and other labor costs. Consequently, the share of business' profit increases proportionally, all other conditions being equal (Bowles, Gordon, Weisskopf, 1983).

3. Increase in productivity of companies, and in profitability of business, through lay-offs, reduction of working time, technological innovation, and faster pace of work (Reich, 1983).

4. Restructuring of industrial sectors, disinvesting massively from those sectors, regions, and companies that become less profitable, and investing in new products and activities, generally in high-technology manufacturing, corporate services, miscellaneous consumer services, and real estate (Bluestone and Harrison, 1982). A major development within industrial restructuring (particularly in Europe and Latin America) is the shrinkage of the public sector, and the alignment of public companies on the logic of profitability.

5. Tremendous growth of the "informal economy," that is, of all kinds of cash economic activities unregulated and uncontrolled by the state, regardless of the legality of their status. This includes the astronomic sum of cash flow in criminal activities (particularly in the production and distribution of drugs), but it mainly refers to undeclared salaried work, unpaid taxes, absence of compliance with health and safety regulations, labor legislation, and so on (Portes and Walton, 1981; Piore and Sabel, 1984). In countries like the United States, massive immigration from undocumented workers fuels the process of the increasing penetration of the center by the periphery. The informal economy today represents a key element of all economies alike, not only for the survival of the poor, but for the dynamism of small businesses, accounting for much of the growth and new employment (Sassen-Koob, 1984; Maldonado and Moore, 1985), and for the transfer of value from the informal sector to large corporations through subcontracting arrangements and networks of decentralized production.

6. Opening of the world market, and increasing internationalization of the economy, taking advantage of the most favorable locations for production, management, and control of the markets, within a system interconnected world-wide. This is a common strategy for both companies and governments, and paradoxically, it simultaneously triggers protectionist reactions, as soon as industrial sectors, regions, or countries, start losing in the cutthroat competition (Bienefeld and Godfrey, 1982; Little, 1982).

7. Relative control of world prices of raw materials and energy from the center, assuring the stability of the price system and exchange flows (OECD, 1984).

8. The internationalization of the world's financial markets caused by

deregulation and advances in information-processing technologies. With the advent of money that can be transferred electronically (e.g. CHIPS), and the further electrical integration of the world's markets and exchanges, any country that has the technology and capital will soon be able to directly interact with major financial institutions around the world (Hamilton, 1984).

Of course, this sketchy presentation of the dominant economic model emphasizes its coherence and internal logic, without considering the contradictions it implies, and the potentially destructive deviations of its own rationality. For instance, in the case of the United States, the claim for fiscal austerity and a balanced budget is translated into a greater deficit, with a shift within the budget from social expenditures to military expenditures (what we call, following Herbert Marcuse, the transition from the Welfare State to the Warfare State). It is financed, without inflation, by the influx of capital from all over the world, thus drying up sources of investment everywhere else, and pushing upward the dollar, therefore wrecking the US balance of trade.

It is important to keep in mind these characteristics of the post-Keynesian economic model of capitalism because the technological revolution has matured precisely during its rise, and it is playing a major role in the model's implementation. In turn, the lines of technological development are now being shaped by the predominant social and economic uses assigned to them.

The new technologies are at the core of the current process of economic restructuring in the following way:

1. They contribute to a qualitative increase in productivity across the board, in manufacturing, agriculture and particularly in services. This impact cannot be equated to a negative effect of new technologies on employment, a more complex issue that we will examine in detail below. But, in any case, the general impact of new technologies on business tends to increase productivity and quality, reduce costs, and improve profitability, thus contributing a great deal to stimulate investment and overcome economic slump.

Because new technologies are primarily aimed at processing information, and this is precisely the subject of most services, the deepest economic impact of the new technologies will occur in services and office work (Noyelle, 1984; Stanback, 1979; Hirschhorn, 1984; Baran, 1985). Yet, for the moment, the most immediate impact in industrial productivity has been in manufacturing, and particularly in the automobile industry. The UNIDO report on the topic (UNIDO, 1984) observes that "The position of the [automobile] industry in the industrial system has altered. No longer will it be a creator of jobs. It will be a pioneer in the introduction and use of technologies and materials of several kinds and in so doing it will transform its inter-industry linkages. These changes are unlikely to be limited to the OECD countries, even though their present force is concentrated in that area" (page 17). In fact, during the 1980s, the automobile industry is experiencing a major transformation in the production process and in the overall logic of industry as a result of industrial robots and CAD/CAM systems of flexible manufacturing. Adding the developments in new materials, it seems that in a few years the automobile industry will have shifted from an electro-mechanical industry to an electronics-plastics industry (UNIDO, 1984) dramatically increasing productivity and reducing employment in production. Similar trends can be observed in key industries such as electronics (Ernst, 1980; Cohen and Zysman, 1986; Jacobson and Sigurdsun, 1983), and telecommunications (Borrus, Bar, and Warde, 1984).

2. At the same time, the potential (or actual) impact of new technologies on job-suppression places management in an advantageous position regarding workers and unions, to obtain concessions in wages and working conditions in exchange for maintaining employment, or of slowing down the phasing out of jobs. Thus, although technology as such is not an instrument of capital, it is being used as a bargaining factor in the redefinition of the power relationships between management and labor, a key component of the overall economic restructuring (Institut Syndical Europeen, 1980; AFL-CIO, 1984; Bluestone and Harrison, 1984).

3. Technological change is also the source of new investment, the main engine of economic recovery, for two main reasons. First, as the 1984 OECD Report states, "Higher than expected growth of non-residential private investment seems to be explained by the increase of marginal productivity of investment in those countries where the share of computers and other high technology equipment in the companies' investments has significantly increased. Thus, it would seem that the profitability for a given investment increases [because of new technologies]. Investments that were previously under the threshold of profitability become profitable now. This phenomenon is particularly important in the U.S. and Japan" (p. 10, my translation from the French version of the Report).

Second, in anticipation of the demand for new technologies, there is a rush of investment in the high technology sectors, thus stimulating the economy out of recession, while deeply reshaping its structure in terms of "sunrise" and "sunset" industries, regions, and countries (Bluestone and Harrison, 1984; Celada, Lopez-Groh and Parra, 1985; Markusen, 1984; Henderson and Castells, 1986).

4. New technologies stimulate markets, particularly for upper income households, by generating new products (such as home computers and new communication devices) or creating new lines of old products by introducing into them informational devices (from cars to kitchens).

5. Last, but not least, new technologies, and particularly telecommunications, constitute the material conditions necessary for the process of internationalization of the economy, probably the key feature of the new model of accumulation. Only through the integrated system of telecommunications and computers is it possible to both integrate and decentralize production, distribution, and management in a world-wide, flexible, interconnected system. The new telecommunication technologies are the electronic highways of the informational age, their role equivalent to that played by the railway systems in the process of industrialization (Nicol, 1985). In addition, world production and distribution is only possible because of the twin processes of perfect standardization of parts (that can be assembled even if produced in very distant locations), and flexible customized production (that can adapt a basic product to specific characteristics targeted on the final market), (UNIDO, 1984; Henderson and Scott, 1986). Both

processes are dependent upon automated production, and flexible electronic tools able to be re-programmed. The world-assembly line and the planetary bazaar, require both the electronic factory and on-line management.

Thus, new technologies are a key component of the process of economic restructuring that determines a new international division of labor whose characteristics are decisive for the making of our future world.

III. High technology, the new international division of labor and the future of the Third World

The new technologies are rendering obsolete the "new international division of labor" that emerged in different areas of the world during the 1970s as a response to the structural economic crisis (Frobel, Henricks and Kreye, 1980). This international division of labor was mainly organized around the policies of multinational corporations that relocated their production "offshore" in countries where low wages, lack of environmental and health controls, pro-business and repressive government policies, and favorable fiscal exceptions substantially reduced production costs in comparison with the core countries (Palloix, 1977; Peet, 1984; Nayyar, 1978; Schmitz, 1984). Thus a new North–South division of labor started to take place between high-technology industries and advanced services in the North and assembly operations, low-skilled manufacturing, and extraction of natural resources in the South (Brandt, 1980). Multinational corporations were important agents in such a process, particularly in the most dynamic industries such as electronics (UNIDO, 1981; Ernst, 1980), and in those sectors that underwent global economic restructuring such as automobiles (Maxey, 1981; UNIDO, 1984). Yet, along with the multinationals, small and medium companies from the newly industrializing periphery, as in Hong Kong (Chen, 1979; Schiffer, 1983), Korea or Taiwan (Browett, 1985), followed a similar strategy of producing for the world market on the basis of their comparative advantage of low-production costs. It followed a realignment of the world economy, an intensification of world trade, and the surge of a group of newly industrialized countries (Browett, 1985; Bradford, 1982; Bienefeld and Godfrey, 1982). So, through a combination of decentralization of productive investment from the core, and of dynamism of indigenous capital in the periphery supported by development-oriented national governments, new economic actors have entered the international arena, increasingly differentiating the so-called Third World.

The development of high-technology industries and technological change are both furthering and modifying this new international division of labor. The transformation of the process takes place along different but inter-related lines that we will analyze sequentially for the sake of clarity.

1. On the one hand cheaper and more effective automation of the work process increasingly allows corporations to retain their factories in the core countries (sometimes relocating in rural areas) while still lowering their production costs (Rada, 1982; Cohen, Zysman and Associates, 1986). In fact, the threat of unemployment, and the policies of economic incentives by regional governments in the depressed regions of the United States and

Europe, are enhancing the chances for an inter-regional rather than an international division of labor (Glasmeier, 1986; Sawers and Tabb, 1984; Massey, 1984). Such a possibility is being extended to sectors such as textiles and garments that were considered to have become the exclusive prerogative of the newly industrialized countries as newer, electronically-based technologies, such as laser-cutting and CAD/CAM production lines are installed in the remaining old industries of Europe and the United States (UNIDO, 1984; Botkin, Dimancescu and Stata, 1984). Furthermore, not only has the migration of core-countries' companies to the periphery slowed down, but there seems to be a process of "relocation back North" (Rada, 1982), apparently induced by a combination of political uncertainty abroad, higher labor costs in the first NIC countries (such as Singapore and Hong Kong), and the need for skilled personnel to handle and repair increasingly sophisticated electronics-based machinery (UNIDO, 1981, 1984).

Nevertheless, there is still a process of productive decentralization across the world that now reaches more countries in the outer periphery. The first ring of NICs (Korea, Taiwan, Hong Kong, Singapore, Malaysia and the industrialized areas of Brazil and Mexico) are now concentrating on more sophisticated and higher skilled production activities, that in the case of Korea and Singapore could even rival some West European countries (Government of Korea, 1985; Botkin, Dimancescu and Stata, 1984). Simultaneously, less developed countries, with a large pool of unskilled, extremely cheap labor, enter the productive line at the low end, particularly Thailand and the Philippines (Henderson, 1986; Lim, 1982; Akrasanee, 1977). Yet, the more automation enters the process of production and management the less low wages play a role in the comparative advantages of a given location. One of the greatest paradoxes of the effects of automation on employment is that the most directly hurt are the Third World countries whose incipient process of industrialization, however exploitative, is based upon the differential cost between unskilled labor in the core and the periphery. Probably the next round of differentiating labor costs will be between skilled labor, including engineers. And this is what countries like Singapore (but also Brazil) are trying to offer. Yet, it is not evident that the training of technical labor could be done rapidly enough, and on a scale large enough to foster a second stage of "off-shore" productive decentralization from the North's industrial base. Thus the fundamental tendency introduced by new technologies is to enhance the role of productivity, instead of focusing on direct labor costs in the overall process of capital accumulation; this therefore reinforces the position of technologically advanced economies in the new international competition.

2. Interestingly enough, while labor costs are becoming a less important factor for the location of companies because of increasing automation, the current trend points toward a greater internationalization of the companies' structure in order to locate closer to their different markets. It thus reverses the tendency of the 1970s, when export-platforms were aimed at the world market (Henderson and Scott, 1986; Lee, 1981; Balassa, 1982; Perlo, 1986). This is a fundamental point that requires some explanation.

The internationalization of the economy and the intensification of world trade in the last two decades led to national economic policies that are increasingly dependent upon their performance on the world scene. International economic competitiveness is a key political factor for any government's fate, domestically as well as in foreign affairs. To reinforce the competitive chances of its national companies, many governments have engaged in restrictive practices of trade, as well as in export incentive programs, so that national corporations can build a home base for their subsequent assault on the world economy (Zysman and Cohen, 1983). This strategy has become known as the Japanese Model (Johnson, 1982), but it is also increasingly true of many NIC countries—Korea (Rosenberg, 1980), and Brazil (Costa Souza, 1985) being the most prominent in this respect.

The EEC has stepped up its control on "unfair competition" of non-EEC countries in Europe, particularly for Japanese exports, and in advanced electronics (there is for instance a 17 percent surcharge on all imported semiconductors). In the United States in the period 1983–86, there has been a dramatic surge of public protest against imports, particularly from Japan, that, in spite of Reagan's free trade philosophy, has led to the imposition of a number of quotas on several products and even to the threat of a commercial war with Japan (*Business Week*, April 8, 1985). Because of the mounting danger of protectionist measures, companies from all countries are positioning themselves to be present in their key foreign markets, often with the support of their own governments, given the strategic importance of the conquest of international markets by national (or nationally-backed) companies. Thus, American and Japanese companies are establishing themselves in increasing numbers in the EEC; Japanese companies (particularly Toyota and Nissan) are locating in the United States; Korean companies settling in Canada; investment from all over the world is pouring into the United States, some of it into securities and real estate, but most of it in setting up new companies or buying old ones, particularly in the West and the Southwest (Schoenberger, 1985; Glickman, 1985).

Large potential markets such as Brazil, Mexico and China are being tapped by foreign investors who are locating there to take over the expansion of new segments of consumers. In sum, the target is still the world market, but the strategy of multilocation is increasingly more important vis-à-vis the export-platform strategy. The consequence for the Third World is two-fold: on the one hand, most investment tends to concentrate inside the economies of the most developed countries, so substituting a North-to-North and a South-to-North pattern for the incipient North-to-South decentralization that was taking place during the 1970s. On the other hand, domestic markets within the NICs, and in the Third World in general, will have to be shared with international companies, at least in those commercial lines considered profitable. Thus, it follows that there will be an increasing dependency, although not necessarily more underdevelopment, of those Third World countries which are somewhat industrialized.

This trend fundamentally alters the current international division of labor because it strongly articulates a new productive location and presence in the market, even though such production facilities will continue to be financially and technologically dependent on the core economies. The development of new technologies plays a major role in this new pattern of the international economy. Let us see why.

3. First, new telecommunications technologies allow the integration of management, as well as internal technological transfer within the same company between its different units, regardless of location (Nicol, 1983; Piercy, 1984). Thus, a country can use a multilocational strategy to penetrate markets around the world, while keeping its own internal coherence, based on easy inter-personal communication and data transmission (UNCTC, 1984). This is particularly important because while "off-shore" production does not require day-to-day contact between the center and the periphery of the company (given that it generally concerns routine assembly operations), productive location close to a market implies a greater coordination of the company's strategy (UNIDO, 1984), something that is only possible thanks to the power, flexibility, and decreasing cost of new telecommunication technologies.

Second, this new strategy of internationalization on the basis of multilocation is largely the result of the opportunity that high technology products and services provide to take over entire countries as protected markets in areas of the world—countries that are in great need of devices that incorporate new information technologies but are still far behind the current leaders in the field of high technology manufacturing. In this sense, Western Europe appears as the most rapidly growing market for high technology companies in the forthcoming years. This is why all multinationals, including the European ones, are striving to position themselves in that market. Yet the United States is still the fundamental market for high technology (particularly considering the current renovation process of industrial equipment in the United States). That explains why many of the US productive facilities of high technology companies will still remain close to their own market. Japanese and European companies are trying to penetrate the US market by investing heavily in it, or setting up joint ventures.

Further, presence in the US technological milieu appears to be a prerequisite for competing in the race for industrial innovation. For instance, the French-government owned electronics giant Thomson, recently acquired the almost bankrupt, highly inefficient American company Mostek, based in Dallas, to gain an additional entry into the US electronics field. Japan is the second largest industrial market in the world (Nazakawa, 1985), but its many ways of disguised protectionism are still keeping it at bay from deep penetration by foreign competition (Borrus, Millstein and Zysman, 1983; Johnson, 1982). Yet, the deregulation of Nippon Telephone Company in 1985, and the monetary and financial policies undertaken in the Fall of the same year by the Nakasone Government seem to signal an awareness by the Japanese establishment of the danger of a backlash in both the United States and the EEC, should their protectionism continue unabated. As a result, it is likely that at least a segment of the Japanese market will join the world economy, further penetrating it along a clearly defined North–North axis. High technology industries, the most dynamic industrial sector today, tend to locate in the OECD countries whose technological-economic lead is thereby self-reinforcing. At the same time, some new potential markets for high technology production appear in oil-producing countries (particularly in the Middle East), and in a few NICs (essentially Korea, Brazil, Mexico, India, and in a few years, China), but they are still very limited in terms of the market, and very distant from the core in their technological capability (with the important exceptions of Singapore and Korea). Much of the Third World (particularly Africa) appears to be left out from the current process of technological modernization, both in terms of markets and of production. The technological revolution for most of the world seems to be limited to the telecommunications networks of some directional centers, or to the enclaves of some large, internationally-oriented companies, and sadly enough, to increasingly sophisticated weaponry. High technology, in its process of uneven development, is profoundly altering the world's economic geography.

Third, the need to access key technologies withheld by multinational corporations has motivated numerous governments to actively seek the location of these multinationals in their countries. Because of the vital need for technology transfer, corporations obtain financial, material, and legislative advantages that amount to a significant bonus to the multinational strategy (UNIDO, 1981; Balassa, 1982). Countries, and regions within countries, enter the competition to obtain the companies' favors. Since in most cases the employment effect of such locations is very limited, and government and local capital financing account for the majority of investments, it seems that the search for technological know-how is the main reason for national governments' efforts to lure high-technology companies. Thus, the technological gap is not only the consequence, but also a major cause of the new process of economic internationalization, by its encouragement of the multilocation of new industries. We are shifting from a strategy based on export-platforms, to a new one relying on the export of the productive platform itself, so that it can penetrate national markets, and be subsidized by national governments, in exchange for some drops of the precious know-how generated by the current technological revolution.

4. At this point we should introduce in the analysis the specific economic policies through which different countries are trying to find their way out of the structural economic crisis. It is only by studying the interplay between current policies of economic restructuring and qualitative changes induced by the diffusion of new technologies that we will be able to understand the emerging international economy.

Three main factors favor the capacity of a given country in the current economic conjuncture to engage in a process of recovery (OECD, 1984; Layard, Basevi, Blanchard, Buiter and Kleppe, 1984): the size of its domestic market; its technological capabilities; and its ability to generate public spending without the high risk of inflation (for instance, by being able to finance a budget deficit with foreign capital buying government bonds). The simultaneous action of the three factors reinforce each other, establishing a strong hierarchical relationship between countries in the international economy. If we consider how these three factors rank countries between themselves (an exercise that we will not undertake here to avoid further complicating this analysis), we find a common sense ordering of the world economy. The United States is at the top, closely followed by Japan; behind them (at an increasing distance) the EEC; further behind are the newly industrialized countries, mainly comprising the growth economies of the Pacific Basin, portions of Mexico, Brazil, and India, and the incipient industrialized areas of OPEC countries; and finally the majority of Third World countries, increasingly deteriorating in their relationship to the center of the world economy, possibly with the exception of China. At the low-end of the structure, a growing number of countries and regions, and therefore of people, have an even looser connection with the overall economic structure. Yet it provides the basic, irreversible framework of their existence.

While this international hierarchy is well known, it is important to remind ourselves of two key facts. First, it is an interdependent *structure*, not just an order of importance; it is made up not just of distance, but of asymmetrical, actual relationships. There is not simply a separation between core and periphery but a highly differentiated, complex structure whose precise workings have to be unveiled in each specific conjuncture. Second, technological capacity is a fundamental factor in the organization of the whole structure. And it is a particularly dynamic one. The technological gap is growing, and will become irreversible in the absence of efforts to reverse the current trends, thus making irreversible the asymmetrical world structure.

This is not only true for the Third World, but for Western Europe as well. The Common Market is in fact rather uncommon because of its imperfect and arbitrary integration. The lack of flexibility of its economies, and the bureaucratization of its public sector have rendered Europe entirely dependent on the pace of the US economy to fuel its own recovery. In the last decade, in spite of the US recession, the American economy created 20 million *new* jobs (admittedly, including fast food teenage workers) while Western Europe lost, in net balance, about 5 million jobs. Furthermore, European high technology industries, with few exceptions, are in a shameful state. The gap between them and their Japanese and US competitors is broadening, at times leading them to surrender to technological supremacy and join the bandwagon of the victors (as in the case of Olivetti). A 1984 official report of the European Community (EEC, 1984, my translation into English) states: "Europe, because of competitive pressure, will have to embrace new technologies, one day or another. If it allows increases in the current technological gap with the US and Japan, the assimilation of new technologies will take place under the worst possible conditions. Its competitiveness will be reduced, unemployment will soar, technological dependency will translate into industrial, economic, and cultural dependency." The prospects are rather grim from a European perspective because, according to the same document, in 1984, "European industry is losing ground in information technologies. Eight out of ten personal computers sold in Europe come from American makers; nine out of ten VCRs sold in Europe come from Japan. European companies have only 30 percent of their national share of integrated circuits and only 13 percent of the world market. In this sector [integrated circuits] Europe as a whole represents one third of the world market, yet it only controls 40 percent of its own market and 10 percent of the world market. . . . The situation continues to deteriorate. All European makers of mainframe computers have had to pass agreements with Japanese or American companies to obtain technology transfer" (page 5). Other estimates are even more pessimistic, and assign to Europe a mere 7 percent of the world market of semiconductors (the core of information technologies), against 53 percent to the United States and 39 percent to Japan (*The Economist,* November 24–30, 1984).

Nevertheless, Europe does have first class scientific institutions and a strong technological base that has been able to keep pace in the fields of avionics, missiles, communications equipment, nuclear power, and, to a lesser extent, biotechnology (FAST, 1984). And yet, two major flaws seem to be causing a decisive handicap for Europe: the first is the inability to translate scientific discoveries into industrial and commercial applications; the second (not unrelated to the first) is the failure of European research and technological development in two key fields: microelectronics and computers. Because they are the core of information technologies, and because it is information technology that commands the current stream of technological innovation, it is doubtful that Europe could ever bridge the existing gap. Some European programs of technological cooperation, such as ESPRIT (FAST, 1984), are now trying to bring together resources and political will to avoid a technological dependency that in today's world will be translated to dependency *tout court.* The launching of EUREKA in 1985 under the initiative of the French government could be a major step in such a direction. Yet, EUREKA is too closely associated with the political battle against the SDI program, a battle many European governments are reluctant to join precisely because of their fear of losing access to a key source of new technologies. Overall, Europe is waking up to the awareness of the key role played by the technological revolution in the restructuring of our world. It remains to be seen if the political priority given to the technological *aggiornamento* can overcome cultural and bureaucratic resistances to the utmost effort of mobilization Europe would require to at least keep pace with the United States and Japan. The issue concerns the entire world, and particularly the Third World. Because only if there is a technologically advanced Europe, will the Third World be able to bargain for its technological development with a plurality of partners, without being immediately confronted with the techno-political rivalry between the two superpowers, or having to choose between American or Japanese economic domination.

5. The impact of the technological revolution on the Third World in the international division of labor is even more dramatic and far-reaching. In fact, together with the process of economic restructuring, the impact of the new technologies has laid to rest the very notion of "a Third World," if it ever existed. The situations of many countries are not only changing (they always were) but are also becoming parts of contradictory processes, whose dynamics pull them apart from each other, into distinct historical constellations.

For the sake of clarity we will risk a highly schematic presentation of the differential impact of the current techno-economic restructuring for several groups of countries with specific positions in the international division of labor:

A. A first group includes the few newly industrialized countries: basically Korea, Taiwan, Hong Kong, and Singapore, with Malaysia striving to join them. They are connecting more and more closely to the core economies, and particularly to the dynamics of the US market. They have used new technologies both as a tool to modernize their industry, making them more competitive, and as a product-line for jumping into the world market, with the increasing sophistication of their electronics industries. For instance, in 1984, Korea's electronics labor force amounted to about 350,000 workers (Government of Korea, 1985), that is, more than all Silicon Valley and Route 128 employees combined, although at a much lower level of skill. Therefore, one can think of the "four Asian tigers" as having joined the industrialized world. They are likely to surpass some European countries in the near future, by shifting from an export strategy based on low-pricing to a new industrial competitiveness based upon the dynamic accumulation of new technologies and new technological products. It must be recalled that such an accomplishment is *not* the result of laissez faire capitalism, or of the beneficial effects of off-shore production by multinational corporations. All four cases are government-led processes of economic development (see Schiffer, 1983, and Castells, 1985, for Hong Kong; Hamilton, 1984, and Luedde-Neurath, for Korea; Wade, 1984, and Lee, 1981, for Singapore; and Chen, 1979, and Browett, 1985, for the overall argument). With the exception of Singapore, the multinationals play a minor role in exports (74 percent of Hong Kong exports and 75 percent of Korean exports come from local, non-subsidiary companies). And the domestic market is decisive for their industrial expansion, with the obvious exception of the city-states (Singapore and Hong Kong). The export-led strategy leaping forward to join the industrialized world by means of the technological revolution is clearly an exception in the overall historical trend, although it is an important exception from which we can learn many lessons about the development process and the potentials for a fruitful assimilation of new technologies. Incidentally, authoritarian regimes such as those governing the four countries are neither a pre-condition nor a consequence of the development process. If anything, they are likely to be undermined by the complex civil society emerging from a developed, highly internationalized economy.

B. A second group of countries corresponds to the model of the so-called "new international division of labor", experiencing dependent industrialization linked to decentralized production by multinationals or their subcontractors on the basis of cheap labor and low government regulations. The second ring of Southeast Asian countries (Lee, 1981) could be included here (Vasquez, 1985), particularly Thailand, the Philippines, and some of Malaysia, along with a number of Caribbean islands, some of them specializing in routine key-punching operations for data-processing services beamed back and forth by satellite. Also, some areas of some countries, basically included in a different position in the world economy, might fit this model: the Mexican border regions (Perlo, 1986), the Chinese Special Economic Zones, and some Brazilian industries (such as shoes and leather) entirely aimed at exports based on low labor costs. For this group of countries, the new techno-economic model has a contradictory, two-fold effect. On the one hand, production can be dispersed across the world and reunited by technological means in a single process. Also, small companies, using data transmission equipment, can actually tap the world market while keeping a lean, flexible organization. On the other hand, automation makes industrial production in the North easier and relatively cheaper, at a moment when political uncertainty and the cost of managerial and technical personnel seem to call into question some of the advantages of off-shoring. Although empirical evidence on the matter is scant, an educated guess would suggest that off-shore production will continue but at a much slower pace. The second round of peripheral industrialization will not take place on a large scale (for instance in the Philippines), and on the sole basis of an export-oriented strategy. Domestic markets still will be fundamental for a lasting process of development.

C. A third category includes those countries whose population size and industrial potential make feasible, at least in theory, a process of technological modernization aimed simultaneously at their domestic market and at the world economy. Generally speaking, it would seem that technology transfer and capital accumulation in these countries will have their dynamic component in an export-oriented strategy, around which the rest of the economy would experience a gradual incorporation. Brazil, Mexico, maybe Argentina, more recently China, and to some extent India, could be examples of this specific situation. For these countries, the eruption of new technologies is a mixed blessing. On the one hand, they can accelerate their pace toward modernization, leaping over the traditional sequence of industrialization. On the other hand, their main comparative advantage (low production costs) is partly offset by automation. Besides, their need to access technological know-how places them in a much greater dependency vis-à-vis the core economies, since autonomous technological capacity cannot be developed in a few years, while the pace of innovation dramatically accelerates. For instance, if we take the example of the most industrialized country among them, Brazil (currently with the tenth largest industrial output in the world), its first item for exports is military equipment, including tanks, armored cars, helicopters, and light planes. Its competitive advantage is low-price for cash-short Third World governments in need of military hardware, along with the absence of any political conditions attached to the sale. Yet, the increasing sophistication of weaponry forces Brazil to enhance its technological level very quickly if it wants to survive in this lucrative market. This will entail considerable efforts to obtain technological licensing and know-how, thus making Brazilian industry more dependent on its sources of innovation in the core economies. At the same time, the modern, multinational sector of the industry will come under increasing pressure to automate to keep its share of the world market; for instance, this is true for the Brazilian automobile industry which is projected to be among the eight largest automobile producers in the world, and the largest in the Third World, by the end of this decade (UNIDO, 1984). Thus, new industrialization will be less labor-intensive, increasing the problem of absorption of the surplus work population whose migration from the countryside will be accelerated by the bio-technological revolution in agriculture.

This process is just beginning, given the incredibly low-level penetration of new technologies in most semi-peripheral countries, even one as industrialized as Brazil. For instance, in 1984, in the entire Brazilian industry, there were only 50 industrial robots, 15 CAD systems, and 850 numerically controlled machine-tools in only 266 industrial companies, out of the 120,600 such companies in the whole country. All companies with some level of automated equipment are either foreign or subsidiaries of multinationals. Concerning services, a similar low-level of information technology appears to exist, for instance, less than 5 percent of banks' branches (the first service industry to use new technologies in all countries) use on-line communications systems (Costa Souza, 1985). On the other hand, because it is aware of the strategic importance of information technologies, Brazil is trying to create an endogenous base for such developments. For instance, it has forbidden the import of mini- and micro-computers, so that Brazilian computer makers can grow on the basis of their domestic market. Nevertheless, it seems doubtful that Brazil, or any other country in the Third World, could develop its own technological base without relying on technology transfer from the multinationals. That is why China is receiving so much attention from American, Japanese, and West European companies. But is it to the advantage of these companies to agree to such a transfer? In exchange for the technological and managerial know-how the Chinese expect to receive from foreign companies, these companies seek, primarily, to position themselves in a market of a billion people that (they hope) will gradually increase its purchasing power.

So, three simultaneous processes are associated with techno-economic restructuring in the largest countries of the Third World: the positioning of the multinational companies in these large, protected markets, using their technological know-how as their primary bargaining chip; the strategy of these large countries to increase their competitive edge in the world economy, with technological modernization in the mid-term while still taking advantage of their low-prices made possible with cheap labor; and the expansion of industrial capability on the basis of large domestic markets that will be served by an increasingly efficient, technologically advanced industry.

What of the compatibility between the three processes? For instance, if the price for technology transfer is opening up the domestic market to the multinationals, it will be difficult for the national companies to build up enough strength in their own country to be able to compete abroad in a second stage (remember that Japan and Korea first developed their industrial might from protected domestic markets). On the other hand, if protectionism arises, it is unlikely that technology transfer will occur at any significant level. Take another major issue: employment, and therefore solvent demand. If large-scale automation is required to compete in the world economy in terms of quality standards, the technological modernization of the industrial base is unlikely to generate enough jobs to stimulate the urban economy and to broaden the domestic market. Instead, it will result in increasing competition by both national and multinational corporations in a relatively small upper-level urban market.

The overall effect seems likely to be the increasing disarticulation of the national economy (and to some extent of society), not between multinational corporations and indigenous capital, but between a highly dynamic sector of the world economy, both as producer and market, and a series of destructured segments that will mix their roles as subcontracting sweatshops for the internationalized sector, as providers of goods and services for specific domestic sub-markets, and as daily inventors of survival strategies.

D. A fourth group of countries comprises the major oil-producers. In principle, their wealth (in spite of the leveling off of oil prices), makes them potential markets for technological modernization and industrialization. In some cases, as in Nigeria and Indonesia, their population size is also a major potential asset. In recent years, these countries have sought to use their financial resources to create an industrial base aimed mainly at import substitution, although still keeping in mind the world market, particularly in petrochemicals. Yet, a number of different elements have fundamentally flawed developmental processes: (a) Exacerbated nationalism and religious fanaticism, manipulated by the superpowers, have pitched countries against each other (notably Iraq and Iran), wrecking their economies, killing their people, and diverting technological modernization from industry to the army. (b) Weak political institutions, widespread corruption, and unstable domestic ethnic and cultural cleavages have channeled resources towards the bureaucracy for the personal advantage of its members. Such seems particularly to be the case of Nigeria during the 1970s (Lubeck, 1985). (c) The attempt to create a national industrial base, in the midst of the opening up of the international economy, turned major public investments into gigantic money losers. Hastily financed by international banks, such ventures transformed oil revenue surpluses into unpayable foreign debt, thus deepening financial dependency and halting the process of autonomous industrialization. Venezuela and Mexico are perhaps the most typical cases.

With the exception of Mexico (whose connection with the US economy makes it more susceptible to direct technological modernization), most of the oil producing countries will be users, rather than producers of new technologies. They are targeted as important potential markets by high technology corporations ready to sell the consumption of the technological revolution at a high price, while those countries maintain, by and large, a dependent economy and a traditional society. In some cases, oil-hungry governments such as France are exchanging technological products for oil, for instance with Nigeria, enlarging the practice of barter that is becoming a major factor in international trade.

But, in general, oil producers have been unable to use their resources to generate industrial development. This is partly because the coincidence of the rise of high technology with the oil bonanza has restructured the international economy. The technological dependence of oil producers on new industrial equipment has deepened and it is now more difficult to enter the world economy with heavy industry which the oil producing countries were trying to build. Political manipulation opened up profitable markets for high tech weapons. Financial greed lent massive capital to the "nouveaux riches" to tie them, and the rest of the world as well, to the "global debt bomb" (Carnoy, 1985). This process refutes the assumption that capital supply is the source of development. Indeed neither the largest inflow of capital in recent history, nor the existence of unlimited technological possibilities, were able to engage countries with archaic, exploitative structures, and tied frequently to the superpowers' geopolitical games, to undertake development seriously.

E. Most of the Third World countries are being largely bypassed by the current technological revolution, except for its military implications, consumer electronics products, and the connection of its directional centers to an integrated network of world telecommunications. Thus, only a few segments of the productive structure and increasingly narrow markets participate in the process of new peripheral industrialization. Furthermore, new agricultural technology is helping to increase labor redundancy in the modern, capitalist exploitations, thus accelerating rural–urban migration. Numerous raw materials are being replaced by synthetic, advanced materials, condemning large areas of the world to economic obsolescence. Functional and social distance is not only increasing between countries, but also between regions of the same country. The downturn of the core economies is also hurting the export capability of most Third World countries, while they are unlikely to enter the competition in the new information technologies (Eward, 1984; Saunders, et al., 1983). High interest rates in the center, and fluctuating exchange rates for national currencies, are imposing an unbearable burden on increasingly depressed economies that are trying to service the interest on foreign debts (Carnoy, 1985). Unemployment, misery, hunger, illness, and individual violence, are on the increase all over the Third World, and particularly in the large urban centers. New technologies by themselves have little influence on such trends. Yet, the peculiar world-wide economic structure to which they contribute relates to the increasing social and economic dislocation of most Third World countries. By interconnecting economically and technologically valuable elements of each country at the world level, and disconnecting social groups, regions, cities, individuals, and sometimes entire countries that do not fit into the new techno-economic system, the current process of restructuring is fragmenting the social fabric of the planet, and recomposing parts of it into a structure that furthers the interests of dominant governments and corporations.

People, regions, countries, and governments, react against such trends. In most cases there is a survival reaction, with the expanding informal economy defining its own rules of the game on the local shop floors of most Third World cities. New unintended forms of connection between center and periphery also take place—for instance, production of and trade in drugs on a huge, international scale. With the collapse of the world's tin markets, and the reluctance of foreign capital to invest in a class-conscious, highly politicized country, Bolivian peasants are tapped by drug traffickers for coca production, making of coca paste the major (illegal) export of the country (Flores and Blanes, 1983). Such a large, uncontrolled cash-economy, in dollars, wrecks the country's monetary system, triggering unsustainable inflation. Colombia, with a stronger, more diversified economy, is at the core of cocaine traffic; Peru, Ecuador, some areas of Brazil and Mexico, are also now entering the race. Thus, new ties are being established between the center and the periphery that pervert the dreams of universal development by means of technological progress. There is still a connection between Silicon Valley and Bolivia, but it takes the form of the technological switch-off of Bolivia from the new international economy and that country's delinquent tie-in with cocaine traffic.

Some countries do react against their internal fragmentation and global marginality, rallying the people around their national governments to strive for political autonomy and economic modernization and thus domestic markets that are responsive to the people's needs. In different contexts, and with diverse ideologies, Mozambique, Nicaragua, and Peru are trying to keep afloat their societies without submitting to the logic of global imperatives. Yet the path is so narrow, and aggression or opportunistic manipulation by both superpowers so blatant, that we still have no example of a country setting its own national development path with relative autonomy vis-à-vis the international economy. As soon as people and nations have to address the issue of their relationship to the world's economic structure, old and new patterns of dependency combine to close the exits, and channel countries toward one of two positions: the international division of labor, currently structured around high technology industries and financial institutions, and political alignment within the power blocs organized around the superpowers striving for strategic supremacy. In both cases, Third World countries will have to deal inescapably with the new technological equation. Thus, new technologies have not yet transformed the world into a global village of communicative fellow humans. Rather, the new techno-economic restructuring is fragmenting people and isolating countries, combining them into a reconstructed image made of the silent fulfillment of invisible structural interests.

IV. High technology, work, and employment: jobless economy or occupational transition?

The potential impact of new technologies on employment is problably the main source of both hopes and fears about the economy, and the future of the majority of the people of which it is composed. On the one hand, productivity gains from the diffusion of the technological revolution into virtually all sectors of activity could pave the way for economic revitalization. On the other hand, the generalization of labor-saving technologies is feared to worsen unemployment, both functional and structural, at a moment when millions of jobs, particularly in manufacturing, are being lost in the OECD countries. In fact, much of the social and political debate around the issue of new technologies concerns the implications for employment. Such a polemical background hinders a serious, objective assessment of the matter, particularly in the absence of solid empirical research on a comparative basis and over a sufficiently long time span. This is why we will proceed with great caution, pinpointing the different questions underlying the more general issue under study.

At the most elementary level, it is clear that new technologies when introduced both in the factory and in the office, considerably reduce working time. Scattered evidence on the basis of case studies points in this direction, for instance, Hunt and Hunt (1983) for the impact of robotics; Maeda (1981), Cockroft (1980), and Drennan (1983) for office automation; and Jansen

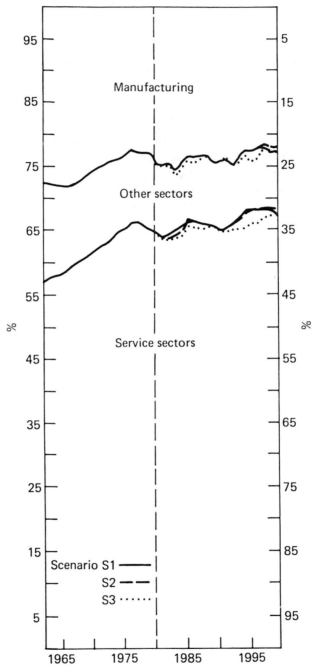

FIGURE 1. Percentage distribution of employment among service, manufacturing and other sectors, 1963–2000, USA.

Note: Manufacturing is defined to include IEA no 12–66 and no 86. The residual category, Other sectors, includes agriculture (IEA no 1–4), mining (IEA no 5–10), and construction (IEA no 11). All remaining sectors are included as Services. Public administration, armed forces, and household workers are not included. Scenarios S1: technology held constant. S2: medium technology change. S3: fast technological change.

Source: Leontieff and Duchin, 1984.

(1984) for the general trends of several industries in Germany). Yet, an evaluation of the overall impact on employment requires the measurement of both direct and indirect effects over a relatively long period of time. The most rigorous of a handful of studies conducted with such methodology is the simulation performed by Leontieff and Duchin (1984) for the impact of automation on employment in the period 1963–2000 on the basis of a dynamic input-output matrix of the US economy. At a general level they found that, taking into consideration only the impact of computer-based automation on the work process, 20 million fewer workers would be required in 2000, compared to the expected number of jobs required for the same output while keeping constant the level of technology. This represents a saving of 11.7 percent in required labor. Nevertheless, the impacts vary among industries and occupations. Interestingly enough, services (and particularly office activities) are predicted to have a greater job loss than manufacturing, due to the massive introduction of labor-saving office machines. Consequently, clerical workers and managers will see their share of the workforce significantly reduced by new information technologies, while that of professionals will increase quite substantially; craftsmen and operatives in manufacturing will maintain their share (Tables 1 and 2).

Yet it is also often argued that, while technological change undoubtedly suppresses jobs (for instance among assembly manufacturing workers, typists, or drafters), the new industries, spurred by demand for new capital goods as well as for computer operations and the handling of automated equipment, will add a substantial number of new jobs, resulting in a structural shift in employment that will allow a technological leap forward comparable in magnitude to the earlier transition from an economy based on agriculture to one based on manufacturing and services (see for instance Lawrence, 1984a; Nazakawa, 1985; and Dosi, 1984). As a matter of fact, Leontieff and Duchin's projections do take into consideration the tradeoff between "old job" destruction and "new job" creation in many instances. They assert, "While the reduction in demand for semi-skilled occupations and laborers, which are directly attributable to robots, is about 600,000 in 1990 and almost 2 million in 2000 under Scenario 3 [the one including fast technological change], the net demand [for labor] is about the same as under Scenario 1 [technology being held constant], apparently due to the offsetting effects of increased production of capital goods" (p. 1.19). Yet, overall, the net effect is the decreasing level of labor requirements for a given level of output and a fixed final demand, as shown in Tables 1 and 2. Furthermore, actual projections of employment changes for the 1982–1995 period show that high-technology employment induced by demand for new capital goods is growing very fast but represents a very small proportion of all jobs—in fact, less than 6 percent (Riche, Hecker and Burgan, 1983). Table 3 provides the BLS projection on the dynamism of high-technology industries in the United States, while putting into perspective their limited role as generators of new employment for the economy as a whole.

Gordon and Kimball (1985) have developed this argument by pinpointing the rapid growth of new technology-based industries, such as electronics, and their inability to account for enough jobs to replace those disappearing as a

TABLE 1. Levels of employment[a] under scenarios S1, S2, and S3[c] in 1978, 1990 and 2000 (millions of person-years), USA

1978	Scenarios S1, S2, and S3	BLS estimates[b]
Professionals	13.9	13.3
Managers	9.5	9.6
Sales workers	5.9	5.9
Clerical workers	15.9	15.6
Craftsmen	11.8	12.0
Operatives	14.0	14.3
Service workers	11.1	10.6
Laborers	4.3	4.5
Farmers	2.8	2.8
Total	89.2	88.6

1990	Scenario S1	Scenario S2	Scenario S3
Professionals	19.8	21.2	20.9
Managers	14.4	14.4	12.4
Sales workers	9.1	8.9	8.2
Clerical workers	24.7	21.2	16.7
Craftsmen	18.0	17.9	17.5
Operatives	22.0	21.8	21.1
Service workers	16.7	16.8	16.8
Laborers	6.6	6.6	6.4
Farmers	4.2	4.2	4.2
Total	135.5	132.9	124.1
2000			
Professionals	25.6	28.4	31.1
Managers	19.0	17.1	11.2
Sales workers	12.4	11.8	10.2
Clerical workers	32.6	25.0	17.9
Craftsmen	23.3	22.9	23.4
Operatives	27.6	26.1	25.8
Service workers	22.3	22.4	23.0
Laborers	8.7	8.6	8.7
Farmers	5.3	5.3	5.4
Total	176.8	167.7	156.6

[a] Includes all private sector employment (jobs) plus employment in public education and health. Does not include public administration, armed forces, or household employees.

[b] Calculated from [US Department of Labor, 1981] using the employment definitions of the IEA Model.

[c] Scenarios: S1: technology held constant. S2: medium technology change. S3: fast technological change.

Source: Leontieff and Duchin, 1984.

result of both technological obsolescence and economic restructuring. Thus, employment in electronics in the United States tripled between 1960 and 1980, jumping from 1.6 percent of the total labor force in 1965 to 2.1 percent in 1974, and to 2.9 percent in 1986. That year, with 2,731,000 people in the industry, electronics accounted for twice as many jobs as the automobile and

TABLE 2. Composition of employment[a] under scenarios S1, S2, and S3[c] in 1978, 1990, and 2000 (percentages), USA

1978	Scenarios S1, S2, and S3	BLS estimates[b]
Professionals	15.6	15.0
Managers	9.5	10.8
Sales workers	6.6	6.7
Clerical workers	17.8	17.7
Craftsmen	13.3	13.6
Operatives	15.7	16.1
Service workers	12.4	12.0
Laborers	4.9	5.0
Farmers	3.2	3.2
Total	100.0	100.0

1990	Scenario S1	Scenario S2	Scenario S3
Professionals	14.6	16.0	16.8
Managers	10.6	10.8	10.0
Sales workers	6.7	6.7	6.6
Clerical workers	18.2	15.9	13.5
Craftsmen	13.3	13.5	14.1
Operatives	16.3	16.4	17.0
Service workers	12.3	12.6	13.5
Laborers	4.9	4.9	5.2
Farmers	3.1	3.1	3.3
Total	100.0	100.0	100.0
2000			
Professionals	14.5	16.9	19.8
Managers	10.8	10.2	7.2
Sales workers	7.0	7.0	6.5
Clerical workers	18.4	14.9	11.4
Craftsmen	13.2	13.7	15.0
Operatives	15.6	15.6	16.5
Service workers	12.6	13.4	14.7
Laborers	4.9	5.1	5.5
Farmers	3.0	3.2	3.4
Total	100.0	100.0	100.0

[a, b, c] See Table 1.

Source: Leontieff and Duchin, 1984.

TABLE 3. Employment and employment growth, by high-tech industries and occupations: 1982 to 1995

Industries Occupations	Employment, 1982 (000s)	Employment growth 1982–95[a]	
		(000s)	(%)
All industries[b]	91,950	25,795	28.1
High-tech industries[c]			
Group I (48 industries)	12,350	4,263	34.5
Percent of all industries	13.4	16.5	
Group II (6 industries)	2,543	867	34.1
Percent of all industries	2.8	3.4	
Group III (28 industries)	5,691	2,029	35.7
Percent of all industries	6.2	7.9	
All occupations[d]	101,510	24,600	25.2
High-tech occupations[e]	3,287	1,508	45.9
Percent of all occupations	3.2	5.9	

[a] Data for 1995 based on moderate-trend projections.
[b] Employment covers all wage and salary workers.
[c] Group I includes industries where the proportion of workers employed in high-tech occupations[e] is at least 1.5 times the average for all industries. Group II includes industries with a ratio of R&D expenditure to net sales at least twice the average for all industries. Group III includes manufacturing industries in which the proportion of workers employed in high-tech occupations[e] is equal or greater than the average for all manufacturing industries; two manufacturing industries that provide technical support to high-tech manufacturing industries are also included.
[d] Employment covers all civilian workers.
[e] Engineers, life and physical scientists, mathematical specialists, engineering and science technicians, and computer specialists.
Source: Richard W. Riche, Daniel E. Hecker, and John V. Burgan, "High Technology Today and Tomorrow: A Small Slice of the Employment Pie," *Monthly Labor Review*, 106, November 1983, Tables 2 and 4.

iron/steel industries combined. And yet, electronics only represented 12 percent of manufacturing jobs, and 2.9 percent of all US employment. In 1984, eating and drinking places were employing almost twice as many people as electronics, government six times more, and non-government services seven times more. Besides, the future rate of growth in high-technology manufacturing is likely to slow down, not to mention the potential losses caused by sharp downturns in the industry (such as that of 1984–1985), and increased international competition, particularly from Japan (Borrus, Millstein and Zysman, 1983). The main high-technology manufacturing industries are expected to create about 830,000 new jobs by 1995. This figure, as Gordon and Kimball write, "constitutes less than half the number of manufacturing jobs lost in the U.S. economy between 1980 and 1983. High-technology industries will continue to expand more rapidly than total employment but nevertheless are expected to contribute less than 9 percent of all new jobs in the period 1982–1995. In other words, all but a small proportion of the new jobs established in the foreseeable future will originate in spheres *outside* high-technology industry while high technology itself will have little impact on reducing unemployment in the U.S., Western Europe, or the Third World" (p. 23).

The real issue, however, is not the direct tradeoff between jobs eliminated through labor-saving technologies and jobs created in the high-technology industries, but the overall effect of technological change on economic growth and, thus, on employment in all activities, especially services. Robert Z. Lawrence (1984a) has built a powerful argument about the beneficial effects of information technologies on employment in the capital goods sector; by increasing productivity, thus alleviating disputes over redistribution; and by extending productivity increases to the service sector. He considers it unlikely that the impact of information technology on the economy will be disruptive, for at least three major reasons: (a) their introduction proceeds at a relatively slow pace—increases in output per worker due to information technology in the United States will not be raised more than 1 percent per year; (b) high rates of investment in new technology will probably take place during expansionary phases of the business cycle, where disruption is less frequent; and (c) even more important, the strongest impact will be during the 1990s, when the rate of growth of the labor force will substantially decline in the United States and in Europe. (The annual growth rate of the US labor force will decline from 3.5 percent in 1970–1982 to 2.3 percent in 1982–1990, and then to 1.4 percent in 1990–1995; for Europe, corresponding figures are 0.9 percent for nine EEC countries in 1980–1985, 0.66 percent in 1985–1990, and 0.37 percent between 1990 and 1995). With these conditions, Lawrence constructs a simulation of employment growth in the United States, from which he concludes that "the decline in the U.S. labor force growth of 2.1 percent is more than twice the rise in output per manhour, but would probably be the maximum due to a rapid increase in information technology. The U.S. economy needs to be no more successful at creating jobs than it has been in the past to absorb the labor potentially displaced by information technology" (p. 31).

Furthermore, it is true that during the 1970s, the two countries that introduced the most information technology in their economies (Japan and the United States) were precisely the countries most able to create jobs, while West European economies, less able to incorporate the technological revolution (*The Economist*, 1984), suffered higher unemployment rates. The case is particularly striking for Germany, which, as of 1980, had a share of high-technology employment in manufacturing similar to that of the United States and Japan, but which performed very poorly in these strategic industries during the 1970s (see Table 4). Thus Lawrence is able to claim that "In European economies, in particular, the new information technologies are viewed with alarm. This alarm is not related to the inherent technological or economic impacts of the technologies, but to the structural problems in European labor markets . . . The key to the superior ability of the U.S. and Japan to adopt the new technologies lies in the flexibility of their labor and capital markets" (p. 48).

Shifting from a comparison of countries to an analysis of industries, the

TABLE 4. Information technology[a]— changes in employment and employment shares in manufacturing

Information technology employment

	1973 (000s)	1980[b] (000s)	Change (%)
United States	2534	2982	17.7
Germany	1321	1149	−13.0
Japan	1789	1708	−1.8
United Kingdom	957	811	−15.3
Sweden	91.4	96.7	5.8

Information technology employment as a share of manufacturing

	1973	1980[b]	Change (%)
United States	13.5	15.5[c]	14.8
Germany	16.5	16.1	−2.4
Japan	15.6	16.7	7.1
United Kingdom	12.7	12.6	−1.0
Sweden	10.2	11.3	1.1

[a] Office computing machinery, electrical machinery, and professional goods.
[b] German data are for 1979.
[c] 16.8 when computer services included.
Source: UN Yearbook of Industrial Statistics (New York: UN, 1979, 1981).

study by Castells and others on the impact of technological change on employment in Spain for the period 1975–1983 (Castells et al., 1986) found no significant correlation between job loss and the introduction of technology for the 64 sectors of the Spanish economy. A more detailed analysis on the evolution of employment in the five automobile companies located in Spain showed a *positive* correlation between the introduction of robots and the level of employment, company by company. The obvious intervening variable was the ability of the company to compete internationally because of stepped-up technological capability, thus enhancing its share of the market and enabling it to maintain its labor requirements in spite of higher productivity. Similar findings were obtained on the relationship between office automation and employment in the Spanish banking sector. As for the United States, a study by Lawrence (1984b) indicates that shifts in employment across sectors in the 1970s (when information technologies accelerated their diffusion throughout the economy) were not significantly different from those in the 1960s.

Thus, it seems that, as a general trend, there is no structural relationship between the use of information technology in the labor process and the evolution of aggregate employment. Jobs are being displaced and new jobs are being created, but their quantitative matching varies across countries and periods, therefore supporting the hypothesis that such differences are probably due to the characteristics of institutional frameworks and the dynamics of each national economy.

Nevertheless, if jobs are created through the dynamism of a newly revitalized economy, they are very different from those phased out. Rumberger and Levin (1984) have shown that, while many of the occupational categories with highest rates of growth in 1982–1995 are directly linked to informational technologies, thus upgrading the skills of future required labor, those occupations with the fastest *absolute* growth, accounting for the bulk of new jobs, are concentrated in low-skilled, low-paid service activities, with little educational requirements. Computer service technicians will grow by 97 percent in 1982–1995, but they will only add 53,000 jobs—while building custodians will increase only by 28 percent, but such a growth will translate into 779,000 new jobs on top of the 2,800,000 building custodians already employed in 1982.

It is on the basis of this trend that many authors (for instance Bluestone and Harrison, 1982; 1984; Markusen, 1983; Rumberger, 1984) defend the idea that the new occupational structure tends to be increasingly polarized, with low-paid service jobs replacing relatively well-paid, unionized manufacturing jobs, and with middle-income groups shrinking their share of the wage-earners' population (Kuttner, 1984; Thurow, 1984). High-technology industries are themselves characterized by a bipolar distribution of skills and ages, with an increasing proportion of employees in electronics (over 50 percent in 1984) being in the non-production category, and a concentration of low-wage, low-skill jobs among production workers (Gordon and Kimball, 1985). In 1984, the average hourly wage of production workers in electronics was $8.89, compared with $13.09 in steel and $12.54 in the auto industry. Gordon and Kimball report usual starting wages in operative work in electronics in the range of $3.50 to $5.50 per hour. Similar trends are reported by Carnoy (1985) for Silicon Valley; by Scott (1985) for Orange County; and by Gordon and Kimball (1985) for Santa Cruz, California. As Table 5 shows, women and minorities account for a growing majority of production workers in high-technology industries, and they tend to be concentrated in the lower end of the occupational scale.

Thus, we observe an evolution of the employment structure of the United States characterized by:

1. A fast rate of growth of high-technology and advanced-services-related occupations, that are accounting for a small proportion of new jobs and an even lower share of overall aggregate employment.

2. A bipolar occupational structure in high-technology employment between a majority of upgraded, professional, non-production jobs (most of them held by white males), and a sizeable minority of low-skilled, low-paid production jobs increasingly reserved for women and minorities, with the greatest share for minority women.

3. A massive increase of service jobs that will account for about 75 percent

Table 5. High technology occupational structure: gender, ethnicity and race

	(1) US high technology industry		
	White female (%)	Minority (male & female) (%)	White male (%)
Production	38.4	24.4	37.2
Technical	15.8	14.3	69.9
Professional	11.9	8.4	79.7

	(2) Santa Clara county		
	White female (%)	Minority (male & female) (%)	White male (%)
Production	30.2	46.4	23.4
Technical	16.7	28.0	55.3
Professional	13.3	14.4	72.2

	(3) Santa Cruz county		
	White female (%)	Minority (male & female) (%)	White male (%)
Production	48.4	29.4	22.2
Technical	25.3	23.0	51.7
Professional	24.0	12.7	63.4

Sources: *1980 EEOI Summary Report of Selected Establishments from the Technical Services Division, OSP,* Equal Employment Opportunity Commission; R. Gordon and L. Kimball, *Small Town High Technology: The Industrialization of Santa Cruz County,* 1985. We are very grateful to Lenny Siegel, Pacific Studies Center, Mountain View for supplying the EEOI raw data from which the US and Santa Clara tables are calculated.

of all new jobs in the period 1982–1995. Most of these jobs will be in low-skill, low-pay occupations, such as janitors, cashiers, secretaries, waiters, and the like. It follows a general pattern of de-skilling and downgrading of labor in the overall occupational structure (Rumberger and Levin, 1984).

4. At the same time, high-level occupations such as professionals and technicians will significantly increase their share of employment, from 16.3 percent in 1982 to 17.3 percent in 1995 (Silvestri, Lukasiewicz and Einstein, 1983), while production occupations will decline somewhat (from 12.8 percent to 12.1 percent). Along with the preceding trend towards the

downgrading of many service jobs, it would seem as though the process of bipolarization will actually affect the entire occupational structure, though the bottom will certainly be larger than the top. Thus, re-skilling and de-skilling, upgrading and downgrading, operate at the same time, with a changing emphasis following different industries and occupations.

Nevertheless, the question arises of the specific relationship between new technologies and the emerging profile of the occupational structure as described. In other words, the secular transformation toward a service economy, and the specific characteristics of such service activities, would seem a much greater source of the new occupational structure, including the process of bipolarization and the occupational segregation by gender and race, than the introduction of information technologies in the process of work.

A serious attempt to answer such a question empirically for the United States has been undertaken by Ronald Kutscher of the US Bureau of Labor Statistics (Kutscher, 1985). Kutscher proceeds in two steps. He first analyzes the specific impact of technological change on employment by industry and by occupation, between 1967 and 1978, comparing the actual level of employment to what would have resulted while holding constant input-output technological coefficients at their 1967 level. He then goes on to evaluate the impact of technology on future employment change by calculating a factor analysis on the 1977–1995 projections by industry and by occupation, sorting out the specific impact of input-output coefficients, once having controlled the effect of other factors, particularly GNP growth. Kutscher's definition of technological change is very broad. It includes all changes in the goods or services required to produce each industry's goods or services. Yet, his findings on the specific effects of technology on the evolution of employment in the 1967–1978 period are a good approximation of what we need at this very general, exploratory stage of our research. His research suggests that technology had a significantly negative effect on agriculture and on manufacturing, a positive effect on construction, a slightly negative effect on wholesale and retail trade (offsetting the positive effects of the increase in output), a positive effect on finance, insurance, and real estate employment, and a very positive effect on "office services." Using data not shown in the Table, we observe that the negative effects on manufacturing have been concentrated in textiles, apparel, iron and steel, and motor vehicles; while positive effects have been concentrated on "other services," primarily in miscellaneous business services and non-profit organizations.

The statistical analysis for occupational change between 1967 and 1978 shows a positive effect of technology on the share of professionals and technicians, a negative effect on operatives and farmers, and a lack of impact on clerical workers. Concerning future trends, the analysis is made more complicated by the projective character of the data. Also, Kutscher has kept a high level of disaggregation to make possible his factor analysis, so that the trends are less clear for the 1977–1995 period. Yet, it does appear that, in terms of decline, traditional manufacturing and manual workers are the most badly hit by technological progress, while clerical jobs do not appear among the 40 occupations with the largest decline. High-tech manufacturing and advanced services are the industries whose employment is most positively influenced by technology. But, the occupations showing the largest increases in employment from technological change are not necessarily the typical high-tech occupations, but service-related occupations. Thus, security-related occupations, household repair and maintenance, and financial experts outweigh communications mechanics or computer programmers in their increase as a consequence of technology. Services are the predominant source not only of job creation, but also of the expanding employment sector as a result of technological progress, once the effects of GNP growth, productivity, and staffing patterns are taken into account.

Such an overwhelming trend for the expansion of service employment does not mean the demise of manufacturing. Manufacturing employment added 4.5 million jobs between 1959 and 1979, though it lost 2.2 million jobs in the 1980–1982 recession, dropping to 19 percent of total employment in 1982. Yet, it will not decline further according to the projections up to 1995, adding another 4.3 million jobs and retaining its current share of total employment. The difference is, of course, that new employment creation (about 23 to 28 million jobs between 1983 and 1995) will take place entirely in the service sector, and predominantly in the "other service" category (including such industries as business services, professional services, medical care, hotels, personal services, and non-profit organizations), which will account for one-third of new jobs. This will put "other services" employment in 1995 at 31 million jobs, or one-fourth of total US employment.

The most interesting point about the factor analysis performed by Kutscher is that the general trend toward employment in services is due, to a large extent, to GNP growth, and, to a lesser extent, to the specific effect of technological change on the structure of employment. Thus technology is having a double effect on the type of jobs created in the new economy: on the one hand, being a major factor in economic growth, it accelerates the shift toward the service economy; on the other hand, it stimulates employment growth in high-tech manufacturing and in new services as a direct effect of technology itself. Therefore, there seems to be a statistical relationship between the characteristics of the current technological revolution and the specific profile of the employment structure emerging in the new economy, at least in the United States. Productivity increases through automation in both factories and offices "frees" labor, which is used by an ever-expansionary service sector, whose lower level, increasingly more important than the upper, concentrates most women, minorities, and immigrants in low-skill jobs. These occupations, lacking in organizational strength, become also low-paid, ill-protected jobs.

So, we can say that high technology does *not* create unemployment by itself, particularly if we take into consideration the declining rate of growth of the labor force. When used to spur economic growth, it frees enough productivity to stimulate profitable investment as a response to expanding final demand, thus also expanding employment outside the high-tech world. Yet, high technology seems to contribute to a new occupational structure characterized by polarization, segmentation, and individualization of labor relationships. It probably does so in spite of the upgrading of much of the labor working in high-technology industries by contributing to the dissolution of the social fabric that for decades protected the wage-earners from the sheer imposition of management's logic. Otherwise, it would be inexplicable why clerical work as such is less well paid than assembly-line work, or why electronics production workers cannot match the wages of their auto industry counterparts. It is the dissolution of old activities, and the subsequent creation of new ones, under the powerful drive of technologically-led economic growth, that accounts for the current structural transformation of employment. New technologies do not necessarily cause unemployment, yet they do transform the kind of employment, and therefore the nature of work and of work relationships.

V. New communication technologies and everyday life

New technologies are transforming all domains of our life, from the schools of our children to the biological reproduction of human life. But perhaps the most important development in the relationship between new technologies and social life is the coming of the "home information revolution" (Dutton, Kovoric, Steinfield, 1983). It refers not only to the increasing use of home computers, but to the transformation of a large proportion of households into real communication hubs (Williams, 1982). By 1984, about 7 percent of US households were equipped with home computers, 21 percent had programmable video games, and 37 percent subscribed to some kind of cable-TV service (up from 25 percent in 1980). The progression in home electronics equipment in recent years is spectacular, in spite of some slump in the home computer market in 1984–1985. Sales of consumer electronic products reached $19 billion in 1983. Home computer sales accounted for $2 billion in 1983, against $1.3 billion in 1982. Even telephone sales increased dramatically (by 60 percent in 1983), reaching 31 million domestic telephone units in 1983. Cable-TV was a $6.1 billion industry in 1983. In 1984, 67 million US homes (above two-thirds of all homes) had been wired for cable, and actual penetration of service had risen to 32 million homes (*Business Week*, 1981; Williams, 1982; Baldwin and McVoy, 1983). The technological development of communications in the field of news and entertainment has an even greater potential impact. To the 150 million television sets in use in the United States (99 percent of homes have at least one set, 50 percent at least two) has now been added the explosion of video-cassette recorders (VCRs) (currently in about 28 percent of US households) and video-disc equipment, along with new developments in specialized radio, video, television and hi-fi musical equipment. The increasing use of satellites and the affordability of roof-top discs will allow reception of literally hundreds of channels, potentially submerging the receivers' capacity of assimilating signals and information.

Yet, if we know what the current developments are (*Business Week*, 1984; *New York Times*, 1984), we are most uncertain what actual use all this equipment will be. Home computing seems to be more diffused among professionals, basically for word processing functions, since more business-oriented activities are generally performed in the work environment. Income tax accounting is a frequent use of personal computers, but it certainly does not use up all the computer's potential. Games seem to be the most general use of the home computer, but, after the initial excitement and novelty leveled off the video-game industry ran into a deep crisis. Thus, while home computers are here to stay, and while their use will develop steadily with user-friendly models and the foreseeable dramatic reduction in cost, their impact on the home (and on society) will be less in terms of their own information-related capabilities than as a piece of a broader communications network.

It is in the field of *on-line information services* that the new function of the electronic home has been most frequently forecast. Though this perspective is generally associated with cable, and with the image of the wired city, a variety of other competing technologies aim at the same target: the delivery of a variety of information, with the possibility of some two-way interaction. Packet-type data radio and television allow sending information in bursts, including codes to identify the signal, thereby bypassing the current cable operators. But the main source of information delivery is likely to be the telephone, once it is reconnected to digital transmission capabilities, and its speed and cost improved through the combination of laser and optical fiber. In fact, these different technologies are not mutually exclusive. Given the cost of two-way cable, cable companies are already planning to set up systems that would allow sending information through the already installed wire and receiving the feedback from homes through the telephone line (Williams, 1982).

But . . . technologies for what? What will be the services provided by all these communications wonders? We are told that, by 1990, about one-third of US homes will have some kind of videotext service. What will be the informational content of such a service? Dorkiek, Bradley, Names, and Martin projected the following adoption of services by the US population in 1995 (*Business Week,* June 29, 1981; Dorkiek et al., 1979):

Type of information delivered	% of all US households
Addresses, numbers, calendars of events	45
Home security (police, fire)	40
Shopping by catalog	30
Directory of goods and services	30
Personal message system	30
Games	30
Public information, such as zoning, regulations, laws	25
Library services	20

Other sources add weather information, electronic banking, electronic mail, energy monitoring, and the like.

One wonders at the real usefulness of the home delivery of these services from the point of view of the consumers, particularly given the current availability of most of this information through the telephone. Are the yellow pages more appealing on screen? Do we really need minute-by-minute updates of the weather forecasts? Is tele-shopping really a viable alternative to shopping centers? Some of the applications of videotext, such as electronic newspapers featured on the TV screen, have already been discounted as being too inconvenient for readership and because people are not able to find any specific use for them after watching TV news and reading the home-delivered morning newspaper. In fact, current experiences of videotext services have been generally disappointing. The French "telematique" system has not really taken off, in spite of the massive support of the French Post Office. The British Prestel system has had a moderate success because of its capacity of conveying a broader range of miscellaneous information. In the United States, the average pay-cable household takes only 1.3 pay services. People are generally reluctant to pay for services for which they do not have a compelling need, or which they used to have free through the telephone line. Electronic mail, already in fast development, particularly in its facsimile transmission service, concerns offices more than homes. Yet it could have some impact on the home-delivery of mail as a result of the increasing cost of personal mail. If this trend develops, we could see a combination of three types of mail: electronic messages through computer hookups; self-pickup electronic mail at neighborhood post offices transformed into computerized transmission centers; and the home delivery service as an elite consumer item at an extra cost.

In fact, the main uses for electronic home services could develop along these different lines:

(a) Home security, with wired systems of alert in case of an emergency. This is actually the hottest item in the cable business, outside of entertainment.

(b) Public information, such as government regulations or available services (i.e., health, education, libraries, children's programs, and so on). This could be provided as a service by public agencies, thus increasing their reach and capabilities, though certainly reducing the level of personal contact with citizens.

(c) Electronic banking, which is already being heavily encouraged by banks. In fact, this development is a good example of what is really happening. It is well known that people prefer to deal personally with a bank teller in all money transfers. Automated banking machines have increased the security risks for handling money, in terms of cashing in the street, potential errors, and the increased risk of misuse of stolen bank cards. Yet banks are reducing personnel, closing branches, and generally automating. With the potential of home electronic banking, this movement will dramatically accelerate—not because of customers' convenience, but because of the dramatic breakthrough in productivity that this will represent for the banking industry. Once some key services are almost mandatorily executed through cable or telephone lines, many others will be branched into the same network. In this sense, we can foresee a slow but steady trend toward the "telecommunicated city." The likely impact will be (as is already being observed) a decrease in functional travelling around urban areas, and a concentration of activities around three major poles: work places, homes, and pure leisure time and places. At first it seems ideal to be able to limit the necessity of going out (outside work) just for the pleasure of doing so. But we know that people are rarely able to take time off to travel for the fun of it: this is the privilege of youth, and of a small proportion of the middle class. Most people use the city in between the functional activities they "had to do," playing on the margins of instrumentalism and expressiveness, without necessarily having to decide on the optimal use of their time. Internalizing functional activities at home and at work apparently leaves more room for the free use of the city in terms of pure choice. But it also increases the functional zoning of time and space in such a way that public space becomes the space of leisure (for those who have the time and the money) *and* the space of wandering (for those who do not fit in the functional assignment of work and residence).

Urban cultures have always been characterized by the mixture of their uses. Land use zoning started to segregate people and activities, thus leaning toward the disintegration of the social tissue of cities. Now, electronic zoning dramatically enhances this tendency, transforming places into uni-functional units, unless an unprogrammed activity can take place. But then there is a chance that spontaneity will become increasingly associated with weirdness (if not deviance).

The real "revolution" occurring at home under the impact of new technologies is actually in *entertainment*. Homes are becoming increasingly equipped with a self-sufficient world of images, sounds, news, and information exchanges (Sabbah, 1985). The most interesting aspect, nevertheless, is that, even if the TV set is the centerpiece of the system, television, as we have known it, is on the decline. In recent years, there has been an increasing demand for a more diversified TV, with more emphasis on entertainment and on specific matters, varying according to subsets of the audience. Cable-TV was supposed to be a response to this demand for a diversified and decentralized TV programming, and this explains the rapid development of local cable systems in the 1970s. Yet, the current state of the industry has not supported the expectations of a community TV, more directly connected to people's everyday life. The same national TV networks, as well as some major corporations, stepped into the new, promising markets, and transformed it into an extension of TV programming, with more targeted audiences. In fact, cable-TV has become one of the most concentrated sectors of the media industry. Instead of controlling the viewers' growing desire for autonomy, the taking over of cable-TV by the big networks has only accelerated their disaffections, actually provoking a crisis in cable-TV itself. Its development leveled off in 1982, and currently, 40 percent of cable-TV subscribers disconnect pay services every year.

Companies have responded by raising fees, concentrating on the most profitable sectors of the market, introducing new pay-per-view technology, and slowing the introduction of new services—all of which results in deepening the crisis. For instance, in spite of all the talk on the promise of two-way cable, and the publicity of systems such as Qube in Columbus, Ohio, only 500,000 homes are equipped with interactive cable. What is really taking the place of traditional television is video (Stark, 1984). In 1985, about 28 percent of US households had VCRs. World-wide, the 1984 figures are 40 million VCRs, with projections for 1990 being 70 million. The same projection estimates that by 1990 home video will be a $10-billion-a-year industry in the United States, which is more than the entire American film and music industries combined. The number of video-cassette stores climbed from 6,000 in 1982 to 14,000 in 1984. Big supermarkets are becoming distribution points. And movie theaters are selling video cassettes of the most popular movies they have shown. Video production is growing. In 1982–1984 about 2,000 titles were released, at an average price of $40, with rentals as low as one dollar a night. "Raiders of the Lost Ark," the leader of the new industry, sold 800,000 cassettes in the first year of its release, distantly followed by "Jane Fonda's Workout," which sold 170,000 copies. Yet the biggest explosion is still in the making: musical video (stereo VCRs and video albums), which, it is estimated, will represent about 25 percent of the entire home-video market by 1988.

The main element in the enticement for video is increased freedom in control over both the time of viewing and content. The possibility of TV recording, as well as of "pirate recording," offers an unlimited field for the accumulation of images, sounds, and information, a new kind of library that finally departs from the Gutenberg Galaxy. Thus television will still be used as a source for news and instant information (from sports to live televised warfare, as in the Falklands war). Homes will increasingly become at the same time instant receivers of planetary information (thus actually creating the global village), and personal refuges of selective consumption of images and sounds. Technologically speaking, most homes will become self-sufficient entertainment centers, thus increasing the tendency toward a home-centered private life (Morfoot, 1982).

Furthermore, the trend is not only toward home-centered entertainment, but toward the individualization of the communication experience. The simultaneous development of highly specialized radio stations, and of "walkman" devices, is perhaps the most spectacular expression of the new trend. Not only will people be able to stay at home, see nobody, and yet receive news from the entire world, or fill their eyes and ears with a large variety of experiences, but they will also be able (as they *are* already) to leave home with their inner experience of sound and information through earphones that protect them from the world outside—which represents everything that is not pre-programmed and, more and more so, not *personally* pre-programmed. Certainly, these are only *tendencies*, and they can be reshaped by purposive action, as well as by the interaction with other elements of our culture and social organization. Besides, there is nothing wrong with the great possibilities that video offers to people who want to control to some extent the audio-visual culture in which we live.

Sometimes the actual social effects are quite unpredictable. For instance, it has been generally assumed that the video explosion would hurt movie theaters as much as TV did. And yet, it does not seem that such is the case. Not only is movie-going still popular in Western Europe, but in the United States the number of screens is actually on the rise (from 16,500 in the late 1970s to about 19,000 in the mid-1980s). The film industry is responding to the video challenge by increasing the quality of exhibition in movie theaters, and video-viewers are attracted to the theaters, much in the same way that LP records are an advertising spot for live performances. Images that lead to images that refer to images . . . of the "reality." Which reality?

The electronic home is, above all, a self-sufficient unit of communication in a world increasingly dominated by images and information. People will be able to stay at home and communicate, though this communication will be selective and specialized. If we add the technology of individualized communication (pocket-type distribution of data, "walkman"-type receiving devices, wrist TVs and receiving stations, portable and disposable telephones, and so on), we can concede that the new technologies lead toward the de-localization of experience in the sphere of private life, as they do for work-oriented organizations. Homes *could* become dissociated from neighborhood and cities, and still not be lonely, isolated places. They would be populated by voices, by images, by sounds, by ideas, by games, by colors, by news. And yet, you (we) could switch it all of in one gesture, as we already do. So, we know that the world (at home) is only there if we wish it so. From a strictly technological point of view, there is no more mediation between the individual and a global culture that is satellite-transmitted, then specialized, and targeted to specific people and to specific moods. Thus, in-between, there is no more society.

Joshua Meyrowitz, in his recent major book on the social effects of electronic media (Meyrowitz, 1985), agues that the electronic environment blurs social roles and identities, separates physical space from social perception, and mixes public and private spheres in the same frame of reference. Francoise Sabbah (Sabbah, 1985) goes even further. For her, the new media *are* our new reality. We construct our categories to interpret what we live through, and by the images we constantly receive from a variety of media. People tend to relate their actual experience to the symbols and meanings constructed in their minds by the pervasive presence of media's messages. It is not only the medium that becomes the message, but also the image that becomes the real experience around which we tend to construct our relationship to the world.

The result is the fragmentation and individualization of human experience, and in the absence of powerful antidotes (such as community life or strong social networks), the dissolution of solidarity ties, the end of shared codes of communication, and, in the last resort, loneliness as a way of life.

VI. High technology and the military connection

There is a close relationship between the origins of the current technological revolution and the military and space programs in the United States (Dumas, 1982; Dellums, 1983; Fallows, 1981; Markusen, 1985). Government support was decisive in the fields of semiconductors, computers, and communications during the take-off period of the 1950s and 1960s (Carlson and Lyman, 1984; Siegel and Markoff, 1985). Generous funding to the universities, and safe, assured contracts for development of new technologies to private companies, created the basis for an industry-research-government partnership that made possible much of the technological breakthroughs in information technologies. Furthermore, the emphasis from the military has always been on performance, rather than cost, thus favoring innovation and long-term investment, rather than immediate success in the commercial market. So, in

spite of all the ideology about the role of small business and entrepreneurial-
ism in the launching of a new technological era, government support and
product specification by the military laid down the organizational basis for
new technologies. The interesting point is that the research undertaken
directly by government institutions failed, while the most successful programs
were those carried out by independent institutions or companies under
government contract (Carlson and Lyman, 1984). Yet the characteristics of
the products required by the military and space programs largely influenced
the informational devices that became the keystones of the new technological
era. Key requirements were *mobility* and *miniaturization* (Markusen, 1985).
That was the beginning of an evolution that will soon end up in a new era of
vehicles which are entirely based on electronics, regardless of the
aerodynamic capabilities of their increasingly bizarre shapes. When Jack
Kilby co-invented the integrated circuit at Texas Instruments in 1959,
practically all of its production went to the military markets (Mutlu, 1979).
Yet, even at that time, that was not an economic imperative. The
simultaneous co-inventor of the IC, Bob Noyce (then at Fairchild, and later
the founder of Intel), did not work for the military, and Fairchild sold only a
small proportion of its production to that market (Carlson and Lyman, 1984).
Thus, one can see, at the same time, the crucial role of the military-induced
contracts in the high-technology industries, and the product diversification of
the industry in commercially oriented products. Carlson and Lyman (1984),
show the *decreasing* share of government markets in the semiconductor
industry, when the industry matured. With the coming of the microprocessor
(by Ted Hoff, at Intel, 1971), and the generalization of chips-applications,
including the development of micro-computers, the demilitarization of high
technology industries accelerated. Along parallel lines, the tremendous
influence of Japanese technology, in the absence of military markets,
demonstrates that there is no necessity for association between information
technology and weapons production (Borrus, Millstein and Zysman, 1983).

Nevertheless, the process of technological discovery in the particular
situation of the United States in the 1950s and 1960s did produce such an
association, and led to a series of consequences in the way high technology
industries developed and in the products and processes they turned out to
generate (De Grasse, 1983). As late as 1970 about 22 percent of all US
electrical engineers, about 50 percent of aeronautical engineers and about 30
percent of physicists were working on military-related projects (Dempsey and
Schurde, 1971; Rutziek, 1970). Defense spending poured into some very
specific regions and industries where a combination of scientific technical
skills and conservative political climate could support the new industries,
particularly in Silicon Valley, Orange County, and Texas (Markusen and
Bloch, 1985). Much of the new dynamism of the Sunbelt since the 1970s is
related to the political support that these areas enjoy from the Defense
Department (Markusen, 1986).

At the same time, the nurturing of technological innovation triggered all
kinds of civilian applications on their own, so that during the 1970s, two
convergent lines of high technology industries developed in the United States:
one closely connected to the military (aircraft, and communication

equipment, for instance), another in which defense spending, while important, represented a relative minority of the trade (about 7 percent for computers, or about 13 percent for semiconductors, in 1982). The situation in the early 1980s has thus become quite mixed (Markusen, 1985). The basic picture is this combination of two trends; one, the original military connection of the 1950–60s period, and the other the second stage, the blossoming of technological civilian applications of the 1970s, spearheaded by the microprocessor, the invention of which was entirely alien to the military market—it resulted from an order by a Japanese pocket-calculator maker—(Braun and MacDonald, 1982; Rogers and Larsen, 1984).

Nevertheless, the tendency is being reversed again, and in quite a decisive manner, because of the qualitatively new military build-up undertaken by the two Reagan Administrations. As far as it is known (*Business Week*, October 21, 1985), since 1981, defense outlays in the United States have increased by 60 percent, and Defense Department spending has more than doubled in real terms, jumping from 2.8 percent annual increase during the Carter Administration to about 7.5 percent annual increase, on average, in the Reagan Administration. Defense accounts for about 30 percent of the annual federal budget, for a staggering amount in excess of 300 *billion* dollars. It is also true, however, that if defense spending has risen from 5.4 percent of GNP under Carter to 6.7 percent under Reagan, it is still lower than the 8.9 percent of GNP it averaged between 1954–1964, and lower than the 7.4 percent of GNP it represented in 1970. Furthermore, some estimate that the Soviet Union spends close to 30 percent of its GNP in direct or indirect military expenses, so apparently justifying the US build-up (Coates and Kilian, 1985). Thus the rate of increase of US military expenditures is significant; the commitment of the current US government to the military is clear to everyone; and, most important, the sheer size of the US economy translates an even moderate proportion of its GNP (between 7 percent and 10 percent) into a colossal mass of resources that, effectively targeted, could ensure military supremacy to the United States.

The economic effects of such a military policy are decisive (Gansler, 1980). Experts consider that between 15 percent and 20 percent of employment gains, and about 0.5 percent of the growth of GNP, generated in 1982–1984, can be attributed to defense spending (*Business Week*, October 21, 1985). More fundamentally, a deficit-financed policy of military expenditures can be seen as the new form of "perverted Keynesianism" that has pumped the American economy out of the recession, as we have argued elsewhere (Carnoy and Castells, 1985). By targeting high-technology industries that produce new military hardware, such a military-industrial policy has done more than stimulate the economy; it has favored new industries, new regions, and new sections of the labor force, skewing it toward white male engineers and technicians (Markusen, 1986). The whole US economy is being restructured under the current process of government-induced, military-oriented, high-technology development (De Grasse, 1983).

Other countries, particularly France, Great Britain, Italy, West Germany, Brazil, Spain, Israel (besides, of course the Soviet Union and Warsaw Pact countries), are following similar paths toward economic recovery, making up for their trade gaps with weapons sales, mostly to Third World countries. Arms sales have already become the number one export items for France and Brazil. Thus, in some fundamental way, the complex effects of military spending and high technology manufacturing have become a key element, if not the backbone of the economies of the most advanced industrial economies, with the exception of Japan. And even for the latter, it seems that Japanese companies are finally making inroads into the US military procurement contracts, with both the attractive quality and the price of Japanese would-be advanced weaponry producers (Coates and Kilian, 1985). We believe this feature will stay in the foreseeable future. While military markets do not represent the predominant share of high technology industries, they are a key component from which technological innovation flows to the entire economy. The tendency is not irreversible, as the case of Japan again shows, but it is a hard fact of our current economic structure.

Nevertheless, it would be a major mistake to believe that high-tech military development is the consequence of an economic policy (implicit or explicit) designed to overcome the crisis of the 1970s, or more specifically, the 1980–1982 recession. To be sure, the economic pay-off of increased defense spending is an important argument for keeping it in most countries. Besides, in countries like the United States defense-related industrial areas such as California and the Southwest are not indifferent to the military build-up and are politically close to the Reagan Administration. But if Reagan has failed to follow his own economic ideology, and endangered the American and the world economies with the largest budgetary deficit in history, it has not been for the sake of a short-term reflationary process. The military build-up is motivated, fundamentally, by a political goal: the re-establishment of US military supremacy. Unlike the military policies of the last three decades, the United States is trying to leap forward, as it did during World War II, by transforming its technological edge (shared only with a non-military power, Japan) into a decisive military superiority. In this sense, the Strategic Defense Initiative (regardless of its technical feasibility or of our own political or moral judgments) is a major indication of the new direction in which military policy, and therefore world policy, has already embarked. This is the really fundamental, historically new connection between the military and the current technological revolution.

So much has been written about the "Star Wars" program, and such a large debate has (rightly) surrounded the proposal, that we are in danger of overlooking its significance. What matters about SDI is not its achievement (which is still in doubt) but the process it triggers by the simple existence of the program on technological and strategic grounds. SDI represents the most spectacular element in an overall effort by the United States to use the technological revolution to achieve strategic supremacy. It could be a program designed to dominate the world, or, on the contrary, to pacify it, making impossible forever the ambitions of the "Evil Empire" and thus allow the improvement of the social and economic well-being of all nations under the protection of a benevolent America. But this is not relevant to my point. The key issue is the transformation of technological superiority into a military one, and thus into political supremacy.

The effort under way is gigantic, and although it goes back to programs in the 1960s, with the formation of the Defense Advanced Research Projects Agency (DARPA), and other specialized institutions, it has received a qualitative impulse during the Reagan presidency. The United States leads all other Western nations in R & D investment, both in absolute terms and as a percent of GNP. In dollar terms, the United States spends more than Germany, Japan, the United Kingdom and France, together. Using the last comparable figures for 1981, the United States invested 2.5 percent of its GNP in R & D, compared to 2.4 percent in Japan, 2.7 percent in West Germany, 2.1 percent in the UK, and 2 percent in France. But most of this research, unlike in other major industrial nations goes for military programs in the United States. In 1978 (a year in which there are comparable data with Japan), 49 percent of US government R & D expenditures were for national defense, with an additional 12 percent for the space program, while Japan only dedicated 2 percent of government's research expenses to defense, and 5 percent to space, against 54 percent for the "advancement of knowledge." In 1984, the shape of US government research expenditures budgeted to defense had jumped to 70 percent (Botkin, Dimancescu, and Stata, 1984). Research for SDI has received, for 1986–1990 a budget of 2.6 billion dollars. Yet, the effort is more than quantitative. A complete reorganization of the defense system is under way. Highly educated, technologically-motivated senior officers have been appointed to key positions of command since 1981 (Coates and Kilian, 1985). DARPA, credited as being one of the most innovative and well-run research agencies in the world, has been given the task of coordinating and funding research efforts to bring together government, industry, and universities in strategic areas, very much based on the Japanese model, but with fundamentally military applications as the major goal. In the fall of 1983, DARPA announced the launching of a strategic computing program, that overshadows by far the resources behind Japan's Fifth Generation computer program. The Strategic Computing Program brings together, under the leadership and funding of the Department of Defense, the two major university–industry research consortia recently formed in the United States: the Semiconductors Research Corporation (SRC), based in North Carolina's Research Triangle Park with the participation of about 30 universities—the "lead centers" at Cornell, Berkeley, Carnegie–Mellon, MIT, Illinois, and Stanford, receiving about $20 million per year on a number of targeted research programs; the second joint-venture is the Microelectronics and Computer Technology Corporation (MCC), established at Austin, Texas, by 13 companies, led by Central Data Corporation (Botkin, Dimancescu, and Stata, 1984; Farley and Glickman, 1985). Such targeted efforts, along with a number of more specific, less publicized agreements, between the Defense Department, industry, and leading universities, are creating the scientific and technological basis for an entirely new form of warfare, and thus of military-political strategy. The information-based technological revolution is now deeply intertwined with the politics of global confrontation. Technology has become, more than ever, the key source of power.

Furthermore, SDI amounts to an integrated program of technological development in which the US government would like to include its NATO allies. Thus, for European countries, the dilemma could be between missing the connection to the most advanced sources of technology and applied science, and being partners in a program with a predominant military emphasis. The French-inspired Eureka program has recently brought together 18 European countries in an attempt to build a different network of technological cooperation focused on civilian applications. Yet, Eureka is, at the end of 1985, little more than a series of already existing cooperative programs (foremost among them being ESPRIT, particularly focused on computers), plus a number of ad hoc joint ventures between governments and leading European firms in electronics, biotechnology, energy, and advanced materials. Few technological breakthroughs will come from Eureka, unless further integration is accomplished and greater financial and scientific resources are provided by European governments and firms. For the moment, it is a political statement rather than a true technological alternative to SDI. This is why most EEC countries (including Britain, West Germany and Italy) are participating *at the same time* in Eureka and SDI, as if they wanted to emphasize their political autonomy, yet maintain a strong connection to a source of technological discovery that, building on the current United States advantage, is likely to accelerate over the next few years.

Critics of the increasing militarization of science and technology in the United States have pinpointed the waste of material and intellectual resources that such an orientation implies, and they have argued that the narrowing of the industrial base to military-related high-technology manufacturing will considerably jeopardize American competitiveness in the international economy (Markusen, 1986; Botkin, Dimancescu, and Stata, 1984; Siegel and Markoff, 1985). Thousands of scientists in all major universities in the United States have stated their opposition to SDI and declared their refusal to cooperate in any such research programs. So the debate is not over, and SDI still remains a specific proposal highly dependent upon the political fate of the Republican party and surrounded with uncertainties about its technological and budgetary feasibility.

Nevertheless, it seems that the close association between the new technological revolution, military programs, and the new drive towards strategic supremacy, will be well established in forthcoming years, regardless of what happens to SDI. It is too tempting for a great power, so vigorously embattled in the last decade, to use the sudden technological lead it is enjoying (only shared in some areas with Japan) to redefine the rules of the game. World power will be largely decided in the research laboratories of the industrially advanced countries of the world. Of course, people's mobilization and consciousness, public opinion, and political coalitions, will still play a major role. And many local conflicts and regional wars will still be decided by the specific political equations underlying them. Yet the major strategic equilibrium will be more and more dependent on the mastering of information technology, itself determined by the capacity of a society to generate scientific research and to apply it to industrial and commercial innovation, ultimately leading to a pool of technological discoveries available for military uses. We are entering a period of transition, in which we will see the emergence of new battles to control the technological revolution for the sake of power, and attempts to reach a new global equilibrium under the terms imposed by the information-driven technological era. This is a particularly challenging and dangerous time. Alternative models for the use of new technologies can still be put forward, but at the same time, the fear of a qualitative rupture of the global equilibrium between the superpowers could trigger reactions that would unleash the devils of the old, industrial, nuclear world before we reach a socially responsible informational age.

VII. Alternative technology or alternative society?

New technologies are not responsible for the shameful state of our world. In fact, paradoxically, while we now have the economic and technological possibility of fulfilling many of humankind's historical utopias, our social and political institutions are the two barriers to their realization. Nevertheless, new technologies are so powerful and so pervasive that they accelerate and emphasize the contradictory tendencies present in our societies. Thus, the economic uses of automation translate labor saving into job suppression, and work flexibility into union busting. Uneven development on a world scale transforms the impulse for technological innovation into an insurmountable technological gap for dependent, impoverished Third World countries. The new media reinforce the tendency toward social isolation and turn the electronic home into an individualistic inner space, open to the sounds and images of the entire planet, yet too often closed to face-to-face interaction. The most powerful innovative technologies are appropriated and kept secret, to be geared toward warfare, keeping our world a nuclear hostage of state terrorism in the competition between the superpowers. While new technologies are based upon free flows of information, hidden bureaucracies tend to utilize them for scrutinizing people to program their lives. On the edge of liberating its creativity with an unprecedented technological revolution, humankind becomes the slave of its own collective monsters, fostered by the greediness of capital and the despotism of state. Under these circumstances, it is understandable that people all over the world have criticized the current technological revolution and denounced its militaristic, authoritarian, and exploitative ramifications. Consequently, some of the critics of new technologies argue for alternative paths of technological development that are closer to "human nature" and more respectful of ecological equilibrium in searching for the harmony of lost, simpler, rural-like communities. In most cases, without taking such extreme positions, the horror of the militarization and bureaucratization of the new technological environment has led responsible professionals and grass-roots groups to resist the inevitability of the current process of technological change, looking for alternative ways to handle work and everyday life. While such reactions are entirely understandable, they are, in my opinion, fundamentally confused. This is for two basic reasons: first, because technologies are not the cause but the instrument of the devastating effects being produced in the current historical process; second, because in order to transform this process, it is crucial to recognize the ineluctability of technologically-induced structural transformations, so as to be able to address our social and political problems in their new historical terms. In other words, instead of withdrawing into the seclusion of alternative technology (which can only be a marginal phenomenon), we ought to struggle for an alternative society that will incorporate, master, and reshape the extraordinary technological discoveries that are taking place. After all, the primacy of information implies the coming of culture and symbols to the forefront of our experience and social organization, making society potentially freer to construct itself around its own desires. This is precisely why, barely out of our pre-historic era, where hunger, illness, torture, and massacres are still the actual problems faced by much of humankind, the level of our technological development is much higher than that of our social development. The solution to this gap is not to downgrade our scientific creativity but to enhance our social organization.

Sociologists know that visions of a better world must be rooted in the historical workings of a given society, to have any chance of achieving the status of human experience. At the same time, such action-oriented visions cannot be reduced to linear extrapolations of current trends. The factor of will, the consciousness and purpose of human subjects, individual or collective, are an objective social process by themselves. Visions are not utopias because they connect with material, historical trends. But they are human matter, that is, a particular form of matter that is self-reflective, and can therefore act upon its own environment.

It is in this twilight zone between utopia and pragmatism that we would like to suggest potential ways to orient the technological revolution toward social uses more humane than those currently in the making. The fundamental idea which we want to put forward is that, rather than alternative uses of technology, what we need are alternative forms of social organization capable of resisting the formidable stress to which our current institutions will be subjected by the ongoing technological revolution.

To be sure, some of the new information technologies could be put to a better use. For instance, communication technologies could be used to enhance interactive systems of popular consultation at the level of local government institutions. Or, instead of using computers for state control of people's private lives, citizens could be authorized to penetrate the informational avenues of *their* government, at whatever level, from their personal computers. Handicapped people could be rendered mobile on a large scale by using currently restricted technologies; and the blind could read by using machines already at work in the intelligence services. Biotechnology could be spread out from the commercial wishes of pharmaceutical multinationals to contribute to Third World agricultural production in the countryside, and to the Third World's serious pollution and sewage problems in its new, sprawling cities.

Yet a few well-intentioned twists to the general pattern of using new technologies will do little in comparison with the fundamental structural transformation to which new technologies are contributing as described in this report. What we require, most urgently, is a social restructuring able to match, and to control, the techno-economic restructuring underway. We will briefly indicate what seem to be the main axes of social transformation required to articulate in a creative way the effects of technological transformation.

The first major domain in which an alternative society must emerge in the forthcoming years is that of work and employment. Instead of eliminating jobs or contributing to the polarization of the occupational structure, new technologies could be used, and should be used, to redefine the social nature of work. Paid working time should be reduced dramatically for everybody, so that everyone has the possibility of being employed. Productivity increases, allowed by widespread automation, could provide substantial pay for less working time, even allowing for a fair increase of private profit for employers in a capitalist economy. What sounds utopian is in fact not much different from the actual historical transition from the condition of salaried work in the nineteenth century to labor legislation in Western Europe in the second half of this century: blue-collar workers have about one-third less working time, while their real take-home pay has increased substantially, let alone their general standards of living. When the German metalworkers' union went on strike for a 35-hour week without reduction in pay (obtaining, in fact, 38½ in the automobile industry), they were putting forward the demand we propose to generalize as the overarching principle of a new social organization of work, made possible with the information revolution: let us share paid working time, so that everybody has, at the same time, a sure job and more free time. Nevertheless, such a goal will be impossible to fulfil on a significant scale, unless it is generalized simultaneously at the international level. Otherwise, competition between countries and companies will wreck the economic foundations of those engaging in the path of social change. The example of France, reducing just one hour per week of working time in 1981, and paying heavily for it in terms of jobs and income, is quite indicative in this sense. But to speak of a generalized international policy of sharing working-time is, in fact, to speak of a fundamental transformation of values and of the principles of social and economic organization. Because for free-time/equal-pay to be more than a countercultural gadget, a number of economic and social issues have to be addressed.

Economically, we have to make explicit the relationship existing between free time and higher productivity in the workplace, so that the reduction of working time does not necessarily mean the reduction of actual production input in the work process. The connection is established precisely by the new, strategic role of information as a source of productivity. The more a worker of the information age is educated, healthy, relaxed, equilibrated, up-to-date on a variety of information and activities, integrated in his or her personal, family and community life, the more her or his brain is alert and innovative. It is as simple as that: in the information economy, the improvement, maintenance, and repair of the human mind is the most important productivity investment that can be made. And because of the social characteristics of our species, the conditions of a more productive intellect, on a sustained basis, are precisely the possibility of enjoying a multidimensional, equilibrated, healthy, everyday life, in which the individual is not wasted but enhanced by his or her way of living. In fact, many high-tech companies already employ this philosophy for their top researchers and designers, trying to accommodate them with flexible time and to provide them with access to health clubs, recreational activities, educational improvement, and the like. Yet most of the scientists and engineers are true workaholics and hardly live a healthy, harmonious life. This is due to the current one-dimensionality of social change. Some individuals can express themselves in work-related innovation while still being incapable of other experiences, with the exception of indulging themselves in compensatory consumption. So, once having bought a second BMW and continually trapped in the same traffic jams to rejoin the dullness of an anonymous suburb, the avenues of technological discovery appear as the only true open road for those human spirits. Therefore, the ability to become a multidimensional human being does not depend only on the free control of our time, but requires a broader cultural transformation that has to be part of the articulated process of social change constructed around the information revolution.

Such changes of the relationship between work and social life are not limited to the top of the productive scale—researchers, engineers, and managers. It could in fact permeate the entire occupational structure, if we consider three elements: (a) Most of the routine work, including services, could easily be automated. (b) Therefore, information-processing will play a major role in almost all jobs, since for each position a number of machines will have to be instructed and a variety of situations will have to be assessed and decided upon. As a matter of fact, research done in our universities on the transformation of work in the insurance companies points to the dramatic upgrading of skills in those few middle-management positions that survive automation. The problem, of course, is the downgrading of life for subsequently laid-off workers, as well as their re-entry in the labor market through even more routine, lower-paid jobs, as we have pointed out earlier. This is why the upgrading of some key working positions, which are not only professionally rewarding but well-paid as well, has to go along with automation of much of the routine work, and with the sharing of the dramatically reduced working time among everyone (assuming, too, that everyone has the skills, or education, to keep up with such qualified jobs). (c) To connect the need for creativity, as generated outside the workplace, with information-processing productivity at work, on a general scale, we also have to abandon the old (yet too-present) distinction between intellectual and manual labor. Many non-scientific, non-high-tech jobs require tremendous cultural skills and professional qualifications, which require a long education and an even more supportive lifestyle to develop.

Thus, from an economic point of view, the loss of productivity linked to the reduction of the quantity of work can be more than offset by the productivity generated by the quality of work in the information economy. And such quality is produced, enhanced, and preserved by the whole development of human creativity, both physical and intellectual, allowed by a multi-dimensional pattern of life that requires freer and more flexible use of time outside the rules of specific organizations. Under the productive conditions of the information age, free time and organized work could complement each other.

Nevertheless, such a profound transformation of work is unlikely to succeed (leaving aside for the moment the political obstacles to fulfilling this vision) in the absence of a dramatic cultural change and of social policies aimed at providing the material conditions for the expression of a new, multi-dimensional personality. The new welfare state would be one emphasizing the accessibility to the arts, to scientific knowledge, to manual work, to languages, to travel, to sports and physical fitness, to outdoor experiences, and to interactive, decentralized communications media for everyone. Many programs for youth in advanced industrial societies already do just that. But there is some implicit conception that this "play time" should be reserved for some short period for the very young and for the left-over time of the very old, once they have finished their period of duty. Why could not general-purpose, free activities, and focused, salaried activities be combined in a different pattern along the entire life cycle? According to sexist social rules, women can stay at home bringing up children for a few years, to work later, once their family duties have been fulfilled. What if we redistribute working time and social time between genders and between ages, reducing constrained activities and making free time productive through the enhancement of creative capabilities?

The main obstacle for the development of a holistic welfare state is not economic but cultural and political. Cultural, because we have equated not being paid with not being worthwhile, and because social services are perceived as a redistributional matter instead of as human capital formation. Political, because we associate the welfare state with centralized, costful bureaucracies, providing services or allocating payments to their passive clientele. And yet the state is us; the services "they" deliver are of our utmost concern. Therefore, citizen participation in the management of state institutions, volunteerism, and free-work contribution could dramatically increase the capacity to generate services and to support activities. Of course, voluntary organizations must not substitute for the services and programs that people are entitled to require from the state. Also, such programs could easily be financed with increased revenues from a highly productive information economy, and decreased expenditures from a much smaller military budget, rendered obsolete by other measures we will discuss below. Thus, what we are suggesting is that *in addition* to a rationalized, flourishing welfare state, citizen participation and users' involvement could greatly expand the range and quality of public services infrastructure, from which would blossom widespread human creativity. Such a decentralized, participative structure requires, of course, a different kind of state; one that would use information technology to decentralize its power, and that would translate democratic principles into full involvement by citizens in the management and control of public affairs.

The cultural obstacles can be the most difficult to overcome. Thousands of years of submissive labor and oppressive politics have created in us the habit of conceding our working time in exchange for the preservation of our own preserved patch. Yet, as most social research on activities of the retired shows, harsh work and a harsh life leave little room for the self-expression of people, even if, and when, they are on their own time. Life is most often dried up from the inside. This is why the structural transformation we are advocating will have to start with the next generation. A revolution must take place in our schools while we set up the institutional framework and the economic policies necessary for the historical reconversion of the productive structure. Our children will have to be provided not only with computers (they will be, anyway, so in fact some major change *is* going on), but with the technical ability to use them *at all levels,* and with the social personality capable of entering the new world. The school system is a strategic ace in the making of the new world. If we just let the spontaneous trends of the technological revolution enter our schools as they are, we will see a dramatic reinforcement of social selection and discrimination by class, by gender, and by race. Our schools are totally obsolete, and not simply technologically, but intellectually and organizationally. The computer in the school, in every class of every school, must be accompanied by a total restructuring of the educational system, to overcome social obstacles to the acquisition of information technology, and to socialize the children of the next generation in the new world of multidimensional personality that the information age makes functionally necessary and socially desirable. To be sure, the education and socialization process does not take place only in the school, and will have to include a reorientation of the relationship between children and the media, community-based programs aimed at children's activities, and a vast educational effort toward the families, so that they can manage the cultural transition.

Visions such as the ones we have outlined in this section might seem inappropriate when we keep in mind the current conditions in Third World countries, and the rather bleak prospects that, as we have shown, the acceleration of the historical tempo of the technological revolution offers to them. And yet, the Thirld World too has to come to grips with the reality that, unless we plan alternative paths of development, the conditions for most people in most countries will dramatically worsen over the next two decades—and this not only true on the economic plane, but also in the overall structure of society, as we tried to explain in Section III. The two basic problems confronting the Third World, in relation to the current technological revolution, are the increasing technological gap and the disconnection/reconnection process that will destabilize national societies while strengthening global power. To avoid the tremendous disruptive potential of such processes, we must develop immediate feasible alternatives that introduce a different dynamic in the relationship between new technologies and the Third World.

Third World countries will have to combine self-reliance while playing the technological game in the international arena. By no means can they afford to be left out of the current technological revolution, with its potential for improving their living conditions much faster and with less effort. On the other hand, such technology transfer should take place under the control and in the interest of Third World peoples, sometimes represented by their national governments. This is a nice, abstract principle, but extremely difficult to be concretely implemented.

An obvious bottom line is the reinforcement of the technological endogenous potential of the Third World by building cooperative advanced research institutions through the joint effort of national governments and international institutions in key areas of the world. Many of the top scientists and engineers of the OECD countries are from the Third World, and a substantial number of them would gladly return home if given the material and institutional opportunities to pursue their scientific endeavors. Furthermore, until such institutions exist on a large scale, it seems useless to continue sending Third World graduates to receive PhDs in the United States or Europe, at great cost, for their own benefit, and resulting in the further concentration of research capabilities in a few world-dominant centers. A program to stop the brain-drain starts with the creation of conditons for these brains to develop in their own countries in the first place. Given the scarce resources of most countries, the building of a few major regional international institutions in the key technological areas seems to be the most fruitful way. The United Nations could sponsor such an effort, but multinational corporations should be called in also to give support, both financially and technologically, in exchange for the access they obtain to markets and locations. If the Singapore government has been successful in building such institutions with the support of various corporations, there is no reason why other countries should not amplify the effort, particularly if they cooperate in it and receive the backing of international institutions. There is no greater priority for Third World development in the next quarter of a century than to create the conditions for the expansion of its human capital.

Along with this effort at the top, Third World governments must be helped to introduce computer literacy at a higher scale in their primary and secondary schools. It may seem ridiculous to propose such a program when schools simply do not exist for a substantial proportion of the population. Yet it is precisely because a new educational system has to be built that Third World countries should leap over the traditional stages of development to create new schools with the help of information tools and aimed at educating their people about the information age—which, as we maintain, goes far beyond just using computers.

On a third level, technological cooperation with the Third World could receive a decisive impetus by using new technologies, particularly in agriculture and health care, to deal with the fundamental problems of survival against hunger and illness. Joint programs between governments, community groups, multinational corporations, and international institutions could target specific areas and problems, and concentrate research efforts and technological training, in the same manner as companies seeking to discover a potentially profitable product. Throughout the process, the implementation of such programs at Third World sites would also train the technicians and scientists who will bring their knowledge, in the near future, to the fulfillment of the self-reliant politics on which the Third World will ultimately have to count.

The fourth fundamental axis of intervention in this area concerns the need to keep the internal coherence of national societies, in their regional context, vis-à-vis the techno-economic pattern of asymmetrical flows of domination and control, as described in Section III. Several lines of policy are available to Third World countries. The most important matter is to reinforce the social fabric at the grass-roots level and to closely connect it to national institutions and policy-making, while accepting the necessary tensions and contradictions involved in such a process. On the basis of widespread citizen participation and face-to-face interaction in the public domain, the historical roots and cultural specificities of societies offer enough resistance to the penetration of electronic flows so that new messages can be assimilated, and reinterpreted, without local cultures becoming diffused into the foreign-controlled networks. Another fundamental element would be a national policy of telecommunications, including the media. This is not necessarily for governments to control messages, but for countries to set up their own systems of communication, enabling them to connect to the world network under their own terms and conditions. Telecommunications and media policies are key components of any process of national development today; yet they are often neglected in order to concentrate on apparently more urgent matters, thus undermining a country's future.

As a last example of how Third World governments could fight to avoid their increasing marginality in the world-wide system of decision flows, governments of different ideologies have an objective interest in reinforcing regional economic and political organizations, with the specific aim of dealing collectively with major transnational corporations. Only in this manner can governments avoid being played against each other in the economic strategies of world-wide organizations. After all, most governments in the Third World have more in common among themselves than with the multinationals. Since cooperation with major companies will still be a necessity for a long time, the only way out of the contradiction is to present a common front, at least at the regional level, and to debate internal differences within the regional institutions. The problem will be to set up such a system without duplicating wasteful, ineffective international bureaucracies. If there is truly a political will, the operational procedure could be extremely fast, with a very light infrastructure. For instance, a system of on-line telecommunications, monitoring several countries' economic activity on a daily basis, with ad hoc teleconferences among the key decision-makers, could reverse some of the direction of decision flows, decentralizing them, and making the world a more complex yet a more diversified and less centralized network.

The Third World must enter the technological revolution with a clear sense of its specific common interests (in spite of the diversity of situations we have shown), or the fragmentation of its societies will become the one-way terminals of a new, invisible colonization.

An then, finally, the major question: war and peace.

On this matter, the obvious vision to reach for is total nuclear disarmament in our lifetime. After all, this is what the majority of countries and millions and millions of people are calling for, in what amounts perhaps to the most significant of current social movements. Nevertheless, I doubt that such a goal could be attained, even in the mid-term, simply by popular pressure and governments' self-responsibility. All historical experience conveys, with force, the lesson that, whenever and wherever there is a State, it will preserve its capability to use extreme violence, as far as it can reach, when faced with a threat to its own existence.

The greatest paradox of all could be that the real limits to nuclear military power as we know it today could come from its technological obsolescence. New technologies, together with historically original political processes, are slowly displacing warfare to different forms that could be (and some already are) a much more immediate threat than a nuclear holocaust permanently adjourned by the balance of terror. Perhaps to address these issues from now on (while keeping up the necessary support of the peace movement, both in the West and in the East) could be a more critical contribution to the cause of peace, if we take a mid-term historical perspective. These are the issues that we consider of most immediate concern:

First, new technologies are rendering conventional warefare equipment continuously obsolete. Because advanced industrial countries (from the West and the East) want to keep up with the latest developments, they heavily invest in weapons production. For such expensive investments to be cost-effective, they must combine production for the national army with arms export. Besides, since these countries control military technologies, and the actual combat zones are in the Third World, weapons exports have become a major element for the industrial economies. The trend is unlimited, since the spread of technological change accelerates over time. This pattern takes a tremendous toll on Third World economies, wastes human and industrial resources in all countries, and risks a relentless stream of widespread destruction (as in Iran and Iraq) that, just because it is not nuclear, receives relatively little attention. But it should be possible to limit the production of much of the new technological warfare equipment, leaving it at the research-and-test stage through a multilateral negotiated agreement. The first beneficiaries would be the Third World countries, since state-of-the-art sophisticated equipment would not be produced in large quantities, and, therefore, would not be available for their potential adversaries. The first effort for arms reduction should concern conventional weapons, which are the ones actually being used, and the ones wrecking Third World economies. If we do not stop this trend now, the level of destructive capability introduced by new technologies in conventional armament will rapidly escalate to being close to the nuclear weapons minus the effects of fallout.

The second major issue refers to the displacement of traditional warfare to what is now called "international terrorism" (which includes, of course, State-sponsored terrorism, whether it be the CIA, the KGB, or the French Intelligence Service). New information technologies, sophisticated weapons and communications equipment, and the very existence of a delicate technological life-support structure for our societies will make this form of political violence (this is what war is all about) the prevailing form of confrontation in the forthcoming years. Its effects are devastating, not only in terms of lives and damage but also because it can trigger a rapid escalation towards major confrontations, since public opinion is increasingly sensitive to the issue, and is likely to embrace a militant, revengeful mood. And, furthermore, because of the interstitiality of terrorism, and because of its impact on the paranoiac imagery of our societies, it could be the most important factor in eroding our liberties, in transforming new technologies into an instrument for policing, and in elevating the "raison d'état" to a way of life. We must contribute to stopping terrorism, all kinds of terrorism, whatever our feelings on the particular causes terrorists defend or believe they defend. An international, multilateral effort against terrorism, including the independent, international monitoring of intelligence services of national governments (to prevent them from engaging in terrorism) is a reachable, fundamental goal that could halt the trend toward living with terror as a way of life in the technological age.

Finally, because the strategic superiority of the SDI program derives from the technological edge the United States has over the Soviet Union, it is almost certain that the United States (and not only the Reagan Administration) will continue with such a program, boosted by each new technological success in its development. SDI opens up an entirely new strategic perspective that could render obsolete much of the current nuclear strategy. This is precisely why, at the Geneva meeting of November 1985, the Reagan Administration appeared to be much more conciliatory toward the Soviets, while not conceding anything on SDI. The more a side obtains a strategic advantage, the more it has an interest in preserving detente, unless a crisis situation develops—a crisis the solution of which would be almost dictated by whoever holds the strategic advantage. The more we engage in this course, the more SDI could become a "casus belli," forcing the Soviet Union to react, once they realize, as we hypothesize, that they do not have the technological capability to keep the warfare equipment race in its new high ground. On the other hand, the United States (and most likely the majority of Western Europe and Japan) will increasingly consider SDI as a cornerstone of their strategy, and, to some extent, of their research programs. In view of this, it is crucial to ensure that the research for such programs, supposedly defensive, would be universally shared, including of course the Soviet Union, so that the global equilibrium is not dangerously altered. Interestingly enough, such was Reagan's initial proposal. The Defense establishment, however, is rapidly backing away from such an idea, and it is most likely that the declared intention will remain a propaganda ploy, unless international public opinion's pressure is put upon the superpowers. In fact, it could be envisaged as a simultaneous interpenetration of advanced military research teams of different countries with a systematic dismantlement of the nuclear arsenal rendered obsolete by the new technologies. It is highly doubtful that we could ever reach true disarmament, or that new technological weapons could be merely defensive. Yet, the movement toward integrating research capabilities would prevent the dangerous phase of strategic transition, in which both sides could react to what they would see as an intolerable modification of the strategic balance of power.

Thus, new technologies do transform our societies and our economies, our source of life and our abyss of death. Their pervasive, powerful influence will require all our lucidity, imagination, and courage to restore the internal equilibrium of a technologically developed, socially underdeveloped, human species. People do make their own history, and ultimately all the visions we have projected will depend on the capacity of social movements and political institutions to undertake the process of structural transformation. Yet, unless people recognize the actual profile of our world, we will be fighting the shadows of our past, instead of planting the seeds of the next historical harvest.

Notes and references

G. Adams, *The Iron Triangle—The Politics of Defense Contracting* (New York: Council on Economic Priorities, 1981).

AFL-CIO, *Deindustrialization and the Two-Tier Society* (Washington, DC: AFL-CIO Industrial Union Department, 1948).

N. Akrasanee, *et al.*, (editors), *Trade and Employment in Asia and the Pacific* (Quezon City, Philippines: Council of Asian Manpower Studies, 1977).

B. Balassa (editor), *Development Strategies in Semi-industrial Economies* (Baltimore: The Johns Hopkins University Press, 1982).

F. Baldwin and D. S. McVoy, *Cable Communication* (Englewood Cliffs, NJ: Prentice-Hall, 1983).

B. Baran, *Technological Innovation and Deregulation: the Transformation of the Labour Process in the Insurance Industry* (Berkeley: BRIE, University of California, 1985).

M. Bienefeld and Godfrey (editors), *The Struggle for Development: National Strategies in an International Context* (New York: John Wiley, 1982).

P. Blackburn, R. Coombs and K. Green, *Technology, Economic Growth, and the Labor Process* (New York: St Martin's Press, 1985).

B. Bluestone and B. Harrison, *The Deindustrialization of America* (New York: Basic Books, 1982).

B. Bluestone and B. Harrison, *The Economic State of the Union in 1984: Uneven Recovery, Uncertain Future* (Boston, MA, 1984), unpublished manuscript.

M. Borrus, F. Bar and I. Warde, *The Impacts of Divestiture and Deregulation: Infrastructural Changes, Manufacturing Transition, and Competition in the U.S. Telecommunications Industries* (Berkeley: University of California, BRIE, 1984).

M. Borrus, J. Millstein and J. Zysman, *Responses to the Japanese Challenge in High Technology Innovation, Maturity, and U.S.-Japanese Competition in the Microelectronics* (Berkeley: University of California, BRIE, 1983).

J. Botkin, D. Dimancescu and R. Stata, *The Innovators, Rediscovering America's Creative Energy* (New York: Harper & Row, 1984).

S. Bowles, D. Gordon and T. Weisskopf, *Beyond the Wasteland* (Garden City, NY. Anchor/Doubleday, 1983).

C. I. Bradford, "Newly industrializing countries in an interdependent world," *The World Economy*, vol 5, no 2, 1982, pp. 171–185.

W. Brandt, (Chairman of Commission) *North-South. A Program for Survival* (Cambridge, MA: MIT Press, 1980).

E. Braun and S. MacDonald, *Revolution in Miniature* (Cambridge: Cambridge University Press, 1982).

J. Browett, *Industrialization in the Global Periphery: The Significance of the Newly Industrializing Countries* (Adelaide: Flinders University of South Australia, School of Social Sciences, 1985).

Business Week, "The Home Information Revolution," June 29, 1981.

Business Week, "The Consumer Rush in on for Anything Electronic," February 27, 1984.

Business Week, "Special Report: Collision Course. Can the U.S. Avert a Trade War with Japan?" April 8, 1985.

Business Week, "Pentagon spending is the economy's biggest gun," October 1985.

B. Camus, M. Delattre, J. C. Dutaille, F. Eymard-Duvernay and L. Vasille, *La Crise du Systeme Productie Français* (Paris: INSEE, 1981).

R. Carlson and T. Lyman, *U.S. Government Programs and their Influence on Silicon Valley* (Menlo Park: SRI International, Research Report, 1984).

M. Carnoy, *Foreign Debt and Latin American Domestic Politics*, Paper delivered at the Institute of the Americas Brazil Conference, San Diego, CA, November 21–22, 1985.

M. Carnoy, *The Labor Market in Silicon Valley and its Implications for Education* (Stanford: Stanford University, School of Education, Research Report, 1985).

M. Carnoy and M. Castells, *Technology and Economy in the U.S.*, Paper for the UNESCO Conference on Technological Change, Athens, September, 1985.

M. Carnoy, D. Sheaver and R. Rumberger, *A New Social Contract* (New York: Harper & Row, 1983).

M. Castells, *The Economic Crisis and American Society* (Princeton, NJ: Princeton University Press, 1980).

M. Castells, *Public Housing and Economic Development in Hong Kong* (Hong Kong: University of Hong Kong, Centre of Urban Studies and Planning, 1985).

M. Castells, A. Barrera, P. Casals, C. Castano, P. Escario and J. Nadal, *Nuevas tecnologias, economia y sociedad en Espana (Madrid: Alianza Editorial, 1986).*

F. Celada, F. Lopez-Groh and T. Parra *Efectos espaciales de los proceses de reorganisacion del sistema productivo en Madrid* (Madrid: Communidad de Madrid, 1985).

E. K. Y. Chen, *High-Growth in Asian Economies. A Comparative Study of Hong Kong, Japan, Korea, Singapore and Taiwan* (London: Macmillan, 1979).

J. Coates and M. Kilian, *Heavy Losses: The Dangerous Decline of American Defense* (New York: Viking Press, 1985).

D. Cockroft, "New Office Technology and Employment," *International Law Review,* vol 119, no 6, Nov–Dec 1980.

S. Cohen and J. Zysman, *Manufacturing Matters* (Berkeley: University of California, BRIE, 1986).

P. R. Costa Souza, *Los impactos economicos y sociales de las nuevas tecnologias en Brasil* (Madrid: Fundesco Seminar on New Technologies in Industrialized Countries, 1985).

R. De Grasse, Jr. *Military Expansion, Economic Decline: The Impact of Military Spending on U.S. Economic Performance* (New York: M. E. Sharpe, 1983).

R. Dellums (editor), *Defense Sense: The Search for a Rational Military Policy* (Cambridge, MA: Balliner, 1983).

R. Dempsey and D. Schurde, "Occupational impact of defense expenditures," *Monthly Labor Review,* December 1971, pp. 12–15.

H. S. Dorkiek, *et al.,* "Network Information Services: the Emergence of an Industry," *Telecommunications,* September 1979, pp. 217–234.

G. Dosi, *Technical Change and Industrial Transformation* (New York: St. Martin's Press, 1984).

M. P. Drennen, *Implications of Computer and Communications Technology for Less Skilled Service Employment Opportunities* (New York: Columbia University, Research Report to the US Department of Labor, 1983).

L. Dumas (editor), *The Political Economy of Arms Reduction* (Boulder, CO: Westview Press, 1982).

W. Dutton, P. Kovoric and Ch. Steinfield, *Issues and Perspectives on Computing in the Home: Towards a Research Agenda* (Houston: University of Houston, International Telecommunications Research Institute, 1983).

The Economist, "How Europe Has Failed," November 24–30, 1984.

R. S. Eward, *The Competition for Markets in International Communications* (Dedham, MA: Artech House, 1984).

EEC, Office of Economic European Community *The Europe of New Technologies,* Madrid Office, 1984 (Spanish text).

D. Ernst, *The Global Race in Micro-electronics* (Frankfurt: Campus Verlag, 1980).

J. Fallows, *National Defense* (New York: Random House, 1981).

J. Farley and N. Glickman, *R & D as an Economic Development Strategy: The Microelectronics and Computer Technology Corporation Comes to Austin, Texas* (Austin: University of Texas, Lyndon Johnson School of Public Affairs, 1985).

FAST, *Eurofutures. The Challenges of Innovation* (London: Butterworth, 1984).

G. Flores and J. Blanes, *?Donde va el Chapare?* (Cochambamba, Bolivia: Centro de Estudios de la Realidad Economica y Social, 1983).

F. Frobel, J. Henricks and O. Kreye, *The New International Division of Labor* (Cambridge: Cambridge University Press, 1980).

R. Gabriel, *Military Incompetence: Why the American Military Doesn't Win* (New York: Hill and Wang, 1985).

J. Gansler, *The Defense Industry* (Cambridge, MA: MIT Press, 1980).

A. Glasmeier, *Spatial Differentiation of High Technology Industries* (Berkeley: University of California, Dept. of City and Regional Planning, Ph.D. Dissertation, 1986).

N. Glickman, *International Economic Change and the Cities,* Paper delivered at the Annual Conference of the American Collegiate Schools of Planning, Atlanta, GA, 1985.

R. Gordon and L. M. Kimball, *High Technology, Employment and the Challenges to Education* (Santa Cruz: University of California, Silicon Valley Research Group, 1985).

Government of Korea, *Current Status and Prospects of Information and Communication industry in Korea*, Paper delivered at the FUNDESCO Seminar on new Technologies in Industrialized Countries, Madrid: FUNDESCO, 1985.

C. Hamilton, "Class, State, and Industrialization in South Korea," *Institute of Development Studies Bulletin*, vol 5, no 2, 1984, pp. 38–43.

J. Henderson, "The new international division of labor and American semi-conductor production in South-East Asia," in: D. Watt, C. Dixon and D. Drakakis-Smith (editors), *Multinational Companies in the Third World* (London: Croom Helm, 1986).

J. Henderson and M. Castells (editors), *Global Restructuring and Territorial Development* (London: Sage, 1986).

J. Henderson and A. J. Scott, *Global Restructuring and Internationalization of the American Semiconductor Industry* (Hong Kong: University of Hong Kong, Centre of Urban Studies and Planning, 1986).

J. Henderson and A. J. Scott, "The growth and internationalization of the American semiconductor industry," in: M. Brehemy and R. McQuaid (editors), *The Development of High Technology Industry: An International Survey* (London: Croom Helm, 1986).

L. Hirschhorn, *Beyond Mechanization* (Cambridge, MA: MIT Press, 1984).

H. A. Hunt and T. L. Hunt, *Human Resource Implications of Robotics* (Kalamazoo, MI: W. E. Upjohn Institute for Employment Research, 1983).

Institut Syndical Europeen, *L'impact de la micro-electronique sur l'emploi en Europe Occidentale dans les annees 80* (Brussels: ISE, 1980).

S. Jacobsson and Sigurdson (editors), *Technological Trends and Challenges in Electronics* (Lund, Sweden: University of Lund, 1983).

H. Jansen, *Information and Communication Technologies in the Growth and Employment Crisis* (Berlin: International Conference Organized by the Government of the Federal Republic of Germany and the OECD on the Social Challenge of Information Technologies, November 28–30, 1984).

C. Johnson, *MITI and the Japanese Miracle* (Stanford: Stanford University Press, 1982).

R. E. Kutscher, *Factors Influencing the Changing Employment Structure of the U.S.*, Paper delivered at the Second International Conference of Progetto Milano, Milan, January 25, 1985.

B. Kuttner, "The declining middle," *The Atlantic Monthly*, July 1984, pp. 60–72.

Robert Z. Lawrence, (1984a) *The Employment Effects of Information Technologies: An Optimistic View*, Paper delivered at the OECD Conference on the Social Challenge of Information Technologies, Berlin, November 28–30, 1984.

Robert Z. Lawrence, (1984b) *Can America Compete?* (Washington, DC: The Brookings Institution, 1984).

R. Layard, G. Basevi, O. Blanchard, W. Buiter and P. Kleppe, *Europe: the Case for Unsustainable Growth* (Brussels: Centre for European Policy Studies, paper no 8–9, 1984).

E. Lee (editor), *Export-Led Industrialization and Development* (Geneva: I.L.O., Asian Employment Program, 1981).

W. Leontieff and F. Duchin, *The Impacts of Automation on Employment, 1963–2000* (New York: New York University, Institute for Economic Analysis, Research Report, 1984).

N. H. Lim, *Policies to Attract Export-oriented Industries: The Role of Export-processing Zones in the Philippines* (Freiburg: Institute of Development Policy, 1982).

I. M. D. Little, "The experience and causes of rapid labour-intensive development in Korea, Taiwan Province, Hong Kong, and Singapore and the possibilities of emulation," in: E. Lee (editor), *Export-Led Industrialization and Development* (Geneva: ILO, Asian Employment Program, 1982).

P. M. Lubeck, *Authoritarianism, Crisis, and the Urban Industrial Sector. Nigeria's Role in the International Division of Labor* (Hong Kong: Paper delivered at the ISA Conference on the Urban and Regional Impact of the New International Division of Labour, August 1985).

R. Luedde-Neurath, "State Intervention and Foreign Direct Investment in South Korea," *Institute of Development Studies Bulletin*, 15 (2), pp. 18–25.

N. Maeda, "A fact-finding study on the impact of microelectronics on employment," in: *Microelectronics, Productivity and Employment* (Paris: OECD, 1981), pp. 155–180.

L. Maldonado and J. Moore (editors), *Urban Ethnicity in the United States* (Beverly Hills, Sage, 1985).

A. Markusen, *High Tech. Job Markets, and Economic Development Prospects* (Berkeley: University of California, IURD, Working Paper, 1983).

A. Markusen, *Profit Cycles, Oligopoly, and Regional Development* (Cambridge, MA: MIT Press, 1984).

A. Markusen, *The Economic and Regional Consequences of Military Innovation* (Berkeley: University of California, IURD, Working Paper 442, 1985).

A. Markusen, "Defense spending as industrial policy," *International Journal of Urban and Regional Research,* January-March 1986.

A. Markusen and R. Bloch, "Defensive cities: military spending, high technology, and human settlements," in M. Castells (editor), 1985.

D. Massey, *Spatial Divisions of Labour* (London: Macmillan, 1984).

G. Maxey, *The Multinational Motor Corporation* (London: Croom Helm, 1981).

J. Meyrowitz, *No Sense of Place. The Impact of Electronic Media on Social Behavior* (New York: Oxford University Press, 1985).

R. Morfoot, *Television in the Eighties: the Total Equation* (London: BBC, 1982).

Servet Mutlu, "Inter-regional and international mobility of industrial capital. The case of the American automobile and electronics industries" (Berkeley, California: University of California. Department of City and Regional Planning. Ph.D. dissertation, 1979).

P. Nayyar, "Transnational corporations and manufactured exports from poor countries," *The Economic Journal,* vol 88, no 1, 1978, pp. 59–84

T. Nazakawa, *Impactos economicos y sociales de las nuevas technologieas en Japon* (Madrid: Fundesco Seminar on New Technologies in Industrialized Countries, 1985).

The New York Times, "Cable Operators Take a Bruising," March 4, 1984.

L. Nicol, *Information Technology, Information networks and On-Line Information Services* (Berkeley: University of California, IURD, 1983).

L. Nicol, "Communications technology: economic and spatial impacts," in: M. Castells (editor), *High Technology, Space, and Society* (Beverly Hills, CA: Sage, 1985).

T. Noyelle, *The Shift to Services,* Paper delivered at the UNIDO Conference on Regional Development and the International Division of Labor, Vienna, August 1984.

J. O'Connor, *Accumulation Crisis* (Oxford: Basil Blackwell, 1984).

OECD, *Economic Perspectives of OECD,* Paris: OECD, Annual Report, December 1984.

C. Palloix, "The self-expansion of capital on a world scale," *Review of Radical Political Economics,* vol 9, no 2, 1977, pp. 1–28.

R. Peet, "Class Struggle, the relocation of employment, and economic crises," *Science and Society,* vol 48, no 2, 1984, pp. 38–51.

M. Perlo, "Exploring the spatial effects of the Internationalization of the Mexican economy," in: J. Henderson and M. Castells (editors), *Global Restructuring and Territorial Development* (London: Sage, 1986).

N. Piercy (editor), *The Management Implications of New Information Technology* (London: Croom Helm, 1984).

M. Piore and C. Sabel, *The Second Industrial Divide* (New York: Basic Books, 1984).

A. Portes and J. Walton, *Class, Labor, and the International System* (New York: Academic Press, 1981).

J. Rada, *Structure and Behavior of the Semiconductor Industry* (New York: United Nations Center for the Study of Transnational Corporations, 1982).

R. Reich, *The Next American Frontier* (New York: Times Books, 1983).

R. W. Riche, D. E. Hecker and J. D. Burgan, "High technology today and tomorrow: a small slice of the employment pie," *Monthly Labor Review* 1983, pp. 50–58.

E. Rogers and J. Larsen, *Silicon Valley Fever* (New York: Basic Books, 1984).

N. Rosenberg, *Inside the Black Box. Technology and Economics* (Cambridge: Cambridge University Press, 1982).

W. Rosenberg, "South-Korea: export-led development—severed and unsevered," *Journal of Contemporary Asia,* vol 10, no 3, 1980, pp. 300–308.

R. W. Rumberger, "High technology and job loss," *Technology in Society* vol 6, 1984, pp. 263–284.

R. W. Rumberger and H. M. Levin, *Forecasting the Impact of New Technologies on the Future Job Market* (Stanford: Stanford University School of Education, Research Report, 1984).

M. A. Rutziek, "Skills and location of defense-related workers," *Monthly Labor Review*, February 1970, pp. 11–16

F. Sabbah, "The New Media," in: M. Castells (editor), *High Technology, Space, and Society* (Beverly Hills, CA: Sage, 1985).

S. Sassen-Koob, *Growth and Informalization at the Core: the Case of New York City* (Baltimore: The Johns Hopkins University Press, June 8–11984).

R. J. Saunders, *et al.*, *Telecommunications and Economic Development* (Baltimore: The Johns Hopkins University Press and the World Bank, 1983).

L. Sawers and W. K. Tabb, *Sunbelt/Snowbelt. Urban Development and Regional Restructuring* (New York: Oxford University Press, 1984).

J. R. Schiffer, *Anatomy of a Laissez-faire Government: The Hong Kong Growth Model Reconsidered* (Hong Kong: University of Hong Kong, Centre of Urban Studies and Planning, 1983).

H. Schmitz, "Industrialization strategies in less developed countries: some lessons of historical experience," *Journal of Development Studies*, vol 21, no 1, 1984, pp. 1–24.

E. Schoenberger, *Direct Foreign Investment in the U.S.* (Berkeley: University of California, Dept. of City and Regional Planning, Ph.D. Dissertation, 1985).

A. J. Scott, *High Technology Industry and Territorial Development: the Rise of the Orange County Complex, 1955–84* (Los Angeles: UCLA, Department of Geography, Research Report, 1985).

Lenny Siegel and John Markoff, *The High Cost of High Tech* (New York: Harper and Row, 1985).

G. T. Silvestri, J. M. Lukasiewicz and M. A. Einstein, "Occupational employment projections through 1995," *Monthly Labor Review*, November, 1983, pp. 37–49.

T. Stanback, *Understanding the Service Economy* (Baltimore: Johns Hopkins University Press, 1979).

P. Stark, "Special Report: VCR Revolution, the Big Changes in Entertainment," *San Francisco Chronicle*, February 27, 1984.

C. L. Taylor (editor), *Why Governments Grow* (Beverly Hills, CA: Sage, 1983).

L. C. Thurow, "The disappearance of the middle class," *The New York Times*, February 5, 1984.

UNCTC, *Transborder Data Flows and Brazil. The Role of Transnational Corporations, Impacts of Transborder Data Flows, and Effects on National Policies* (New York: North Holland, 1984).

UNIDO, *Restructuring World Industry in a Period of Crisis. The Role of Innovation* (Vienna: UNIDO Division of Industrial Studies, Working Paper, 1981).

UNIDO, *International Industrial Restructuring and the International Division of Labor in the Automotive Industry* (Vienna: UNIDO Division of Industrial Studies, Working Paper, 1984).

N. D. Vasquez, *The impact of the New International Division of Labor on ASEAN Labor: the Philippine Case* (Hong Kong: Paper delivered at the ISA Conference on the Urban and Regional Impact of the New International Division of Labour, 1985).

R. Wade, "Dirigisme Taiwan-style," *Institute of Development Studies Bulletin*, 15 (2), pp. 65–70.

J. Walton, *The IMF Riot*, Paper delivered at the I.S.A. Conference on the Urban Impact of the New International Division of Labour, Hong Kong, 1985.

F. Williams, *The Communications Revolution* (Beverly Hills, CA: Sage, 1982).

J. Zysman and S. Cohen, *The Mercantilist Challenge to the Liberal International Trade Order* (Washington: US Congress, Joint Economic Committee, 1983).

New Understandings of Peace and Security

Peace Movements in History

NIGEL YOUNG

Introduction

The idea of peace is probably as old as humanity. But secular or political movements for peace—what we have called peace movements—are not more than two hundred years old, and have evolved largely in the western and northern countries. Those peace movements with religious orientations are older and have arisen in many different periods and in all parts of the globe. In this paper, the peace movement refers to social or political movements which consciously, explicitly or implicitly, concern themselves primarily with peace as a term, concept or title, which define themselves (or are defined) as part of the "peace movement," or are overtly opposed to war, militarism or the organized use of violence.

Before the first modern popular mass movements against war emerged in the late nineteenth century, there existed a myriad of peace sects and traditions (almost all religious) which included peace and the renunciation of war as a principle or goal. The history of anti-war sentiments or peace ideas, actively expressed in the resistance to war by various sects and groups from the early Christian period onward, is thus much older than even the first secular peace groups in Europe (circa 1815). In many countries, ethnic and other groups have opposed specific wars and conscriptions on political or cultural grounds without necessarily being "anti-war" *per se*, or without having any conscious orientation to peace or peace movements. Although such groups were widespread in the nineteenth and early twentieth centuries, they are not included in this survey as peace or "anti-war" *movements*. Equally, more broad religious movements and churches, such as Buddhism, have concepts of peace as part of their doctrines without as a whole ever becoming part of an active peace movement. They too are marginal to this discussion, except when a section self-consciously creates or becomes a peace or war-resisting church, such as the Unified Buddhist Church in Indo-China after 1960, or Hinduism, which clearly contributes elements to the Gandhian movement without ever itself being a "peace movement" or tradition. Furthermore, one has to distinguish between peace and anti-war *movements* as broad, amorphous, and somewhat ephemeral social phenomena, and the

Commissioned by the Committee for a Just World Peace for presentation at its Lisbon Conference, March 1985. First published in a revised form in *Alternatives* XI:2. Research for this article was supported by the North American Program of the Peace and Global Transformation Project of the United Nations University.

specific peace *traditions* expressed in often small but prophetic groups providing ideas, initiatives and motivation for the entire peace movement.

Aims and objectives

This paper deals with the peace movement as it has evolved for over two centuries in the industrial societies: a social formation fundamentally concerned with the problems of war, militarism, conscription, and mass violence, and the ideals of internationalism, globalism and non-violent relations between people. Therefore it does not incorporate the contemporary concerns of the South with hunger, development and related repressions, nor does it explore the linkages of peace, democracy and human rights. Yet the peace movement *has*, to varying degrees, incorporated these concerns and, it will be argued, as the movement becomes more global in its scope and appeal, and the threat of species-death more of a reality, these issues will become more explicitly part of the peace programme of peoples' struggles everywhere.

One purpose of this paper is to lay out the historical sequence of the major peace traditions so that their goals, social bases, strategies and their inter-relationships in the great periods of anti-war feeling can be examined: 1890–1914, 1916–21, 1930–39, 1957–63, 1965–70 (Vietnam), 1979–86. Another is to ask why coalitions fell apart—why do peace movements rise and fall? As can be seen in Figure 1, the history of the peace movement is a history of peaks and troughs. A further objective of the paper is to analyse the objectives and aspirations of anti-war movements both immediately before and during the emergence of mass warfare after 1800. In so doing, one can assess the degree to which the sects and minority traditions follow the upturn of mass peace movements, or conversely, initiate and inspire them.

The overall approach of this paper is typological. In order to gauge the growth of peace programmes, the movements will be analysed in relation to certain larger ideological or religious traditions to show the impact of intellectual trends of the period: socialism, liberalism, internationalism, etc. The constituencies mobilized around such ideas are themselves significant. If the peace movement is more than the sum of its organizational parts, what makes it up? What is its popular appeal? Some attention will be paid in each case to the social bases of recruitment for the various peace groups, and the degree to which they are related to the oppressed or agents of social change. In this regard, two phenomena have prominently influenced different social groups in different countries and, indeed, the peace and anti-war movement itself: most recently, the threat of mass destruction by nuclear war; and earlier, the almost universal introduction of compulsory male conscription by 1915.

Toward a typology of peace traditions

Before one can judge the entire peace movement's history in terms of its achievements or goals, its impact on state and society, and its success or failure, one has to ask a question: in what sense can one talk of *the* peace movement as a continuous global or unitary social phenomenon? It is

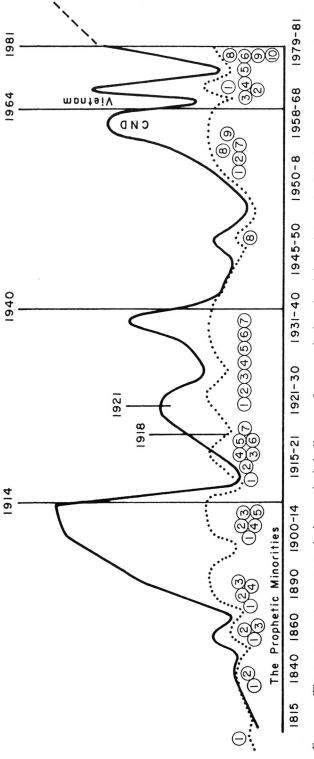

FIGURE 1. The mass peace movements. An impressionistic diagram of peace cycles based mainly on data on the British peace movements—but incorporating other European and North American sources. Waves indicate support as *relative*/ratio of population, at each time period. National variations *not* represented. Top line indicates mobilized support (demonstrations, memberships etc). Dotted lines indicate organizational continuities (for numbers see Fig.2). (Not to scale)

arguable that there is no such thing as a single peace movement, but a variety of peace traditions: religious pacifism; liberal internationalism; the women's peace movement; anti-conscriptionism; conscientious objection; socialist anti-militarism; socialist internationalism; the peace fronts associated with the Comintern; radical, secular pacifism; anarcho-pacifism; Gandhian non-violent revolution; unilateral nuclear pacifism of parts of the nuclear disarmament movement; the transnational anti-war New Left of the 1960s; and the ecologically inspired movements of the seventies and the eighties. Each has made a contribution, sometimes in coalition, sometimes as separate sects or sub-groups. Yet at times a peace movement has arisen that is more than the sum total of these traditions or the organizations that represent them. At such times it has attracted a mass base.

To be sure, there have been moments of popular activity on issues related to war and peace when various strands and traditions, immensely diverse in character and often contradictory in their stance, have joined with the politically mobilized. But these minority traditions which coexist, within the broader peace movement for much of the period have distinct histories and successes and failures of their own. Their impact on the larger peace movement, accordingly, must be analysed separately; some, for example, *grew* during World War I when the peace movement generally receded. Prophetic minorities and peace sects are able to survive and even flourish in periods of war and movement decline. Yet at other times these diverse fragments have had little or no contact with society or one another, and have all but disappeared from the historical scene; they have fought bitter feuds or retreated into alternative strategies, or even emigrated and escaped. In other words, the history of peace movements, as with so many other social movements, is one of discontinuities and divisions.

I have attempted to break down the peace movement into its constituent elements developed over the past 180 years (and some which precede the first modern peace movements). A set of "ideal-type" clusters of ideas and strategies has emerged sequentially with differing goals and methods and varying degrees of salience and influence, both within and beyond the peace movement. Understanding these developments is hindered by the lack of systematic knowledge and analysis of the peace movement: its history, social character, political strategies, ideologies, and social base. There are many excellent monographs and detailed studies, but what is really needed is some holistic approach to appreciate and gain strength from the variety and richness of peace movement traditions. Many peace efforts in the 1980s are seen as novel, but often they are not. For example, few know of the internationalist, feminist, anti-militarism of 1914–16 on which research is now being done, or of the massive anti-war feeling among the armies in Europe in 1916–20.

But before analysing the mass popular peace movements 1880–1914, 1920–36, and 1957 and beyond, it is necessary to examine the growth of the constituent parts of these movements as they developed mainly during the nineteenth century. By the 1890s, a number of major peace traditions had emerged with their own clear organizational expressions. Co-operation and contact between the various wings and strands were often minimal; their visions, strategies and social base differed widely.

The religious peace traditions

The religious tradition is certainly the oldest of the major peace strands and predates the growth of the concept of a peace movement, that is, as a largely secular and political force independent of churches or the representatives of states. Even before the fourth century the tradition of religious pacifism was associated with individual witness and principled war resistance of an absolute kind. Later, conscientious objection to military service was claimed as a right as conscription spread, usually invoking both a universalistic ethic and moral critique of war, and was often rooted in a communal religious base. In some cases these collective values led to a withdrawal of the group from the world into monastic contemplation or quietist and retreatist sects, and this continued to play a role even in the twentieth century. In other cases these groups were confronted by state and military authorities, rebellion, emigration, and persecuted and repressed to the point of extinction.

Peace ideas, if not absolute pacifism, in Christianity, as in other major religions, certainly predate the era of the European religious Reformation. They can be found in the less orthodox social undercurrents of the Catholic Church and monastic movements which precede both the Anabaptist revolt and the cosmopolitan humanism of Erasmus. But it was out of that crucible, and the extensive warfare of the seventeenth century, that one group emerged that has played a virtually continuous role on peace issues both in England and elsewhere, providing witness against war since the English civil war: the Quakers.

The Society of Friends, or "Quakers," merit analysis despite their small numbers. They have had an influence on the sustenance and growth of the peace movement for more than 300 years in the English speaking countries and beyond that is truly remarkable and quite out of proportion to their size. Their activities combine a number of root elements which remained a key part of the broader movement as it grew. The Quakers draw together a number of elements found in earlier religious peace traditions for their particular contribution to peace visions, symbols, strategy and social organization, both religious and secular.

The first element is the desire not merely to oppose but to actively resist war, both collectively and through individual witness or non-cooperation with military service. The second element is the belief in the ultimate possibility of the abolition of war through non-violent unarmed relations between peoples and groups as well as individuals. This utopian vision is based on non-violence or non-resistance as both an ethical principle and an ultimately practical basis of order. The third element is a religious notion of universalism—unity as people under God or in the spirit. It stresses the ultimate identity of all human beings, using it as the basis for a moral critique of war as a collective crime against the species itself. This leads to a transnational loyalty beyond states and national borders which characterizes most religions but has special meaning for peace churches. The fourth element is a belief in the necessity for social and structural change. Peace and human fairness and compassion are perceived to be linked; an unequal world or society leads to violent conflict and death. Intrinsic in this idea is that change in the individual and the community is possible.

These four dimensions of Quaker peace ideology passed into many of the traditions and movements which followed—including the more secular liberal and socialist ones. This fostered an intimate relationship that allowed productive alliances and coalitions among them.

Liberalism and internationalism: proposals for reform

A second major tradition of peace activity tried to prevent war through the reformed behaviour of states: peace plans, treaties and proposals, negotiations, or international law and arbitration between all groups and peoples. This search was developed further through the concepts of civil disobedience, mediation, conflict resolution, and non-violence. In the 1890s, there was a great surge of support for such initiatives. Elite plans and proposals for peace and disarmament had emerged even before the Quakers took them up and became widespread in European ruling circles during the carnage of the Thirty Years War (1618–1648). The Quakers (for example, Penn) adopted some of these ideas in America and combined them with ideas of positive peace and a non-violent social order (Woolman), and international harmony

1. Religious Peace Traditions	Religious Pacifism, Society of Friends (Quakers), International Fellowship of Reconciliation, Pax Christi, Unified Buddhist Church of Vietnam
2. Liberal Internationalism	League of Nations Associations, Peace Councils, Peace Society, World Disarmament Campaigns, Union of Democratic Control
3. Anti-conscriptionism	(Single issue lobbies) No Conscription Fellowship, War Resisters' International
4. Socialist War-resistance	War Resisters' International, CGT (France)
5. Socialist Internationalism	Second International
6. Feminist Anti-militarism	WILPF, Women's Peace Party, Women Strike for Peace, Women for Peace
7. Radical Pacifism	War Resisters' International, No More War Movement, Gandhi's Congress, Movement for a New Society
8. Cominternationalism	World Peace Council; Peace Committees, Mouvement de la Paix
9. Nuclear Disarmament	Campaigns for Nuclear Disarmament, SANE, "The Hibakusha", Freeze, END
10. The "new peace movement" (?)	The Greens (?)

These categories are neither exhaustive nor mutually exclusive—some are much larger, more continuous and important than others—some of the sub-segments e.g. of religious traditions are themselves continuous parts of the peace movement (Quakerism). The anarchist anti-war tradition is arguably distinct, but it overlaps with anti-conscriptionism; socialist war resistance; radical pacifism; feminist anti-militarism; and the new peace movement and was also involved in socialist internationalism and nuclear disarmament; and certain religious peace tendencies (Catholic Workers, Radical Quakers, Tolstoyans). This shows the hazards of such classification.

Figure 2. A typology of peace traditions (some examples/organizations)

to parallel the more cosmopolitan and visionary ideas of the Enlightenment humanists. The ideas of liberal internationalism gave the peace plans of the seventeenth and eighteenth centuries a broader base: public opinion on war began to coalesce and to matter.

The first peace societies were formed in the early nineteenth century. Preventing war though international organization was closely linked to a concept that was to remain basic to peace movement activity and thought: universalism, the cosmopolitan ethic that sprang from both the Enlightenment and earlier religious ideals of a universal or transnational church. With the growth of socialism, a new form of this internationalist ethic emerged to complete a peace perspective based on the relativity of national boundaries and frontiers and the ultimate limitation of the sovereignty of states.

These developments did not provide a united strategy or ideology for the early modern peace movement, but they did lay the foundations for a simple lowest common denominator of action and aims: namely, the survival of the species, the eventual elimination of war, and the basic unity of human society. It was this common platform that spurred the long delayed but deeply rooted reaction to the arms race in the early twentieth century.

Liberal internationalism has often been termed *pacificism* since it aims to avert war but never renounces its use, or participation in it, as absolute *pacifists* do. This distinction did not become clear until 1914 when the peace movement shattered—split between its "pacifist" and "pacificist" wings. The latter and more numerous segment was willing to support war in most cases. The liberal internationalists had formed the International Peace Bureau (1892), associated with the great peace conferences at The Hague, and agitated for a League of Nations (after 1920, supporting it through the League of Nations Unions). They also stressed civilian democratic control of war (via the Union of Democratic Control in Britain) with the protection of civil liberties, as against military autocracy.

What hindered the liberal internationalist dream were the geopolitical developments which preceded the 1914–18 war. After the American and French revolutions, Europe witnessed the spread of nation-states, mass conscripted armies, and industrial bases for militarism and imperial expansion. One of the key intellectual debates in the peace movement was between a non-conformist, free-trade liberalism that saw global capitalism as creating a new war-less world, and socialism, which saw capitalism as the engine of a highly militarized, exploitative and centralized state system of enormous destructive capacity. Nobel's peace prize symbolized this basic conflict.

Conscription and war resistance

The peace movement's third major tradition, anti-conscriptionism, was often linked to liberal issues of civil rights or the liberty of the individual. But it also coincided with religious non-conformity, such as the Quaker's witness against war (conscientious objection), and with socialist resistance to war especially by left labour unions (the CGT in France). But even before modern conscription began in France in 1793, war and military service had in many countries at different times been opposed by the poor and the illiterate: inarticulate peasants and crafts people; persecuted religious sects and communities; emigrants and immigrants. Whilst not formally part of the peace movement, these people constituted a vast reservoir of discontent that was drawn into religious and political activity by certain intellectual currents in socialism (for example, Anarchism and Syndicalism) and the charismatic anarcho-pacifism of Tolstoy in the Slav countries. A substantial following had developed by 1900, influencing Gandhi and millions of religious pacifists in Tsarist Russia.

From early Christian times, many religious communities have resisted war, or at least distanced the religious group and the individual from the institution of war and the performance of military service. This constituted one of the moral and political foundations for the more modern "civic right of conscientious objection;" a right which secular liberal internationalists, socialist war resisters, members of other churches (including other peace sects), and international organizations came to support in different ways, at different times, and to different degrees. By the twentieth century, conscientious objection was being claimed as a basic human right. During the 1914–18 war, this was to prove of crucial importance in sustaining the peace movement and anti-conscriptionism in wartime, and in building the new anti-war movements at the end of the war. However, as will be seen, these nonconformist inspirational roots did not produce a single or uniform socialist response to war and conscription. Socialists were deeply divided over the progressive character of conscription and the justification of progressive war.

Socialism and the peace movement: militarism and anti-militarism

The rise of socialism highlights the fourth element in the inspirational roots of the peace movement: the necessity for social and human change, given that war is linked to problems of economic injustice and political repression, to the selfishness of narrow élites and powerful ruling groups, and to national and imperial as well as racial chauvinism. Marxists and non-Marxists alike continue to be divided over the role of the nation-state as an apt vehicle for socialist change, on the necessity for revolutionary violence, and the desirability of socialist participation in existing capitalist governments. And by no means were all socialists anti-conscriptionist or internationalist (or even anti-militarist). It is no wonder then that all the debates and proclamations of the Second International came to nothing in 1914, despite the rhetoric of the Stuttgart Resolution of 1904.

The socialist peace tradition can be best broken down into two main dimensions: "socialist war resistance," as typified by the CGT in France, and "socialist internationalism," that was largely co-opted by "communist internationalism" after 1917.

Socialist war resistance opposed, through direct grass-roots actions like the Barcelona Strike of 1909, militarist governments, conscription, and war preparations, which they perceived to be integral aspects of capitalism, imperialism and class rule. Whilst some Marxists such as Liebknecht and Luxemburg may be identified with this first dimension, it was mainly non-marxist socialists, anarchists and syndicalists (often from outside the Second International) who organized this proletarian anti-conscriptionism (usually through the labour unions) into an anti-war movement. In the period before 1914, socialist anti-militarists like Keir Hardie in Britain, Karl Liebknecht in Germany, and Domela Niewenhuis in Holland, tried to link their socialist critique to the idea of practical war *prevention*. If the organized producers, now numbering tens of millions in Europe, could strike in unison across national frontiers against war, then the militarists and nationalists, generals, emperors, tsars and capitalist-backed governments would be immobilized by mass non-cooperation. Anti-militarist strikes did take place before, and also after, 1914; the dream of a general strike of workers of all countries against war did not die with the August mobilizations, but led to other political action during the war and after.

In the anti-war opposition from 1880–1918, one can distinguish the existence of a socialist, Marxist anti-militarist tradition. Admittedly Marx himself contributed little to this position, particularly for those revolutionary Marxists like Liebknecht and Luxemburg who were among the socialists most resolutely opposed to the war in 1914–18. Liebknecht had opposed the idea prevalent amongst many socialists that conscription created a "people's army." Rather, he argued, it created "an army against the people" and could not be an instrument for socialism. Luxemburg questioned whether progressive national wars between the increasingly militarized states were possible any longer, though Lenin advocated nationalist "wars of defence." (Marx had established a tradition of seeking to establish the more "progressive" of military antagonists in each war, one that many Marxists continued to follow.) Luxemburg, however, was far more critical than Lenin of the effect that revolutionary war could have on revolution itself, and believed that opposition to violence was (like freedom and democracy) essential to socialism.

Yet the Marxist anti-militarist tradition, despite the courageous sophistication of Liebknecht and Luxemburg, was always a weak one. The rich socialist anti-militarist tradition was ovewhelmingly non-Marxist and often anti-Marxist. Niewenhuis, Proudhon, Herve, Keir Hardie, Debs, De Ligt, and the mass syndicalist anti-militarists before 1914 often found themselves opposed by the Marxists in the Internationals. Marxists supported the expulsion of libertarian anti-militarists, and Marxist support for the Stuttgart Resolution was actually a tactical shift in emphasis from practical steps to *prevent* war. The basic problem was not the horror of war but who was fighting for whom. Indeed since Engels campaigned for conscription, war as an institution has been discussed little within Marxist theory.

Socialism was divided between its anti-militarist and militarist traditions. Since the Russian Civil War, the latter has predominated. In the fifty years before that, a heroic anti-militarist tradition had evolved, and at the turn of the twentieth century appeared to be in the ascendant. Socialist anti-militarism preceded Marxism, and was often in tension with it during this crucial half-century. However, the national mobilizations of August 1914 and the military consolidation of the Russian state after 1918 reversed that relationship and made socialist militarism a key factor in world politics.

Revolutionary socialists like Lenin and Luxemburg saw in the war a new chance to organize the mobilized producers against their officers and rulers as war weariness grew. At the Zimmerwald Conference, the notion of revolutionary defeatism was born, turning the armed conflict between states into a conflict between classes—a war within a war. In a number of European countries, and a number of armies, the idea grew that peace would have to be made by attacking those ruling groups responsible for war (Peace through Revolution). Later in the war, in the French and British armies, massive mutinies occurred; by 1917, the mood in the Russian army and, by 1918, the German army had gone beyond mutiny to revolutionary discontent and mass desertion.

But part of the reason for the failure of 1914 was due to that other socialist peace tradition, socialist internationalism, and its inability to act in a practical transnational way. Unlike socialist war resistance, it was a movement of intellectuals, party leaders and organizers, not so rooted in popular movements and local communities. Moreover, it was more closely linked to the sentiments of national parties and union leaders. Like the socialist war resisters, it indulged in the rhetoric of war prevention and anti-militarist strikes, and it was much less convinced than liberal internationalists about the possibilities of agreements between existing states.

On the other hand, socialist internationalism took the nation-state for granted and was largely wedded to advancing within that framework. In 1914, one socialist party after another succumbed to the call for national unity and voted war credits. Only a minority of socialist anti-militarists and internationalists defied this debacle. When the socialist movement might have become more fundamentally anti-militarist given the appalling experiences of 1914–18, it turned in the opposite direction because of the perceived need to defend the Russian revolution. The revolutionary tradition had become militarized as well as "state-" and nation-centred.

Emergence of the modern peace movement

In the wake of the butchery of the Napoleonic wars, the religious, liberal and internationalist traditions jostled each other in a somewhat unresolved and kaleidoscopic scatter of peace societies and pressure groups. Whilst retaining its religious heritage, the peace movement became more influenced by the secular ideas of the *Auklärung*, the development of modern ideological formulae. The idea of a "workers' strike against war" was heard for the first time. With the French revolution and the *levée en masse*, the reality both of the "peoples' army" and the ambiguities of the French "wars of liberation" in Europe soon became apparent. The latent dilemmas of violent social change were answered in part by utopian and communitarian views of social change without violence, or at least without resort to arms. From now on the peace movement would be divided over the ethics and issues of "just wars," whether by progressive states or progressive oppositional groups. In the 1860s members of the peace movement, and indeed pacifists such as the Quakers, found themselves divided over a war that could emancipate black slaves in 1863. Time and time again in the nineteenth and twentieth centuries, such divisions would be repeated. The peace movement split over whether a war was "just" or "progressive," whether the evil to be overcome was any greater than the injustice and violence needed to succeed and whether military service—the "democratization of the means of violence" by conscription—might itself be a progressive phenomenon.

One can term these nineteenth century groups "modern" not because they were secular, since they overlapped with religious non-conformity, but because they sought to organize public opinion in society either to create new institutions—like the Interparliamentary Union (IPU), the Red Cross and the Postal Union—which would have a bearing on peace, or to pressure existing politicians and structures to change their ways or introduce new policies or institutions. Although reformists, they inevitably paved the way for the new socialist oriented peace and anti-militarist concern which aimed to mobilize peoples to create a new war-less world society—even if it meant the violent overthrow of the old order. As the public involvement with war grew through conscription, the killing of civilians, and new communications, so too did the reaction against war of organized public opinion.

The twentieth century peace movement: new traditions

Two of the major peaks of the peace movement in terms of mass public support occurred before and after the first (1914–18) "Great" European war. From the late 1880s until 1914, and from the 1920s until the mid-1930s, one can talk of a mass peace movement certainly in Europe and the United States (as one can again in the late 1960s and 1980s). The western peace movement as it reached the first peak of support between 1890–1900 reflects, as we have shown, the traditions upon which it was based and the development of peace-related groups and organizations, some of which initiated this impressive growth and some that jumped on the bandwagon.

Both socialist internationalism and anti-militarism suffered near terminal defeat in 1914, but socialist war resistance continued (sometimes illegally) in many belligerent countries. In fact, certain new peace traditions emerged as an understanding of the nationalist mobilizations grew. During the war these various traditions overlapped, co-existed and fused, or were renewed. War resisters in prison included religious pacifists, anti-conscriptionists—in Britain where conscription was introduced in 1915–16, they were organized into the No Conscription Fellowship, an organization headed by Fenner Brockway, Bertrand Russell and Clifford Allen—and socialist anti-militarists of various hues.

A major new force was feminist anti-militarism. Even before 1900, a new transnational women's peace movement had begun to assert an identity of its own. It created groups and brought together Marxist, socialist, anarchist and liberal women, feminists and non-feminists, those involved in the suffrage movement and those from Christian backgrounds, all united by the ideal of a distinctive role for women on the issue of peace and female unity across national boundaries even in wartime. Inspired by women such as Adams, Pankhurst, Jacobs, von Suttner, Schwimmer, Eastman, Luxemburg and Goldman, by 1914 they had created a uniquely feminist peace tradition. The war-time meeting at The Hague in 1915 of over 1000 women to inaugurate the Women's International League for Peace and Freedom (WILPF) exemplified this new transnational movement.

Despite the hardships and traumas of 1914–22, a number of peace traditions went through a period of renewal. Several key international peace organizations such as the WILPF, the IFOR, and the War Resisters International (WRI) emerged. The secular pacifism of the war years grew in the 1920s into movements like the No More War Movement in Britain (and later the PPU of the 1930s). Liberal internationalism regrouped in organizations such as the League of Nations Union and the German Peace Society. Protestant religious pacifism was now co-ordinated by the International Fellowship of Reconciliation (IFOR) with Quakers continuing in key roles. Small numbers of Catholic pacifists were also now grouping in Pax Christi. Moreover, a new form of integral pacifism was born that was largely secular (and often socialist) in character. It drew on all the previous traditions and was more radical than pre-1914 pacifism, linking international war resistance, anti-conscriptionism and civil libertarianism with schemes of utopian social (if not always social*ist*) change. These changes were to be brought about by the new non-violent direction action techniques of Gandhi that were publicized by Rolland and others in Europe after 1918, rather than by the violent class war still advocated by many socialist anti-militarists. In many countries, branches of the WRI were formed which expressed this radical synthesis, both socialist and anti-conscriptionist, forged during the war and now related to minority strands (conscientious objection, feminism and libertarianism).

As for socialist anti-militarists and internationalists, they submerged themselves in the broader peace coalitions (and in Britain in the ILP). Socialist internationalism tended either to merge with social democracy, liberal internationalism and the League, or to identify with the socialist militarism and the geopolitical interests of the Soviet Union after 1920. As communism retreated to its Russian base, a new internationalism dominated by that of the Comintern, occupied the vacuum left by the Second International and played a leading role in the mass peace fronts emerging in the late twenties and thirties. With the domination of the pro-Russian communist parties and the rise of fascism in Italy and Germany, the independent socialist anti-militarist tradition became a minority one. Comintern nationalism practised effective "entryism" in the peace movements of the twenties and thirties, but by 1936 had switched to anti-fascist rather than peace activity. However, it did establish national peace committees, later linked to the World Peace Council, which played significant roles.

By 1932, the peace movements in Italy, Germany, Russia, and to some extent Japan, had already been crushed or had disappeared. But in the United States, Britain, the Netherlands, and to some extent France and Scandinavia, mass peace movements still thrived.

Two paths of evolution

The European and North American peace movements gathered strength during the arms race that lef to the war of 1914–18. In its wake, a new mass movement based on revulsion at the nature of the conflict arose. But by the 1930s the peace movement was focused on the renewed arms race and the rise of fascism. However, two opposing tendencies were articulated after 1918. One was to organize public opinion to reform the world system of nation-states either through a League of Nations or through a global hegemony by an enlightened power or powers. The other was to stress increasing claims against the state system, using extra-parliamentarist strategies of social change: extension of the rights of conscience, resistance to conscription, civil disobedience, and anti-militarist direct action (radical non-violence and transnational and subcultural identification).

In the short-term both of these tendencies were doomed to failure given the context of national rivalries and the nascent period of political autocracy. Indeed the peace movements in this period achieved few manifest victories. The establishment of the League, the creation of a new socialist state, the Kellog-Briand Pact, the widespread acceptance of peace propaganda, all could not arrest the drift towards militarization and the war of 1939.

The latent effectiveness of the peace movement in preventing even worse militarist excess from occurring is impossible to measure. All that can be claimed is that the peace movement adopted new perspectives from the disaster of 1914, maintained a moral critique of war, accumulated new peace traditions, and acquired (but only temporarily) a new mass base. It failed to halt the arms race after 1930, as it had after 1900, and failed in most of its other stated goals. In addition, several key peace traditions suffered dramatic discontinuities.

Still, ideas and organizations were created in these three decades which remained alive and active. They provided links to strategies for peace and disarmament in the later years of the twentieth century, when a broad coalition of peace constituencies—like that which grew in the years between 1900 and 1914—re-emerged to form the contemporary movement.

The peace movement as a global movement

The rise of fascism and the cataclysm of the 1939–45 war led to another profound disjunction in the peace movement. Peace organizations and ideas remained, but not a peace movement. Indeed, the period from the growing peace protests against civilian bombing in the 1940s until the rising tide of concern in the mid-fifties is the longest single caesura in the two hundred year history of the peace movement. It can best be explained by the partial relegitimization of war in the face of fascism, East and West, and by extending the defence of liberties against autocracy by force of arms. In the period before and after the war of 1914–18, it is plausible to argue that the silent majority had become sceptical of war as an instrument of politics and that at best most nation-states were considered quasi-legitimate. Ironically the subsequent democratization or "self-determination" of a number of states and the establishment of socialism in one country led to a more widespread legitimization of war, disseminated by socialism and liberalism through an expanding communications network and increased global literacy. The anti-fascist fronts of the thirties laid the groundwork for the "just war" theory of World War II. The silent majorities before and after 1945 supported the war alliances: the "unjust" stereotype of war from 1918 was replaced by a grudging acceptance of big battalions, and apostasy from pacifism and anti-militarism lasted beyond 1945. This is the only way to explain the delayed reaction to nuclear weapons (except in Japan where there are some additional specific circumstances). The state system itself shared in the general legitimization of the peace of the victors despite the bloc bifurcation and the new arms race. This acceptance of a "just nuclear peace" was paralleled by the shift of liberation movements to anti-colonial wars in Asia and Africa.

During the hiatus, perhaps for the first time, events, movements and ideas outside the white western and industrial countries became significant in the peace movement. Gandhi's movement to liberate India came to fruition in 1947 through an overwhelming non-violent social movement that linked itself explicitly to peace. The first use of atomic weapons took place on an Asian country, Japan, whose earlier peace movement had been shattered by fascist militarism. A new peace movement arose that was partly inspired by the witness of the atomic victims, the "Hibakusha." In many countries peace became identified again with social justice, and the end of racial and colonial oppression. Many countries tried to follow India's example, some like Gandhi through non-violent or peaceful means. The repression of Indo-Chinese independence led to a global anti-war reaction. Nuclear testing in the Pacific was responded to by transnational peace voyages. There were international protests in the French Sahara. The movement of non-aligned states emerged after the Bandung Conference in 1955 with great expectations, and involved mostly less developed states. Tanzania and Cuba were hailed as new models of development.

So far the peace movement has largely been analysed as a phenomenon developing in the western or Christian countries, in the industrial democracies, or the English-speaking world. But it is also arguable that Gandhi's movement, the response to Hiroshima and Nagasaki, and the influence of socialism—first Russian, then Chinese and other more indigenous forms— on liberation movements such as the Indo-Chinese, began to shift the locus of the peace movement to a more global plane. Rising radiation levels throughout the world that were due to nuclear testing by several countries, especially in the Pacific, led to a global outcry. Certainly the emerging peace movements of the northern hemisphere were beginning to find new echoes and counterparts in the South. Also, human or civil rights came to be seen as integral to peace, as in the massive US movement for black social justice which was associated with Martin Luther King, Jr. and his advocacy of non-violence, and which linked itself to struggles for black Africa.

The initial lack of opposition against the growing atomic arsenal of the United States provided a vacuum for the World Peace Council to step in with its Stockholm Peace appeal in 1950, a move that gained mass support despite its aligned origins given the US monopoly of the genocidal weapons. Most of the old peace traditions had survived by the late 1950s, when the upsurge of public opinion against nuclear arms grew in Europe, North America, Australasia and elsewhere. It can be argued, however, that the then "nuclear pacifism" of groups like the broadly-based British Campaign for Nuclear Disarmament (CND), founded in 1958 while drawing on the old traditions was actually itself a *new type*—reflecting the drastically altered character of war and weaponry. By 1965, US involvement in Indo-China and the repression of non-violent movements there led to the formation of an international coalition, and the birth of the contemporary peace movement.

The contemporary peace movement

More than any other single event, the spontaneous yet co-ordinated mass demonstrations in twelve European capitals and several other major cities in 1981 seem to have galvanized political negotiators, both East and West, and given new life to the global peace movement. With several million participants, the upsurge of anti-nuclear activity between October and December 1981 in Bonn, Brussels, Paris, Athens, London, Bucharest, Rome, Madrid, Amsterdam, Helsinki, Oslo, East and West Berlin, Stockholm and Copenhagen engendered a sense of transnational unity and a vision of success. These demonstrations revealed a common political purpose rarely seen before; some observers looking back as far as 1848 for a comparable trans-European movement.

The new peace movement fanned out from the Netherlands to Germany, Britain, Belgium and Italy; it elicited signs of an independent peace mood in Eastern Europe; it steadily expanded through Scandinavia and the Mediterranean; it reached Canada, New Zealand, Australia and the United States; and, almost last of all, touched France. In Europe, these campaigns, in the context of a new cold war, had their decisive catalyst in the December 1979 NATO decisions to deploy a new generation of missiles, and the abandonment of serious disarmament negotiation after SALT II was left unratified.

The churches were more intimately involved than they had been in the first mass nuclear disarmament campaigns in Europe twenty years earlier. Following the example of the Dutch churches, both congregations and religious leaders, East and West, took considerably more radical stances. In all, this was a more transnational and massive protest than anything in the sixties, involving a broader political coalition with new elements from the Vietnam war period and the women's ecological and anti-nuclear power movements. It had a regional as well as international dimension, new forms of political organizing, less reliance on formal structure and leadership, and a greater political awareness of the need for autonomy.

The result of this second awakening of public sentiment against nuclear weapons—as in the 1958–63 period—was a revival of critical appraisals of the role of war and military change in socialism, even hints of, the revival after sixty years, of a genuine socialist anti-militarist tradition. During the years of its dormancy, especially since the 1930s, the tensions between socialism and pacifism had multiplied. But now a resumption of dialogue foreshadowed in the 1960s between radical pacifists and varieties of revolutionary socialists seems to be occurring. The absurdity of nuclear war and nuclear weaponry, and the serious problems of militarized national revolutions, make such a reappraisal inevitable, and *rapprochement* possible. In this second awakening, twenty years more of Third World wars of liberation, with their questionably socialist character and results, have added further dimensions to the debate.

A new peace strategy

Developing a new peace strategy requires a certain detachment from the various, fragmented, reactive, and sometimes divisive peace traditions that provided the core of the peace movements since the early nineteenth century and whose descendants are still prominent in the ostensibly "new" peace movement.

Despite discontinuities, the previous traditions each have contemporary equivalents and organizational expressions; especially the religious dimension which overlapped with the more secular movements in the mass pacifism of the 1930s. Liberalism came to be represented by the World Disarmament Campaign, the United Nations Association, various disarmament lobbies and some National Peace Councils. An anti-militaristic tendency survived in many of those countries with military conscription. Single-issue organizations like the Campaign Against the Arms Trade, the National Council for Civil Liberties, or Amnesty International also represent this tradition (as does perhaps the British Campaign for Nuclear Disarmament). In many countries, branches of the WRI represent a synthesis of both socialist and anti-conscriptionist tendencies, with feminist and libertarian influences. The most dramatic transnationalist movement against a specific and barbarous "conventional" war was the draft-resistance organized in response to the war in Vietnam (1964–74).

Despite the continuous existence of the WILPF since 1915, the continuity of a broad women's anti-militarist coalition only became clear in the late 1970s with its independent role in the new peace movement, for example, the transnational marches and peace camps. Its contributions include an emphasis on spontaneity, radical destructuring, and new forms and models of participation. Radical non-violent traditions tended to become submerged in the counter-culture movements of the 1960s. But it retained strong links to groups such as the WRI and is now closely identified with the environmentalist and anti-nuclear power lobby, and feminism. It tends to be globalist in orientation, yet has strong community roots. The internationalism of the Comintern, "Cominternationalism" (later communist international-ism), declined in importance after the mid-fifties. In the 1960s, it practised effective "entryism" in some mass peace and anti-nuclear movements, highlighting and opposing specific United States or western actions. The national peace committees (that is, those linked to the World Peace Council) have only played a key role in a few countries, but their significance since 1979 has declined except in France and Eastern Europe, and even there they are now challenged.

From this diversity, an important new model of what a grass-roots movement can be and how opinion can be organized effectively against the arms race and nuclear war, has emerged (or is emerging). But it is hardly perceived as such by the older peace traditions, nor by many "nuclear pacifists" (for example in CND), or by the politicians who oppose or manipulate these orientations. Indeed peace researchers themselves may constitute one particular minority tradition as they have played a disproportionately important role in the intellectual leadership of the new peace movements since 1979, especially in END. This new model will be discussed in the rest of the paper.

Grass-roots movements as "subjects" of action

In comparing the contemporary peace movement to those of the past, we can distinguish between movements that have been essentially objects of mobilization by political élites and those that have been subjects. The difference between the mass peace movements of the 1930s or 1950s and those of the pre-1914 and post-1958 period, is that the latter were much more subjects of their own activity. In the contemporary peace movement, manipulation is a less dominant feature; synthesis emerges from the bottom-up. This is not to say that tensions do not exist—especially in END between the visionary programmatic approach of the intellectual leadership versus the down-to-earth pragmatism of the grass-roots—but the gap between those who mobilize and those who are mobilized has closed compared with many earlier movements. Indeed this may explain superficial activation of concern in the United States and Japan during the same period. The bottom-up, "subject" movements are not immune from co-optation or manipulation, but they are less vulnerable. Of course, beneath the large, visible and superficial mass mobilizations may lurk the potential for localized "subject activism"—the United States, Russia, and Eastern Europe may be applicable here.

Several elements are particularly important in understanding the re-emergence of widespread militant and usually non-aligned opposition to nuclear weapons in Europe after sixteen years: the revival of unilateralism as a tactic; the prior strength and organizational experience of the anti-nuclear power movement; the subsequent acceptance of direct action; and the participatory character of the new movement rooted in local communities. The latter three elements were not as dominant in the anti-nuclear weapons campaigns of the late 1950s. The movement then was much more sponsored and created by hierarchical organizations; when direct action was more controversial, and when opposition to civil nuclear energy was lacking.

Civil disobedience has become a much less divisive issue than in 1960–61. There is an overwhelming consensus that massive direct non-violent action and training for it are necessary. This shift in opinion arose partly because of the civil disobedience campaigns of 1953–63 and the direct actions against Polaris submarines and US bases (for example, in Britain) and, also, partly because of the agitation against nuclear power plants in the seventies. Civil disobedience has also won new respect because of the symbolic witness of the strongly feminist camps at Greenham Common and Molesworth in England, and Cosimo in Sicily (one of the first sites for cruise missiles). These are among dozens of peace camps now established in Britain, Germany, Italy, Holland, Denmark and the United States.

A new dimension of the contemporary peace movement is a grass-roots movement for peace education within and outside schools organized by parents, pupils, teachers, local councillors and churches. It has gained such strength that one government has attacked it publicly as "appeasement" education, and widely circulated its own counter-propaganda. This movement is closely linked to the growing public concern in many countries and the transnational linkages of professional groups inside and outside education concerned with peace.

The European Nuclear Disarmament (END) movement

Probably the most significant new strategic ingredient in Europe is the European Nuclear Disarmament (END) movement, which stemmed from an appeal drafted by British historian E. P. Thompson and Ken Coates. END campaigns for a nuclear free Europe or a nuclear free zone or zones in Europe (for example, Nordic, Balkan, Central European), adding the new dimension of transnational linkage and non-alignment to the nuclear disarmament movement. They seek to link the national unilateralist and multilateralist groups into a common third force transcending national boundaries, bridging East and West with slogans like "No Cruise, No SS-20s," "An end to NATO and the Warsaw Pact," a "nuclear free zone from Poland to Portugal" (or "the Atlantic to the Urals").

Perhaps not surprisingly, it has been accused of being crudely naïve about the possibilities of unfreezing the cold war or generating an independent peace movement in the East. END contends that such a political realignment is an essential part of any strategy to disarm Europe: forcing both of the superpowers back into their national fortresses of mutual assured destruction makes a lot of strategic geopolitical sense. In fact, the same is true for the politically frozen situation within each European country. For decades the social democratic, labour, and communist parties have been party to the cold war and have inhibited any new breakthroughs, especially in northern Europe. END has had to work outside them as an autonomous and extraparliamentary force, although some left wing socialists and, especially, the Greens in Germany have responded to the new initiatives.

For END, "greater Europe" is now a prime target with theatre nuclear weapons deployed alongside the battlefield weapons already in place. With Europe paralysed by both the Communist Party governments in the East and even the Social Democratic governments in the West, only a cross-national and non-governmental European campaign challenging the hegemony of the nuclear monoliths and the lesser "independent" nuclear powers of Britain and France can alleviate the situation. Major debates within the Western peace movement remain, as in the sixties, on the issue of alignment, NATO membership, the role of peace activity vis-à-vis Eastern Europe, and its relationship with the labour movement (where the unions and the left wing are influential but have taken varying positions against nuclear weapons).

However, and unlike the fifties or sixties, a multitude of local peace groups, women's peace programmes, peace camps, anti-cruise missile campaigns, European disarmament, World Disarmament, and others have arisen in each locality. In Britain, CND's membership grew from under 3,000 in 1979 to over 100,000 by 1984, increasing by 35,000 in 1980–81 alone; with hundreds of local groups it is beginning to rival the main political parties.

END has stimulated non-alignment between East and West, broadened the national movements to an international and European approach, and also opened up a dialogue between unilateralists and multilateralists around the ideas of reciprocal initiatives and regional nuclear free zones. European transnationalism has created a special role for the six non-aligned or neutral countries—Finland, Sweden, Austria, Yugoslavia, Switzerland and Ireland—at the governmental and non-governmental levels as a third force outside the blocs. To be sure, movements like CND question whether "multilateral" approaches, and calls for "general and complete disarmament" by negotiation, and bilateral arms control or limitations are either sincere or effective campaign platforms. This applies even to movements in the United States and the USSR where peace movements are not significantly unilateralist. In Europe, NTA (Norway, Denmark), CND, IKV (Netherlands), Svenska Freds (Sweden), each of whom has called for major action by each country *regardless* of what others do, tend to be alienated from those who argue for conditional steps related to bilateral or multilateral negotiations such as missile trade-offs. Clearly "unilateralism" has been a necessary force in the rise of the European peace movement, although it is certainly not sufficient for its success.

Unity and diversity: the search for synthesis

It is necessary to build a pattern of unilateral, graduated steps across Europe—East and West—as a programme and strategy that is multilateral not only at the level of the movement but also at the level of political leadership. Each country and region has aspired to direct the European movement: in the Netherlands through the IKV or IPCC; in Germany through the Greens; in Britain through CND/END; and elsewhere through the WDC, the IPB, and the Eurocommunists (Italy). END seems to present the best hope for a synthesis out of all the movements. While recognizing the special role of national movements like the German, British and the Dutch—theoretically and practically—END also encourages local grass-roots movements to create their own *local* nuclear free zones. Hundreds of municipal authorities (including the whole of Wales) have created community nuclear free zones, and then paired them with other nuclear free municipalities on the European continent. Through END, many local peace activists have come into contact with the grass-roots activism and ideas of the whole European movement. This has been a critical factor in internationalizing movements (like the British) which are insular and inward looking, and thus broaden their programmes and outlooks and strengthen their commitment to non-alignment.

The movement in West Germany illustrates clearly the community basis of opposition to nuclear weapons. Because Germany, East and West, is the likely first victim and atomic battlefield of any theatre nuclear war, protests there have special significance. Die Grünen, the Greens, offer a fresh programmatic approach to peace politics with a synthesis of anti-militarism, ecology, feminism, local and worker democracy, and political decentralization. Its source of synthesis, or at least pluralistic dialogue, is based on the grass-roots coalitions of autonomous local groups. Counter-cultural politics runs stronger in Germany than anywhere else, and the influence of the extraparliamentary New Left of the sixties and seventies, especially in Berlin, remains strong. Being so close to military, political and psychological frontiers, the German movement is sensitive to problems of East/West alignment and non-alignment, or reunification and separate development, which are so complex and bring the dangers of escalation closer to reality. Predictably, the demonstrations in Germany have been some of the largest and most dramatic.

The "ploughshares" movement and the Berlin Appeal, based in the largely evangelical Lutheran churches of East Germany, are especially significant. Initially springing from Protestant and youth opposition to military service (opposition that is also widespread in West Germany) and support for conscientious objectors, the movement has also shown support for the END position favouring military disengagement and the denuclearization of Central Europe, including both Germanys and possibly Czechoslovakia.

More than in any other European country, conscientious objectors in both East and West Germany have formed a movement with their own organization. BRD applications for conscientious objector status have run at a massive rate since the Vietnam war, reaching over 50, 000 a year (between 12 and 15 per cent of those eligible for military service). In the East, 4,000 young Germans have written to ask for similar status, although no exact parallel exists. In the Netherlands, and to a lesser degree in Belgium and West Germany, peace ideas have spread into the armed forces, with a group of dissident generals, soldiers and officers in uniform appearing in demonstrations in Brussels, Amsterdam and elsewhere.

An indication of the broad constituency of the new movement is the mobilization of women from many different social contexts and milieux. The women's marches from Scandinavia, first to Paris and then to Moscow, played a key part in spreading the movement both symbolically and literally in establishing cross-border links. These events and others, such as the symbolic human arm-chain linking the United States and Soviet embassies in Stockholm, made *transnationalism* more real, inspiring groups elsewhere, as at Greenham, to take bolder steps in direct-action, and to create women's groups in Eastern Europe.

As this brief survey suggests, the new peace movement in Europe is complex and varied. It certainly is better informed, more plural, probably larger, and clearly ready to move towards a more political and militant strategy than was the peace movement of the 1960s. It also appears that non-violence is taken a great deal more seriously, both in relation to its own actions, and as a potential alternative form of resistance to aggression at the local level, than by previous movements.

Of course, to talk of a "new" peace movement is only to say that the movement is a coalition of new and old elements. It includes in fact the various prophetic minorities, the full range of accumulated peace traditions with a rich historical experience: liberal and socialist internationalists, communist internationalists, religious and radical pacifists, non-violent (Gandhian) revolutionaries, independent Marxists, anarchists, anti-militarists, feminists; and new organizations like community groups, ecologists and the anti-nuclear power groups. To all of these one must add a new generation of activists, many of them young and new to protests or resistance politics, and many active in the women's peace camps and movements. It is clear that the new professional, technical class is highly involved, and to some there are distinct parallels in the range of participants between the peace movement and the emerging labour movement of the nineteenth century.

Current challenges: some negative features

Many key problems remain not only in Britain and the United States, but also in France and even in the Netherlands and Scandinavia, not least of them being the residual tendency to narrow peace campaigns to purely national and single issue movements focusing on one party (for example, in Britain usually the Labour Party, and in Italy, the Communist Party), one weapon system (cruise, the neutron bomb, Trident, or SDI), and one national political arena (for example, "Little Englandism"). To "refuse cruise" (or Pershing) is simple and emotive, but problematic both tactically and ideologically.

It is here that the new consciousness-raising and peace education works is most critical in sustaining a transnational and indeed global consciousness, a sense of the larger Europe—not only NATO or the EEC, but also the neutral and non-aligned strip (Finland, Sweden, Switzerland, Austria, Yugoslavia, and Ireland), as well as Eastern Europe and European Russia. It is here that third party intervention and initiatives for disengagement and *détente* are crucial, enlarging the strategic vision of more parochial peace groups and forcing them to confront the cultural and political underpinnings of a unified and non-nuclear "greater Europe." The Italian and Greek campaign for the Mediterranean as a "sea of peace" involving nuclear free initiatives (Sicily, Malta, Greece, etc.) complements this development. Strong parallels emerge in the North Atlantic and Pacific Rim movements.

The peace movements between 1958 and 1963 lacked (and this is where END's non-aligned populism is so relevant) a practical neutralism with an activist and non-governmental base. Thus when the Rapacki plan emerged in the fifties, it could not easily be linked to ideas of campaigns of "positive neutralism" or popular protest because it was a plan for political negotiators. When CND tried to adopt a similar proposal in 1963—Steps Toward Peace—it lost touch with its own rank and file. But now the situation is different; the plans can be linked to a grass-roots upsurge of protest and pressure. The idea of a Europe free of the nuclear giants now has great unifying appeal, the potential for linking different national movements across frontiers exists in an entirely new way because, since 1963, the world has been affected by the Vietnam war, the experiences of the New Left (for example of 1968), the Russian incursion into Czechoslovakia, and the repression of "Solidarity." The nuclear free zone is no longer a concept remote from popular understandings and movements. Transnationalism rests on a much more solid base, as the women's peace marches across Europe and various international gatherings have demonstrated. Such ideas are echoed in the movements for a nuclear free Pacific and the successes in Australia and, above all, New Zealand.

But the difficulties of sustaining the peace movement are immense; the struggle over non-alignment is a continuing one. The shift by sections of the traditional left to an anti-NATO position in several NATO countries like Britain might prove premature and divisive, as well as tactically disastrous, unless a policy of opposing the Warsaw Pact is pursued equally vigorously. Even END supporters, however much they dislike NATO politically, consider it tactically wrong and publicly unnecessary to call for the withdrawal from NATO when a majority of the public supports the peace movement on the nuclear weapons issue in many or most West European (NATO) countries, and yet also identifies with the western alliance (at least as long as the Warsaw Pact exists).

Other crucial obstacles include the repression of the peace movements in Germany (East and West), Soviet Union, Czechoslovakia, and Turkey; the problems raised by events in Poland; the issue of human rights in all these and other countries; the tentative survival of the unofficial peace movement in the GDR and Hungary; the "top-down" character of the officially sponsored peace movement in Romania; the lack, until recently, of a significant non-aligned grass-roots peace movement in France; and the official suspicion of an autonomous peace orientation in Yugoslavia. All these factors make transnational strategies and linkages at times seem utopian. The actions in Grenada and the Falklands, as well as events in Central America, ruptured many internationalist hopes in the United States and Europe, just as the Afghan conflict and repression in Poland and the USSR had dashed the hopes of a massive political thaw in the East. These events, and the militaristic speeches of western defence spokesmen and women at the SSD II in 1982 confirmed the continuation of cold war hostility, tension, and national chauvinism. Yet the peace movement has survived this. The spectre of an arms race in space is a further campaigning issue to sustain public concern.

The changing context in the West

The position of the peace movement is now almost unrecognizable from that of the mid-1970s. The official centre of gravity, of conventional wisdom, has moved towards the peace movement's platform: in a small way this is shown in Europe by the dramatic move in moderate opinion from 40 per cent to 60 per cent against "cruise," Pershing and Trident, between 1981 and 1983. Such shifts give much greater "democratic" legitimacy to civil disobedience and direct action. Moreover, the non-violent campaigns shift the focus back from the negotiating table to the communal grass-roots level from where the long-term visions and strategies spring. At Greenham and international camps, with mass confrontations, transnational debate and dialogue, the peace movement has made a strategic leap from a communal base to global strategy.

Across the Atlantic, the issues of the American peace movement such as the Nuclear Freeze Campaign are difficult to integrate within the new European peace movement because they represent a substantial step back for almost every peace group. That the US movement is also concerned to prevent further Vietnams in Latin America is also a key difference. Of course, there is much activity in the United States on NFZ's and the MX, on SDI, on "first strike," or "first use," and on deployment in Europe that is complementary to the European movement.

To some degree, the two movements understand each other's different contexts. Tactical differences in the short-term do not necessarily disguise the fundamental solidarity of the long-term vision. In parts of the movement, there does exist a somewhat unstable peace alliance among religious pacifists (including Quakers), nuclear pacifists, pro-Moscow peace fronts and old style communists, which fails to grasp the real political issues. The danger is that simple, national campaigns like those against deployment or for the freeze could reproduce the mistakes of the past and founder on leadership splits. For many countries, the pressures against "going it alone" will be massive both domestically and, from the United States, internationally. Only broad internationalist stances with an alternative foreign and defence policy, can sustain such a move. But while "alternative defence" commissions and other groups have worked feverishly to provide such policies and to help educate public opinion for such options, the peace movement has largely shunned such platforms for a variety of reasons. Thus the emergence of the European Nuclear Disarmament movement has a distinctly independent and cross-national character more reminiscent of pre-1917 internationalism. Its great danger remains that it too will be a Eurocentric movement, rather than one of community and grass-roots impulses.

The ebb and flow of mass peace protest

At this point it is possible to make some estimate *not* of the success of the peace movement in terms of goals, but in terms of popular mobilization at given periods over the last 150 years. Despite successive defeats in which the movement was reduced to prophetic minorities, it revived, and with it further traditions accumulated. Using such world-wide data as the reported size of demonstrations and anti-war strikes, the circulation of peace newspapers, numbers arrested for anti-militarist activity, organizational memberships of peace groups, and the overall number of "war resisters," legal conscientious objectors and draft evaders, it is possible to come to some quantitative (*not* qualitative) estimate of numerical peace movement strength in each period.

Of course, such data are highly problematic. The "troughs and peaks" in numbers appear at different times in different countries: the peace movement was very large in America and Britain *after* 1932, at the very time it was being crushed in Germany, the Soviet Union, Japan, Italy and elsewhere. Gandhi's movement in India (1917–46) has a profile quite different from peace movements in the West. The 1950s anti-nuclear movement in Japan emerged some years before the first western ones, as did its second wave in the 1970s. The Dutch movement was stronger in the early 1920s than in the 1930s. And in the 1970s, Greenpeace Pacific activity had little northern or western support or attention paid to it.

The profile in this paper is based mainly on historical evidence from the northern and western movements and the English-speaking areas, and even so cannot reflect all the variation, or depth and quality of participation accurately. For example, 6,000 conscientious objectors ("subjects") willing to face imprisonment *may* have more impact on a society than 600,000 organized but transitory demonstrators ("objects"). A number of sources show also that the decline in the peace movement in 1939–40—for some countries in 1914–18—was neither as sudden, dramatic nor complete as conventional wisdom once held. The external environmental shifts so dramatically, however, that in a period of war mobilization a peace movement can *seem* to "disappear" when it may only be "underground" or as in the case of the pacifism in Britain between 1939–41, still growing organizationally.

Nevertheless, it can be seen that there is a tendency for peace movements to gather their greatest strength before wars—at the time of accelerating arms *races* rather than after wars (1912 being one major exception). However, the *new* peace traditions tend to emerge during or immediately after wars (1815, 1915, 1920, 1965, etc.). What such a profile does not show is the degree of feeling, new ideas, or commitment expressed in each period. In some periods, for example, the United States in the thirties, or the active years of the Soviet-backed movements, one gets the impression that large numbers are mobilized but that they have a superficial segmental commitment, or segmental attachment. In retrospect, size of mobilization is an unsatisfactory indicator of either effectiveness or success, as the popular mass movements of the 1930s and the 1950 Stockholm Appeal indicate. One can measure effectiveness because in most cases the peace movements made explicit a particular objective or goal: some sought to abolish war (pacifism or pacificism); some opposed particular wars on liberal or socialist grounds; some aspired to limit or prevent war by negotiated disarmament, international law and peace treaties; and some opposed specific dimensions or armaments and war (such as conscription). In some cases, such as with the socialist movements, anti-war movements fused with movements for social change to abolish the war-making society and associated institutions. These and a number of later peace movements (for example, the Gandhian) had positive as well as negative objectives of peace; they wished not only to create a non-violent or more just, equitable and harmonious society, but also to link with utopian and communitarian movements.

With peace movements, as with other social movements, the results of public activity are always ambiguous. Like other great social change or social protest campaigns, they have both latent and manifest consequences. They may actually prolong the wars they aim to stop. They may alienate public opinion. Their relative success or failure always depends on other independent or external factors, not just the degree or level of activity achieved. This has always been one of the weakening illusions of peace movements: the structural and historical context of the deeply humanist abolitionist movement against slavery, for example, was just as, or more, important than the efforts of the abolitionist campaigns themselves. Moreover, the abolition of slavery left or even produced *new* evils, and involved the injustices and carnage of a terrible civil war that split and virtually destroyed the American peace movement, whilst racist oppression soon grew in virulent forms.

A further variation of this critique is the theory of "cycles" or of political "generations." For each wave of the peace movement, commitment appears inevitably cyclical. A theory involving "cycles of protest" argues that movements have an inherent limit, such as the energy, time and resources people will devote to a single issue or movement unless institutionalization takes place. Generational explanations stress the span of youthful involvement from age 17 to 25, roughly the years of compulsory military service for males. These years may be relatively free of social ties and commitments and therefore can be spent in radical movements where risks may be taken in social protest. Youth involvement in peace politics is undoubtedly a generational experience, as transient as military service in most countries—a few intense years and it is over. A movement that can institutionalize youth involvement, however, can capture a generation, the attendant dangers of such a development are inflexibility and dogmatism, an introverted, "retreated" sectarianism, where the generational experience is frozen into dogma and slogans which are damaging to the peace movement. Thus people "drop in," and out, of anti-war and other movements in large numbers—but may and do return ten or twenty years later. Evidence of the two phases of nuclear opposition shows recruitment from both the new younger age groups and the earlier generation. The cycles may vary from three or four, to ten or even fifteen years, but the time span appears to be getting progressively shorter. Without success, and after a few years, fatigue, cynicism and despair may predominate; or people may turn to other issues.

Another factor often cited to explain failure has to do with social class. It has been typically argued that peace movements have drawn from too narrow a social base to succeed (for example, they have been "middle class"). The Marxist charge that much *individualist* pacifism was originally "petty bourgeois" has some truth. Equally, liberal internationalism or "pacifism" was overwhelmingly middle class and "respectable" or professional and also male, white, and middle-aged most of the time. Yet other peace traditions, like anti-conscriptionism, have appealed in *all* countries and to all classes. Socialist anti-militarism was overwhelmingly working class, and socialist internationalism represented both the labour aristocracy and the independent intellectuals. Equally, many fundamental peace sects have been found amongst the very poor, the peasantry, and ethnic minorities.

It is true that only in rare periods has a really broad social coalition been forged. This issue of "coalitions" and why they fall apart is also related to whether peace movements have too narrow or too wide a programme. Are they single issue (or single war or weapons) movements, or broad ideological and programmatic movements with manifestos for social change? The temporary coalitions of the mass peace movements have usually included both tendencies, as does the current anti-nuclear movement. As a result, basic splits are likely on tactics, methods, goals and alignments. They occur most when the specific, concrete successes sought are lacking—for example, if a movement fails to prevent a new weapons system from being deployed, having pledged to do so.

The "lowest common denominator" movement aims to avoid such splits by demanding consensus on two or three simple demands that cut across other allegiances, religious or political: "Refuse the Missiles," "No Visits of Nuclear Armed Ships," "End the Draft," "No to Napalm," "Ceasefire Now," "Troops Home," "No Nuclear Weapons on Our Soil" and so on. Yet these movements can easily be coopted or defused by alternative policies or conventional weapon systems. Or temporary delays can allow the movement to subside (as may be an official tactic in Europe). Either way, the coalition can still fall apart, even if the aims or goals remain narrow. The obverse is not much better. A diffuse general programme of peace has often been successful in mobilizing broad masses, but unsuccessful in making any political impact. It is often one, more visionary, *element* in a diffuse coalition—for example, the Greens in Germany, draft resisters in the United States, women's peace camps in England—that provides the most dynamic thrust or represents the symbolic leading voice for the movement.

There is also a sociological approach which dismisses much peace protest at the grass-roots as "expressive" or millenial rather than "instrumental" or pragmatic; as being not really about war or nuclear weapons, but a channel of expressing personal or social alienation. Whilst such an argument tends to be conservative and can be abused, it would be wrong to dismiss the possibility that latent motivations for involvement in peace politics exist, especially among the prophetic minorities. Certainly the division between the "blind activists" of the grass-roots and the "pure theorists' in the leadership can produce charge and counter-charge of impure (or anti-intellectual) motivation. Certainly the lack of a strategy for popular political change can compound such frustration, and movements that are reactive rather than creative fall victim to this type of introversion and in-fighting, especially when success does not come as quickly as is hoped.

A general problem for social and political movements in opposition has been that of participation in government through individual cooptation or group incorporation. Individuals can be manipulated and bought off; protests can become ritualistic; an élitist leadership may not wish to lose its prestige, its organization, its money or its position. The elevation of leaders into any national establishment or parliament can weaken and discourage the grass-roots who feel betrayed; or raise false hopes that are quickly shattered as has happened wherever local peace movements have looked to established leaders and politicians within the structure of the state.

As a result, several of the peace traditions analysed have displayed a deep ambivalence or distrust about operating within the state system—or have attempted to transcend it. This was most marked before and after World War I, and again in the 1980s. Movements in this situation can become a safety valve, rather than a challenge to the war-making system. A clear case is where conscientious objection is drawn into the actual machinery of the war effort as in the United States during World War II; or where socialist MPs vote for war credits (World War I) or nuclear bases (after 1963 in Britain), having been previously pledged to oppose them.

Peace movements can of course also be repressed and severely harassed—leaders jailed, even killed. The American anti-war movement of 1917 was virtually destroyed physically by police raids, arrests and vigilante action (1917–20), and the leaders were given long terms in prison. The civil disobedience campaign in Britain was badly shaken by long-term imprisonment of a few of its leaders (1961–62). The South Vietnamese Buddhists were attacked, imprisoned and killed by both sides (1965–75). The independent peace movements in the Soviet Union and Eastern Europe, and the peace movement in Turkey, have recently suffered similar setbacks. In Nazi Germany and other fascist countries, a number of peace leaders were executed; likewise with some pacifists after the Russian Revolution, and in Japan before World War II. But this does not provide a general explanation of the failure of peace movements. Surveillance, the limitation of human rights and censorship *are* key issues for peace movements, but do not constitute a sufficient, only a contributory, cause of decline.

Of course the role of media suppression or opposition is equally crucial; adverse conditions can pre-empt the emergence of peace movements, as illustrated in many developing countries. However, the experiences of the last peace movement since the "conspiracy of silence" of the late fifties are that the movement can have an impact on the communications systems of some societies and that such media are not permanently monolithic. The censorship and bias attending the peace movement, and which culminated in the banning of a major anti-nuclear film in Britain in 1965, was countered especially in the Vietnam years by a number of alternative strategies. The movement first established its own media or was reported in an alternative media (reaching over two million people in the United States, for example). This had an impact on the dominant media itself by outflanking its newsgiving function, but also trained individuals who would later "enter" the more established networks and presses. The diversity of roles and functions at different levels proved after the Indo-China experience that there was always potentially another voice. As a real alternative, the movement's media was limited, but as a lever on existing channels it was significant.

Finally, but not least importantly, is the sense of *impotence* or paralysis that sets into many movements. This is the feeling of social despair, that nothing can be done, that the problem of war is beyond human control. Despondency and cynicism, even suicide or other forms of self-destruction, are common responses to the weakness and sense of failure that accompany many peace and social change movements as they enter their "troughs" or suffer major defeats. Among other solutions, this has led to a self-conscious attempt at "empowerment" based on the therapeutic politics of group affinity and solidarity.

Conclusion: building a permanent and globalist peace movement

In the contemporary peace movements of Europe, East and West, and of Canada, the United States, Australia, Japan, India and beyond, many old problems have survived with the sectarian traditions and have helped sustain divisions and ideological obstacles to building a permanent movement for peace and human survival. In particular, the tension between the broad social programme of a New Left or the Greens, and the single issue politics (or single *weapon* politics) of an "MX," "B1," cruise, or neutron or Trident campaign is growing. The clash between blind activism and pure theory, between the aligned and the non-aligned, the programmatic and the single issue, the parliamentarist and extraparliamentarist, especially over issues of alliances, alignment and direct action may yet tear the peace movement apart.

If one were to be pessimistic, one could conclude from this that in peace politics, people have learned (and can learn) little from the past; that there is no sense of history. For once again we see a broad social movement with multiple issues but too narrow a social base, lacking strategy and direction, obsessed with negative propaganda and conspiracy threats of war. If there are major setbacks, fatigue, and feelings of powerlessness, defeat and despair will predominate in the coming years.

On the other hand, there are dimensions of the movement which are profoundly empowering; there are signs that the very character of the new peace movement makes it different from the past, that its transnational linkages are more real; that its non-alignment is more firmly understood and articulated; that its grass-roots are more firmly planted. In 1982, many abandoned, after SSD II, their last illusions about interstate charades of disarmament dialogue. Its communal dimensions and transnational linkages make the movement ready for a systematic programme of alternative defence rooted in localized civilian resistance. Civil disobedience is now accepted by much of the peace movement and can be linked to the non-cooperation at the heart of the war resistance tradition and Gandhian ideas. Moreover, since the 1960s, the acceptance of a just social programme (for example, socially useful production, not an arms export economy) has become more widespread and is now part of the larger programme (for example, of the Greens and of the New Left). In other words, the dominant tendency is beyond both the single issue and the national framework, beyond state and parties, beyond old alignments and sectarian traditions, whilst building an autonomous and new tradition and a model of action that draws from all of them.

Attempts to be realistic about the discontinuities and fragmented character of the historic peace movements need not lead to an entirely pessimistic prognosis in the present. If one denies the very possibility of success of such human endeavour, further study or action might have very little justification. But because as a species we cannot afford the luxury of a people's peace initiative which ebbs again in the coming years, it is essential that the peace movement use its collective intellect to forge an analysis of present strengths and past weaknesses that can enlighten strategic and programmatic debates and help deemphasize certain actions, policies and linkages as against others.

This does *not* mean evolving some monolithic, unitary or reductionist strategy or ideology, as sectarians would hold—the peace movement is as plural as it is international. Pluralism is a source of unity as well as fragmentation: the very diversity of the peace movement discribed here may be an expression of an inner strength, of a containment of potentially open dialectic, not the clash of blinkered orthodoxies, each contemptuous or dismissive of the historical role and contributions of the next. Within the new peace movement, there is growing understanding of both national and cultural peculiarities and transnational solidarity and symmetry; the potential complementarity of local and global, of a mass autonomous movement *and* focused pressure within specific structures and institutions; the single issue campaign and the programmatic long-term direction. Peace, women, environment, participation, economic well-being, the secular and the spiritual—the synthesis in people's movements is from the communal base.

Research on the history and social character of war resistance reveals that ordinary people are able to oppose and resist war, militarism and war mobilization on a sustained basis most typically when they have both a strong local communal base of organization *and* an identity, as well as certain social factors or orientations (ideology, religion, ethnic linkage) which *transcend* national boundaries and the sovereign edicts of the state. Within the peace movements themselves, as this essay has tried to illustrate, such vision and strategy linking localism and globalism, cosmopolitanism and communalism, has sometimes descended into a narrow parochialism or become a form of rootlessness. But in groups such as the Quakers (or, later, the War Resisters International) the idea of linking the local and the global has often given vision and practical support to peace groups over a period of more than three centuries.

Certain factors (the opposite of "transnational and communal" ones) have been specifically noted in the foregoing analysis as contributing to the failure of the peace movements. The following two sets of ideal type forces are by no means exhaustive but constitute the main dimensions, both positive and negative, of the contemporary movement.

1. State centrism (chauvinistic nationalism, ethnocentrism).
2. Limited pressure-group concepts of politics (reformist, secular).
3. Alignment (to parties, states, or state-centred ideologies or blocs); for example, cooptation by the social democratic left.
4. Reactive and short-term character (lack of social programme resulting in despair).
5. Lack of social alternatives (no strategy for political change); disempowerment.
6. Gap between leadership (intellectual/political) and grass-roots base (élitism); this may be a generational gap.
7. Lack of a strong communal base (amorphous superficial coalition character).

The above are the negative features of the peace movement. But as the new peace movement, or parts of it, especially the new women's peace movement, illustrate, these are exactly the problems that are now met by giving greater prominence to such alternative mediums as the following:

1. Localism and communalism (networks or human relationships).
2. Transnationalism/globalism, networking, linkages (peace as a species issue).
3. Autonomism and spontaneity (initiative from below).
4. Direct action and affinity groups (non-violence).
5. Unilateral initiatives (action first).
6. Activation of affinities (bonding across borders).
7. Non-alignment (the peace movement as an independent force).

Although they clearly overlap significantly in terms of empowerment and species identity, these seven elements expressed in diverse activities such as international marches and camps, twining communities and nuclear free zones, indicate that a growing disempowerment has taken place and that the evolution of violent structures has occurred. For feminists this may be explicitly linked to seeing the origins of war and the monopoly of violence particularly in patriarchal conquests. It also suggests a potential understanding of the history of resistance to that disempowering process; both old peace groups and the new constituencies are drawn together by affinity and potential, by the growth of a sense of history in the long human struggle for peace, in developing a synthesis that is analysed and understood in a creative way.

In the historic clash between state and civil society, it was those entities under attack, the smaller communities, the churches, smaller political units, intellectual sub-cultures and autonomous cultural and economic entities, which became the vessels of anti-militarist activity and perspective. These are now regaining their salience as a base for a popular world view. Indeed they are much more than ideas. They have been realized in specific public events and people's movements which are no longer obsessed with altered national policies alone, but grasp the necessity of activating the affinities across military borders, not least of all the East/West divide: mobilizing groups on the basis of personal exchange and grass-root reciprocity; linkages of activists as well as leaders: twinning communities, municipalities and nuclear free zones; and diplomacy between cities.

The East European strategy, for all its setbacks, is not by any means a lost cause. The swords and ploughshares groups, the trust groups and groups for dialogue, the conscientious objectors, women's groups (sisters across the iron curtain), the youth culture, and the entrenched churches, remain a base for future growth. Despite the repression of the Moscow Trust Group, the human rights issue has created space, and the end of European division is crucial in relation to the East European state. The ecologically oriented groups can also organize in a way that poses less of a threat than military oriented groups. All these are platforms for further take-off. There are limits to the cooptation of the peace issue by the state.

This can be seen as part of the globalization of what is a species problem, of the breaking with both state-centric and inter-state centred approaches to disarmament. It offers not symmetrical patterned interactions which move up and down with political pyramids of state power, but a slow draining away of legitimacy and attention from state-centred solutions and national frames of reference. Of course, it does not exclude unilateral, national or governmental reciprocity, but "unilateralism" need not be a monopoly of national governments. The new peace movements have shown that from the smallest community to multi-nation, regional zones and proposals, unilateralism as a popular initiative gives a certain power that many peace movements have lacked in the past. It does not forgo pressure on governments, but acts from the outside, from the portents of a peace politics that like some radical movements of the past begins to move outside the state system—the dominant features of legitimization—by building non-governmental, cross-frontier linkages and strategies.

Such a reality, based on the "true worlds" disguised by 400 or more years of territorial state-growth, offers new insights both to activists and researchers and a fruitful interchange of both. They can empower and give continuity to a sequence of peace movements which has a series of heroic experiences as well as a history of tragic defeats. However inchoate, the present movement holds within it the potential for such a strategy which could bring both continuity, growth and effectiveness.

This survey has indicated how more and more peace traditions have accumulated over the past 200 years—in that sense there has been continual growth. But it has also shown that the mass support of organized public opinion has regularly and dramatically declined: in most countries in the period after mobilization for war, such as 1914 and 1940. The relation between this public involvement and the small peace groups or sects is itself a problematic one, but in general one can state that as a ratio of population there has been no clear quantitative growth in peace movements since the late nineteenth century. In addition, there is in any case, no clear correlation between the numbers mobilized, and impact on society or the state.

Clearly the multiple stranded peace traditions described here have so far patently failed to do more than marginally affect the arms race spiral. If they follow the patterns of the past, they are likely to fail again. State policies and public attitudes have been significantly shifted on such issues as certain war (for example, Vietnam) and types of weapons (e.g. nuclear), or specific actions (bomb-testing) or conscription. But no twentieth century state of any size has shown any serious inclination to substantially demilitarize itself, and it is clear that increased pressure will have to be largely external to the state apparatus and the system of states.

The peace movement has been divided over aims, methods, analysis and strategy, but has occasionally been forged into a strong coalition by particularly atrocious wars (such as Vietnam) or weapons (nuclear). But its failure has been the central one of failing to achieve a visionary synthesis, a new model and strategy that is appropriate to a changing global society. It has not been able to effectively harness even those emerging social tendencies such as communal and transnational growth which favour it.

The threat of the breakdown of nuclear deterrence into a global nuclear war gives humanity one last chance to sustain a movement for our global species survival that will emphasize those aspects of society which can save us: the ability to live cooperatively in relatively small human societies; our ability to diffuse and limit political power and control the use of violence; and our ability to act as species-beings rather than territorial or national animals. The peace movement contains within its present character these elements and the potentiality for such a "permanent and global peace movement." The question remains whether it has the time, the will, and the imagination to realize that potential.

Some key sources on the peace movements

Frank Barnaby and Gwyn Thomas, *The Nuclear Arms Race: Control or Catastrophe* (London: Frances Pinter, 1982).

Peter Brock, *Pacifism in the United States: From the Colonial Era to the First World War* (Princeton, NJ: Princeton University Press, 1968).

Peter Brock, *Twentieth Century Pacifism* (New York: Van Nostrand Reinhold Co., 1970).

Peter Brock, *Paifism in Europe to 1914* (Princeton, NJ: Princeton University Press, 1972).

April Carter, *Direct Action in a Liberal Democracy* (Henley, England: Routledge & Kegan Paul, 1974).

Martin Ceadel, *Pacifism in Britain, 1914–45* (Oxford: Oxford University Press, 1980).

Charles Chatfield, *For Peace and Justice: Pacifism in America 1914–41* (Knoxville, TN: Unversity of Tennessee Press, 1971).

Charles Chatfield, *Peace Movements in America* (New York: Schocken Books, 1973).

G. D. H. Cole, *History of Socialist Thought*, vol III, part 2 (London: NY: Macmillan, 1953–60).

Merle Curti, *Peace or War: The American Struggle, 1636–1936* (New York: W. W. Norton & Co., 1936).

James Finn (editor), *Protest: Pacifism and Politics* (New York: Random House, 1968).

Paul Goodman (editor), *Seeds of Liberation* (New York: George Braziller, 1964).

A. Paul Hare and Herbert H. Blumberg (editors), *Nonviolent Direct Action, American Cases: Social-Psychological Analyses* (Washington, DC: Corpus Books, 1968).

James Joll, *The Second International* (London: Routledge & Kegan Paul, 1974).

George Lakey, *Strategy for a Living Revolution* (San Francisco: Freeman, 1972).

Staughton Lynd (editor), *Nonviolence in America: A Documentary History* (Indianapolis: Bobbs-Merrill, 1966).

David Martin, *Pacifism—an historical & sociological study* (London: Routledge & Kegan Paul, 1965).

Peter Mayer (editor), *The Pacifist Conscience* (Chicago: Henry Regnery Co., 1967; New York: Holt, Rinehart & Winston, 1966).

John Minion and Philip Bolsover (editors), *The CND Story* (London: Alison & Busby, 1983).

Geoffrey Nuttall, *Christian Pacifism in History* (New York: Seabury, 1971).

Bob Overy, *How Effective are Peace Movements?* (Boston: Beacon Press, 1983; Toronto: Harvest Books, 1985).

Peterson and Gilbert C. Fite, *Opponents of War* (Seattle: University of Washington Press, 1968).

Lillian Schlissel (editor), *Conscience in America: A Documentary History of Conscientious Objection in America, 1757–1967* (New York: Dutton & Co., Inc., 1968).

Gene Sharp, *Poliics of Nonviolent Action* (Boston: Porter Sargent, 1973).

Martin Shaw (editor), *War, State and Society* (London: Macmillan, 1984).

Mulford, Q. Sibley (editor), *The Quiet Battle: Writings on the Theory and Practice of Nonviolent Resistance* (New York: Beacon Press, 1968).

Richard Taylor and Colin Pritchard, *The Protest Makers* (Oxford: Pergamon, 1981).

Arthur Weinberg and Lila Weinberg (editors), *Instead of Violence: Writings by the Great Advocates of Peace and Nonviolence Throughout History* (New York: Grossman Publishers, 1963).

Lawrence Wittner, *Rebels Against War: The American Peace Movement, 1941–1960* (New York: Columbia University Press, 1969).

Nigel Young, *War Resistance and the Nation State* (Ann Arbor, MI: University of Michigan, 1976, xerox microfilms; UC Press forthcoming).

Nigel Young, *An Infantile Disorder? The Crisis and Decline of the New Left* (London: Routledge & Kegan Paul, 1977; Boulder, CO: Westview Press, 1978).

Nigel Young, "New Strategies for Disarmament; Perspectives for Peace Action and the Role of the Peace Traditions," *Bulletin of Peace Proposals* (Oslo, 1981).

Nigel Young, "Sensing their Strength—Towards a Strategy for the New Peace Movement in Europe," *Bulletin of Peace Proposals* (Oslo, 1981).

Nigel Young, "The Contemporary European Anti-Nuclear Movement: Experiments in the Mobilisation of Public Power," *Peace and Change*, Summer 1983, vol 14, no 2, issue on peace movements (Kent State University, Ohio).

Nigel Young, "Transnationalism & Communalism," *Gandhi Marg 52*, vol 5, no. 4, July 1983 (New Delhi).

Nigel Young, "Why do Peace Movements Fail? An Historical and Sociological Overview," *Social Alternatives*, Spring 1984, special issue on contemporary peace protest (Melbourne).

Library: *Garland Collection on War and Peace*, 328 volumes, edited by Blanche Cook, Charles Chatfield and Sandi Cooper (New York, 1971).

Culture, Discourse, Insecurity

R. B. J. WALKER

I.   Introduction

There is a special urgency about the developing patterns of military relationships that are visible in the modern world. This urgency is expressed through a wide range of ideological and philosophical prisms. It is felt rather differently depending on geographical region. Sometimes concern is raised over highly specific weapons systems. At other times there is no more than a vague sense of broad historical trends. In whatever way this urgency is understood or expressed, it has undoubtedly become one of the most pressing themes in political life in the late twentieth century.

The most obvious concern, at least in more prosperous societies, arises from the deployment of nuclear technology. The promise of final annihilation has transcended the bounds of religious eschatology to become an all too real possibility. This concern is heightened by instabilities in the geopolitical and strategic relations between the superpowers. The changing configurations of global power and multiple systemic and regional crises are made even more complex by a spectacular capacity for technological innovation in weapons systems. Whatever logic there has been to the way nuclear weapons have been managed over the past few decades now appears increasingly fragile. The teasing rituals of arms control negotiations and the constant resort to technological solutions for political problems do not inspire confidence.

While the so-called nuclear arms race between the superpowers claims most attention, many analysts now point to a more general and insidious tendency to resort to military solutions to social and political conflict on a global scale. Military force, it is suggested, is becoming both more violent and more thoroughly integrated into different arenas of human activity. Armaments are becoming more and more lethal, even when non-nuclear. More significantly, they function not only as weapons, but also as commodities, as both military and economic artefacts.

In his classic study *On War*, published in 1832, Karl von Clausewitz depicted war as "a remarkable trinity"

> of primordial violence, hatred and enmity, which are to be regarded
> as a blind natural force; of the play of chance and probability within
> which the creative spirit is free to roam; and of its element of
> subordination as an instrument of policy, which makes it subject to

This essay was first published in a revised form in *Alternatives* XI: 4.

> reason alone. The first of these three aspects mainly concerns the
> people; the second the commander and his army; the third, the
> government.
>
>   These three tendencies are like three different codes of law,
> deep-rooted in their subject and yet variable in their relationship to
> one another. A theory that ignores any one of them or seeks to fix an
> arbitrary relationship between them would conflict with reality to
> such an extent that for this reason alone it would be totally useless.[1]

In the century and a half since that time, the social structures that allowed
Clausewitz to make these distinctions have altered considerably. The
phraseology that now accompanies analyses of preparations for war is likely
to be dominated less by differentiations than by aggregations and hyphens, by
complexes of military-industrial-bureaucratic and technological forces. This
reflects the internationalization of production as well as changing patterns of
state conflict. The processes of militarization visible in the modern world
engage as much with the categories of political economy as with those of
strategy and geopolitics. Where the logic of interstate relations may still bear
some resemblance to tendencies already identified by Thucydides, Kautilya
or Machiavelli, contemporary forms of militarization also have to be
understood as an integral aspect of the historical development of
industrialization, capitalism and modernity.

Suspicions have been aired that this is leading us to a novel phase in the
organization of human affairs. Terms like "militarism," "militarization,"
"exterminism," "nuclearism," and "war system" have been used to capture
and probe a new set of global determinations, in which military production
and deployments play a central role in constituting new forms of social life. At
the very least, it is possible to identify interrelated processes at work between
the so-called "military-bureaucratic-industrial complexes," superpower arms
deployments, regional arms deployments, arms transfers to less affluent
states, and the use of armaments as an instrument of repression within states.[2]
It is not difficult to find indicators of the way massive resources are being
channelled in military directions, suggesting that something structurally
significant is going on. To take one symbolic example—the material resources
spent annually on armed forces around the globe currently exceed the total
income of the poorest half of the world's people.

Military forces, arms races, armaments production, and so on are matters
not only of exotic hardware being deployed on behalf of conflicting "national
interests," but also of cultural forms and discourses: of "strategies," fantasies,
rhetorics, symbolic orders and languages. In fact one of the most striking
aspects of our current predicament is the extraordinary gap between the
sophistication of the technologies of destruction and the banality of the
rhetoric, sophistry, values and "psychology" that accompanies its deployment. This has led a variety of commentators to stress the particular
"competence" of students in the humanities in this context, not only as
representatives of "humanity," but also as specialists in the textual and
discursive character of contemporary preparations for war.[3] Certainly, much
of the rather sparse literature on the cultural context of contemporary

militarization suggests that cultural forms—ways of thinking and expressing ourselves—are increasingly conditioned by military structures. Conversely, the cultural sphere is often an important source of legitimacy for tendencies towards militarization.

This cultural dimension is of primary concern here. More specifically, I want to explore the connection between two theoretical problematics that have generally been treated in isolation. On the one hand, there is the empirical analysis of contemporary processes of militarization. On the other hand, there is a concern with the conceptual and theoretical coherence of our understanding of these empirical processes. Culture, I will argue, is crucial in both. An emerging body of literature has begun to delineate ways in which processes of militarization engage with, produce, and transform particular cultural forms and identities. I want to use this literature to examine some ways in which our *understanding* of these processes is mediated at the cultural level.

To grasp what is at stake here, it is only necessary to think briefly about such an apparently simple phrase as "the arms race." It is far from being a simple phrase. It resonates at many cultural levels, all the way from sporting metaphors to deeply rooted assumptions about the essentially competitive nature of human existence. And as a theoretical category it is seriously misleading. The term suggests a race to some well-defined end, in which the critical issue is the perceived relation between the contestants: *A* does something, *B* responds, *A* responds in turn, and so on. There is something to this image, but it ignores the way that recent arms deployments have been largely the result *not* of what the other side has done, but of the available technology, the state of the economy, allocations made for defence budgets, pressure from the armed services and bureaucratic institutions, intra-alliance politics and Murphy's Law. This is a process in which competition between states as such plays a relatively small role.[4]

Meditation on examples like this, and the broader connection between cultural processes and forms of understanding that they imply, is especially important given the somewhat fragile state of our knowledge about contemporary patterns of militarization. Detailed analysis abounds, yet there is considerable disagreement about even the most fundamental of categories. There are many blunt assertions about the way things are and what ought to be done. Yet this is an area in which it is more appropriate to admit the tentative quality of what we claim to know and what we think possible. This is so in at least three important respects.

First, and most obviously, it is partly a matter of inadequate theoretical concepts and lack of research. At best we have indications of apparent trends and a variety of more or less plausible explanations of some aspects of a very complex affair. Some fundamental theoretical disputes are of significance here, especially about whether these trends are best understood as an outgrowth of the logic of the states-system, imperialism, *kapitalogic* or some more complex combination.

In this context, culture enters the picture primarily in terms of the relationship between militarization and cultural production. From this direction it is possible to suggest ways in which the cultural realm participates in the construction of the specific political, bureaucratic and economic structures through which a resort to military force is encouraged. It is also possible to examine the broad cultural contexts in which militarization is interpreted and legitimized.

Second, it is partly a matter of our limited capacity to speak meaningfully of war at all in the contemporary context. Here the advent of nuclear weaponry is crucial. A nuclear war, it is often said, simply cannot be—at least not in any sense in which the concept of war still carries any meaning for us. Nuclear weapons undermine our conception of what war is and under what conditions it might be legitimate. These limits are already at play in the early formulations of nuclear deterrence theory. They are expressed in Bernard Brodie's classic claim that "thus far the chief purpose of our military establishment has been to win wars. From now on the chief purpose must be to avert them."[5] Nuclear weapons were quickly recognized as introducing a major disproportionality between ends and means. Only the *threat* to use, not the actual use of nuclear weapons was assumed to be understandable—and then only marginally—as the continuation of politics by other means. Even so, while this cliché of deterrence has played a significant role in the development of declaratory policy, the counter-assertion that nuclear weapons have not really changed things has continued to be very influential in practice. Recent controversies between deterrence and war-fighting theorists reflect a fundamental disagreement on the question of whether the limits of our understanding of the place of war in human affairs have been reached. The suspicion that they have is re-enforced by the fact that nuclear war itself is discussed in terms of a chilling melange of instrumental technique, utilitarian models of rational choice, and apocalyptic religion—all discourses in which the moment of politics is neatly evaded.

In this context, culture enters from a rather different direction. The limits on our ability to speak coherently about war and the scale of our capacity for destruction further expose—and intensify—a number of contradictions already visible in the cultural traditions of Western modernity. Here it is possible to frame the issues less in terms of specific instrumental structures than of the more general critiques of rationalization, reification and bureaucratization that have been central to an understanding of political life in this century. From this direction we can see how processes of militarization impinge on a number of fundamental values we have come to take for granted—specifically reason, democracy and security—in a way that undermines many of the categories through which political and military affairs are understood.

Third, it is not clear how it is possible to enter into an effective *critical* engagement with the emerging trends that have been tentatively identified. While it seems obvious that we live in a world in which military structures have become increasingly dangerous—unstable, irrational, wasteful, repressive and inhumane—weapons continue to be produced as if there were no tomorrow. We are confronting structures that seem to be beyond the bounds of effective political action.

In this context culture enters primarily in connection with changes in the character and especially the location of political life. Three levels of movement are involved here. There is an expansion of political reference from the state to some broader "community." Culture as such becomes less important than cultures. Attention is drawn to the manner in which different societies respond to emerging military structures in ways that reflect their location within global divisions of labour and power. At the same time there is a contraction of political reference to the level of the individual. Global patterns of militarization now bear upon the most immediate and local aspects of everyday life and consciousness. In between, the conventional focus of political identity the state is increasingly implicated in the construction of global military structures. Indeed, the state has become the crucial point of integration between the geostrategic and economic forces that give rise to modern forms of militarization. In this respect, therefore, culture enters as a quest for human identity.

It will be quite apparent that the term culture is being used here in a variety of ways. This is intentional. Culture is a multifaceted concept, bearing traces of a complex historical lineage.[6] I propose to use the scope and flexibility of the term to draw attention to the range of current research being conducted in these three contexts, and to use this research to explore how our understanding of contemporary militarization participates in a variety of cultural processes. I will then draw upon this analysis to explore the relationship between militarization and language or discourse, illustrating how processes of militarization enter into the very categories through which they are analysed and understood.

All these themes converge in our understanding of the modern state. The paper will therefore conclude with a reading of the cultural politics of the state in the context of contemporary forms of insecurity. It will do so by reflecting on the theme of bureaucracy introduced by Max Weber early in this century and by suggesting ways in which Weber's own formulation of the politics of the modern state must be challenged.

IIA. Militarization and cultural production

The most systematic analysis of the relationship between militarization and culture is currently focused on changing patterns of cultural production in the affluent industrial societies. In these societies, weapons systems are among our most sophisticated artefacts. As products of modern science and technology, they reflect the character and self-identity of the society that produces them. It is therefore not surprising that weapons have become symbols, woven into a great variety of myths and fantasies. More than this, they have become cultural commodities and an intrinsic part of the process of cultural production. Several observers have begun to speak of the fetishism of the weapon, with the term "fetish" taking on both a Freudian and a Marxian interpretation.

To enquire into the cultural roots of this particular obsession undoubtedly raises deep issues of cultural interpretation, and in this respect the names of Marx and Freud suggest a rich vein of interpretive possibilities. Yet it is not necessary to invoke deep theoretical insights to see that military iconography has become very important in a wide range of modern cultural forms, from explicit military propaganda (parades, adverts, air-shows) to games, sports, toys, clothing, films, videos, science fiction, war and spy novels, and so on. Video games, for example, now simulate everything from Custers Last Stand to the most robotic of space wars. Such forms are not entirely new. Neither can they all be analysed as simple legitimations of militaristic tendencies; here, as elsewhere, the relationship between cultural forms and political life is a matter of considerable complexity and dispute. But it is possible to take seriously Robin Luckham's suggestion that we are witnessing the novel development of a specific "armaments culture."[7]

Luckham's analysis is essentially synoptic, and provides the most powerful classification of a growing and potentially rich field of research. For Luckham, the issue is not just the effect of armaments upon cultural forms, but the way in which armaments have entered into the process of cultural production and reproduction, becoming both producer and product of the manifold forms of cultural activity. Luckham attributes special importance to the scientific estate, the security intellectuals, security managers, and various interpreters and publicists. He also suggests that the relationship is institutionalized and controlled through four principal instruments: direct state ownership of the means of cultural production; private ownership of such means, particularly through advertising; systems of professionalization and occupational regulation; and the structure and operation of the markets for cultural commodities. Other writers have focused their attention more specifically on the defence intellectuals,[8] the mass media,[9] war literature,[10] the special cultural characteristics of the nuclear imagination,[11] gender relations,[12] the science-military technology nexus,[13] and the complex cultural factors at work in particular societies.[14]

In the broadest terms this research suggests the necessity of being highly sensitive to the way thinking about militarization occurs in a cultural milieu partly produced by the processes of militarization. This is particularly apparent in the structure of public debate on questions of war and peace, which often takes on a highly ritualistic quality. Complex technical and political issues are obscured behind clichés and slogans. Constructive dialogue is swallowed up in hardline platitudes. This is also apparent in the more rarefied sub-cultures that specialize in military matters. While military strategists and specialists in international politics often pride themselves on their hardnosed approach to the supposed realities of inter-state conflict, their portrayal of those realities is thoroughly permeated by textual and interpretive codes. Whether in terms of the structures of public debate of the specialized discourses of military élites, the relationship between militarization and cultural production cannot be ignored. The major challenges here concern the appropriate theoretical conceptualization of cultural production, and the need for more comparative research in a wide range of different societies.

IIB. Militarization and the contradictions of modernity

Emerging military structures, in addition to their participation in cultural production and reproduction in the modern world, also have an important impact on the value systems expressed by different cultural traditions.

Cultural sociology gives way to more philosophical considerations. Here the emphasis is less on culture as a product than as the expression of philosophical, ethical and even theological options.

Take, for example, some of the cultural values of Western modernity, particularly our claim to be part of a rational, progressive and civilized society. Looking backwards, we see ourselves in part as a product of the Enlightenment, the promise of emancipation from myth, superstition and barbarism. This was a promise of progress made possible by reason, science and technology. Uncertainties and contradictions arise once we recognize that our deadliest weapons are also products of scientific progress. This has been a century of total wars and mass exterminations. The prospect of nuclear war simply underlines a fundamental tension between the promise of scientific reason and the threat of ultimate barbarism. The structures of contemporary militarism heighten still further the suspicion that the heart of our civilization and culture is not reason but irrationality and force. This suspicion has long been a reiterated theme of political, social and cultural theory.[15] It is arguably one of the major cultural themes of the twentieth century. But with nuclear weapons, the tension between Enlightenment and Despair is pushed to an extreme.

A similar line of thinking arises out of our self-understanding as a democratic society. The move towards democratic forms of politics has undoubtedly been one of the greatest achievements of our age. Nevertheless, theories of democracy usually come in qualified forms. One classic qualification involves the tension between political democracy and economic inequality. Another involves that between political democracy and the instrumental requirements of an efficient administration. A third concerns the way in which questions of "state" and of "national security" ought to be exempt from the unruly pressures of "public opinion." Different societies have struggled to resolve these tensions in different ways. They now find that the dynamics of contemporary militarization have further exacerbated them.[16]

A number of themes are significant here. Nuclear weapons in particular have been linked to a growing sense of powerlessness on the part of citizens in Western industrial states. The scale of the forces at work, and the complexity and technical nature of the debates about appropriate policies, lead to a fundamental withdrawal from participation in questions of life and death, a capitulation to expertise and specialists. Contemporary strategic debate is spectacularly arcane. Decisions are made—or at least justified—on the basis of esoteric forms of information which only a small élite can successfully claim to know. This is one realm of modern life that has been most receptive to the lures of a purely instrumental reason. This in turn involves a high degree of centralization in decision making, a centralization that is reinforced by direct connections with specific economic interests. Contemporary military structures embody both a concentration of power and an acceleration of the translation of politics into technique and administration. Not only is the state increasingly impervious to democratic pressures in this way, but the state itself comes to play an increasingly important part in the structuring of civil society. The "bomb," after all, is not a single inert object safely stored in its silo. It is a complex system involving research, production, processing, reprocessing, servicing, modification, and transportation, not to mention the structures necessary to preserve secrecy. The state intervenes in economic policy in order to "defend the national interest." It enhances its ascendancy over the institutions of civil society under the same pretext. Consequently, the pressures that result from the processes of militarization seem likely to resolve the central contradiction between state and civil society in favour of the former. This is a resolution that necessarily undermines the state's claim to legitimacy as a guarantor of liberty and democracy, at least in those societies where this liberal distinction has been historically important.

Contemporary forms of militarization also throw our understanding of security into serious question. Unlike reason or democracy, security is a neglected category of political analysis. Where reason and democracy have been the subject of sharply contested interpretations and even political struggles, the concept of security has had a relatively quiet history. It played an important role in classic texts (like Hobbes' *Leviathan*) which sought to justify the legitimacy of the state in the early-modern period. And for the most part the claim that the state is in fact able to provide security for its inhabitants has been accepted. Most political thinkers have simply assumed security to be a given, and have then gone on to discuss more elevated values like justice, freedom, community, and the like. Security has become the preserve of theorists of relations *between* states. The assumption that security means national or state security has thereby been reinforced. But this division between life within states and relations between states embodies a fundamental schism between the claims of citizens of states and the claims of human beings as human beings. These claims are intrinsically in tension with each other. And, of course, with contemporary military technology, the pursuit of security by states in the name of their citizens increasingly implies the insecurity of all human beings as human beings. State security threatens global security. The more security is defined in terms of the interests of the citizens of states, the more it is undermined for the inhabitants of the planet.[17]

None of these contradictions is novel. They may be said to be constitutive of the cultural and political traditions of Western societies for a few centuries at least. But they are contradictions. The destructive power that is incorporated into contemporary military structures makes them very tense contradictions indeed. As with the concept of war itself, reason, democracy and security have become ambiguous in the context of our modern capacity for mass self-annihilation.

IIC. Militarization, cultures and everyday life

Nuclear weapons have a universalist finality about them. They do not discriminate among the many cultural divisions through which we have managed to differentiate ourselves from each other. Similarly, no matter how the specific characteristics of military production and deployments are identified and understood, it is not possible to ignore their global scope. Modern forms of militarization have begun to cut across political and cultural boundaries. And yet one of the more striking characteristics of contemporary life is that the recent clamour for nuclear disarmament, within Western industrial states, has had little resonance within other societies. Eqbal Ahmed has offered a compelling explanation for this:

> Since the mid-19th century, nearly every significant trend in the West—of the right, center, and the left—has been reflected in non-Western societies. Sometimes, as in the case of nationalism, Marxism and statism, the non-Western derivations have had as great or greater impact on modern history than their Western originals. The anti-nuclear is one of the rare Western movements to have had no influence in the Third World—intellectually, politically, or morally. An explanation for this is to be found in its own limitations. It is, in effect, a woefully narrow and parochial response to a universal challenge.[18]

Here the cultural horizons of our understanding of militarization take on the guise of ethnocentricism. Emerging military structures may well be global in reach. Nuclear weapons may well threaten species extinction. But these things are not understood or interpreted in the same way in different societies. Ethnocentricism, the projection of parochial assumptions as universal categories, is not just a matter of cultural relativism. It also involves relations of power. In this case, the emergence of global military structures and even the possibility of global war, is characterized differently depending on one's location within the international political and economic order.

For some, mainly in the West, the problem is posed by specifically nuclear weapons. Hope for the future is pinned on the achievement of nuclear disarmament. For others, the most pressing concern is the role of military force in maintaining repressive regimes or structures of international hegemony. Hope for the future is then seen more in terms of enlarging the scope of human rights or national autonomy. For others still, the concern is for immediate survival. The question of peace is seen as meaningless unless framed as a matter of economic well-being. Peace is interpreted through categories of development. This is not simply a question of different cultural or philosophical traditions suggesting different understandings of what peace and security might mean, although this is an interesting consideration.[19] It is more that global structures of military power affect different people in different ways, leading to contrasting accounts of appropriate political action.

The very diversity of forms of contemporary militarization might be great enough to inhibit effective theoretical articulation of the general processes involved. Yet the concept of culture itself provides a crucial insight into the underlying theoretical problem involved here. In the European context, the concept of culture took much of its meaning from its historical association with the Romantic reaction to the cosmopolitan claims of the Enlightenment. The particularist and subjectivist sensibilities of culture opposed the universalist claims of science and reason. To think of the processes of militarization in terms of cultural differences is to engage once again with the old dialectic of universalism and pluralism embedded in the concept of culture itself. On the one hand, we can see a universalization of the problematic of militarization and an internationalization of the armaments culture. On the other hand, we can see significant differences in the way these processes are interpreted and resisted. But where this dialectic has so often led to the formulation of political options in strongly either/or terms—states or world order, nationalism or cosmopolitanism, tradition or modernity—the key question for a critical engagement with emerging processes of militarization concerns the possibility of acting in a way that recognizes *both* the universality and the particularity of those processes. Temporal and spatial considerations are important here.

Nuclear war is usually posed not only in terms of universalist finality, but also as future event; as a convergence of present tendencies, perhaps, but nevertheless a danger located at a time still to come. Yet it is increasingly clear that the problem is not only the possibility of future conflagration but also the present and ongoing consequences of militarization has for people now living. This has begun to be obvious in two ways. First, we have become aware of the central role the military sector plays in the economic life of modern societies. The old "third man" theme about war as the engine of human progress now takes the form of "military Keynesianism"; the production of weapons of mass production is legitimized by the promise of greater employment, not to mention profits. Again, this is hardly new, but the real human cost of the processes through which military production is integrated into economic life has become a matter of increasing controversy.[20] Second, we have become aware of the immediate fear, alienation and sense of helplessness engendered by present tendencies.[21] The work of a number of psychologists on children's attitudes to nuclear war is particularly instructive here. In both cases, the conventional distinction between future war and present peace dissolves. Contemporary militarization has to be understood as a process that affects both the future and the present.

Similar considerations arise in terms of spatial categories. Warfare is conventionally posed as a foreign affair arising from the *external* relations between states. This convention is deeply rooted in the major traditions of Western social and political theory. As with security, so also with the good life—justice, legitimacy and freedom. These things are depicted as occurring *within* the spatial boundaries of the state. Relations between states, by contrast are characterized in terms of contingency, perpetual conflict and the clash of powers. War has been understood as a phenomenon that occurs "out there" in the space between states, a space of power and opportunism, of *realpolitik*, original sin and the pursuit of power and security at almost any cost. Of course this has always been an exaggerated view. Relations between life within states and interaction among them has always been a more complex matter of dialectical processes, contradictions, projections and penetrations than the conventional dichotomy allows. The distinction has also been blurring for a considerable time as war has become more and more "total." But with the kind of militarization that seems to be emerging it becomes even more important to stress both the temporal and spatial immediacy of preparations for war, the contraction both from then to now and from there to here. We cannot escape the fact that war is an intrinsic part of our everyday life. We live in a world, a civilization, in which preparation for war has become embodied in everyday practice and institutionalized as bureaucratic routine.

III. Militarization, language and discourse

Language is arguably the heart of any cultural process, so it is not surprising that the relationship between militarization and language has recently become the subject of a growing critical literature. As one might expect, primary attention has been directed to language in the context of the relationship between militarization and cultural production. Here the changing rhetorics of mystification and propaganda have been of particular interest. But there has also been some concern with the way particular words and discourses embody, obscure and disclose some of the key cultural contradictions of Western modernity. It is also possible to see how these words and discourses imply a specific location for critical political practice. In all three contexts, language reflects and constitutes significant horizons within which we understand and respond to contemporary processes of militarization. Here I want to suggest briefly one way in which a sensitivity to language enables some connections to be made between the three styles of cultural analysis that I have drawn on here.

Language is a medium of both communication and mystification. Therein lies much of its political power.[22] At the simplest level, politics offers considerable scope for the use and abuse of euphemisms, jargon, metaphors, clichés and what George Orwell called "double think" and "newspeak." Some of the linguistic ploys that have accompanied the accumulation of nuclear weapons are now well known. There is the jargon of sterile technologism through which massacre turns into "collateral damage." Other jargons deflect our attention through allusions to theatre and sport, or the use of anthropomorphic, animal or mythical names. Some terms have gone through a complete reversal of meaning. The destabilizing MX missile has become the "peacemaker." Secrecy and force are justified in order to "defend democracy." Exhortations are made about "peace through strength" or joining the peace movement through joining the army.

More systematic research has uncovered a wide range of linguistic usages through which our understanding of contemporary military affairs has been filtered. Paul Chilton, for example, has examined early attempts to describe the bombs that exploded on Hiroshima and Nagasaki.[23] Reports by eye witnesses were couched in terms of "awe-inspiring" religious images. Very soon, press reports were expressed in terms of the power of nature or the revelation of the secrets of nature. The mushroom cloud became a symbol of vast mysterious power. The whole event was quickly assimilated to natural or supernatural processes and thus located beyond human control. The language was more appropriate to the experience of scientific discovery than of mass annihilation.

Metaphors have also played an important role in shaping our understanding of military affairs. Glen Hook has written of how the metaphor of a "nuclear allergy" has been used to undermine resistance to nuclear weapons in Japan; the metaphor portrays a political position as an illness to be overcome by careful treatment.[24] Similarly, tendencies towards political neutralism have often been dismissed as an unfortunate case of "Hollanditus." Many who oppose the accumulation of nuclear weapons also persist in using simple-minded medical metaphors.

The language in which modern weapons deployments are portrayed requires particularly careful examination. As noted earlier, the term "arms race" is especially misleading. Similarly, the term "deterrence" brings with it meanings and implications that both elucidate and obscure what is going on. Consider, for example, the way deterrence theory incorporates the term "balance," as in balance of power, which can mean both preponderance (as with a bank balance) or equilibrium. This difference is crucial to the debate between deterrence and war fighting schools of nuclear strategy. In conventional military terms, the more and bigger, the better. For classical minimum deterrence, enough is enough.[25] Similar ambiguities arise from the use of terms like "modernization," or the quantitative rather than qualitative depiction of strategic deployments.

The prevalence of "nukespeak," as such usages have come to be called, does not exhaust the importance of language in this context. Indeed, as some of the terms already mentioned may suggest, what is important here is less the linguistic characteristics of particular words or the propagandistic intentions of specific usages than the discourses about military affairs in which particular words and intentions participate. Two terms with very deep historical and cultural roots are particularly suggestive here: the "enemy" and "peace."

The concept of the "enemy" invokes a very complex theme within Western culture concerning "the Other." This theme comes in many forms, from the dialectical logic of master and slave to the projections of psychoanalysis. In its crudest forms, a Manichaeism prevails; we have truth, reason and God, they have superstition, barbarism and the devil. This theme is familiar enough in many of our categorizations of the so-called insane, in the social construction of gender, and in relations between the West and the rest, whether this has been the Ottoman Empire, the Soviet Union, or the Third World.[26] It has been particularly pronounced in the recent rhetoric of the Cold War.

The wider implications invoked by references to an enemy are closely related to the highly problematic nature of the concept of peace. Here problems arise from false distinctions between war and peace in an era in which preparations for war are an increasingly important aspect of peacetime activity. Problems also arise from definitions of peace as the mere absence of war, or from attempts to reconcile peace with other cherished values like "justice." But perhaps most significantly, our commonest understandings of the meaning of peace in Western societies embody conceptions of universalism that reflect a culturally specific philosophical tradition. Most obviously, peace has been associated with claims to unity, with universalist claims about the priority of order over conflict. The philosophy of Immanuel Kant is symbolic in this respect. With Kant, the possibility of peace is explicitly linked to the realization of universal reason. This connection in turn grows out of a commonly perceived philosophical tradition that goes back to classical Greece. In fact, the conceptual opposition between war and peace reflects a wider philosophical discourse in which the moment of unity or identity is linked with the good, the true and the beautiful. Diversity and difference are then treated as the inferior negations of these privileged values. And, of course, whether one understands this cultural tradition in terms of the rise of secular rationalism, or of the convergence of rationalism with religious monotheism, the postulation of a single moment of unity, identity and truth allows for a sharp distinction between those who can and those who cannot claim to have access to it. A concept of peace that is firmly attached to extreme universalism easily permits a rapid slide into a Manichaean world of friend and foe.

In short, to examine terms like "enemy" or "peace" is to recognize the depth and complexity of the broader discourses in which specific linguistic meanings are constituted. Manipulative rhetoric and propaganda become less important than the capacity of such discourses to generate and limit our understanding of the way the world is, and even to specify the options available for the world to become. Something like Michel Foucault's analysis of the discourses through which our understanding of madness and sexuality have been constituted, is therefore called for here.[27]

The starting point for any such analysis must be the way our understanding of modern military affairs is caught up in a culturally and historically specific discourse dominated by a sharply dichotomized account of the relationship between the principle of identity or unity and the principle of difference or pluralism. I have argued elsewhere that it is precisely this account that informs the most influential modern theories of international politics.[28] More specifically, it underlies both the contrast between political realists and political idealists, and between forms of political realism informed by a sense of history and change (Machiavelli) and those informed by a structuralist account of inter-state relations (Hobbes). This has predisposed analyses of change in international politics to pose possibilities for the future as either a tragic continuation of the same old game of power and war or an historic leap towards a universalist global community. It is not immediately obvious that this either/or choice is warranted by the historical evidence or by the indicators of current trends available to us. Nevertheless, this formulation continues to have a powerful grip on contemporary thinking about international politics. It informs both textbooks and policy prescriptions. And it is clearly visible in public debate between "hawks" and "doves" on military issues, at least in the North American context. A critical assessment of these predispositions is essential.

These discourses constitute one of the most powerful expressions of the connection between culture, broadly conceived, and emerging processes of militarization. On one level, they can be understood as participating in the processes of cultural production. They generate popular images and meanings as well as inform the interpretive codes of specific research communities. On another level, they reflect and obscure deep tensions within the dominant cultural traditions of Western modernity. Our thinking about the nature of war and the possibilities of peace, for example, is frequently structured by an underlying tension between the philosophical principles of identity and difference. It is not difficult to show that the limits to our understanding of reason, democracy, and security are implicated in similar tensions. On a third level, they reproduce assumptions about the location of human identity and political action. Where modern forms of militarization demand greater and greater attention to their impact on both global structures and the local activities of everyday life, these discourses reproduce a vision of politics as either the presence or absence of the state. Unfortunately, while the state has long been the form of political community that has been able to claim legitimacy and obligation precisely because of its capacity to provide security for its citizens, contemporary forms of militarization have begun to turn the state into a primary source of insecurity. It is in terms of the theory of the modern state, therefore, that the connection between culture and insecurity must be established most clearly.

IV. Insecurity and political practice

The discussion so far has surveyed the number of ways our understanding of contemporary forms of militarization is caught up in the complex webs of our inherited cultural assumptions, ongoing cultural practices, as well as our linguistic usages and discursive structures. The relationship between militaristic and cultural processes is felt all the way from the slippery rhetorics of militaristic propaganda to the philosophical assumptions that inform attempts to comprehend militarization within more systematic theoretical categories. I have argued that in addition to the more obvious connections between militarization and cultural production, it is necessary to examine how contemporary forms of militarization intensify still further some major tensions within the cultural traditions of modernity that have been problematic in political life for most of this century. They also put into question our capacity to resolve these tensions within the political structures of the modern state and states-system. At each level, it is possible to specify possible implications for political practice.

At the first level, the implications of the connection between militarization and cultural production are perhaps the most straightforward, at least in principle. They suggest the need for a cultural politics of resistance, and the delegitimization of militarization through cultural activities. This can involve satire and ridicule, as in the case of, say, *Dr. Strangelove*, or attempts to emphasize the sheer horror of war, as in the genre that goes back at least to Tolstoy's *War and Peace*. It requires skill in the decoding and demystification of rhetorics, and the clarification of the hard realities—both military and economic—behind the cultural forms.

At the second level, militarization can be linked both to the tensions within the cultural traditions of Western modernity and to the sophisticated discursive structures about war and peace that have arisen within these cultural traditions. On the one hand, this suggests the need for a cultural politics aimed at uncovering these tensions. That we live in a society that claims Enlightenment but advances barbarism, that claims democracy but enhances the secret state, that claims security but accumulates the power of mutual suicide, are fundamental points that demand constant exposure. On the other hand, there is the need for a cultural politics aimed at defusing the dominant discourses about war and peace. In the Western context these discourses reflect a heritage of Western rationalism. Consequently, the critique of militarization inevitably becomes trapped in the familiar logic of identity versus difference, order versus conflict, universalist community versus pluralist conflict. This logic issues in the co-optation of dissent and the continued legitimation of present practices. Hence the crucial importance of refusing any simple dichotomization of the claims of identity and difference.[29] Where militarization is often justified by the claim that human societies are different, and therefore inevitably in conflict, and where opposition to militarization coalesces on propositions about the essential unity of human existence, it now seems necessary to stress the claims of both unity and diversity as a starting point for any formulation of more peaceful possibilities.

Both levels lead on to the third, and it is here that the most important issues arise. In this context, the relation between culture and militarization appears as a reconstruction of the horizons of human identity. On the one hand this is felt as an expansion, a recognition of the global structures in which we all participate, whether we wish it or not. On the other hand, it is felt as a contraction, a fusion of the most global structures with the minutest activities of everyday life. Yet the processes are occurring at precisely the same time that the currently most powerful focus of human identity—the state—is becoming ever more powerful. In the more prosperous societies, processes of militarization seem to be enhancing the power of the state at the same time that the state is less and less able to justify its claims on human identity. In less prosperous societies, the state retains legitimacy in part because of its role in resisting more powerful states. It does so by entering further and further into the structures of militarization that render human security in general increasingly problematic.

Perhaps the sharpest way of posing these connections between culture, insecurity and the state is in terms of the broad problematic announced by the term "bureaucracy." It is here that many of the themes raised so far begin to come together.

In the context of cultural production, questions of war and peace now engage very large bureaucratic institutions. Where it is tempting to analyse modern weapons deployments through general theories about the logic of deterrence or the determinations of technological innovation, it is often much more instructive to enquire into the detailed analysis of the bureaucratic routines and rivalries that mediate specific decisions.[30] One of the most interesting issues here concerns the way modern military-bureaucratic structures reach out into a very broad sector of the intelligentsia. In the American case, for example, we can point to the symbolic early case of the Rand Corporation, the development of deterrence theory by ex-economists, and the proliferation of research institutions and university research projects dependent on defence funding. Conversely, modern American social theory continues to reflect an understanding of social life through metaphors and models stimulated by military research, as with cybernetics, game theory, operations research and systems analysis. Here it is possible to analyse the relationship between particular bureaucratic institutions and the more general processes of cultural production and reproduction. It is also possible to examine the specific way in which policy is constituted through particular discursive structures.

But the problematic of bureaucracy is a matter not only of administration or the institutional apparatus of the modern state but also of the trajectory of politics in the twentieth century. As announced by Weber, this latter theme is double-edged. Rationalization has become the defining characteristic of Western culture and socio-economic life. Yet ironically, rationalization, particularly as manifested in bureaucratization and industrialization, has produced more efficient ways of realizing specific goals only by neglecting the fundamental values which guide human conduct.

In this context, contemporary patterns of militarization appear as a particularly depressing footnote to the theme of the iron-cage. Whether as the fate of Western civilization or as the peculiar technological domination characteristic of capitalism, the bureaucratization of mass murder confirms a grand philosophy of history. It is, of course, a philosophy of history that has long been troubled by the problem of political practice. Weber's own formulation is the most troubling of all. For Weber, the escape from the snares of rationalization is provided by the non-rational and quasi-existential commitments of individuals in a world of inevitable conflict, whether between individuals or nation-states. It is an appeal that serves to resolve the paradoxes of Weber's own moral universe but which merely amplifies the contradictions in his own cultural heritage.[31] History as rationalization issues in politics as the irrational assertion of power. In the late twentieth century, power politics offers little escape from rationalization. It promises only its probable completion.

The connection between bureaucracy and the state occurs both as institution and as philosophy of history. To invoke the name of Weber is in both cases to portray the connection in the most pessimistic way. No theory of the processes of militarization can avoid an account of the participation of state bureaucracies in both the strategic and economic aspects of modern processes of militarization. And it is at the level of the state that the contradiction between Enlightenment and Despair occurs as the abandonment of reason in favour of irrational power in its most dangerous form. It is also in relation to the state, whether as labyrinthine institution or as national power, that the ideological role of cultural forms is strongest and the counter-hegemonic potential of cultural politics seems weakest.

A less pessimistic conclusion emerges from the third reading of the connection between culture, insecurity and the state. Here the crucial point is that the patterns of contemporary militarization suggest that the state no longer has a monopoly on the provision of security. The state itself is viewed increasingly as a source of insecurity. And this insecurity is now felt acutely both in terms of the grandest of global structures and of the minutiae of everyday life in local communities. It is precisely these two contexts that are excluded in favour of the state by the discursive traditions that have dominated thinking about matters of war and peace. They have been treated as mutually exclusive realms, as political analogues of the philosophical principles of identity and difference.

The state has continued to monopolize the terrain of security precisely because it has been possible to appeal to abstractions like national interest—abstractions that reify both the moment of difference between communities and the moment of identity within communities. Whatever layers of complexity are added to this basic reification by the specific characteristic of cultural production in particular societies, it is this connection between security and the state that has become increasingly vulnerable. The fact that insecurity is now felt both locally and globally is a danger; but it also provides an opportunity to redefine security in ways that stress both its local immediacy and global reach, and thereby undermine the legitimacy of contemporary processes of militarization.

In the context of the contradictions of Western modernity, the recognition that insecurity is felt both locally and globally acts so as to undermine the very discourses in which those contradictions have long been embedded. The tension between Enlightenment and Despair is itself a form of the reified opposition between identity and difference. Weber is symptomatic in this respect. The conventional progressivist view of history is deprived of its capacity to attain some universal truth. Meaning and value are denied the possibility of any universalizing integration and are then distributed to the relativism of pluralistic and irrational decisions. Because identity is denied, difference is embraced. The impossibility of their reconciliation then takes the form of the tragic view of history that has guided so many appeals to *realpolitik* in this century. Contemporary forms of insecurity suggest that all this is based quite simply on a false bifurcation. In fact, we have common insecurity which manifests itself in quite different ways. It is a matter of us *and* them. In this context, therefore, there is considerable space for deconstructing and reconstructing the discourses and traditions that reproduce a view of security as us *or* them.

The recognition that insecurity manifests itself simultaneously in both global and local forms is of particular significance for the cultural politics of human community. Historically, the state has been the political form through which the projects of security and of human community have converged. The paradigm of this convergence has been the nation-state. Contemporary forms of insecurity put this convergence into question. If those who claim to be realists are right in suggesting that human communities are in the end rooted in the search for security, then we should expect an increasing concentration of political activity at both the local and global levels. The interesting question that then arises concerns neither the priority of the one over the other, nor the necessity of resolving the claims of unity and identity with those of particularity and difference in an eternal reification of the state; but rather the way in which political space is likely to be disarticulated into a variety of different levels both above and below the state.

The relations between culture and insecurity thus appear in the form of cultural production, in the form of discursive articulation, and in the form of political practice. In the last case, the key moment now involves the exploration of new forms of political community and identification, and of the possible connections between them. If there is to be a space for creative politics in the face of the kinds of structural determinations that induce the bureaucratization of mass murder, it is these connections between communities responding to different forms of a shared insecurity, that will have to be explored and encouraged.

Notes and references

1. Quoted in Michael Howard, *Clausewitz* (Oxford: Oxford University Press, 1983), p.73, from *On War*, ed. and trans. by M. Howard and P. Paret (Princeton, NJ: Princeton University Press, 1976).

2. This classification is taken from Yoshikazu Sakamoto and Richard Falk "World Demilitarized: A Basic Human Need," *Alternatives*, vol VI, no 1, 1980, pp.1-16. Recent literature relevant to this general theme includes: Asbjørn Eide and Marek Thee (editors), *Contemporary Militarism* (London: Croom Helm, 1979); Mary Kaldor and A. Eide (editors), *The World Military Order* (New York: Praeger, 1979); Kjell Skjelsback, "Militarism, Its Dimensions and Corollaries: An Attempt at Conceptual Clarification," *Journal of Peace Research*, vol XVI, no 3, 1979, pp.213-229; Seymour Melman, *The Permanent War Economy* (New York: Simon and Schuster, 1974); E.P. Thompson, *et al.*, *Exterminism and Cold War* (London: New Left Books, 1982); Martin Shaw (editor), *War, State and Society* (London: Macmillan, 1984); Nicole Ball and Milton Leitenberg (editors), *The Structure of the Defence Industry: An International Survey* (London: Croom Helm, 1983); Helena Tuomi and Raimo Vayrynen, *Transnational Corporations, Armaments and Development* (New York: St. Martins Press, 1982); S.G. Neuman, "International Stratification and Third World Military Industries," *International Organization*, vol 38, no 1, Winter 1984, pp.167-197; Andrew J. Pierre, *The Global Politics of Arms Sales* (Princeton, NJ: Princeton University Press, 1982); David Holloway, *The Soviet Union and the Arms Race*, 2nd edn. (New Haven, Conn: Yale University Press, 1984); the special issue on "Militarization and Society" of *Alternatives*, vol X, no 1, Summer 1984; and *World Armaments and Disarmament: SIPRI Yearbook 1985* (London: Taylor and Francis, 1985).

3. For a version of this argument see Jacques Derrida, "No Apocalypse, Not Now (full speed ahead, seven missiles, seven missives)", *Diacritics*, vol 14, no 2, Summer 1984.

4. For a short discussion see Lawrence Freedman, "Nuclear Weapons in Europe: Is There an Arms Race?" *Millenium: Journal of International Studies*, vol 13, no 1, Spring 1984, pp.57-64.

5. Bernard Brodie (editor), *The Absolute Weapon: Atomic Power and World Order* (New York: Harcourt, Brace, 1946), p.83.

6. My usage of the term culture here is informed by the historical stance adopted by Raymond Williams, for whom it is less a clearly definable concept than the site of unresolved historically constituted contradictions. See Williams, *Marxism and Literature* (Oxford: Oxford University Press, 1977); *Culture* (London: Fontana, 1981); and *Keywords: A Vocabulary of Culture and Society*, 2nd edn (London: Fontana, 1983), pp.87-93. See also R. B. J. Walker, "World Politics and Western Reason: Universalism, Pluralism, Hegemony" in: Walker (editor), *Culture, Ideology and World Order* (Boulder, CO: Westview Press, 1984), pp.182-216.

7. Robin Luckham, "Of Arms and Culture," *Current Research on Peace and Violence*, vol 7, no 1, 1984, pp.1-64 and "Armament Culture," *Alternatives*, vol X, no 1, Summer 1984, pp.1-44. Luckham's analysis can usefully be read in conjunction with Joel Kovel, *Against the State of Nuclear Terror* (London: Pan, 1983), and Stuart Ewan, "Mass Culture, Narcissism and the Moral Economy of War," *Telos*, vol 44, Summer 1980, pp.74-87.

8. The connection between strategic theory and American strategic policy has been of particular concern here. See e.g. Lawrence Freedman, *The Evolution of Strategic Thought* (London: Macmillan, 1982); Fred Kaplan, *The Wizards of Armageddon* (New York: Simon and Schuster, 1983); Robert Scheer, *With Enough Shovels* (New York: Random House, 1982); Desmond Ball, *Politics and Force Levels: The Strategic Missile Program of the Kennedy Administration* (Berkeley and Los Angeles: University of California Press, 1982); Ken Booth, *Strategy and Ethnocentricism* (New York: Homes and Meier, 1979).

9. Crispin Aubrey (editor), *Nukespeak: The Media and the Bomb* (London: Comedia, 1982); Noam Chomsky and E. Herman, *After the Cataclysm* (Boston: South End Press, 1979).

10. Warren W. Wagar, *Terminal Visions: The Literature of Last Things* (Bloomington, IN: Indiana University Press, 1982); I.F. Clark, *Voices Prophesying War, 1763-1984* (London: Oxford University Press, 1966); Nicholas Humphrey and Robert Jay Lifton (editors), *In a Dark Time* (London: Faber and Faber, 1984).

11. Shiv Visvanathan, "Atomic Physics: The Career of An Imagination," *Alternatives*, vol X, no 2, Fall 1984, pp.193-236.

12. Cynthia Enloe, *Does Khaki Become You? The Militarization of Women's Lives* (London: Pluto, 1983); Brian Easlea, *Fathering the Unthinkable: Masculinity, Scientists and the Nuclear Arms Race* (London: Pluto, 1983).

13. Mary Kaldor, *The Baroque Arsenal* (London: Deutsch, 1982).

14. Some analyses include Anthony Barnett, *Iron Britannia* (London: Allison and Busby, 1982); Alan Wolfe, "Nuclear Fundamentalism Reborn," *World Policy Journal*, vol II, no 1, Fall 1984, pp.87-108; Richard J. Barnet, *Roots of War* (Baltimore: Penguin, 1971); Jerry W. Sanders, *Peddlers of Crisis: The Committee on the Present Danger and the Legitimation of Containment Militarism* (Boston: South End Press, 1982).

15. The classic text here is Max Horkheimer and Theodor Adorno, *Dialectic of Enlightenment*, J. Cumming trans. (New York: Seabury Press, 1972). More accessible discussions relevent to this general theme are Geoffrey Hawthorn, *Enlightenment and Despair: A History of Sociology* (Cambridge: Cambridge University Press, 1976) and Langdon Winner, *Autonomous Technology: Technics-out-of-Control as a Theme in Political Thought* (Cambridge, MA: M.I.T. Press, 1977).

16. On this general theme see Richard A. Falk, "Nuclear Weapons and the Death of Democracy," *Praxis International*, 1982, pp.1-12; Falk, "Nuclear Weapons and the Renewal of Democracy," *Praxis International*, 1984; and Joel Kovel, *Against the State of Nuclear Terror*. Interesting discussions of the British case include John Dearlove and Peter Saunders, *Introduction to British Politics* (Oxford and Cambridge: Polity Press, 1984), pp.115-168; G. Pryns (editor), *Defended to Death* (Harmondsworth: Penguin, 1983); and Duncan Campbell, *War Plan U.K.* (London: Hutchinson, 1982). An additional complexity is added by the way in which large states intervene in smaller states; a particularly interesting case here concerns American–Australian relations; see e.g. Richard Hall, *The Secret State* (Stanmore, N.S.W.; Cassell Australia, 1978); and Desmond Ball, *A Suitable Piece of Real Estate* (Sydney: Hale and Iremonger, 1980).

17. For a recent attempt to rethink the meaning of the concept of security in the international context see Barry Buzan, *People, States and Fear: The National Security Problem in International Relations* (Brighton: Harvester Press, 1983); and Buzan, "Peace, Power and Security: Contending Concepts in the Study of International Relations," *Journal of Peace Research*, vol 21, no 2, 1984, pp.109-125.

18. Eqbal Ahmed, "The Peace movement and the Third World," *END: Journal of European Nuclear Disarmament*, vol 15, April-May 1985, p.14. For a parallel set of considerations see Ferenc Feher and Agnes Heller, "On Being Anti-Nuclear in Soviet Societies," *Telos*, vol 57, Fall, 1983, pp.144-162. See also R.B.J. Walker, "East Wind, West Wind: Civilizations, Hegemonies and World Orders" in: Walker (editor), *Culture, Ideology and World Order*, pp.2-22.

19. For a useful brief discussion, see Johan Galtung, "Social Cosmology and the Concept of Peace," *Journal of Peace Research*, vol 18, no 2, 1981, pp.183-199.

20. For brief discussions of this theme see Dan Smith and Ron Smith, *The Economics of Militarism* (London: Pluto Press, 1983); and Tamas Szentes, "The Economic Impact of Global Militarization," *Alternatives*, vol X, no 1, Summer 1984, pp.45-73. For an important recent addition to the large literature on the historical relationship between military requirements and economic development see Gautam Sen, *The Military Origins of Industrialization and International Trade Rivalry* (New York: St. Martin's Press, 1984).

21. Robert Jay Lifton and Richard Falk, *Indefensible Weapons* (New York: Basic Books, 1982); Lifton, *The Broken Connection* (1979); Kovel, *Against the State of Nuclear Terror*.

22. For a good selection of writings on this complex theme see Michael Shapiro (editor), *Language and Politics* (Oxford: Basic Blackwell, 1984).

23. Paul Chilton, "Nukespeak: Nuclear Language, Culture and Propaganda," in: Aubrey (editor), *Nukespeak: The Media and the Bomb*, pp.94-112. See also Paul Chilton (editor), *Language and the Nuclear Arms Debate: Nukespeak Today* (London: Francis Pinter, 1985).

24. Glenn D. Hook, "The Nuclearization of Language: Nuclear Allergy as Political Metaphor," *Journal of Peace Research*, vol 21, no 3, 1984, pp.259-275. See also Hook "Making Nuclear Weapons Easier to Live With: The Role of Language in Nuclearization," International Peace Research Institute, Oslo, Report 9/84; and Hook, *Language and Politics: The Security Discourse in Japan and the United States* (Syuppan; Kurosio, 1986).

25. The broad context of this issue is discussed in Hans J. Morgenthau, "The Fallacy of Thinking Conventionally About Nuclear Weapons," in: David Carlton and Carlo Schaerf (editors), *Arms Control and Technological Innovation* (London: 1977). On some of its contemporary consequences see Ken Booth and Phil Williams, "Fact and Fiction in U.S. Foreign Policy: Reagan's Myths About Detente," *World Policy Journal*, vol II, no 3, Summer 1985, pp.501-532.

26. The best known statement of this theme in the context of international politics is Edward Said, *Orientalism* (New York: Random House, 1978). See also Lata Mani and Ruth Frankenburg, "The Challenge of Orientalism," *Economy and Society*, vol 14, no 2, May 1985, pp.174-192.

27. Michel Foucault, *Discipline and Punish: The Birth of the Prison*, trans. A. Sheridan (New York: Vintage, 1979); *The History of Sexuality*, trans. R. Hurley (New York: Pantheon, 1978 and forthcoming).

28. "Realism, Change and International Political Theory," *International Studies Quarterly* (forthcoming); "Contemporary Militarism and the Discourse of Dissent," in: Walker (editor), *Culture, Ideology and World Order*, pp.302-322; "The Territorial State and the Theme of Gulliver," *International Journal*, vol 39, no 3, Summer 1984, pp.529-553. See also Richard K. Ashley, "The Power of Power Politics: Toward a Critical Social Theory of International Politics," forthcoming in: T. Ball (editor), *Social and Political Inquiry*.

29. In this context see the important discussion of the cultural politics of Indian resistance to colonialism in Ashis Nandy, *The Intimate Enemy: Loss and Recovery of Self under Colonialism* (Delhi: Oxford University Press, 1983); and Nandy, "Oppression and Human Liberation: Toward a Third World Utopia," in: Walker (editor), *Culture, Ideology and World Order*, pp.149-179.

30. See, as just one example among many, Robert J. Art and Stephen E. Ockender, "The Domestic Politics of the Cruise Missile Development, 1970-1980," in: Richard K. Betts (editor), *Cruise Missiles: Technology, Strategy, Politics* (Washington, DC: Brookings Institution, 1981), pp.349-415. More generally see Desmond Ball, "Nuclear Strategy and Force Development," in: Ball (editor), *Strategy and Defence: Australian Essays* (Sydney: George, Allen & Unwin, 1982).

31. For a succinct account of this theme see Rogers Brubaker, *The Limits of Rationality: An Essay on the Social and Moral Thought of Max Weber* (London: George, Allen & Unwin, 1984). A comparative reading of two of Weber's seminal political essays is particularly instructive in this respect: "The National State and Economic Policy" (1985) *Economy and Society*, vol 9, no 4, 1980, pp.428-449; and "Politics as a Vocation," in: *From Max Weber: Essays in Sociology*, trans. and ed. H.H. Gerth and C. Wright Mills (New York: Oxford University Press, 1946), pp.77-128. See also David Beetham, *Max Weber and the Theory of Modern Politics*, 2nd edn (Cambridge: Polity Press, 1985).

The Challenge of the Peace Movement: Civilian Security and Civilian Emancipation

ZSUZSA HEGEDUS

The significance of transnational protest

When on October 10, 1981, some 300 000 people rallied in Bonn to protest the installation of Pershing II cruise missiles in Germany and Western Europe, peace suddenly emerged as the most powerful mobilizing issue in Europe. This massive protest, the largest since World War II, was merely "the beginning" of a transnational protest in the West and of a wider struggle on both sides of the Atlantic. In the course of a few weeks, hundreds of thousands of people—in Rome, London, Madrid, Copenhagen, Milan, and Amsterdam—marched against the deployment of new intermediate range missiles in Western Europe. The protest exploded on the European scene not when the decision to deploy the missiles was made, but rather when United States President Reagan declared that his administration would use such weapons to fight and win a "limited nuclear war" in Europe in the event of a Soviet threat.[1]

A "pacifist wave"?

Appearing first in Holland, the protest swept across Europe (with the exception of France) like a tidal wave. Indeed, it was immediately labelled a "pacifist wave," an epiphenomenal act of refusal, i.e. an opposition to these particular missiles and/or the general rejection of nuclear arms and war. This "pacifist" label further suggested that the protest was dictated essentially by a reactive, irrational, and irresponsible fear of those weapons which were

Commissioned by the Committee for a Just World Peace. An earlier version was presented at the Committee's Royaumont Conference in December 1985. This article utilizes the results of sociological research carried out by the author in the United States and West Germany on the orientations and dynamics of the peace movement. The results of this research, including the analysis of one hundred interviews conducted among activists belonging to various currents in the movement, will be published in a forthcoming volume.

supposed to defend the West against the USSR and protect our liberties against the menace of totalitarianism.

This interpretation likens the mobilization against the missiles to the ban-the-bomb movement of the 1950s, which was taken over by communists for the purpose of redressing the nuclear balance in favor of the Soviet Union. It has also been compared with the prewar pacifist movement, which was indirectly responsible for the "spirit of Munich," and hence for the collective retreat of the Western democracies in the face of Hitler's onslaught.[2]

This protest supposedly leads, if not to complicity with the USSR, then at least to collective retreat before the menace of totalitarianism. In short, it has been seen as a reflex action incapable of going beyond mere opposition to these missiles, unable to question both the aims and the consequences of security policy, or to challenge the power behind them. Moreover, since Germans, Scandinavians, or West Europeans have been stereotypically characterized as being inclined towards passivity, the protest was also seen as nothing more than a defensive action, emanating from specific situations defined by geopolitical, cultural, or historical circumstances.

Strangely enough, such explanations have been maintained even though the hypothesis of a reaction of the "periphery" against the "center," the only one that could account for the manifestly European dimension of this protest, has been singularly weakened by events. These two interpretations of the peace movement as either a pure act of refusal or a specific reaction still prevail today outside France (where debate continues to revolve around the "wave of pacifism").[3] Recent events have discredited these theories.

The wave of protest in Europe did not diminish but rather experienced an unprecedented upsurge. Even before new demonstrations mobilized hundreds of thousands in West Germany, Great Britain, Italy, Belgium, Spain, Denmark, the Netherlands, and Greece, the "fever" reached the United States. Although originating in the "periphery," the protest had reached the "center." At the same time the campaign against the Pershing II and cruise missiles experienced unexpected success on one side of the Atlantic, while the campaign for the "freeze," launched the year before by a diverse group of scientists and professionals, took on new dimensions on the other side of the Atlantic.[4] On June 12, 1982, New York City witnessed the largest mass demonstration in its history. Heads of State from all over the globe, who had assembled that very day at the United Nations for a conference on disarmament, were deprived of their monopoly of initiative in the domain of security. Close to a million people challenged them directly in the streets, calling for a halt to the arms race and a freeze in nuclear arsenals, their demands being presented as the indispensable precondition for any security policy responsible to present and future generations.

Within a few months, the mobilization took on undeniable global dimensions not only in geographic scope but also in its effects, its political impact, and, especially, its mode of action. "For our children, for your children, for their children, stop the madness! Reverse the arms race!" chanted on that historic day in New York City now echoes throughout the world, underscoring not only the global character of the movement but also suggesting that the present movement was more than a mere behavioral response, or even less a reflex refusal. For having generated a demand outside the realm of official security policy, the protest has shown its potential to challenge the policy behind armaments and especially to question the ultimate aim of those policies—in the name of future generations.

The birth of a new struggle

The mass demonstrations which marked the first phase of mobilization were only the tip of an immense iceberg. These demonstrations, organized around precise and limited objectives, brought together feminists and archbishops, ecologists and trade unionists, Nobel Prize winners and ministers, scientists and housewives, members of religious communities and former members of the counter-culture, the churches and activists from the "new" social movements, "militants" from social and political struggles and ordinary people from the nonpoliticized mainstream, conservatives and radicals, voters on the left and on the right. Moreover, these demonstrations were accompanied by a veritable explosion of diverse citizens committees, associations, and activist groups. Such groups have proliferated since 1981 on both sides of the Atlantic, coordinated through an immense and informal system of multiple and multiform networks, both nonhierarchical and diversified, patterned after those of the feminist and ecologist/antinuclear movements.

Indeed, through this multitude of groups, a new social fabric is being constructed which cuts across age, sex, class, occupation, political ideology, and religious affiliation. Moreover, the mobilization is transnational because these people are involved in a praxis that, while different in content from country to country, is identical in its mode of organization and action, namely, it is nonhierarchical and grass roots in its structure, nonviolent, and expressive in its methods. In other words, this diverse social movement is engaged in an autonomous protest similar to the activity of the "new" social movements of the 1970s.

In fact, the "active minorities" of the "new" social movements have played a central role in this new protest.[5] In most cases, these activists, along with diverse Christian groups, scientists, and professionals, have initiated the new protest. But even when this was not strictly the case, the activists very quickly appropriated the socio-organizational infrastructure built up by the social movements of the 1970s. The experience gained during these earlier struggles, both at the level of organization and at the level of action and collective reflection have proved invaluable.

The present peace movement is the combination of two types of action. The first is directed toward informing people and mobilizing public opinion across national boundaries through single-issue campaigns aimed at maximizing the impact of the movement. This type of action seeks, on the one hand, to win the greatest number of people and, on the other hand, to maximize the movement's visibility in the streets and in the media through massive and well-timed demonstrations.

The other type of action seeks to involve informed people in a praxis which is genuinely "basist" and antihierarchical in its mode of organization, nonviolent, and expressive in its mode of action, even if it is as diversified in its content as the people who are involved in the movement. While the single-issue campaigns are being carried out to rally public opinion around "limited" objectives such as "No to the Pershing II" or the "nuclear freeze," the grass-roots peace movement that has arisen in the past five years across the Western world (except France) involves people through a multiplicity of networks and in different, more radical actions. Such actions include local informational efforts, "blockades," petitioning local representatives, referenda to establish nuclear-free zones (ranging from neighborhoods to entire nations), and civil disobedience.

The single-issue campaigns follow an essentially political logic. They seek to inform and mobilize public opinion and thereby force political parties to address the problem and respect majority opinion. In contrast, the movement emerging from the actions of citizen networks follow a different logic. In fact, this movement differs from the feminist, ecologist, or antinuclear movements only in its theme and problematic. It shares with the latter movements a heterogenous and nonintegrated structure, a very diverse "constituency," an autonomy *vis-à-vis* political parties, and a certain mode of action and organization. However, its impact and dimensions go far beyond that of the "old" social movements: it is different from them in its intensity within each country and its presence within all the Western countries (except France), in its unprecedented capacity for mobilization, and in its extraordinary influence on public opinion and, consequently, on the political system.

One may ask if these protest movements bear any similarity to other movements in the past so as to warrant being construed as an historically interconnected whole, particularly at the level of praxis? More importantly, does the present struggle have the capacity to recognize and address problems that may be qualitatively different from the problems raised by the earlier movements? Do these new movements raise or articulate new questions and challenges?

Posing the questions in this way suggests an affirmative answer and underscores a core hypothesis for further research on the nature, significance, orientations, and dynamics of the peace movement. However, before asking how the praxis of this struggle relates to a nascent social movement and to its capacity to address problems which pose central questions to the meaning of life in the modern world, we must ask whether it is justified to speak of only *one* movement? In other words, are the single-issue campaigns and the mushrooming networks which have varied content but identical structure part of a larger whole that can be theoretically delineated? Or are we simply witnessing "events" that are independent from one another and whose simultaneous occurrence within a specific nexus seems to impart to them a semblance of unity? Can these two types of activity be defined and analyzed as different "faces" or elements of a single movement that, as in the past, is a "melting pot" of meanings and levels of activity that are often contradictory?

A new social challenge: security

Even those who do not reduce this movement to a series of distinct events address these questions essentially at the level of content. What they emphasize is the presence of either a minimum shared objective, or a common act of refusal. In short, the protest is reduced to its lowest common denominator, and defined as a single issue activity.

However different these two types of action are in their orientation and logic, they constitute the two sides of a single movement. Whatever distance or tension there may be between an action that strives to rally public opinion behind limited objectives and a contestatory praxis that seeks social transformation (which, by definition, is in the beginning a minority action), all these campaigns and actions focus, in one way or another, on the same problem: human security in the modern world. This direct or indirect yet constant reference to the problem of security gives to this protest its novelty and its unity.

The emergence of a new social issue

In fact, the issue that has prompted this transnational protest, and which, in the past five years, has mobilized public opinion and dominated political debates in the West (with the exception of France) is not, in the first instance, the concern for peace. Of course everybody is speaking of peace: "winning" the peace in West Germany or searching for its "makers" in the United States.[6] However, the real question is how to insure the peace, or more generally, how our security may be assured in a world of nuclear weapons and totalitarian structures—a world divided into two blocs, where the balance of power between two different political systems rests on nuclear armaments.

Of course, security itself means different things to different people. For some, the major risk is that of an eventual nuclear holocaust which, even if it did not immediately destroy human life, would undoubtedly threaten the survival of the species. For others, the major danger is the outbreak of "limited" nuclear war. Some ask how Europeans can be guaranteed protection simultaneously from the latter eventuality and against Soviet tanks. Still others are disturbed that politicians and military officials have discarded the idea that nuclear war would be unwinnable and now seem to believe that nuclear confrontation is a "reasonable" gamble precisely because such a war is winnable.[7]

For the Germans, it is first and foremost a matter of ensuring their own security when faced with the intermediate range missiles of the two contending sides: the SS-20s and the Pershing IIs. The Germans in the postwar era have direct experience of the division of Europe into two blocs; today they are threatened with total annihilation in the event of a nuclear confrontation between the two superpowers. In this context, some people have criticized the doctrine of graduated response and have demanded a different nuclear strategy. Others go so far as to reject any nuclear defense, advocating instead either a "classical" defense or civil defense. Still others demand a noninterventionist policy. Finally, there are those who put the moral demand that we build a nonviolent world.

This wide range of criticisms illustrates the complexity of the security issue and the diversity of the debate which the movement has opened up. Under the influence of this protest, the issue of security has been raised—sometimes in its moral/political aspects and at other times in its technical/economic aspects—in a very limited or overly general manner. However, the debates (whether taking place in the streets or presented in the press) and the various forms of action (from mass demonstrations to symbolic protests) all center on the same problem and address directly or indirectly the same question: what does security mean in today's world and how should it be insured?

The new centrality of security

The centrality of the problem of security differentiates the current protest from any reflex of refusal or pacifist-type action, and affirms its openness to the future. That it has been able to bring into the open the problem of security lying behind the deployment of the Pershing IIs and the arms race demonstrates the originality of this protest in terms of the influence of its past experiences and its ability to shape the future. Moreover, the constant reference to a common problematic, which transcends national frontiers, gives to this protest a real unity borne not out of refusal or common "waves of pacifism," but rather out of a fundamental challenge to deal with the problem of security in the contemporary world.

Thus, this protest can be differentiated both from pacifist actions, which reject armaments or war in general, and from the various mobilizations against nuclear weapons that have taken place over the last 40 years. All these previous movements have challenged the problem of nuclear weapons but have failed to address the problem of security in the last quarter of the 20th century in way that deals simultaneously with its two dimensions: that of nuclear arms *and* totalitarianism.

The peace movements of the 1950s were directed against the A-bomb and were usually led by communist parties whose objective was to change the balance of power in favor of the Soviet Union. The movements of the late 1970s were directed against the neutron bomb and were led by feminists, Christians, advocates of nonviolence, and extra-parliamentary opposition without any relation to the USSR. Nonetheless, while these two examples highlight major differences at the level of objectives and actors, certain common elements can be discerned. Despite varying objectives—one strictly political, the other essentially moral—earlier oppositions to nuclear weapons failed to address the problem of security necessary in a world both nuclearist and totalitarian without subordinating one to the other.

In contrast, the current protest addresses precisely this problem by explicitly rejecting the arms race as a means to defend the West against the Soviet menace. Not only does this differentiate it from past practices, but it also demonstrates its determination, if not its capacity, to tackle the problem of security in a new way, and, more significantly, to assume direct responsibility for the future. Of course, this intention and determination in itself is not sufficient to delineate in a positive fashion the possibility of transformation nor the specific orientation of the protest in the realm of security. But this intent is sufficient, in and of itself, to allow us to distinguish this protest from previous protests. The association, be it weak or strong, of a "No" with the demand for a different security policy suggests that the dimension of refusal, preeminent in the initial stages of protest, has always been related to a more fundamental concern. The essentially oppositional orientation of this protest has always been linked to a counter-offensive, i.e. to the will to take charge of the future, to invent a new way of dealing with the problem of security which does not subordinate the protection of humanity against nuclear weapons to the defense of the West against the East.

Democratic protest and social movement

Indeed, the peace protest, at least in Europe, has transformed the problem of security into a collective issue. In the first place, it was brought into the "public arena," whether in the streets or in the media. In the second place, it introduced the security issue as a subject for public debate. Thus, despite their limited and basically negative objectives in the realm of security, the single-issue campaigns produced a major opening within the broad arena of the democratic process and served as a vehicle for democratic protest.

More significantly, in opening up debate, these campaigns have also created the terrain for a new movement which has transformed the once closed and unidimensional field of security into a field of conflictual action. The process has already engendered transformations analogous to those produced by the feminist and ecologist/antinuclear movements in the socio-political realm.[8] The movement, born of a refusal and bolstered by fear, has taken the power latent in its protest and utilized it to open up new public space on the question of security, to exert control, and to promote socio-political transformation. This is accomplished by seizing upon an issue, over and above that of peace, that raises questions about one fundamental axis in our type of society, namely, one's security in this world of conflict and the security of this world in a nuclear era. In fact, the movement has challenged the largely nondemocratic process that has surrounded discussions of security, a discussion which has largely remained the monopoly of states, governments, politicians, and military experts—and thus has escaped any collective democratic control.

This protest movement, which no longer defines itself through its constituency, ideology, or the political affiliation of its activists, but solely through its activity, has a double focus: the development of a new collective capacity to deal with the problem of security, and the invention of a new problem-solving process. Moreover, it is transnational not only in terms of its scope and similarity from country to country, but because of the centrality of the problematic and challenge which they share in common. More importantly, these new protests are neither peace nor disarmament movements, but a *movement for human security*.

This learning process, this work, and this self-transformation are headed in two different directions, corresponding to the two principal orientations of the movement. Already they are bringing about two major transformations, both within the socio-political space of the nation-state and beyond it, i.e. at the level of the management of transnational and global relations. These two orientations, while analytically distinct, at times appear to complement each other and at times seem contradictory. Yet, they are intrinsically linked "from above" by their common problematic and, even more so, "from below" by the very real unity of their praxis.

The emergence of a new transnational public space

The major effect of the first orientation (dominant between 1981 and 1983) was to open up a major debate, extending across national boundaries, on the issue of security. Through a variety of actions undertaken in various Western countries around more or less similar objectives—actions whose very expressiveness is an instrument of political practice—this protest directly addressed (without resorting to intermediaries) governments, political parties, public opinion, and individuals. As a result, decision-makers and politicians in most countries are now held accountable for ensuring the kind of security that is inseparable from the collective destiny of our planet. Whereas the debate on security was once confined to the cabinets of national governments, today it is as much in the streets and in the media as it is in Western parliaments (with the exception of France). Massive demonstrations and public discussions, citizen-sponsored referenda and symbolic protests, press conferences and delegations, letters and telephone calls to local, regional, national, and international representatives are the main forms taken by the debate.[9] The actors may be ordinary citizens and heads of state, military strategists and Roman Catholic bishops, scientists and artists, politicians and mothers. The major result of this protest is to extend the democratic process so that the military–statist realm of security is transformed into a transnational public sphere.

An end to the military–statist monopoly

After five years of the "pacifist wave," it is obvious that this protest has not undermined the West's capacity for defense, but only the ability of Western governments, politicians, and military experts to monopolize the decision-making process concerning our security. As a result, security has become a public good: to be debated and decided on by civil society itself.

More importantly, in this debate a public hostile to nuclear arms is not lined up against a political elite vested with the responsibility for security; nor are experts, counter-experts, military men, and politicians of various stripes pitted against one another.[10] In contrast to the past, the protagonists of the present debate are, on one side, decision-makers and political representatives of all stripes, and on the other side, all those who through their activities oppose existing security policy and who, for the first time, are no longer content merely to express their opinion but instead put forward their own demands in the realm of security.

The issue of security is now articulated in ways which challenge directly the experts and nonexperts, civilians and military men, heads of state and citizens alike. In short, security has ceased to be the business only of experts, military strategists, and the political elite. Civil society has asserted its desire for control and its capacity for initiative in a domain that was previously monopolized by the state. In this context, the demand to reverse the arms race is not only autonomous and novel with respect to its content. It is even more so as a *process* which breaks with the military–statist problem-solving process in the security field and challenges the military–technocratic management of the arms race.[11]

Furthermore, the peace movement has developed a capacity for initiative outside the framework of the state. This framework, within a system of blocs in a nuclear era, guarantees the security of populations less than it preserves the states' monopoly over the management and organization of relations between various regions, countries, and continents. In contrast, the transnational scope of the movement, which goes together with its essential local organization undergirded by millions of grassroots groups coordinated through regional, national, and continental networks, is creating a new transnational public sphere and simultaneously constituting a new social fabric both within and beyond national borders. In short, civil society is developing a new capacity to debate openly the stakes and the choices that are critical to its future, discovering the ability of people to "control their history,"[12] and acquiring a new freedom and capacity for action that is no longer defined by a national framework.

Capacity for initiative and political representation

The development of this new capacity has also shed new light on the significance and impact of this protest on the political system, i.e. on political parties and on the political process.

The anti-Pershing and pro-freeze campaigns have become an obligatory reference point for all political elites and parties on both sides of the Atlantic. Be they for it or against it, politicians are forced to take a stand (or else face sanctions in the next elections) with respect to this demand, propelled and demanded by an autonomous and mass protest (supported in West Germany by the majority of public opinion and in the United States by at least 50% of the population).[13]

Due to its high degree of openness and unusual sensitivity to public opinion, the US political system reacted first. In 1982, the Kennedy–Hatfield motion took up the "freeze" idea and was immediately endorsed by a significant number of representatives, mostly Democrats but also Republican. In the Spring of 1984, the US Congress voted in favor of the "freeze" resolution. Whatever the real merit of his zero-option plan or his more recent endorsement of "Star Wars" (which would ostensibly permit the elimination of nuclear weapons), President Reagan, under pressure from public opinion and faced with congressional reticence about his military projects and, especially, the military budget, has been forced to abandon his previous aggressive stance. Finally, while not paramount during the presidential elections, the "freeze" nonetheless proved to be an important issue during the primaries and one on which all candidates for the Democratic nomination had to take a stand.[14]

Due to the rigidity and hierarchical organization of its political parties, the European political systems reacted more slowly. Nonetheless, the import of the eventual changes largely made up for this slow response, especially in the

German case. The major event came with the SPD's special congress in October, 1983. Although SPD Chancellor Schmidt initiated NATO's double decisions, the SPD congress reversed itself and came out overwhelmingly against the deployment of the Pershing IIs. Moreover, it issued a general condemnation of the arms race and especially of those policies that had dangerously heightened East–West tensions. The fact that the SPD had lost control of the government and that Schmidt was no longer party leader in no way diminishes the importance of this turn of events. Here we find the largest party of a major country forced to radically alter its policy, in a domain wherein the state exercises exclusive authority, as a result of a demand imposed from without by an autonomous protest movement, which henceforth had the capacity to compel the political system to represent it.

Moreover, the de facto denuclearization of New Zealand by the government of David Lange under the influence of a massive and very successful movement demonstrates that the struggle is not only transnational in scope, but also underscores its differences. For, indeed, New Zealand's case cannot be explained by the specific situation of Germany. Might not this major turn of events indicate that this protest is essentially a reaction by civil society against the state? Conversely, do not these formidable victories indicate that, rather than constituting an autonomous action, these protests seek to develop only the ability to exert political pressure?

Those who have advanced such interpretations are not entirely wrong. The presence, or even the force, of such an orientation is irrefutable given a protest movement that opposes the state and acts on political terrain. However, the major weakness with such explanations is their inability to account for precisely that which is unique to this current protest, namely, its capacity for autonomous initiative, manifested through the praxis of citizens' initiatives.

A new, autonomous praxis of citizens' initiatives

The campaigns against the Pershing II and for the "freeze" are considered by most activists as points of departure and as a minimal consensus around which their movement is constituted—a movement which, however, cannot be reduced simply to the achievement of these limited objectives nor to the search for some form of political pressure. Rather than degenerating into mere political pressure, these campaigns are accompanied by, and even give birth to, a multitude of citizens' initiatives which relate these issues to both local concerns and to broader issues such as economic and social questions (unemployment, poverty, the growth of the military budget at the expense of spending on social welfare, education, or health services) at the domestic level, or the disarmament issue at the international level.

One form this campaign has taken is the formidable multiplication of referenda, organized through popular initiative, usually around themes determined autonomously. These referenda are organized at the national, regional, and local levels and may or may not be capable of being expressed within a legislative framework. They deal with questions ranging from endorsement of the "freeze" to rejection of the Pershing IIs to the creation of nuclear-free zones, from a reorientation of local budgets to continued membership in NATO, from bans on installing or transporting nuclear weapons through a city or region to prohibitions on production or related research on such weapons.[15]

Along with these referenda at the national level came ones at the local or regional level. With respect to the former, prevalent in the United States, the "Jobs for Peace" campaign resulted in numerous local referenda. In Europe, the latter were more common, as referenda proliferated on the denuclearization of different zones: communes, cities, counties, or regions (e.g., Greater London or the Hesse laender). The referendum organized at Cambridge probably best exemplifies this trend. It is also significant that the protest in Spain, rather than demanding that Gonzalez's socialist government take a position on this particular issue, pushed instead for a referendum on Spain's continued participation in NATO.

These referenda are not designed to monitor public opinion; rather, they aim to open debate on issues related to security at the level of local, regional, or national collectivities. The goal is to create new spaces and autonomous forms of civil praxis: not "participation" but rather "empowerment" is at stake.[16] Indeed, this new practice of citizens' initiatives has already established a new autonomous social sphere which can be directly represented at the level of the political system through activities that are autonomous in content, form, and "destination."[17] The entire political system is called upon not to represent some "being," i.e. a specific or particular population or interest, but rather a problematic and a debate.

Thus the peace movement involves more than a mere reaction or form of political pressure; it also shows us the new shape of political debate. The debate is not over just one but rather a set of policies: the choices for the future and the organization of the social form in which such choices are made.[18] Both the initiative and organization of this debate belong to a new social fabric which has been produced, articulated, transformed, and enlarged continuously through a multitude of actions. Having generated a new autonomous social space, have not these actions also engendered a new social debate unique to a self-creative society, defined by its capacity to create, invent, and choose its own future?[19]

This is the central question that must be addressed with respect to a movement whose capacity to transform the democratic process and the socio-political sphere is beyond any doubt. Having produced a new political praxis, at the level of democratic protest, is the movement equally capable of producing a new social praxis? Is it able to open up the domain of security and of challenging the power of those who make the choices which are realized by a specific security policy? Is it capable of engendering a social conflict where the model of security, even the model of the organization and management of relations and conflicts between countries, regions, continents, or blocs, is the crucial issue? In short, the challenge posed by this question, which seeks to understand the presence and power of a social movement, is not only theoretical. It is a matter of determining whether or not the model of security can become the object of social debate and whether the orientation of this model can be generated in a democratic manner.

Opening up a new field of action

As a consequence of the "new" peace movement there is little disagreement that the issue of security has become recognized by people across the world as a collective public issue, if not the major issue of our age. However, by extending the space for democratic debate within Western societies, has not this peace movement increased the risk that this very space may be curtailed by threats from forces external to these societies? In other words, having opened up debate on the problem of security, is this protest really capable of opening up the field of *choices* within what is to date a closed and unidimensional theory and practice of security?

The strategic controversy: challenging the rationality of the arms race

While the most visible effect of the anti-Pershing II and "freeze" campaigns has been the opening up of public debate on security policy within the very world of military experts and "establishments," their immediate effect has been to bring to light the controversy about the strategic operationality and rationality of the arms race. The military, technical, as well as strategic and political aspects of security policy are today being questioned. The debate ranges from questions about the efficacy of single weapons systems to the doctrine of flexible response, to the "first strike" option, and to the rationality of military strategy. Thus, the Pershing II, as well as the MX, have been criticized for being offensive weapons—despite the military's claim that they are primarily defensive armaments. In addition, some military criticisms of the doctrine of flexible response as well as the overall strategy that is essentially but not exclusively nuclear, have underscored their unfeasibility and their dangerous, uncontrollable consequences.

Moreover, the controversy touches on the issue of alternative proposals which range from "no first use" and "lesser retaliation"[20] to the denuclearization of military policy and the demilitarization of defense policy. The proposed alternatives call for a reduction in the role played by nuclear weapons within security policy. In short, across this controversy, both the consequences and the rationality of security policy are being challenged.

Once the logic of military strategy has been criticized, it loses its esoteric character and its univocal construal of security policy no longer appears inevitable. Once its methods have been scrutinized and its rationality challenged, security policy becomes a matter of debate on alternative options and not some ineluctable response to a nuclear world or to the reality of totalitarianism. As a consequence of this critical process, our defense policy towards the USSR can be understood differently. By rejecting the present security policy as the sole and unique solution to confrontation with a totalitarian empire, the strategic controversy makes it clear that far from being a necessity, the arms race is nothing but a consequence of prior choices made about our relationship to the USSR. That is, what is at stake is not solutions but rather the choices that such solutions put into practice. The controversy is not about means, but, more important, of ends.

Hence, the real question concerns the capacity of this protest movement to challenge security policy, i.e. its capacity to take charge of this new debate, by transforming it into a political, social, and ethical debate rather than simply a strategic one. We may finally ask whether the protest, by raising the issue of security, has broken the monopoly exercised by states and governments in matters of public life? More importantly, beyond this opening up of the unidimensional realm of security, is the protest movement capable of challenging the dominant problem-solving process which has led to the nuclear arms race?

The articulation of a new field of action

The peace movement today is dominated by two debates which address in different ways the same question: *How can we proceed otherwise?* The first challenges the rationality of security policy that gives absolute priority to the balance of nuclear terrors. The second challenges the moral legitimacy of a system which provides protection of some at the risk of destroying everyone—a "security" which is unacceptable because it is irresponsible with regard to humanity and to the future.

The first orientation searches for different policies that would ensure our security in today's world by reducing the risks of annihilation. Its focus is on means. However, since it goes beyond mere opposition to weapons and challenges a specific security policy, this debate takes on the powers behind those orientations. Thus, through this political debate a potential conflict emerges.

The second orientation involves a search for a "new political practice" which would be able to assure our security in a responsible and morally acceptable manner. This second position is an ethical one which focuses mainly on ends and elaborates a new model where the security of one would necessarily be the security of all. However, in going beyond a moral refusal to challenge one set of values in the name of another, i.e. the principle of nonviolence as opposed to that of violence and the war system, this debate brings into view the specific goals and limits behind security policy. It attempts to define a praxis appropriate to this new value. Nonviolence is translated into a new praxis which, individually and collectively, seeks to handle conflicts in a new way. Thus, from the ethical debate an opposition emerges between two approaches, two opposing ways which deal with the problem of security.

Building the movement

From opposing policy to challenging entrenched power

Both the tone—more pragmatic on one side, more dramatic on the other—and the content of the debate on security policy differs in the United States and West Germany. While conducted in specifically national terms in the United States, the debate in Germany is ineluctably tied to the problem of dependence. German territory would be the theater of a nuclear battle according to the security policy elaborated and decided upon by the USA and the USSR, both of whom are ready to wage a nuclear war. This reality explains the ambiguity of the terminology utilized in the German and European debate and sets the concrete limits within which alternatives can be sought. Nonetheless, if opposition to a security policy decided upon by the United States often takes on an anti-American tone, the logic behind this protest is not anti-American. Similarly, while the problem of dependence of Europe and especially Germany is formulated in "national" terms, the debate does not evoke nationalist solutions.

We should not mistake the trees for the forest, nor miss the real meaning behind the words employed. Behind the anti-American, "national" rhetoric, one can discern the logic of a conflict that does not merely counterpose the United States to West Germany and Western Europe. Rather, one particular territory that depends for its survival on a particular security policy opposes the power that defines the orientation and goals of that policy. This territory encompasses more than just Germany, and the power in question encompasses both the superpowers.

Behind a policy that gives absolute priority to the balance of military and nuclear forces between the two superpowers and jeopardizes the very survival of Germany and Europe lies the two superpowers whose security policy is designed to maintain and reinforce their hegemony over the world. And behind Western Europe and Germany lies the whole territory whose destiny depends on that security policy, and hence on the two superpowers: a territory whose "identity" is defined negatively and cannot be properly understood in national, political, or cultural terms.

In other words, the debate on the dependency of the Federal Republic of Germany and of Western Europe has brought to light the power relationship between a periphery defined precisely by that dependence and the two superpowers who, in the name of a policy of security, assure their hegemony on this territory and subordinate the fate of the entire planet to that end. Thus, a situation specific to Germany serves to illustrate the dependency relationship that traverses, in reality, the two blocs. It is the opposition between the two superpowers and the whole periphery, both transnational and transbloc, which is, de facto, submitted to their military hegemony. Defined solely by that dependency, this periphery can acquire an identity and capacity for emancipation only on the basis of a new solidarity that transcends not only political frontiers and national and cultural differences, but also the division of the planet into three worlds.

Dependency and emancipation: the political limites of the German debate

The very real opening up of a new arena of conflict (both transnational and global) and the appeal for an indispensable new solidarity nonetheless cannot easily be translated into a practical stance within the ongoing political debate in West Germany. While these seem to refer to positions within an ethical debate, they indicate first and foremost the limits of the German political debate and the ineluctable ambiguity of any search for concrete alternative solutions or immediately realizable political goals. Since dependency cannot be overcome solely within Germany, any autonomous effort presupposes either a commitment to and a capacity for identical action within the Soviet empire (an impossibility given its totalitarian nature) or a commitment to and capacity for action at the very center (where those security orientations, upon which Germany is dependent, are elaborated). Hence the debate on security policy which is taking place in the United States is of crucial importance. It is here that the choices and goals can be challenged.

This situation creates the real limits for the political debate and the ambiguous content of the alternatives put forward within West Germany. Dominated as they are by (a perfectly legitimate) resentment of Germany's dependence in the realm of security, all the alternatives put forward attempt to increase the autonomy of different territories, whether defined in political (the Federal Republic), national (Germany), or regional (Central Europe) terms. On their own these proposals, such as a reinforcement of *Ostpolitik*, a denuclearization of Central Europe, or even unilateral acts, cannot be achieved. Rather than helping to overcome the system of two blocs and the dependence of every nation on one or the other superpower, these proposals would serve only to increase the relative autonomy of West Germany, at the price of either turning inward or becoming "finlandized"—either of which would be highly dangerous and politically unthinkable.

However, if such a trend (more a turning inward than "finlandization") can be discerned in the German debate, it is neither strong nor the product of a conscious submission to the USSR. Rather, it can be explained by the situation of dependency to which the Federal Republic has involuntarily fallen victim. The search for specific German solutions, more symbolic than actual, expresses a desire for emancipation that takes into account the dual constraints on the German policy: on the one hand, the totalitarian nature of the Soviet bloc, and on the other, its dependence on US security.

From challenging the ends toward conflict

The internal US debate has questioned both the general consequences and the particular thrust of US security policy. This debate began with the strategic controversy and was broadened to include both foreign and domestic policy. What started as a challenge to the strategic rationality of US policy became a challenge to its political, economic, and social rationality. In contrast to the German case that highlighted the opposition between the military hegemony of the two superpowers, and the vital interests of that transnational territory dependent upon it, the basic opposition in the US case arose between that same goal and the security of the US people as well as between that goal and the socio-economic interests of the nation.

From an external perspective, the policy of security is criticized as dangerous because it aggravates conflicts and military tensions around the world. Moreover, because nuclear weapons are uncontrollable and are operative in a period when they have become "banalized," they might degenerate into a generalized nuclear confrontation. Accordingly, this essentially military foreign policy is called into question for its inability to preserve the position of the United States in the world and for protecting its positive image. Finally, these criticisms question the very goal of the security policy of the two superpowers, whose result has been a heightening of tension and the multiplication of military conflicts in the Third World. The Third World appears to have been increasingly transformed into two spheres of military influence where the superpowers, via proxies, confront one another. Thus, they can be held accountable both for the deaths by war and famine in the Third World and for the increasing risk of an eventual nuclear confrontation between the First and Second Worlds.

Domestically, US security policy is criticized for its detrimental impact on the social, economic, and financial realms. The unprecedented increase in military outlays (at the expense of social programs) has been denounced for contributing to the massive poverty in the world's richest nation. Budgetary favors for the military sector are attacked for their deleterious social, economic, and financial consequences.[21] Hence, the specific orientation of US security policy has been challenged for subordinating civilian interests and ends to strictly state and military ones.

By assigning priority to reinforcing US military hegemony abroad, this policy in effect strengthens the power of its domestic engineers, i.e. the military–industrial networks.[22] This assures their monopoly and control over the choices and decisions behind US security policy—a policy that in fact compromises both the security and well-being of the US population. As the internal consequences and means of this security policy have been so contested, it becomes more evident that this policy is the result of specific choices and options that serve a particular goal and societal group.

The stakes: the model of security

While the German debate is dominated by an external opposition to the two superpowers, in the United States the conflict is internal between a military and a civilian orientation of security policy. This opposition is always very pragmatic and is accompanied by alternative ways of dealing with the same problem of security, although the attempt is made to handle it in a more effective, rational, and responsible manner. Notwithstanding their diverse content, these counter-proposals always advocate a reversal of current policies as the pre-condition for implementing a more rational and responsible security policy.

In this way the US debate transcends specific US interests. The reversal of civilian and military priorities in US security policy means a call for a new orientation that could only be demanded of Germany. This would entail a US security policy that, rather than reinforcing the balance of military forces in the world, would replace them with a balance of civilian forces—with the aim of not only assuring the security of civilians but also the capacity of civil society to regain control over its future.

The debate brings out the conflict between two courses of action, two ways of dealing with the problem of security, which differ in their means and are opposed in their aims. The military–state problem-solving process serves, in fact, to maintain the balance of military forces in the world and to reinforce the power of nation-states in and on the world. In contrast, the civilian-oriented problem-solving process promotes the security of civil societies in the world and their capacity to control their destiny everywhere in the world.

Toward a transnational movement of civil emancipation

By calling for a "civilized" model of security and by making it the indispensable condition for any collective mastery of the present and of the freedom of the future, the political debate connects with the ethical debate. It is no longer a matter of saying that we must "do"—but rather to *do it in a different way:* to develop a new model, a new praxis which deals with the problem of security in the world in a new way which transforms the military–state relations between nations into civilian relations between people who live in different parts of the planet.

A new ethic of civilian responsibility

The political debate, which allows the movement to work out its orientations, practices, field, and problematic, has in no way deprived this protest of its moral fervor. Rather, it is through this work that the moral refusal (of weapons and of a dangerous, diabolical, and profoundly immoral world) and the appeal to basic values (such as life, children, the species, or the human persona) is transformed into a new ethic of civil responsibility. This new ethic is not simply grounded in a refusal of nuclear weapons and is no longer oriented toward the past; instead, it prepares the future and to the ability of peoples and individuals to assume complete responsibility for their destiny and for those of the others here and now. More than just saying "No" to the arms race, it is the ability to tackle directly and in a new way the whole problem of security in the contemporary world.

This ethic of civil responsibility provides the linkage between three problems and three worlds, between the arms race, famine, and the absence of freedoms—all of which result from the dominant problem-solving process in the security field. Hence the imperative to acquire the capacity to invent and to apply a new civilian model of security, which is the only way to achieve collective mastery over the present, to assume the responsibility for the management of the future, and to open up the range of choices in the three worlds.

Moreover, this new peace movement affirms that where the stakes involve the other two "worlds," the responsibility lies entirely in the First World and belongs to all those who are privileged enough to live in it. The West has the capacity to undertake initiatives around the globe; it possesses that unique good not found anywhere else: freedom of action. In other words, out of this ethic of civil responsibility emerges the figure of a transformational movement of civil emancipation. Acting in the name of a new civil solidarity, both transnational and global, this movement can take the responsibility for inventing and applying practices that challenge the military–state problem-solving process and which undermine the dominance of the state and military powers in the world today.[23]

A new praxis of transnational civil emancipation

In contrast to earlier protests characterized mainly by mass demonstrations, the new protest is today dominated by a multitude of actions, called civil disobedience in Germany, noncooperation or radical nonviolence in the United States. Whatever the label, this is a new autonomous social praxis that converts an ethic of civil responsibility into actions that are both responsible and autonomous, radical and nonviolent. By combining the symbolic and the efficacious, noncooperation and empowerment, expressiveness and instrumentality, this new autonomous praxis permits us to define a movement identified not by its content but solely by its values, its orientation, and its way of action. The praxis of the ethic of civil responsibility has been directly transformed into a praxis of civil emancipation.

Unlike nonviolent utopias, this new praxis of civil responsibility has been translated into actions that tackle concretely the problems of the Third World, and especially, the issue of freedom in the Second World. This connection develops at the level of praxis through actions carried out in support of, and in cooperation with, "pacifists," Solidarity supporters, and dissidents in the Eastern bloc.

If the movement, as in Germany, is limited in the ways it can politically respond to the question of how peace, freedom, and famine are connected, it relates these issues, nonetheless, at the level of practice. In fact, the German peace movement is fighting for the same self-determination which is at stake, admittedly in different circumstances, for Solidarity in Poland. Both are creating an emancipatory process which combines noncooperation and civil disobedience, resistance and empowerment. This process, we have argued, seeks to retrieve the capacity of civil society to control its future: either through trade union liberties (Poland) or security (Germany).

In the United States, the ethic of civil responsibility has been translated into an analogous practice, although in a less dramatic way. The United States is recognized as responsible for the dominating problem-solving process and for this statist–military model of security. It must therefore be held responsible for transforming and "civilizing" it. In other words, while in West Germany this ethic translates into a praxis that is above all one of protest, in the United States it is dominated by the articulation of civilian, nonviolent alternatives.

Civilizing the model of security: civilizing transnational relations

In Germany the question of security, liberty, and famine are linked on the basis of a new solidarity common to all dependent people, which is translated into a praxis of civil emancipation. In contrast, in the United States, these problems have led to the search for new ways of dealing with the problem of security, the invention of a new model based not on power and hostility, but on interdependence, and on a new way of constituting transnational relations. Three elements inform this new model of security: the security of one is the security of all; the primacy of civilian and nonviolent resolution of conflict; and the centrality of the reduction of the causes of tensions around the world through the emancipation of civil spaces around the world. Together these three pillars delineate a new way of dealing with planetary problems whereby the civilian, nonviolent resolution of conflicts is intrinsically linked to a policy of development that would guarantee the means necessary for the autonomous development of the Third World and would intensify cultural, economic, scientific, and technical relations with the Second World, in order to promote autonomy of both the South and the East.

What is at stake is more than replacing military means with civilian ones; it aims at the civilizing of transnational relations through the emancipation of civil spaces. The development of these civil spaces is the only means of reducing tensions among nations and of loosening the grip of the statist–military powers of some nations. Only the autonomous development of the Third World can open up the closed space that the planet has become as a result of the security policy pursued by the two superpowers (which, in turn, guarantees their power and precludes other spheres of influence). Reducing tension in the world and promoting autonomous development would limit the military hold of the two superpowers over the globe and the power of generals in the Third World. Similarly, only renewed civil relations with the East could mitigate the external power of the Soviet military–statist establishment, since autonomous relations with non-Soviet nations increases the autonomy of civil society within the Soviet sphere.

Will this effort to civilize transnational relations through a transnational movement of civil emancipation which practices an ethic of responsibility and transnational solidarity be able to transform effectively the statist–military world while addressing the problems of peace, freedom, and famine? The answer is far from clear. Yet this movement has at least brought this challenge to light and has made manifest our responsibility to meet it.

Notes and references

1. The NATO double decision relative to the deployment of intermediate range nuclear missiles in Europe dates to 1979, at which time it provoked no real mass response. The installation of the missiles was scheduled to take place in late 1983.
2. The first interpretation dominated the press during the 1981–1982 period. Subsequently, the second view began to prevail when it became increasingly evident that the communist parties played a relatively minor role in the protest movement.
3. I have discussed the French debate in "Vague pacifiste ou renouveau democratique," PASSE-PRESENT No. 3 (1984).
4. Here it is important to note the new and important role played by medical doctors especially Randall Forsberg and the Physicians for Social Responsibility in launching the "freeze" campaign.
5. The term "active minority" is employed here in the sense given it by Serge Mascovici in his *Social Influence and Social Change* (London: Academic Press, 1976).
6. For example, "Peace in Search of Makers" was the title of a colloquium organized by Riverside Church in New York City, 4–5 December 1978, on the subject of reversing the arms race. See Jane Rockman, ed. *Peace in Search of Makers* (New York: Riverside Church "Reverse the Arms Race Convocation," 1979).
7. See for example the many declarations issued by the Reagan administration in 1980–1982 to this effect.
8. For a re-examination of these movements and their results, see Zsuzsa Hegedus, *Il presente e l'avvenire: Nuove pratiche e nuova rappresentazione sociale* (Milan: Franco Angeli, 1985); and

"Riflessioni sulla natura e sulle condizioni di articolazione di un nuovo spazio sociale," in *Le imperfette utope* (Milan: Franco Angeli, 1984).

9. If at the beginning this protest most usually took the form of mass demonstrations, these were soon followed by referenda, the spread of which is of paramount importance.

10. The movements of the 1950s tended to follow the first pattern, while the "test ban" movement of the 1960s resembled the second.

11. On this subject see Sally Zuckerman, *Nuclear Illusion and Reality* (New York: Vintage Books, 1982); and Daniel Ford, Henry Kendall, and Steven Nadies, *Beyond the Freeze* (Boston: Beacon Press, 1982).

12. This was the call issued by actor Paul Newman in the highly successful film "War Without Winners" produced by the Center for Defense Information.

13. Opinion polls show that in Germany over 60% of the population oppose the deployment of the Pershing II. In the United States, referenda on the "freeze" held in a number of states during the 1982 mid-term elections showed that 50% of the population favored a freeze on nuclear arsenals. The referendum organized by the movement in Germany to coincide with the European elections registered 80% as opposed to the installation of the Pershing II (i.e., among those 60% of the electorate that voted).

14. That this issue did not prove to be central to the presidential campaign cannot be taken as proof of its exhaustion. In my opinion, this can be explained, on the one hand, by the importance of economic issues, and, on the other, the failure of the Democratic Party candidates (with the exception of Jesse Jackson) to advocate a reversal rather than a mere "freeze" of the arms race. The latter became in the discourse of the various candidates somewhat akin to "Mom and apple pie," i.e., devoid of any content (as had been predicted by Randall Forsberg).

15. Beginning in 1981, referenda on the "freeze" were organized in most states. In 1983, referenda on the Pershing II were linked with demands for popular consultation ("Pershing Nein, Volksbefragung Ja!"). The latter, organized through the initiative of Peace Coordination, was to coincide with the June 1984 European elections.

16. This question, while of greatest importance, cannot be dealt with here. I take it up in my book on the peace movement, and it is the central issue in a forthcoming book on social movements and their activists. See note 8.

17. The Greens experienced this autonomy in the recent Saarland elections. The "pacifist" vote, supposedly controlled by the Greens, went instead to Oskar Lafontaine, a Social Democrat, who could deal with the German debate in all its diversity. His success points out, in addition, the major inroads this debate, stimulated through protest, has made within the SPD.

18. Hegedus, *Il presente e l'avvenire*, note 8.

19. Alain Touraine, *Production de la societe* (Paris: Seuil, 1973).

20. Robert McNamara, "The Military Role of Nuclear Weapons: Perceptions and Misperceptions," *Foreign Affairs* Vol. 61, No. 1 (Fall 1983), pp. 59–80.

21. Such criticisms, emanating from unions and business executives alike, undermine the myth that military investments contribute to economic recovery and the creation of jobs.

22. John Kenneth Galbraith, *The Voice of the Poor* (Cambridge: Harvard University Press, 1983). Also, Richard Falk, *Nuclear Weapons and the Future of Democracy* (Totowa, New Jersey: Rowan and Allenheld, 1986).

23. The formidable and unexpected proliferation of popular initiatives in support of Africa and the alleviation of famine show that this new ethic of civil responsibility and transnational solidarity has transcended this particular movement and has made major inroads into civil society. Their actions reject any connotation of charity. Instead, they claim to act out of an obligation and responsibility, and they call for a new transnational and global solidarity, e.g. "We are the world."

New Understandings of Development

Building Utopias in History

ELISE BOULDING

Historical overview

The human capacity to visualize *The Other* as different and better than the experienced present is found in archetypal form in all civilizational traditions through visions of the Elysian Fields, the Isles of the Blessed, Zion, Valhalla, Paradise. However, these visions are more ancient than civilizational. Anthropologists report that blessed isles are part of the dream-world of tribal peoples. Nor are they confined to the West. Utopian elements are found in Taoism, Theravada Buddhism, medieval Islam, and in Chinese, Japanese and Indian stories about imaginary havens of delight (Manuel, 1979, p. 1).

Under the pressure of social upheaval, the archetypal vision is transformed into concrete imagery that answers to specific social needs and dissatisfactions. Thus Plato's *Republic* was a response to the upheavals of the Peloponnesian Wars. The hundreds of desert communes established by Christian men and women in Egypt and Syria in the first few centuries of the Christian era were a response to the corruption of urban life in Imperial Rome, an affirmation of an alternative human potentiality that has continued as a viable monastic tradition for 2000 years. The millenialist crusades and utopian communities that erupted by the hundreds in the Middle Ages were a series of responses to plague, famine and the gradual breakdown of the feudal order.

It is ironic then that utopia ("no place," as Thomas More named his pattern-setting *Utopia* in 1516) has come to be synonymous with a flight from reality. All the great utopians have been masterful critics of their own time. Utopians have many forms and functions, but one enduring function is to satirize society as it exists; another is to describe a more desirable way of organizing human affairs. One key problem of utopia-writing is that all utopias have implicit political goals, but few utopianists are able to devise political strategies to achieve their utopia which do not destroy these very goals. Historically, the theoreticians of utopia and the practitioners have not been the same people, and when they have, the results have been disastrous. On the other hand, the theoreticians have to be in touch with the currents of

Commissioned by the Committee for a Just World Peace for presentation at its Royaumont Conference, December 1985. First published in a revised form in *Alternatives* XI:3. Research for this essay was supported by the North American program of the Peace and Global Transformation Project of the United Nations University.

the times in very special ways. The evidence for this, as Manuel (1979) points out, is that "virtually every one of the major slogans that expressed the hopes of French and English working-class movements of the first half of the nineteenth century was plucked from the gardens of the printed works of utopian writers" (p. 10).

Although utopianism is found in all cultural traditions, its modern equivalent has a very Western flavor. Since it is modern utopianism, beginning in the sixteenth century, which is our focus here, we will have to pay particular attention to the differential experience of utopianism between Euro–North America and the rest of the world.

The particular set of upheavals which ushered in modernism originated in Europe and provided the ingredients for the great utopias of the past three centuries, including: (1) the voyages of discovery, which brought news of many different lifestyles and cultures and produced a rash of literary island utopias; (2) a rapid rate of scientific discovery and technological invention, which gave a new sense of control over the environment to human beings; (3) urbanization and industrialization, which introduced the concept of class interests for new social groupings—industrial workers, and the bourgeoisie; and (4) the rise of the modern nation state and the military expansion of the industrial order through colonization. All four of these factors contributed to the sense of social progress and control over the future. The four major ideologies of socialism, marxism, liberalism and anarchism, which developed in different contexts within different social formations, all worked to realize their respective utopias.

However, the path of utopianism has not been smooth. Utopia became an increasingly bad word during the world revolutionary movements of the mid-nineteenth century. Marx himself was a relentless anti-utopianist. Even Toynbee saw utopian thinking as a symptom of a descending stage of the civilization cycle. It was not until Mannheim published *Ideology and Utopia* (1929, English translation 1936) with its conceptual clarification of the function of utopian thinking as a response to pressing social problems, and its typology of kinds of utopian thinking from chiliastic to socialist-communist, that the concept was restored to respectability. Nevertheless, the Mannheimian discussion was a very western-oriented one. The Third World in the meantime was experiencing the upheavals of modernism very differently. For the Third World, the voyages of discovery led to conquest and colonization; science and technology came with no context, and was seen as magic; urbanization and industrialization meant the destruction of traditional patterns of landholding and agricultural production and the replacement of village self-sufficiency with landless urban poverty. National liberation movements alternated between a feeling of empowerment—that they could shape the future—and a feeling of helplessness and dependency in the face of alien political and economic forces they could not control and technologies they could not understand. In short, utopianism has had very different contexts and dynamics in Euro–North America and the rest of the world. The dominant Eurocentric concepts about utopianism are not easily applied to the Third World, where most of the utopian practices of the past century have taken place.

Concepts and issues

The rage for order and the longing for nature

Two key aspects of utopian thought that are continually at war with one another are the rage for order and the longing for what is "natural." The rage for order is the powerful drive to impose rational, efficient, just and peaceful behavioral protocols and structures on irrational, inefficient, untidy and impulsively aggressive human beings. Science and technology offer the tools for creating this rational and peaceful order. Boguslaw (1965) points out in his *New Utopians* that automation systems are designed to reduce as far as possible the number of responses that humans can make (i.e., reduce human error) while increasing as far as possible the number of responses the machine makes (the machine being immune (!) to error). Behavioral modification provides the same effect with the use of psychological tools. Nowotny (Mendelsohn and Nowotny, 1984), in a grim assessment of science and utopia, speaks of the overloading of utopian thought with a "surplus of order" in order to keep the incoherence of actual societies at bay.

Society as a perfectly functioning mechanism is an attractive idea. Planning becomes the central function of such a society. Everything becomes do-able. Authoritarianism and military organization slip in easily. Fourier's phalanx system (Fourier, 1876) is a good example of this type of utopia—a completely formalist design that provides for everything that can happen in the society. And that is what Huxley's *Brave New World* and Orwell's *1984* were written to denounce.

Clashing with the rage for order is the longing for the spontaneous untidy abundance of nature. This organic approach sees nature as evolving in its own way, a way with which humans can beneficially cooperate. A transformation is taking place, and a new consciousness is needed on the part of humans to recognize the transformation and work with it. The millennialist Joachim de Fiore (see Manuel, 1979: pp. 56–59) wrote in the thirteenth century about that transformation. He declared that the Age of the Holy Spirit had arrived to replace the age of the bureaucratic institutional church. People needed only to follow the paths laid by the spirit to enter into this new age. The Anabaptist tradition which grew from Fiore's teachings is utopian in the best sense of the word. Anabaptists taught egalitarianism, both between classes and between men and women. Working for the ideals of social justice and peace in the post-feudal era, they empowered peasants and workers alike with the tools of literacy and the skills of craft and industry. But their openness to promptings of the spirit left them vulnerable to a charismatic leadership which violated their own intentions. Norman Cohn's *Pursuit of the Millennium* (1957) vividly documents the chiliastic uprisings of peasants and workers in the late Middle Ages in the name of the Holy Spirit—uprisings which turned into nightmares of cruelty and bloodshed as charismatic leaders carried themselves and their followers away in an excess of emotionalism. The 1534 Anabaptist seizure of Muenster under the leadership of John of Leyden which ended in the death of most of its inhabitants illustrates the tragic distortion of a noble vision. Twentieth century charismatics have on the whole remained more peaceable, though transformation of consciousness can still be accompanied by great violence, as in the Jonestown massacre.

The concept of attunement to nature and organically evolving processes has been a continuous tradition, both in religious and secular form, from the time of the Anabaptists. Religiously, we see this in the historic peace churches of the Quakers, Mennonites and Brethren—the direct descendants of the Anabaptists. In the social sciences, we find it in the theories of Herbert Spencer (1884, 1896) about society as an organism, evolving over time from savage tribalism through military order to the highly differentiated peaceable industrial society that Spencer saw as an evolutionary end-product.

Oddly enough, both the mechanistic and the organic models of utopia were based on deep convictions about continuing social progress. The mechanists saw progress as coming through the application of scientific principles to the designing of social structure. The organicists saw progress coming through an awareness of the nature of living systems, including human and social systems, and working with that nature to achieve the good society. Both models were vulnerable to the distortions of authoritarianism and militarism. Spencer's theory of evolution toward a peaceable industrial society depended on a voluntaristic, non-bureaucratic relationship between industry and the state which did not come about. The growth of government machinery, which he feared as an inevitably pathological distortion of organic processes, has instead produced a world military order which is the antithesis of the industrial society he visualized.

But there is a special utopian tradition in the organic mode which stands as a critique of the vulnerability to authoritarianism, and that is the feminist utopian tradition. The feminist tradition is based on a carefully disciplined attunement to the structures and processes of the natural order which enables individual actors and social groups to work with the potentials in any organic entity without doing violence to those potentials. The shaping of the individual and the social order according to such principles is seen as a task demanding the utmost effort, both intellectual and intuitive. Charlotte Perkins Gilman's *Herland* (1979) exemplifies this approach to social evolution, as do the novels of Ursula LeGuin. On the scientific side, the work of Barbara McClintock (in Fox, 1983) demonstrates the kind of breakthroughs in understanding possible when this kind of disciplined attunement, drawing equally on the intellectual and the intuitive, is practised in scientific research on living systems.

Both the mechanistic and the organic models suffer from the deep ambivalence represented by the metaphor of the machine in the garden, a recurring motif in western writing, particularly American. Part of the ambivalence stems from the double perception of America as the new Eden, the garden of the New World where life is to be shaped anew and America as the pioneer in the application of science and technology to the good life. Washington Irving's description of edenic Sleepy Hollow, a quiet pastoral place suddenly invaded by the thundering roar of a nearby passing train, is symbolic of the sense of invasion which machines bring with mobility, productivity, and progress. The doubts about the machine are clear already in the writings of Carlyle, who called attention to the dangers of reliance on mechanisms for the development of the inner life (Leo Marx, 1964). Karl Marx's concept of alienation also reflects this ambivalence, though no one relied more heavily than he on the machine to further human progress. The suddenness of the entry of the machine into the garden heightens the trauma. Industrialization is sometimes thought of as a slow gradual experience in the West, and only sudden in the context of the Third World; but in fact the machine by its very nature erupted with explosive sudden force, whether in the textile mills of Britain or New England, or the trackless prairies of the United States.

In the United States, Emerson, Thoreau, Mark Twain and Henry Adams all wrestled with the problem. At the very beginning of the Gilded Age in the 1870s, a group of American writer-activists attempted to develop populist political movements that would preserve the human scale and community values in the face of the machine's onslaught. Henry George, Henry Lloyd and Edward Bellamy were three such writer-activists (see Thomas, 1983). Their evangelical zeal petered out with the decline of populism, but the country-life movement, the community planning and garden city movements of this century, along with the more recent bioregionalism, continue to deal with the problem of the machine in the garden.

In Europe the same movements exist, although with less intensity. Europe, after all, has experienced urban population densities for a long time, and the factory predated industrialism. The romantic tradition from Rousseau to Ruskin, and the village utopia novels of nineteenth century England by authors such as Morris and Hudson, kept the issue of how to deal with the machine alive. The back to the land movement in Europe, however, took a different form than in the United States—back to the land meant emigration, colonizing other people's land on other continents. The same movement that brought emigrating Europeans closer to the land deprived many native peoples of their land through the process of colonization. Most of the migrations were personal ones to better individual circumstances. Some, however, were purposeful in the utopian sense. Best known are those that migrated for reasons of religious persecutionand who established a series of religious utopian settlements in North and South America. Similarly, a smaller group of social utopianists, such as the Owenites set up new communities in the United States. In each case these ventures were seen as contributing to the reconstruction of society by setting up working models, but their efforts were confined to the microlevel. They will be further discussed below in the section on microlevel utopias.

The important thing to bear in mind in considering the conflict between the rage for order, which relies heavily on science and technology to create that order, and the longing for the "natural," the organic connectedness with nature, is that the two impulses usually coexist in each camp. The failure of utopias, insofar as they can be said to have failed, lie to a considerable degree in their inability to resolve this particular set of dilemmas.

The role of violence in revolutionary change

Because utopia is always *The Other*—something totally different from existing society, a radical restructuring of the existing order—the changes implied by utopia are in effect revolutionary whether based on a commitment to gradual evolutionary change or sudden restructuring. This is why revolutionary violence keeps appearing in many utopian efforts, even when there is a commitment to peaceableness as with the Anabaptists. If the goal is a total restructuring of how humans live, whether on the micro or macrolevel, then the destruction of existing arrangements, including the physical destruction of the human beings who maintain it, may come to be seen as a necessary wiping clean of the slate. In *The Magic Mountain*, Naphta sees the utopianism of Settembrini, "the man of progress, liberalism and middle-class revolution" as monstrous, and declares that "the task of the proletariat is to strike terror into the world for the healing of the world, that man may finally achieve salvation and deliverance and win back freedom from law and from distinction of classes" (in Lasky, 1976, p. 626). It was Napoleon who said there could be no revolution without terror, a theme re-echoed in revolutionary change.

Violence has been particularly important in certain Third World settings. Frantz Fanon, speaking of the process of liberation in Algeria, writes that "for the native, life can only spring up again out of the rotting corpse of the settler." And again, " . . . violence is a cleansing force. It frees the native from his inferiority complex and from his despair and inaction; it makes him fearless and restores his self-respect." (Fanon, 1963, pp. 93, 94). In the West, the very size of the challenge posed by the abstract globalism of a revolutionary commitment to free all humans everywhere would seem to necessitate violence to prepare the ground for change. During the crisis, when the time is ripe, anything goes. There is time enough later for the gentler human virtues to reassert themselves. This argument operates as strongly for religious as for secular revolutionary change. A distillation of this reasoning is found in the *Reformatio Sigismundi* (in Lasky, 1976, p. 626) on the eve of the Reformation. The argument goes: The final crisis is now; this is a time for anger; our cause is just so we must succeed; refuse to bow to present authorities, and listen to the prophetic revelation that gives us a mandate for action (cite favorite scriptural reference here). It is a call to holy war, and there have been many such calls to war in all religious traditions.

It is an oversimplification to say that the resort to violence has been the operative cause of utopian failures, since nonviolent utopias also fail. The same problems of human learning beset both types of utopia. It is true however that the visibility of revolutionary violence, and the pride and fear it engenders, affects deeply our assessment of radical change, and indeed the assessment of utopias in general. With rising tides of violence in industrial countries (to say nothing of the Third World), there is a loss of faith today in the capacity for peaceful change. Cotta (1985, p. 1) writes that "violence hides in the antinomies of our very ways of life, which are lawless and mass-dominated, intellectualized and emotive, artificial and natural, torn apart between the pressing urge (often brought about artificially) for productive activism and a spreading desire for amusement and happiness." In short, generalized violence endangers the utopian commitment.

The centralization–decentralization debate

The centralization–decentralization debate mirrors the mechanistic organicist debate. Shall the new order be centrally designed by those with competence and skill, and imposed on people who could not in their present state of being achieve this way of life unaided, thus helping them in spite of themselves? Or shall the seeds of the new order be planted wherever the fertile soil of existing structures can be found at the local level, thus allowing the old to be gradually transformed into the new? Again, both positions are held within each camp, frequently even by the same person. Marx, who identified historical conditions necessary for the emergence of socialism, had nothing but contempt for the tinkering of his fellow socialists, which he saw as standing in the way of unfolding historical processes. It was the identification of these processes that rendered his socialism scientific, in contrast to "utopian" (read unscientific, unrealistic) socialism. Did this lead Marx to study existing associational structures available to peasants and villagers at the local level which might participate in that emergence? No, both Marx and Lenin consciously avoided using local structures, relying on a theoretically based social design, and on the manipulation of economic and political variables without regard to local structures, to achieve the changes they sought. In their view, local structures could only safely be used *after* revolutionary reconstruction had taken place. This refusal to work from the beginning with the social materials at hand was certainly one of the failures of Soviet communism. We will see in the next section how differently various revolutionary utopian efforts dealt with pre-existing traditional structures.

Buber (1958) takes the position that no revolution can succeed unless it has already happened, that the taking of power by a new group can only be the formal legitimation of a process that has already taken place. He focuses on the pre-existing traditional structures in every case, and shows how the richness of those associational structures determines the capacity of a society to engage in participatory change that is responsive to local situations and local needs while fitting into a larger societal picture. The panchayat, kolkhoz, ejido, ujamaa, tauhid, shramadana and many other traditional village associational forms are all potentially revolutionary change agents when brought into full participation. Kropotkin emphasized the importance of the fluidity and spontaneity which localism makes possible. As we will see, the centralist-localist dialectic is important in all macrolevel utopian experiments.

The development of the new human for the new society: the restructuring vs. the re-education debate

The last major issue to be dealt with here is the formation of the new human being who is to function in the new society. Again we see the now familiar division between the mechanists and the organicists. The mechanists place their faith in structural redesign to create the new type of human being. When oppressive conditions are removed, and humanly facilitative conditions created, individuals will automatically engage in constructive and desirable behavior. Essentially, this theory presupposes the "innate" goodness of humans. The organicists take the position that humans have to evolve along with the society. If they belong to the automatic transformation school, nothing has to be done to facilitate individual transformations. Some organicists, however, see re-education as an important part of the evolutionary process, involving spiritual, intellectual and emotional development. Generally, it is the religious utopianists who take seriously the re-formation of the individual. Their attention to this process has clearly paid off in the longevity of many religious utopias.

The educational experiments of many secular utopianists have not been successful. One could argue that this is because of an inadequate understanding of the human learning process. Even the behavioral modification techniques of the Walden II experiment in Twin Oaks (Kinkade, 1972) do not seem very successful, although in part this is because of hesitation in applying them. Squabbling and greed destroy most "organic" utopias. The restructured societies on the mechanistic model are notorious for failing to produce the desired behaviors, even though educational systems are in theory included in their design. Political power struggles swamp altruistic behavior every time. The significance of human functioning for both types of utopia is matched only by the inability of any model to produce people who can function effectively in it.

How utopianists have dealt with their conceptual dilemmas

As we look in turn at macrolevel and microlevel utopian efforts to design and implement utopias, we will see how differently various experimental groups have dealt with the tension between the rage for order and the longing for the spontaneity of organic processes; between the desire for central control, and the recognition that locality has its own competence; between the desire to destroy all traces of oppressive structures and wipe the slate clean before beginning anew, and the impulse to nurture the seeds of the new within the shell of the old, trusting that gentleness, not violence, will free the goodness in humans; and finally the tension between structural redesign and trying to produce new kinds of human beings to achieve the new society. We will see that macrolevel utopias have generally placed less faith in organic local processes, but where they have, they have been more successful. The microlevel utopias, favoring the organic, have tended to fail on the order side. But neither group has been able to confine itself to one set of strategies or the other, and what we will be observing in the descriptions that follow is a variety of strategic mixes. Because the emphasis in this paper is on utopian solutions in the real world, theory and action are more closely linked in what follows than is normally found in writing on utopias. Utopias which never reached the praxis stage, of which there are legion, are not discussed.

Macrolevel utopian experiments

In this section, we will look at society-wide efforts to institute revolutionary utopias. By their nature, they have a political component that micro-utopias do not, since they are working at the level of the nation state. This both reduces their degree of freedom to experiment, and makes them more answerable to the public eye. The failure of a local utopian commune is not considered a major event, but the nation state utopian experiment is watched like a hawk by the rest of the world. There is a stong desire on the part of most observers to cry "Failed!" when the experiment runs into trouble. But surely no macrolevel experiment should be pronounced an irrevocable failure as long as it is continuing to develop, modify and change its mode of operation. The word experiment itself is crucial here; indeed every political leader in a socialist utopian state emphasizes the experimental nature of the venture.

An important point to keep in mind is the statement made by both Marx and Lenin that no one can really know what a fully socialist society will look like. Buber calls this an irresponsible refusal to fantasize, to explore future directions in the mental experiments so strongly recommended by Weber, but that refusal can also be seen as reflecting an openness to what the future may bring. Not one of the socialist utopian experiments to be reviewed here is a completely closed system. Not only can outsiders learn from the experiment, but clearly those inside the society are also learning, no matter how slowly and imperfectly.

The Soviet experiment

Marx himself would have been horrified to have the Russian socialist experiment called utopian. However, by our broad definition, which includes both designed and evolved utopias with varying degrees of historical readiness for the experiment, the Russian experiment is utopian. Marxist theory gives a lot of attention to the economic and political forces that will have to be controlled in order to construct a socialist state. The early Soviet leaders tried to compensate for the fact that Russia did not have a sufficiently well developed industrial proletariat for revolutionary purposes. The irony is that, by Buber's standards, many of the preconditions for social revolution were there. A number of autonomous local soviets had been formed, partially built on the village kolkhoz model, partially by urban workingmen's associations. Crucial village-urban alliances had been made. But the problem was that these local associations had their own ideas, which did not match the ideas of Lenin and his planners. *Lenin's Last Struggle* by Moshe Lewin (1968) documents how the overwhelming scale of the problems which faced Lenin at the close of World War I—feeding a famine-stricken nation, organizing production and distribution of energy and goods—repeatedly drove him into the arms of hardened army professionals and bureaucrats from czarist times who were least likely to implement revolutionary goals. At the same time, he turned away from all the local revolutionary associations already committed to socialist goals because they were too spontaneous, too untidy, and could not be dealt with in the time he felt he had available. Too late he realized that he had made the wrong alliances, and his final months were a tragedy of realized failures. He had created a monstrous new bureaucracy, and he was helpless to modify or control it.

The Stalin era consolidated all the worst features of the new state, in which the term Soviet had become a parody of itself, a controlled mouthpiece instead of an autonomous entity. Yet the utopian ideals of the socialist society, and the reminder of its ultimate open-ended future in which the state itself will have withered away, have not disappeared from socialist rhetoric. A massive reconstruction of the educational system to give universal education to a hitherto illiterate population may have unforeseen effects in another generation or two. Societal change in large-scale societies has to be seen in terms of generations, not decades. It could be argued that the massive change in bureaucratic structures required to pursue the original intentions of the Russian experiment would require another revolution. What is clear is that the original excitement, which lasted for some decades after the revolution, about being the leading edge of what was to be a world-wide revolution and liberation of oppressed masses everywhere (see for example the Statement of World Communist Leaders in November 1960 (Marshall, 1960)) has now been seriously modified. Yet pride in a society that "cares for everyone" and a sense of contrast with what is perceived to be a set of uncaring capitalist societies, may still provide a dynamic for further growth. Just as the panchayat tradition has survived longterm violent attempts at eradication in India, so the kolkhoz may survive the current Soviet system. All in all, to call a superpower a utopian experiment is a contradiction in terms. It may be more accurately described as a society which is beginning to learn from its mistakes.

The Spanish experiment

The extraordinary anarchist utopian experiment that took place in Spain in the 1930s, documented in vivid if fragmentary ways by Franz Borkenau (1963), is one of the few twentieth century examples of a utopia that definitively failed in the sense of going completely out of existence. Yet it remains one of the most inspiring stories of this century, and affected a whole generation of men and women around the world who fought for the revolution in Spain as members of the International Brigade. What was the utopian experiment for which they were fighting? Because there were so many factions in Spain at the time, many Brigade members had only a confused idea of the social experiment they were trying to help. I will focus here on the CNT, the Confederacion General de Trabajo, the only large-scale anarchist union in the world, because it did in fact establish anarchist political structures in some parts of Catalonia. The Asturian revolt, in which anarchists joined with communists and socialists to maintain a commune comparable to the famous Paris Commune of 1870, is one example, out of many, of the organizational skills of anarchists.

The anarchist tradition of complete local autonomy and total participation in local communes, with the radical abolition of private property, actually worked for short periods of time in urban industrial areas as well as in some rural areas where local autonomous traditions were strong. The reason the anarchist model worked at all, for admittedly short periods of time, was because of the high skill level of anarchist communities. In industrial areas the anarchists were the most skilled workmen in Spain, and could easily run factories more efficiently than their alien bureaucratic managers. In rural areas, similarly, they were excellent farmers, with strong traditions of mutual aid, and could effectively administer resources in common. But as soon as the anarchist groups tried to include people without their skills and training in their political domain, the whole thing fell apart. The lesson in this story is the importance of organizational skills and associational traditions of sharing and consensual decision-making. Whole villages and urban areas had been trained in these skills. Within the confines of their familiar territory, they could handle complex social operations very efficiently. The problem was that there was no basis for translating these skills into cooperative activity with non-anarchists.

The tragedy of the Spanish experiment is that there were too many competing utopias, and not enough cross-cutting traditional structures to enable different trade union and peasant associations to work together. Spain is very different from the rest of Europe in that it had its industrial revolution without a "French Revolution" and therefore never developed strong statist structures. This gives utopian experiments in Spain a different flavor from elsewhere, and makes Spain an important source for alternative approaches to industrialization.

The Cuban experiment

What is not unusual about the Cuban experiment is that the effort to produce an instant socialist reconstruction of Cuban society on the Russian model created the same kind of disasters for Cuba in miniature which the Soviet Union experienced after its revolution. What *is* unusual is that Castro publicly described the disaster and took personal blame for it in his famous July 1970 speech (Lockwood, 1970). He confessed to poor planning, organizational inefficiency and just plain ignorance on the part of the leaders of the actual situation in local communities. The Cuban experiment is of particular interest because Castro seems to understand that the society needs strong local workers' associations in order to function effectively. While there has been some devolution of power to the local level since 1970, Castro's charismatic central role limits that process. This meant that the skills so important and necessary in the anarchist communes of Spain were not given room to develop in Cuba. In short, that important process of forming the new humans to work in the new society is incomplete. Literacy alone, and more equitable resource distribution in comparison to the pre-revolutionary society, is not enough.

The Chinese experiment

Two issues are of particular importance in the Chinese experiment. The first is that the revolution was built on a traditional peasant associational infrastructure, including the age-old peasant secret societies, and adopted the structures that made the Taiping rebellion a significant, if failed, political event. The second is that Mao Tse Tung, the charismatic leader of the revolution, was in touch with that infrastructure. He first walked the length and breadth of China (metaphorically speaking) well before the revolution, becoming familiar with village life. He later led the Long March with a group of loyal followers that turned the tide of the revolution and again provided continuity with the tradition of local involvement. Watching the film of the Long March made to honor Mao's eightieth birthday, one realizes that village involvement in an otherwise remote part of China has bound the mystique of the revolution directly to the people in a way that no other type of activity could. Unlike other revolutionary leaders, Mao was familiar with local conditions in many parts of China, and had confidence in local associational structures (block-by-block neighborhood committees in every city can be seen as a contemporary continuation of those structures).

But what neither Mao nor anyone else in any country had was the organizational know-how to create a manageable administration for a country that encompassed one quarter of the world's population. His experiments, such as the Great Leap Forward, were bold. So were his admissions of failure, though they were not quite as forthright as Castro's. When the burgeoning of unworkable bureaucracies produced the chaos that led to the Cultural Revolution, Mao in one sense got out of the way, in another sense rode with the tide. The consequence was that the continuity of that revolution was thrown into local hands. By western standards, terrible things happened during the Cultural Revolution. Nevertheless, travellers in China will hear not a few stories from intellectuals who were sent to pig farms, providing a moving picture of a new kind of learning experience—a learning about the lot of the poor peasants of their land. The closing of schools, universities and scientific laboratories was disastrous in terms of cutting off precisely those skills most needed to get on with China's further development. Yet the full story of both the Great Leap Forward and the Cultural Revolution has yet to be told. In both there was a major effort to involve people at the local level in their own development.

That these efforts took place in the context of an authoritarian state that reserved for itself the power of life and death over entire populations makes the experiments in localism both puzzling and interesting. The current policy of allowing more private economic initiatives to farmers and urban workers is a further experiment in localism which is difficult to interpret in the light of a fluctuating overall economic policy. One strength of that policy is the effort to develop village industry to maintain a viable rural-urban nexus, and thus prevent the emptying of the countryside into the cities.

The twin Chinese traditions of active peasant secret societies at the local level and the mandarin system—one of the world's oldest imperial bureaucracies—at the national level probably have something to do with the fact that large-scale social experimentation is possible at all in the world's largest country. The groups left out of that equation—the tribal minorities— have not benefited from the experiments, at least not by their own lights, and they may become a serious force to be reckoned with in future developments. However, the spirit of utopian adventure continues to pervade one major element of Chinese society—the huge Chinese Women's Federation. This associative structure has been active from the 1870s on, and is a substantial force since it reaches into every household in China. The Federation to a degree makes up for the deficiencies of the educational system, which falls far short of educating the population to the skill levels needed. It organizes local training and employment opportunities for youth who fall between the cracks in the larger system. If the Chinese utopian experiment succeeds in the long run, it will to a significant degree be due to what Buber would call the associative richness of that society.

Other Third World utopian experiments:
Tanzania, Mexico and Iran

Nyerere's efforts to build a socialist utopia in Tanzania based on the concept of a village economy—the ujamaa—has run into serious problems. This is despite the fact that the principle of building on traditional local structures was apparently followed. The maji-maji, active in the independence movement, have been involved. Nevertheless, many local structures suffered from bureaucratic decision-making at the national level, and there have been persistent and widespread reports of village demoralization. Here is a case of what appears on paper as a very attractive utopian design running into serious economic and political difficulties.

The ejido system of communal land ownership which was revived by the Mexican government in the 1915 land reform represented a utopian experiment that could not survive the competition of traditional landholding interests and urban-based political power. The ejido system is present as a tradition in all Spanish cultures, and has Indian equivalents as well. Periodic efforts to revive it are undertaken by peasant groups in different Latin American countries (Mar in Meynaud, 1963; Infield, 1947), but the associative structures are not strong enough to withstand centralized political opposition.

It is not exactly common to think of the recent Iranian revolution as an experiment in utopia, but in fact by Shiite Moslem standards it is precisely that: an experiment in the construction of an orthodox Islamic republic with the obliteration of church–state distinctions under twentieth century world-economy conditions. There is little doubt that the rich associative structures of local mosque communities with local Imams facilitated the revolution. While western-oriented Iranians have suffered greatly, a large sector of the population, male and female, have adopted the traditional practices of devotion, seclusion of women and the strict ascetic and stewardship practices which *shia* orthodoxy requires. The rewards of establishing a vigorous non-western identity are apparently great enough to outweigh the many sacrifices which this path entails, at least for the present. The utopian aspect of this experiment is that in spite of the fact that the new orthodox regime does not provide the promised economic, social and political wellbeing of its citizens, it creates an environment in which a satisfactory social and spiritual fulfillment is apparently possible for many devout Iranians. While the government appears extremely authoritarian to western eyes, it also has a strong participatory structure for men, and strong family structures for women.

While this venture is so far unique, movements to institute similar orthodox

Islamic republics exist in most Arab countries at present, with varying degrees of political strength. If these developments turn out in fact to be viable adaptive responses to the stresses of westernization, we may see more such experiments.

The Indian refusal of a utopian experiment

If utopian experiments are instructive, so are refusals to experiment. At the time of India's independence from Britain there were several revolutionary nationalist movements which had helped gain that independence and offered local community development models for India to utilize. Gandhi and Sri Aurobindo were the two revolutionary leaders who had the most highly evolved community development models, based on some years of experiment and practice. Both offered educational systems which provided for the holistic development of the individual in terms of intellectual, spiritual and craft skills; both offered small-industry community development which could serve India's economic needs without denying the advantages of modern technology. Both offered experience with the traditional panchayat village councils and their participatory mechanisms. The first parliament was dominated by Congress Party members who had been associated with the Gandhian movement. The first prime minister was Nehru, a Gandhi associate although *not* a disciple. Yet the policy India chose was one of intensive urban-based industrialization. The government rejected a unique indigenous development model in favor of following the Western path. It simply ignored the panchayat system, and Hindu traditional methods of education. Education continued to be based on the British model.

It would be interesting to compare the achievements of China and India in terms of the relative success of their very different choices. China chose the utopian experiment, India chose a highly pragmatic westernization. Yet today India is increasingly seeking to assert its identity as a Third World nation with its own tradition and its own ways of conducting foreign policy. It has become a strong leader in the nonaligned movement. Its decision not to engage in a utopian experiment, even when all the conditions for that experiment were apparently in place, warrants further studying.

Israel: successful utopia?

Martin Buber has called the Israeli experiment, specifically the kibbutzim, one of the world's few successful utopian experiments. In the case of the kibbutzim there can be no doubt that they are a unique invention of the modern era. Complete communal ownership of the means of production and communal arrangements for childrearing and family maintenance have produced a new generation of Israelis who are indeed the "new human beings" and who can function productively in the new society—that usually elusive goal of all utopias. Research indicates that kibbutz-reared youth are more sensitive to group processes and to the needs of those around them, and participate more effectively in group decision-making, than non-kibbutz-reared young people. (They are also reported to make better soldiers.) The experiment at the state level of creating an ingathering of peoples with a common religious heritage who have been spread throughout the globe over the centuries, and constructing a socialist society in which these diverse people can labor productively together is an unusual achievement. The idealism evoked by the concept of Zion, Jehovah's holy mountain where none shall hurt nor destroy, where the lion shall lie down with the lamb and where a little child shall lead them, has to a degree been translated into a workable social order with a strong welfare infrastructure. However, this society has an internal minority to which it denies citizenship—the Arab population, which is native to the land. This refusal to acknowledge the civic status of a sizeable sector of the population makes it impossible to call Israel a successful utopia.

Furthermore, external relations with the region in which Israel is situated could hardly be worse. Often utopias can successfully isolate themselves from the larger world in the short term, but rarely in the long. The degree of attention given to building features into the experiment that allow for development of crosscutting associational structures with Arab populations, both within Israel and with surrounding Arab nations, will determine the longer-run success or failure of the Israeli utopian experiment.

Utopia in Western Europe and North America

While the United States cannot be technically regarded as a utopian experiment, for many, historically, the United States *was* utopia. As indicated earlier, it was seen as the new Garden of Eden. It became the home of many utopian experiments that could not take place in Europe because there was not enough room both physically and socially. If the United States is the home of many utopian experiments at the microlevel, it could be said that Europe has been a prime exporter of such experiments. The United States has always rejected socialism, but its values of individualism have enabled it to give space to socialist, anarchist and religious experiments of every kind. Europe has gone much further with socialism, but few states would conceive of themselves as utopian experiments. Sweden is an exception. The Swedish experiment is comprehensive in terms of providing a welfare state without parallel in Europe. At the state level it has been possible because Sweden has the richest associative structures of any country on the continent. Early in the nineteenth century, it had a country-wide adult education program at the village level, and village debating forums, which would be the envy of any western country today. It was those structures which enabled Sweden to develop the first effective, country-wide participatory population control policy of any country in the world. These local structures continue alive and well as Sweden moves into the twenty-first century.

Microlevel utopian experiments

Microlevel utopian experiments are much easier to initiate than macrolevel ones, since the responsibility of the experimenters is only to a limited group of people operating on a small scale. Microlevel utopias are thought of as a western phenomenon, but in fact there are many village-level utopian experiments in the Third World. They have a special characteristic of reaching into the past to find traditional local structures which can be redeveloped to make a better life at the village level under contemporary conditions. The sarvodaya movement, which builds on the panchayat tradition in India, and incorporates Gandhi's ideas of local development using local resources but is also open to appropriate uses of high technology for local betterment, has now become an international movement with linkages to comparable groups in other Third World countries. In Sri Lanka, the counterpart institution is the shramadana (Macy, 1983) village worksharing with a strong spiritual component. The sarvodaya movement has now become a transnational nongovernmental association, as has the World Council of Indigenous Peoples, with international congresses held in Geneva. These transnational bodies provide support for local experiments and legitimation for nonwestern approaches to community development. Another source of legitimation operating at the international level is Unesco's program for the New International Cultural Order (Shore, 1981) which encourages and funds efforts by Third World governments to identify traditional practices of cultural transmission, education and community decision-making. Long discouraged, these practices, when brought back to life, frequently have the character of a utopian experiment for the people involved. Many of these practices involve women's associations; indeed women have particularly benefited from reaching into the past to find the utopias of the future.

Microlevel utopias in the First World

When Charles Nordhoff (1875) did his survey of *Communistic Societies in the United States* in the early 1870s, he found there were eight societies for the promotion of communes and 72 communes which had developed between 1794 and 1852. The oldest had been in existence 80 years, the youngest 22 years. Some are still in existence 100 years later. Religiously based (or with a doctrine held with religious intensity), they had differing patterns of communal ownership but a similar work ethic, high craft skill level, and good basic schooling for their children. The standard of living was generally higher than that in the immediate neighborhood. Peaceable, with a high standard of morality, and generous in sharing with the local and transient poor, communal lives were so well ordered that Nordhoff found the communes unutterably dull. The culture was very limited, and no one had higher education. But they were all good farmers! Nordhoff pointed out that the commune members seemed to enjoy life, and find pleasure in amusements which looked tame to him.

What do such communes achieve? A demonstration of a more serene and humane way of life, with a higher level of altruism than in the outside world. These utopias do not set out to change the world, only to show that it is possible to live differently in it. Economic forces should not be ignored in considering the founding of this type of commune. Its members are working class people who frequently have a hard time making it alone. More new communes are founded during times of economic depression than at any other time. Many single women who could not find a place in the economy joined these communities and prospered. These religious communities were primarily agrarian. During this same period there were 47 socialist experiments, studied by John Humphrey Noyes (1870), all of which failed in rather short order. Unlike the religious communities, the socialist utopians tried to develop a model which could change the world. Their founders were, as Noyes says, "high-minded, highly cultivated men and women, with sufficient means, one would think, to achieve success" (p. 407). Unlike their religious counterparts, the socialist utopians were rarely skilled farmers. Equally unlike their counterparts, they were highly individualistic. Brook Farm, New Harmony, Nashoba and New Lanark were among the secular failures.

The concept of building a working model which can spread to the larger society continues to be sufficiently compelling to attract new utopian efforts in each generation, based on the style of that generation and the needs of the times. Many utopian ventures started in the depression, reminding us again of the relevance of economic forces. Among the most interesting and least known of these ventures are the 22 cooperative farms organized by the Farm Security Administration that operated between 1937 and 1942, when Congress closed down the project (Infield, 1947). These were cooperative corporation farms established for poor farmers regardless of race. In those where the members psychologically took ownership of the project (some never did), a much higher level of living developed; members took re-education seriously, there was a lot of mutual aid, and substantial economic betterment. When other factors were held constant, these farms were more productive than the average for the state in which they were located. This uncelebrated depression experiment on the part of the US government should be explored further. Similar ventures were undertaken during the depression by the governments of Wales and Australia.

Other depression-generated utopian experiments included the Quaker community of Penncraft in Pennsylvania for unemployed workers; the Delta Farm in Mississippi; the Macedonia Cooperative in Georgia; Saline Valley Farms in Michigan; Celo Community in North Carolina; Koinonia in Georgia, and the Borsodi (1933) back-to-the-land movement. Many of these communities have continued to the present, some with highly diversified activities such as Celo with its school, summer camp, pharmaceutical cooperative, and various craft products. They began out of economic necessity, but have continued as a demonstration of a viable alternative way of life within a capitalist society.

The next generational wave of communes grew out of the conscientious objectors of World War II. They came out of the alternative service camps and prisons determined not to return to the same old society, but to establish their visions of the good society in experimental communities. Some of them joined the communities founded in the depression. Others joined religious communities such as the Bruderhof, which belonged to the older German tradition but, under the stress of wartime conditions, had finally fled to North and South America. Still others founded their own new communities. Like the socialist communities before them these were short-lived, but they provided a transition for the eventual re-entry into mainstream life. What they also provided was a continuing associational structure, deeply embedded in the peace movement, which enabled these conscientious objectors, their wives and eventually their children, to continue sustained peace action over a lifetime. These are people from my own generation, who are in leadership positions in the peace and senior citizen movements everywhere.

The last round of utopian experiments came with the so-called hippie communes in the 60s and 70s. Lacking the social disciplines which the religious and social communitarians were able to establish, most of them disintegrated rapidly. However a few have survived, usually through the persistence of an articulate leader. The Farm, a controversial 1500-person community founded by Stephen Gaskin (1981), carries out many peace and development projects in Central America. These communitarians are poor by middle class standards, but well off compared to the areas in which they work. Secular communes which survive have achieved some minimal degree of work discipline, and a critical mass of altruistic members with some vision of a society for which they are willing to keep working for. This vision includes the abolition not only of militarism, but also war itself, and (frequently) the end of the nation-state system as we now know it. It includes a sense of social justice, a strong environmental ethic, and (usually) a discerning attitude toward science and technology. Most communes are rural because it is easier to live simply and cheaply in such a setting, and not just because of a desire to escape the city. The longer-lived ones all have active urban–rural networks. The misuse of power is a major issue with communitarians. Most of them find that leadership is important, but insist on a highly participatory process, with strong checks against authoritarianism.

None of these communities, whether long- or short-lived, act as powerful social forces in contemporary society. Very few of them do overtly political work, and there seems to be a huge gulf between their very small-scale efforts at human betterment and the state-level utopian designs discussed earlier. Are they therefore insignificant failures? Or are they laboratories functioning as laboratories do: providing a more or less controlled environment for discovery? I would argue the latter. However, studies of micro-utopian experiments tend to focus on human relationships per se, and therefore fail to uncover the connections between the micro and the macro.

Connecting the micro and the macro: the future of utopianism

One context in which the micro–macro linkage of utopian experiments should be seen is the rapid development of transnational nongovernmental organizations in this century. Over 4000 transnational nongovernmental networks bring diverse peoples together through common interests and concerns, and are today a major new set of actors in the international system. Compared to nation states they have few resources and little power. Yet most of the world's intellectual resources and many of its craft and social skill resources are concentrated in these organizations, particularly in the scientific, cultural and social welfare associations. Research on major world problems, such as the threat of nuclear war, environmental deterioration, malnutrition, disease, and climatic change, is done by scientific NGOs with support from the United Nations and largely nongovernmental sources. Governments would be helpless without the policy recommendations NGOs are able to make, based on their research and experience, although the advisory process is nearly invisible to the general public. Most major policy initiatives at the international level of the UN and governments in recent decades have been based on the work of transnational nongovernmental organizations. Many of the most innovative community development projects at the local level are also NGO projects.

Because NGO networks are information networks as well as face-to-face people networks, local utopian ventures today have a very strong probability of being recorded and transmitted over a variety of channels, and eventually of being incorporated into policy recommendations. NGOs represent a new level of associative richness which potentially connects local communities everywhere in ways of which we have not yet dreamed.

Another context for viewing the micro–macro linkage is the new international order. The old order was shaped by less than 50 nations, mostly of the West. The new order is being shaped by the 150 nations who more adequately represent the diversity of human experience on the planet. This has extended the range of social experimentation enormously. It is mostly the new nations, and not the old ones, which have tried state-level utopias. It is mostly the new nations, and not the old ones, which are blending tradition and modernity in their utopian experimentation to soften the abruptness of the changes experienced in this century. Out of the pain and suffering of colonialism and in response to the trauma of finding a machine they didn't understand in a garden they no longer owned, Third Worlders have forged a creative utopian response to the Toynbeean challenge of the West. Third World blends of tradition and modernity deal precisely with those persistent dilemmas discussed earlier: mechanistic versus organic change; centralism versus decentralism; violence versus nonviolence; the redesigned robot versus the reconstructed human being.

The socialist countries play a special role in utopian experiments, since they are neither First nor Third World, but are usually given the separate designation of the Second World. They belong to the West, but their social clocks have run at a different speed. Because they faced the opportunities and traumas of modernization later than the rest of the West, and have not yet experienced the traumas of "overdevelopment," their images of the future are more like those of the Third World than of the First. In a Unesco study undertaken in the early 1960s of images of the future of selected countries (Ornauer et al., 1976), there was noticeably more optimism and a sense that the future was more open-ended in the Second and Third Worlds than in the First. This was before the more recent world food crisis and general realization of the failure of the development models which First World economists had been providing to the Third World. It was also before the significance of the nuclear threat and the extent of world militarization was recognized. Some of the optimism recorded in the 1960s will be gone now.

Does this mean that it is time to declare all utopias of East and West a failure? The question of success or failure of a utopian experiment may not be relevant to our deeper concerns. If, as Kenneth Boulding says, our most significant learnings are from failure, not success, then each utopian experiment is successful to the extent that learning from its failures takes place. Many of the macro-utopias—the Soviet Union, China, Israel, Cuba—might be considered to be in active learning phases right now. Have the micro-utopias lasted long enough for learning to have taken place? Even very short-lived utopias represent thoughtfully chosen responses to upheaval and change, and presumably have enabled the experimenter to move on to other more sustained responses.

The message about the importance of associative richness as the basis for utopia-building on anything beyond the local scale has gotten across to the extent that "networking" is a word almost as common as Coca Cola. The message about the importance of a focus on learning has not had equal promotion. There is still a tendency to believe that designing the situation will produce the desired behaviors. People may denounce Skinnerian philosophy, but they prefer manipulation by design to venturing out on the uncharted seas of human learning.How does anyone learn a really new thing? Since utopias are by definition "new," "not-yet," "other," how will human beings be able to function in them in ways that do not throw us back to the old order if we do not pay more attention to learning? Wishful thinking about the desired transformation of consciousness as an inevitable historical process distracts us from studying the difficult disciplines that will make transformation possible.

The real test of whether we have learned from the failures of past utopias is whether we can develop a theory of utopia-building that solves the problem of scale in human organization in a new way. Weber's theory of bureaucracy carried us from feudalism to industrialism, but it cannot carry us to the post-industrial society. We are paralyzed by the centralist-decentralist dilemma, since efficiency appears to require lines of hierarchical authority, yet the need to match policy to local terrain requires local participation. Buber's theory of associative richness as the basis for effective responses to social change beyond the local level, and the phenomenon of an increasingly dense network of transnational nongovernmental associations on a global scale, suggest new solutions to the old dilemmas. The overall theory has, however, yet to be formulated.

Most writers on utopia focus on only one type. An examination of the whole range of utopian experiments in their highly diverse settings, going beyond the very broad generalizations I have made here in the interest of length, may lead to a more sophisticated theory of utopia-building. Such a theory will have to deal witht he problematic fact that utopia is at once a vision, a way of life, and a tool.

References

Robert Boguslaw, *The New Utopians: A Study of System Design and Social Change* (Englewood, NJ: Prentice-Hall, 1965).
Franz Borkenau, *The Spanish Cockpit* (Ann Arbor: University of Michigan Press, 1963).
Ralph Borsodi, *Flight From the City* (New York: Harper & Row, 1933).
Martin Buber, *Paths in Utopia* (Boston: Beacon Press, 1958).

Norman Cohn, *The Pursuit of the Millennium* (New York: Oxford University Press, 1957).

James E. Connor (editor), *Lenin: On Politics and Revolution* (New York: Pegasus, 1978).

Sergio Cotta, *Why Violence?*, trans. Giovanni Gullace (Gainesville, FL: University of Florida Press, 1985).

Frantz Fanon, *The Wretched of the Earth* (New York: Grove Press, 1963).

Charles Fourier, *Theory of Social Organization* (New York: C. P. Somerby, 1876).

Stephen Gaskin, *Rendered Infamous* (Summertown, TN: The Book Publishing Co., 1981).

Charlotte Perkins Gilman, *Herland* (New York: Pantheon, 1979).

Henrik F. Infield, *Cooperative Communities at Work* (London: Kegan, Paul, 1947).

Evelyn Fox Keller, *A Feeling for the Organism: Life and Work of Barbara McClintock* (New York: W. H. Freeman, 1983).

Kathleen Kinkade, *A Walden Two Experiment* (New York: Morrow, 1972).

Melvin Lasky, *Utopia and Revolution* (Chicago: University of Chicago Press, 1976).

Moshe Lewin, *Lenin's Last Struggle* (New York: Pantheon, 1968).

Lee Lockwood, "This Shame Will Be Welcome . . . ," *The New York Review of Books*, September 24, 1970, pp. 18–33.

Joanna Macy, *Dharma and Development* (West Hartford, CT: Kumarian Press, 1983).

Karl Mannheim, *Ideology and Utopia: An Introduction to the Sociology of Knowledge*. Published 1929 in German. Reprint (New York: Harcourt, Brace, 1986).

Frank Manuel and Fritzie Manuel, *Utopian Thought in the Western World* (Cambridge: Belknap Press of Harvard University Press, 1979).

Charles Buton Marshall (editor), *The Communist Manifestoes* (Washington: School of Advanced International Studies, Johns Hopkins University, 1960).

Leo Marx, *The Machine in the Garden* (New York: Oxford University Press, 1964).

Everett Mendelsohn and Helga Nowotny, *Nineteen Eighty-Four: Science Between Utopia and Dystopia* (Boston: D. Reidel, 1984).

J. Meynaud, *Social Change and Economic Development* (Paris: Unesco, 1963).

Thomas More, *Complete Works of St. Thomas More. IV Utopia*. Edited by Edward Surtz and J. H. Hexter (New Haven: Yale University Press, 1965).

Lewis Mumford, *The Story of Utopias* (New York: Viking Press, 1962).

Charles Nordhoff, *Communistic Societies of the United States*. 1875. Reprint (New York: Dover Publications, 1966).

John Humphrey Noyes, *History of American Socialisms* (Philadelphia: J. B. Lippincott, 1870).

H. Ornauer with H. Wiberg, A. Sicinsky and J. Galtung, *Images of the World in the Year 2000* (The Hague: Mouton, 1976).

Fred Polak, *Images of the Future*. Trans. E. Boulding (Dobbs Ferry, NY: Oceana Press, 1961). Also one volume abridgement by E. Boulding (San Francisco: Jossey-Bass/Elsevier, 1972).

Howard P. Segal, *Technological Utopianism in American Culture* (Chicago: University of Chicago Press, 1985).

Herbert Shore, *Cultural Policy: UNESCO's First Cultural Development Decade* (Washington: US National Commission for Unesco, 1981).

Herbert Spencer, *The Man Versus the State with Four Essays on Politics and Society*, 1884. Reprint. Edited by Donald Marcal (London: Penguin, 1969).

Herbert Spencer, *Principles of Sociology* (New York: Appleton, 1896).

John L. Thomas, *Alternative America* (Cambridge: Belknap Press of Harvard University Press, 1983).

Alternative Development as Political Practice

D. L. SHETH

Introduction

The idea of development that informed much of the thinking and analyses in the social sciences of the 1960s and early 1970s is on its way out. The view that development is a linear, universal process involving different time-lags for different 'developing countries' is no longer academically respectable. Development theorists are no longer confident about the check-lists of 'do's' and 'don'ts' they once issued from time to time for the benefit of planners and policy-makers in the so-called underdeveloped countries.

Paradoxically, this loss of optimism and confidence in the model that promised development of all nations and for entire populations within nations, albeit with varying time spans and costs, has grown in direct proportion to the growth in the conceptual elegance and methodological sophistication of theory. While books on the conceptualization of development proliferated in the 1950s and 1960s and while countless papers devoted to the perfection of methods and techniques of comparative development were choking spaces in professional journals, poverty in Africa, Asia and Latin America became both more acute and more intractable than ever for these societies. In the course of the last two decades the reality of under-development has moved ahead of the theory of development. The various dispensations sanctioned by the theory, and administered by the rich and powerful countries in the form of aid, advice and even arm-twisting, have proved counter-productive for the very survival, let alone development, of the poor countries and their peoples.

It has become an embarrassing situation which has induced development theorists to shift their ground and change their tone. But it has not deterred many of them from continuing to assume their post-war role as custodians of the international economic order conceived at Bretton Woods. With the abandonment of the original expectation of 'development for all', a new set of terminologies was introduced in the early 1970s in an attempt to preserve the

The author is grateful to R. B. J. Walker, Bharat Wariavwala and Giri Deshingkar for their very useful suggestions on the earlier drafts.

political force of the original theory. Instead of growth we hear of 'growth with distribution'. Instead of foreign investments for stimulating endogenous factors of growth within the underdeveloped countries, we hear of interdependence and an international division of labour. In reality, however, the international division of labour signifies a hierarchy of positions and values. It underscores an unequal and unjust economic and social order among nations and among populations within nations.

It is not surprising, therefore, that the study of comparative development, once a vibrant academic pursuit, has now lost much of its attractiveness, especially for the social scientists in the Third World. Looking back, the academic discourse of the 1960s on comparative development, in which the social scientists of the Third World joined in awe and expectation, now appears to have been a wasted effort. Development is now increasingly perceived by them as a theory not about economic growth and elimination of poverty, but as an ideological and institutional device used by the rich and powerful nations to monitor economic and power relations *vis-à-vis* the underdeveloped nations in order to maintain the former's political domination and to establish cultural hegemony.[1]

At no time since the birth of the Bretton Woods system in 1944 has the rich industrial North made such a concerted attempt to dominate the poor South as in recent years. The developmental prescriptions the North offers and today presses on the South are reliance on the 'magic of the market' and the implementation of the IMF 'stabilizations' plans. It seems that with the onset of the economic recession in the North in the early 1970s the entire content and policy thrust of the developmental paradigm has changed. The concern is no more with the development of the South, as it probably had been in the 1950s and 1960s, but with fiscal issues such as debts, interest rates, investments and reciprocal tariff advantages. Paradoxically, the reach of capitalism has become truly global just at a time when its centre, the industrial North, has experienced the worst recession since the Great Depression of the 1930s.

Yet, the idea of development as a linear and universal process still holds sway in the minds of the ruling élites of the Third World. As an article of faith it helps them to keep false hopes alive among the poor masses. As a theory of international power, mediated through the economic and social policies of the ruling élites of the Third World countries, it effectively curbs any economic, political and cultural initiatives by the poor, the non-state actors and their organizations aimed at attaining a modicum of political autonomy, economic self-reliance and cultural vitality.[2] This article aims at exploring the political possibilities of such initiatives in acquiring a durable basis of knowledge and action. It is for this purpose that I shall, in what follows, examine various strands of what is generally described as the thinking on alternative development.

Alternative development and political practice

The old, inductively oriented, post-war model of comparative development which emphasized stimulation of the internal processes of growth within the nation-states and in which both the 'stimulation' and the outcomes of growth were being monitored under the direction and by the diktats of the victor states, led by US state power and by the various international agencies established under its aegis, has itself undergone significant changes.[3] In place of the initial US hegemony there has now developed a sharp differentiation in the international power structure between military–political power and economic power. The very 'success' of the Bretton Woods system has given rise to an economically powerful West Germany in Europe and Japan in Asia. By the early 1970s, some countries of Latin America and East Asia had emerged on the world economic map as industrial countries. NICs, as they are called, arrived at this stage by extensive interaction with, even dependence on, the capitalist countries of the North. Their path of development, the export orientation, is now proffered by the mainstream developmental theorists and policy makers as the growth model for the entire South.

The 'success' of the old order has brought new problems. How to manage the extensive economic interdependence among the North and NICs is one crucial problem. In addition the high level of interdependence, accompanied by global economic contraction, has created a set of problems for the North: social welfare versus social Darwinism of the market economy, protection versus comparative economic advantages, growth versus environmental protection. This change has far reaching implications for the hitherto semi-industrialized and un-industrialized parts of the world. Having reached a state of almost full capitalization of their own respective economies, the countries of the North have now turned to the various non-capitalized milieus of the Third World. In place of the earlier idea of enlisting various countries, especially of the North, for a 'partnership in growth', the new strategies of the model aim at colonizing the resources of the Third World countries by bringing them into the organized sector of the global capitalist economy.[4]

The shift has also given rise to a series of internal critiques of the model and to new proposals for its adaptation and modification. These critiques, such as the ones made by the Club of Rome and the Brandt and Palme Commissions, often use radical rhetoric to persuade the economically powerful nation-states of the North to curb their rapaciousness in dealing with the underdeveloped parts of the world. The over-riding concern, however, is to keep intact the basic foundations of the post-war model of world development. It is a mistake to identify these critiques and proposals as belonging to the category of thinking on alternative development.

The alternative structuralist approach

A more fundamental critique of the model has emerged from scholars in Latin America, Africa and Asia. They do not address themselves to the issue of reforming the model, but question both the workability and desirability of the model. As such they offer alternative perspectives for reordering the world economic system. These can broadly be identified as 'alternative structural analyses', and include the 'dependency' thesis developed by Latin American scholars, the 'centre–periphery' analyses of some African scholars and a series of structural analyses of poverty by some Asian and African scholars. These have been further systematized in global terms in the literature on the world capitalist system and its impending crisis.[5]

Much has been written on the issues raised in this genre of literature which we have broadly characterized as alternative structural analyses. I have no intention either of repeating the oft-repeated views and positions contained in this literature, or of explicating the finer conceptual and theoretical nuances among them. Nor do I want to go into the—often considerable—academic merits of these intellectual and analytical exercises.[6] My purpose here is to discern what theory of political action, if any, is suggested by such alternative structural analyses.

These exercises have succeeded in exposing the claims of universality and justice of the post-war model of development and, in the process, have demystified the concept of development itself. But like the mainstream model, they consider the nature of the economic activity of individuals and of collectivities fostered by the state to be the chief determinant of all other transformations. And even there their proposals, like those emanating from within the mainstream model, are addressed to the changes required in the economic policies of the countries in the North. The view of the Third World is still taken to be that of an entity responding to the state policies of the countries in the North. While this may be relevant empirically, the proposals do not suggest any need for, or any capability of, active agencies or movements within the Third World to counter these processes. By almost completely externalizing the sources of crises in the Third World, the ruling élite of the Third World countries remain, for good or bad, the only relevant actors for any strategy of action which the counter-proposals of the alternative structural analyses may have to suggest.

These 'alternative' analyses lack the theoretical capacity to guide action by the victimized population and their own organizations. By emphasizing *structures* they view human intervention in abstract terms as an interplay between various systemic forces. Disagreements between the proposals issuing from the mainstream model and those from alternative structural analyses are, thus, generally about attributing different degrees of salience to the various 'objective' forces operating within the overall system (which is essentially conceptualized in economic terms), both in terms of identifying the nature of the present crisis and in assessing how decisive a particular force is in determining its outcome. While the mainstream model emphasizes improving communication and distribution systems for the effective functioning of the model, the alternative structural model locates the source of the Third World predicament in the workings of the world capitalist system.

In both cases the locus of action necessary either for reforming or transforming the system is the *state*. Both place great reliance on the reconstitution of state power (though not saying how and through what process), rather than on changing forms of other (non-state) organizations in the society, or on changing the consciousness which legitimizes the perpetration of injustice and encourages its sufferance by the victimized populations. The mainstream model explicitly recognizes the state as the only relevant agent of reform. With the alternative structuralist analyses, the question of the agency of transformation is submerged in the discussions of 'objective' forces which work inexorably towards intensifying the crisis, thereby precipitating the collapse of the world capitalist system, in whose place, it is hoped, would emerge something like a world socialist system.[7]

I do not mean to suggest that the structuralist analyses lack the power to explain the phenomena of underdevelopment or of restricted economic growth, and consequently of poverty, in Third World countries. On the contrary, given the positive (as against normative) nature of these analyses, their explanatory power is superior to many other theories of development. Especially since the 1950s, when neo-Marxist scholars began to treat the Third World economies not merely as an undifferentiated feudal mode of production but as manifesting various specific forms of capitalist develop-ment, they have generated a series of empirical explanations of poverty in Asia, Africa and Latin America. But if the point of these analyses was to *change* (and not merely to *explain*) the course of history, they fell short of this basic expectation.

The singular implication for political action that emerges from these analyses is the recommendation to the Third World élites and their governments to break away from the imperialist economic and political structure of world capitalism, by delinking their economies and politics from the prevailing system of domination. But this is as far as it goes. The crucial questions are: what are the viable strategies of delinking and what kind of politics is required—at the international, national and local levels—for effecting the delinking process, and what alternative economic and political structures need to be evolved to sustain it? To be effective, the delinking process must begin at the grassroots level of the local communities, which then may eventually compel the respective governments (as is evident from the ecology movements, particularly the *Chipko* movement in India) to move in the right direction—a classical Gandhian strategy of withdrawing legitimation through forms of struggle based on militant non-violence and non-cooperation. The politics involved in this process is more to articulate and work through a series of dualisms created by the working of the conventional development model, than to confine the action only to the class dimension of the struggle.[8]

In contrast, the economy-centred analyses of the structuralists fail to suggest any concrete idea about the politics of delinking. Given the highly systemic understanding of world capitalism, the prevailing linkages are viewed as vertically superordinated, structurally determined and involuntary in nature. In such a view delinking is possible only with a change in the global power structure. But the time span for this is almost epochal. To match this perspective of change with the time-space matrix available for action on the ground is not just a difficult task: it is almost an impossible task. Consequently, the activist movements and organizations engaged in the delinking process find it difficult to locate their politics in the global perspective of the structuralists. They evolve their own forms of organization and micro-ideologies which often clash with the Marxist and neo-Marxist structural analyses of social and political change which inform the political parties. Those at the grass roots, who still persist in locating themselves in the structuralist perspective, spend their energies in ideologically countering the other alternative movements rather than taking up concrete issues of social transformation.[9] They simply wait for changes to take place at the apex of the system and adjust their action, finding new rationales as and when such adjustments are made in respect to any minor change that may take place at the global level.

In brief, the political agenda of the structuralists does not flow from their analyses. Very often, it is extraneous to their analyses and hence lacks viable strategies of action that may enable the political activists to calculate the costs and possibilities of delinking at every level—regional, national and local.

The alternative normativist approach

The recent thinking about alternative development has emerged in explicit contrast to both of the above approaches—the mainstream and the alternative structuralist. While such thinking is often short on sophisticated theoretical formulations and systematic analyses, it takes the question of *practice* very seriously indeed. This question is approached less within the conventional categories of economics or statist politics than in terms of evolving conceptions of basic human needs, alternative life-styles, self-reliance, ecological appropriateness, and so on.[10]

These new conceptions point to a more substantive and non-linear understanding of human *wellbeing* than the one suggested by the structuralist analyses. They emphasize the satisfaction of basic human needs, both material and non-material, rather than the 'growth' that is central to the conventional models. Economic activity is interpreted in the context of self-reliance and the autonomy of cultures and societies. Structures of genuine interdependence and cooperation are assumed to require self-reliance and autonomy rather than the existing patterns of competition in which the weak exist in a relationship of either dependency or subjugation with the strong under an overall structure of domination or conflict. They lead to a critique of the contemporary ethos of over-consumption as a consequence of growth-mongering development, and to the affirmation of life-styles that restore the 'inner boundaries' of the person and the outer-limits of nature; the former prevents enchroachments on the material world that violate the inner self and the dignity of a human person, and the latter prevents rapacious exploitation of nature.

While it is necessary for an emerging theory of alternative development to start from such value premises, it cannot hope to provide a real *alternative* on the ground unless it addresses itself to the question of making the values a basis for a new consensus in the various national societies of the North and the South and at the micro-level of the local communities. Without a theory of political action, such thinking on alternative development will continue to remain at the level of global normativism, confined to the narrow circles of the counter-élites in the North and their jet-setting counterparts in the developing countries.

The crucial question, therefore, is whether such a normativist theory of alternative development suggests political action that is consistent with the values that underlie its theorization, and whether it adopts methods of analysis which yield propositions amenable to such action. Let us examine, briefly, the kind of action that the current theorization of alternative development has to suggest. Many normativist theorists of alternative development have limited themselves to demonstrating the unworkability of the existing system which, in their view, is heading towards a collapse. The only issues are how soon, and what happens afterwards. There is little thinking on this issue in political terms. All we get is an eloquent logical demonstration of the impending collapse and the doom it will spell for the entire humankind. It neither suggests any politics of transition nor any action aimed at damage limitation, in which the activist non-party political groups can engage themselves, nor does it come up with a new politics into which the idea of alternative development can be built. Obviously, this is not the stuff on which the activists of the grass-roots movements can base their struggles. The only action possible to them, if they locate themselves in such a normativist theoretical framework, is to amplify the message of doom, hoping that it will sensitize the ruling élites at national and global levels to the need for caution and, hopefully, to the need for changing the present disastrous course of development they have set upon. The local grass-roots activists, however, cannot even do this. They can no longer scare the scared and the doomed for whom and with whom they work. They cannot persuade them to engage in any action involving delinking from or non-cooperation with the various manifestations of the 'doomed system' they confront every day and which threaten their very survival. The activists, in fact, are in need of ideas which would infuse a sense of hope and possibility in the people. They need to win a battle, even a small one, every day, to keep at least some hope alive. Little by way of politics is available for this from the current normativist thinking on alternative development, except in the form of an alternative value system to which many of them are, in any case, already committed. For their day to day political struggles, however, they are left to their own wits for devising the modes of struggle and for organizing people to that end. And, in this pursuit of self-reliant theorization many activists are showing remarkable ingenuity. But this is despite, not because of, the theory.

There is one strand of normativist theorization which is addressed not only to the ruling élite, but also to the people at large. It holds that the people fail to act in the right direction for want of information and lack of rational thinking. The argument goes that if the desirability of the alternative value system is established through normative–analytical studies of the present crisis and if the people are shown, with the help of rational–mathematical models, the feasibility of achieving such values, they would then move in the direction of alternative development. This approach stresses the need for the dissemination of ideas and the training of change-agents in systematic normative thinking based on feasibility studies in order to impart a direction to organizational and mobilizational activities. However, the fact is that the process of arriving at a consensus on values in any society is not merely a rational–analytical exercise. It involves a conception of action appropriate to the goals of the alternative development that is being sought.

The alternative structuralist analyses, as was pointed out earlier, largely rely on mainstream politics in order to acquire control of the state-apparatus, either through electoral and party processes or through direct revolutionary action. The normative model of alternative development also, by and large, addresses itself to changes in the direction of state policies. It has yet to evolve a notion of politics that can activate non-state social and cultural movements towards achieving a new consensus based on the values of alternative development at the popular level and towards evolving institutional mechanisms embodying these values. Both approaches relate primarily to the confrontation of forces at the apex of the system, leaving the transformative forces on the ground more or less untouched.

Alternative development and democracy: the problem of the knowledge system

The fact that thinking on alternative development still fights shy of raising questions about political practice is not simply due to a lack of theoretical ingenuity. It is also important to understand the way in which the prevailing conceptions of knowledge, especially those informed by the positivist analysis of social sciences, systematically reinforce conventional ideas about the nature of development.[11]

The key link between the conventional theories of development and the alternative models is the presumption of universalism that characterizes the concepts of knowledge that inform both. This continuity is expressed in three different but interrelated, ways: (i) in the assumption of the universality of the alternative value system; (ii) in the failure to conceptualize alternative development in terms of the political processes through which it is to be achieved; and (iii) in the amnesia about the differences between societies to be involved in the process of alternative development. Each of these themes is important for understanding the connection between conceptions of alternative development and theories of democracy.

The global models of alternative development tend to assume universality for the alternative value system, with the result that the need to achieve a political consensus on these values at various levels does not figure as an item on their agenda. By an almost exclusive reliance on a normative–ideological approach in their analyses, thinking on alternative development seems to posit *another* centralizing universal principle that is expected to counter the established model of development. In the process, the alternative global models ignore the vital points of difference in the existential conditions of different societies. In this sense the alternative paradigm (however radically differentiated it may be from the conventional model) views such differences as problems arising in the process of universalization of values of alternative development. They simply become problems resulting from the distortions introduced by the processes of conventional development rather than as either expressions intrinsic to the traditional pathologies of these societies or as manifestations of their potentialities for alternative development that may be different for different societies. Hence, instead of viewing alternative development as a process through which a plurality of competing models can emerge and coexist, current thinking on the subject views it in terms of the emergence of one universal model of alternative development which would replace the conventional one.

The implied shift turns out to be from one kind of linear universalizing principle (embodied by modernity) to another such principle embodied in a vision of the 'post-industrial' or 'post-modern' society. The quest for universality ignores the fact that the historical, cultural and civilizational continuities that characterize different societies throw up different *universal* models around which their respective development may be shaped; and that it is through the interactions based on these empirical experiences of development that a new perspective on alternative development has to emerge. Whether these various alternative development experiences of different societies (as different as Gandhi's India is from Khomeini's Iran) conform in reality to a single vision of *the* 'post-industrial' society is an empirical question for which the visionaries of alternative development have no patience.

The normative–analytical orientation of the alternative development theorists does undermine the conventional development paradigm by attempting to replace instrumental rationality with critical reason as the criterion for evaluating the developmental processes. Yet, without reference to the empirical facts and processes that have a role in shaping norms, the whole exercise only reinforces the traditional norm-setting activity of the élites—however benevolent and radical they may be. The root of élitism, either of the Right or of the Left, as we in India have known for centuries, lies not so much in society's existing opportunity structures but in the legitimation of the intellectual role of a small élite in determining the terms of self-definition for their societies. The fact of the matter is, the consumers of development cannot be kept out of the process of formulation of norms of alternative development—however inconvenient this might prove for the theorists' own 'critical reason'.

Concepts of alternative development still suffer from the kind of sociological determinism that informed the conventional development paradigm. Development was conventionally treated as a function of the overall structure of modernity; it had no dynamics of its own in the larger paradigm. Similarly, in conceptualizing alternative development, it is often forgotten that the reformulation of norms is essentially a political process.[14] It is not merely an epistemological exercise, nor is it the discovery of some self-evident truths about alternative development. It is, therefore, not surprising that so much literature on alternative development remains unconcerned about the role of politics—national or international—in preventing or facilitating the vision of alternative development on the way to its becoming a reality. By focusing exclusively on para-political events and processes, this approach shuts out consideration of the forces intrinsic to various political systems, forces that may engender crisis points in a particular process of alternative development.

Furthermore, the new global thinking on alternative development often obscures the differences in the political systems through which the idea of alternative development would have to acquire content and meaning in different societies. It is often forgotten, for example, that limiting wants, identification and satisfaction of basic needs and emphasizing communitarian living would mean one thing in a society where the decision-making processes are embodied in a political democracy and quite another in societies where political democracy is either explicitly rejected as a framework of decision-making or where it has not yet evolved. In the former, the norms of development would be subject to negotiation and consensus-making and in the latter they serve as prescriptions handed down from above; a certain life-style is presented *ex-cathedra* as a given preference to the people. In the latter case, the rejection of one life-style and the acceptance of another does not come about through changes in consciousness. Put differently, by choosing to be apolitical, the theory of alternative development fails to recognize the fact that democratization is an integral part of the process of alternative development.

The solution, however, does not lie in marrying a pure normative model of alternative development to another pure normative model of democracy. *All pure normative–analytical models lend themselves to élitism of one kind or another* (either of the Left or of the Right) and by their very nature negate, in the long run, the idea of alternative development itself. Such models, devoid of empirical and political thrust of their own, are easily amenable to élite manipulation and are subject to the exercise of power by the minority over the majority. They disregard the empirical criteria for sorting out the norms of alternative development from among the plurality of existential preferences and goals as well as the criteria for evaluating the functioning of democratic institutions which make such choices possible. In addition, the pure normative–analytical models often find the practice of democratic decision-making to be a distraction for implementing the proposals of alternative development, and they, thus, are prone to become authoritarian in their politics. Since democratic decision-making at any given time is inevitably riven with all kinds of contradictions and compromises and since, above all, it usually lacks intellectual and operational clarity about the direction of development, the *pure normative–analytical* models all the more tend to orient their politics towards authoritarian solutions.

Democracy may be said to be a model of 'deliberate' imperfection, a model that tolerates various loose ends in the system, vast sectors of under-socialized or unsocialized activities of individuals and groups (the sectors that do not always fall in line with the dominant social thrust or with 'raison d'état'). Democracy recognizes the existence of non-unitary multi-purpose organizations and a multiplicity of possible courses open to the system at any given point of time. The crux of any politics for alternative development, in my view, lies in integrating into its theory an empirical model of democracy which treats the *legitimation* of values and institutions as an open process. In contrast to the normativist, Utopian and structural–historicist models of alternative development in which the dominant (or counter) élites can pass off their ideology as the only legitimator of the institutional and normative structures in a society, in the democratic model, with its inbuilt pluralism, the seeking of alternative development must depend, both for the articulation of values and their realization, on a participative democratic process. The latter always presumes a society that allows *various* legitimation processes to test themselves out on the ground—through critical analyses *as well as* through real-life conflicts, struggles and integrative movements of ideas and action.

For the politics of alternative development to emerge, the corresponding theory should be primarily rooted in the *problematique of democratization*. More specifically, the idea of alternative development must be explicitly integrated with the idea of democracy and such integration must allow the criteria emerging from the ground to shape the very conception of alternative development.

Alternative development and grass-roots movements

What, then, should be the politics for alternative development? Can we turn for an answer to the other level at which thinking on alternative development is being articulated, namely the phenomenon of grass-roots movements? The assumption held by the grass-roots movements is that a theory of action for alternative development will emerge from the concrete struggles of the people themselves.[12] Insofar as the peoples' organizations and movements address themselves to the prevention of damage and destruction wrought by the so-called developmental policies of the ruling élites, it is believed, they create new political spaces for movements of alternative development to emerge; and from these may emerge a new convergence between theory and action. So far this does not exist. Currently, the thinking seems to be that a theory of action will be formulated by the objective, non-participant thinkers observing this new phenomenon. This view implies a dichotomy between knowledge and action, between theory and intervention. It assumes that two different sets of people are involved in the process of social transformation: the producers of knowledge and its consumers; the socially concerned but politically inactive 'thinkers' and the politically engaged but theoretically disinclined activists.

Although some division of labour and differences of proclivities are inevitable in any enterprise, an alternative theory of action requires that grass-roots thinking and movements must move away from such a dichotomy. It is possible for them to do so only if the activists of the movements become their own theorists and the theorists find authentication of their thinking through their own role located within the movements. When this happens, knowledge ceases to be viewed as the pursuit of expertise, and action as 'implementation' of somebody's idea. Instead, it sets in motion a participative process which obliterates the distinction between the subject and the object, between the producers and the consumers of knowledge.

What is preventing this from happening so far is the fact that, with some exceptions, the grass-roots movements have, in my view, failed to evolve an alternative to conventional politics. Although at the level of values many of these movements share the critique of development—variously characterized by them as capitalist, imperialist or generally anti-poor—and are inclined towards the thinking of alternative development, they operate in a state of ambivalence with regard to the political action required for achieving these values. In fact, the scene of grass-roots movements is quite heterogenous and one cannot expect from among them the emergence of a single theory of action. This being the case, the task of creating a politics for alternative development through the grass-roots movements is as difficult as creating it from normative analytical thinking at the global level. Nevertheless, it is necessary that a theory of alternative action emerge through the process of grass-roots movements making their impact on the global thinking, rather than the other way round. It is with this view in mind that I would like to identify some specific problems of grass-rootgrass-root organizations and movements that prevent the emergence of a new theory of action for alternative development.[13] I shall confine my comments to two broad types of grass-roots movements: non-political developmental and non-party political formations.

First, many grass-roots organizations are apolitical in nature and as such are subject to the official government policies which either keep them in a state of permanent mobilization for enlisting their support to the regime or depoliticize all voluntary action and segregate developmental activity from the political activity. Both make them available for the legitimation process of the state. Such organizations function as voluntary agencies in charge of implementing 'development programmes' which their governments have often got from the international development or credit agencies. The political space within which they can operate is explicitly or implicitly defined by the governments and is, in effect, quite restricted. If on the other hand they get their funds directly from a foreign government or a foundation, their political role becomes odious from the start. Unless they have frequent occasion to participate in a wider field of interaction with different types of grass-roots movements, especially the politically oriented ones, these organizations cannot evolve a mode of politicization for themselves which is relevant for alternative development.

This is not to deny the fact that these non-political developmental organizations are of significant help in providing succour and relief to the poor in times of man-made calamities. They perform this task in a manner that, left to itself, the development bureaucracy of the government cannot. But their role even in the conventional development model is of doubtful effectiveness. This limitation is largely due to their apolitical nature. Several studies show that their efforts do not result in taking the benefits of development to the poorest among the poor. Crossing the barriers of social structure and reaching the poor calls for a political process which they are not equipped to initiate or handle. Their actions, therefore, remain by and large confined to the dispensation of goods, rather than to creating assets and entitlements for the betterment of the poor. For example, they often try to get monetary compensation to the poor peasants and tribals for land that has been submerged by reservoirs but do little to prevent the money from being dissipated without much collective benefit. They work on schemes for disbursing money to help the poor to buy cattle but have no plans to ensure that the recipients can maintain the animals; they often help to disburse money to buy tools which produce unmarketable goods; or they work on schemes that result only in temporary employment among the poor without securing for them a durable means of livelihood. All this is not the result of any lack of motivation and effort. It is the lack of political content because of which their programmes fail to achieve the intended results. The result is frustration among the activists and disillusionment among the poor.

Secondly, there are the politically oriented grass-roots movements and organizations, usually called non-party political formations.[14] Although they distance themselves organizationally from the mainstream politics of political parties and elections, they have yet to evolve a distinctive pattern of politics characterized by thinking on alternative development. It is probably too premature to judge the nature and direction of their politics which is only now beginning to evolve. But precisely for this reason it is necessary to formulate some issues arising from their style of functioning. Non-party political organizations are in danger of being absorbed into mainstream politics unless they are aggressively clear about the political direction of their work. They generally invest their energies in issues affecting the poor, issues usually not taken up by the political parties. In this sense the issues they take up naturally belong to the politics of alternative development. But their concrete political action on these issues is often located in conventional politics—the politics of mobilization of public opinion on specific and disparate issues, and of pressurizing the government to respond to popular demands. In the process, they often end up being no more than spade-workers for the political parties.

The crucial question is whether such actions can move beyond the politics of pressure-groups, away from the power of the state and towards the creation of peoples' own power and organizations. Creative action for alternatives is most unlikely to come either from experts or expertise-oriented developmental groups or from any kind of political mobilization active within the state system. In my view, it can come only from non-state actors operating at the interface of the state and the society, the interface between politics and culture. Some experiments in this direction are being undertaken by various groups in Latin America and Asia. They focus primarily on generating new social knowledge for alternative development, and on activating networks of peoples' organizations for working out their own solutions for the problems they face. The method employed is of dialogues, interactions and participative action research (PAR). Such initiatives are, however, still in their formative state and are confined to only certain types of movements in these countries.[15] It will take a long time before their impact is felt at the global level in terms of creating a new politics for alternative development.

Conclusion

As we have seen, the structuralist and the normativist analyses being carried out at the global level in search of an alternative to the mainstream development theory have contributed to new initiatives and movements. They have provided an understanding of the vertical linkages of power structures that perpetuate the present unjust and oppressive national and international orders; perhaps even more importantly, they have formulated goals and value commitments consistent with the idea of alternative development. However, as we have shown, they badly lack a conception of transformative political action. The result is that such analyses, even if by default, lead to the location of the activities of the new movements in the conventional politics of pressure groups. It is to overcome this impasse that some grass-roots movements for alternative development, especially in Latin America and Asia, seek to go beyond questioning the legitimation claims of the conventional development model. Instead, they emphasize withdrawal of legitimation by delinking themselves from the institutions of mainstream politics: elections, parties, trade unions and so on. They do take the democratic framework of institutions as an important condition of their functioning; they cherish democracy as a value which they would fight for if it were sought to be undermined. But, in doing this they want to shift their battleground to a larger arena of society and culture. In this sense they do not view the mainstream political institutions as instruments of transformation. Their political agenda, instead, is of further democratization not only of the political institutions but of the family, the community, the workplace and society at large.

It is for this reason that their political thinking does not stop at transforming the *structures*; it invariably goes beyond to achieving integrity of values and action at a personal level, practising life-styles appropriate to their idea of alternative development and, above all, to seeking authentication of their values and politics in their individual biographies. Such a conception of politics can best be described as *societics*—political activity of individuals and organizations addressed to transformation of consciousness and of organizational forms, especially of the non-state organizations in society which only ultimately may lead to the transformation of the state itself.

The grass-roots movements for alternative development, at present limited as they are in their geographical spread, have nevertheless acquired significant intensity and persistence. The challenge facing them is how to work this new politics from the bottom up so that its impact is felt at the national and global levels. This calls for a greater degree of interaction and communication among them than now exists. They need a knowledge base that not only prevents their cooptation into mainstream politics but also enables them to acquire geographical spread and political intensity in their actions.

This indeed is a difficult path for the new movements to negotiate. More difficult is to assess the potentials of these initiatives to grow and spread in the future. But if desertion by sizable numbers of professionals (in the countries of Asia and Latin America) from their conventional professions and their participation in various types of people's organizations is any indication of the strength of these initiatives, and if the extent to which the people organized through these initiatives are becoming less and less available for conventional politics, gives any indication of their growing political influence, these movements are bound to pose a serious challenge to the political establishments in these countries in the years to come.

Whatever the future brings, these movements have a far more profound significance beyond the realm of institutional politics. Insofar as they address themselves to changing the forms of consciousness and transforming (non-state) organizations in society, in the long run they have implications for providing a new basis for transforming the prevailing unjust and oppressive economic and social orders underwritten by the power of the modern state. This new basis is to be found in a new theory of knowledge, a new pedagogy of democracy and a new conception of politics itself.

Of course, given the embryonic and dispersed character of these grass-roots movements for alternatives it would be unwise, indeed unreasonable, to assume that the challenges they pose to mainstream development theory and practice would be decisive or that the success of the transformative projects they are engaged in, is assured. For either to happen, a macro theory of transformative political action is required which is based on the values and practice of democracy and which has synthesizing potentials for integrating the perspectives and actions of various issue-based movements in a larger framework of transformation. The current global thinking on alternative development represented by the structuralist and normativist approaches falls short of this basic expectation. The need is to reconceptualize alternative development in terms of democratic practice. And to reconceptualize democracy in basic socio-cultural terms and in respect of opening up spaces within the institutions of society itself. Meanwhile, as we have shown, it would be a serious mistake to underestimate the long-term transformative potential of these alternative movements on both the global and local levels. Indeed, these are embodiments of the rediscovery of new agents of social change, new 'subjects of history'. They are the cutting edge of the process of democratization which can be the only source and context of fundamental political and social transformation.

Notes and references

1. See for example, Claude Alvares, 'Deadly Development', *Development Forum*, Vol. 9, No. 7, (October 1983); Ashis Nandy, 'Development and Authoritarianism', *Journal for Entwicklungspolitik*, November 1986.
2. The recent tendency of some Third World governments to bring the voluntary sector closer to the administration of conventional development projects and to delegitimize their political role of protest and action for alternative development is best illustrated by the new policy of the Indian government towards the voluntary and non-governmental organizations. For details see 'On Threats to Non-party Political Process: A Report on a Lokayan Dialogue', *Lokayan Bulletin*, Vol. 3, No. 2 (April 1985). For a more extensive debate on this issue see *Lokayan Bulletin*, Vol. 4, No. 3/4, pp. 1–51.
3. For a detailed analysis of changes in the post-war model of development and their implications for the world economy see Folker Fröbel, Jurgen Heinrichs, Otto Kreye, 'Dead End: Western Economic Responses to the Global Economic Crisis', in Herb Addo *et al.*, *Development as Transformation: Reflections on the Global Problematique* (United Nations University, 1985), pp. 86–110.
4. On implications of the new strategies of the conventional model for the Third World countries see, Folker Fröbel, Jurgen Heinrichs, Otto Kreye, 'The Global Crisis and Developing Countries', in Herb Addo *et al.*, *Development as Transformation, ibid.*, pp. 111–124.
5. For want of a better term I have characterized here the neo-Marxist reformulations of the dependency thesis, the literature on 'internationalization of capital' and on the crisis of the world capitalist system as 'structuralist alternative'. I have ignored some important nuances among various positions within this genre of literature. For, lately, they all seem to converge in viewing alternative development in the context of the crisis of the world economy.

   For some representative writings on the dependency school see F. H. Cardoso, 'Associated-Dependent Development: Theoretical and Practical Implications' in Alfred Stefan (ed.), *Authoritarian Brazil: Policies and Future* (New Haven: Yale University Press, 1973); C. Furtado, *Economic Development of Latin America: Historical Background and Contemporary Problems* (Cambridge: Cambridge University Press, 1970); Andre Gunder

Frank, *Capitalism and Underdevelopment in Latin America* (New York: Monthly Review Press, 1967). For a Marxist reformulation of the dependency thesis see Samir Amin, *Accumulation on a World Scale: A Critique of the Theory of Underdevelopment*, 2 Vols. (New York: Monthly Review Press, 1974).

With the emergence of newly industrialized countries the dependency thesis was reformulated, even transformed. This gave rise to different theories of internationalization of capital. See, for example, H. S. Marcussen and J. E. Torp, *The Internationalization of Capital: The Prospects for the Third World* (London: Zed Press, 1982). Instead of unequal exchange and trade terms these theories emphasize export of capital from the centre to the peripheries. While this brings the peripheries under the domination of the world capitalist system, it is held that such internationalization of capital does not enhance the growth possibilities of the peripheral countries; it only enhances the centre's sphere of operation internationally. By far the most substantive contribution in this regard is: Folker Fröbel, J. Heinrichs, Otto Kreye, *The New International Division of Labour: Structural Unemployment in Industrialized Countries and Industrialization in Developing Countries* (Cambridge: Cambridge University Press, 1980).

Lately, there seems to have emerged among the writers in the dependency tradition a broad consensus on the issues of world economy. Recent works of Andre Gunder Frank and Samir Amin indicate a movement towards the world system approach associated with the work of Immanuel Wallerstein. Admittedly, there are some important differences among them, marked by the different ideological origins of these writers and the intellectual journeys made by them in arriving at the respective crystallizations of their positions. Hence, for example, the differences between Wallerstein and Amin with respect to the role of class struggle and the salience of modes of production in their analyses. Nonetheless they share a common perspective on the working of the world capitalist system and its impact on the Third World countries. Both the area of convergence and the differences among them are made explicit in a book co-authored by Samir Amin, Giovanni Arrighi, Andre Gunder Frank and Immanuel Wallerstein: *Dynamics of Global Crisis* (New York: Monthly Review Press, 1982). That there is continuity of the basic dependency thesis in the literature on internationalization of capital and on world system analyses and that they all share a certain structuralist perspective is shown by Magnus Blomstrom and Bjorn Hettne in their *Development Theory in Transition: The Dependency Debate and Beyond* (London: Zed Books, 1984), pp. 182–192.

6. For a comprehensive treatment of issues raised in this genre of literature see Magnus Blomstrom and Bjorn Hettne (note 5).

7. Unlike even orthodox Marxism, which had an explicit theory of revolutionary action and an agency of revolution, these analyses do not have any notion of an actor or an agency for implementing their political agenda. Lacking political criteria for evaluating action, they often view the new popular movements in reductionist terms and characterize them as 'retrogressive'. See, for example, Samir Amin's recent article, 'Apropos the Green Movements' in Herb Addo *et al.*, *Development as Social Transformation*, (note 3), pp. 271–281.

8. Both on the analysis of emerging multiple dualisms and on the need for evolving politics addressed to multiple dualisms by the grassroots movements see Rajni Kothari, 'The Non-party Political Process', *Economic and Political Weekly*, Vol. 19, No. 5 (February 1984); 'Flight into the 21st Century: The millions will be stranded', *Times of India*, April 27, 1986; 'Masses, Classes and the State', *Alternatives*, Vol. 11, No. 2 (April 1986), pp. 167–183.

9. This tendency is best illustrated in a recent article published by an official journal of the Communist Party of India (Marxist) attacking the grass-roots movements. See, Prakash Karat, 'Action Groups/Voluntary Organizations: A Factor in Imperialist Strategy', *The Marxist: Theoretical Quarterly of the Communist Party of India (Marxist)*, Vol. 2, No. 2 (April–June 1984).

10. The literature on 'normativist alternative' comprises a variety of conceptualizations emphasizing different normative elements of theory, and also actions in terms of initiating and supporting movements. It is difficult to take account of all these in the present paper. For our purpose the term 'alternative normativist approach' refers to the literature identified as such by Bjorn Hettne in his monograph reviewing the literature on development theories. See, Bjorn Hettne, *Development Theory and the Third World* (Sarec Report, 1982), Ch. IV, pp. 75–98.

11. For a detailed treatment of this issue, see my 'The Knowledge-Power System and Action Groups: The Role of Participative Research', *Social Action*, Vol. 34, April–June, 1984.

12. For a detailed analysis of ideologies, organizations and activities of the grass-roots movements, see my 'Grass-roots Stirrings and the Future of Politics', *Alternatives*, Vol. 9, No. 1 (March 1983), pp. 1–24.

13. For more details on the problems faced by grass-roots movements and their political role, see my 'Grass-roots Initiatives in India', *Economic and Political Weekly*, Vol. 19, No. 6, February 1984.

14. For elaboration of the concept of non-party political movements and on the transformative potentials of these movements, see Rajni Kothari, 'Non-Party Political Process', (note 8).

15. While one can find several such organizations and movements operating on the ground in these countries in specific geographical areas and while they have found some expression in the theoretical literature on alternative development and in the form of 'case studies', this phenomenon has not yet received the recognition and treatment it deserves by the social scientists as well as by the writers on alternative development.

    For the literature on movements and initiatives referred to here see, for Latin America, Orlando Fals Borda, *Knowledge and People's Power: Lessons with Peasants in Nicaragua, Mexico and Columbia*, International Labour Office, Geneva, 1985; Gustavo Esteva, 'Generating People's Spaces', *Alternatives*, Vol. 12, No. 1 (April 1987), pp. 125–152. For Asia see, Vandana Shiva, 'Ecology Movements in India', *Alternatives*, Vol. 11, No. 2 (April 1986), pp. 255–273; Anisur Rahman, 'The Theory and Practice of PAR', in Orlando Fals Borda (ed.), *The Challenge of Social Change* (Sage Publishers, 1985), pp. 107–132. For an earlier pioneering study in the field of PAR see, Niranjan Mehta, Md. Anisur Rahman, G. V. S. De Silva, Ponna Wignaraja, 'Towards a Theory of Rural Development', *Development Dialogue*, 1979:2. Also see Ponna Wignaraja, 'From the Village to the Global Order', *Development Dialogue*, 1977:1. For a cross-section of reportage on the new initiatives see the special issue of *Development: Seeds of Change, Village Through Global Order* (SID, Rome), 1981:1. Also see *Development*, 1985:3.

People's Ecology: The Chipko Movement

VANDANA SHIVA

The 1970s witnessed the emergence of grass roots ecology movements searching for a new kind of peace—peace with nature. In spite of differences in the stage and in the actors, these movements shared the common objective of a search for an alternative development that is more in harmony with nature's rhythms, patterns and processes. In India, ecology movements went a step further. They emerged as movements for a just peace. The simultaneous search for justice and peace through a restructuring of man's relationship with nature has been a characteristic of India's ecology movements because of her cultural, historical and natural heritage.

India is a large country, with a large population and an ancient history. Every ecological niche is occupied in one way or another. The balance between nature's productivity and people's needs is a delicate one and can be easily upset in such a context. The replication of the industrialization patterns of the countries of the North in countries like India cause rapid resource depletion and the diversion of resources from people's basic needs to industrial raw materials. Ecological disruption and economic exploitation are intrinsically linked; and this linkage stares everyone in the face when resources are scarce, people are many, and new modes of production are resource intensive and resource wasteful and consume resources needed for survival.

The ecological implications of resource-intensive and labour-displacing production forms were understood in ancient India. This understanding was revived by Gandhi in modern India. And it has been revitalized by the contemporary ecology movements.

In India, to be civilized is to practise "Dharma" (the Sanskrit word for right conduct). Etymologically, Dharma means the stabilizer. It is the source of stability of human societies. And this social stability is related to stability of natural resource and of ecology. According to the Indian cultural heritage, the three values of life which guide human activity are Artha (which stands for resources), Kama (which stands for needs and desires of human beings), and Dharma (which denotes right conduct or the proper utilization of resources to fulfil or satisfy the needs and desires of human beings). According

Commissioned by the Committee for a Just World Peace for presentation at its Lisbon Conference, March 1985. First published in a revised form in *Alternatives* XI:2.

to the Isavasyopanishad, Dharma consists in restricting use of resources to satisfaction of basic needs, because using resources beyond one's needs would be appropriating the resources of others. According to the Isavasya, a selfish man utilizing others' resources to satisfy his own ever increasing wants is nothing but a thief. Justice and ecological and social stability are therefore intrinsically interlinked in the Indian world-view.[1] "Dharma" is the mediator between resources and needs and is thus a secular category, not a religious one. It implies rational economic and technological choices. It involves a conscious rejection of resource-wasteful production.

In Gandhi's view, the Indian civilization opted for another development not because of technological inadequacy, but because of ecological sophistication. "We have managed with the same kind of plough as existed thousands of years ago. . . . It was not that we did not know how to invent machinery."[2] This relationship between restraint in resource use, ecological stability and social justice was also emphasized by Gandhi who said, "Earth provides enough to satisfy every man's need but not for every man's greed."[3] This creed of political economy, in which restraint in resource use is a precondition for justice and peace, is best substantiated in land use. If we co-operate with nature's processes and its cycle of life, the soil renews its fertility indefinitely and provides sustenance. But when the exploitative and predatory attitude takes over, nature's balance is upset and there is an all-round biological deterioration. Upon the balance between man and nature depends the stability of and peace in society. The philosophical recognition of the nexus between ecology and a just peace is contained in the concepts of Dharma and Ahimsa (non-violence) on which the ancient civilizations of the East were based.

Contemporary ecology movements in India are informed by this philosophy. They also respond to the existential reality of the wanton destruction of the life-support system of a very large number of people. They realize that the criteria for choosing life-styles and matching technologies inherent in the Indian heritage are now the only criteria that can assure survival. And survival is the elementary and fundamental right of every human being—as much of the poor (who have to suffer the gruesome consequences of the pillage of nature) as of the rich (who perpetrate this outrage in pursuit of a wickedly affluent life-style, inimical to justice and peace).

Ecology movements in India are struggles of the dispossessed, the marginalized, the victims of discrimination. They include women, tribals and non-commercial farmers. These movements are aimed at conserving nature's balance in order to conserve their means of survival. In this sense they are the keepers of the residual Indian cultural and economic heritage.

Although grass roots ecological struggles are seemingly local episodes, their reverberations have global significance. Survival on the local plane now depends on forces that are non-local in origin—such as the dominant proselytizing scientific and technological culture; the development paradigm forcibly imposed through conditionalities of loan and aid and trade; and overarching all this, the hard national-scientific state. Local struggles are part of the process of global transformation currently under way. They are modest manifestations of a search, non-theorized and non-verbalized, for an alternative scientific and technological culture; an alternative development paradigm; an alternative concept of state and security; and, with their stress on non-violence and justice and peace, an alternative civilization.

The survival imperative and ecological movements

For all the long tradition of ecological consciousness in India, instances of ecological abuse were not wanting. They also invariably provoked people's resistance. Some three centuries ago, for example, the entire Jain community of Vishnois of Rajasthan sacrificed their lives to prevent felling of green trees by the royal forces of Jodhpur.

More systematic large-scale destruction of forests for commercial-industrial purposes and misuse of other natural resources began, in the colonial era. They also almost invariably met with resistance. A confrontation that became a landmark in the history of the national struggle for freedom from colonialism occurred in the Champaran, district of Bihar in 1917. In Champaran every tenant was bound by law to plant indigo on three out of twenty parts of his holding for the landlord (the British planter). Simmering discontent came to a boil when Gandhi (made well-known by his historic struggle against racism in South Africa and now plunged into Indian public life) was persuaded to take up the cause of the exploited farmers of Champaran. He led them to victory and indigo planting was abolished. Gandhi had scrupulously avoided giving the struggle a political colour by keeping the Indian National Congress and non-Bihari Congress leaders out of it. Another struggle in 1930, centred on the use of commons and the people's right of access to them, was frankly political. It was an open country-wide defiance of the salt law which, for the first time in the history of India, had made it illegal for the citizens to collect salt on the sea shore or make it anywhere in the land. It had vested total monopoly of making and marketing salt in the state. What began as an assertion of the people's right of access to the free gifts of nature became the assertion of people's right to independence.

India did become independent. But even in independent India, ecological abuse has not ceased. Neither have the struggles for ecological conservation. In fact, the intensity and range of the ecology movements in independent India have kept on increasing as predatory exploitation of natural resources has increased in extent and intensiveness as a consequence of the huge expansion of energy-intensive and resource-consuming industrialization and development projects, and the narrowing resource base of the economically poor and powerless. Ecology movements came up as people's response to this threat to their survival and as demands for conserving vital natural resources. The most vital resources that were being destroyed are soil, water and vegetation systems, and these have therefore been at the centre of ecology movements in the last few decades.

The Chipko movement is the most well-known ecology movement in the country. It is a movement of the forest dwelling communities to save the forest cover from destruction. Movements with the same end, though not with the same means, have been occurring in other vulnerable mountain systems like the Western Ghats, the Aravallis and the Vindhyas. They have occurred in all tribal belts of the country. Most notable among them are the Singhbhum (Bihar) and Bastar region (Madhya Pradesh) where people's movements were aimed against the conversion of mixed natural forestry into monoculture of commercial species such as teak or pine, a sure recipe for the destruction of the tribal modes of life.

There has been resistance wherever forest and agricultural lands have been threatened by inundation, waterlogging, salinity resulting from the construction of large dams and large irrigation projects—for example, in Tehri in the north, Koel Karo in the east, Sirsi in the south, and Inchampalli in central India. Another significant ecological movement has evolved round the threat to marine resources as well as to indigenous fishing from mechanized fishing. It has surfaced all along the Indian coastline. One in Kerala has received additional attention because of the involvement of the radical section of the Catholic clergy.

Ecological conflicts, regardless of where they take place and how they are conducted, have things in common. They all centre around the right of access of the poor to natural resources, and they all focus on three interrelated conflicts:

1. Economic: conflict between two types of economic activity—one aimed at ensuring survival for the people in a sustainable manner through a genuinely collective management; and the other aimed at maximizing the growth rate even at the cost of bare survival of many.

2. Technological: conflict between two types of technology—vernacular and labour-intensive, one aimed at minimizing ecological costs to ensure survival; and the other borrowed from abroad regardless of its suitability in the local context, aimed at "modernization" of the productive process.

3. Scientific: conflict in the politics of knowledge—one open to all, non-dogmatic, not ruling out other ways of acquiring knowledge; and the other a closed system, drawing a sharp dividing line between the expert and the non-expert.

"Chipko" movement

The "Chipko" (hug-the-tree) movement,[4] which derives its name from the novel method it invented, is the most powerful ecological movement of India. An analysis of Chipko shows that it is a civilizational response to a threat to survival. Beginning as a grass roots local movement, it has spread into the national and the transnational arenas, challenging global paradigms of resource use. While the first global environment meeting of the élite was taking place in Stockholm in 1972, the first grass roots ecology movement was emerging in remote villages in the southern foothills of the Himalayas. The villages were totally unaware of the global event. Their awareness was born of their own existential experience of increasing floods and landslides caused by deforestation; it was rooted in their cultural heritage that has instilled in them a deep respect for the lofty, luminous, awe-inspiring Himalayas, as also for its magnificent forests and sparkling frolicking streams.

The first Chipko action occurred in March 1974 in Reni village of the

Garhwal Himalaya. A group of village women led by one Gaura Devi hugged the trees, challenging the hired sawyers, about to cut down trees for a sports-goods company, to saw them alive first. In July 1970, the Alaknanda valley, in which Reni village is located, had experienced a disastrous flood, when the Alaknanda inundated 1,000 sq.km. of land and washed away a large number of bridges and roads. The cause, they knew was deforestation. The women resorted to the novel method to protect their forests in order to protect themselves from future landslides and floods. The occurrence of landslides had increased dramatically through the 1970s largely as a result of road expansion and timber extraction. In 1977, the Alaknanda disaster was followed by the Tawaghat tragedy. In 1978, the holy Ganga was blocked at Kanodiagad, 50 km. down stream from Gangotri, by a massive landslide. When the dam burst, the entire Gangetic plain was flooded all the way down to Calcutta.

These ecological disasters had prepared the ground for a grass roots popular movement to protect the forests; the Chipko movement spread rapidly in the valley. In February 1978, Chipko activists in Henwal valley saved the Advani forests; and in December 1978, the forests of Badyargad were saved through Chipko. The news spread beyond the geographical boundaries of Garhwal; and in 1983–84, the Chipko strategy was used by environment activists of the Western Ghats to save the forests of the other ecologically vulnerable mountain systems of India.

Ecological world-views and Chipko

The ecological crises to which these village communities responded were new, yet the ecological perception with which they responded was centuries old. The illiterate women of the hill villages did not need professional forest hydrologists to tell them of the role of forests in protecting the land and water stability of mountain watersheds, they had drunk this knowledge with their mothers' milk, and had it reinforced as they grew with religious myths and folklore. One of the best descriptions of the hydrological role of the Himalayan forests is contained in the myth of the descent of the mighty and sacred Ganga. Reiger, the eminent Himalayan ecologist, describes the rationality of the myth in the following words:

> In the scriptures a realisation is there that if all the waters which descend upon the mountain were to beat down upon the naked earth, then earth would never bear the torrents. In Shiva's hair we have a very well known physical device which breaks the force of the water coming down . . . the vegetation of the mountains.[5]

The Chipko strategy draws on these ecological modes of perception by readings from the scriptures. Tactically, too, this mode of mobilizing people by appeals around the ecological messages from the religious heritage is effective because it uses an ancient and spontaneous form of gathering village communities together. Another tale from the scriptures which communicates the ecological value of trees and is used in Chipko mobilizations is from the Bhagwad Geeta; it drives home the life-sustaining role of forests.

Chipko and conflicts over forest resources

The conflicts and tensions from which the famous Chipko movement has emerged can be traced to the far-reaching changes in forest management introduced in India during the colonial period. Until then, forest resources, like other vital natural resources, had been managed as common resources with strict, though informal, social mechanisms for controlling utilization to ensure sustained productivity. Besides the large tracts of natural forests that were maintained through this careful husbanding, village forests and woodlets were also developed and maintained through careful selection of appropriate tree species. Remnants of commonly managed natural forests and village commons still exist in pockets and these provide knowledge of the scientific basis underlying traditional land management.[6]

Colonial impact on forest management undermined these conservation strategies in two ways. First, changes in the system of land tenure through the introduction of the zamindari system transformed common village resources into the private property of newly created landlords. People who satisfied their domestic needs from the collectively owned village forests and grasslands had now to turn to natural forests. Secondly, large-scale felling of trees in natural forests to satisfy non-local commercial needs—such as shipbuilding for the British navy and sleepers for the expanding railway network—created an extraordinary process of destruction. After about half a century of uncontrolled exploitation the need for controlling it became obvious.

The colonial response to this was to vest ownership in the state and set up a forest bureaucracy to regulate commercial exploitation and conserve forests. What the bureaucracy protected in practice was forest revenues, not the forests themselves. This typically colonial interpretation of conservation generated severe conflicts on two levels. On the level of utilization, the new management system catered only to commercial demands and ignored local basic needs. People were denied their traditional rights, which, after prolonged struggles, were occasionally granted as favours.[7] On the conservation level, since the new forest management was concerned solely with forest revenues, ecologically unsound silvicultural practices were introduced. This undermined biological productivity of forest areas and transformed renewable resources into non-renewable ones.[8]

With the reservation of forests and the denial of the people's right of access to them the villagers created resistance movements in all parts of the country. The Forest Act of 1927 sharpened the conflicts, and the 1930s witnessed widespread forest satyagrahas as a mode of non-violent resistance to the new forest laws and policies. Villagers ceremonially removed forest produce from the reserved forests to defy forest laws that denied them their right to forest products. These satyagrahas were especially successful in regions where survival of the local population was intimately linked with the access to the forests—as in the Himalayan foothills, the Western Ghats and the Central Indian hills. These non-violent protests were suppressed with the might of arms. In Central India, Gond tribals were gunned down for participating in the satyagraha. In the Himalayan foothills dozens of unarmed villagers were killed and hundreds injured in Tilari village of Tehri Garhwal on 30 May 1930, when they gathered to protest against the forest laws. After enormous loss of lives, the satyagrahas were finally successful in regaining some of the traditional rights of the village communities to various forest produce. But the forest policy and its revenue-maximizing objective remained unchanged.

In independent India the same colonial forest-management policy was continued, but enforced with greater ruthlessness and justified in the name of "national interest" and "economic growth". The threat to survival having become more sinister, the response of the people has changed. Sporadic protests have become organized and sustained movements. Chipko is the most spectacular of these.

Global implications of the Chipko movement

Chipko has generally been viewed merely as a forest movement, and sometimes as an environment movement. But it is more than this.

Ecology movements like the Chipko call into question the dominant paradigm of thinking and living in all its aspects: ontological, epistemological, scientific, technological, social, economic. In effect, they call for a redefinition of science and rationality, of technological choice and economic development. Above all, they call for a reconceptualization of what is meant by a good life.

Scientific and technical knowledge of forestry in the existing model of forest management assumes that forests are nothing more than so much timber—for industrial-commercial use, of course. This inevitably leads to manipulations of the forest ecosystem for furtherance of those species of trees that yield commercial wood. Hence the encouragement given to replacement of ecologically valuable oak forests by commercially valuable conifers. This leads to the destruction of other biomass forms that have low commercial value but very high use value for the people. In its present form, scientific forestry depends on an essentially *reductionist* system of knowledge that ignores the complex relationships within the forest community and between plant life and other resources like soil and water. By ignoring the systems linkages within the forest ecosystem and its multiple functions, this pattern generates instabilities in the ecosystem and leads to irreversible soil erosion and uncontrollable floods. The Alaknanda disaster in the Garhwal region was an exceptionally grim reminder of this. The lesson was lost in the reductionist science; but the people of Garhwal rose to the defence of forests because their life-support system was at stake. The two conflicting perceptions corresponding to two conflicting interests are captured in the two slogans used in the Chipko movement. The establishment perception of the forests went as follows:

> What do the Forests Bear?
> Profit, Resin and Timber.

The people's perception was summed up as:

> What do the Forests Bear?
> Soil, Water and Pure Air.

It is this conflict of interests and of perceptions that lies at the heart of the Chipko movement. It has now turned into a national movement, spreading into forest areas of Karnataka, Himachal Pradesh, Rajasthan, and Bihar, laying the nebulous foundation for an alternative science and technology and an alternative development strategy for sustainable and equitable development. Similar conflicts have arisen in the case of mineral resources in Doon Valley at the base of the Himalayan foothills. An ecology movement has grown up there directed against limestone quarrying. The Doon Valley is well known for its rich water resources as well as rich limestone deposits. In the reductionist view of a market economy (where the only value that matters is exchange value), the most efficient use of the limestone deposit is its extraction for the satisfaction of commercial-industrial demands. In the ecological view limestone in its fractured form provides the best and largest aquifer that sustains the rich water resources of the valley. The most efficient economic use of the mineral in this perspective is its conservation for the sustenance of the water resources on which the whole economic life in the valley is dependent. The reductionist view of minerals is blind to their other functions and therefore destroys them for maximizing short-term benefits.[9]

Like Chipko, the Dehradun movement has emerged from the ecological perspective of the people whose survival depends on the continuing ecological functions of natural resources. It carries within it the seed of an alternative knowledge system. In the words of Paul Feyerabend:

> . . . in a free society intellectuals are just one tradition. They have no special rights and their views are of no special interest (except, of course, to themselves). Problems are solved not by specialists (though their advice will not be disregarded) but by the people concerned, in accordance with the ideas *they* value and by procedures *they* regard as most appropriate. This is how the efforts of a special group combining flexibility and respect for all traditions will gradually erode the borrowed and self-serving "rationalism" of those who are now using tax money to destroy the traditions of the taxpayers, to ruin their minds, rape their environment and quite generally to turn living human beings into well trained slaves of their own barren vision of life.[10]

The politics of forestry science and the dialectics of nature

Ecological perceptions of nature provided by Chipko and other ecology movements are based on the recognition of interrelationships and interdependence among the various material components of nature. They are aware that these relationships are crucial and have to be preserved to ensure survival of plant and animal life. A direct implication of this ecological perception is that the properties of individual components of the ecosystem will differ according to the other components it is seen to be related to. Relationships thus define the context for knowing the properties of nature. What properties are perceived depends on the context, which, in turn, is fixed by priorities and values that govern the pattern of the use of natural resource. The context is therefore created by a value system. Properties perceived in nature depend on how one looks at nature; and how one looks depends, in turn, on the economic interest guiding the use of nature. If one looks at them as ecosystems, one sees their productive role in soil, water, fertility, nutrition.

Looking does not itself create properties in a causal sense. It creates them by creating conditions for perception. As Feyerabend argues:

> We no longer assume an objective world that remains unaffected by our epistemic activities, except when moving within the confines of a particular point of view. We concede that epistemic activities may have a decisive influence even upon the most solid piece of cosmological furniture—they may make gods disappear and replace them by heaps of atoms in empty space.[11]

The thesis that there are no objective facts of nature independent of their context of perception is not peculiar to ecology movements for preservation of nature's resources. It is also supported by the ontological implications of the physics of quantum mechanics which suggests that the properties of systems change when the context of their observation is changed.[12] The Einstein–Podolski–Rosen paradox arises from the fact that measurements on one system can influence the properties of a related but separated system.[13] The paradox is resolved when it is recognized that these changes in properties are not "results of a causal interaction between object and observer but of a change in the very conditions that permit us to speak of objects, situations, events."[14] The Kochen–Specker theorem makes the same point in a different way.[15] The value of a particular magnitude changes according to the context in which it is defined. Quantum mechanics confirms at the micro level some of the ontological implications of an ecological world-view.

This contrasts with more conventional or reductionist views of science in which the components of a system are perceived in isolation from their interrelationships. Properties and facts about nature arrived at through the reductionist approach are therefore specific to the context created by reductionist ontology and epistemology. Since the context is not explicitly mentioned in reductionist claims about nature, such claims are presented as neutral factors about nature independent of the contextual value. The dominant system of knowledge of forest resources is linked with the wood-based industry such as paper. However, its value commitment is implicit, and it is called "scientific forestry". Forestry science practised by forest dwellers, such as tribals, who see trees as living entities providing them with conditions of life are declared unscientific in the reductionist framework. In spite of being restricted by their particular context, reductionist knowledge of "scientific forestry" is projected as universal and objective. However, as Feyerabend has pointed out:

> The appearance of objectivity that is attached to some value judgements come from the fact that a particular tradition is *used* but not *recognised*; absence of the impressions of subjectivity is not proof of "objectivity" but an oversight.[16]

This oversight leads to the exclusion of the possibility of alternative contexts of perception of nature. A non-reductionist ecological perception of nature, as provided by Chipko, leads to the awareness that reductionism is a particular way of looking at nature, in which only certain facts of nature are picked out while denying the existence of the others. Ecology provides the foundations for an alternative philosophy that recognizes that there is a plurality of ways of knowing nature; it provides the ontological possibility of an alternative framework for science and technology.

Ecology also provides an epistemological framework that shows that alternatives to reductionist science and technology are preferable because, unlike exclusivist reductionism, they provide a holistic view of nature. Reductionist forestry is silent about the hydrological role of tree species. Because Chipko treats ecology as an issue of survival, it is also rooted in a materialistic philosophical position, though a materialism that is dialectical rather than mechanistic. In this, they follow Marx and Engels. As Engels put it, mechanistic analyses of nature may have provided

> the fundamental conditions of the gigantic strides in our knowledge of nature which have been made during the last four hundred years. But this method of investigating has also left us as legacy the habit of observing natural objects and natural processes in their isolation detached from the whole, vast interconnection of things and therefore not in their motion but in their repose, not as essentially changing but as fixed constants, not in their life but in their death. In considering individual things, it loses sight of their connections; in contemplating their existence, it forgets their coming into being and passing away, in looking at them at rest it leaves their motion out of account because it cannot see the wood for the trees.[17]

In practice, "scientific forestry" becomes a prescription for desertification.[18] Ecologically based alternatives in science are an imperative because they alone ensure human survival by preserving the life-support system.

Reductionism is not an epistemological accident. It is the answer to the need of a particular form of economic organization. The reductionist world-view, the industrial revolution and the capitalist economy were the philosophical, technological and economic components of the same process. This nexus is substantiated in the dominant paradigm of forestry.

Reductionist forestry was born with the increasing need for transportation and communication in an emerging global capitalist economy. Teak was exploited for shipbuilding; sal and deodar were felled for the railway network. The purpose of forestry science was, and still is, to generate revenue for the state and profits for industry. Trees ceased to be seen as vital parts of a living and essential ecosystem; they became commodities. This economic value is built into the very concepts, basic terms, definitions, of the science of forestry.

The conflicting economic objectives guiding the utilization of natural resources are generated by social groups with conflicting economic interests; and they are reflected in conflicting perceptions of nature. And it is in this sense that Chipko as an ecology movement converges with movements for alternative sciences.

The politics of development

The earlier forest satyagrahas as well as their contemporary form, the Chipko movement, should be seen as civilizational responses to a development model based on ecological destruction, on the one hand, and poverty creation, on the other. They have been inspired by the Gandhian world-view which recognizes that prosperity of the ordinary citizens of India can only be based on an ecological development that is just and sustainable. The imitation of a pattern of development which had evolved elsewhere in a different socio-economic and historical context could not, in Gandhi's view, solve India's economic problems:

> Why must India become industrial in the western sense? What is good for one nation situated in one condition is not necessarily good for another differently situated. One man's food is often another man's poison. Mechanisation is good when hands are too few for the work intended to be accomplished. It is an evil where there are more hands than required for the work as is the case in India.[19]

The demand for wood of forest-based industry has been a major source of conflicts to which ecology movements like Chipko are a response. In the Himalayas, at the heart of the conflict over forest resources is the need of forest-based industries for species like pine, on the one hand, and the basic need of local villagers for species like oak, on the other. Responding to the needs of organized industry, the forest department has been planting pine at the expense of oak. Pine, unlike oak, is not useful for fodder or fertilizer; it upsets the hydrological balance of the mountain slopes, leading to increased floods and erosion, and decreased infiltration into subsoil and ground water sources. The drying up of springs and water sources has been a major cause of changes in vegetation. Chipko activists have been removing pine seedlings from forest department nurseries and replacing them with seeds of oak and fruit-bearing trees.

In other regions of India, too, the demands of forest-based industry have led to drastic changes with severe ecological consequences. In the Western Ghats rich natural forests were felled to plant eucalyptus for the pulp industry. This was justified on the grounds that eucalyptus planting would increase the "productivity" of the site—productivity for the cellulose-based industry. For the village communities the cultivation of eucalyptus was counterproductive. Large-scale eucalyptus monoculture upset the ecological equilibrium, since in the tropics stability is related to biological diversity.[20] Eucalyptus plantations in the Western Ghats, raised after clearfelling dense evergreen and moist deciduous forests, have themselves been devastated by fungal diseases; and the consequent low productivity has defeated the very purpose for which they were raised. In the Western Ghats the movement, known as "Appiko" aims at stopping the destruction of natural forests which are critical to the survival of the agricultural community.

The needs of pulp-based industry cannot be satisfied without turning renewable land and vegetational resources into non-renewable ones. It may be noted that the conversion of fertile croplands into wasteland has the official

sanction and international funding for so-called "social forestry" programmes. Here is a glaring example of collusion between politicians and
private interests to undermine the equitable and sustainable use of resources
for—development! A campaign called "Munna Rakshana Koota" (Save the
Soil) has been initiated to counter the threat posed to people's survival.

Technological development and resource under-development

Technological modernization is sold as a means of increasing productivity.
Productivity here means productivity of labour (more production with less
labour); it does not care for increasing the production of raw materials (that
is, natural resources) which are an indispensable input for even the most
sophisticated industry, nor does it care for making increasing production
sustainable; it cares less for an equitable sharing of what is produced.

This limited definition of productivity, evolved in a specific context, has
been universalized, and the ruling élites in entirely different societies avidly
subscribe to it in the name of "national interest". Labour-saving and
resource-guzzling technology has been introduced in societies where labour is
abundant and resources scarce. The development-planner has been
brainwashed by education and training to believe that resources and resource
processes that are not produced through excessive technological and capital
inputs are valueless. This economic doctrine leads to a thoughtless
destruction of natural resource which is the survival base of millions. The
assertion in action of the simple truth, not self-evident to the planner, that
human survival is a precondition for development, is the central contribution
of Chipko and other ecology movements to development alternatives. Chipko
stresses the fact that for survival, satisfaction of two basic needs is enough: (i)
the need for food and water, quantitatively and qualitatively enough for
healthy biological survival, and, (ii) the need for clothing and shelter
necessary for physical survival.

Traditional economies with a stable ecology, share with affluent economies
the ability to use natural resources to satisfy these basic needs. The difference
between them is twofold: (i) in affluent societies the same needs are satisfied
through longer technological chains requiring higher energy and resource
inputs; and (ii) affluent societies generate new and artificial wants to create a
demand for increasing production of industrial goods and services.
Traditional economies may not be advanced in the creation and satisfaction
of non-basic needs; but in regard to the satisfaction of basic needs they are,
barring natural disasters, what Marshall Sahlins calls "the original affluent
society".

Economies based on indigenous technologies have been viewed as having
lower productivity because of the distorted concept of productivity. With a
sensible view of productivity as optimum use of natural resources and
adequate labour these traditional technologies are usually very productive
and efficient. The destruction of these technologies, along with the destruction
of their material base, is generally the reason behind the poverty in societies
which have been made to bear the cost of resource destruction for economic
growth.

New technologies and new production processes are often merely new ways of satisfying basic needs or generating new non-basic needs. In societies where most resources are already being utilized for satisfaction of basic needs, diversion of resources to new uses for the satisfaction of non-basic wants threatens survival and therefore generates conflicts between the demands of growth and the demands of survival.[21] When, for instance, forest resources are already being fully utilized to stabilize soil and water, and to provide for the basic needs of food, fodder, fertilizer, fuel, and so on, their diversion to the pulp industry makes no sense to the people living in the society.

Growth or destruction?

The much used metaphor in the dominant paradigm of economic development is that the national cake must grow bigger if everyone is to get a bigger slice. Modern technologies are believed to increase the size of the cake, never mind if it does not achieve justice and peace.

Ecology movements challenge this paradigm by showing that modern technologies involve high ecological and social costs. In many instances— such as in forestry—it is plain that the cake is actually shrinking because of the spread of resource-intensive, resource-wasteful, resource-demanding technologies.

The assumption of the technological solution to underdevelopment and poverty is related to the historical metaphors guiding the received view of economic development. Development is equated with economic growth, which is then reduced to the growth of technologies and hardware. Linear progression is the guiding principle; resource endowments, resource scarcity and resource conflicts are just ignored. W. W. Rostow's famous version of this model as a series of stages of economic growth, for example, simply assumed that resources are unlimited.

The first stage in this model is the traditional society whose structure is developed within

> limited production functions, based on pre-Newtonian science and technology and on pre-Newtonian attitudes towards the physical world. . . . The central fact about the traditional society was that a ceiling existed on the level of attainable output per head.

The fact that such societies had consciously chosen to adopt limited production functions to ensure sustainability and justice is not recognized. The second stage of growth in this model embraces societies in the process of transition from the traditional to the take-off stage. During this period of transition, it is assumed, the traditional society persists side by side with modern economic activities. It is this stage of transition which provided the backdrop for the common characterization of contemporary India as a "dual sector" economy. The third stage is the take off

> when the old blocks and resistance to steady growth are finally overcome. The forces making for economic progress, which yielded limited bursts and enclaves of modern activity, expand and come to dominate society.[22]

The Rostowian model of economic growth assumes that the process of modernization ensures economic development for all groups because "the economy exploits *hitherto unused natural resources*". The new methods of production are therefore viewed as generating increased employment and consumption in an absolute sense. Growth and development are assumed to be the same thing.

However, it is only in very exceptional cases that the natural resources consumed by modern production processes have been "hitherto unused". Their traditional utilization has remained invisible to modern technologists, economists and planners for two reasons.

1. Traditional utilization of natural resources has been predominantly for use and not for exchange. Since it is only the exchange value that gets noticed in modern economics, resources are declared unused or useless if they do not have exchange value, even if they have high use value. The role of forests as a common resource providing fuel, fodder, fertilizer is not internal to forestry science or forestry economics; only their commercial yield is.

2. The traditional utilization of natural resources is calculated, not only by the extent of their consumption but also by their ecological function in maintaining the productive processes of nature which make sustained supply of resources possible. The failure or refusal to recognize these ecological functions of natural resource leads to their being viewed as unused even while they are being utilized economically in conservation. The invisible function of forests in soil and water conservation had to be made visible by the Chipko movement. It was not perceived by foresters.

Modernization based on resource-hungry processes materially deprives communities which use those resources for survival, either directly or through their ecological functions. The growth of pulp industry does not ensure development for all. On the contrary, it hits those communities who need water and land for agriculture. It causes underdevelopment of those affected negatively by resource diversion or destruction. Conflicting demands on resources lead to economic polarization through growth brought about by modern technology. It is therefore necessary to evaluate the role of new technologies in economic development on the scale of their resource demand. The productivity of a technology in the perspective of human survival must distinguish between basic and non-basic needs. It is on the satisfaction of basic needs that human survival depends. As Georgescu-Roegen points out:

> There can be no doubt about it. Any use of the natural resources for
> the satisfaction of non-vital needs means a smaller quantity of life in
> the future. If we understand well the problem, the best use of our
> iron resources is to produce plows or harrows as they are needed, not
> Rolls Royces, not even agricultural tractors . . .[23]

Indicators conventionally used for measuring economic growth rate are insensitive to the difference between the satisfaction of vital and non-vital needs as well as to the differential contribution of economic growth to the diverse social groups and classes. These indicators focus on increasing the total consumption of non-vital commodities irrespective of how this increased consumption is linked with a decreasing availability of resources for the satisfaction of vital needs. In forestry, for example, while the major thrust in economic growth is towards production and consumption of non-vital industrial products like pulp, cement or steel, there is no serious attempt to stop the alarmingly quick rate of the destruction of natural water resources, for drinking or irrigation. In a world of finite resources, if the emphasis is on the satisfaction of non-vital needs, it can be done only at the cost of satisfaction of vital needs.

Civilizations that have survived without denying others the right to survival have always been guided by criteria of technological choice which are sensitive to nature and man. The unit of assessment of technological productivity is the entire chain of technologies that transform natural resources into goods and services for human needs. Contemporary technology, however, leaves both nature and man out of the growth calculus. Technologies are considered fragments of value in themselves, not as a means for satisfying human needs. The technological shift that has taken place is a shift based on changing the value referents for human activity. Accelerating erosion of resources and poisoning of ecosystems are the inevitable outcome of this self-serving technology. The values of "Artha" (resources) and "Kama" (needs) are no longer primary. And there is no place for "Dharma"—the stabilizer.

Ecology movements are an attempt to shift value back to nature and people. They are also an attempt to revive the earlier criteria for choosing technology. Peoples' ecology movements like Chipko attempt to do just that by redefining development in terms of different concepts of "economic value" and "productivity" in which symbiotic survival of people and nature is the central consideration.

The underdeveloped societies are not those that have yet to fall prey to the ideology of growth and development. The really underdeveloped societies are those in which a small section appropriates whatever benefits accrue from growth and a much larger section is made to pay for it. Rostow's take-off is integrally linked to this syndrome. Britain's take-off at the end of the eighteenth century was made possible by its forcing three continents into a state of underdevelopment. The destruction of Indian textiles industry and Indian agriculture and much else besides, the slave trade from Africa and the genocide of the indigenous North American people provided the scaffolding for building modern industry in Britain. The Rostowian fiction of take-off for the whole society with improved quality of life for all appears seductive because, under the historical conditions of colonialism, the costs of growth were borne by the colonies, while the entire population of the ruling countries benefited from the gains, notwithstanding the internal inequities in distribution. The vast geographical spaces separating the benefiting and the losing countries in the process of colonial exploitation made the resource destruction of the colonies invisible and led to the superficial impression that absolute growth was taking place. The model has been invalidated by the experience of countries which have attempted to follow it: increasing poverty alongside economic growth. In the process the odious features of colonialism have emerged: interior and resource-rich interior areas of the country bear the costs of destruction of their resources while a small minority appropriates all the benefit. Communities living in these regions and supporting themselves on local resources are pushed to the wall. Ecology movements are a warning that when life is at stake even those on the margin can fight—non-violently, of course—with their backs to the wall. They are a reminder, too, that a radical shift in the received wisdom about economic development is overdue.

Societies have not always progressed on the Rostowian linear path. Societies that have been careless about their resource base for sustenance have collapsed after an initial spurt of prosperity. The collapse of the Mayan and the Mesopotamian civilization was associated with a collapse of their life-support systems. The threat to the survival of the sub-Saharan countries is again rooted in the destruction of life-support systems. History falsifies Rostow.

The ecological consciousness of ancient civilizations was based on cyclical progress, not along a linear path. But just as classical physics is incapable of explaining or understanding the motion of the electron, so is conventional economics incapable of understanding stable and ecologically sound development. It interprets stability as stagnation and ecologically sound development as "limited production functions" (that is, without any movement whatever). Capturing this civilizational conflict between stable and unstable societies, Gandhi observed:

> modern civilisation seeks to increase bodily comforts, and it fails miserably even in doing so . . . . This civilisation is such that one has only to be patient and it will be self destroyed . . . there is no end to the victims destroyed in the fire of (this) civilisation. Its deadly effect is that people come under its scorching flames believing it to be all good . . . .
>
> . . . It is a charge against India that her people are so uncivilised, ignorant and stolid that it is not possible to induce them to adopt any changes. It is a charge really against our strength. What we have tested and found true on the anvil of experience, we dare not change. Many thrust their advice upon India, but she remains steady. This is her beauty, it is the sheet anchor of our hope.[24]

The contemporary ecology movements like Chipko are a new Gandhian attempt to establish that steadiness and stability do not mean stagnation, and that balance with nature's innate ecological processes is not technological backwardness but technological sophistication. At a time when a quarter of the world's population is facing starvation due to erosion of soil, water and genetic diversity of living resources, running for the mirage of unending growth is a major source of genocide. Killing people by murdering nature is no longer an invisible form of violence. Claude Alvares has called it the Third World War—"a war waged in peace time, without comparison but involving the largest number of deaths and the largest number of soldiers without uniform."[25]

Ecology movements are a non-violent intervention in this Third World War which threatens the survival of humanity, including even the victors. They are political movements for a non-violent world order in which nature is conserved for conserving the options for survival. They are movements on which issues of peace, development and environment converge.[26] These movements are local, but their impact is bound to be felt far beyond their small geographical boundaries; for the right of survival that they are demanding can be ensured in a just and peaceful world. That is how these grass-roots movements are linked with the global issue of peace. Unless the world is restructured in its social-political-economic organization, in its world-view, in its life-style, peace and justice will continue to be elusive. As the Vedic poet realized, peace for man cannot be isolated from peace in the universe. He prayed:

> Peace of sky, Peace of earth, peace of waters, peace of plants, peace
> of trees, peace of the universe, peace of peace, may that peace come
> to me.[27]

Grass roots ecology movements are basically striving for the realization of the old concept of "Vasudhaiva Kutumbakam" (earth-family), in which peace means peace not only for man but for all living organisms.[28] Such a peace is not inconsistent with development; it is a precondition for a just and sustainable development.

Notes and references

1. Mahamopadhyay Laxmithatachar, "Srivaisnavite precepts practice concerning environment," paper presented at a seminar on social and religious basis of environment policy, Bangalore, 1984.
2. M.K. Gandhi, *Hind Swaraj* (1938), p.61.
3. Pyarelal, *Towards New Horizons* (1959), p.12.
4. J. Bandyopadhyay and Vandana Shiva, "The evolution, structure and impact of Chipko," paper prepared for the UNU Himalaya-Ganges project, 1984; and Sunderlal Bahuguna, *Chipko: A Novel Movement to Re-establish Cordial Relation between Man and Nature*.
5. H.C. Reiger, "Whose Himalaya—A study in Geopiety," in: T. Singh (editor), *Studies in Himalayan Ecology and Development Strategies* (1980).
6. M. Moench and J. Bandyopadhyay, "Dynamics of resource degradation in the Himalaya," paper presented at a seminar on Ecological Crises and Legislative Safeguards, New Delhi, 1984; and Bandyopadhyay and Shiva (Note 4).
7. Bandyopadhyay and Shiva (Note 4).
8. C.T.S. Nair, "Crisis in Forest Management," paper presented at a seminar on Ecological crises and Legislative Safeguards, New Delhi, 1984.
9. J. Bandyopadhyay, et al., *The Doon Valley Ecosystem* (1984).
10. Paul Feyerabend, *Science in a Free Society* (1978), p.10.
11. Ibid., p.70.
12. Vandana Shiva, "Hidden Variables and Nonlocality in Quantum Mechanics," Ph.D. thesis, University of Waterloo, Ontario, Canada.
13. A. Einstein, B. Podolski and N. Rosen, "Can quantum mechanical description of physical reality be considered complete?," *Physical Review*, 45, 1935, pp.777–780.
14. Feyerabend (Note 10), p.70.
15. S. Kochen and P. Specker, "The Problem of Hidden Variables in Quantum Mechanics," *Journal of Mathematics and Mechanics*, vol 17, 1967, pp.59–87.
16. Feyerabend (Note 10), p.83.
17. Friedrich Engels, *Anti-Duhring*, 1947 edition, p.36.
18. J. Bandyopadhyay and V. Shiva, *Ecological Audit of Eucalyptus* (EBD, 1984).
19. M.K. Gandhi, *Young India*, 25 July 1929, p.2444.
20. J. Bandyopadhyay and V. Shiva, *Ecological Audit of Eucalyptus*, (1984).
21. J. Bandyopadhyay and V. Shiva, "Political Economy of Technological Polarisations," *Economic and Political Weekly*, vol XVIII, no 45, 1982, pp.1827–32.

22. W.W. Rostow, *The Stages of Economic Growth* (1979), p.4.
23. N. Georgescu-Roegen, *The Entropy Law and the Economic Process* (1974), p.2.
24. M.K. Gandhi, *Hind Swaraj*, p.61.
25. C. Alvares, "Deadly Development," *Development Forum*, vol XI, no 7, 1973, pp.3–4.
26. S. Bahuguna (personal letter).
27. Krishna Chaitanya, "A profounder ecology: The Hindu view of man and nature" (mimeograph).
28. E. Lott, "India's religious resources for developing a global eco-theology," Paper presented at a seminar on social and religious basis of environmental policy, Bangalore, 1984.

Regenerating People's Space

GUSTAVO ESTEVA

From "development" to "hospitality"—peasants' perspectives: some historical notes*

"Mexicans," mostly peasants, numbered in the millions at the beginning of the 16th century. While scholars cannot agree on the exact number, estimates varying between seven and 25 million, one thing is clear: one hundred years later, only one million remained. Those remaining survived by the slow recovery of—and, wherever possible, sought the regeneration of—their spaces, hosting the new gods brought by the Spaniards to their land and into their culture.

They grew to around four million (80 percent of the total population of Mexico) by the end of the 18th century, most of them living in municipalities of colonial design, then called "Indian Republics" after their autonomous form of government. They enjoyed an opportunity to advance along a path of their own during the first part of the 19th century because of the instability and weakness of the central government, through the Revolution of Independence (1810–1824), and through the social and military convulsions that followed.

A group of enlightened liberals, who re-established the Republic after French and US military interventions (1861), conceived a democratic dream for Mexico cast in the French and US molds. They were unable to bring the dream to life but the dictatorship that overthrew them undertook a similar task. Its project meant depriving the peasants, especially the Indians, of their spaces: physically, the commons—the communal land—was to be turned into private property; and culturally they were condemned to be transformed into "citizens," individually embedded in an abstraction, the so-called "national society."

At first glance, it might seem that the project was almost completed after thirty years of dictatorship for by 1910, there was a social organization that resembled a nation-state and society. Most of the land of this "nation" was by then in private hands; one percent of the population (the *hacendados*) owned 90

---

*This section which was intended by the author as an appendix is being placed here by the editors as an introduction to provide the reader unfamiliar with Mexican history a context for the essay. *Editors*

Commissioned by the Committee for a Just World Peace.

percent of the land. Most of the peasants were reduced to forms of slavery, serfdom, or labor, usually as destitute individuals. The apparent success of the dictatorship in conventional economic terms ran parallel with the social and political success of dissolving the peasant and Indian traditional communities. Because of the historical nature of the peasant culture, however, it was able to show its resilience at this point. A revolution, triggered by a liberal call for political democracy in 1910, exploded soon after in a myriad of peasant revolts. The peasant armies that dominated the scene for several years organized themselves around claims to recover "the commons," and to regenerate the physical and cultural spaces which had been damaged but not destroyed by the liberal dream.

In 1917, the Constitution gave legal sanction to the peculiar and strong entitlement of the Indians to their *original* communal land, if and when it was recognized by the Spanish Crown. In the constitutional article that assigned to the "nation" full rights over the land, it was provided that there would be a *possibility* of constituting limited private property of the land, but it also enshrined the *obligation* to give land, in the form of *ejidos*, to any group of peasants who claimed it.[1]

The early revolutionary governments reluctantly followed the constitutional rule. They saw the *ejidos* as a political compromise with the peasants which had to be accepted, but taken as a transitional step toward a more "modern" form of exploitation. Instead of *haciendas* and *ejidos* they dreamed of small private farms, patterned after the then existing US model. The peasant reaction to the anti-agrarian winds prevailing in government around 1930, paved the way for the pro-agrarian administration of President Lázaro Cárdenas. Under it, by 1940, the *ejidos* and the Indian communities covered more than half of the agricultural land of the country.[2]

In 1938, at the height of the agrarian reform of the Cárdenas government, the *Confederación Nacional Campesina* (CNC) was founded. It soon became a powerful and well-rooted peasant organization, perhaps the biggest and strongest that ever existed on the continent. In the post-war era, however, in the service of the development dream, it became a tool for control and manipulation of the peasantry. This function weakened it, as the peasants lost control over its direction and practices, and the national balance of forces became mostly adverse to peasant interests. Even so, the CNC has been, and is still today, the most important peasant organization at the national level.

During the following decades, as the "Green Revolution" progressed, destroying both peasant economy and culture, the peasants tried to replace the CNC with other national, class-oriented organizations. Each one enjoyed a short period of success, more regional than national, before joining the CNC because of its brokerage function.

In the 1960s, when the Mexican "agricultural miracle" started to fall apart, the peasants tried once again to advance their interests through all forms of political struggle, including revolts and guerrilla activity. At the same time, they also broadened their claims. In the 1970s, the populist regime of Luis Echeverría tried to federate all "national" peasant organizations. It submitted the peasants to a form of permanent mobilization from the top down which was actually much ado about nothing, insofar as their basic claims were concerned. But, at the same time, it opened for them new spaces and opportunities.

By the early 1970s, the "Green Revolution" had lost its charm, but the conventional modernizing ethos still prevailed, gradually corrupting peasant dreams. After 1976, a vigorous modernizing program was launched, clearly supported by the World Bank and other international institutions. That orientation, stubbornly maintained, and made worse by bad weather, precipitated a disastrous agricultural year in 1979 which intensified peasant unrest. In reaction, the government launched, in 1980, a new and ambitious food strategy. For the first time in 40 years, the official policy focused on food self-sufficiency and recognized the key role of the peasantry in achieving that goal. This jeopardized the conventional developmental orientation, which was religiously attached to the idea of "comparative advantages," following the World Bank catechism. Oil and loans gave the Mexican government the opportunity to implement the new strategy by generous subsidies to the peasants, without forcing the government to abandon its traditional clientele in the "modern sector." But the impressive results of this strategy in terms of production were not enough to give the policy a long life. In 1982, when a new Administration took office, in the midst of the so-called crisis of the Mexican economy, more conventional policies were implemented again, with budgets reduced due to the "adjustment process" prescribed by the IMF for countries like Mexico.

Since 1975, the peasants have concentrated on the regeneration of local and regional organizations which have been effectively controlled by the peasants themselves, and not by the "national" organizations. These local and regional organizations are constantly multiplying and intensifying their horizontal contacts, relationships, and alliances, but they have carefully avoided the temptation to federate themselves into bigger "national" organizations. In 1978 some peasants made what may turn out to be the last attempt to build a new "national" organization to replace the existing ones which were weakened, corrupted, or co-opted. The limited success of this effort corresponds not only to the prevailing mood of the society and the present balance of forces, but to a change in the orientation of the peasant movement. Some of the peasants follow the conventional lines of class struggle, or make economic and political claims, and are usually linked to political parties. They struggle for a better piece of the economic pie, and look for the goods and services usually associated with "development." Many others, however, even though they are still attracted by the myth of "development," are no longer paralyzed by it. They are subordinating, more and more, conventional economic struggles to focus on the regeneration of their spaces.

Regenerating people's space

I want to tell a story and elaborate on it. I do not know, however, *whose* story it is. Am I really talking of *one* story with a defined subject? Who is the real teller? Can I ascribe to one subject the different theoretical insights that cross my mind?

I can imagine my audience. I am writing for my friends who are looking for a just world peace. I am writing for those interested in peace and security, redefined in peoples' terms, and for those examining modern social movements actively striving for these and other claims. I am writing for social activists, for those interested in the recent evolution of "grass-roots activism," and for the people "activated" by the activists, or who are in motion by their own impulses.

Since I cannot use my own vernacular language to tell my story, I will try to overcome that handicap by using simple images. I hope that this will enable my readers to represent, in their own terms, what I have to say. Paradoxically, at the level of a theoretical elaboration of the experience, where a logical common ground can be expected to be found, I am not equally confident in my ability to find it and at the same time make my point.

I am explicitly trying to avoid two extremes: to describe my story as extremely peculiar and absolutely unique, closed in itself, and thus irrelevant to others; and, even worse, to introduce overtly or surreptitiously something like a "model," a "paradigm," a "methodology," a "social experiment," a "case study" to be imitated or reproduced by others. But I do not know how to accomplish my task.

After this puzzled introduction, a puzzling text will follow. It cannot be but an essay, juxtaposing, through explicit ruptures, two different modes of perception. Two modes of perception that I, for one, cannot merge.

Trouble with being a "we"

During the 1970s, the Mexican peasants concentrated their efforts on rebuilding their organizations at the local level, and on the regeneration of their local spaces. I can hardly explain the phenomenon in a few words, but the introduction to this essay offers some historical background for interpretation.

People coming from the other extreme of the educational scale then began to join them in a new way. It was not to get affiliation to a political party or ideology, or to give the peasants technical assistance or charity. It was to explore new life projects, side by side with the peasants. We were some of those middle-class professionals looking for another path. We were disenchanted with development and its institutions, with political parties, and bureaucratic or academic careers. We tried to participate in building new and diversified forms of social institutions that flourished at the time. Highly decentralized webs of heterogeneous organizations proliferated before our eyes, transforming us into de-professionalized intellectuals. And now, an expanding circle of ex-economists and one-time sociologists or industry managers that we are, we find it increasingly difficult to make our former peers grasp what we learned near the grass-roots, namely, that no indicator can reflect the pain caused by the loss of local self-reliance, of dignity and solidarity which is the inevitable shadow of any measurable progress. Similarly, no indicator can tell the story of human *remediation* and profound joy that "we" are finding in the more hospitable world to which "we" have started to belong.

I cannot use indicators to describe the process but it is perhaps useful to offer some landmarks. In the mid-1970s, "we" were no more than a collection of individuals unified both by our involvement with the peasants and by frustration with our ambivalent institutional success: the higher up we were in the hierarchy, the more distanced we were from the peasants and from what we wanted to do. We felt the need to create an autonomous space for our activities. To begin with, we created a couple of non-profit organizations offering some support and professional services to peasants. We built in them democratic representative bodies, managerial hierarchies, and coordination centers to render our professional services. However, we soon discovered that these organizations were not as autonomous as we wanted them to be. In the process of earning our living, on the one hand, and "giving" our services, on the other hand, we were practising a form of hidden paternalism. We also perceived that our institutional design was blocking initiatives and inhibiting vital and creative impulses. We were probably just imitating the managerial scheme we were used to. Such a scheme can be useful as an exogenous intervention in peasant life—for their good, of course. It seemed inappropriate, however, for projects looking for autonomy and endogenous action.

Gradually, we changed our institutional form and started to build *webs*. Networking was fashionable at that time, and we liked the idea behind the image of a web: it provided a pattern for building institutions while at the same time avoiding an internal or external center (political, ideological, or administrative). A web can be constructed through horizontal linking and by creating linkages that only linked adjacent "points," thus also avoiding the need for linking everyone with everyone else. But after some time we started once again to feel uncomfortable with the web design. We resented the "integrative" principle, which appears as a tendency within any web, because it implied homogenization and heteronomy, and invited adhesion, affiliation, belonging—the opposite of what we wanted. We discovered that the webs—as fishermen and spiders know very well—are designed to trap. But we were not trying to trap or catch anyone or anything. So we started to use the image of a *hammock* to represent, metaphorically, our vocation.

Like a web, the image of a hammock holds the idea of horizontality and lack of a center (except for its center of gravity). But it opens other possibilities. The hammock is there, where it is placed: one is not inside it, nor part of it, nor a member of it. It can be used or not used when necessary, and for whatever purpose. One can change its location and carry it along when travelling. The hammock, above all, has the quality of adopting the shape of its user.

"We" *are not* a web nor a hammock. "We" *have* a hammock: a flexible construction that "we" use when "we" need or want. But who are "we"? Usually our answer is that "we" are around 400 groups of peasants, urban marginals and de-professionalized intellectuals. "We" know what "we" are not: an organization, a party, or a social movement (if we assume that a movement requires some kind of political steering towards common goals).

The stuff that keeps the stability of relations between and among all "our" groups is friendship and trust. These remain even if "we" do not see or deal with each other every day—as in any friendly relationship. Obviously, this does not mean that everybody is friends with everybody else. (We are speaking here, perhaps, of half a million people.) It means that the members of a group are friends with those of another group, and some of these are friends with a third group and so forth. Thus, "we" are intertwined through links of friendship and of trust. "We" met each other along the way, and became friends: *compañeros*. "We" decided first to build organizations, formalizing our ties, but when "we" saw that they limited and hindered us (and sometimes damaged our friendship), "we" abandoned such design and "we" built webs. But "we" had not advanced much on that road when "we" realized that the web naturally tended to become too formal to rebuild organizations. That is when "we" built the hammock, which does not stand between one another; it is there to be used when needed by any friend who needs it.

But who are "we"? That problem still remains. We have no representative bodies that can speak in the name of all. Nobody expresses a unique and all-encompassing voice. Isolated representatives of some of the groups that are the "owners" of the hammock cannot represent the others. I cannot speak in the name of the hammock. It is inappropriate for me to do so. It may be that some of the de-professionalized intellectuals who use the hammock identify themselves with my discourse more than other users. But I can only speak on my behalf even when, for practical purposes, I assume my formal affiliation: the position I have on the boards of some of the non-profit organizations embedded in the hammock (e.g., Opción, S. C.; Copider, A. C.; Fondo de Cultura Campesina, S. C.) or even on the board of the coordinating space of all these organizations, where most of the de-professionalized intellectuals living in the hammock or using it are working (e.g., Autonomía, Descentralismo y Gestión, A. C.—formally and legally constituted for some practical purposes in 1982).

At the same time, I know very well that I am not just expressing my personal views or presenting my own experience. The "we" that I use is a very diffused one. It is not a majestic "we," like the Pope's. It is not a rhetorical "we," like a populist politician's. It is not the formal "we" of anyone invested with a formal representation or mandate. It is analogous to the "we" used by members of a cultural group (blacks, women, the Eskimos, the French, neighbors), but the analogy is imprecise. I hope that the inability to explicitly define "we" will not be an insurmountable obstacle for telling the story I want to tell here.

Trouble with being a "self"

I was born and brought up in Mexico City in a middle-class family. I was brought up with the idea that I was an *individual* member of my father's family. I can remember my efforts to give concrete meaning to the abstraction of a 200-year old genealogical tree. I was also led to believe that I "belonged" to a homogenized physical and social space—Mexico City, Mexico, humankind—which I could acquire only after my affiliation with "concrete communities": my neighborhood, my school, my class, my creed, my party. . . . One cannot be a real member of the most populous city in the world. By the same token, one can avoid communion with the people living in the same place or sharing a similar role or function (school, neighborhood, etc). One *can* and *must* choose a "community" if one wants to belong.

For a long time, together with my friends—now de-professionalized intellectuals—we applied this constructed perception of the world and the conventional lenses of formal categories of social science to understand peasant actions and reactions. We failed time and time again. Then we began to suspect that conventional wisdom inevitably reduced the peasant world to a mechanical structure and, in the process, lost the keys to understand that world. So we started to trust our own noses more than the experts' scientific analyses, and thus we smelled another possibility. Could it be that we were standing face-to-face with an entirely different mode of perceiving things?

My mother's mother, a Mexican–Indian, was supposed to be hidden from my father's sight when she visited us in Mexico City. I do not know why. But the fact established two clear-cut worlds during my growing up years.

At home, in Mexico City, I used to go to the store around the corner, and later, to the supermarket or to Sears and Roebuck. When on holiday, I asked to be taken to my grandmother Dolores's—in Oaxaca, where her family tended a stall in Oaxaca's traditional market. I played around the market place with other kids. Since I was a well-mannered child, I could not ask my grandmother to buy me a lovely knife displayed at the market which I admired day after day. One morning, my grandmother said to me: "I will buy you *your* knife." She took me by the hand to exactly *the* place, and started a long conversation in *Zapoteca* with the stall-keeper. Then we just left. Of course, I could not say anything. The next morning, after another long conversation with the man, now in Spanish, she said: "My grandson wants *his* knife." "Good," he answered, as he placed my cherished knife on a table by his right. And once again we left without the knife. Morning after morning, during that holiday, my grandmother chatted with the man. But I did not get my knife. One year later, on my second holiday in Oaxaca, my grandmother took me by the hand exactly to the same place and told the stall-keeper: "My grandson has now come for his knife." The man took the knife from the table where it had remained for one year, my grandmother paid the price apparently settled the year before, and finally I got my knife. I still have it.

Obviously, I had been looking at this event through the eyeglasses of my schooldays. So, I saw my grandmother's world as an illustration of the pre-modern mind described by conventional wisdom. It was, for me, but an "insufficient conscience." She just lived in her underdeveloped world—one that I respected and loved, but which I rejected for myself and for my children, and for my country. It was a world which needed to be "developed"—or so the logic went.

As I have said before, "we," the restricted "we" of the now de-professionalized intellectuals, failed to understand the peasant world through conventional wisdom. But the smell of another possibility brought me back to my childhood. I tried to remember the *mystery* of that time, and also tried, for the first time, to unveil it. I took this as a challenge, a venture of discovery, not as something new, but as something that I could reduce to my conventional perception. I was challenged both by the mystery itself, and by the miracle of its persistence. Was it not possible that we were standing face-to-face with a real mystery, that is, something that we cannot see through the lenses we were conditioned to use? I wondered. And then, just for a change, I took the glasses off. I suddenly saw my grandmother again and was able to realize that I had seen her before, with these same eyes, but that I was forced to suppress or forget that vision of her.

I know now that I cannot see simultaneously with and without the conventional lenses. My eyes and the lenses give me completely different pictures. I cannot reduce one to the other.

Everybody knows what is seen through the lenses of conventional wisdom, since they are constructed in such a way that everybody sees the same picture. (Some even think that by using them one can only see the lenses, not through them.) It is useless, then, to say here what "we" saw through those lenses, though for a time "we" felt very happy with our contributions to the literature, which "we" considered original theoretical insights. This is why my story, in contrast, talks of what "we" *actually* saw with our own eyes.

With this new vision, "we" found that the *Mexican peasants continue to be a people born in a concrete, collective space, both physical and cultural, to which they belong and which belongs to them.* Their spaces are *localized*—located in a specific place—but *unlimited*, i.e., without defined limits. They travel a lot. Some of them settle for years in another town or city, or even in another country, but they always keep, as a point of reference, that commons to which they belong and which belongs to them.

As is obvious, this insight appeared immediately to us as an inverted symmetry of our conventional perception. In the world in which we were educated, our spaces are *non-localized* but *limited*. In that world, following the Western tradition, "we" see *frontiers*, both physical and cultural, that define our relations with the "others" living beyond those frontiers: the aliens, the strangers, the barbarians. But that space does not have formal and permanent location. Everyone can define it and relocate it, within given limits. In the peasant perception, following our insight, the outer space is perceived as a *horizon*, not a frontier. A horizon is not a geographical or topological concept, but an historic and cultural metaphor. It is a collective conscience completely independent of geography, a "collective memory"—as Roger Bastide would call it—in continual transformation. Steger points out that the competition between the hierarchical principles of the "frontier" (ascription), and "horizon" (movement) is a constant (among certain cultures).[3]

With this in mind, "we" defined our challenge in institution-building as the need for complete openness to differential realities and perceptions. "We" needed for our tools a built-in flexibility that fully assumed the ignorance of who the other is and what he or she wants, paving the way for the smooth co-existence of radically different beings or entities. "We" selected the image of a hammock to represent metaphorically the very specific kind of pluralism "we" had started to fully assume in our practice.

Now, every institution and organization, even an informal web or network, has *rules of access*: the member or user must adapt himself or herself to those rules, taking the shape imposed by the institution or organization, be it a public agency or a service, a private business, a church, a political party, a non-profit or a charity institution. The hammock, in contrast, does not pre-determine the shape of the user, but adapts itself to any shape. And the hammock is used for joy and rest, to get support; there is no pre-condition but only that of knowing how to use it. This knowledge, in addition, can be learned independently by anyone, once he or she has discovered what the hammock is all about.

Instead of rules of access "we" have trust and friendship. This is the basic stuff that links all these groups of peasants, urban marginals, and de-professionalized intellectuals, and organizes the successful circulation of ideas or goods among them. The hammock, for example, constitutes a fund of around half-a-million dollars to support peasant projects or initiatives and for use during emergencies. Any morning, a peasant group can come to the fund's offices to ask for "credit." They may be already known to the "hammock" or they may simply be friends with one of the hammock occupants. No more than two hours later they get the cheque. If the fund is depleted, they are informed of the date on which they may return; this is estimated on the basis of the repayment dates of the money "lent." The whole transaction is conceived as a form of donation: for the peasants, it is a donation when they receive the cheque, and for the fund it is also a donation when they pay back. When being given the cheque they are told that the fund can "donate" to the same group only once. (If they have a permanent need for credit, the hammock can arrange to get it from a banking institution.) They are also told that the fund was created to support peasant groups and that it is maintained through the recovery of the "credit" granted. Now, after five years of operation, the original fund has revolved four times, "recovering" more than 95 percent of the "credit" granted. No peasant group has, until now, refused to pay back. The outstanding 5 percent corresponds to groups confronting especially difficult circumstances. The fund, of course, does not press them to pay back.

To many observers, building only on trust and friendship looks like a utopian, romantic fantasy. They think that such an "institution" cannot operate in the "real" economic world; though they admit it can work only in limited and marginal spaces. The people, in contrast, believe that these foundations are not only sound "survival strategy," but also define a joyful, promising, and fully pragmatic way of life. To depend for their livelihood on the promises of development, or to be dependent on market forces, or on public institutions to make a living, seems to them to be not only foolish fantasy, but a dead end. They know well that they have very limited access, if at all, to the goods and services associated with development. With the so-called crisis, they can see more and more that they are dispensable for the economic, formal world; a world which is, in any case, falling apart and in the process revealing the ugly side of progress that has been, for the so-called poor, its only real side. They also know that the so-called national economy is but an abstraction. The peasants have also discovered that *homo economicus* can survive only when help is given by friends. And perhaps they share with Plato the social environment that made him say: "The first and highest form of State and of government and of law is that in which there prevails, most widely, the ancient saying that 'Friends have all things in common'."

I must recall at this point that in the "real" world I am ranked as a *mestizo*, a man of mixed blood. I am not so sure that I am one. I do not have mixed perceptions of the world. The hammock does not need to reduce all its users to one shape. Similarly, I am not forced to adopt only one mode of perception, even though I need to be conscious of my switching from one to the other. Just as I am changing from a "we" to an "I." I also need to specify, in writing, when I am wearing the glasses and when I am not.

A living hammock

The range of activities supported by the hammock is almost inexhaustible. The hammock is used by its "friends" to improve corn cultivation practices; to examine the impact of fertilizers and pesticides on land and people and to experiment and use alternative practices, like those of organic agriculture; to install latrines, with original technologies, in urban or rural settlements, and to organize a world congress on the experience of latrines; to disseminate techniques for the independent construction of ovens in rural areas that care both for the forest and for women's dignity and space; to organize and operate the direct exchange of goods and services between peasant groups and urban consumers; to finance small peasant projects for the return of migrants to the countryside from the cities; to rebuild the houses of the victims of the 1985 earthquake with original, participatory, and creative designs, around communal patios and services, in downtown Mexico City, and with traditional materials and designs in rural areas; to conceive and implement small productive workshops of many different kinds in urban or rural areas; to conceive and publish journals expressing the views and experiences of individuals or groups related to the hammock; to establish and operate an urban space for informal encounters, including a library, a documentation center on alternative technologies and rural issues, a bookstore, a room for lectures and exhibitions, and a small restaurant (where the cook is a French anthropologist); to collect old traditional musical instruments and songs, to play them for different audiences in rural and urban areas, to organize their reproduction by peasant and Indian groups and to experiment with their use in combination with modern musical instruments; to rescue forest land for the original peasant owners and to organize and implement the ecological and productive use of forests and of wood; to organize and implement practices against soil erosion and deforestation; to experiment with and implement alternative practices for intercropping and crop diversification; to reinforce traditional practices of healing; to test, improve, and disseminate the use of medicinal plants; to technically and politically support the world of traditional midwives; to complement local knowledge and practices of healing with modern doctors' advice; to experiment with and organize alternative methods of learning; to establish or enrich libraries; to talk informally with others about ideas and insights; to autonomously redefine capacities and needs; to struggle for human rights; to organize cooperatives; to finance and support participatory action research and disseminate its results; to export honey and ceramics to Swiss friends; to test and disseminate practices for backyard vegetable plots, in rural or urban areas, to achieve family sufficiency in basic staples; to improve the collective use and care for water resources, including water purification projects to make water potable, small dams, etc.;

to build roads connecting isolated rural villages; to organize spaces where the elders and teenagers can care for each other. . .

I can fill one hundred pages with a list of activities supported by the hammock, but they would lose their meaning if reduced to only a taxonomic list. The arbitrary selection of examples I have given offers only a quick glance at our hammock's world.

For a while, "we" used the image of a barrel full of holes to represent the peasant economy as "we" saw it. The peasants were pouring into the barrel their living work, but everything leaked out—including the peasants themselves—to finance, among other things, the industrialization of the country. When the barrel began to run low, endangering the food supply in the cities already congested by peasant migration, the government started to pour money and projects into it. The faster it poured in, however, the easier they came out of the barrel through the holes. What "we" have created, following peasant initiatives, is a diversified and flexible collection of small plugs, one for every kind of hole. "We" have also organized a very informal system of communicating vessels to keep the level of the living fluid in all the barrels interconnected. The holes themselves are well-known; the literature is filled with examples: financing, marketing, transporting, voting, obtaining public services, using the media, travelling, applying "modern" technology . . . almost every contact of the peasants with others is an occasion for being damaged. The hammock is there to be used when trying to stop or reduce the damaging process. It can also be used in different ways for the regenerative process that naturally appears when the barrel starts to fill up again.

If "we" were forced to use just one word to describe the hammock's activities, "we" would perhaps use the image of *remedies*. But this requires some theoretical elaboration.

Beyond development, what?

In the peasant world, for a long time now, "development" has been recognized as a threat. Most peasants are aware that it has undermined their subsistence based on centuries-old diversified crops. For a while, through the "Mexican Agricultural Miracle" and the oil boom, this threat was masked by illusions. The so-called crisis has laid the threat bare.

In Mexico, you must be either numb or very rich if you fail to notice that "development" stinks. The damage to persons, the corruption of politics, and the degradation of nature which until recently were only implicit in "development," can now be seen, touched, and smelled. The causal connection between the loss of healthy environment and the loss of peasant solidarity, both of which had been hitherto taken for granted mainly by the poorest, has now been documented by a new, expert establishment. The so-called crisis in Mexico has now provided the peasants and others with the opportunity to dismantle the goal of "development."

After 1982, the Rural Development Bank of Mexico no longer had enough funds to induce the peasants to plant sorghum for animal feed. As a result, in many places, peasants have returned to the traditional practice of intercropping corn and beans. This has not only improved their diet, it has restored some of the traditional village solidarity (which, in turn, allows available cash to reach farther).

The damage to the peasant economy and culture, which was a by-product of the Green Revolution, forced many peasants to emigrate. In the cities, already congested by the demographic explosion (also created by "development"), they did not find the promised land. Very few of them were able to secure even a livelihood; instead they became social atoms, as they were placed in a very low position in the homogenized and hierarchical world that defines urban life. They, thus, became the true "marginals" in every conceivable sense. Many of them, however, drew upon their tradition as a survival strategy. They re-created, in the city, physical and cultural spaces—the *barrios*—and maintained links with their original communities. And so they were able to resist the permanent threat of urban development, which attempts to replace the living and lively social entities that the *barrios* are with homogenized and specialized spaces to sleep, work, buy, or use free time, enveloped by the speedways which are created for cars and not for men and women.

For a long time, the slum-dwellers had realized that development had made their skills redundant, and their education inadequate for the jobs that were available. The truly marginal groups know very well how painfully "development" has forced them, in ever new ways, into the cash economy. The so-called crisis, however, has occasioned new opportunities for many of them. Production cooperatives are springing up in the very heart of Mexico City, and they thrive thanks to the decreasing purchasing power of the formerly employed. A phenomenal increase in next-door catering has been observed in many places. Street stands and tiny markets have returned to the street corners from where they had disappeared years ago. As some rural communities start to flourish again, some "marginals" are returning to the spaces to which they once belonged.

By now, "we" are ready to present a very good case against development. In addition to our own experience, we can use the extensive documentation and literature produced by expert establishments around the world, including the United Nations and other international institutions. These materials, however, do not derive any coherent and pertinent conclusions from the facts they document and examine. For years, the literature arrived at the analytical conclusion that a missing factor or tool, or the perverse, corrupt, or inefficient use of something, could explain the damage done by development to people and their environments. These "analyses" have come to a dead end. They move in a vicious circle, like a dog chasing its tail. The conclusions of some studies are the premises of the others and so on. Every development "strategy" or "approach" has been tested, again and again, under widely different conditions but with the same frustrating results. When "we" talk about the archaeology of the development myth, assuming that its cycle and promises are over, "we" are just offering a different insight about known facts, in the context of our own shared experience. We are now using our own eyes and noses, not those of the experts.

It is now becoming more easy to arrive at a consensus on the evaluation of the damages wrought by development. It is not so easy, however, to convince others of the logical consequences "we" derive from the evaluation, namely, that the experiment is over, that development is dead. We can now successfully present our case in public as a radical critique of existing development theories and practices. (To my surprise, after my July 1985 presentation before the World Conference of the Society for International Development in Rome, my paper was immediately reproduced and commented on in a dozen countries.) Interestingly enough, "we" are immediately asked to produce an alternative strategy. That is certainly not our enterprise. "We" are opposed to any attempt by the "alternative" establishment to grant the notion of development a new lease on life through new labels: "alternative," "another," "humane" development. Indeed we get incredulous looks when we say that all these forms of "alternative" development are nothing but a deodorant to mask the stink of development.

"We" are not promoting a new banner or ideology. "We" are just trying to be honest about our shared experience, i.e., accepting with responsibility a radical, well-known, and sound critique of development history which covers the experiment of the past 40 years, as well as rejecting the preceding myths about progress and modernization. When "we" refuse to talk about any form of development or progress, however, "we" are immediately accused of wanting to return to the Stone Age even by people who have successfully escaped the traps of all the evolutionisms that still prevail in much of development discourse. It is not enough to counter this accusation by arguing that we are, in any case, returning to the Stone Age or hastening the Apocalypse by our refusal to put an end to the nuclearist phase of development. Nor is it enough to show our sophistication and pragmatism by using in our own "expert" ways the "best" that modern science and technology can offer, after carefully examining the implications of such technology and assuming that the most "modern" technology is only the last one tested in a concrete space and not the latest electronic gadget produced by the Japanese or the most recent agricultural experiment in Iowa or Wisconsin. The stark fact is that we are not taken seriously unless we accept some version of "development."

For the past few years, with a group of friends, I have been trying to ask: After development, what? To be more precise: Beyond development, what?

Recently, forced to use only one word to express my views, I answered: *hospitality*. The Western ethos, of which development is the most recent expression, views the world as inhospitable. Immersed in that perception and embedded in the construct of being an individual living in a world culturally and politically divided by frontiers but without concrete, defined, and collective spaces of belonging, nobody can really be a host to others. One can *tolerate* them, but tolerance is the opposite of hospitality. To be a host to others is not to follow them, to opt for them, or to affiliate one's soul to them. It is just to acknowledge and respect the others, to be hospitable to them.

My friend Yoshi Sakamoto did not much like the idea of hospitality as a notion beyond development. He preferred the notion of *sacrifice*. By this he perhaps meant the recent mood in some industrial countries that conceives the need of sacrificing the present standard of living because of the so-called crisis. (Of course, he may also have in mind other meanings that "sacrifice" seems to evoke in Japanese culture.) I demurred about the notion of sacrifice. My peasant thinking says that to do without something in order to be hospitable to someone, to give him or her gifts one has (everything one has is a gift!), is no sacrifice; it is a joy. Of course, "sacrifice" could mean hospitality towards oneself even more than to others. This is not hospitality but self-serving self-interest.

In "our" hammock, "we" are not trying to promote development. 'We" do not accept any form of *aid*. "We" do not aim to reach any common, universal goals. We just live with the different hopes and projects of everyone, hosting them all. We do not even take as guiding principles any general "values." I know what they are. I was brought up and educated to believe in them by my father's family. They are Western values. But then these values were challenged by my grandmother's world, where the concrete cultural patterns that orient collective behavior were so fully embedded in daily life that it was impossible to isolate them as abstract definitions. My grandmother was completely unable even to perceive, let alone understand, the values of modern culture, those abstract constructs formulated long ago in Western Europe. She could not be educated in those values and died happily having ignored them. I am now more than convinced that if one fully accepts cultural relativism—and we need to after Louis Dumont—one must also accept its consequences, i.e., the dissolution of universal values. This does not mean, of course, having no guiding principles to live in community. It means exactly the opposite: to have them fully rooted in the perception and attitudes of daily life, instead of supplanting them with artificial constructs which are hypothetically universal and more or less ahistorical.

Because of the damage done by development, it is not enough to be hospitable. This can be dangerous at times. In addition to redefining rules of hospitality so that we become hosts to inhospitable peoples and ideas, "we" need to apply *remedies*, in order to repair our damaged lives and environments and to regenerate them. While doing so, "we" need to change the nature of the tools "we" use. (I use the word in the Illich sense.) There was an epistemological transformation when the *commons* was turned into *resources*. While applying remedies, we need to bring about a new epistemological transformation, restoring to the so-called resources their quality as commons.

As "we" are immersed in an inhospitable world, "we" have been forced to struggle. So, in addition to localized struggles, to rescue or protect our old or new commons, "we" have periodically felt the need to organize public campaigns. For example, the Latin American chapter of the Pesticide Action Network and the hammock actively circulated information against the use of these dangerous materials. The relative success of this chapter and other networks in banning the production and use of pesticides, however, started to produce a boomerang effect. Some companies, that for some time now have been restricted in their production of pesticides in the industrialized countries, and which they can no longer sell in our country, have created the scarcity of some varieties of pesticides which the peasants traditionally use for pest control. If they succeed in monopolizing these varieties, "we" will confront serious difficulties later. The hammock, therefore, is now being used to protect those varieties and to popularize their use, after testing and improving them.

"We" do not wish to talk about the many public campaigns "we" have successfully launched. "We" do not want to appear as their promoters and pay the price for the accumulation of "political power" that can come after their success. "We" have found that it is easier and better to diffuse the political "merit" of any campaign; sometimes the issue becomes common knowledge and nobody can claim the "ownership" of the campaign; at other times "we" gladly accept the claims of other organizations for the "patent rights" of the issue, so long as the campaign achieves its objectives.

For the hammock to operate smoothly, an appropriate umbrella is needed. "We" have discovered that the so-called representative democracy provides a good one and "we" actively support it, as well as the efforts to improve it. "We" need to confess, however, that our support of representative democracy rests on the assumption that it is not "real" democracy nor an ideal to follow or defend. Rather, for this historical moment, it is the appropriate umbrella of "our" activities; it offers more advantages in comparison with a dictatorship.

In many ways, our actions seek to dissolve State and market institutions, specifically their centralism. This does not mean that "we" have something like an anarchist design for "society." ("We" cannot even perceive what "society" means since we reject formal abstract categories. In any case, "we" believe that "anarchism" is a contradiction in terms.[4]) "We" recognize that both State and market institutions are what our social environment comprises and that they set limits to our lives and projects. "We" also recognize the need to transform them, as "we" are doing. But "we" do not want to go farther and pose, propose, or impose a "global design" for the national or international arena. "We" feel more or less comfortable under the democratic umbrella "we" have now, and probably would like something of that kind to emerge at the world level. "We" feel uncomfortable, in contrast, about plans or projects struggling for a *specific* shape of a national or world government. "We" prefer to see the "realities" as our horizon—not as our frontier—and to be hospitable to them.

As I have said earlier, the physical and cultural spaces which originally defined the peasant world are *localized*—located in a specific place—but *unlimited*, i.e., without defined limits. The outer space is perceived as a horizon, not as a frontier. Under such conditions, hospitality defines the basic attitude towards *the other*. The pre-Hispanic peasants are oriented thus. The modern Mexican peasants are also so inclined in their rural communities and in the cities. They have learned, by their centuries-old experience, the need to re-define some rules for hospitality: to be a host to foreign ideas, tools, goods, and the practices of people who ignore hospitality and tend to pose, propose, or impose on others what they have and assume to be of universal value. But by extending hospitality to the Spaniards, the people were colonized. By hosting other gods, their own gods were destroyed. By hosting "development," their environment and livelihood were seriously damaged. By hosting "improved" seeds, for example, they lost the genetic richness of their centuries-old pool of seeds, seeds which were able to respond to the constant variations of their micro-climates. It seems to be a miracle that after all such experiences they could still retain hospitality as a defining trait. They have done so because they know that it is not only a condition for survival, but also *the only way to live*. Since the complete failure of this monstrous experiment called "development" can now be recognized for what it is, the peasants are determined to regenerate a hospitable world, following their traditional paths which are now enriched by the lights and shadows of modernity. *Homo sapiens* and *homo ludens* are celebrating their awareness of having awakened from the nightmare created by the impossible attempt to establish *homo oeconomicus* on earth.

Looking for new grounds

In a recent workshop held in Mexico City, in which representatives of more than 40 "networks" of Central and South America participated, I heard a beautiful story about a man asking what Juan Chiles was like in his time, how he went about fulfilling his epic Indian exploits in the early 18th century. An old Indian participant gave the following cryptic answer: "Juan Chiles was a wise man," he said. "He knew how to untie the *quechua*, to read Charles the Great's writings and to *labrar a cordel*."[5] The answer impressed all of us. During the discussion that followed, I realized that the cryptic definition of the wisdom of Juan Chiles could be used as clues for our present theoretical pursuits.

Learning to untie the quechua

Language, they say, is the matter of thought. (Matter comes from *mater*.) Language is the progeny of thinking and thinking guides action. Language can be, therefore, a determining factor for action.

But words do not come from thin air. In order to identify the nature and meaning of our thoughts and actions, we need to dis-cover the genesis of our words. We must elaborate on their formulation—establishing the conditions in which they were historically and culturally constructed. And then find out how they came to be placed amongst us, with what purpose they were pro-posed to us, under what conditions they were im-posed upon us. We need to write the history of our words to find out, among other things, whether those words taught to us are truly ours.

The history of words, of language, of perceptions, is an urgent venture for all of us who are committed to life. It is not a task to be entrusted only to academicians and experts. It is a fundamental act that involves all of us including the professionals. Undertaking this venture does not doom us to silence. It allows, at least, for two things:

1. *To take a critical distance from the words with which we have been educated.* Having seen their origin, the conditions of their generation, we may re-cognize and de-cognize them. Most important, we are enabled to run away from those words which masquerade before us as truths, postulates, and laws, of universal and necessary nature which are for general and permanent application.

2. *To learn how to untie the* quechua. In Mexico, over 50 ethnic groups

speaking as many different dialects coexist. Every popular neighborhood of Mexico City has its own distinct and unique vernacular speech, mastered only by the people in that neighborhood. All too frequently—and dangerously so—revolutionaries from top to bottom, from the left and the right, activists and social promoters—these agents for change, know only the alien language in which they were educated. They very rarely wonder about the concrete substance and validity of the categories used by Tyrians and Trojans. They usually take the formal categories of State and Civil Society, for example, as "scientific" expressions without recognizing their association with a particular project of domination that imposed these words upon us, turning our social existence into something which we have never really wanted and which many of us continue not to want.

We can undertake the regeneration of *quechua*, of vernacular speech and language. We can respect the other's world. We can give up the idea of educating others (i.e., programming them with the code with which we were educated). We can combat all proposals for a common discourse (of groups, of classes, of nations, of regions, of "South . . . ," etc.). And if we are able to recover fully our vernacular speech, perhaps we could strive to re-discover how to untie the *quechua*, like the wise man Juan Chiles.

Reading the writings of Charles the Great

The world is no longer a dream, a prophecy, a project. It has become real. Fortunately this does not mean that there is a world already unified and homogeneous, even if this is the project and design of what we call the West. The dream of the "global village" persists (McLuhan); instead of unifying the world, as in the past, through ideology (religion and civilization, for example), now the attempt is to unify it through production: the global farm, the global factory, the global market. While the Western project appears to have been successful, it is far from being fully implemented. Some of us have even begun to suspect that it has already failed, that historically it is exhausted and dead.

To say that the world has become real means that cultural isolation is a thing of the past. There are no groups, peoples, ethnic communities, cultures or societies living without "contact" with the "outside." In addition, it means that there is intertwining, that we are a social mesh on a world scale. Hence inter-action, inter-penetration, inter-dependence is inevitable.

This reality is reinforced by another, namely, the *totalitarian* regime, a political invention of the 20th century, which has already been globally implemented with a wide range of nuances and conditions. The *polis* of the distant past was a space in which citizens converged to discuss matters of interest to all, including issues of the city's administration. For many centuries, politics had its own stage: political actors discussed the contradictions and conflicts inherent to politics in certain privileged spaces that were clearly different from those of daily life with its own spaces and actors, and from which strictly political activities were excluded. The political regime that is characteristic of our time has politicized daily life which is, in all its expressions, directly, immediately, and radically political.

In this context, the localism vs. globalism opposition appears to be a short-sighted perception. The "local" perception that cannot see itself in "global" terms and dimensions fails to see itself with sufficient *local* depth. (The local decision of cultivating a certain crop, on certain land, with certain technology, runs the risk of being short-sighted without some knowledge of the national and world markets for foodstuff, the modern nature of land tenure, the class conflict in which production activities are immersed, the ecological implications of agriculture, and the knowledge of the technological options that are open.) A "Global" perception that cannot be expressed in local terms (in all possible locations) lacks true reality: it is mere speculation; it becomes ideology. (Such radically abstract expressions as "the law of value" or "class struggle" acquire meaning only when they act as conceptual catalysts which illumine concrete and local contexts. What, for example, is the meaning of the "North" and "South" polarity in this context? To become concrete and local we must talk about the Norths of every South and the Souths of every North. But then, we would be speaking a very different language.)

Charles the Great's writings are well worth reading, following the wise man Juan Chiles. Reading them will make us realize that once one becomes a real "we," there arises the need to re-cognize the others. Only by trying to understand the other can one really be a host to him or her. And by knowing how intertwined "we" all are in the way we come into being, we may perhaps, discover the other in ourselves. The other, then, will loom on our own horizon, here and there, which is not his or her frontier.

Learning to labrar a cordel

We have been taught to live *for* something (having something in mind), not *by* something. (To live in order to get a diploma or a job, to make money or to have more, to make revolution, to save the soul or change the world.) We have been taught to go in a certain direction and not to be here. In the process, the present has been turned into an ever-postponed future. Because the present has been concealed or stolen from us, we have been installed on a bridge between the past and the future. This is nothing more than ideology.

I know nothing of the future, except that it is what does not exist and may or may not have an existence for me. I can say nothing about it and I do not want its shadow to blur my present perception. I do not know what will become of me in a few days or a few years, much less what I will want, how I will want it, whom I will love. Planners from top to bottom, left and right, from governments to revolutionary movements, tell me that they know what will happen, what I will want, and what we will all want. They say they know what the interests and will of the people are, what they "really" want, where they—all of them—want to go. They say they possess a particular enlightenment: they are the governments enlightened through democratic representation or popular polls, or they are the enlightened vanguards for what they call the "scientific analysis of reality." I do not share the faith they have in their own enlightenment, nor am I enlightened by them. In my daily experience I constantly discover that my friends and colleagues have enormous differences in their projects, wills, and designs. I have learned to appreciate the value of these differences. I do not want to suppress them, to cast them into a single and common project, least of all when such projects refer to things that are so deeply alien to us—like the nation, the continent or the world.

Instead of *expectations*—the theoretical and practical category of an economic nature, through which we have been taught to postpone the present into the future—I have *hopes*. I hold them close to my heart in order that they do not freeze. I mold them according to my will and change them constantly with the passage of time.

I have been learning to live my life day by day. Along the road of Juan Chiles, I try to learn how to *labrar a cordel*. I want to know well what I have to do and also what I want to do.

In the path of dis-covering

"We" already feel comfortable with the insights associated with the idea of the hammock as a remedial venture. "We" are dis-covering that beyond development lies hospitality. "We" are also enjoying the constant surprises "we" find in the path of Juan Chiles, cleaning up our words (and perceptions), meeting the other again, recovering our space, and our present.

To give a more complete picture of our present status, however, it will be useful to mention some of the difficulties "we" have also encountered in our agenda of puzzles.

Language revisited

It might seem academic and arrogant, in addition to being innocuous, to state that three thousand years ago in the West the names of the days in the week belonged to the gods: Moon (*Luna*) turned into Monday (*Lunes*); Mars (*Marte*) into Tuesday (*Martes*); Mercury (*Mercurio*) into Wednesday (*Miercoles*) and so on. But the story of other names is not so innocent—and it had nothing to do with academia.

By delving into the history of the body, we will find out perhaps, that our present perception of it seems to have been created under precise historical circumstances, during the 18th century, when it was considered necessary to control the bodies of workers and of women. In the case of the former, it was to make them productive units in factories; in the case of the latter, they were seen as fertile reproducers to guarantee the continuance of the labor supply. It became possible to program the body when men and women became a quantifiable *population*, a useful *resource*, an *object* of professional attention. The insights "we" have found in the doctoral dissertation of Barbara Duden, which is a careful examination of the "body experience" in Germany at the turn of the 18th century, requires that we reconsider the whole perception of the self and its relationship with its environment.[6] If the "body experience," that is, the way the body is experienced in every historical period and culture, is seen as a condensation and as a mirror of that whole period and culture, then "we" need to re-examine the modern "body experience" to identify what modernity is all about. By exploring the historicity of the body "we" can reformulate our present experience in a new light.

"We" are by now quite well acquainted with the history of *development*. That is why I want to undertake the archaeology of that myth. As Mexicans, "we" (this is a new "we" I am using here) are used to living with sinking monuments which are built on ruins constructed upon ruins. But the ruins of development have no comparable foundations. In Spanish, at least until well into the 19th century, *desarrollo* meant the "unrolling of a scroll." It denoted "giving back to an object its original form." In the mid-19th century the life sciences co-opted the word as a metaphor to describe an organism that is growing into its proper form. After Darwin, it came to mean growth into an ever more perfect form. Schumpeter, in the first decade of this century, made an effort to introduce the word into economics, but it never became a useful technical term. The result is that development economists are not people with a specific technical competence, say in monetary theory or econometrics, but are people who make their living from funds that politicians earmark for "development."

After a century, the term *desarrollo*, that had originally meant unscrambling, had migrated through at least three scientific domains and, at the end of the road, had re-emerged in ordinary language with contours that are about as precise as those of an amoeba. It can now be used to mean a housing project, or the logical sequence of a thought, or the awakening of a child's mind, or the budding of a teenager's breasts. It has become one of the amoeba words that my colleagues and I try to ban from our conversations. It is one of those words without recognizable denotation which one cannot use without evoking powerful connotations. And what "development" connotes is always, at least, one thing: escaping from a vague, unspeakable, undignified condition called *sub-desarrollo* or underdevelopment, a term which was invented by Harry Truman on January 10, 1949. Seldom has a term been accepted around the world as this word has been, ever since the very day it was coined. Truman used it to diagnose a particular misery which affected most human beings and communities outside the United States. He used it to designate a social condition that almost anybody might claim to be in, without having to identify with the personal stain that it leaves on the majority to which it refers. But he used it as a name for that which was un-American that even anti-Yankees would recognize as something undesirable. It also became a term that spawned irrepressible bureaucracies.

Since Truman, development theories have followed each other at ever-shortening intervals. In all of them "development" appears like an algorithm, an arbitrary sign that is defined by the theoretical context in which it is used. However, the more varied and contradictory the definitions of development become, the stronger its connotation. Development implies that one has started on a road that others know better, to be on one's way towards a goal that others have reached; to race up a one-way street. Development means the sacrifice of environment, solidarities, traditional interpretations, and customs, in the name of ever-changing expert advice. Development promises enrichment, although for the overwhelming majority, it has always meant the progressive modernization of their poverty: growing dependence on guidance and management. While Mexico's predicament is called a crisis by others, "we" call it an opportunity. It is our chance to share with others, now forever out of a job, the ten thousand modern techniques which have been claimed by a parasite class as its property in the service of development, and which they have used to trick the common people. The crisis is our chance to de-link well-being from development.

The word *decentralization* now in vogue was a fundamental ingredient of the administrative theories of the British and French empires that played an important part in the domination by the metropolii over the colonized territories. Efforts to put into practice this idea has not overcome the dominative traces of decentralization. This is why "we" use the term very carefully. In our hammock, "we" preferred "decentralism" to decentralization, although we are not completely happy with the substitution. Our discussions of the issue have frequently left us unsatisfied.

Popular participation and *popular communication* are expressions which many "alternative" groups have adopted to describe their intentions and practices. On our part, "we" feel that these so-called participatory theories and practices are tainted by the theological origins of participation (to take part in God) which has overtones of submission and subordination.

On the other hand, "communication" which has emerged only in the last quarter of a century, implies, in its modern meaning, the intent—which has become almost an attempt—to *plug* men and women into a common, simplified code: the code of domination. Observation and experience allows "us" to discover that the people—if "we" are able to recover this beautiful word—do not "participate" or "communicate." Indeed, promoting their participation or communication implies their submission, their subordination to an alien design.

Structural change is another fall-out phrase from the language of science that has invaded ordinary language. As in the case with other amoeba-words (development, energy, communication, sex, etc.), it circulates without any precise meaning; it is a vague but positive-sounding term which is assumed to be readily understood and accepted by everyone but whose definition is left in the hands of experts. When they are consulted, the experts find no difficulty in reducing the expression to a mere algorithm which acquires meaning depending on the context in which it is used. Thus, the term "structural change" has become a theoretical scapegoat and a tool for manipulation which urgently requires a complete overhaul.

The history of *education*, specifically the emergence of *homo educandus*, i.e., a new kind of human being that needs to be educated in order to exist, can give us clues about the conditions which allow for the generation of this new kind of human being, different from *homo sapiens* or *homo faber*. Through this "method" it is possible to approach the history of the *text*, as a period of history when vernacular speech has been reduced to a code and a memory: the time in which the words were separated from the subjects who pronounced them and circulated as such, as "loose" objects. "We" may dis-cover that *homo educandus* perceives reality as if it were a text and sees himself or herself as if she or he was a text, torturing his or her own being in order to reach an identity through his or her identification with a text. The previous reduction to the Cartesian individual (individual: that which cannot be divided, the homogeneous atom) fosters living-in-a-context (the individual, as a text, communicating with others; encoded, reduced to a code).

Like Foucault, "we" perceived that *power* does not exist as "something" that is someplace which some people, groups, or classes, own. We accepted, with him, that it is but the *name* given to a strategic situation, to fix the "relations of force" existing in it. "We" also followed his idea of concentrating on the autonomous production of truth, assuming that it is not the production of true statements but of statements through which people govern themselves and others. By localizing the critique—making it local—it is possible to start with the solid ground of the insurrection of subordinated knowledges. By coupling scholarly knowledge with local memories, something like a "historical knowledge of struggle" can be constituted. But Foucault did not write the history of power and domination. He left many questions open. One of them is that *power*, in the political sciences, may be playing the role that *phlogiston* (the principle of combustion) played in chemistry in the 18th century.

A fresh look is also needed in the case of categories like *social classes* and *class struggle*. We all know, though many do not see, that social classes never existed *as such*. The struggle of *the* classes never occurred in history. While the abstraction of class struggle has historically proven its validity by explaining some of the social conflicts in the so-called class societies, the category is essentially economic. Indeed, to speak of classes is to refer to the economic *classification* of society. But men, women, or "society" cannot be reduced just to the economic sphere, even though this has been done in theory and has been attempted in practice. Economics is only one dimension or facet of reality, not reality itself. So, the value of class analysis, which examines the nature of concrete social contradictions, becomes an obstacle for action when it is taken as an organizational principle. Concrete social struggles are much more than class struggles, though the former always express class contents—whether they want to or not, whether they know it or not. Once "we" are able to establish the limits of economics—another item on our agenda—to celebrate the unfeasibility of the existence of *homo oeconomicus*, "we" will need to revisit class analysis and the theory of class struggle.

Returning from the future

"If you don't ask me what time is, I know what it is; if you ask me what time is, I won't know any longer" Saint Augustine.

It is often said that it is not possible to take away from the people their faith in the future. History, it is said, is with the people. It is also said that we do not know when "victory" will come, but that we know it will come. According to legend, when Sandino began his struggle for freedom, he did not know *when* he would win, but he knew that the people, in the long run, would "triumph." "We" can no longer trust this linear vision of history. "We" find such blind faith quite dangerous. What "we" do know is that whole peoples have been defeated and have disappeared from the earth. They would turn in their graves if they could hear these phrases. To say, for example, that the American people will "win," that they are the owners of their future is sheer demagoguery. Most of the peoples who occupied the territory that is today the United States disappeared into oblivion. These people were not triumphant. The "victory" of peoples elsewhere will not be theirs; nor can it compensate for their defeat. Moreover, to use the term "people" is an abstraction of the highest order. To refer to all the people that in all times have been exploited or oppressed, and then to say that they will, at some uncertain date in the future, leave oppression behind and that their triumph will belong to all—including those who were exterminated before them—is to engage in cruel manipulation of sentiments. Such phrases lack real and historical meaning.

Being the owners of our space is what "we" are all about. This, it seems to me, is what Indians, peasants, and "marginals" have been trying to do. In their space (which is at once physical and cultural) they carry out their projects, which are nothing else than to lead their own lives. They have dreams and hopes and they know quite well what the consequences of their actions are (that is why they care for the land, ecologically speaking). But they know they do not own the future. With them, "we" have learned that groups that call themselves the owners of space and time are totalitarian oppressors. (The extreme example, of course, is Hitler who formulated a plan to possess a world space, as well as a millenium. Incumbent governments all over the world remain attached to the same notion, even if they apply it with a wide range of nuances and conditions, some of which create the illusion that there is no oppression.)

In the past, one knew about the future from one's own people. Since in the world today societies are intertwined, any prediction about the future implies knowing, beforehand, what will happen in the whole world. Government planners and revolutionary or "alternative" groups gamble with the future. Acting on behalf of that future, under the assumption that history or science is with them, they actually play with the real hopes of the people and give them promises or instructions. (Populists transform hopes into promises; technocrats do not deliver promises, but give instructions.)

"We" were educated to believe in the illusion of being able to master time. In exchange, we were persuaded to lose interest in mastering space, which was then occupied by all and therefore by no one. (The world has been turned into a hotel; the city has been pitted against the neighborhood; "human units of production" have been automated, homogenized, and transported from one place to another without ever remaining in one place long enough to establish roots: no space is theirs because they belong to no space.) "We" are learning once again to first rescue and then to master our space. And in the course of learning "we" have realized that what "we" are achieving, as far as the autonomous production of truth is concerned, does not suffice; in fact, even the hammock turns out to be inadequate. Of course, what "we" are doing enables "us" to become radically de-linked from the institutional and ideological world that attempts to control us and which antagonizes and blocks us. But such de-linking can become effective, it seems, only through authentic cultural creation (by recovering its shape: by *anastomosis*). This, in turn, requires protecting umbrellas. When trying to build these umbrellas "we" stumbled into the campaign form of collective action. Instead of second level organizations (federations, unions, associations, parties, etc.) with which "we" have had bitter experiences, "we" are trying to organize *ephemeral* or *issue* campaigns in concert with others; the former, through short meetings, well defined in time and space, for the exchange of ideas and experiences or for specific "battles" that are shared; the latter, through the adoption of common decisions on a systematic effort related to a very specific, well-defined issue, over which "we" have the clear conviction of a common and shared interest. ("We" have found that these "specific" agreements are shared by many when they refer to what "we" do *not* want: "we" do not want repression, oppression, exploitation, licence, violence. As to what "we" *do* want, it is possible to reach complex agreements in very small groups. As the group grows, agreement becomes less and less specific. At the level of the "masses" one has only the "sparkle of life" and all one needs is to drink it.)

Among those who are in "webs" or "networks" there seems to be points of convergence, heterogeneity, and divergence. They converge as far as "radical change" is concerned, although they are not sure what this means; they easily agree to oppose oppression, exploitation, injustice, violence; they also agree on the necessity of accompanying the people in their struggles and conflicts; and of committing themselves to life. Though ill-defined, one can discern the convergence in general spirit and in the conviction that the "webs" they are building are useful regardless of how formal or informal they may be. There is clear heterogeneity, a very welcome heterogeneity, as to the concrete procedures and styles of relationships, and above all, regarding the dreams of a "new society," regarding what they *do* want. There is divergence, finally, about the concrete role of these "webs." Some see them as useful tactical aspects of global strategies whose main significance lies in creating organizations of a different kind: vanguards, political steering groups, parties, second level organizations, fronts, etc. Those who think along these lines tend to separate the means from the ends. They think, for example, that peace may be achieved through war or that democracy may be established after applying a "temporary" vertical, non-participatory strategy. Others, like "us," think that our "webs" or hammocks are ways of life, of action. "We" do not trust second or third level organizations, nor vanguards nor enlightened leaderships. "We" believe it is impossible to separate the means from the ends. And many of "us" are determined to change today, to whatever extent possible, and the issue of the extent of change has to be discussed today, not tomorrow. "We" also think, that "we" must not only change. "We" must change the way to change. And the way to change will contain the drive and meaning of the change that we want and must bring forth.

This is where "we" stand, along the road of Juan Chiles.

Looking for a new commons

Let me conclude where I started: Who are "we"? As I have explained, I do not feel at ease speaking on behalf of the hammock, thus reducing to one single "we" the many we's "we" are. I have also explained our insight about how peasants and ex-peasants are born and brought up as belonging to a *commons* which defines their mode of being on Earth and their mode of perception. I felt something like that, unknowingly, while being with my grandmother. But she has passed away. I can no longer be with her, except when I recognize her in myself. I can immediately perceive the difference between that feeling and the one I have when relating with my "modern" friends—the now de-professionalized intellectuals of the hammock, for example. How can the status of the restricted "we" of the now de-professionalized intellectuals be described?

In the hammock's design, the stoppers to plug the holes of the barrel and, in general, the activities of the de-professionalized intellectuals, are always *on the hinge*. Through this image "we" want to say several things:

a. *From pro-motion to co-motion.* To promote something is always to try to move something in a predetermined direction. In connection with people, this usually implies that they are not in motion or that they are moving in the wrong direction. Our experience tells us that there are no people without motion, and "we" cannot presume the role of a *primum movens* for the people. "We" are also not trying to take the people some place, to mobilize them, to organize mobs. "We" cannot presume that "we" know what they do not know and should know; or what they want or do not want, or what they need to do for their own good. To be on the hinge means that instead of promotion, "we" look for co-motion; "we" move ourselves with them. "We" move just by being with them; "we" also accept being moved by them.

b. *Nonintervention.* As Mexicans, "we" are proud of the stubborn defense of the principle of nonintervention in the internal affairs of other peoples which has been embedded in the foreign policy of our country for the past one hundred years. Benito Juarez, after the French and US military interventions in Mexico, formulated the apothegm: "Respect for other people's rights means peace." Of course, today, the world needs to repeat this apothegm tongue-in-cheek to avoid any form of cynicism. However, after learning hospitality from the peasants, "we" have learned to be hospitable with them. "We" avoid, consciously and carefully, any form of intervention or even participation in the "internal affairs" of any group within the hammock. This posture gives "us" more freedom to take initiatives and create options from the outside, from the hinge.

The hammock is not really *creating* space for people, for peasants or urban "marginals," but *regenerating* it. Following our insights, they constitute a commons; they belong to a space both physical and cultural that belongs to them. By using the hammock they are first enabled to stop or reduce the damage done to them by development and then to start the regeneration of their lives and projects.

The hammock is also used, from time to time, by some "affinity groups." They are the survivors of the communal movement of the 1960s and 1970s. A few of them are quite successful in the "communities" they have created and their experiments in social change are often fascinating and certainly always interesting. They are not, however, the open or preferred option for those in the hammock since they do not have a commons as their origin.

Something like the commons of a new kind is emerging through the trust and friendship that define "our" relationship with the commons of the peasants and the "marginals." Step by step, the groups of professionals who still have the institutional designs "we" started with a decade ago or who are yet unable to de-professionalize themselves, are changing their attitudes and trying to adapt their original organizational schemes to the spirit of the hammock. Those of "us" who can already be properly called de-professionalized intellectuals constantly look for the creation of new commons.

These new commons simultaneously have and do not have a concrete, collective space which is both physical and cultural. They have a space: they are located. But "we"—the ones who are a specific commons—do not permanently live there, as "we" also have other spaces, other commons. It seems to "us" that the option open for people, already "individualized" through economics and modernity, is not to replicate the traditional commons, but to invent new *multiple* commons. Commonality can be constituted and lived within different spheres of reality. Some of "us" share a common interest in one specific kind of activity, inside the hammock, living and working in the same region, a rural town or *barrio*, doing similar things for the same people, or regenerating conviviality in the same physical and cultural spaces. Others prefer sharing commonality across many of these things.

Some of the spaces in the process of being our new commons engage just one "point" for most of the time during the lifetime of some of us. Something like a new commons emerged, for example, for a good number of de-professionalized intellectuals who were associated last year, inside the hammock, with the life regeneration process of the victims of the September 19, 1985 earthquake in Mexico City, Guerrero, Oaxaca and Jalisco. But other "institutions" of a different nature can also emerge.

Perhaps the gatherings organized every Monday by Lee Swenson in Virginia Street, Berkeley, to talk about common readings is an example of a commons of a new kind. The get-togethers, twice a month, by Gerard Tolck of Les Fonges near Delemont in South Jura, Switzerland, to talk about the meaning of "Beyond Development" for Jurasians, now that the Japanese have a monopoly on clock and watch production, is another example. And the Thursday *tertulias* that "we" have in our place, El Disparate, with the cuisine of our French anthropologist, where "we" no longer use words like development, communication, structure, sex, problem, crisis, or funny slogans like revolution, structural change *arriba y adelante*, we, the people of the United Nations, constitutes yet another example.

For the time being, I do not want to say more about these "new commons" except about their limits. As I have said before, "localism" reflects for "us" a short-sighted perception which fails to recognize the very nature of local processes and their linkages with global ones. "We" confront other difficulties as far as "globalism" is concerned. "We" are worried here, most of all, because "we" cannot conceive of any possibility of a "global design" that is not an inhospitable reduction of the perception of others to the shape of our own.

Some years ago, "we" renounced the use of the beautiful word *socialism*, as it exploded into a myriad of meanings, many of them contradictory, because of its economic bias. "We" did that, it seems to "us," without losing any of the vital impulses behind the word. Our present difficulty is of a more general kind. "We" cannot imagine a single word or slogan which has a really universal and clear meaning and content. Today, *peace*, one of the best words in any language, means so many different things to different people that "we" cannot trust that word any longer, nor the efforts undertaken in its name. It is no longer the people's peace of the medieval wars. It means different things to Reagan or to Gorbachev; to the French or to the Japanese; to Nelson Mandela or to Gandhi; to the *Sandinistas* or to the *Contras*; to our Zapotecas or to the Angolans. Development is just *pax economica*; it has become a state of permanent war waged by its promoters and suffered by its victims.

"We" can easily see that the same difficulty would apply to our own *hospitality, remedy*, and *horizon*. "We" are not proposing these words as new slogans. "We" are just describing "our" attitudes, sharing our experiences with others. The so-called transnationalization of economies and societies appears as the product of tendencies inherent in the compulsion of the growth of corporate capital. (Some would say: as an expression of the nature of world capitalism.) Whether this is so or not, and even though the opposite symptoms are proliferating, there seems to be a trend to dissolve, through economics, the established frontiers. But the people were doing exactly this a long time ago, and they are now using the spaces created by economic compulsions for their own purposes. "We" like that. "We" nourish the hope—not the expectation—that it is possible to recover the perception of horizon and to regenerate hospitality.

I hope my spontaneous statement will not be interpreted as a plea for a new, fashionable slogan such as "a more hospitable world," that will be added to the collection of more recently fashionable ones like "a peaceful and sustainable world" which are manufactured for alternative audiences. With such slogans, their perpetrators are trying to construct a mobilizing myth that will appeal to the "masses" all over the world who belong everywhere and hence nowhere.

I wanted to tell a story and to elaborate on it. This is just my story. I hope it can be read like that and no more than that.

Notes and references

1. The word *ejido* comes from *exitus*, exit. In the 15th century, it designated in Spain the common land located at the exit of rural towns. The Spaniards used the word to refer later to the Indian communities they found in America. Struggling against the colonizers for the recovery of their spaces, the Indians got used to the word, which they firmly incorporated in their vernacular speech during the 19th century. The revolutionary claim in 1910 took the form of a recovery of the *ejidos*.
2. In an *ejido*, the land still belongs to the nation but its usufruct is given to a group of peasants, while individual rights to the exploitation of a specific plot of land are recognized. The right is not equivalent to private property, since it is restricted to the direct exploitation of the plot. Legally, the *ejidatario* cannot sell, rent or mortgage his land. Moreover, inheritance is regulated by certain legal provisions which may prevail over the explicit will of the *ejidatario*. Organization of production in the *ejidos* may take different forms, on the basis of the *ejidatario's* decisions, within the limits and restrictions laid down by the law.

3. Frontiers may separate and/or join. But they cannot be here and there at the same time. The frontier between France and Germany is either "here" or "there," but not here *and* there at the same time.

   In contrast, horizons may overlap and may be "here and there" at the same time: Augustus the Strong was a Lutheran "here" (in Dresden, as the Prince Elector), and a Catholic "there" (in Warsaw, as King). Therefore, the Prince-Elector–King of Saxony, a Catholic, was, up to the dissolution of the Old Empire in 1806, the representative of the Lutheran party before the Assembly of the Empire of Regensburg (and still until 1918, as an individual, he was truly a Catholic, but as the King of Saxony, he was a Protestant bishop).

   In the realm of horizons one could be one thing, but at the same time, the other, *if* one wanted, and without losing one's identity. But if not wanted, one could fight against oneself to the point of self-annihilation. In this case, one always preserved the *commonality of horizons*. One could (and can) break away from common horizons without resigning to them. Endless examples of this could be given. Hans-Albert Steger, "Horizontes contemporaneos," Introductory paper presented at the International Colloquium on the Problematique of Central Europe, held in Regensburg, March 5–7, 1986.

4. One cannot really believe in no government and then actively and even violently try to govern other's lives with one's own perception of what life without government can be. Of course "we" have tried to enrich ourselves with the beautiful and complex insights embedded in anarchist thinking and experience. But "we" cannot follow any of their catechisms.

5. A very refined and sophisticated traditional form of cultivation whose equivalent in English I am unable to find.

6. Barbara Duden, "Die Praxisleiten den Vorstellungen eines Eisenacher Arztes vom Koerperinnen und die Klagen Seiner Patientinnen um 1720–1750," (Berlin, 1985).

A Peoples' Quest for Authentic Polity: the Philippine Case

LESTER EDWIN J. RUIZ

It is an experience of incomparable value to have learned to see the great events of the history of the world from beneath: from the viewpoint of the useless, the suspect, the abused, the powerless, the oppressed, the despised—in a word, from the viewpoint of those who suffer.*

Introduction

The "February 1986 Rebellion" that dislodged the Marcos dictatorship and captured the imagination of the international community has once again focused attention on the Philippines and its struggle to establish an authentic democratic society. While it is too early to predict the outcome of such a struggle, optimistic observers have noted that the dislodging of the Marcos dictatorship by the "legal opposition" represented by the Aquino leadership will give the Philippines another chance of a peaceful, non-violent solution to the Philippine crisis. Such an observation suggests that, indeed, a "liberal democratic" solution still is the most acceptable way of moving the country into a post-Marcos era.

Such an analysis, however, may conceal more than reveal the depth of the crisis in Philippine political, economic, and cultural life. Indeed, despite the initial success of the "February 1986 Rebellion," and as I have argued elsewhere,[1] the Philippine crisis cannot be reduced simply to a crisis in political leadership. Too narrow a conception tends to ignore the structural character of the crisis understood within a domestic–international nexus of the global political economy dominated by East–West geopolitical and "security interests." Consequently, it is well to dwell on the nature of this crisis for a while longer. Indeed, it may prove helpful in the long term if we are better able to uncover and/or re-state some of the fundamental assumptions that inform the nature of the contending political forces in the Philippines today. Such a task underscores the plurality of these political forces which,

---

*From Dietrich Bonhoeffer's *Gesammelte Schriften*, vol 2 (Munich: Kaiser, 1965) p. 441

This is a revised version of an earlier essay which appeared in *Alternatives*, vol XI, no 4, 1986, pp. 505–534.

prior to the demise of the Marcos dictatorship, were constitutive of a "politics of opposition," but which since then, is largely being transformed into a "politics of reconstruction and reconciliation."

This essay, therefore, explores the thoughts and sentiments that constitute the self-understanding of these contending political forces in the Philippines. By uncovering their character, and by identifying the underlying themes that shape both their theory and practice of politics, I hope to re-state the questions with which we must be concerned if we desire to comprehend fully the crisis in the Philippines. This, in turn, could offer some guidelines for a political praxis that would lead beyond not only the Marcos legacy, but beyond the "liberal democratic" self-understanding that gave it birth. My main concern is to re-interpret modern Philippine history as a quest for authentic political subjecthood which is the *soul* of a politics of transformation. This essay is a meditation on the historical emergence of this quest in the Philippines.

Crisis: the context of the quest for authentic political subjecthood

The historical dimension of the crisis

In the late 1960s, Filipinos began to experience a growing sense of collective national agitation not felt before, at least in its depth and magnitude, in the history of the Republic. The historians Teodoro Agoncillo and Milagros Guerrero perceived this national agitation as a "critical situation of widespread discontent and pessimistic forebodings" for which the Marcos government, while not solely responsible, was certainly accountable.[2]

This collective national agitation was due, in large measure, to the fundamental contradictions in Philippine society arising from its experience of colonial and neo-colonial domination. The Spanish *encomienda* system established a landed aristocracy which eventually formed the politico–economic infrastructure for a "culture of patronage," a *padrino* system, that continues to shape Phillipine politics today. This "culture of patronage," which bears affinities to what Max Weber described as "patrimonialism," was altered, at the turn of the century, by the "American experiment in democracy" which proclaimed, on the one hand, a vision of liberal Lockean democracy, while modifying, on the other hand, the landed aristocracy into a client–elite within the US neo-colonial system.[3]

It was partly the failure of this *padrino* system to deliver what it promised that led to the growing "critical situation" in the nation. Despite the rhetoric of political and economic democracy, the continued success of the "culture of patronage" required the maintenance of an oligarchy in which political and economic power had to be absolute, not unlike the concept of absolute ownership underlying the *encomienda* system. In short, the 1960s and early 1970s found the Philippines in the midst of a "revolution of rising expectations" for which the possibility of fulfillment was, in reality, limited only to a few.

The "parliament of the streets"

Perhaps the most telling event of the national disillusionment was the widespread existence of a "parliament of the streets," involving different sectors of the nation, primarily though not exclusively students in the various metropolises of the archipelago, where the dissenting voices of the people found a forum. These fora challenged the government's self-serving disregard of the basic needs and interests of the *common tao*. This extra-parliamentary phenomenon marked a shift in the political understanding of a large segment of the Filipino people. On the one hand, it showed both a discontentment with the consequences of the "culture of patronage" and a skepticism about its adequacy to their political, economic, and cultural aspirations. On the other hand, the "parliament of the streets" evidenced the breakdown of what then Chief Justice Roberto Conception called "libertarian assumptions" which valued "freedom without responsibility," and indicated the emergence of a political consciousness that valued citizenship, i.e., public responsibility, on a wider scale.

Needless to say, this extra-parliamentary and extra-legal activity was encouraged and in some cases orchestrated by different interest groups in the nation.[4] However, knowing who are responsible for the "parliament of the streets" may be less important than perceiving its significance. For its existence was not only an expression of a widespread "crisis of confidence" in the ability of the Marcos government to provide the responsive and responsible leadership for an agitated nation, but, also pointed to the existence of a far deeper crisis which a "crisis of confidence" could not adequately explain.

The imposition of martial law

On September 21, 1972, Ferdinand E. Marcos, then President of the Republic of the Philippines, placed the entire Philippine archipelago under martial law. The immediate reasons for what some "liberal democratic" Filipino political thinkers like former President of the Philippines Diosdado Macapagal and former Senator Raul Manglapus considered a constitutionally questionable measure,[5] were meticulously stated in Proclamation No. 1081 "Proclaiming a State of Martial Law in the Philippines," which read in part:

> . . . it is definitely established that lawless elements . . . have entered into a conspiracy . . . for the prime purposes of . . . undertaking and waging an armed insurrection and rebellion against the Government . . . in order to . . . forcibly seize political and state power . . . overthrow the duly constituted government, and supplant our existing political, social, economic, and legal order with an entirely new one . . . [their activities] have seriously endangered and continue to endanger public order and safety and security of the nation . . . [and] have assumed the magnitude of an actual state of war against our people and the Republic of the Philippines . . .[6]

There was no meaningful consensus among political observers about the appropriateness of Proclamation No. 1081 although the events surrounding its declaration seemed to suggest the existence of a situation that fulfilled the requirements for its imposition. The "First Quarter Storm" triggered by police firing on unarmed student–peasant–labor demonstrators which led to bloodshed and destruction of property, the famous student barricades and take-over of the University of the Philippines, the infamous 1971 bombing of the "*miting de avance*" of the Liberal Party at Plaza Miranda, nearly wiping out the leadership of the opposition to the Marcos government and which precipitated the suspension of the privilege of the writ of *habeas corpus*, the dubious 1972 "Digoyo incident" in the north and the Moro secessionist movement in the south, all seemed to warrant the temporary imposition of martial law.

In the years following the declaration of martial law, particularly between 1978–1983, the national agitation experienced in the decade of the 1960s and the early 1970s was gradually transposed into *the existence of martial law itself as the national crisis*. Considering the enormous weight of the political, economic, and cultural changes which the institutionalization of martial law brought about or intensified, this shift is understandable.

For example, the war of liberation waged by the Moro National Liberation Front/Bangsa Moro Army in the southern Philippines, while consistent with the 450-year history of the Moro struggle for self-determination, came to be focused against what Abdurasad Asani called the Marcos dictatorship's "barbaric campaign of genocide" against the Moro people.[7] The consolidation of the Communist party of the Philippines/New People's Army leadership in the "liberated zones" and their steady gains in new "guerilla fronts" was not only one more indication of what some international observers had called the Philippines' "drift to the left" but evidence that the Marcos dictatorship was steadily losing legitimacy not only in these areas, but more significantly, in the whole Philippines as well.[8] The increasing deterioration of the economic conditions in the country, while generated by the pressure of both domestic and transnational corporate–capitalist interests was perceived, not altogether incorrectly, as having been exacerbated by the Marcos dictatorship.[9] Finally, despite the fact that the national agitation has deep roots in the colonial and neo-colonial heritage of the nation, the dictatorship, being seen correctly as an inextricable part of that heritage, was therefore held responsible for the crisis.

The intensification of the crisis not only received careful scrutiny and documentation from domestic observers, but confirmation from international observers as well. The unconscionable violations of human rights, for example, have been recorded by reputable organizations such as Amnesty International, the Lawyers Committee for International Human Rights, and agencies of the United Nations, the Vatican, and the World Council of Churches. Moreover, international "solidarity groups" have documented their own eyewitness accounts of the situation in the Philippines.[10]

In a different, though related context, the 1980 Session on the Filipino People and the Bangsa Moro People of the Permanent Peoples' Tribunal, an international "Third System" tribune, after hearing extensive evidence presented before it,[11] called upon world public opinion to support the Filipino and Bangsa Moro Peoples' struggle against the governments of Marcos and the United States. By its actions, the Tribunal not only re-affirmed the normative character of established rules and principles of international law, particularly as they are embodied in the "Universal Declaration of the Rights of Peoples" (The Algiers Declaration), it also asserted that leaders of governments are responsible for acts deemed as "attacks on humanity itself" and therefore must be brought to account before an international legal instance. Moreover, the Tribunal's decision exposed and confirmed internationally the intensification of the national crisis in the Philippines.

Perhaps the most damning confirmation of the deteriorating political, economic, and cultural conditions in the country, since martial law was imposed and despite its formal/procedural lifting in 1981, damning not only in its documentation but for its very existence, was the controversial secret World Bank Document on the Philippines, the "Ascher Memorandum," a report confidentially circulated in order to "sensitize Bank staff to the potential problems that could affect the viability of the Bank's approach and operations in the Philippines."

The memorandum included, among other things, the recognition of the precariousness of the Marcos government arising from its failure to overcome the increasing disparities in income distribution, the acknowledgement that the World Bank programs in the Philippines and their underlying strategy of "export-led industrialization" had either failed or backfired, and the admission that foreign control of the economy had increased sharply, which was due in part to the policies of the Bank itself. The memorandum, therefore, underscored the culpability of both the Marcos government and of the transnational corporate–capitalist structure. It served to illustrate what Robert Stauffer calls the "political economy of refeudalization," a structural dynamic of the Philippines' dependent–authoritarian status in the larger global political economy.[13]

The Aquino assassination

Benigno "Ninoy" Aquino, Jr.'s assassination on August 21, 1983, marked what many observers believed to be the "beginning of the end" of the Marcos dictatorship. Indeed, Aquino's assassination transformed the Philippine political landscape both on a domestic and international level. It provided the occasion for the "rebirth" of the "parliament of the streets," forced a serious "re-thinking" by Washington of its attitudes towards the Marcos dictatorship, and re-awakened a renewed determination by the different opposition forces to dislodge Marcos from power and to establish a regime more in tune with the sentiments of the Filipino people.

While the "parliament of the streets" has a long historical tradition in the protest movement in the Philippines, its post-Aquino assassination re-birth within the context of a publicity-sensitive dictatorship had a different *Geist* captured by these poignant words:

> By the millions, people poured onto the streets, marching for hours in the hot sun and cold rain. Day after day they came out, braving Marcos' threats and police bullets to protest the murder [of Aquino]. Workers in worn clothes, nuns in billowy habits, students in T-shirts, business executives in coat and tie.

From the time, eleven years ago, when Marcos declared Martial Law, the number of people who dared to oppose the dictatorship increased steadily. Others continued to be intimidated by government repression. No more. The murder of Ninoy Aquino destroyed the wall of intimidation that held back the pent-up anger of millions of Filipinos. Ninoy's sister, Lupita Kashiwahara said it all: "The Philippines is never going to be the same again."[14]

As the Aquino assassination "tore into the very fabric of Philippine life" it rekindled the sentiment of protest in the majority of the Filipino people and catapulted the largely "silent" bourgeois sector into an open conflict with the Marcos dictatorship. Whereas earlier the business community was willing to "overlook" the blatant abuses of the dictatorship, particularly where the emergent "crony capitalists" were concerned as long as business opportunity was open to all, the Aquino assassination rudely awakened them to the realization that the Marcos regime was "bad for business."

Such a realization, however, cannot be attributed to the Aquino assassination alone. Indeed, the roots of the growing disaffection between the Philippine business community and the Marcos dictatorship lie deeper in the political and economic organization of the latter, including its "dependency status" in the global political economy and its adoption of a "World Bank–International Monetary Fund" model of economic development. As Robin Broad suggested, "Aquino's assassination may prove to have been the spark . . . [but] it was [the] long-growing economic desperation which brought poor, middle and upper classes into massive protest demonstrations."[15] The most immediate result of the Aquino assassination was its de-stabilizing effect on the Marcos dictatorship and its capacity to hold the country together. In retrospect, the Aquino assassination marked the "point of no return" in the growing de-legitimization of the Marcos dictatorship.

The Aquino assassination, which in my understanding includes its infamous conclusion in the acquittal of Armed Forces Chief of Staff General Fabian Ver along with the 25 other defendants despite overwhelming evidence implicating them in a conspiracy to murder Aquino, also occasioned a serious "re-thinking" by the United States and Washington, in particular, of its foreign policy towards the Marcos dictatorship. It is no secret that Washington's support for the Marcos regime was unequivocal in the pre-Aquino assassination period. The now famous toast of Vice-President George Bush is paradigmatic: "We stand with the Philippines, we stand with you sir, we love your adherence to democratic principles and to the democratic process, and we will not leave you in isolation." This was followed by President Reagan's own statement in the 1983 presidential campaign in which he outlined US foreign policy options in the Philippines as largely between Marcos or the communists. By arguing that the Marcos government, despite its dictatorial character, had a better record than any communist regime—and therefore, deserved US support—Reagan was affirming a Kirkpatrick vision of foreign policy that saw nothing worse than the possibility of a communist takeover. Unequivocal support of "the democratic process" gave way to support for anti-communist regimes regardless of "adherence to democratic principles."

With the Aquino assassination and the public outcry that followed, the Reagan administration was forced to cancel a visit to the Philippines in November of that year, then its strongest expression of displeasure with the Marcos dictatorship. The growing "communist insurgency" and the apparent failure of the Marcos government to control it, along with its inability to discipline and reform the members of its armed forces, and the continued decline and contraction of the economy in the post-Aquino assassination period, forced Washington to re-evaluate even its Kirkpatrick approach to the Marcos dictatorship. Indeed, Washington's displeasure with its "protege" in Asia was, in reality, evidence of a growing recognition within Washington circles that the Marcos regime was losing its credibility and legitimacy, not only with its own people, but with the American people as well. The renewed vigor in Congress to halt further (military) aid to the Marcos government, the visit to the Philippines of Senator Laxalt as a personal emissary of the President, and the pressure put on Marcos to hold elections, all signalled a growing concern with regard to the capacity of the Marcos dictatorship to "keep its house in order," that is, to maintain an effective counter-insurgency program in order to safeguard the national security interests of nations within the western camp, particularly that of the United States. The most telling evidence for this growing disaffection, however, was expressed in a National Security Directive completed in November 1984 in which Washington, contrary to its previous endorsement of the Marcos dictatorship, admitted the need for other "democratic" alternatives to it. Part of this confidential document is paradigmatic:

> Our [US] support is one of Marcos' largest remaining strengths. Our assets, particularly at the people to people level, could be lost, if we come to be seen as favoring the continuation of the Marcos regime to the exclusion of other democratic alternatives.[16]

The Aquino assassination, however, was only the "tip of the iceberg" in the intensification of the crisis in Philippine political life. For example, the work of the New Peoples Army, which primarily was a movement in the countryside, though not limited to it, was not eclipsed by the political ferment generated by the Aquino assassination since the latter was largely an urban phenomenon. The "February 1986 Rebellion" has confirmed this observation. Political observers have pointed out that such an urban movement, in the long run, would benefit the total struggle against the Marcos regime. Clearly, the NDF/NPA/CPP opposition has continued to grow indicating that the intensification of the crisis, was more profound than what the Aquino assassination underscored.[17]

My own argument has sought to underscore the broader structural whole, understood in terms of a political–economic–cultural dependency, as the context not only of the Aquino assassination, but of the whole crisis itself. Indeed, the 1986 "snap" elections, a consequence of the growing protest movement which the Aquino assassination inspired, was only the "legal," i.e., constitutional face, of the opposition to the Marcos dictatorship, a largely "liberal democratic" attempt to dislodge Marcos through the electoral process. In a country whose people were largely held captive by their own government, the optimism in the possibility of dislodging the Marcos government by the very process to which he appealed, did not seem to be warranted. As Joel Rocamora pointed out, "the murder of Aquino starkly shows that Marcos will use all means to defend his monopoly of power. It also shows the limits of reformist strategies in the anti-Marcos struggle and the need to develop the capability to fight Marcos in his own terms, with armed, underground forces."[18] In fact, I argue below, the dislodging of the Marcos dictatorship cannot be attributed exclusively to the February presidential elections, but rather to the confluence of domestic and international factors, including the international de-legitimization of the Marcos dictatorship, the ongoing work of protest and resistance movements in the Philippines particularly of the Left, and the mobilization of "people's power' through the Church.

The "February 1986 rebellion": gateway to democratic transformation or anti-democratic reform?

At the heart of the "February 1986 Rebellion" was the re-discovery of a particular understanding of democracy.[19] It was, in the first instance, a break with a concrete expression of domination, a "great refusal," infused by the spirit of courage, passion, hope, though happily not of Promethean heroism, of people from all walks of life—thus, the broad reference to what is now popularly known as "people's power." In those decisive days, the unequivocal support of the Roman Catholic Conference of Bishops and of the Vatican, as well as the public outrage both in the United States and the Philippines expressed in such actions as the US Congress moving to cut all military and economic aid to the Marcos regime, the public recognition by the White House of the "loss of legitimacy" of the Marcos government, the resignation of top level advisers within the Marcos dictatorship, and the defection of high cabinet and military officials in the country as well as abroad, suggested that the repudiation was widespread, even total.

There was, however, a second level repudiation of the Marcos dictatorship symbolized in the presidential leadership "style," both in form and in substance, of Corazon C. Aquino. Contrary to the Marcos dictatorship characterized by a non-participatory, unilateral leadership committed to the priority of "order," manipulation, and control, which is reminiscent of the Eurocentric politico-philosophical tradition of Machiavelli, Hobbes, and Locke, and which the Philippines inherited through the United States,[20] Aquino continues to embody a deliberative, participatory, and compassionate leadership style committed to an open society shaped by freedom and justice. She has been able to offer the kind of political leadership which can provide a metaphor for a truly transformative politics if it is nurtured, sustained and allowed to survive the demands of *Realpolitik*.

Anti-democratic problems

While the crisis in the Philippines cannot be reduced to the question of political leadership, the appointment to key government and military positions of some individuals who had either served faithfully under the Marcos dictatorship or who have not been unsympathetic with the underlying "liberal democratic" philosophy of both the Marcos and the Aquino regimes, continues to raise the danger not only of the superversion of the coalition Aquino government, but also of the continuation of the militarist and corporate–capitalist commitments of the previous government. An analysis of the recent resignation of Defense Minister Juan Ponce Enrile and his replacement by General Rafael Ileto, hailed by many as a hopeful step towards "liberalization," suggests that the change is more apparent than real. Enrile endorsed the appointment of Ileto, one of the military's top counterinsurgency experts.

The Aquino government's seemingly contradictory stance *vis-à-vis* the communist insurgency is illustrative. Recent events indicate a growing if not abiding frustration and impatience within the 230,000-strong New Armed Forces of the Philippines towards the progressive elements within the Aquino government. On the one hand, while the Aquino government has finally entered into a "ceasefire agreement" with the National Democratic Front as part of a broader "peace process' aimed not only at the reconciliation of the contending forces in the country, but more importantly, at the solution of the political and economic problems of the country, public pronouncements from some high government and military officials, as well as continuing counterinsurgency operations in the countrysides, suggest a lack of "good faith" towards the NDF. Aquino herself does not appear to be maximizing her moral and political leadership—which even "the Left" and "the Right" forces recognize—in setting the *direction* for social and political change in the country. Indeed, some of the key persons in her government have been reluctant to publicly acknowledge or deal forthrightly with the key problems which divide the moderates and the radicals. These include both the dominance of foreign interests and the domestic structures of inequality in the political, economic, and cultural life of the Filipino peoples. For example, the abrogation of the US–Philippine Bases Agreement, as well as other treaties and agreements prejudicial to Philippine interests, and the underlying commitment to a non-aligned, independent foreign policy it pre-supposes, have been largely postponed to 1991. The democratization of the state, both in form and substance, with its concommitant commitment not only to the primacy of civilian over military authority but especially to the real participation of the people in the process of governance, remains a point of contention, particularly in the light of Aquino's growing dependence on elements of the New Armed Forces and the continuing violations of peoples' rights by military and paramilitary units practically. The transformation of the political economy, both domestically and internationally, which requires a commitment to the de-alignment of the economy from the corporate–capitalist world economy and the immediate dismantling of an inequitous land-ownership structure in the country remains largely untouched, in the face of countervailing pressures from multilateral and multinational interests as well as domestic power elites to maintain, at the very least, a pre-1972 situation. On the other hand, some significant sectors of the military establishment, chafing under Aquino's personal commitment to a comprehensive approach to the solution of the communist insurgency which the former perceives as an unrealistic and militarily unwise approach, has exhibited not only a progressively hardening militarist stance towards the NDF/NPA/CPP, but has adopted what appears to be a strategy of "low-intensity conflict" to complement its ongoing counterinsurgency campaigns.

While these contradictions may simply be the consequences inherent in any coalition government, the message it communicates, in the absence of realistic and long-term "peace negotiations" and a reluctance to publicly recognize the right of the NDF/NPA/CPP to exist on its own terms within the larger body politic, is that the Aquino government is unwilling to entertain fundamental structural changes. This, in turn, may foreclose the possibilities of meaningful dialogue beyond the 60-day ceasefire agreement. If the Aquino government chooses the military's hardline anti-communist stance it could prompt the NDF/NPA/CPP to seek international recognition of a "status of belligerency" resulting in a war that would prove too costly for the Filipino peoples to bear. What must not be lost to public view is the fundamental political question, namely, whether the post-Marcos era will be characterized by a broad, nationalist, and pluralistic democratic structure which recognizes the "Left" and what it represents, or whether it will be an alliance of groups that fall only within the orbit of elite "liberal democracy." In this context, the "ceasefire" and the larger hoped-for peace negotiations of which it is a part, is of fundamental significance, perhaps second only to the "February 1986 Rebellion," not only because it has opened a dialogue between the so-called insurgents and the Government, but, more importantly, because it has inaugurated a political ethos in which, for the first time in 20 years or more, alternatives ranging from authoritarian rule to "liberal democracy" to national democracy are being discussed on the popular level.

Moreover, a vocal minority of "Marcos loyalists," whose significance lies less in their attempts to re-instate Marcos than their adherence to a "rightist" authoritarian view of politics, continues to threaten the fragile democracy which the peoples' rebellion inaugurated. They appear more concerned with preserving and protecting their own interests than with being involved in the much needed reconstruction of the country. Furthermore, the "overwhelming" ratification of the 1986 Constitution, which includes provisions that could provide the moral and political space for meaningful transformation and enhance democracy, remains circumscribed by the new government's insistence on its exclusive legitimacy. This compromises the crucial democratic "right to dissent" and disenfranchises the NDF/NPA/CPP and other resistance movements and their constituencies from the *body politic*. This, no doubt, will discourage those who historically have been excluded from "liberal democratic" politics, but who have demonstrated their commitment to the Filipino peoples, especially the "poor and the oppressed," and who, without question, represent them, from fully participating in the new government.

Unhappily, the economic advisers of the Aquino government, including Jose B. Fernandez, who as Central Bank Governor has significant oversight of the financial aspects of the economy, still prefer to replace the "crony capitalism" of the previous regime with a largely "free enterprise" capitalist philosophy. Such a choice confirms the liberal bourgeois orientation of many in the new government and raises the specter of continued transnational corporate intervention in the Philippine economy. The experience with capitalism in the Philippines has demonstrated that as a peripheral country integrated in the capitalist world system, its economy is subject to the dictates of multinational corporations and/or multilateral agencies whose interests are best served by keeping the country dependent. These anti-democratic elements, if not changed, will make it difficult for significant members of the Filipino body politic to support the new government. A founding member of the Communist Party of the Philippines put it: "You may see some different faces in the government, but the same repressive system remains in place."[21]

Also disturbing was the earlier self-congratulatory attitude of Washington towards the Aquino government. Not unlike its preemption of Spanish surrender in 1898, the US government took credit for the demise of the Marcos dictatorship, obscuring the fact that it consistently supported the dictatorship from its inception in 1972. There is no doubt that the United States played a decisive role in dislodging the Marcos dictatorship. Such support, unfortunately, was premised on the preservation of US military and economic "security interests' in the region. Indeed, by its public and private actions before, during, and after the 'post-election crisis," and despite its explicit withdrawal of support for Marcos during the "February 1986 Rebellion," Washington has remained largely supportive of Marcos who it sees as "an old ally and friend." Moreover, despite its public support of Aquino against Juan Ponce Enrile's "de-stabilizing activities," Washington's silence about the Aquino government's 60-day ceasefire with the NDF/NPA/CPP, its tacit approval and support of General Rafael Ileto's appointment as Defense Minister, and its unequivocal preference for the retention of the US bases in the Philippines, suggests that Washington remains committed to its over-all anti-communist foreign policy towards the Philippines. What is ironical is that this very policy, created in the name of democracy, is that which may foreclose the very possibility of democracy in the Philippines.

Democratic transformation or anti-democratic reform?

The "February 1986 Rebellion" presents a political choice. As a repudiation of the Marcos dictatorship it is a choice that departs both from the statist, militarist, and corporate–capitalist ideology of Philippine "Constitutional Authoritarianism," and the Western "liberal democratic" tradition that gave birth to it. This Euro–American legacy of "liberal democracy" valorized the State as the *locus politicus* along with the normative separation of its procedural and substantive dimensions. It upheld the "possessive," self-interested bourgeois subject as the fundamental unit of politics. And it understood the Western democracies as the exclusive bearers of "modern," "civilized humanity" in a world of self-serving "barbarians," a legacy of "messianism" that reaches as far back as the "marriage" between the warrior tribes of northern and Western Europe and Christianity,[22] expressed more recently in Reagan's apocalyptic-filled obsession to rid the American continent of "a cruel clique of deeply committed communists at war with God and man [sic]."

In contrast, the "February 1986 Rebellion" marks the re-discovery of a democracy that upholds the primary of the peoples' dwelling as the *arche* and *telos* of political life, and affirms the capacity of persons in community to transform their lives and society in the light of their shared values. As a political choice it is rooted in, and committed to, a vision of democracy as a *way of life* that upholds the intrinsic connection between State and Society while subordinating the statist assumptions of liberalism to the populist/ participatory assumptions of democracy. In fact, it is a refusal to reduce democracy to the administration and adjudication of competing claims, a rejection of the logic of liberalism in the name of democracy. In the post-Marcos era it will be crucial to discern whether the structural questions are being addressed, whether meaningful political and economic participation is encoded into the institutions of government, whether intervention by foreign governments, multinationals, and multilaterals is disallowed, and whether the commitment to dialogue, plurality, and community remain central to the new government's theory and practice. In short, whether progressive elements of the Aquino government can keep democracy alive and prevent the impetus for democratic transformation from being turned into anti-democratic reform.[23]

From a politics of opposition to a politics of transformation: legitimacy, authority, tradition, people

Contending political forces: between "liberal democracy" and national democracy

In the context of the demise of the Marcos dictatorship and the euphoria that has accompanied the beginning of the Aquino regime, it is important to pause and evaluate our options for the long term. Clearly we are witnessing the dismantling of the Marcos dictatorship and its ideology of "constitutional authoritarianism" in favor of "popular democracy." What may not be as clear are the fundamentally different assumptions that shape the latter. Thus, while it is important to underscore the unity of these political forces, it is necessary to identify their major contours, i.e., the points at which there is continuity and change, collaboration and conflict, among these contending political forces.

While these political forces in the Philippines today continually align and re-align themselves making classification difficult, it is possible to identify several "groups" by their declared politico-philosophical and organizational commitments: 1) the "authoritarian liberals" which include the Kilusang Bagong Lipunan, the Nacionalista Party, the Marcos loyalists, and individuals like Enrile, who are not necessarily pro-Marcos but who share his political philosophy; 2) the "liberal democrats" including the Liberal Party, the Partido Demokratiko ng Pilipinas/Laban ng Bayan, President Aquino herself, who are largely, though not exclusively, anti-Marcos but not anti-US; 3) the nationalist, communist/Marxist front under the aegis of the National Democratic Front/New People's Army, which was declared "illegal' by the Marcos dictatorship and continues to be so under the Aquino government, but which appears to have the clearest socio-political alternative to 'liberal democratic" politics; 4) the Muslim front of the Moro Liberation Front/Bangsa Moro Army, similarly declared "illegal," which is concerned primarily with establishing in the southern Philippines a structure of self-governance based on Muslim politics and culture; 5) the Cordillera Peoples' Liberation Front concerned also with self-governance of cultural minorities in the northern Philippines; and 6) the "open Left" and 'cause-oriented groups," which are informed largely by nationalist and democratic philosophies and organized around specific causes, including Ang Bayan, a broad coalition of cause-oriented groups, Gabriela (women), Kilusang Mayo Uno (labor), Kilusang Magbubukid ng Pilipinas (peasant), National Ecumenical Forum for Church Response (church), the Cordillera Peoples' Alliance (minorities), and more recently, the Partido ng Bayan, a left-oriented political party, to name only a few.

It is not possible in this essay to deal exhaustively with the similarities and differences of these different "groups." Indeed, a comprehensive perspective on Philippine politics requires one to attend to the plurality of forces that constitute an inextricable whole. It is important, however, to begin with some of these contending "groups" or forces especially those that appear to play relatively significant roles in the transformation of Philippine political life today. These contending political forces, particularly those that are characterized by a "liberal democratic" and "national democratic" orientation, reflect differing fundamental pre-suppositions of the character of human dwelling, i.e., how peoples are constituted as historical and political communities. These presuppositions, sometimes consciously and/or unconsciously excluded from critical reflection, are the historical prejudices of these political communities which continuously shape and guide their thought, feeling, and action.[24] Hence, in order to understand more fully the nature of the crisis, it is necessary to identify these different fundamental presuppositions, and to explore them in the historical context of their challenge to, and transcendence of, the "US–Marcos dictatorship."

The question of legitimacy

Our inquiry into the nature of the contending political forces in the Philippines begins with what is generally perceived to be the most crucial political problem, namely, legitimacy. Indeed, the first challenge to the Marcos dictatorship and its philosophy of "constitutional authoritarianism" was a two-fold challenge posed to its juridico-procedural and substantive legitimacy, what Walden Bello, one of the critics of the "liberal democratic" perspective, calls the "dual crisis of political legitimacy and economic development." This question of legitimacy, or the normative (legal) acceptability of a political institution or leadership, is important not only because most "liberal democratic" critics of the Marcos dictatorship see the "loss of legitimacy" as crucial, but also because the question of legitimacy illustrates the fundamental differences within the shared consensus of these contending political forces.

Almost ten years after the declaration of martial law, Senator Jovito Salonga, one of the more populist-oriented liberal democrats, reiterated the "liberal democratic" challenge. After pointing out that the principle of the "emergency" character of martial law is inviolable and applicable only where there is a great magnitude of peril, namely "invasion, insurrection or rebellion," Salonga declared:

> When President Marcos declared Martial Law on September 21, 1972 to "save the Republic," he did so in apparent obedience to this principle. But when he frankly admitted later that what had been installed was a system of "authoritarianism", a polite term for dictatorship, it became abundantly clear that he had repudiated a principle he was reportedly upholding . . . . It is the violation of this principle that is at the root of our present difficulties.[25]

The "establishment" or elite "liberal democratic" opposition did not challenge the Marcos government for invoking the constitutional provisions on martial law in order to "maintain public safety and order." Rather, they challenged its constitutional validity when the relevant provisions were invoked for the "establishment of a new society." As Macapagal had argued earlier, the illegitimacy of the Marcos government was in its continued use of martial law where the conditions which justified its use no longer existed.

The unconstitutionality of both Proclamation No. 1081 and the Marcos Martial Law government that imposed it was further challenged when the constitutional ground on which the edifice was built, i.e., the 1973 Constitution, was deemed to have been improperly ratified by the people. Thus, martial law and the Martial Law government, especially after December 1973, were in total violation of the 1935 Constitution, which, for many of the "liberal democratic" opposition, was the only valid "fundamental law of the land."

The challenge to the legitimacy of the Marcos Martial Law government is based on a particular interpretation of the "rule of law," a principle shared very deeply by the "liberal democratic" opposition with Marcos' "constitutional authoritarianism." It emphasizes a juridico-procedural perspective which challenges the law in the name of Law. It questions the Marcos interpretation of the law, while presupposing the normativity of Law as such. In short, it is a challenge to the identification of "the Law" with the State. While this challenge underscores the seriousness of a "legitimation crisis," it remains a partial challenge insofar as it assumes the unquestionability of the "rule of law." The notion implies an acceptance of a particular vision of how political life should be organized, namely, that State and Society must be subsumed under the Law, which is the "objective" expression of the "will of the people." Thus, the question of whether or not a positive internal relationship exists, in reality, between the Law and the People, a precondition for the adequacy of the "rule of law," does not arise. While this question needs to be raised, the unconditional acceptance of the Law as the

Archimedean point from which "the rule of law" is understood militates against such a task.

With the convening of the Batasang Pambansa and the 1984 elections that saw the coming into office of a significant though greatly outnumbered "elite" opposition, however, this earlier unequivocal position that deemed the Marcos government unconstitutional gave way to a more pragmatic approach to "legitimacy." While many "liberal democrats" privately questioned the Marcos government's "constitutional legitimacy," many chose to de-emphasize it and focus their attention on changing the political leadership through the very electoral process that under Marcos was considered "illegitimate." Thus, the 1986 "snap" elections, in contrast to the 1984 elections and the huge "boycott movement" that accompanied it, received wider support from the "liberal democratic" forces through their fielding of a "unified" Aquino–Laurel ticket.

It may be argued that participation in an electoral process that is deemed illegal, and therefore, illegitimate, undermines any further formal/procedural challenge to the process. Such a challenge has largely been superseded by the conviction that "legal" considerations must give way to the larger commitment to the "will of the people." This is not inconsistent with the "liberal democratic" tradition, particularly in its Lockean form. Indeed, as the "February 1986 Rebellion" has shown, the earlier challenge to the Marcos government which emphasized a juridico-procedural perspective has progressively become tempered by the extra-parliamentary cry for substantive changes in the status quo. In short, the "rule of law" is being challenged in the name of the "people." Formal/procedural legitimacy is relocated within the context of substantive legitimacy. Indeed, the "liberal democratic" understanding of "constitutional legitimacy" rests on the "will of the people." As Salonga put it poignantly:

> In the final analysis, our hope is not in any foreign power, nor in a Constitution, nor in any statute or law, nor in any court of justice. Our true hope is in our own people who, thanks to current developments, including the so-called lifting of Martial Law, are asserting their right to be free—with increasing boldness and courage.[26]

Unfortunately, this hopeful transformation within the "liberal democratic" challenge is undermined by a deep tension. For while it challenged the Marcos dictatorship in the name of the people, its commitment to the "rule of law" constrains it to seek alternatives within the framework of the rule of law. In short, legitimacy is not only a function of consent and/or representation, but, more importantly, it becomes a condition of order. Thus Aquino's open invitation to the NDF/NPA/CPP to "rejoin the wider society" rests on the latter's willingness to adhere to the "rule of law" as it is interpreted by the new government. It implies not only the qualification of dissent, but also the suppression of other aspects of socio-political life which the NDF/NPA/CPP forces represent. In this context, the underlying commitment of the "liberal democratic" front to what elsewhere I have called the "liberal bourgeois subject" that is constituted by the principle of individuality,[27] tends to reduce the reasons for the crisis in the Philippines to one man's greed or avarice, i.e., to Marcos and his cronies. It tends to understand the crisis as one of political leadership, emphasizing what Johan Galtung calls an "actor-oriented" perspective at the expense of a "structural-oriented" one. While the former cannot be disputed, the challenge tends to repress the structural dimensions of the crisis and, not unrelated to this non-structural perspective, implies that the Marcos dictatorship was simply an aberration in an otherwise acceptable "liberal democratic" polity. As I have argued elsewhere, there is evidence to strongly suggest the contrary. That is to say, the Marcos dictatorship was the logical end, not an aberration, of "liberal democratic" polity.[28]

In contrast, the National Democratic Front/New People's Army/ Communist Party of the Philippines raises a different though not unrelated challenge, namely that the "US–Marcos dictatorship" lost its legitimacy because its anti-nationalist, imperialist, and bureaucrat[ic] capitalist self-understanding is a betrayal of the Filipino people. As stated in its "Ten-Point Program" of April 23, 1973, the NDF/NPA/CPP seeks to

> . . . build a broad unity of patriotic and progressive classes, groups and individuals all for the purpose of overthrowing the US–Marcos dictatorship. . . . In the process, we must create a vigorous anti-fascist anti-imperialist and anti-feudal movement. The anti-fascist struggle must lead to genuine national independence and democracy.[29]

This programmatic assertion is grounded in the earlier works of Amado Guerrero, chairman of the Revitalized Communist Party of the Philippines, who pointed to the "three historical evils" that afflict Philippine society—US imperialism, feudalism and bureaucrat[ic] capitalism which are responsible for the society's semi-colonial and semi-feudal character.

The NDF/NPA/CPP challenge to the "US–Marcos dictatorship" went beyond the "liberal democratic" challenge of *constitutional* legitimacy. It challenged the political legitimacy of the dictatorship on the basis of what is perceived to be its politico-economic illegitimacy. Moreover, it not only challenged the Marcos regime but also the historical-structural forces which have shaped and allowed such client-states as the Marcos dictatorship to exist, namely, US imperialism. Marcos, therefore, was viewed as only one of many "enemies of the people."

Despite its polemical language, the NDF/NPA/CPP challenge correctly frees the question of legitimacy from its juridico-procedural moorings and locates it on the substantive level, especially within the decisive framework of political economy. "National liberation, unhindered national industrialization and genuine land reform," the "Ten-Point Program" notes, "are the solution to the economic problems of the people." Political legitimacy is dependent on politico-economic validity.

The NDF/NPA/CPP challenge rightly underscores the significance of the politico-economic *structure* for the legitimacy of any government. Their criticism of "market relations" as an unjust form of economic exchange highlights the failure of the present economic paradigm and points to the need for a different kind that can "liberate the peasant masses from feudal and semi-feudal exploitation" in order to "improve the people's livelihood, guarantee the right to work and protect national capital against foreign monopoly capital."[30]

This critique of political economy is also a challenge to the legitimacy of the state–society relation as it is presently constituted. For the NDF/NPA/CPP, the Philippine government is an oligarchy that serves its own class interests. Only a state that "serves the people" is legitimate. Hence, the quest for a new paradigm of economic exchange, a quest rooted in the understanding of the human as *homo faber*, is simultaneously a search for a new state-society paradigm, namely, that the state must be a *tool* for the realization of the proletarian interest from whence it derives its legitimacy. The challenge points to the "proper" relationship of political legitimacy, political economy, and the people. Thus, while "the Left" may have suffered strategic setbacks with the dislodging of the Marcos dictatorship by a moderate, centrist government, and despite its having entered into dialogue with the new government, its challenge will continue to place it at variance with some of the members of the Aquino government making it difficult for meaningful collaboration to occur. This is unfortunate since the state–society relation even under the new government is in disrepair and in desperate need of theoretical and practical reformulation.

It is not difficult to see why the "liberal democratic" (bourgeois) understanding of legitimacy is viewed with profound suspicion by those whose commitments fall outside the orbit of "liberal democracy." Indeed, the NDF/NPA/CPP challenge in its unequivocal repudiation, from a nationalistic Marxist–Leninist–Maoist position, not only of the legitimacy of the "US–Marcos dictatorship" but also of the elite "opposition," which it construes as a structural whole, offers the possibility of an alternative to the status quo. Because of "exteriority," particularly to the formal/procedural sensibilities of the "liberal democratic" heritage, it is able to envision radical changes, indeed, even through armed struggle, in Philippine life. This contrast between the "liberal democratic" opposition and the nationalist communist/Marxist opposition is underscored by the Filipino political scientist Joel Rocamora when he notes that "where elite oppositionists are mainly opposed to Marcos and his immediate circle of allies, popular organizations demand the dismantling of the entire US–Marcos dictatorship, including both key personnel and policies. The elite opposition would be pleased if the United States would stop supporting Marcos and in fact continues to hope that US support will be transferred to its leaders. Popular forces demand the radical restructuring of US–Philippine relations away from US dominance and control."[31]

Indeed, much of the discussion of social change, especially in the post-Aquino assassination phase of the crisis, has revolved around the question of the place of armed struggle in fundamental change. We will return to this crucial, even subversive, question in the latter part of this essay. For the moment, it is important to simply point out that for the NDF/NPA/CPP, the question of parliamentary change, including the 1986 "snap" elections, belongs to the genre of "reformist" change, and therefore is inadequate to the complete overthrow of what they perceive is the total bankruptcy of US imperialism and its client states. Contrary to those who see this as terrorist anarchy, even as an atheistic anti-humanism, the NDF/NPA/CPP challenge, stems from a deep conviction that the "US–Marcos dictatorship," and now including, I suspect, what may be called the "US–Aquino alliance," lacks legitimacy because of the injustice it perpetuates, albeit more sanguinely in the latter, on the Filipino people. It comes as no surprise, therefore, that the more radical forces in the Philippines view the Aquino-led rebellion with guarded skepticism. Indeed, it fears a consolidation of US and Filipino elite interests against the interests of "the poor, the deprived, and the oppressed" classes.[32]

In the light of this fundamental challenge it is unfortunate that an equally important critical task, one recognized by communist-Marxists in other contexts, has been largely ignored: the challenge to the metaphysical/philosophical presuppositions of political economy that undergird its political theory and practice. Perhaps because of deep-seated suspicions of "superstructural questions" which tend to be disjoined from "infrastructural questions" in "reformist-bourgeois" reflection, the official NDF/NPA/CPP challenge has remained self-consciously within the political-economic realm. In this sense, the NDF/NPA/CPP challenge is also a partial one. Nevertheless, since these "ideological supports" are decisive for the continued existence of oppression, they require challenge and deconstruction. It is worthwhile to note that Marx himself argued against a positivistic/economistic understanding of political economy.

The question of authority

The question of legitimacy points to the fundamental question of political authority: the triadic *relationship* among the people, its government, and the normative goals which they share. Indeed, it may be said that the "crisis of legitimacy" is symptomatic of a fundamental loss of political authority. When Salonga asks on what basis the Marcos dictatorship maintains martial law, presupposing thereby an understanding of legitimacy that goes beyond its identification with the existing government, he is challenging not only the *legal* basis of its claim but also, more importantly, the very configuration of the relationship between the Marcos dictatorship and the people within the commonly held values of the nation.

For the "liberal democratic" forces, authority is meaningful only if it is acknowledged. Something is authoritative insofar as it is able to freely generate a person's confidence and commitment on the basis of its normative claims. This is the sense in which authority is said to reside in the people and vested in the Law. Authority, in other words, is not primarily the prerogative of a ruler but a relationship of participation, authorization and representation between the ruler and the ruled. Not unlike "constitutional authoritarianism," the "liberal democratic" forces identify this relationship as being structured by the juridico-procedural mechanism of the law and its underlying "legal mentality."[33] Unlike the Marcos dictatorship, however, it tends to emphasize the representative character of the relationship rather than its authorization, and unfortunately affirms a formal/procedural view of participation. Thus, when the Marcos government juridically violated the "will of the people" in the use of martial law and the "ratification" of the 1973 Constitution, both of which were deemed illegal, it was said to have "lost" its legitimacy and its authority.

Similarly, for the NDF/NPA/CPP, the authority of government which lies in its being the instrument of class interests resides in the consent of the people and the truth of their claims. Here, the *proletariat* is unequivocally identified as the "people" and its truth claims as resting on a (structural) scientific analysis of the "objective conditions of society." Since the proletariat was effectively excluded from participation under the Marcos dictatorship, thereby dismissing the proletariat's claims to truth, legitimacy was thrown into question and authority was lost.

Central to both the "liberal democratic" and nationalist communist/ Marxist conceptions of authority is the notion that political authority is relational and dialogical, i.e., it is the giving and receiving of confidence and commitment between persons who recognize and affirm a "common humanity"; it is not an independent variable that creates or imposes the values that constitute this "common humanity." The breaking of this *triadic* relationship, i.e., when the three elements no longer inhere together, signifies the loss of authority. Legitimacy/legality, in other words, is conferred by authority, not the reverse. Authority precedes the law. Relationality precedes Authority.[34] Legitimacy rests ultimately on the existence of a political community with commonly held values. It may be concluded, therefore, that both the "liberal democratic" and nationalist communist/Marxist forces are fundamentally democratic, that is, they affirm the primacy of "the people" as the "source" of political life. Indeed, the "February 1986 Rebellion" may be understood precisely as the re-discovery of democracy, i.e., paraphrasing Manfred Halpern, the "power of the people" as the cornerstone of politics.

The question of tradition

Yet, the question of political authority cannot be abstracted from the reality and concept of Tradition. For traditions, as the horizoning prejudices that shape and guide human thought, feeling, and action,[35] provide the sources for normative values within the political community. For this reason, the question of authority is fundamentally a question of tradition. Here, jurisprudence, religion, culture—the cumulative experience of peoples, i.e., history—become the crucial sources of authority.

However, the question of tradition is inextricably related to the question of "the people" which is not simply a matter of concretely identifying who embodies truth and gives consent but, more importantly, a matter of defining the character and significance of "the people": how peoples are constituted as historical and political communities. Thus, ideology, socio-economic location, the proletarian interest, as well as constitutional law, bureaucracy, political charisma—all of which are questions of tradition—come to rest on the question of "the people." For while tradition cannot be reduced to a "human project," but is, in fact, that which makes human dwelling possible, a *living* tradition is possible only as it is embodied, i.e., temporalized and spatialized, by a people. As the Minjung theologians of Korea have clearly pointed out, traditions are borne by the people, i.e., fundamental assumptions and normative visions are embodied in political and historical communities. In this sense, the question of tradition is politicized in the question of "the people" and becomes more fully historical.

The question of "the people"

The question of "the people" arises because Philippine traditions are breaking. The fundamental presuppositions which have shaped society, and which have been institutionalized, have become contradictory—even meaningless. It is, therefore, not simply a crisis of institutions but a crisis precipitated by the breaking of the foundations on which these institutions are built. Moreover, it is a crisis in the relational fabric of human dwelling, a breaking of human–human, human–nature, and human–divine relationships, a phenomenon of incoherence not limited to the Philippines, but, as Halpern has noted, is characteristic of the modern world.[36] In short, the crisis of tradition is a crisis of what it means to be a people. It is a question of political identity, and its participatory and empowering character. That is, a question of *authentic political subjecthood*, of which "people's power" during the "February 1986 Rebellion" is only one expression.

Coming to a meaningful consensus about *what* or *who* "the people" are is a difficult task. After noting that "people is a reality and concept that has become an indelible part of the social and political landscape everywhere," the Filipino social ethicist Feliciano Cariño, delineates the major perspectives on "the people" in the Philippines: the religio-cultural and the politico-economic, about which there is much controversy and little consensus. Cariño observes:

> For some, the reality of people need not and cannot be defined; it needs only to be described . . . the obvious thing about the present social situation is that a very large majority of the population is "deprived, oppressed and poor." The primary, though not exclusive, reality of people therefore must be understood in terms of this political and economic fact.
>
> For others, however, the fact of the political and economic deprivation of people cannot and should not be isolated from and should be linked with other dimensions of their existence. While the fact of and commitment to the "deprived, oppressed and poor" may not be questioned, the manner in which the linkage of this fact with other dimensions of existence is less a matter of description, but more of interpretation.[37]

Cariño goes on to argue that these two apparently divergent perspectives may not necessarily be mutually exclusive and that any attempt to reduce the reality of "people" to single-factor explanations may become "unproductive in grasping the reality of people." A similar question is raised by Antonio Lambino who asks, rather polemically, "People according to Christ? Or people according to Marx? Which one for the Philippines?"[38] Lambino asserts that the religio-cultural dimension of "people" is, at least, equally decisive for a full understanding of Philippine political reality.

This discussion, which is only one of many,[39] is significant because it reflects the immediacy of the crisis of *political identity*, i.e., of authentic political subjecthood. It also underscores the plurality of perspectives that are vying for dominance in providing solutions to the crisis. Moreover, it indicates a growing awareness on the part of the Filipino peoples of the comprehensiveness and complexity of the crisis. However, the bifurcation of the religio-cultural and politico-economic understanding of the people, implied in most of these discussions, is misconceived. Such reductionism leads to disastrous consequences, not least of which is the failure to comprehend the depth and multi-dimensional character of human dwelling, and consequently a misleading and inadequate vision for the transcendence of the crisis of "political subjecthood."

Nationalism as a question of authentic political subjecthood

The crisis of "the people" and the discourse it has engendered has taken various shapes in the history of the Republic, an indirect testimony to the depth and breadth of the question of political identity. In the 1950s and 60s, the question was formulated in terms of nationalism. Questions about the meaning of nationalism and its roots in the cultural values of the Filipino heritage posed a serious challenge to the colonial past of the Philippines. For example, Renato Constantino, the dean of Filipino nationalism, in his classic essay on "The Mis-education of the Filipino,"[40] underscored the deep fissures in the Filipino national psyche due to the onslaught of US colonialism which sought to benevolently assimilate the Philippines into the US system.

Constantino's essay on mis-education, while dated, is paradigmatic. It demonstrates the extent to which "liberal democratic" values were imposed on a largely non-liberal culture. It already suggests what later historical research confirms, namely, that Philippine historical experience was largely a struggle against the imposition of a "bourgeois vision" of human life. The essay laments the eclipse of Filipino religio-cultural values and underscores the destructiveness of US colonialism, illustrating thereby the nature of the crisis as a deep clash between Western and non-Western values.[41] In a different though related context, nationalism interpreted positively as a question of community pointed to the existence of a rich and diverse tradition. It is this "national tradition" to which Horacio de la Costa, the Filipino Jesuit historian, appeals in arguing for a truly Filipino society.[42]

More recent discussions, particularly the "revolt of the masses" thesis,[43] have underscored not only a more fully religio-political understanding of the question of people, but a more explicit commitment to viewing "history from below." Reynaldo C. Ileto, the Filipino historian, radicalizing Constantino's nationalist argument, has shown the interplay of religious traditions and political projects particularly of peoples who have traditionally fallen outside the orbit of the dominant Western "liberal (bourgeois) democratic" assumptions operative in Filipino understanding. The significance of this view lies not only in its having decisively demonstrated the religio-political character of (populist) people's movements, but also, and more importantly, in its articulation of a view of "the people" that does not sacrifice either the religio-cultural or politico-economic dimensions of "the people," and in its shifting of the level of discourse from bourgeois and Western assumptions to non-Western indigenous and "proletarian/populist" assumptions.

Development as a question of authentic political subjecthood

In the late 1960s and early 1970s the question of "people" was transposed into the question of "development and liberation." Here, the question of "people" moved from discussions of "cultural values" and "US colonialism" to a broader largely "world-systems" perspective that included questions of the "deprived, the oppressed and the poor." C.G. Arevalo, one of the major proponents of the discussion captures the spirit of this move:

> Development is to try to bring each man [sic] and each human community to the point where all that we have said about equality and participation will be true of them. Development is about man [sic]—where man [sic] can be truly free and responsible and where every man [sic] is a brother [sic] to the other. The purpose of development is not promoting chicken-breeding but humanizing society.[44]

The question of development, and to a lesser degree of liberation, had as its *arche* and *telos* the humanizing of society. It presupposed normative values of what it meant to be human, drawing these normative values from the religio-cultural ethos of a predominantly Roman Catholic Philippines which included, therefore, the social teachings of the Roman Catholic Church as rooted in the humanist tradition of the Enlightenment. The commitment to the values of equality and participation, for example, marked what Vitaliano Gorospe called the emerging "new morality" of post-Vatican II.[45]

This question of "development" as a question of political identity located the religio-cultural perspective of people within a *modernizing* politico-economic perspective. The move seemed to suggest that the crisis was rooted in a politico-economic crisis and emphasized identity as a question of *populus* rather than *ethnos*. Happily, this shift provided a larger framework of discourse, allowing for elements of a more radical persuasion to be included, and broadened the question of "authentic political subjecthood" to include the crucial economic and political factors that shape identity.

Liberation as a question of authentic political subjecthood

With the intensification of the crisis brought about by the "US–Marcos dictatorship," along with the shifting trends in the global political economy which the *Dependencia* school helpfully illuminates, the question of "people" was radicalized into the question of liberation, already presupposed, though not thematized, in the earlier discussions of "development." Here the notion of development, particularly in its "liberal democratic" form popularly known as developmentalism, was repudiated. Thus, Carlos Abesamis, the

Filipino Jesuit theologian, can write:

> Asian theology, aiming to respond to the imperative put to it by
> Asian reality, has two basic characteristics: its "Third-Worldness"
> (with its thrust towards socio-political and total human liberation of
> the poor, the deprived, and the oppressed) and its "Asianness" (the
> peculiar character, whatever that happens to be in our different
> situations respectively). Both . . . are essential . . . and inseparable.
> However, the main and principal characteristics . . . is its "Third-
> Worldness". . . [which] is the substantive, while "Asian" is the
> adjective . . . The primary thrust and concern, therefore . . . is
> liberation . . . which, of course . . . must be inculturated . . .[46]

With the question of liberation the centrality of the politico-economic
understanding of "people" was established. This particular understanding
owes much to the Marxist–Leninist–Maoist perspective of human dwelling,
particularly in its commitment to transforming the oppressive socio-political
structures of Philippine society. Not surprisingly, its appropriation in other
realms of discourse including theology has led to the recognition of the
seriousness of the claims of the NDF/NPA/CPP whose vision of "the people"
has consistently been "the poor, the deprived, and the oppressed."

This understanding of "people," set within a liberation perspective, and
tempered by a non-Western indigenous "proletarian/populist" commitment,
meant the radicalization of the crisis of political identity. It signified the
repudiation of the *Ilustrado* interpretation of "national self-determination,"
"popular sovereignty," "liberty," etc., but affirmed a fundamental critical
solidarity with the Marxist–Leninist–Maoist project which, itself, tends to be
Ilustrado in its "rationalist" form.[47] It pointed to a view of political identity
that involved not only the important religio-cultural dimensions of identity,
but also its politico-economic dimensions.

This meant, in the first place, a break with the political and economic
assumptions of developmentalism as an ideology of domination.[48] Capitalism
in its various forms, though with its common *consumerist-acquisitive* mentality,
was viewed as inadequate to sustain economic viability within a world of
scarcity. "Liberal democracy," particularly its valorization of "possessive
individualism" as a way of understanding the human being, on the one hand,
and the reduction of politics to the practice of statecraft, on the other hand,
was viewed with skepticism and disappointment. In the second place, it
revealed the oppositionary character of the question of political identity. The
struggle for liberation was set within a framework of opposition to a
dominating reality, particularly against a government that was seen as having
violated its mandate by usurping, through domination and force, the rightful
place of "the people" in political life. It highlighted, therefore, the history of
the Filipino people, viewed from below, as a history of opposition. In the third
place, as shown above, it provided the context for a strategic alliance in
struggling against the "US–Marcos dictatorship."

It is precisely on the question of "the people" that political forces in the
Philippines are most seriously divided. Indeed, despite the agreement on the
"primacy of the people" and the clear unanimity regarding who or what the

"enemy" is, at least prior to the "February 1986 Rebellion," there are profound differences about *who* the people are, and therefore, *what* direction must be taken in the process of social change. The question of "people" implies a "theory of social change," namely, who are the bearers of the possibility of fundamental transformation? and; how does fundamental transformation come into being? For the "liberal democratic" forces, "the people" is largely understood in terms of citizenship, i.e., as individual citizens whose identities are constituted mainly through their rights and obligations *vis-à-vis* State and Society and guaranteed by the Law. The citizens have the responsibility for social change. Not surprisingly, adherents of such a view see "parliamentary struggle" as the paradigm for transformation.

For the nationalist communist/Marxist forces, the "people" is the proletariat which, as a class, has been excluded not only from the decision-making processes of the State, but, more significantly, from the fruits of their labor which, together with their capacity to create and re-create species-life, constitutes their identity. Thus, any fundamental change, they have argued, must begin by affirming the constitutive character of the proletariat for social change, and the unequivocal commitment to the transformation of the relations of production and reproduction, returning to the proletariat their original unity with the fruits (products) of their labor. Since the present "order of relations," both on the political (state) and economic levels, is built on the expropriation of the laborer's fruits, and since the proletariat has been effectively excluded from participation in the "legal" process, the only option for social change is a non-parliamentary, indeed an armed, revolutionary struggle.

With the "results" of the February presidential elections, it is crucial to put to rest the "liberal democratic" illusion that only a parliamentary struggle offers the solution to the crisis of social and political transformation in the Philippines. At the very least, it has taught us that transformation through the electoral process must presuppose freedom and non-coercion before, during, and after the actual voting. In brief, the dismantling of the dictatorship must precede any process that seeks to ascertain the authentic "will of the people." In the context of our discussion, the struggle for justice will have to be a long and protracted one in which both parliamentary and non-parliamentary forms of "struggle" are subsumed within a larger more inclusive vision of political activity that sees in these forms a rightful and appropriate place for the achievement of a "just, participatory, and sustainable" society.

In fact, the "February 1986 Rebellion" points to the broader, more pluralistic, convergence of these contending political forces in the Philippines today. It demonstrates the efficacy of both parliamentary (the electoral process) and non-parliamentary (the military/popular resistance) forms of struggle for transformation. While other fundamental implications remain to be unfolded, it is clear that the successful "overthrow" of the Marcos dictatorship was brought about largely by the rediscovery of the "power of the people" embodied in a common struggle for liberation, rooted in the shared values of freedom and justice, and expressed within a community of peoples committed to a common vision for the future of the Filipino peoples.

Conclusion: the quest for authentic political subjecthood

Thus, it may be argued that the question of "the people," which I prefer to call a "quest for authentic political subjecthood," is situated within the framework of, and constituted by, contending political forces, where the political (politics) is defined simply as "all that we can and need to do together."[49] This quest for authentic political subjecthood is characterized, in this instance, by the interplay between the oppression of the "US–Marcos dictatorship" and the people's resistance to it; the latter taking on both parliamentary and non-parliamentary forms. Consequently, violence, while distinctly reduced to a minimum, was unavoidable. For this reason, it is crucial to be clear on the distinction between violence and counter-violence and to subsume it within the larger question of the kind of transformation that is being sought.

The crisis that is faced by the Filipino people today reflects a profound heightening of self-understanding, namely, a recognition of the arbitrariness of present political–economic–cultural relationships and a growing confidence in the human capacity to shape and to be shaped by history. It is, philosophically put, the comprehending of the historical character of human dwelling, i.e., *the coming into being of peoples as subjects of their own histories.*[50]

I conclude this discussion by retelling an event that not only sheds light on the *Geist* of this historical emergence, but also unequivocally underscores the fundamental commitment that shapes and guides my reflection. Sometime in 1974, the Marcos dictatorship began a multi-million dollar modernizing enterprise called the Chico River Dam Project, which envisioned the construction of four huge dams in the Chico River Basin for the purpose of generating hydroelectric power for practically all of northern Luzon. However, this meant the relocation of the Bontocs and Kalingas, national minorities, who have inhabited the region for centuries.

In the initial stages of the project's implementation the Marcos dictatorship met fierce non-violent resistance, which in turn it met with military force. Why did the Bontocs and Kalingas resist? Through the years, their struggle against the Marcos dictatorship was intensified and radicalized. Their own story, recorded by one of their own people, is evidence of the continuing crisis of dwelling and is paradigmatic of a politics of transformation as a quest for authentic political subjecthood.

> Everything we have in life is from Him who dwells above. He put us here and this is where we will live and die. Only He can take what He has given us, our lives included . . . Our fathers built all the ricefields you see . . . We cannot give up [this] heritage. It is something holy and we must hand it intact to our children . . . We are planted here, rooted in sacred land. All our dead are buried here . . . Now we are asked to allow our dead to be covered over by the waters of the Chico. This is an impossible request. Separated from our dead, we will die. The government assures us it will spare no effort nor expense to disinter the dead . . . It does not understand. The very soil we tread on—this is the dust of our fathers.
> The president assures us that the government will recompense us

double whatever we lose . . . But our *ukhali* [traditions]—this cannot be replaced. And its loss will be our death as a people . . . our *papatayan* [burial grounds] cannot be transferred with us . . .

The government thinks it is easy to rebuild our terraces . . . [but] building rice terraces is not simply a matter of putting up stone walls. The paddies have to be watered, nursed along, coaxed into bloom, but this takes years, generations even, before they start producing well . . .

Even if the dam is not built here in our area but is built farther down among the Kalinga, we should be just as concerned. For we are all one people with them; we are all *Igorots*. This should mean solidarity with them at all times, especially in their need.[51]

"Authentic political subjecthood," therefore, is not an "intelligible essence" but a *vision* that seeks historical justification. It is not simply "historical consciousness" but a way-of-being-in-the-world, a praxis, that is constituted by what Hannah Arendt, the political theorist, called communities dwelling "between past and future." It is persons together shaping, creating, transforming their present situations in the light of their experience of the past and their normative visions of the future. It is intentional communities involved in personal and political transformation who understand politics as creative and critical participation in the bringing into being those dimensions of human species-being that are repressed and suppressed in modern life but have not yet been obliterated.[52] Philippine historical experience, particularly when viewed from the perspective of the "poor and the oppressed," suggests that history is a story of liberation and transformation towards a future of freedom and justice. It is the historicizing of a counter-tradition of transformation in conflict with the dominant tradition of oppression and repression. For this reason, the "quest for authentic political subjecthood" is a history of struggle, a "permanent revolution" in the service of a "friendlier tomorrow" for all the Filipino peoples.

This emergent "revolution," which is not only institutional, is Janus-faced, i.e., it has both a "bourgeois" and a "popular" face.[53] Any politics of transformation, therefore, as this essay has sought to underscore, must come to terms with the significance of this reality and recognize the normative implications of how these "faces" are to be prioritized so that the "fundamentally new and better," the just society, may be created. Strategically, this means creating and nurturing, both domestically and internationally, a broad, pluralistic, nationalistic, anti-interventionist, sectoral coalition of political communities that include "liberal democratic," nationalist communist/Marxist, and other "cause-oriented" forces. Comprehensively, it means creating and re-creating populist structures of representation, decision-making and accountability; it means focusing on fundamental structural changes in the political economy that aim not only at the re-distribution of wealth but also at the transformation of the country's economy away from its status of dependency within the international capitalist system to an independent, though not autarchic, political economy committed to meeting basic human needs and the full "democratization of wealth," i.e., equity in sharing *both* gains as well as losses; it means developing a profoundly nationalist, though global, anti-militarist public philosophy that is committed to the "self-determination of peoples," and to the liberation of the "poor and the oppressed" within a normatively pluralistic framework that not only recognizes but also affirms the necessity of conflict and collaboration, continuity and change, and the creation of shared values, i.e., freedom and justice. It also means, however, that on the politico-philosophical level, we must refuse the temptation of unity for the sake of "realist political expediency" at the expense of forgetting what we have learned from our history, namely, that "liberal democracy" with its anti-democratic consequences, as a way of life, has been one of the most deceptive and elusive obstacles to radical transformation in the Philippines.

From the perspective of politics as the quest for authentic political subjecthood, the "February 1986 Rebellion" opens to the theoretical and practical possibility of creating a truly *democratic* society. This will depend, in large measure, on whether the Rebellion is understood in the light of a "liberal/bourgeois" or "populist/popular" commitment. The choices that are made will determine whether the "February 1986 Rebellion" and the transformations it has inaugurated will move the Philippines beyond "liberal democracy" or whether it will return the country to it, and thus to the origins of "constitutional authoritarianism." Transcending the latter requires that the spirit of democracy, of "people's power," be given normative priority in the very creation of a transformed and transforming Philippines.

Notes and references

1. Lester Edwin J. Ruiz, "Philippine Politics and the 'February 1986 Rebellion': Democratic Transformation or Anti-Democratic Reform?" Lecture delivered at the 1986 IMPACT Annual Spring Briefing, Rochester, New York, 17 April 1986.
2. Teodoro A. Agoncillo and Milagros C. Guerrero, *A History of the Filipino People*, 5th edn (Quezon City, Philippines: R.P. Garcia Publishing Co., 1977), p.642; see also Amado Guerrero, *Philippine Society and Revolution* (Oakland: International Association of Filipino Patriots, 1979); Renato Constantino, *The Philippines: A Past Revisited* (Quezon City: Tala Publishing Service, 1975).
3. See William Pomeroy, *American Neo-Colonialism: Its Emergence in the Philippines and Asia* (New York: International Publishers, 1970); Noam Chomsky and Edward Herman, *The Washington Connection and Third World Fascism*, vol 1 (Boston: South End Press, 1979), pp. 1-104, 230-241; Jose Maria Sison, *The Struggle for National Democracy* (Quezon City: Progressive Publications, 1967), pp. 56ff.; Miguel Bernad, *Christianization of the Philippines: Problems and Prospects* (Manila: The Filipiniana Book Guild, 1972); Renato Constantino, *The Nationalist Alternative* (Manila: Foundation for Nationalist Studies, 1979), pp. 1-22, 23-64; Alejandro Lichauco, "The Lichauco Paper: Imperialism in the Philippines," *Monthly Review*, July-August 1973, pp. 14-52 passim; Walden Bello and Severina Rivera (editors), *The Logistics of Repression and Other Essays: The Role of U.S. Assistance in Consolidating the Martial Law Regime in the Philippines* (Washington, DC: Friends of the Filipino People, 1977).
4. The notion of "parliament of the streets" was commonly understood as referring to the massive student-led demonstrations of the mid-60s and the early-70s which involved industrial and agricultural workers, tenants and small farmers, fishingfolk, slum-dwellers, professionals, employees and students, and, small and medium business-people.
   This notion must be broadened to include "popular movements" such as the 1967 revolt of the *Lapiang Malaya* against the Marcos government which many "modern" Filipinos

dismissed as "fanaticist," "nativist," or "millenarianist." Their disclosive possibilities challenge the dominant interpretations of Philippine society heretofore interpreted through *middle-class values*. See Reynaldo C. Ileto, *Pasyon and Revolution: Popular Movements in the Philippines, 1840-1910* (Quezon City, Metro Manila: Ateneo de Manila University Press, 1979), pp. 3-15.

For additional documentation of these "popular movements" see David Sturtevant, *Agrarian Unrest in the Philippines* (Athens, Ohio: Ohio University Center for International Studies, 1969); see also the bibliography in Ileto's *Pasyon and Revolution*, pp. 332-340. See further Southeast Asia Resource Center, "Tribal People and the Marcos Regime: Cultural Genocide in the Philippines," *Southeast Asia Chronicle*, 67, October 1979, pp. 1-32.

5. Diosdado Macapagal, *Democracy in the Philippines* (Ontario, Canada: Ruben J. Cusipag, 1976), pp. 28-29; Raul Manglapus, *Philippines: The Silenced Democracy* (New York: Orbis Books, 1976), pp. 13-20; see also Rolando del Carmen, "Constitutionality and Judicial Politics," in: David Rosenberg (editor), *Marcos and Martial Law in the Philippines* (Ithaca: Cornell University Press, 1979), pp. 85-112.

6. Proclamation No. 1081 "Proclaiming A State Of Martial Law In The Philippines," in: Ferdinand E. Marcos, *The Democratic Revolution in the Philippines*, 2nd edn (Englewood Cliffs, New Jersey: Prentice-Hall International, Inc., 1979), pp. 335-351.

7. Abdurasad Asani, official spokesperson of the MNLF, in a speech delivered at the Fifth Oil Workers World Anti-Monopolist Conference, Tripoli, Libya, 26-30 March 1980; see also Richard Vokey, "Islands Under the Gun," *Far Eastern Economic Review*, 8 May 1981, pp. 36-42; Cesar Adib Majul, *Muslims in the Philippines*, 3rd edn (Manila: Saint Mary's Publishing House, 1973); Southeast Asia Resource Center, "400 Year War—Moro Struggle in the Philippines," *Southeast Asia Chronicle*, 82, February 1982, pp. 1-28.

8. Rodney Tasker, "Philippines: The Drift to the Left," *Far Eastern Economic Review*, 21, August 1981, pp. 17-22; see also Southeast Asia Resource Center, "The Philippines in the 80's—From Normalization to Polarization," *Southeast Asia Chronicle*, 82, April 1982, pp. 1-28.

9. Walden Bello, David Kinley, and Elaine Elinson, *Development Debacle: The World Bank in the Philippines* (San Francisco: Institute for Food and Development Policy/Philippine Solidarity Network, 1982), pp. 1-66, 165-182; "The Philippines: American Corporations, Martial Law, and Development," *International Documentation on the Contemporary Church*, 57, November 1973, pp. 8-83; Guy Sacerdoti, "Cracks in the Coconut Shell," *Far Eastern Economic Review*, 8, January 1981, pp. 42-48.

10. Report of an Amnesty International Mission to the Republic of the Philippines, 11-28 November 1981, (London: Amnesty International Publications, 1982); *The Philippines: A Country in Crisis* (New York: The Lawyers Committee for International Human Rights, 1983); "Preliminary Report on a Fact-Finding Mission to the Republic of the Philippines, 28 November–17 December 1983," sponsored by the American Association for the Advancement of Science, American College of Physicians, American Committee for Human Rights, American Nurses' Association, American Public Health Association, Institute of Medicine of the National Academy of Sciences, January 1984. (Mimeographed)

11. For full documentation of the Permanent Peoples' Tribunal Session on the Filipino People and the Bangsa Moro People, see *Permanent Peoples' Tribunal, Philippines: Repression and Resistance* (London: Zed Press, 1983).

12. William Ascher, Central Projects Division, World Bank cited in: Walden Bello, "Secret World Bank Document on Marcos: An Alliance Coming Apart?" *Counterspy*, 5, February-April 1981, pp. 30-38; see also "The World Bank Philippine Poverty Report," Confidential first-draft version obtained by the Congress Task Force and *Counterspy* Magazine, Southeast Asia Resource Center, Berkeley, California.

My interpretation of the Ascher Memorandum is drawn largely from Walden Bello's "The World Bank in the Philippines: A Decade of Failures," *Southeast Asia Chronicle*, 81, December 1981, pp. 3-9.

13. Robert Stauffer, "The Political Economy of Refeudalization," in: *Marcos and Martial Law in the Philippines*, pp. 180-218. Also, Robert Stauffer, *The Philippines Under Marcos: Failure of Transnational Developmentalism* (Sydney: University of Sydney, TNC Research Project, 1986), pp. 171ff.

14. Joel Rocamora, "Is Marcos a Lameduck Dictator?" *Southeast Asia Chronicle*, 92, December 1983, pp. 2-11.

15. Robin Broad and John Cavanagh, "Disintegration of an Economic Model," *Southeast Asia Chronicle*, 92, December 1983, pp. 14-17.

16. US National Security Directive, cited in: Richard A. Falk, "Breaking the Deadlock: Redefining the U.S. National Security Interests in the Philippines," speech delivered at the Philippines: Crisis and Opportunity Conference, Washington DC, 22 September 1985; see also Walden Bello, "The Pentagon and the Philippine Crisis," *Southeast Asia Chronicle*, 95, pp. 20-24.

17. The intensification of the Philippine crisis, particularly since 1983, is well known. See for example, Resource Center for Philippine Concerns, *Solidaridad II*, 9, April-September 1983, pp. 2-49; Guy Sacerdoti and Philip Bowring, "Marx, Mao and Marcos," *Far Eastern Economic Review*, 21 November 1985, pp. 52-62; Guy Sacerdoti and Jose Galang, "The Seeds of Change," *Far Eastern Economic Review*, 31 October 1985, pp. 103-110; Steve Lohr, "Inside the Philippine Insurgency," *The New York Times Magazine*, 3 November 1985, pp. 40-60; *Lawyers Committee for Human Rights, Salvaging the Philippines: Violations of Human Rights Under Marcos* (New York: Lawyers Committee for Human Rights, 1985).

18. Rocamora, "Is Marcos a Lameduck Dictator?" (Note 14), p. 10.

19. Manfred Halpern, "Choosing Between Ways of Life and Death and Between Forms of Democracy: An Archetypal Analysis," *Alternatives*, Vol. XII, No. 1, 1987, pp. 5–35. For Halpern, "democracy" does not refer to the "rule of the people," but to the "power of the people," i.e., "the persistent re-opening of the process of participation by the people as they discover new grounds and new capacity to reshape their life together and as they join in nourishing what they hold to be good."

   In this context, Washington's obsession of urging countries where the democratic process is in question to hold elections (including the 1986 Presidential "Snap" Elections in the Philippines), is illustrative of its preference, particularly in the Philippines, for a policy of "liberalization," as part of its overall commitment to an interventionist, anti-communist counterinsurgency program in its foreign policy. In short, democracy, is reduced to the electoral process. See for example, Walden Bello and Edward S. Herman, "U.S.-Sponsored Elections in El Salvador and the Philippines," *World Policy Journal*, vol 1, no 4, Summer 1984, pp. 851-869. Also, Walden Bello, "Edging Toward the Quagmire: The U.S. and the Philippine Crisis," *World Policy Journal*, Winter 1985-1986, pp. 29-58.

20. Lester Edwin J. Ruiz, "Towards a Transformative Politics: A Quest for Authentic Political Subjecthood" (Ph.D. dissertation, Princeton Theological Seminary, 1985).

21. *New York Times*, 28 February 1986.

22. Roberto M. Unger, *Knowledge and Politics* (New York: Free Press, 1975), pp. 1-145; C.B. Macpherson, *Democratic Theory: Essays in Retrieval* (London: Oxford University Press, 1973); C.B. Macpherson, *The Political Theory of Possessive Individualism* (London: Oxford University Press, 1962); William McNeill, *The Rise of the West: A History of the Human Community* (Chicago: University of Chicago Press, 1963).

23. Feliciano Cariño, "Illusions and Reality: Some Questions and Reflections on the Aquino Ascendancy and People's Power," *Tugon*, vol. XI., No. 2, 1986, pp. 77–86. United Church of Christ in the Philippines, "A Statement of Protest Against U.S. Interventionist Policy Towards the Philippines," *Oikos: Mission Update*, 1/8-10, February-April 1986, pp. 20-22.

24. See Lester Edwin J. Ruiz, "Power, Justice, and the Concept of Human Development," paper presented at the 23rd Annual Convention of the International Studies Association, Cincinnati, Ohio, 26 March 1982; see also Lester Edwin J. Ruiz and Charles Amjad-Ali, "Terrorism: A Logocentric Moral Issue or an Expression of the Plurality of Human Dwelling?" *Chitty's Law Journal* (Forthcoming).

25. Jovito R. Salonga, "Reflections on the Constitution, Human Rights, and the Rule of Law: After Martial Law," Speech delivered at the Symposium of the Greater Manila Region of the Integrated Bar of the Philippines, held at the Philamlife Auditorium, U.N. Avenue, Manila, Philippines, 10 February 1981.

   Included in this broad "liberal democratic opposition" is a "leftwing" *nationalist* faction headed by prominent politicians like Jose Diokno (recently deceased) who advocate an unequivocal anti-Marcos, anti-Washington position.

26. Jovito R. Salonga, "The Democratic Opposition and its Vision of the Society Our People Want," Speech delivered before the Manila Rotary Club held at the Manila Hilton, Manila, Philippines, 9 October 1980, p. 7. (Mimeographed.).

27. Ruiz, "Towards a Transformative Politics," (Note 20).

28. Lester Edwin J. Ruiz, "Constitutional Authoritarianism as State Terrorism: The Case of the Philippines," in: Michael Stohl and George Lopez (editors), *Development, Dependence and State Repression* (Greenwood Press, forthcoming).

29. National Democratic Front, "Ten-Point Program of the National Democratic Front in the Philippines," (Oakland: Union of Democratic Filipinos and the International Association of Filipino Patriots, 1978), p. 1.

30. "Ten-Point Program," ibid., pp. 12-14; Joel Rocamora, "The Structural Imperative of Authoritarian Rule," *Southeast Asia Chronicle*, 65, November-December 1978, pp. 7-19.

31. Rocamora, "Is Marcos a Lameduck Dictator?" (Note 14), p. 10.

32. Walden Bello, "Reflections on a New Era in the Philippines: 'Third Force' Myths and Realities," *Christianity and Crisis*, April 7, 1986, pp. 111-113; Institute of Religion and Culture, "A Major Battle Won: But the Struggle Must Continue," *Kalinangan*, vol 6, no 1, March 1986, pp. 30-31.

33. This is clear from the nature of the "liberal democratic" opposition's challenge to the Marcos martial law government, namely, the emphasis on constitutional legitimacy which presupposes what Max Weber called "legal rationality." Cf. Roberto Unger's notion of "legal mentality" in *Knowledge and Politics*, pp. 69-71.

34. Iredell Jenkins, *Social Order and the Limits of Law: A Theoretical Essay* (Princeton: Princeton University Press, 1980), pp. 153-191. I have addressed the significance of the "eclipse of relationality" in other essays. See, for example, Ruiz, "Towards A Transformative Politics," (Note 20).

35. My interpretation of the relationship between tradition and authority is largely founded in the work of Hans Georg Gadamer, *Truth and Method*, trans. Garrett Barden and John Cumming (New York: The Seabury Press, 1975), pp. 235-374; however, it will be argued further that the notion of tradition can be rendered more fully "political" and, therefore, more fully historical, by transposing it into the question of "authentic political subjecthood."

36. See, for example, Manfred Halpern, "Beginning in Incoherence," in: "*A New Theory of Transformation for Explaining and Overcoming the Great Breaking in All Human Relationships*," (Princeton, New Jersey, Spring 1984), (Mimeographed.) pp. 1-52.

37. Feliciano Cariño, "Church, State and People: The Philippines in the '80s," in: *Church, State and People: The Philippines in the '80s*, Report and Papers of a National Theological Dialogue, Manila, Philippines, November 10-13, 1980, ed. Feliciano Cariño (Singapore: Christian Conference of Asia, 1981), p. 67.

38. Antonio Lambino, S.J., "Theology in the Philippine Context: Two Views of People," *Tugon*, 2, March 1981, pp. 31-38.

39. See for instance, "Theology in Action," Manila, 1-12 September 1972, proceedings reported in: *Theology in Action: A Workshop Report*, eds. Oh Jae Shik and John England (Tokyo: East Asia Christian Conference, 1980); Cf. "Human Rights in the Philippines: A Christian Responsibility and Asian Solidarity," Manila and Tokyo, September 1979, proceedings reported in: *Human Rights in the Philippines—A Christian Responsibility and Asian Solidarity: Report of a Regional Conference on Human Rights in the Philippines* (Hongkong: Resource Centre for Philippine Concerns, 1980); "People Against Domination: A Consultation Report on People's Movements and Structures of Domination in Asia," Kuala Lumpur, Malaysia, 24-28 February 1981.

40. Renato Constantino, "The Mis-Education of the Filipino," *Weekly Graphic*, 8 June 1966. See for instance Horacio de la Costa, *The Background of Nationalism* (Manila: Solidaridad Publishing House, 1965); Leopoldo Yabes, *Rizal and National Greatness and Other Essays on Nationalism, Liberalism, and Democracy* (Manila: Rangel Publishing, 1966); Mauro N. Zialcita, "The Filipino Identity," *Solidarity*, 4, September 1969, pp. 31-43.

41. See also Jaime Bulatao, "Split-Level Christianity," in: *Split-Level Christianity, Christian Renewal of Filipino Values,* Jaime Bulatao and Vitaliano Gorospe (Manila: Ateneo de Manila University Press, 1966), pp. 1-18; Miguel Bernad, "Philippine Culture and the Filipino Identity," *Philippine Studies*, October 1971, pp. 573-592

42. Horacio de la Costa, "The Filipino National Tradition," in: Raul J. Bonoan (editor), *Challenges for the Filipino* (Quezon City: Ateneo Publications, 1971), pp. 42-60.

43. Reynaldo Ileto, *Pasyon and Revolution*, (Note 4), pp. 1-10; Renato Constantino, *Neocolonial Identity and Counter-Consciousness: Essays on Cultural Decolonization* (London: Merlin Press, 1979).

44. C.G. Arevalo, "Notes for a Theology of Development," *Philippine Studies*, 19, January 1971, pp. 65-91.

45. Vitaliano R. Gorospe, *The New Christian Morality and the Filipino* (Manila: Jesuit Educational Association, 1973).

46. Carlos H. Abesamis, "Faith and Life Reflections from the Grassroots in the Philippines," in: Virginia Fabella (editor), *Asia's Struggle for Full Humanity* (New York: Orbis Books, 1980), p. 134.

47. There is a long and dynamic history of this debate within the communist/Marxist opposition. From the early formation of the communist parties with their millenarian-populist dimensions to a highly sophisticated and "rationalist" Marxism within the party leadership in more recent times, the debate is evidence of the continuing quest to develop an authentic *Filipino* Marxism. A major point of contention has been the positive or negative evaluation of the millenarian-populist dimension particularly as it is practiced by the rank-and-file. The tendency to evaluate negatively this dimension suggests the "rationalist" and "economist" bent of contemporary Philippine Marxist thinking. See for instance, *Marxism in the Philippines: Marx Centennial Lectures* (Quezon City: Third World Studies Center, University of the Philippines, 1984). Moreover, the emergence of "Specific Characteristics of our People's War" is a hopeful sign that the significance of the specifically Filipino character of the struggle, including its archipelagic context, and therefore of its populist/pluralist dimension, is finally being recognized. See Amado Guerrero, "Specific Characteristics of Our People's War," in: *Philippine Society and Revolution*, 3rd edn (Oakland, California: International Association of Filipino Patriots, 1979), pp. 179-216.

48. See for instance, C.G. Arevalo, "The Task of the Church: Liberation and Development," in: Vitaliano Gorospe and Richard Deats (editors), *The Filipino in the Seventies* (Manila: New Day Publishers, 1973), pp. 233-283, esp. pp. 262-265; cf. Gustavo Gutierrez, *A Theology of Liberation: History, Politics, Salvation*, trans. Sr. Caridad Inda and John Eagleson (New York: Orbis Books, 1973), pp. 32-42; Immanuel Wallerstein, *The Capitalist World-Economy: Essays by Immanuel Wallerstein* (New York: Cambridge University Press, 1979), pp. 152-164.

49. I am indebted to Professor Manfred Halpern of Princeton University for this definition of "politics."

50. *Moving Heaven and Earth: An Account of Filipinos Struggling to Change their Lives and Society* (Manila: CCPD/WCC-Philippine Writing Group, 1982); Southeast Asia Resource Center, "The United Front in the Philippines"; Southeast Asia Resource Center, "Cultures of Resistance," *Southeast Asia Chronicle*, 70-71, March-April 1980, pp. 1-36.

51. Francisco Claver, "From my Father's House: A Letter to the President," in: *The Stones Will Cry Out: Grassroots Pastorals* (New York: Orbis, 1978), pp. 135-145.

52. This "transformative politics" which is both a "theory and practice," is not limited to the Philippine situation. See, for example, Sharon Welch's notion of "communities of resistance and solidarity," Cornel West's "Afro-American revolutionary christianity," Leonardo Boff's "Church as Sacrament of the Holy Spirit," Manfred Halpern's "counter-tradition of transformation," and Kim Yong Bok's "Minjung theology," Sharon Welch, *Communities of Resistance and Solidarity: A Feminist Theology of Liberation* (New York: Orbis Books, 1985), pp. 15-92; Cornel West, *Prophesy Deliverance! An Afro-American Revolutionary Christianity* (Philadelphia: Westminster Press, 1982), pp. 15-26, 131-148; Leonardo Boff, *Church: Charism and Power: Liberation Theology and the Institutional Church*, trans. John Dierksmeier (New York: Crossroads, 1985), pp. 125-164; Manfred Halpern, *Transformation: Its Theory and Practice in Personal, Political, Historical, and Sacred Being* (three volume work-in-progress, Princeton University), but cited in this essay; Kim Yong Bok (editor), *Minjung Theology: People as the Subjects of History* (Singapore: Christian Conference of Asia, 1981), pp. 77-118, 185-196.

53. By "face" I mean, paraphrasing Unger, a way of thinking about social life, a mode of consciousness that is bound together with both a doctrine and an experience of social life;

See Unger, *Knowledge and Politics*, pp. 72-76. Cf. Enrique Dussel, *The Philosophy of Liberation* (New York: Orbis Books, 1985) passim. See also, Lester Edwin J. Ruiz, "Towards a Theology of Politics: Meditations on Religion, Politics and Social Transformation", in: Feliciano Cariño (editor), *Theology, Politics and Struggle* (Manila: National Council of Churches in the Philippines, 1986), pp. 1–46.

The Challenge of Connections

Grass-roots Initiatives: The Challenge of Linkages

CHADWICK F. ALGER AND SAUL H. MENDLOVITZ

> Some of my most depressed moments are when I feel we have won an issue on the local level, making life better for some people in this town, but nothing has been done to transform the world into a better place.
>
> *A Member of the City Council of a small California town.*

Introduction

Despite the transformational potential of the widely used phrase—"think globally act locally"—it has often become a trite shibboleth. Indoctrinated by the ideology of the state system, most people still accept the notion that matters beyond the state border will be taken care of by small elites that have been specially trained and authorized to attend to "foreign affairs." Scholars share responsibility for the inability of most local activists to develop strategies that would enable local people to cope with the problems that transcend state borders. The ideology of the state system has permeated scholarship no less than action, placing on one scholarly domain the institutions and activities in local communities, and placing in a separate domain the institutions and activities in international/global affairs. Connections between the two, particularly in terms of purposeful action through local initiatives, have been made *unthinkable*.

Particularly regrettable has been the degree to which those espousing global transformation have failed to provide roles for local activists in their visions of the future, as they focus their attention on proposals for new kinds of world organizations. This omission has significantly isolated, and often alienated, local activists from those espousing global transformation. It is unfortunate that globalists and localists working on the same problems— whether it be poverty, social injustice, ecology or violence—tend to work in

Commissioned by the Committee for a Just World Peace for its meeting in Lisbon, Portugal, March, 1985. This is the second report of the Grass-Roots Activism: Global Implications (GRAGI) program of the World Order Models Project. The first report, sections of which are reproduced here, were published in *Alternatives*, vol 9, no 4, 1984, pp. 447–474. The authors wish to thank Ronald Slye and Lester Edwin J. Ruiz for their valuable assistance in the writing of this essay.

isolation of each other. As a result, the potential impact of both localists and globalists is diminished.

The gap between localists and globalists actively concerned about similar social issues is a worldwide phenomenon, but the context varies across societies. In the United States, for example, there are many people who are concerned with global issues (e.g., the arms race, communications, ecology, militarization, poverty, and war). At the same time, there is considerable grass-roots activity on social issues focused on local communities. Yet, with notable exceptions for short periods of time (e.g., the nuclear freeze movement, Sanctuary, anti-apartheid movement etc.), there appears to be a lack of response by grass-roots activists to global issues. In the end, the often trite shibboleth turns out not only to be a characterization of a possible transformative posture, but more importantly, an occasion to explore the problems that have given rise to the disjunction between the "local" and the "global."

The authors of this essay have developed an ongoing research project that explores the character of this problematic gap and seeks to identify ways to overcome it. At its core, the project is a series of interviews/dialogues conducted with grass-roots activists from different parts of the United States, involved in a variety of issues ranging from local problems to global issues. This essay presents the preliminary results of the project.

Part I states the methodological concerns of the authors including their assumptions, definition of terms, and research procedures, as a way of clarifying the context of the research project. Part II describes the contours of present grass-roots activism in the United States in order to provide the background for the major theoretical and practical concerns of the authors, namely, the local/global problematique. Part III summarizes the findings of the research in terms of two issues: the apparent lack of reciprocal connections between local and global activists; and the concerns they seem to have in common. Part IV examines in greater depth two groups of grass-roots activists, those who explicitly avoid global issues, and those who blend local and global activism. Because these activists have made a conscious choice *vis-à-vis* the local/global problematique, we felt that their insight would help us understand better the issues with which we are concerned. Finally, Part V offers some tentative generalizations on the local/global problematique, especially as it concerns globalists who are trying to integrate both perspectives in their work and lives.

It is important, at the outset, to indicate that Parts I through III of this essay are derived largely from our study of grass-roots activists who think, feel, and act within a horizon that may be characterized as "local," Part IV of this essay, on the other hand, builds on this study but examines further these activists in the context of their stated commitments—or lack thereof—in integrating local and global concerns.

Part I. Methodological concerns

The authors. Our field of specialization is traditionally labelled "international relations and international organizations," although both of us have redefined the field such that one of us tends to focus on the need for transforming global structures, and the other on the need for transforming local participation in world systems. Common to both approaches is a global perspective informed by a set of interrelated humane world order values, namely ecological stability, economic well-being, meaningful participation, peace, and social justice, for all polities and all members of the human race.

Recognizing our distance from large numbers of groups and individuals in the United States who are concerned with issues of social and economic justice for their locale within the national polity, we decided to become involved in interviews/dialogues with selected social-change activists, community organizers, "the Movement," etc., to see if we could learn what their agenda was, and so more meaningfully relate to it. Two assumptions underlie this intentional activity. First, there is an ongoing transformational process taking place on the face of the globe labelled by some as interdependence and/or interpenetration. Secondly, and more importantly, if this transformation is to achieve the values noted above, it will require a global social movement informed by these values; otherwise the transformation is highly likely to be destructive of these values, and indeed, harsh, repressive and degrading for large numbers of the human race.

Each of us is convinced that the nation-state system as it presently operates is unable to deal with the problems of alienation, ecological instability, poverty, social injustice, and war. But we have a major difference in emphasis, yet to be resolved, on the manner in which this is likely to or should occur. One of us, drawing on some aspects of "small is beautiful," emphasizes the need for decentralizing and bypassing the state by articulating the already existing relationships among the various local communities, cities, and regions of the world. This maximizes them so that the power of national elites to determine the policies and practices of these cities and regions are diminished, making room for larger local participation in the decision-making processes. The other author emphasizes the necessity and feasibility of centralization at the global level in order to adequately attend to the global problems with which we are confronted. He is not a "World Federalist type," and his major theoretical and political thrust has been the attempt to insinuate a structural—indeed, a struggle—theory of history into world-order thinking and praxis. Thus, our work together has produced continual creative tension centering on the merits and deficiencies of decentralization and centralization.

Definition of "grass roots." It is important to recognize the absence of consensus where the term "grass roots" is concerned. Indeed, there is no generally accepted definition, let alone analytic precision, in its usage. However, it may be this very ambiguity that gives the term its vitality which invites more attention to the reality that it symbolizes. In this context, exploring its various uses may be helpful.

The term "grass roots" is of relatively recent origin in the US political scene. According to Hans Sperber and Travis Trittschuh, the term is said to have been used in Ohio around 1885, but is most firmly fixed with the presidential campaign of Theodore Roosevelt in 1912, when it was characterized as a "campaign from the grass roots up."[2] The first widespread use of the term, however, began in 1935, when the Republican Party began using "grass roots" in preparation for the 1936 presidential campaign.

Of course, the term "grass roots" was not limited to its use by the major political parties in the United States which narrowly construed it to mean any citizen in their districts who can vote; or to the relatively nuanced definition, reflected for example in the *Dictionary of Social Reform*, of "heartland America" with its "progressive" and conservative ideologies;[3] nor even to the broader societal and literary/journalist perspective that includes in its definition the Rotary Club, the church, the school board, the professionals in the small town and medium-size cities, as well as what remains of rural America—a Main Street, Babbitt, America of sorts.

There is another kind of "grass roots" which stems from populism and has as its underlying rationale equity, participation, and challenge of bigness in business and/or government. It is Jacksonian in origin and has a strong cultural dimension of countryside against urban city slicker, and especially that kind of culture that emanates from or integrates effeminate European ways. Influenced and shaped by the left, anarchists, wobblies, socialism, communism, etc., its heroes are Big Bill Haywood, Eugene Debs, Sacco, Vanzetti, and the like. Its ambience, however, is "heartland America" and its goal equity, equality, and participation.

More recently, the development of the neighborhood movement in the United States initiated by Saul Alinsky has added to the meaning of "grass roots," particularly in its self-understanding that mutual aid groups work to empower the urban poor, disadvantaged ethnic minorities and blacks in order to permit them to "get a share of the action." While the organizers of these movements have a general affinity for the political left, many of these grass-roots individuals and groups are concerned mainly with breaking down dismal urban ghettos, assisting decimated and hapless individuals in the more degenerative regions of the city, and empowering the downtrodden and ordinary people, both to get a better economic deal and some participation in the political process of the present system. As Harry G. Boyte puts it:

> The citizen movement represents, indeed, an alternative popular democratic thread of insurgency in modern society—what I believe can be called a "populist" heritage . . . and it incubates an alternative view, different than the conventional wisdom of either left or right.[4]

Thus, "grass roots" seems to cover everything from the individual who may be apathetic—even hostile—with regard to electoral politics, to the highly focused and organized political cadres working from a fixed Marxist ideology, who, as a matter of strategy or tactics, has decided to work within a confined, generally circumscribed territorial political entity. (Although in this latter case there may be a theoretical or actual linkage to similar cadres in other territorial jurisdictions.) To the extent that there is an *operative meaning*, it is "working at the local level." However, social activists who have a populist or political/ideological left perspective tend to use the phraseology "working from the bottom up."

Information sources. The prime source of information for our project were interviews/dialogues, carried out between May 1982 and September 1986, with some 75 people "working at the local level," predominantly in middle-sized cities and small towns in the United States. In attempting to deal with the vast variety of ways in which individuals defined their "cause," we found ourselves thinking along five dimensions: 1) the extent to which the activists saw themselves as dealing with a single or a set of issues; 2) the extent to which the social activists who were involved saw their identity as being involved in a particular territorial context, and the extent to which this identity reached to the entire globe; 3) the extent to which the change being called for was seen as reform or transformation *from their own perspective*, albeit the authors undoubtedly had standards of evaluation which colored their interpretations of their definitions; 4) whether the style of change involved violence or non-violence, and, if non-violent, the extent to which electoral politics, movement politics, and civil disobedience were involved; and, 5) the time span over which the cause or problem might be dealt with.

A second source of information was the research of one author on the worldwide connections of local places to world systems and his efforts to discern, and experiment with, possible ways through which local people can become autonomous participants in these systems.[5] His work has been based in Columbus, Ohio, but has been infused with experiences in other cities, both in the United States and in other countries. His work has probed the characteristics of transnational activity with local roots: Who is involved? What is their agenda? How is the quality of involvement affected by perceptions of the world, of the state system, of obligations of citizenship? This work offers insight on why most people involved in local issues tend to confine their interests and activities to the territorial space of the United States.

A third source of information has been a growing body of literature on social movements and on local activism, including the work of Aronowitz, Boyte, Ferguson, Freeman, Kotler, and Veysey.[6]

Characteristics of interview/dialogue universe. We defined the universe from which we would draw our respondents as individuals active in groups who felt that there was something "wrong" with the world and who had committed themselves to changing their society and the world into a better place for human beings. Initially we identified some 15–20 causes as comprising this universe, including alternative lifestyles, anti-nuclear, ecology, gay rights, handicapped, indigenous peoples, insurgent labor, internationalists (from UNA to World Federalists), left-wing church, senior citizens, Vietnam veterans, and women. The bases for selection were that these groups were understood by the informed public, as well as the group members themselves, to be political and cause-oriented.

These groups, of course, included people with a global perspective. But in selecting individuals to be interviewed we made certain that their activities were firmly rooted in grass-roots activity. They ranged from persons focusing on local single issues to activists with a global perspective who were working on local concerns. While we made an effort to obtain respondents from a number of these causes, no effort was made to obtain a systematic sample.

Instead, in keeping with the character of our inquiry, we allowed opportunity and intuition to guide us to individuals who had a relatively high intensity of feeling about wrong, who tended to be very active, and who were reported to be good sources of information on their group's activity.

It is important also to note whom we did *not* attempt to include. Most significantly, we did not reach out to people who were attempting to bring about reform within the traditional practices, guidelines and rhetoric of the Republican and Democratic Parties. The other major groups with whom we did not engage were the conservative social-change agents, running from the Committee on the Present Danger to the Moral Majority; nor did we deal with such radical movements as the Libertarians, let alone white-supremacy groups. While much could be learned from an analysis of their perspectives and from dialogues with them, this will have to wait for another occasion. We realized that understanding progressive, social-change activists was a large task by itself.

Part II. The contours of present grass-roots activism in the United States

It is obvious that grass-roots activism in the United States today has a diversity of origins, running from Thomas Paine, to varieties of populism, to wobblies and abolitionists; it includes prohibitionism, women's labor, gay, anti-nuclear and anti-war movements. Some activists identify strongly with this heritage, or with part of it, as when some women see their action evolving out of the achievements of their antecedents who won them suffrage. Other activists tend to be moved to action out of their own unique experiences with injustice, while often unfamiliar with similar endeavors in earlier times or even in other places at the present. There are also many working on a diversity of issues who tend to perceive their activity as a continuation of "the Movement." By this they mean a movement that developed out of the civil rights movement in the late 1950s and eventually extended to welfare rights, anti-Vietnam, feminism, environment, gay rights, anti-nuclear and other issues. Jo Freeman defines "the Movement" in this way:

> The term "the Movement" was originally applied to the civil rights movement by those participating in it, but as this activity expanded into a general radical critique of American society and concomitant action, the term broadened with it. To white youth throughout most of the sixties, "the Movement" referred to that plethora of youth and/or radical activities that started from the campus and eventually enveloped a large segment of middle-class youth.
>
> The imprecise use of the term is illustrative of the imprecise definitions of the Movement. In some ways, it was several movements operating under the same rubric with a certain affinity, if not always agreement. In other ways, it was an ill-matched pairing of a social base in search of an ideology and an ideology in search of a social base. The Movement is also referred to as "the student movement" and "the New Left," reflecting the respective social base and ideology.[7]

"The Movement" stemmed initially from the incompatibility of racism with the ideological thrust for equality, equity, and political participation in the United States. While there were a variety of ideological perspectives brought to bear in the struggle against racism, the predominant strand in this struggle was the call for major change *within* the system. Blacks were to be given the same opportunities and treatment as the white majority; but the political, economic and foreign relations of the society were to remain the same. It was a "single-issue" focus but, because it covered all of social life, it was at a minimum a broad single issue. Indeed, for many blacks and partisans of this cause, it was considered a change of the system and genuinely transformational.

These broad single-issue areas were seen by many to have transformational potential. Thus, for example, three other issues that, in part, evolved out of the civil rights movement—rights of the poor, feminism, and sexual preference—based on the ideological underpinnings of equality, equity, and adequate participation, have this potential. Environment is also one of those single issues which, while not building directly on equality, equity and participation, has within its ambit the conditions for a major transformation. It therefore should be singled out as another cutting edge for "the Movement."

It needs to be noted that the vast majority of single-issue activists tend not to perceive themselves as part of "the Movement" and are concerned only with bringing about reform in their particular area. "The Movement" has a hard core of individuals who are into transformation over a wide variety of issues. And they see the specific single issue as a focal point for building a larger movement that will make system transformation possible.

Social activists, whether they personally identify with "the Movement" or not, tend to emphasize one of five approaches to transformation: 1) the ideological and political left (including some populists); 2) spiritual transformation; 3) community-organizing, neighborhood empowerment groups; 4) life-style change; and 5) interpersonal transformation. These categories are based on themes strongly emphasized by particular activists. Obviously, there is much overlap in actual practice. For example, some feminists believe that it is essential to become involved in spiritual transformation, while others believe that radical political economy change is essential for the achievement of their goals. And the trend, as we shall elaborate below, is in the direction of combining all five postures even where there is some tension and conflict among them. But here there is value in a prototype statement of each of the approaches.

The ideological and political left (including some populists). In many ways the ideological and political left are inherently non-localists. That is to say, almost all of them have a global system view, whether they are doctrinal Marxists or not. They tend to see the world as being a part of a capitalist structure which is a dominant source of the suffering on the globe. (Of course, there are large numbers of the ideological/political left who see the Soviet society and Eastern Europe in a very unfavorable light and would argue that the Eastern bloc no longer represents progressive change.)

However, the people on the ideological/political left, by and large, place a high premium on grass-roots activity, beginning with labor and then through workers to housewives, to minorities, migrant workers, and the like. The ideological/political left want to engage *masses* of ordinary people by sophisticating their view of their oppression and needs.

One of our sources provides the clearest example of this strategy. He is a 33-year-old man for whom the Vietnam war was an important influence in his formative years. Coming from a small coal-mining town in eastern Pennsylvania, with a Republican, conservative background, he found himself attracted to the anti-Vietnam war movement and became a member of the Socialist Workers Party. As a member he took on the assignment of getting a job in various factories, first in North Carolina, and then in the Philadelphia area, where he would engage workers in discussion and dialogue and then, hopefully, act on a wide variety of problems. He would discuss such matters as race relations, inflation, energy and the like, and, as he puts it, "wait for the opportunity to connect these issues to the broader historical problems."

It should be noted that the ideological/political left are strong believers in state sovereignty, are very much opposed to world government, or any centralized authority, and do have some underlying anarchical strain in the sense of "the withering away of the state." This group no longer sees violence in the United States as a way of achieving transformation. Still, they are very much in favor of assisting decolonizing struggles, "wars of national liberation, wars against capitalist imperialism," and believe in providing an ethical rationale for armed struggle in others parts of the world. But in the United States, work stoppages, perhaps civil disobedience and even electoral politics, which would include coalitions with what they would regard as conservative forces, are all part of their view of appropriate social change processes.

There is a split in the ideological/political left between Marxist-oriented and populist-oriented views of the world. The Marxists still adhere to some notion of class struggle in which the working class must take over the reins of government, and there is some inevitable flow of history in the direction of socialism and communism. The populists are by and large involved in the struggle of small against big, poor against wealthy. They see it as a continual struggle, do not adhere to any particular mind-set *vis-à-vis* the progression of history, and are interested in maximizing participation of ordinary people in the political processes.

The more general journals of this group run from *Mother Jones* through *The Progressive*, and the *Nation*. There are a host of specialized journals on multinational corporations, anti-nuke perspectives, race and apartheid, etc. Occasionally, they will form coalitions with the liberals, i.e., the *New Republic*, *Atlantic* and *Harpers* constituencies, but their heart and spirit are not in it.

Spiritual transformation. If the ideological/political left is concerned with large groupings of people attempting to seize power and control of the social structure as a way of transforming the globe, the prototype spiritual transformer presents a fundamentally different view of transformation and how it can be achieved. In a way it is the split between the yogi and the commissar, that is to say the spiritual transformationalist believes in individual transformation into a genuinely good and decent person. As one of our respondents put it, "Greed is the enemy; greediness in myself, in my family, in my group and in my country. Each of us must learn how to overcome greed."

While the essential priority of life is to become a better person, at the same time there is an underlying theory of social change. It assumes that if each of us would become a better person by learning how to control our venalities and evil impulses, and achieve some harmony in ourselves, that harmony would be reflected in the way we treat other human beings, other groups, and indeed the planet itself.

There is a major split, evidenced by skepticism if not derision, between the ideological/political left and the spiritual transformationalists. The ideological/political left believes that spiritual transformation is at best fantasizing and not even very good mythology, and at worst bourgeois and futile nonsense. The spiritual transformationalists tend to see the ideological/political left at best as denying their own human capacities in pursuit of false goals, and at worst an expression of power-hungry individuals.

The spiritual transformationalists do have, in addition to internal growth (whether it be of yoga, Maslowian, or humanistic psychology), some collective orientation. That is to say, there is a kind of politics of spiritual transformation and the journal *New Age*, or the book *The Aquarian Conspiracy* by Marilyn Ferguson, pronounces and describes this politics.[8] It encompasses such matters as vegetarianism, organic gardening, frugal living, reverence for other life, no smoking, meditation, all of which can be done individually, but are also perceived as collective enterprises. There is an emphasis on eco-ethics, egalitarianism between the sexes and non-hierarchial arrangements, either in social life or workplace. While some of them have recently become involved in the anti-nuke movement, both with regard to civilian use and military arsenals, "New Age" people are very conscious of the danger of becoming "political." Emphasis here is on achieving the elimination of these evils by living their own lives in an exemplary fashion.

Community organizing/neighborhood empowerment groups. The basic tenet of this position is "ordinary peoples' power is beautiful." The community organizing/neighborhood empowerment position stems from Saul Alinsky's work, which originated in the 1930s and 1940s in Chicago as an attempt to help the downtrodden of Chicago to organize their own lives so as to become an effective political force for jobs, police, schools, etc. While it began in some ways with the working class, an overriding notion was that local communities could organize themselves so that they could bring pressure to bear on local government and the industrial/business financial institutions of their own area to get a share of the action. While there is a strain of ideological left in this movement, it would be more appropriate to characterize this movement as populism in urban centers. Furthermore, for many of the practitioners of this community empowerment movement, it is crucial that ordinary citizens determine their own agenda and own goals and, in the end, their own ideology. Furthermore, there is a belief—indeed faith—that if ordinary people are given the opportunity to determine for themselves how they should live and work and play, this will ultimately lead to the good life.

The modern ideologues of this movement are to be found in Harry Boyte, Milton Kotler, William Miller (trainer of community organizers), the journal *Social Policy*, and national organizations such as ACORN.[9] Also included are activities such as electoral registration, street lights, fighting heroin, and even gardening in the city.

There are a fair number of individuals who are professional community organizers; they are sensitive and indeed sophisticated with regard to the global political-economic system. Nevertheless, as one respondent put it (and this was in 1982 and early 1983, the height of the Reagan recession), "98% of my work is involved in unemployment, street lights, kids on heroin, and while occasionally I get a chance to think about the world, there is not much I can do about bringing it into my daily work, but I think it is probably important to do so, and I would like to continue to talk about it."

For this group, community empowerment could lead to major transformations in society. They hold the view that it is the big power groups which run society, so that if community groups were to really take hold it would mean a major transformation in decision-making and power centers.

Life-style change. "Small is beautiful." The fundamental premise of this position really stems from the Schumacherian view of the intentional small community, self-reliant and hopefully even self-sufficient. It has an ecological ethic which inveighs against rapacious industrialism and its capacity to not only destroy the fauna and flora of the Earth, but also to extinguish life on the planet. It is the small community in which the needs (as contrasted with wants) of human society are met, where face-to-face relations determine burdens and benefits, rather than profit maximization, where attention to life processes go hand in hand with sensitivity to each other. The Schumacher books are the sacred literature of this movement and there are all sorts of practitioners, such as the New Alchemy, or Clam Shell Alliance, concerned about experimental low-energy living to political action against pollution and despoilation.

Interpersonal transformation. This view of transformation bases its fundamental premise on fairness, equality and participation. It is transforming because it challenges institutions supporting male chauvinism, parental domination and heterosexuality as the only permissible expression of sexuality in human society. It should be noted, however, that though the success of these challenges would permit the victims of the system equal treatment within the present system, there is no intrinsic reason to say that the war system, the pollution system, or even the injustice system would be eliminated. Thus, for example, in our interviews/dialogues, two women—one from Columbus, and one from Gettysburg—are strong advocates of ERA, and yet neither of them moves toward transformation of the political-economic system, with the important exception that they want women to receive equality. The same, incidentally, is true of most gays.

Part III. Grass-roots movements: some initial findings and interpretations

Although our findings are admittedly impressionistic, we have found a movement (we now use the term in a broader sense) of dissent, protest and transformation in the United States that embraces a broad spectrum, running from traditional electoral politics to spiritual transformation. It includes mainstream liberals and confrontational radicals; and there is a subculture of local community organizing which is part of the movement but never has been completely integrated into it.

Within the movement there is a central core of activists who have participated in many protest and dissent groups, who are veterans of electoral as well as confrontational politics, and increasingly large numbers of individuals who have been involved in civil disobedience. The movement is widespread and diffused throughout the country. Indeed, it has left the main urban centers of the east and west coasts, and there are now individuals and cadres of cells in small and medium-sized communities and cities in the United States who carry on the movement ideologically as well as politically. The movement is very wary of national leadership.

The ideology of those who identify with "the Movement" at this point seems to be best exemplified by those individuals who are attempting to carry on a life-style change with direct confrontation as well as dissociation from authoritative structures. They are individuals who hotly contested the Vietnam war—by draft resistance, civil disobedience, tax denial, and the like—and are now agitating for ecological ethic, male/female equality, interpersonal sensitivity, and decentralization. They meditate and mobilize; they pray and protest. They act as a bridge between the wealthy, affluent, spiritual and eco-types, and the protest, dissent movement people.

There is no agreed-upon coherent vision for which they are striving. There seems to be a general consensus that we need to decentralize and make certain that there are participatory processes in organizing, mobilizing and establishing institutions. The local, territorial-based group has become central to this way of thinking. At the same time, many of them have some knowledge of the global structure that impinges upon them.

There is no agreed-upon strategy of transition, although "Movement" activity rather than electoral politics, or at least "Movement" activity as a way to prod electoral politics, is the main focus of their work. There is no significant individual, let alone group, promoting the use of direct violence.

Racism and black participation have now a peculiar place on the agenda of "the movement." In the late 1970s and the early 1980s, especially during the Reagan depression, many activists claimed these matters almost dropped from the agenda completely. The blacks we spoke with suggested four reasons for this. First, blacks had made an almost incredible advance in electoral politics in 20 years. In the 1960s, there were only five elected black officials; today there are close to 6,000. Secondly, this advance had its draw backs—the "sell out." Put in another way, once blacks achieved power, they behaved like anyone else. Third, the system is too difficult to overcome—and even black power will not do it. Fourth, the Reagan depression had fragmented the black community. Apathy, despair, hopelessness and overwhelming use of drugs are part of the inner-city black experience. In addition, the rift between the blacks and the Jews over Israel has been a severe detriment to the blacks and to the entire movement itself.

These points made by blacks were qualified, in some ways, by the ever-growing presence of black elected officials. There was the belief that somehow despite the first three problems noted above, a critical mass of black politicians might make a difference. Perhaps the most significant new element in all of this was the presidential campaign of Jesse Jackson and the organization of the National Rainbow Coalition. The interpretation of both of these processes ranges from the blacks as insinuating themselves into the political process as just another interest group, to the development of a new and significant black potency, to a serious new coalition which has transformational potential for the entire US polity. This is yet to be tested.

Finally, local activists tend to completely dismiss labor as a force of political innovation.[10] The three groupings that are now looked upon as potential leaders are the church, students and self-styled middle-class transformationalists.

Given our characterization of "the movement" in the United States, we now turn to our findings on the local/global problematique. Our focus initially addresses the questions why localists and globalists who are active on similar issues work in isolation with each other; and, in what way do they have common concerns.

On the issue of isolation, several reasons present themselves. First, while not explicitly recognized, state ("nation") boundaries are a very real barrier between localists and globalists. When we asked local activists to describe their activities, and their successes and failures, they primarily talked about local problems and local activities. But eventually they would reveal that they had found the need to link up with those involved in similar movements in other places, in order to share ideas and to build strength through regional, state (province) or national coalitions. But their expressed need to move beyond the local did not transcend state ("nation") boundaries. Nor did their discussion of issues recognize the fact that most local issues are affected by world systems. On the other hand, when pushed to assume a global perspective, respondents tended to easily relate to people beyond their national boundary in two senses. They recognized that many people in other countries face the same kinds of problems as those confronted by people in their own community. And they tended to feel some kind of identity with humanity that includes concern for the welfare of others who, like themselves, are facing difficult social problems. Also, when pushed, most would cite military expenditures as a problem taking resources away from local social programs. But our respondents confined their activities within the boundaries of their country and did not perceive this to be a problem. There was widespread ignorance of governmental and non-governmental international institutions with issue agendas similar to those of local citizen movements. And there seemed to be no awareness of groups working for global transformation with respect to the same kinds of issues.

Second, the current emphasis on decentralization is accentuating the traditional gap between globalists and localists. Many involved in local activities have recently moved from activities national in scope in primate cities to a new local scene. They are going through a period of transformation in which they must become acquainted with the local contexts in which they are working, establish common ground with local people and even learn a new vocabulary for social action. This often involves abandonment of earlier involvement in international/global issues.

Third, at the same time, globalists have been losing touch with local communities as they tend to spend more and more time in dialogue with globalists from other parts of the world. This too has required becoming acquainted with new contexts and vocabularies, about dependency, new international economic and information orders, and other processes on the global level. But action implications that flow out of this context are changes in global structures, in contrast to the changes in local structures that occupy the localists.

Fourth, the efforts of some local activists to combine action styles, ranging from confrontation to change in interpersonal relations and spiritual transformation, may also contribute to the wide gap between localists and globalists. There seems to be a greater tendency on the part of most globalists to keep separate their personal lives and their prescriptions for global transformations, often resulting in personal behavior that even denies espousal of global social justice. Perhaps it is more difficult for local activists, under the scrutiny of local people, to be blatantly inconsistent in various dimensions of life. It might also be that action in smaller space, where the impact of individual actions is more obvious, motivates peoples to a fuller commitment of their lives to social goals.

Whatever the causes, what some might call the more "spiritual" aspect of some multi-action style, local activists distinguishes them from many who advocate global transformation. This could have its origin in earlier experiences of global transformationalists, with those people who exude goodwill for humanity, often based on some religious belief, but who tended not to be involved in action that would put this goodwill into action. Indeed, the globalists often perceived, perhaps as a result of an understanding of global systems not shared by these people, that their actions contradicted their professed identity with the sufferings of humanity.

Lest we be misunderstood, we are aware that there are those working for global transformation who do combine lifestyle change with other modes of action; simply, we are trying to make the point that this seems to be more prevalent with local activists than with globalists. Also, we encountered in our interviews/dialogues cases in which religious belief was a fundamental factor in local social action, and sometimes seemed to be an important source for action that combined local and global action. Nevertheless, we feel that the role of what is often called "spiritual transformation" in the United States is far more pronounced in local movements than in the movement for global transformation.

Fifth, while there are great variations in visions of the future of globalists, there is a strong tradition of the invention of global futures. In contrast, we encountered a lack of visions on the part of local activists. Most respondents, when asked to talk about expected or preferred futures, were very hesitant and even unresponsive. Their visions rarely extend beyond their local places and their specific issues. Perhaps another way of stating it is to say that whatever their vision, it is decentralized, by implication rather than by articulation.

This leads to a sixth difference, in that globalists tend to see the need for new institutions and approaches in their arena of action, and this usually implies centralized institutions, at least in some issue areas. The localists tend to see the need for new institutions and approaches in their arena of action, and this usually implies new local institutions and approaches. Perhaps we globalists have become so accustomed to visions of the future involving centralized elements that we have difficulty accepting decentralized visions as viable alternatives. Perhaps the localists have become so frustrated by state centralization that they reject, without probing throughout, all global visions that would include elements of centralization.

Despite this isolation, i.e., this lack of connection, localists and globalists appear to have common concerns. Indeed, both localists and globalists seem to share a severe criticism of the performance of national governments, which could often be perceived as anti-statism. The anti-statism of the globalist tends to produce global transformation strategies that go around, and perhaps beyond states, whereas the anti-statism of the localists tends to promote local transformation that ignores states. We did not uncover either serious anarchist or world-government positions; and the line of attack on the state was ambivalent in that our respondents would frequently talk about taking over the reins of power. Nevertheless, it seems fair to say that the criticism of national governments had an underlying logic that went to questioning the capacity of the state to meet the needs of human beings, both locally and globally. Because globalists and localists are working in different arenas, often involving different priorities and vocabularies, this shared anti-statism tends to be obscured. There is even a tendency for some localists and globalists to disparage the work of the other. The localists may believe that "globaloney" is at best premature until grass-roots transformation is achieved. The globalist tends to think that local transformation is impossible as long as powerful states and corporations control world systems. These differences aside, localists and globalists clearly share common concerns in redefining the role of states. Both have a very important role to play, perhaps in collaboration, in this redefinition, and in its implementation.

Moreover, although very few local activists are involved in, or even perceive, activity that transcends national borders, there does tend to be a widespread tendency for local activists to be concerned about, and to identify with, those suffering injustice everywhere. (We encountered some exceptions in local activists working on senior citizen and environment issues.) This is a concern that is shared with those desiring global transformation. It would seem that this shared unbounded identity with those suffering from injustice offers important common ground for collaboration between those people working for local transformation and those working for global transformation.

While it seems important that local activists tend not to be activating, or even informing local people with respect to suffering on a global basis, it could be significant that military expenditures and anti-nuclear campaigns are the most prominent examples where local social action and international/global issues have been joined. The military expenditures issue raises local concern because of the perception that these expenditures take away resources that could be devoted to local programs. The same could be true of the anti-nuclear issue, although this may be primarily out of fear of a nuclear holocaust. Whatever the reasons, this does suggest that local activists are beginning to have some success in linking local issues to efforts to control direct violence in international relations. But there seem to be no similar successes with respect to social justice worldwide.

Part IV. The local/global problematique: perspectives from the grass roots

Our investigation revealed that the vast majority of grass-roots activists in the United States were not concerned with global matters or issues and that, relatively speaking, there was only a small minority which had a globalist perspective. At the same time, we did dialogue with a sufficient number of grass-roots activists who had consciously concerned themselves with the local/global problematique. They provide a rich and variegated source of information and insight on these matters. We have found it useful to classify them into two broad categories: those who have chosen to focus their activity on local problems and ignore global issues; and, those activists who integrate local and global issues. In the second group, we will look carefully at a small number of individuals and groups who have made the conscious decision to "think globally and act locally" and are involved in developing strategies for global transformation through local initiatives.

"Shrinking the world"

As we turn to an analysis of these grass-roots activists, we do not underestimate the obstacles, many of which are discussed in the previous section, that confront these activists. The conclusions of Manual Castells in his cross-cultural study of urban movements, *The City and the Grass Roots*, underline the challenges to be confronted.[11] Castells emphasizes the difficulty of bridging the "local" and the "global" in meaningful ways, although he also underscores the significance of the task and the potential for overcoming the difficulties. He asserts that today's urban social movements do not have transformational potential because they "are not agents of structural social change, but symptoms of resistance to the social domination even if, in their effort to resist, they do have major effects on cities and societies." Because urban movements face two overwhelmingly powerful forces, namely, worldwide economic systems and powerful states, they often find themselves powerless:

> . . . to handle satisfactorily the production and delivery of public goods and services, [any historical actor] has to be able to reorganize the relationship between production, consumption, and

circulation. And this task is beyond any local community in a technologically sophisticated economy that is increasingly organized on a world scale and, at the same time, increasingly disguised within the labyrinths of the underground economy . . . Furthermore, how [is one] to advance grass-roots democracy when the state has become an overwhelming, centralized, and insulated bureaucracy, when the power game is being played all over the planet with nuclear stakes . . ? The more locally based urban movements aim at local governments, but local communities are, in reality, powerless in the context of world empires and computerized bureaucracies.

It is Castell's belief that the overwhelming forces arrayed against them have driven people to local action: "So when people find themselves unable to control the world, they simply shrink the world to the size of their community."

Castells' conclusions on this matter are supported by our own research. Those who explicitly avoid global issues recognize that there are global issues significant to local communities, but have chosen to work exclusively on local issues. We found that many of these people have earlier been involved in international/global issues, often through national organizations in Washington and sometimes in other large metropolitan areas. Many have now moved their scene of activities to smaller cities in order to build movements from the grass roots. But why have they explicitly avoided focusing local activity on global issues? Why, indeed, have they "[shrunk] the world to the size of their community?"

Local activists who explicitly avoid global issues. With respect to this group, we found five reasons why people defer active concern for global issues. Individual activists tend to give greatest emphasis to one of these reasons, although most refer to more than one. First, and most fundamentally, there is the belief that local communities have to be built before any kind of meaningful community-based action can take place. Harry Boyte, who earlier assumed that social action could be based on existing communities now thinks that local communities have to be "reconstituted and simultaneously democratized" because the United States is a transient society. He sees this as the only viable basis for a challenge to "corporate culture and institutions and to broad dehumanizations of the modern age regardless of economic system."[12] We asked Boyte whether reconstituting communities based on ethnicity might not lead to parochialism and greater distancing from global issues. His response to that (with a kind of prefatory apology of being "too intellectual") was that:

> It is in particularity, as Hegel pointed out, that one discovers universality. In other words, it is when people find their own roots that they are able to sympathize and be tolerant of other people similarly looking for roots.

Second, there are those who concentrate on empowerment, believing that people who learn to organize themselves will eventually come to the right political perspectives in broader domains. We encountered two views on the necessity for providing some image and ideology for local groups. Some individuals believe that getting people to organize themselves so that they are able to demand of city officials a stop sign for their corner is a major success for it enables—empowers as it were—these individuals to go on to other matters. At the same time, there are individuals who, in concentrating on empowerment, do have a specific image, such as solidarity; that is, they aspire to create a broad-based popular movement which would be constantly monitoring governmental authority and practice. Indeed, they measure success or failure in those terms, and one of them said, "If I look forward to the next five years, it is with the hope that we will be able to produce a Solidarity for the San Francisco area." But even with this broader image, they are unwilling to focus on global issues unless they come from the populace itself.

Third is the view that there are lot of people working on global issues and too few working at the grass roots to help ordinary and poor people. Thus, for example, a man in his late 50s, who had been very active in the Eugene McCarthy presidential campaign in 1972, on the eastern seaboard and who had made enough money so that he was able to retire from business, moved to California and decided to spend his time working on local problems. He started with an environmental issue, but within a year had become very active in low-income housing and rent control, on the grounds that "There were too few people in my position who were working on these matters." At the same time, he was certainly aware of global issues. He brought out a list of his end-of-the-year financial contributions and they included donations to groups working on a nuclear freeze, Latin American policy, combatting apartheid, the UN Association, and similar organizations.

Fourth is the concern that adding global issues would overwhelm an already loaded local agenda. A woman in Chicago, who was a major figure in community organizing, and who had a background in movement politics in the 1960s, responded to the question about her concern for the abolition of war in the following way: "I don't want to hear about that because I am afraid it will add to my agenda." That is to say, she found the idea sufficiently attractive that she felt that if she were to discuss it she might become involved with the idea. But she feared that this would overwhelm an already loaded local agenda. She is concentrating on empowerment activities through specific issues that she considers to be winnable.

Another woman, who runs a small foundation in Southern California, found species identity and human identity congenial to her way of thinking. In fact, in response to questioning as to why nuclear freeze was on the agenda of "a local" foundation, she replied: "Well, as a citizen of the world, I feel we have an obligation to deal with this." Yet, when asked about her concern for poverty around the world, she replied, "The whole thing is so overwhelming, I just don't think I would be able to cope with it whatever."

This same woman revealed a fifth concern, shared by a number of informants: suspicion and fear of world movements and organizations. When asked how her board members would react to the possibility of participating in a movement for global change, she said that they "would respond in very suspicious fashion. Their concern would be that they were being taken over, being made part of some over-arching organization that would destroy their autonomy." We sense that this fear of world movements and organizations comes partly from the assumption that they are linked to the idea of world government, and also out of the expectation that such a government would be dominated by states. What is feared, then, is yet another layer of government that would frustrate local action in solving local problems.

What is to be learned from people who deliberately ignore global issues when working in local contexts? Is the message that it is necessary to put aside, if only temporarily, global issues until local people have the necessities of life and have acquired organized competence that would make participation in global issues feasible? This would be a reasonable conclusion in the light of the fact that dedicated activists have gravitated to the grass roots in order to get a meaningful grasp on problems that seemed incapable of solution in broader vistas. This would demand that local activists await the solution of local problems and the completion of a certain degree of local mobilization before attempting to enter some kind of alliance with globalists.

On the other hand, could this approach reflect subtle capitulation to state ideology that would wall off local people from deliberate and self-conscious participation in international/global issues? Can local activists really cope with the local problems they face without confronting the global dimensions of these problems in their local community? Taking the five reasons why people defer active concern for global issues in the same sequence as above, we might ask the following questions.

First, to what degree do global economic institutions and processes account for the transient nature of US society and the resulting destruction of local communities? What is the impact of the flight of manufacturing plants abroad, of plant closures and flight of refugees from economic squalor and repression? Can local communities be built and sustained without coping with the global economic institutions and processes that cause people to flee their local communities?

Second, we turn to those attempting to empower people with the confidence that out of this empowerment will come the power and perspectives that enable people to deal with problems in larger domains, perhaps extending to the entire world. It cannot be denied that learning through participation in small space seems to be prudent preparation before proceedings to larger domains that might overwhelm the new activist. But is there not a danger that this learning will once again incapacitate people for dealing with international/global issues? Does not the setting aside of these issues until later, unwittingly accept the continuance of state ideology, i.e., leaving the international/global issues to others presumed to be more able to deal with these issues? Is it not necessary, right from the beginning of local participatory learning, to recognize and deal with the fact that the global is part of the local?

Third, the concern that there are relatively too many local people working on global issues and not enough working at the grass roots suffers from the same traditional perception of the local and global as two separate domains. We would not in any way wish to disparage the sacrifices made by the local activist who made monetary contributions to certain global causes. But it seems important to ponder why he chose to address apparently distant issues by sending money to be spent by people in other places while responding to local issues with local mobilization. Can issues such as apartheid, nuclear technology, infant formulas, and intervention of Central America, really be dealt with in ways that respond to human needs without local mobilization?

Fourth, those local activists who avoid global issues out of concern that they would be overwhelmed seem to fit Castells' observation that "when people find themselves unable to control the world, they simply shrink the world to the size of their community." But Castells also counsels us that ignoring global institutions and processes is an intellectual sleight of hand that distorts reality. We are required to ponder yet again whether the apparent overwhelming nature of global issues is partly a creation of incompetence generated by the traditional practice of leaving international/ global issues to distant experts. Can globalists help to present global issues to local activists in ways that do not overwhelm but rather generate an added sense of power for dealing with the local manifestations of global issues? There are, of course, global manifestations of the some issues on the agendas of globalists.

Fifth, why are many local activists suspicious of global movements and organizations? This is a critical issue which globalists must confront. Is fear caused by the fact that much global thinking has traditionally espoused world government, or a world state? Is this fear based on knowledge about world government schemes or only on vague impressions? Is it known that present thinking is far more flexible, offering a diversity of options? Of course, another problem is that globalists have rarely consulted localists when devising alternative futures. As a result, local roles are absent from the future images of globalists. It should not be surprising that local activists feel they might be threatened by these global schemes.

Local activists who work on local and global issues. Now we turn to our second group of local activists, those who blend local and global issues and do it in a variety of contexts and styles. Virtually all of our dialogues were with individuals who are working in local citizens organizations, with the exception of two local elected officials and a former member of the Socialist Workers Party employed in a factory. These local activists can be further divided into four categories: 1) localists who conceive of a specific global issue as a local matter; 2) those attempting to create a world network of communities serving peoples' needs; 3) individuals who pursue a single issue throughout the globe from a local base; and 4) people who are simultaneously attempting to deal with an array of both local and global issues.

Treating global issues as local issues. First, by localists who conceive of a specific global issue as a local matter, we have in mind those individuals who have as their ideological and political thrust the betterment of the local territorial polity as a way of achieving major reform and transformation in their society. At the same time, there are certain "foreign policy issues" which are of such overwhelming significance that they become local matters.

The most obvious illustration of this in recent times has been the nuclear freeze. Thus, a councilman and former mayor of a conservative California city sees nuclear freeze as a local issue. It is a local issue because the problems of physical survival and economic misuse of resources are matters which local officialdom must taken into account if they are to service their own community properly.

Mayor:	I just don't think we are going to get any progress out of them [Congress and the President] without getting ourselves squared away locally to the point where we tell these guys, "Either you could build a more secure world or get out of the way for people who are going to build a more secure world."
Interviewer:	And by build "a secure world"—fill that in.
Mayor:	Well, obviously we have got to get nuclear weapons control.
Interviewer:	And that's a local issue?
Mayor:	It is. I spend a lot of time on that. You make the obvious point, which is, that as local elected officials we deal with health and safety all the time. Two hundred people at a time come to a council meeting petitioning us for a stop sign to keep some little child from being killed. The obvious point is, public health and safety in the largest possible sense is in immediate danger from the nuclear arms race. Everybody recognizes that. But we go beyond that, to the economic issue. As budget balancers here at the local level, as people who have to make the resources meet the human needs in our cities and towns where people live, we know what the arms budget means in terms of deprivations to the cities and to the towns, and that's a message that I find that you can take to more conservative mayors and council members and make some real headway.

Unlike people in the third and fourth categories that follow, this local official does not perceive a continual linkage between one or more local and global issues. Instead, he believes global concerns should be tended to after putting the United States in order:

> Well, I think if we begin to get our own priorities straightened out here in this country, then there would be an opportunity for those of us who do care about the rest of the world to say, Well, you know, maybe we ought to do something more than loading up every corner of the world with military hardware. Maybe we really ought to be exporting some of our technology, our know-how. I mean, the Peace Corps was not a bad idea. It was just a little thing instead of a big investment in improving the world. We think of just stopping the United States from doing all the horrible things in Central America instead of going down there with millions of dollars and skilled

personnel and really being a helpful neighbor. That seems now, in
the present context, to be visionary, of course, but I see it as a step in
getting things beyond just a measure of control here in this country.

Despite this strong local emphasis, he does have a vision of a transnational
"Elected Officials for Social Responsibility." In this sense he has mild
tendencies toward the distinguishing characteristic of our second group,
which sees the world as a network of local communities serving people's
needs.

Other examples of localists who see a specific global issue as being a local
matter are, for example, people who become involved in the advisability and
constitutionality of the War Powers Act, asking the question: should the
President of the United States be monitored by Congress in terms of his use of
armed forces in the manner prescribed in the War Powers Manual? Or, in the
black community, apartheid is seen as illustrative of continuing racism on the
part of a US white power structure that is insensitive to blacks in the United
States.

While some involved in global issues such as arms expenditures, war, and
racism do not conceive of themselves as transforming the world, other people
involved in these issues see themselves as transforming the global political
system. Tensions may exist between those taking a more local perspective and
those approaching an issue from a more global perspective. We will encounter
this in our third group.

Creating a world network of communities serving people's needs. Another approach to
linking global and local concerns is one which creates local institutions that
serve people's needs and simultaneously views the world as a network of such
local institutions. Thus, for example, there are individuals who are involved
in the co-op movement. They see themselves as servicing the local community
in terms of bringing better food at lower prices, information about
appropriate nutrition, dealing with corporate advertising that is misleading,
and, at the same time, engaging the co-op membership in a variety of global
issues. Thus, one particular co-op director has helped initiate a program in
which members may meet their time quota for service at the co-op by
demonstrating their participation on a variety of issues running from local
environment to "keep the United States out of Central America." In addition
to broadening the substantive arena of the co-op from economics of the poor
and nutritional issues to these other areas of political and social action, this
particular co-op director sees the co-op movement as a global one. She spends
a few months every two or three years travelling to various parts of the world
so as to be able to make contacts with other co-ops and to begin to develop a
common agenda not only for the co-op movement proper, but for
transformation in general.

Pursuing from a local base a single issue throughout the globe. The global issue that
has probably received the greatest attention in the United States in the past
decade has been that of food and hunger. The goals of individuals and groups
involved in this issue range from straight emergency relief to major social
change. Thus, there are groups who become activated, let us say, by the

famine in Ethiopia and Red Cross appeals; others who become members of Oxfam, World Neighbors and the like, who worry not only about emergencies but sustaining development in other parts of the globe; and perspectives like that of Frances Moore Lappè, whose "Food First" is not only a slogan but also an analytical concept of the way societies ought to develop.

One particular group, The Hunger Project, which is a creation of an interpersonal transformation group, EST, based on self-awareness training within the context of intensive weekend retreats, has involved somewhere between 5,000,000 and 10,000,000 people since 1975. Some four years ago its founder, Warner Erhardt, decided it should be possible to mobilize people around issues facing the world, and devised The Hunger Project. One of our respondents, who is a liaison coordinator for a small community on The Hunger Project, explained that grass-roots participatory activity permitted individuals and small groups to develop their own program and to decide what efforts they should engage in to make certain that hunger is eradicated by 1997. Their efforts are mainly educational, with each group trying to promote local education which would involve people in the United States in eradicating the sources of hunger worldwide. These people are in no way committed to transforming the globe along other lines. This is in contrast with the Food First group who conceive of their program as involving major transformation of the priorities and social systems of the societies of the globe.[13]

Embodying the local/global problematique

Individuals who simultaneously work on an array of local and global issues. We turn now to an inspiring and potentially very significant, albeit small number, of local activists who are devoting their lives to bridging the local and the global. This group defies the widespread acceptance of statist ideology, the primacy of the state in foreign affairs, the pervasive influence of worldwide economic institutions on the quality of life locally, and the failure of scholars and politicians to recognize their transformative potential. Castells' study which we cited earlier provides insight into the importance of this group. Despite his brutally frank appraisal of the limitations of urban movements, Castells concludes that today's urban movements somehow contain the "embryos" of a movement that can transform states and worldwide economic structures:

> Thus, urban movements do address the real issues of our time, although neither on the scale nor the terms that are adequate to the tasks. And yet they do not have any choice since they are the last reaction to the domination and renewed exploitation that submerges our world. But they are more than a last, symbolic stand and desperate cry: they are the symptoms of our contradictions, and therefore, potentially capable of superseding these contradictions . . . Urban movements do, however, produce new historical meaning—in the twilight zone of pretending to build within the walls of a local community a new society they know to be unattainable. And they do so by nurturing the embryos of

tomorrow's social movements within the local Utopias that urban movements have constructed in order never to surrender to barbarism.[14]

While Castells' observations are helpful, the group that we discovered transcends this characterization of grass-roots movements, for they are not only the "embryos of tomorrow's social movements within the local Utopias," but it seems fair to say that they actually embody in their lives the local/global connection. Indeed, they are the precursors of local/global community. What can we learn from their efforts?

These individuals all have a global perspective which they are trying to bring to bear in local contexts. Continually attempting to link local and global concerns, they see themselves as working on social issues which involve the betterment of humanity. At the same time, they feel that they must be concerned with local communities, not only because they are a base for transformation of the globe but also because there are people in local communities who are deprived and need assistance. A good deal of time is spent, in fact, in trying to determine how much weight should be given to local vs. global issues. For example, there is a woman who helps run a peace and justice center in Pittsburgh. She is a housewife who has three children and has been involved in the civil-rights movement, unemployment issues, draft resistance, anti-war movement, and now, the anti-nuclear movement. The staff also deals with such issues as crime, schools, drugs, and there is frequent discussion among them as to whether their time should be devoted to the immediate issues facing the neighborhood or on civil disobedience and protest against nuclear weapons.

In sharp contrast to the locally elected official already discussed, is a city councilman in another California city who asserted that he had become a councilman as a means for changing the global system. He believes that local mobilization is essential in bringing about structural change. A veteran of "the movement" of the late 1960s and early 1970s, he is a self-proclaimed socialist and, at the same time, has developed a coherent vision of simultaneous mobilization and organization on three levels—establishing a mass base, creating progressive coalitions, and promoting and even erecting alternative visions of local and global structures. He sees the necessity for the interaction of these three levels and recognizes the limitations of each. Thus, for example, he declares that in establishing a mass base one must "listen hard to what ordinary people want and help them get it." At the same time, he is concerned that in the attempt to be successful one tends to become very pragmatic and therefore settles for winning change in traffic flow or even major change in police enforcement. Thus, he states: "Some of my most depressed moments are when I feel we have won an issue on the local level, making life better for some people in this town, but nothing has been done to transform the world into a better place." He observes that the second level, bringing people together into coalitions—environmentalists, feminists, the gay movement, the peace movement, and the like—is an important way of building organization, but runs up against the problem of opportunism. He uses this as an illustration: voting for a local congressperson who is more liberal than the other candidates running, but who really is only a reformist. "He is the lesser of two evils."

It is when he is talking about the necessity of insinuating alternative visions into the local scene that he feels he is fulfilling his mission. Since 1980, for example, he has been introducing resolutions in the city council on such matters as apartheid, draft resistance, nuclear freeze, and Central American policy. Here he believes there is the possibility of making a major change. As he sees it, we are at a moment when it is necessary to continue the work of mobilizing and organizing so that when the opportunity presents itself, there will be people trained and ready for the action which would be necessary to implement major social change:

> Right now, we don't have the political climate, that is, we don't have the organization necessary to bring about change, but we need to continue at all three levels to work on progressive issues to learn not only to win a few of them but to learn how to work with them. When the change comes, it may not be gradual because, by then, the necessity for change will be understood and there will be groups of people who know how to take advantage of the opportunity to bring about change.

One might say, in the words of Manuel Castells, he is "nurturing the embyos of tomorrow's social movements."

We spent an entire day in dialogue with six people working with the Movement for a New Society (MNS) in Philadelphia, whose goal is to be helpful with local problems while constantly bearing in mind that they have global dimensions. They work in transition neighborhoods, on the borders between blacks and whites, between poverty and affluence. They espouse non-violence, both locally and globally. Most of these people have had experience in working on global issues in other cities, some in service abroad. There is a strong emphasis on combatting the arms race through a local jobs with peace campaign, including dissemination of explicit information on the impact of military expenditures on the local satisfaction of human needs, and local hearings with members of Congress. There is also strong emphasis on Central America, including involvement in the Emergency Response Network which aims to deter escalation of US military involvement in Nicaragua. As part of this effort, the Nicaraguan Ambassador to the United States was invited to speak to a community group. There is also an effort to discern what kinds of relief projects in Third World countries contribute to long-term development, defining development as the reduction of vulnerability to hazards. Other issues that receive attention are: involvement of local banks in South Africa, contributions by local food banks of a certain percentage of their income to the hungry in other countries, draft resistance, and an exchange of grass-roots leaders in different countries.

In one line of questioning we asked the six people present to share with us their visions of a desirable future. This question was deemed significant because in our earlier report we found that local activists tended not to be able to explicate future visions and even found it difficult to respond to questions on the subject. In contrast, future visions are a standard part of the intellectual activity of those concerned with global transformation. Because MNS people had had substantial experience abroad, largely before coming to MNS, we also expected that, unlike most of our other local informants, they would have visions.

We were not surprised, because of the disinterest of our other local sources in visions of the future, that the MNS people did not see that offering local people explicit visions of the future would be useful in their work. One said, "Much has to happen before local people accept our vision." But when we pressed for information on their visions we found them somewhat different than expected. One person responded that the important thing is to "keep values clear," then the vision will unfold. Another responded that visions are needed on what can happen in the next five years, not long-term visions. Another response was that we have much consensus but it is not spelled out in detail. When pressed further, one person responded that their vision is not a vision of organization or structures but a "process vision." This vision includes such processes as non-violence, a high degree of participation, non-sexism, self-reliance, and non-racism.

These responses are in sharp contrast with the tendency of those espousing global transformation, particularly those in the West, to have concrete global visions that often include explicit global structures or organizations. Instead we found visions emphasizing values and processes, and a tendency to focus on the short term. There was also a tendency to assert that they had a larger vision but were either unwilling or unable to explicate such a vision. This dialogue raises fundamental questions about the nature of visions, and their role in global transformation strategies.

One possible conclusion is that globalists must make a determined effort to translate and adapt their global visions so that they can become meaningful to local people. Another possibility is that global visions are premature, and indeed arrogant, in that they have been constructed by cosmopolitans before most of the people of the world have had an opportunity to contribute to them. It would seem that the MNS group, with their emphasis on values and processes, is taking a position between these two extremes. This approach too merits careful consideration in that it seems to have been born out of the day-to-day experiences of people with deep global concerns who are immersed in efforts to mobilize local people on global issues.

The second main question in our dialogue was to ask the MNS people what they meant by transformation. Here again their responses were not what we expected. We assumed that there would be some emphasis on the global aspects of transformation. But their perspective was very local and tended to consist of strategies for mobilization, a theme to which they returned often in our dialogue. We have compiled a list of their strategies for linking the local with the global:

    1. Take *issues of the moment* in which the adrenaline is flowing.
    2. Use satisfaction of *human needs* as a platform for working.
    3. The motive appealed to is important. Work with *enlightened self-interest*, not guilt or compassion.

*   *   *

4. We have to know our *personal stake* in the struggle in order to struggle well. The stake gets larger as the self gets larger.

5. Lead people to *experience* so they can use their own wisdom.

6. Better than talking about suffering is talking about people *acting*. It is empowering.

* * *

7. *Trust* comes first. People are more likely to change their minds if they trust the social change person.

* * *

8. *Alliances* are needed that cross race and class lines.

The first three, taking issues of the moment, satisfying human needs, and appealing to enlightened self-interest, accentuate responsiveness to local situations. This is in contrast to the tendency of globalists to attempt to put *their* issues, and solutions, on local agendas as a means for bridging the global and the local.

The next three, knowledge of personal stake, leading people to experience, and emphasizing people acting, are all strategies for local empowerment. In employing these strategies MNS would ask globalists to help by demonstrating for them how global trends affect a specific neighborhood, through phenomena such as runaway shops that result in plant closings. The MNS approach here reflects a confidence in local values and wisdom that is greater than that of most globalists. The message they imply is somewhat similar to that espoused explicitly by Rajni Kothari out of the Indian context. He calls for a review of ideological positions that continue to locate "vested interests" in local situations and liberation from them in distant processes.[15]

The seventh strategy, an emphasis on trust, would seem to be very significant to globalists attempting to establish working relationships with local people. Relevant here is the previously discussed fear that globalists are involved in schemes that would produce "some over-arching organization that would destroy local autonomy." The message from MNS seems to be, establish trust with local people before expounding on global issues and visions.

The eighth strategy, alliances that cut across race and class lines, is certainly nothing new to globalists, yet they have had limited success. The MNS offer a useful caveat to the fact that globalists entering local communities are likely to find it easier to establish contact with cosmopolitans whose race and class is inclined to be quite similar to their own.

Part V. "Thinking globally acting locally": what have we learned?

Although based on a limited set of local activists, this foray into local approaches to global issues has uncovered rich resources for pondering both the difficulties and potentialities for transforming the world by "thinking globally and acting locally." From local activists explicitly avoiding action on global issues, there are caveats for globalists who might have a tendency to believe that media and educational campaigns are sufficient for developing global consciousness and action in local communities. It cannot be assumed that local communities actually exist. Action is virtually impossible without efforts to create local empowerment. If the impression is created that global issues are being given more attention than pressing local issues, resentment may be created. Global issues may be introduced in ways that simply overwhelm, and thereby turn away people with loaded local agendas. Global schemes and visions may threaten local people who are struggling for autonomy. It is particularly important that we be conscious of these difficulties because they were raised not by people with a basic antipathy to global issues; but by people who recognize the significance of global issues and see the need to make choices, at least temporarily, between the local and the global. It might be said that their actions implied this motto: "Act locally now and globally later." We need to better explore the degree to which this could be a prudent deferral of global engagement. And, if we find that it is not, we need greater insight on how to overcome this strategy for delay.

Variation in the approaches of those simultaneously involved in global and local issues offers rich food for thought. The insistence of some localists that issues that others call global are intrinsically local is challenging. At first those with primarily a global view are inclined to perceive this view as parochial. After all, these localists are grappling with but one local manifestation of global systems of production, the arms race, and racism. But it would seem that the truth here is that these issues are indeed both local and global. Neither label is more accurate than the other. The globalist must accept this fact. As we noted in our earlier study: "Events seem to be leading the globalists and localists toward an increasingly common agenda. The broadening of the agenda of the globalists over the past two decades from more traditional war–peace issues onto concurrent concern for global justice, economic well-being, and ecological balance has involved them in the same issues as the localists, albeit from a different boundary perspective. At the same time, localists have become involved in war–peace issues as they have challenged rising military expenditures in the interest of applying tax dollars to the fulfillment of local needs."[16] This still leaves the question of what combination of local and global strategies are required for dealing with these issues. But it seems that recognition of these issues as both local and global is a prerequisite for successful action.

The view that sees the world as a network of communities serving people's needs is reflective of the Gandhian approach and reminiscent of the tenets of anarchism. Of course, this tendency may seem somewhat naive in the light of the existence of powerful global military, political, and economic institutions. Yet, it can be viewed as a healthy challenge to the widespread assumption that only centralized world institutions can deal with global issues, and the equally widespread notion that the constituent units of these world institutions will necessarily be states. Have we thought enough about the potential contribution of global networks of local communities as an approach to fulfillment of species identity, and for mobilizing widespread participation in efforts to solve global problems? This approach may satisfy a need people have to make global identity a reality through personal contact with people in distant communities. Does present technology in communications, linking all communities directly to the world, not make this more feasible than most global visions recognize?

Those that are working simultaneously on an array of local and global issues fulfill to the greatest extent the admonition to "Think globally and act locally." In this respect they may offer the richest insights into the problems and possibilities involved. The city councilman who despaired about the fact that local victories do not necessarily transform the globe, brings us face to face with the extraordinary demands that people attempting to link the local and the global may make on themselves. It seems that this councilman aspires to "Act globally and act locally." Perhaps his despair suggests the vital necessity of defining reasonable goals. His "depressed moments" could be healthy recognition that victory in one place may not have an immediate impact or long-term significance around the globe. Yet they could also lead to burnout and withdrawal.

There is a tendency for globalists approaching the local community to perceive the task as one of placing a global issue on a local agenda, with globalists tending to assume that their powers of persuasion alone can achieve that task. But our encounters with those actually struggling to put global issues on local agendas made the task seem much more complicated. These local activists were spending much time in establishing trustful relations with local people, working on empowerment, and helping people cope with locally defined issues. As a result, our questions about transformation and visions did not bring the kinds of responses usually received from fellow globalists. Our initial reaction was that these activists had largely acquired their local acceptance by abandoning much of their global commitment. But on reflection, we discern that they were also illuminating our overly simplistic notions of what in reality is required if the local and the global are to be bridged. They thus provided a valuable four-part guide for globalists who are trying to bridge this gap.

First is recognition that the global is in reality but a vast array of local places. One way of dealing with global needs is by satisfying them in the individual communities in the world. This is an important response to the despair of the city councilman noted above.

Second, our sources underlined the significance of empowerment. There is a tendency for globalists to seek to transform the world by changing the policies of those in power, or at least to presume that others that might help are already mobilized and simply need to redirect their activities. But many people active locally on global issues find that mobilization is a vital part of their work.

Third, there is a strong tendency of globalists to approach local communities with solutions to global problems. We found those working in local communities more willing to let the solutions emerge. While not expressing the phrase explicitly, they were saying, far more than globalists, "Trust the people." This seems to be difficult for globalists, who have spent years in devising strongly held solutions to global problems, to accept.

Fourth, the fact that our local informants either had no concrete visions of the future, or were unwilling to explicate them, was deeply surprising. Indeed it seemed almost like a betrayal of the expected practice of people with serious concern for the future of the world. Instead there was an emphasis on values and processes. While they did not put it exactly this way, perhaps what those immersed in local situations were implying is that they were building capacities to create visions. Were they saying that the few empowered to have global visions should not push so hard to implement their visions until many more in local circumstances have had a chance to enter the fray? Whatever the answers, there is tension between giving priority to the propagation of visions and giving priority to the development of a more widespread capacity to generate visions.

Undoubtedly, there are many more areas that need to be explored to fully understand and appreciate the relationship between the local and the global. This study, however, illuminates several important areas of concern and, we hope, provides new and innovative insights that will enable localists and globalists to better understand the concerns and motivations of each other. We are even more convinced now than when we started that a sensitive and understanding alliance between those who call themselves localists and those who call themselves globalists would provide a powerful base for a transformational movement aimed at creating a more human and just world.

Notes and references

1. Chadwick F. Alger and Saul H. Mendlovitz, "Grass-roots Activism in the United States: Global Implications?" *Alternatives: A Journal of World Policy*, vol IX: no 4, pp. 447–474.
2. Hans Sperber and Travis Trittschuh, *American Political Terms* (Detroit: Wayne State University Press, 1962).
3. Louis Filler (ed.), *Dictionary of American Social Reform* (New York: Philosophical Library, 1963).
4. Harry G. Boyte, *The Backyard Revolution: Understanding the Citizen Movement* (Philadelphia: Temple University Press, 1980), p. xiv.
5. Chadwick F. Alger, "Columbus in the World: The World in Columbus," *Transnational Associations*, 8–9, pp. 393–405. See also Chadwick F. Alger and David G. Hoovler, *You and Your Community in the World* (Columbus, Ohio: The Ohio State University, Consortium for International Studies Education, 1978).
6. Stanley Aronowitz, "Remaking the American Left, Part I: Currents in American Radicalism," *Socialist Review*, vol 13, no 1, pp. 9–51; "Socialism and Beyond: Remaking the American Left, Part II," *Socialist Review*, vol 13, no 3, pp. 7–42; Boyte, *The Backyard Revolution, op cit,* note 4; Marilyn Ferguson, *The Aquarian Conspiracy* (Los Angeles: J. P. Tarcher, 1974); Jo Freeman, "On the Origins of Social Movement," in *Social Movements of the Sixties and Seventies,* Jo Freeman (editor) (New York: Longman, 1983); Milton Kotler, *Neighborhood Government* (Indianapolis: Bobbs and Merrill, 1969); and Laurence Veysey, *The Communal Experience: Anarchist and Mystical Counter-cultures in America* (New York: Harper and Row, 1973).
7. Freeman, *Ibid,* p. 13.
8. Ferguson, *op cit,* note 6.
9. Boyte and Kotler, *op cit,* note 4.
10. From mid-1983 through 1984, some grass-roots activists began to explore again the possibility that Labor might be important for more than bread-and-butter issues, although much of the impetus for contact with Labor resulted from grass-roots involvement in unemployment issues. Furthermore, Labor's support of Walter Mondale suggests that it may re-emerge as a major force in grass-roots politics. However, the extent to which these trends will become important in transformation has yet to be determined.
11. Manual Castells, *The City and the Grass-roots: A Cross-Cultural Theory of Urban Social Movements* (Berkeley: University of California Press, 1983).

12. Harry C. Boyte, *Community is Possible: Repairing America's Roots* (New York: Harper and Row, 1984), pp. 88–89.
13. F. Moore Lappe and J. Collins, *Food First* (New York: Ballantine Books, 1979).
14. Castells, *The City*, pp. 329, 331.
15. Rajni Kothari, "Party and State in Our Times: The Rise of Non-party Political Formations," *Alternatives: A Journal of World Policy*, vol IX, no 4, 1984, pp. 541–564
16. Alger and Mendlovitz, *op cit*, note 1, p. 471.

The Global Promise of Social Movements: Explorations at the Edge of Time

RICHARD A. FALK

A focus on social movements with restructuring agendas itself incorporates a political judgment on how drastic global reform can best be achieved at this stage of history. Implicit in this judgment is the view that conventional party politics, even in functioning democracies, have lost their restructuring capabilities, and further, that violent forms of revolutionary politics are not likely to enhance the overall realization of world order values. In this regard, the new social movements seem at present to embody our best hopes for challenging established and oppressive political, economic, and cultural arrangements at levels of social complexity, from the interpersonal to the international.[1]

One feature of these social movements is to connect practices in everyday life with the most general aspirations of politics, including global restructuring. Thus, when Solidarity or Charter 77 leaders call for trust and integrity as operative principles for relations among citizens confronted by authoritarian governments, their call if heeded has itself transformative reverberations at all levels of political life. Or, when inquiry is directed toward overcoming abuse in interpersonal settings (male/female; parent/child; teacher/student), a political engagement arises that alters the perception of the character of abuse in the public sphere of politics. The new social movements, and the theorizing that accompanies their emergence and evolution, change our understanding of "the political" and "the global." By bringing "peace and justice" into our intimate relations we pose a revolutionary challenge which itself is a subversive threat to all modes of oppression. And contrariwise, by refraining from addressing the oppressive element within ourselves, we cast grave doubts upon any claim to play liberating historical roles by leading movements purportedly dedicated to emancipation in one form or another. Both by enlarging our sense of "the political" and by insisting that everyday practices are an element of "the global," the new social movements are dramatically altering our sense of what the pursuit of a just world order entails in a variety of concrete situations.

Commissioned by the Committee for a Just World Peace.

Notes on perspective

In assessing the global political potential of various social movements it is necessary to take account of their overall, yet not unconditional, rejection of *violence* as a means and *state power* as the principal end. Although generalizations are risky, these movements are also skeptical about the procedures of *normal* politics even in societies that possess an operative liberal democratic framework of rights, political parties, and elections. One accomplishment of the peace movement in Europe is to restructure and radicalize the leadership of social democratic parties in several countries, including West Germany and Great Britain, especially in relation to defense policy. As well, these movements and their adherents are predominantly skeptical about the animating creeds of the pre-1960s: socialism and nationalism. Furthermore, they do not have confidence in the capacity of the trade union movement or the welfare state to address the fundamental challenges of societal distress.

These social movements at the core of the new politics (democracy, human rights, feminism, ecology, and peace) are associated mainly with the West. There are important parallel developments in the East and South, especially in India and Latin America. The overall outlook reflects, of course, the specific setting, especially the presence or absence of a "high tech" economy. In general, nationalism (as a counter to colonial memories and interventionary policies) is a more positive ideology for social movements in the South, especially if it upholds the political, economic, and cultural autonomy of a country, than it is for the North where it is associated with imperial projection, the arms race, and war-making. The South, as later discussion of context suggests, is less concerned with strategic trends and nuclearism than with development, peace, order, and security within a continental or regional setting.

The place of religion is also uncertain and contradictory. In general, the holistic emphasis of the new movements evolves in the presence of spiritual interpretations of the human situation that is attracted by the liberation potential of established religious tradition. In this regard, solidarity between rich and poor, between the anti-interventionists in the North and the nationalists in the South, and between ecologists and peace people is often most militantly expressed by those who devoutly profess a religious faith. At the same time, those who are threatened by the transforming demands of the new politics and the uncertainties of the world situation invoke fundamental validations of traditional values, including notions of separatism ("chosen people") and moral absolutism (holy war against various categories of infidels). Both these polar manifestations of religious consciousness are relevant to the new struggle to shape the cultural setting (values, beliefs, myths) that condition politics.[2]

Also, in emphasizing social movements as political actors, our concern is limited to those that possess a liberating orientation. This orientation can be established in many diverse forms, but it generally renounces *violence* as means and subordinates the control of *state power* to other goals. What, then, is the relationship of such struggles to the quest for democracy in South Korea and

Chile or the anti-apartheid movement in South Africa? In these settings, violence enters as a tactic of challenge, although the political challenge mainly arises out of mass upheaval, and state power is definitely a principal and immediate goal, although often subordinated to a programmatic commitment to social, economic, political, and even cultural reconstruction. In this regard, state power is a tactical necessity rather than an end-in-itself. If unexamined in that role, however, the dangers of statism are immense. The new order will expect too much from state power, and can easily be tempted by repressive options as disappointment sets in and enemies are identified to account for the failures of "the revolution." These struggles to dislodge dictators and corrupt leaders do bear centrally, however, on the process of achieving humane governance and equitable development, and also bear somewhat upon the character of "security" (especially if state-centered militarist repression is at stake).

As the Sandinista or Aquino movements suggest, there are elements of tactics and outlook that connect these developments significantly with the normative priorities of the new social movements that have emerged in the North. The situational factors require a broad encompassing framework if our most abiding concern is with global-scale tendencies that work for or against transformation.

At the same time, without a formal democratic framework the constraints on social movements seem far greater, although the capacity of Solidarity to persist in Poland suggests an heroic example of what can be done in a political setting that treats nonviolent oppositional politics as criminal activity. The wider significance of social movements with transformative agendas is definitely associated with the existence and quality of democratic process. Indeed, one shared ingredient of these movements is their anti-state, anti-bureaucratic character, which is a negative way of expressing their confidence in "the people" as progressive agents of history. The essence of democratizing is to increase the political space to mount pressure for change from "below."

Movements have no illusions left about violence and armed struggle, but their confidence in the will of the people often remains romanticized. Evidence suggests that vengeful and authoritarian sentiments are often embedded in a political culture. The Iranian masses have evidently endorsed Islamic terror, as well as the anti-democratic style of leadership associated with Ayatollah Khomeini's rule. Harry Eckstein's study of "civic inclusion" (extending democratic participation, especially education, to the poorest sectors of American society) confirms the prevalence of anti-democratic orientations.[3] To grant power to the people has no assured beneficial normative consequences. It depends on conditions, the experience and outlook of those who have endured exploitation and suffering, and the quality of leadership. In South Africa, for instance, the anti-apartheid movement can either proceed in a vengeful, violent direction or in a more humane direction; tactical and normative support for both directions appears to exist at present. There is no single pattern of human nature, but many potential configurations.

The militancy of these movements is also a reflection of existing oppressive structures, a feedback effect of the sense that established self-corrective mechanisms are futile, too feeble, or not available; that if women and men are to be liberated then they must act themselves on behalf of a liberating process; and similarly, that if future generations are to inherit a resource base and biosphere of comparable quality to what now exists, then environmentalists must protect endangered aspects of nature with their own bodies if necessary. That is, the originality of these movements is, in part, their realization that conventional political options are not available and that defensive action is indispensable, and might not meet with defeat.

By their nature, however, the results achieved by social movements are difficult to assess. There is the problem of suppression of effects arising from the unwillingness of existing leaders to acknowledge the legitimacy or significance of these new fields of action, and the degree to which the mainstream media reinforces this assessment. It is a tribute to the potency of the freeze movement, although a problematic one, that it evidently helped to induce Ronald Reagan to break with mainstream deterrence by proposing the Strategic Defense Initiative (SDI); of course, this causal link was never officially acknowledged, presumably because it would foster "ungovernability."[4] Also, the repudiation of deterrence was mainly rhetorical; it never was consummated at a policy level. As a result, the activities of movements are either perceived as entirely local and seem fragmentary at the level of interpretation, or they are polemicized, as in East/West discourse, to expose the weakness of the adversary, and discredited as more widely relevant. Yet, perhaps, this assessment is too superficial. The rise of the new social movements may be part of a process of mobilizing latent discontent with prevailing forms of order and authority within a given civilization. In the end, it is this latent energy that offers the best hope for a realistic challenge directed at existing oppressive structures.

Moreover, there are problems of cohesion and communication. These new movements are exploratory, include quite a range of outlooks among their adherents, and easily fracture under the pressures of either success or failure. These fractures are "news," and give an often exaggerated impression of demoralization and disunity, an impression that itself may be influential in promoting still further disunity. To overcome fracturing, especially by loss of contact or demoralization, requires contact and communication, which in turn depends upon adequate resources. Many social movements operate on tiny budgets and cannot possibly afford to create transnational networks of like-minded groups and individuals. These organizational obstacles are made even more formidable by hostile institutional responses, including efforts to manipulate such movements by insinuating informers, or even provocateurs, or by obstructing movement of adherents by questioning travel credentials, and the like.

Perhaps, the greatest perplexity of all is associated with the great weight of various distinct contexts, relating to cultural setting, political system, historical circumstances, and stage of development. So many societies are seemingly preoccupied with problem-solving at the level of a given state or region, or even at the level of an immediate political and economic community, that wider preoccupations seem virtually irrrelevant. In the

Middle East, for instance, the political struggles between Arabs and Israelis and between modernizers and fundamentalists take up virtually the entire political space. There is little disposition to question more widespread patterns of reliance on violence or to give up the traditional political goal of control over state power as an end-in-itself. Africa, too, seems beset by immediacy: famines, masses of displaced persons, race war, acute indebtedness, and an array of demoralizing secular problems arising out of corruption and incompetence. The eschatological concerns of nuclear war or ecological collapse seem, by comparison, remote and abstract in such settings.

The situation in China seems similar, yet for quite different reasons. The problems of Chinese relations with foreign countries seem of paramount concern to its entire population, as does the struggle to balance population, resources, and technique in a successful developmental approach. There is present a formidable Confucian disposition to let leaders work out practical and reasonable solutions. Similarly, the peoples of Latin America seem overwhelmingly concerned with issues of democratization, poverty, and indebtedness. That is, the pressures of context constrain the political imagination rather rigidly, yet concentrates available resources of activists on work that needs to be done.

It remains correct to insist that shared vulnerabilities are now of a global character, that we cannot genuinely escape a shared destiny, given degrees of interdependence and probable effects of nuclear war or ecocatastrophe. But many social movements operating within various specific settings are too preoccupied with immediate challenges within very local times/spaces. Of course it is notable when Bishop Tutu journeys to Hiroshima for the 41st anniversary observances or when Petra Kelly or E. P. Thompson speak up on behalf of East European and Soviet dissidents, but these are gestures of commitment that do not go to the essence of what animates their respective movement members back home on a day-to-day basis. In some instances, leaders with a more cosmopolitan outlook lose influence, being regarded as more interested in their own wider image than the concrete struggle back home.

Furthermore, where political systems and cultural settings do not regard social movements as natural modes of popular participation, then their existence tends to be nominal, if at all. Such a characterization applies to much of the non-democratic portion of the world political system, and especially the two state socialist giants, the Soviet Union and China. To accentuate the decisive role of social movements in relation to the larger world issues is to write off these power/influence centers. Such an effect is not inevitable. A more sensitive account of the various roles of actors in promoting positive change under varying circumstances needs to take account of contributions being made by people and governments in societies that apparently exclude or marginalize the role of social movements.

An emphasis on global implications tends to derive from those portions of the planet that harbor imperial dreams, although this does not imply that the globalism of social movements has a secret imperial agenda. However, the less burdensome context of the immediate reality, together with the globalist undertakings of corporations, governments, and media, infuses the imagination of reformist first-worlders with a global-scale conception of problems and solutions, and a correspondingly reduced feeling for the overwhelming intensities of legal and regional preoccupations. In effect, there exists ideological unevenness on matters of perception which restricts communication and effectiveness. Such restrictions cannot be eliminated, although better mutual understanding can help to establish the foundation for more useful types of dialogue and social action.

There is one final element present. The guided transition to the future as promoted by post-industrial statists, modernizers, anti-modernizing fundamentalists, and by disruptive violence-prone groups ("terrorists") can only produce two responses, both unsatisfactory: the first is breakdown and chaos as a consequence of conflict, technology, and failure to adhere to limits; the second is managed order that excludes the poor and marginal from participation, and over time widens and hardens gaps separating those who are saved and those who are damned. Whether these dismal prospects come about gradually or rapidly they cannot be eliminated by either evolutionary reform of existing state and market structures or by revolutionary reversal through violent uprisings from below. To overcome this dark destiny depends on what takes place on the commanding cultural heights of values, beliefs, and policy orientations in the years ahead. Only fundamental shifts in worldview can produce a flow of adjustments that has enough magnitude and coherence.

Social movements are *one* important source of exploration and enactment relating to worldviews associated with the whole planet, with spiritual and ethical solidarity, with reverence for nature, with an outlook of stewardship toward the future, and with new modes of humane governance. But they are not the *only* source. Others include cultural and technological activities; crises, accidents, and education; "silent revolutions" in life style and ambitions; enlightened behavior by governments that solve problems and provide models; cultural artifacts in the form of music, painting, literature; the transnationalizing character of international institutions and professional associations.

The optimistic view is that this process of cultural revisioning is more basic than the variations of context, and is helping establish almost invisibly a series of new political possibilities at *all* levels of social organization. An aspect of the message of the new movements is that "politics" concerns human relations, including especially those within the family, and that the state can rarely control these domains by its coercive apparatus. The state is not as domineering as many fear even in highly authoritarian political arrangements. More space exists for "political" reform than had been understood. In this regard, the cumulative impact of social movements may remain largely "underground" until it erupts at an opportune moment to reshape the relation of forces in many parts of the world as to the character of challenges and responses. To be ready requires conceptions of process (means), visions of end-states (alternatives), and an overall image of human nature and freedom that affirms self-transcending energies. To imagine how we can survive and develop with dignity as a species, given the resources and technologies at our disposal, and given the risks and dangers we confront, is the essence of the speculative challenge. This requires acknowledging limits, while recognizing opportunities, in the continuous multi-faceted struggle to fashion a future that engenders hope and spontaneous support from as many sources as possible.

A five-dimensional guide to practice: an agenda for the 1990s

It is pretentious, and even arrogant, for intellectuals to prescribe from the safety and isolation of their ivory tower. Besides, such prescriptions are sterile and fall on deaf ears.

Yet to relate and interpret ongoing patterns of social struggle is the essence of any engaged political life. In this section the main attempt is to heed and learn from the social movements that are at the front lines of exploration, to find ways to improve the quality of life throughout the planet at various levels of endeavor, as well as to participate in the search for an understanding of hopeful paths to the future. The final section will touch upon "the promised land," the outcome of the present journey, which itself is a resting place for a further voyage. In this crucial respect, our understanding of human nature and social fulfillment is associated with a continuous process of self-transcendence. Such provisional perfectionism may be deceptive at an historical moment when the most obvious imperatives are "defensive"—to stop our world, our society, our cities and countryside, our families and personal lives, from falling apart. Yet the distinction between defensive and creative social action is artificial, and breaks down. The message from the fields of battle is that no defensive strategy will work unless it rests upon dedication to an affirmative vision of human relations at every level. It is not useful to get slightly less sick; the social movements of renewal draw their energy from restorative imagery and experience of genuine health. These movements also realize that getting the opportunity to administer the state on behalf of a radical vision is not the answer either, unless there is a dramatic reconstruction of practice with respect to relations between men and women, industry and nature, politics and violence, and rich and poor. In this sense, the "politics" of the movements are to build a new order from within at the most profound levels of thought, feeling, and action that shape individual and group behavior.

Yet such radical and personal modes of exploration risk becoming precious if cut off from more traditional responses to human suffering. If workers strike or persecuted minorities demonstrate, their privations properly solicit responses from all those who identify with the aggrieved, including the new social movements. When the Green Party adopts the cause of Turkish quest workers it is expressing its conception of human solidarity in a tangible form; to ignore such concrete circumstances impairs the clarity of symbolic communication. One of the problematic features of such traditional perspectives of renewal as, say, the World Federalists or the Bahai's is their failure to exhibit compassion by joining in resistance activities occasioned by concrete abuses of state or communal power.

In this transitional decade of reaction against the dying, obsolescent order evolved in the West by way of state power, technological innovation, consumerism, and the prevalence of military and paramilitary modes of conflict resolution, it is possible to ground a programmatic outlook around the contours of a five-dimensional agenda of interrelated *public sector* concerns.[5]

Denuclearization: steps to lessen the risk of nuclear war and to repudiate reliance upon nuclear weapons as instruments of interstate conflict, as well as challenges directed toward reliance on civilian nuclear power; the Chernobyl tragedy disclosed that the difference between civilian nuclear accidents and the military use of nuclear weapons is, at best, a matter of degree.[6]

Demilitarization: steps to reduce the role of military personnel and military methods in governance structures, particularly at the level of the state; such an emphasis stresses civilianization and greater dependence on persuasion and consent in the relations between the state and civil society.

Depolarization: steps to moderate the ideological and geopolitical rivalry between the two nuclear superpowers, as well as efforts to substitute regional patterns of self-determination for such current arrangements associated with bloc cohesion; seeking, above all, to end highly moralistic and fatalistic views of a struggle between good ("we") and evil ("they") and of an inevitable violent conflict to assess the historical verdict.

Development: steps to assure positive use of renewable and nonrenewable resources to satisfy human needs in various countries and regions, as well as to diminish damage to the natural environment or risks associated with ultra-hazardous technologies; the Bhopal disaster in 1984 suggested that multinational corporations that operate under conditions of lax and incompetent regulations confront society with extreme, if hidden, threats to security and well-being.

Democratization: steps to end governmental abuses and to give greater voice and influence to the preferences and attitudes of civil society, as compared to those associated with the special economic and bureaucratic interests that now dominate the structures of state power; the specific shape of democratization varies with the character of current state/society relations, as well as with the situation of a given country in relation to global conflict.

Action plans, the effectiveness of social movements, and overall patterns of political behavior can be assessed in relation to these five dimensions of world order process. This normative framework is geared to a practical and realistic orientation toward action, and is not intended to identify the outer limits of normative potential, the topic for section III. The remainder of this section will discuss some strategic arenas of encounter during this transition period in which the outlook of the new social movements is becoming manifest.

Resistance

The strength of existing structures, and the threats posed by their main lines of policy, continue to generate exemplary actions of resistance by individuals and groups. The purpose of such resistance is symbolic communication beyond the framework of lawful activity. Resistance implies negation, and it expresses both the urgency of the challenge and the impotence of mainstream responses.

In the setting of human rights, peace, ecology, and feminism, the more severe challenges help generate a culture of resistance. Resistance may be intended to mobilize mass sentiments, as in movements for formal democratization, or to block deployment of nuclear weapons systems, but not necessarily. The main objective may be to heighten consciousness, to challenge the complacency of adherents to the status quo, and to give those who act for militarized dominance structures an opportunity to behave differently. Anti-nuclear resistance has taken numerous forms in the United States, Europe, and the Pacific Region.

In this transition period, the characteristic tendency of resistance activity is to work from a radical overall orientation to that being opposed, to embody the values and prefigure the social forms of a promised land. Connected with this is an oppositional style that converts resistance into an appeal to "the other," seeking conversions not casualties in the course of struggle. A great faith in normative potential is revealed, as well as patience to let it unfold slowly over time. In this regard, when Ground Zero (in the Seattle region) blocks the tracks of trains carrying components of Trident missiles, it is also manifesting an overall rejection of violence, an acceptance of nonconsumerist life styles, a refusal to rely upon patterns of hierarchical organization, an insistence on feminist and spiritualized politics, and a seriousness of commitment that sustains and builds energy without depending on the lure of "victory." This joining of issues and perspectives suggests that "action" includes the construction of cultural foundations for a politics of the future that lives up to the full range of normative pretension, grounded in an implicit sense that the peoples of the world must assume direct responsibility for the overall stewardship of the planet. Also implicit is a transcendence of intra-human boundaries—as between generations, genders, races, and nationalities; human solidarity is so deeply accepted that it is taken for granted.

It is exhilarating to notice how universalistic these forms of resistance, spontaneously enacted in grass-roots settings, have become in tone and symbolic content, despite the unevenness of the situation that exists in various countries and regions. The song of the Swedish Great Peace Journey ". . . we are gentle, angry people" expresses the paradoxical attitudes that underlie a decisive rejection of what is and an equally decisive refusal to fight fire with fire. Of course, in many critical parts of the world there is no space, as yet, for public forms of resistance, or, at least, popular forces have yet to discover "hidden" spaces. As "politics" is extended to the "personal" and "private," resistance can never be altogether precluded, no matter how totalitarian the intentions of the rulers.

Delegitimation

Closely connected with resistance activities is a wide array of movement undertakings that casts doubt directly or indirectly on the legitimacy of existing governmental procedures and institutions for assessing guilt and innocence. The most tangible expression of this doubt is the formation of "tribunals" by which to judge official policies. The pioneer exploration was undertaken in the 1960s under the aegis of Bertrand Russell to inquire into the legality of the policies being pursued by the United States in Vietnam.[7] The rationale for the Russell Tribunal was a self-proclaimed finding that neither governments nor international institutions were protecting the sovereign rights of Vietnam and thus creating a normative vacuum that could be appropriately filled by individuals of high moral standing. At the time, the substance of the allegations against US war policies was what made the tribunal controversial, but in a more profound sense, its radical quality was bound up with the implicit rejection of statist views of a monopoly over the forms of governance. Individuals and groups setting up a tribunal to consider issues of public policy represent an effort to wrest control over the wellsprings of legitimacy from the state.

What is suggestive here is the dynamic of this process. Since the Vietnam War there have been dozens of tribunals in Europe established to reach decisions about controversial issues of policy. The League for the Rights of Peoples, with headquarters in Rome, set up the Permanent Peoples Tribunal in 1976. This tribunal has conducted some 13 sessions during its first decade of existence on such diverse matters as repression under Marcos in the Philippines, intervention in Central America and Afghanistan, the Turkish genocide against the Armenians, and Indonesia's policies in East Timor. The judgments and supporting materials have been published as a way of challenging the legitimacy of policies and elites.

A series of ad hoc tribunals have been organized, especially in Germany, during this same period. Among the most notable were a 1982 tribunal on the nuclear arms race in Nuremberg, organized by elements of the Green Party, and a 1985 tribunal on the international law status of nuclear weapons and strategies, organized by a group of lawyers in England.

Along similar lines are commissions of inquiry that are constituted by private initiative. There have been a large number of such commissions in the area of human rights. "The MacBride Commission", established by a group of prominent citizens in England, investigated the Israeli invasion of Lebanon in 1982 and issued a report on international law aspects.[8] Again, the commissions are not important in themselves so much as they disclose a frustration with the capacities of governments to uphold expectations about compliance with international law and morality.

Unlike the creativity of forms associated with mid-1980s resistance, the tribunals and commissions tend to adopt the characteristics of the prevailing political order. There are few evidences of a political domain that extends beyond being for or against the practices of the state. The new social movements do not directly play a large part here, and male/female relations, organizing patterns, and dress codes conform to the mainstream. The dynamics of withdrawing legitimacy may encourage a kind of rivalry in which the initiative from civil society seeks to reproduce in style the operations of the "legitimate" institution.

Accountability

The fragmented political organization of the planet is in tension with the radius of harmful effects associated with the activities of sovereign states. As a consequence, issues of environmental protection and conservation, of ultra-hazardous technologies, of anti-militarist peace initiatives are illustrative. These reactions involve the response of social movements in civil society to the activities of foreign governments.

Consider first, the July 1985 bombing of the Greenpeace vessel *Rainbow Warrior* while the ship was moored alongside docks at Auckland. This was a French intelligence operation, carried out with approval at the highest level of government.[9] The efforts of the New Zealand government to hold France accountable were rather feeble, especially considering that a member of the *Rainbow Warrior* was killed, reflecting in part France's economic leverage as a major importer of some specialty exports from New Zealand (e.g. lamb brains). This instance of state-sponsored terrorism illustrates the accountability gap, especially where the principal culprits are safely situated in a distant capital city and at most only intelligence operatives, as here, were temporarily detained. Through a mediation effort by the United Nations Secretary General, New Zealand at least received a monetary award and the assurance that the agents would be confined by French authorities on a remote Pacific island for several years.

The Greenpeace provocation was to monitor and protest French nuclear testing in the region of the Pacific islands. Here, again, the statist refusal to desist from such testing which is harmful to health, environment, and resources indicates the impotence of the established procedures of international society to challenge official French behavior. Only a private transnational actor has been able to pose such a challenge. It operates within a framework of militant nonviolence, but it generates a violent style of reaction. Without a political system for making governments accountable, it is only possible to raise the issue by action undertaken without official sanction.

In its effect, World War II created a momentary flourish of commitment by the victorious powers to an ethos of accountability. This flourish climaxed in the form of war crimes trials, especially of defeated leaders of Germany and Japan, held in Nuremberg and Tokyo. These trials produced a body of law, generalized in the form of "The Nuremberg Principles," that affirmed the importance of holding governmental leaders internationally responsible for crimes of states. Yet the impulse here remains suspect, as it was always intertwined with a grand display of victors' justice and was never implemented by the establishment of procedures and institutions. And yet with these gestures of imposed accountability a seed was planted, however unintentionally.

Revival and appropriation of Nuremberg. Social movements have been drawn recently to the symbolism and rootedness of this unfulfilled Nuremberg promise, and have sought to gain control over its symbolic appeal to conscience. A Nuremberg Pledge, prepared in December 1985, has been circulated among professional lawyers groups throughout the world, committing individuals within the sphere of their life as citizens and professionals to uphold the Nuremberg Principles and to extend its application to new areas.

More significant is the use of Nuremberg in the setting of citizens efforts to question the legality of foreign policy initiatives, whether relying on illegal weaponry or overall patterns of military action. In Europe and the United States, many peace activists have engaged in "civil disobedience" under a claim of right, namely that international law binds governments and that individual citizens have a duty to secure compliance. Courts and judges have generally repudiated these challenges to governmental supremacy in the war/peace and human rights areas, but there are beginning to be some significant successes for this movement in extending the domain of constitutionalism to encompass foreign policy. This reliance on law against government is a definite reversal of outlook for political radicals, contrasting with Marxist–Leninist dismissals of legal institutions and procedures as tainted by their class origins and affinities.

Dealing with deposed dictators. Ever since the Shah fled Iran in early 1978, there have been calls for some kind of legal process to punish the perpetrators of alleged crimes of state, as well as to recover national wealth wrongfully converted to private use. "The ghosts of Nuremberg" underlay the resolve of the post-military government in Argentina to proceed against those military and political officials responsible for atrocities such as torture or disappearances.

Protecting peoples and resources from technological breakdown. Bhopal and Chernobyl suggest the complex phenomena at issue here. Individuals are vulnerable to harm, and the distant perpetrators can withdraw behind the safety of national boundaries. Governments are either implicated in the event or fail to respond adequately. As a consequence, civil society is challenged to fashion effective humanitarian and political responses. Questions are raised about whether governments and corporations can be entrusted with full authority to deploy and regulate those ultra-hazardous technologies that are increasingly being relied upon in modern sector productive enterprise. This type of concern gives way, in turn, to issues of life style, values, and meaning of life. It also has stimulated "volunteers," and organizing from below. Young people in India have spontaneously organized arrangements in Bhopal to help victims do physical therapy over prolonged periods to recover the use of their lungs. The Soviet rivals for a world championship have both donated all of their winnings from a match in 1986 to disaster relief for Chernobyl victims.

Of course, it is better to prevent an accident than to assure a constructive reaction, but once there is a breakdown, existing modes of extra-statal response seem weak and ineffectual. There is a need to reach the various layers of authority at issue, ranging from local to governmental or corporate decision. The political sense that governmental and corporate actors be made accountable is becoming a strong mobilizing issue.

The Soviet government has exerted a sanctioning kind of authority to fix responsibility for the Chernobyl events. It has deprived some of those charged with negligence of their communist party status. This entails a loss of privileges and possibly a kind of social ostracism as well. What is relevant here is that such an imposition of accountability makes use of an extra-legal mechanism and is, partly, intended to reassure the citizenry that individuals who act on behalf of bureaucracies will be held responsible. This reassurance would seem associated with the new awareness by all governments, even those who reject liberal democratic forms of accountability via elections, checks and balances, and the like, that their legitimacy is being drawn into question by their inability to protect society from the ghoulish dangers of technological breakdown (whether by accident or subversion).[10]

Religious politics

Not all forms of religiously-oriented activism are relevant here. Excluded are those religiously-oriented initiatives that rely on violence, seek to transform the state into a theocracy, and fail to incorporate the whole of humanity into their professed imagery of salvation. Obviously, fundamentalisms are excluded, but so are liberating struggles that rely on violence in a systematic fashion, except possibly in circumstances where violent resistance is the only alternative to acute oppression. How to assess the Sikh movement for autonomy, the Sandinista struggle against Somoza's forces, or the current anti-apartheid movement is complicated, even uncertain; surely, Archbishop Tutu's efforts to promote a militant nonviolent struggle in South Africa is definitely relevant. Perhaps, the complexity of connection between nonviolence and liberation is captured by the decision of the Colombian revolutionary priest Camillo Torres back in the 1960s to carry an unloaded gun in guerrilla combat situations.

What seems to be arising out of the efforts by social movements to reshape the cultural grounds of politics is a new set of challenges and opportunities for churches. It is a challenge because it jeopardizes the protected status of church and clergy; it is an opportunity because it invites churches and clergy to join in the process of resistance and renewal. Throughout the period of the 1980s churches and clergy have provided resources, facilities, and crucial encouragement to the social movements themselves, providing an invaluable kind of reassurance that the new militancy was not alien to widely felt mainstream values and traditions. A religious element also is congenial with the anti-materialist, anti-secular character of the new movements, as well as with their universalistic sense of human identity. Even those movements' adherents who are anti-ecclesiastical welcome spiritual awakening.

Enclaves. Religious institutions are in a position to provide sanctified space that can claim the right to engage in activity based on conscience regardless of what the state and the legal order prescribe. The Sanctuary movement involving several hundred churches in the southwestern region of the United States is an appropriate example—offering Central American refugees, especially from El Salvador, sanctuary despite efforts by the United States to deport such "aliens" under authority of immigration laws. Clergy have risked prison terms for these acts of defiance. The effect is to provide protection for human rights, although in a precarious form, for those who are especially vulnerable.

Another type of "enclave" is provided by churches to circumvent an authoritarian political atmosphere. In both Poland and Chile the Catholic

Church has lent its symbols and facilities in support of democratizing social movements of a generally nonviolent character. Part of this support is to connect the oppositional activities with a tradition that enjoys unquestionable legitimacy with the society as a whole and cannot be credibly portrayed as an alien or hostile tendency (the efforts by right wing states to discredit by calling an opposition "communist" or Marxist–Leninist and by left wing states to discredit by labelling "capitalist" or Western).

Religious leaders have enormous stature and political leverage. By refusing to validate Marcos' fraudulent elections, Cardinal Sin may have tipped the balance against the regime in the Philippines. Pope John Paul II's anti-Sandinista posture has undoubtedly complicated the political struggle in Nicaragua.

Sacramental politics. This new (very old and hallowed) path is largely nonviolent, seeking to gain secular goals by spiritual means. It is illustrated most vividly by the words and acts of Miguel d'Escoto, the Nicaraguan Minister of Foreign Affairs and one of the three priests in the Sandinista cabinet. As Father d'Escoto describes his own urge toward creativity as a high governmental official: "We Christians have our own special arms that we must use—prayer, fasting, processions with hymns, vigils . . .."[11] Such a perspective led to what d'Escoto called *"la insurreccion evangelica"* (the "evangelical insurrection") and produced his celebrated *"el ayuno por la paz"* ("fast for peace") that went on for thirty days in July 1985, initiated as a protest against US aid to the *contras* and seeking to gain the upper hand in the "spiritual war" going on with the upper echelons of the Catholic clergy in Nicaragua, especially Cardinal Miguel Obando y Bravo. D'Escoto succeeded in endowing his fast with symbolic content and political significance. For any close observer, such a sacramental approach to power completely contradicted the propaganda of the Reagan Administration and of the anti-Sandinistas which was that the leaders in Managua were hardened Marxist–Leninists. The fast attracted attention in many places, especially in church circles throughout Latin America. There were displays of "prophetic solidarity," including many endorsements by Catholic bishops and Christian leaders.

Subsequently, Miguel d'Escoto initiated *"el Via crucis por la paz"* ("The Way of the Cross for Peace"), a traditional expression of popular piety in Nicaragua, drawing on the symbolic resonance of Jesus' suffering and vindication during the last days of his life. This *Via crucis* started on the first Friday of Lent, February 14, 1986, in Jalapa, near the Honduran border, and processed to Managua, some 300 kilometers away, over the next two weeks. The procession of pilgrims, including the Foreign Minister, stayed at peasant homes en route and took part in religious gatherings at churches. At Esteli, the local bishop embraced and blessed d'Escoto before 20 000 people. The entire procession was an effort to sanctify the Sandinista cause and to win popular support.

In a larger setting, d'Escoto's approach represented an overall Sandinista search for survival, given the hostility of the United States, and a mobilization of support within and beyond Nicaragua. It complements Nicaragua's recourse to the World Court, an appeal to international law as a way of resisting the efforts of the United States to destroy the Sandinistas. Both sacramental politics (and recourse to international law) rest on the assumption that it matters to have the moral advantage in a struggle between adversaries of unequal wealth and destructive capacity. As such, this "faith" arises out of the same sources as do the new social movements who seek to prevail, but without reliance on destructive force. A distinct concept of struggle is implicit, one that depends for its outcome on an inner dynamic—how "strong" the will to resist and endure pain on the "weak" side, and how "strong" the will to inflict pain on the "powerful" side.

Closely connected are undertakings with religious backing that involve witnessing and vigils. "Witness for Peace," organized by churches, has sent several thousand ordinary Americans to dangerous war zones in Nicaragua to report upon the real character of combat. As well as an expression of conscience, it is an attempt to discover "the truth" that is so often a casualty of state-organized disinformation and propaganda campaigns.

In this period the images and forms of religious traditions are being deployed on behalf of peace and justice, to challenge a purely military conception of political struggle. To the extent that spiritual and moral energies are mobilized, the cultural setting of politics shifts.

Feminist religion. The spiritual resources of tradition are themselves deformed by patriarchal features and structures. The pursuit of a new cultural ground summons a wide variety of efforts to embody gender equality, but more than this, to overcome the patriarchal bias of scriptures and practices. A new language of the spirit is needed, and being sought, as well as practices that accentuate nurturing and mothering, and that specify the sacred as a reflection of the feminine also.

Empowering transnational arenas

The global scale of some basic trends induced even governments to seek global frameworks for assessment and prescription. As a consequence and starting at Stockholm in 1972 with environmental issues (followed by population, food, and human settlements), inter-governmental conferences were held to clarify substantive challenges, using the organizing capabilities and formal auspices of the United Nations. These occasions aroused media interest, generated a considerable body of specialist literature on the topic, and revealed vividly the enfeebling constraints on effective action if conceived in state-to-state terms. These events exhibited not only the severity of the problems emergent in international life, but also the paralysis of capabilities on the international level. As such, the conferences created an impression of empty rhetoric and impotence.

What vitality did emerge was associated with the so-called counter-conferences—various assemblages of individuals and groups concerned about the subject-matter, drawn to the place by the formal event, but expressing an anti-statist attitude toward what was needed. The counter-conference outlook was instinctively based on human solidarity and on the understanding that an invisible planetary polity existed in nascent form.

The most recent event of this character was the July 1985 United Nations World Conference on Women held in Nairobi. The event brought together women from all over the world, gathered as official delegates of governments, to discern the actualities of gender discrimination and fashion responses. According to accounts by participants, the feminist energy dissolved the characteristic formalism of international governmental events. Yet far more exciting for participants were the informal, counter-conference events, including for instance, "the peace tent" (a large blue and white striped tent at the University of Nairobi set up by Feminists International for Peace and Food "to provide the women of the world with a space for frank, informal discussions, sharing, singing and dancing; the rules stated that, when anyone addressed a group, there was to be no clapping or cheering, no booing or hissing; each woman was to be accorded equal respect").

In a statement prepared by the organizers the undertaking was described as follows: "The Peace Tent is the international feminist alternative to men's conflict and war. It is the place where finding peaceful solutions to conflicts, both in personal lives and in the public arena, is the priority . . .. In the Peace Tent, women can substitute women's truths for patriarchal lies through dialogue, films and exhibits, women's joy for patriarchal pessimism through song, dance and art. The aim of the Peace Tent is to bring women's peacemaking will and consciousness to the world which so desperately needs it."[12] Evident here, is the reliance on cultural forms to attain political results and the expansion of the political to include what was hitherto regarded as personal and private. As such, feminism adopts a holistic view of action that defines its positive energy by contrast with masculine reliance on violence, war, and hierarchy.

The women who participated in Nairobi reported back their sense of excitement and empowerment, arising directly from the experience of women from diverse cultural and class backgrounds discovering powerful affinities associated with their shared experience of both the predicament of women and the transforming possibility of feminism.

In general, these global occasions create networks of individuals and groups across existing boundaries that facilitate the claims of the new politics. Additionally, the impotence of governments in the face of evidence about problems and suffering, contributes to the work of delegitimation. Indeed, these negative reactions have become so prevalent that governments have grown reluctant to sponsor such occasions as they realize that the good effects of displaying concern about the shortcomings of the world is more than offset by the bad effects of exhibiting impotence. As a result, the creation of networks and global arenas will have to be staged by the new movements themselves, not an easy task, primarily because of funding problems.

Envisioning the long revolution

> Once the inevitabilities are challenged, we begin gathering our resources for a journey of hope.
>
> RAYMOND WILLIAMS
> *The Year 2000* (New York: Pantheon, 1985), p. 268.

Whether or not the process of transformation is self-sustaining is a matter of controversy. Does it deepen the motivation of activists to clarify the contours of the promised land? Or is it dispiriting because it can never be specified with enough plausibility, consensus, and vibrancy? The evidence is conflicting, yet it seems worth drawing out some shared normative expectations about the character of a transformed world, if only to improve communication among the many different social actors, and to strengthen the overall sense of a unified direction of radical reformist efforts. Such reflections are conditioned by the caveats earlier set forth, especially the limiting validity of specific context in a world of uneven experience and the provincial character of the perspective of any particular observer.

In actual undertaking, the new social movements are losing some of their particularity by expressing a certain overall commitment to the future that draws on common elements: repudiation of markets and quantitative yardsticks of productive excellence; repudiation of war and technologies of violence as inevitable instruments of social conflict; adoption of identity patterns and affinities that arise from shared commitments; support for the claims of oppressed peoples and groupings to equal stature, and possibly beyond this, to a role of leadership; imagery of wholeness as expressive of the liberation process and as compatible with nationalist goals of self-determination; skeptical and selective attitudes toward technology and modernizing forms of development; coalitions and support activities in transnational arenas and networks; a refusal to regard access to state power as the prime stake of political activity, even if formal procedures of democracy are established; emphasis on local, personal and grassroots mobilization and engagement as the crucial test of political potency; protection of and communion with nature as part of the new political space; promotion of democracy and human rights at the state level to assure minimum decency and to provide political space for exploration, reconstruction, and alternative forms of relationship, production, management, and organization; an emergent awareness that the decisive political battleground for the remainder of this century is associated with an activation of cultural energies with regard to the content of prevailing attitudes, myths, beliefs, virtues, vices, worldviews, and underlying assumptions about the character of human nature.

The presentation of the more visionary content implicit in the new politics is not meant to remove it from present relevance. This material informs present activity by being latent in the consciousness of most participants despite the realization that the prevailing order is antagonistic, and may remain so for a long time. At the same time, this visionary perspective is intended to prefigure (without prescribing) the content of the promised land and to facilitate clarifying dialogue from various rooted circumstances in the world. In the prior section, the discussion related to the identification of normative progress along a five-dimensional field during a transitional period of involvement that is ongoing and of indefinite duration. This section is removed from history in the limited sense that it prefigures a desirable future that can unfold out of an altered cultural setting.

Envisioning a future implies a coherent claim to regard as possible within history alternative ways of organizing and of conceiving basic life structures.

The importance of coherence encourages a mutually reinforcing set of predominant features. To set this forth, five aspects of the interrelated societal whole will be discussed: security; development; environment; governance; and worldview. Such a classificatory scheme seeks only to highlight critical features, not to exhaust or reduce the overall social reality.

Security

The ideal is to protect individuals and groups with minimum reliance on violence, implying a substantially disarmed military establishment and a weaponless police force. There is a subjective side (feeling secure), and an objective side (being secure). Hostile propaganda can create gaps in either direction in this connection between feeling secure and being secure. A secure social order feels secure and is secure.

The current focus is upon security as specified by the government, what has come to be called "national security." Such a focus emphasizes the security of elites and regimes, not necessarily the security of society and people. The visionary imagery of security emphasizes people, society as a whole, and does not confine the scope of protected persons to a specific group. Desirable forms of security emphasize interdependence—we cannot be secure unless others are secure, and vice versa.

Such an understanding of security is almost diametrically opposed to current strategic forms of security associated with the logic of deterrence. According to this logic we deter better if we intimidate others, making them feel and be insecure, at least in relation to ourselves. Since both sides in international (or other) conflict relations subscribe to such thinking, an arms race ensues, especially if resources are being devoted to military research and development with the objective of gaining the upper hand, or at least of not being relatively disadvantaged. In a revised security atmosphere, reassurance about intentions and capabilities would be a major undertaking. It would be helpful at all times to avoid others either being or feeling threatened by any kind of violent behavior.

Implicit in the new social movements is a double sense: violence does not protect in an acceptable manner, especially at an international level; it is practical in an altered cultural setting to achieve security nonviolently.

Of course, there are many intermediate stages, varying with the character of local, national, and regional circumstances. Of great importance is the demilitarization of state/society relations within given countries, and the shift toward nonprovocative defense postures, doctrines, and capabilities in state/state settings, especially in those strategic settings where nuclear weapons are deployed and relied upon.

The attainment of peoples security as outlined above cannot be separated from other transformations that undercut the character of current patterns and modalities of conflict. What makes people secure in a happy family is dependent, above all, on an atmosphere of love and gentleness. Whether a deepening experience of human solidarity and adoption of an ecological ethos can enlarge the social unit that experiences happiness is, of course, unknown, but there is no solid evidence to draw into question the possibility.

Development

The ideal here is to encourage the efficient and sustainable use of resources to assure production flows that will satisfy basic human needs and will not cause too large a gap between classes, regions, and societies. Development can be shaped in many satisfying, acceptable directions, but the constructive use of resources for positive human ends is a unifying theme.

This ideal contrasts with current actualities: wasteful use of resources, and environmentally-destructive patterns of production; dedication of resources to military and paramilitary purposes, and to luxuries despite large sectors of acute poverty within existing states and in certain regions. The prevailing forms of social accounting and market mechanisms allocate resources in a manner that frustrates efforts to use resources for human betterment in an ecologically-sustainable manner.

A major obstacle in the path of such a vision is the tendency of organized labor to buy into market capitalism. Another obstacle is the bureaucratic ineptitude of state socialist planning that appears to erode motivation and to encourage low quality production in deference to quantitative yardsticks of output. In this regard, capitalist societies require more sensitivity to ethical factors. There is no need to conceive of development in an austere form that reduces the world to a common subsistence standard, an ordeal of grayness. As with security, this visionary view of development cannot become established within materialist, acquisitive culture surroundings.

It seems possible to conceive of the emergence of developmental pluralism that is constrained by a shared cultural notion of human need and dignity. Without sentimentalizing the distant past, indigenous peoples seemed to achieve such developmental balance in a variety of societal and tribal forms, in settings informed by reverence for nature and by an underlying ethos of stewardship and conservation.[13] Whether post-modern society, and societies at various stages of industrialization, can reconstitute such a cultural grounding for positive development is uncertain. At the very least, social movements seem alive to this crucial reorientation based on values, not on lifting encumbrances from the operations of the market or assuring that production processes are nominally controlled by the working class.

Environment

Closely associated with security and development is the relation of the overall productive and consumptive process to the maintenance of environmental quality. The modern industrial era, spurred on by the illusions of limitless growth, an ascending curve of profits and productivity, and ever higher standards of living, paid virtually no attention to harmful environmental effects until the early 1970s. Then a variety of forms of pollution, especially of underlying renewable resources (air, water, land), caused a momentary cultural tremor, possibly climaxed by the Club of Rome's study *The Limits to Growth*.

Unfortunately, this upsurge of concern was closely linked to an apocalyptic view of history and emerged without benefit of either a politics of positive adjustment or an ethics of empathy. As a result, environmental warnings have been treated as largely exhortatory, although some governmental efforts at regulation of toxic effects and disaster response were significantly initiated. No fundamental changes of the humanity/nature equation have been initiated in critical areas of energy use, ultra-hazardous technology, petrochemicals in agriculture, waste disposal, city planning, and mass transport.

Because of the absence of any explicit normative outlook, many who identified with the poor in the North or with the South dismissed environmental concerns at first, even regarding those concerns as a sinister technique to perpetuate hierarchy and exploitation in the post-colonial era. As detrimental environmental impacts have been felt around the world, this attitude has dramatically shifted, and now in the 1980s those who most closely represent the grass-roots poor in the Third World are convinced that the control and protection of local resources in all aspects is at the core of political action. India, for instance, has emerged as a hotbet of grass-roots environmentalism with hundreds of separate, independent groups as well as organizations more generally concerned. The upsurge of respect for the cultural perspectives of indigenous peoples has also grounded environmental issues in a variety of interpretations about the right livelihood for individuals and groups.

The ideal of environmental policy is related to preserving, and even enhancing, not only the resource base of the planet as a whole, but also those of distinct communities. This attitude is more than a matter of preserving the material conditions for life on the planet. It also expresses an important feature of the new religious consciousness that endows nature with a sacred and spiritual quality, closely associated with human fulfillment; to destroy nature, or poison it, is to manifest an acute type of alienation. The entry into space exploration has reinforced this kind of awe in the face of the vastness and splendor of nature. As such, there is a rediscovered sense of human limits that is less anguishing than that revealed by such high technology frontiers suggested by the chilling metaphor "nuclear winter."

Emphasizing the visionary revitalization of environment also expresses the intimate connection between local action and general disposition of mind and spirit. To view resources, including human labor, as a valued end, and not just as a means to more abundant production, is of the essence in achieving a social order based on freedom and mutual respect.

Governance

Not necessarily government, but governance, seems an ingredient of an envisioned promised land. The quest is for the gentlest forms of authority that do not intrude on freedoms, do not create a huge gap between citizens and institutions established for their benefit, and yet facilitate the security, development, and environmental quality discussed in prior sections. Obviously, core concerns arising out of oppressive governmental structures have to do with bureaucracy, violence, and technology. In the present world political setup, the most general forms of authority are closely associated with the war system, the arms race, and an anti-democratic style of upholding "national security" even in political atmospheres that otherwise enjoy some form of constitutional governance.

The minimal elements of humane governance include the following: responsiveness to citizenry; unconditional respect for human rights; reliance on education and persuasion to achieve order; mechanisms for alleviating grievances at pre-crisis stages; acceptable ethical standards involving welfare for those who are deprived; and the absence of discrimination among diverse ethnic, religious, and racial groupings. More essential, yet more difficult to envision, is the weakening of existing political boundaries, many of which were established by conquest and sustained by violence and intimidation, while at the same time, strengthening the boundaries surrounding what Christian Bay has usefully identified as natural political communities—those held spontaneously together by bonds of affection and affinity. To enjoy this sort of political participation is not at all incompatible with a simultaneous process of acknowledgement in relation to species identity, an acknowledgement spurred on by both practical and normative considerations. The possibilities for governance of this type depend on a substantially transformed cultural setting along the lines already specified.

Because of our emphasis on new social movements and global-scale problems, governance patterns must be receptive both to planetary requirements and to those of a local and personal character. Space cooperation as a metaphor for the obsolescence of action that is the exclusive product of the political will and technological prowess of a given territorial fragment can be treated as a metaphor for an emergent holism. At the same time, issues of sexual deviance and child abuse suggest the obsolescence of a political domain that excludes the private and personal. Such an enlargement of politics should not be confused with the advocacy of intrusiveness. On the contrary, the essence of governance might be the deepening of respect for privacy and the encouragement of practices of tolerance.

The idea of governance as an ideal ultimately implies self-governance and spontaneous governance. As in Marxist visionary thought, it implies a withering away of the state, especiallay of crude forms of governance (in the mask of "government"). Unlike the Marxist tradition societal preparation for humane governance involves transforming the cultural grounding of politics rather than awaiting the ascent of the proletariat as the last, and most inclusive, liberating class. The flaw at the root of state socialist disappointment is to suppose that self-dissolving power structures embodied in institutional bureaucracies can be established within the current framework of materialist civilization and a geopolitical order that rests on capabilities for violent self-help (that is, on war).

Our view of humane governance is tied to cultural preparation, a process by which the legitimacy and resolve associated with current structures of government are eroded, as other modes of governance gain prominence, at first, in the exploratory domains of the new social movements (for example, in peace arenas such as Greenham Common or Mutlangen; or in religious arenas such as "the base communities" of the Church of the Poor in Latin American countries).

Ethos

By ethos is meant values, worldview, and the ground upon which normative positions stand. It is necessary to have some kind of reinforcing metaphysics to clarify why particular value preferences are selected and why their realization is so fervently desired. This grounding also helps deepen an affirmation of human solidarity and explains why species identity is a source of both pride and hope, and not just a sentimental wish at this time of evolving human consciousness. The cosmopolitan direction of new identity patterns is taken for granted by the social movements without necessarily repudiating more particular and local identities.

In a sense, the ethos of a promised land is the consciousness that manifests itself in all domains of existence including expectations about security, well-being, and fulfillment for individuals and groups. This ethos is necessarily deferential to the local and diverse, as a positive element in the vitality of cultural interaction, and at the same time sensitive to the historical occasion for cooperation, interaction and shared exploration based on mutual benefit. An important dimension of this ethos is a genuine attitude of stewardship toward the future, not only preserving the prospects of generations to come, but also enacting through policy and behavior respectful attitudes toward ecological limits of human endeavor, including a conservatism about risking the long-term effects of ultra-hazardous technologies.

This ethos implies a reorientation of citizenship that goes beyond loyal and diligent participation in the collective life of society. The citizen sensitive to the claims of this emergent ethos needs to extend his or her notions of participation in both dimensions of space (beyond the territory of any particular state) and time (beyond the present, reclaiming past wisdom, and safeguarding future generations). Citizenship so conceived is not meant as an affirmation of a nonexistent global community; to become "a world citizen" by self-proclamation is both too easy and ineffectual. Rather, implicit in the ethos is an outlook elsewhere described as that of the citizen/pilgrim, one who is embarked on a journey of deliverance that is centered upon the ongoing struggle to create a future that approaches normative horizons that now seem mere aspirations.

This envisioned ethos is also an aspect of emergent "realism" that awaits transition from government to governance.

Concluding observations

A big uncertainty is whether the new social movements will be able to adapt, evolve, and grow, possibly reemerging wearing different masks, but born out of the same current of normative energy. Moreover, it is not clear whether their techniques of political action will challenge established, oppressive structures, or will coexist by occupying space at the margins that is accepted as a safety valve, or as a supplement to processes of cooptation. In assessing prospects, it is important to resist the trap to determine relative capabilities by measurable strengths. The potency of the new movements is normative, without tangible substance, but capable of effecting sudden conversions and symbolic leaders and of changing the composition of cultural soil. This potency may also be disguised, being borne invisibly or latently by the culture until it erupts as an unexpectedly powerful tendency. The political possibilities are connected with the gradual establishment of a new foundational ethos, a kind of "continental drift" associated with the unknown geology of cultural transformation.[14]

There is another distinguishing trail here. Positive expectations about the future depend no longer on staying with what Raymond Williams calls "Plan X," that is, guided management at the state level that proceeds on the basis of the given to seek calculated advantages for the self.[15] Nor do they depend on the mystical liberation of violent challenge, whether by terrorist or social revolution. Nor do they suppose a sudden *satori* of practical wisdom by trauma at the brink, the apocalyptic view either of responding or succumbing. Nor do they place much confidence in the fear-driven imagery of "the four horsemen" grimly galloping across the planet spreading disease, famine, war, and misery.

The social movements are confident because of their faith in cultural creativity and the "power" of a new ethos to transform the old order. In this drama unfolding in our time, these new movements need reinforcement from a revived labor movement that relocates its understanding of both the means and goals of struggle (in the manner of Solidarity) and of a resurgent religious activism that finds its spiritual significance in adherence to an envisioned ethos of cultural transformation. As citizens/pilgrims carry forward these struggles in various spheres it is likely that new images of political community will take shape in the imagination of participants, reestablishing our sense of what is possible and desirable. From such a perspective the sharply demarcated managerial style of politics will seem an archaic, yet dangerous and destructive, approach to organizing the collective life of the planet.

Notes and references

1. A helpful assessment of social movements from a variety of angles is found in a symposium issue of *Social Research* edited by Jean L. Cohen: "Social Movements," *Social Research*, Vol. 52 (1985), pp. 664–890.
2. There is here an apparently semantic choice that relates in a basic way to substance: do we encompass the new social movements within an expanded conception of "politics" or do we regard this activity (following Gramsci's lead) as a struggle for the cultural terrain that conditions politics (conceived as mainly governance structures of a formal institutional character)? In this article, an intermediate posture is adopted.
3. For confirmation see Harry Eckstein, "Civic Inclusion and its Discontents," *Daedalus*, Vol. 113, No. 4 (Fall, 1989), pp. 107–145.
4. The phrase and orientation are taken from the Trilateral Commission's notorious publication *The Crisis of Democracy* (New York: New York University Press, 1975).
5. This framework has benefitted from collaborative work with Mary Kaldor under the auspices of the United Nations University. See for example our joint introduction in Mary Kaldor and Richard Falk, eds., *Dealignment for Western Europe* (Oxford: Basil Blackwell, forthcoming).
6. This point is dramatically made by Robert Jungk: ". . . there is no fundamental difference between atoms for peace and atoms for war," at p. vi. See generally Jungk, *The Nuclear State* (London: John Calder, 1979).

7. For text of proceedings, etc., see J. Duffield, ed. *Against the Crimes of Silence* (Flanders, New Jersey: O'Hare, 1968).

8. For text of the report see *Israel in Lebanon: The Report of the International Commission* (New York: Ithaca Press, 1983).

9. For accounts see *Rainbow Warrior*, Insight series of the Sunday Times (London: Arrow Books, 1986); David Robie, *Eyes of Fire: The Last Voyage of the Rainbow Warrior* (New Zealand: London Publishing, 1986).

10. Of course, parallel to reassurance is the counter-terrorist campaigns to uphold the security functions of government.

11. Quoted in Conor Cruise O'Brien, "God and Man in Nicaragua," *Atlantic* (August 1986), pp. 50–72, at 63; this section draws on O'Brien's perceptive account.

12. Both quotations from "Focus on Women," *Breakthrough* (Summer 1986), p. 14; material in special issue includes illuminating accounts of the Nairobi Conference.

13. For broader cultural, political, and economic reflections see S. Diamond, *In Search of the Primitive* (New Brunswick, New Jersey: Transaction Books, 1974).

14. These metaphors are creatively explored in another kind of inquiry by Russell Banks in his fine novel *Continental Drift* (New York: Harper & Row, 1985).

15. Raymond Williams, *The Year 2000* (New York: Pantheon, 1985), pp. 243–48.

Masses, Classes and the State

Rajni Kothari

It is commonplace these days to say that we live in an age of turbulence. What is not clear is the source of this turbulence and the reasons why despite so much of it, it is not being allowed to change the world we live in by those who wield power and authority. What I propose to do in this essay is to explore precisely this relationship—between an increasingly defensive status quo, desperate to retain its power, and the forces of change and transformation that are getting increasingly restive. These forces are conscious of the shackles that bind them and the need to move out of them. They are frustrated and disorganized, yet they seek ways to cope with the growing repression and terror from the status quo.

There is nothing new in this undertaking. All social commentators, at least since the middle of the nineteenth century, who have cared to look at the larger dynamics that lie behind the myriad expressions of the human condition, have sought to deal with this very problem: the encounter between the forces of status quo and those of change. What is new in examining the same problem in our time (and by that I mean the eighties of the twentieth century) is the deep confusion and uncertainty about what really is under way on both sides of the equation—on the side of the global, regional and local forces of status quo and on the side of the agents of change and transformation from the very local and "micro" to the global and planetary "macro" level.

It is by seeking to unravel this deep uncertainty about the directions in which the world—both the dominant structures and those opposed to the dominant structures—is moving that we may be able to at least begin to understand what is at work, what new factors have emerged or are emerging, how these are likely to shape the future and what counter-trends, if any, may be in the offing and may perhaps work. At present no clear framework of understanding, far less of explaining, reality exists, not even a method of coming to grips with it. There has taken place an obsolescence of ideological frameworks, grand theories, and of any clear guide for formulating a praxis. There is a striking decline of confidence among all but the most naïve dogmatists. And this pervading sense of uncertainty has given rise to insecurity, helplessness, bewilderment, withdrawal, cynicism and apathy.

Periods of uncertainty in history, to a large extent, are occasioned by major changes in the structure of reality, changes at so many thresholds of human organization and so simultaneous that their impacts on consciousness leave

This article is based on the N.M. Pereira memorial lecture, Colombo, Sri Lanka, August 1985.

the latter adrift and without any firm anchor. In the contemporary situation we see this at so many thresholds or levels of human endeavour and organization. At the larger political level of the world power structure, both the rise of the Third World in the post-colonial period and the replacement of a world structured around the European balance of power by a bipolar world structured around the two superpowers have unsettled all earlier understanding of international relations. While each of these two events is recognized, the two have not been considered together in an adequate manner. Once one does that, one can immediately see how a colonial kind of bondage was replaced by a much greater and stronger integration into either the global capitalist market or into the strategic straitjacket fashioned by the struggle for world hegemony by the two superpowers. Our existing conceptual categories of historical analysis are somehow ill-equipped to grasp the full implications of this split in the human community occasioned precisely by its greater integration, globalization and homogenization. Most existing ideologies and their off-shoots were born in the typical European setting of nation-states, during the process of first generation industrialization and against the background of essentially class-based identities. These seem to be ill-equipped to deal with a transnationalized world in which the dominant currency is technological, distinct from economic and military and political currencies. It is a totally different human setting.

Again, this is also reflected at the level of the organization of the productive forces. Today, we are confronted with a completely different model of world capitalism, a switch from the European to the American model in which technology as a system, propelled on the one hand by the communications and information order conditioning the minds of men, and on the other by the corporate form of organization conditioning the behaviour of States, makes all other relations of production subordinate. This has generally forced all other "systems"—the socialist system, the Third World, the Japanese system—to fall in line and to measure success in terms laid down by the American cultural syndrome (technology being the only unique cultural feature of the United States).

The growing autonomy of the technological estate has found its greatest manifestation in the military field and the field of military–civilian relationship. We live in an age not just of growing militarization of the whole globe—from the powerful nuclear powers to the powerless Third World countries—but of a model of militarization that is essentially technological. Nation-states are at the mercy of the growing menace of military R & D which marches inexorably and forces every major and even minor country to discard existing weapon systems and adopt ever new ones, with escalating costs and with increasingly hazardous effects on social and ecological systems. It is a new version of militarism, autonomous of the will of the rulers and of course of the peoples.

This dominion of technology and its pervasive impact on politics, economics and security, each of which has become vulnerable to its design, has in turn produced a massive erosion of the ecological basis of human civilization. It has destroyed the resource base of the people, and especially of the millions of rural, tribal and "ethnic" poor who have just been made surplus and therefore dispensable populations by the aggressive march of high-tech capitalism, and their traditional access to natural resources and non-commercial products taken away from them. The usual syndrome facing even the most remote hill peoples is one in which the military builds roads, the urban and tourist traffic moves in with its artefacts and consumerism, modern communications "hardsell" these products, followed by modern technology and its commercial arteries, drawing away all the bounties of nature that were traditionally free for these peoples.

With all these forces impinging on traditional societies, forcing them to fall in line and accept the dominant mode and ideology of forced modernization and, what is more, with the supposedly independent States, too, being forced to fall in line instead of providing new lines of defence to civil society, a deep socio-cultural crisis has ensued, especially in older civilizations. As the State, in effect, withdraws from its responsibility and surrenders its autonomy, civil society in these lands is thrown on its own resources. And this has happened precisely when these societies are experiencing deep convulsions, thanks to the powerful impacts both of the modernizing juggernaut immanent in the aggressive thrust of ruthless technologism which is the form that world capitalism has assumed and, in a different way, the impact of the social and ethnic conflicts generated by formal electoral democracy in which wresting a majority at the time of elections has become the main thrust of politics. Such a formal apparatus of democracy as a vehicle of modernization worked somewhat smoothly so long as it was controlled by an alliance of feudal and bourgeois elements. But with the rise and assertion of the masses, which in good faith had believed in the formal pretences of bourgeois democracy, a big backlash arose from both the feudal landed interests and the industrial bourgeoisie. This backlash has found its expression in massive repression of the poor on the one hand, and the promulgation of a depoliticized technocratic State impervious to the social and political aspirations of the masses on the other.

It is the bewildering interface between these powerful trends—each heralding a strong current of domination and destruction—with which we need to come to grips if we are to comprehend, assess and hopefully steer the counter-trends that are emerging on behalf of the affected masses and peoples of the world. Crucial to such an understanding are two prerequisites. First, we must give up the specialized, single-issue oriented approach to problems and crises that has characterized the dominant method of both the hard sciences and the social sciences. Second, we need to identify the emerging ideological elements in the current praxis of the counter-movements and weave them into a whole which, while drawing upon the best in earlier ideologies, empowers the masses towards a liberating process of their own creation and volition. If ours is an "age of the masses", then it is the masses and their leaders that must evolve a relevant ideology. The task must not be left to some ivory tower intellectuals—they may serve as aides but not as "vanguards"—nor to the wielders of state power who, all indications suggest, have scant interest in the masses except when they have to "mobilize" them from time to time for their own perpetuation in power and self-glorification. Hitherto ideological claims or pretences have been made either by intellectuals in their role of being "vanguards" or by rulers of States and leaders of ruling parties, in which the masses were treated as mindless followers with no ideas of their own, indeed with no capacity for cognition. At least in our age, this presumption must go. For all the élites, including revolutionary élites, have failed to grasp the reality on the ground. On the other hand, one notices some refreshing and original ways of thinking among the masses from which all can learn.

The need to consider the multiple dimensions of domination, exploitation and marginalization in their interrelated manifestations and the need to similarly interrelate and integrate the large variety of counter-trends and their new ideological underpinnings can best be met by focusing on the central issue of our time: the changing nature of the State and its role in civil society, especially as it impinges on the masses and the peoples of the world, particularly of the Third World. We need to re-examine our assumptions about the State and its presumed role as the liberator, equalizer, "modernizer" and mobilizer. As we do this we shall be able to uncover a series of simultaneous dimensions. The State and its relationship to the people come through in this analysis as not just a relationship between classes and the masses, but also between the principal carrier of modern capitalism and technology and the social order. This relationship, it will be noticed, marginalizes a large part of the social order. Between the military and the civil order, the latter emerges the loser. Between the development policies of the State and its transnational sponsors and the economic and ecological catastrophes that are hitting the masses and affecting the sheer survival of large numbers of people, one can easily guess which emerges as the winner. Between the global information order and the citizen reduced to a package of consumption, social prejudice and dazzling circuses organized by the State and corporate intelligence, the citizen is the victim. And, finally, between dominant races and ethnic communities that have control of the State on one side, and those at the periphery, presumably still members of the civil order but progressively being pushed out of it by repressive and genocidal policies, on the other, the former emerge victorious every time. It is this capture of the State by a convergence of class, ethnic, technological and military actors, developmentalists, communicators and managers, including managers of votes, that has set the stage for the contemporary confrontation between the "classes" and the "masses".

There has been with us, especially in the post-colonial world, a presumption of the State as a mediator in ameliorating the harshness of traditional social structures for the purpose of ensuring justice and equality. The State has been looked up to as a protector of vulnerable peoples, the liberator of oppressed and colonized populations, and as an engine of growth and development that would usher in a new civil order based on progress and prosperity and go on to confer rights to life and liberty, equality and dignity on the people at large. There was a further presumption of the State having relative autonomy from entrenched interests and classes, of the State as an independent actor with preponderant powers to influence, discipline and, where needed, even to coerce established interests and estates to accept State policies aimed at transforming, either incrementally or through rapid strides, the status quo. For a while it did seem that the bearers of power in the new States meant to act as autonomous actors and to use their authority for the pursuit of declared policies. The written Constitutions, the fundamental statutes that were enacted and the wide array of social legislation that followed were designed to do this. The vigorous pursuit of economic models that then ensued, whether in achieving greater self-reliance through import substitution and the building of a substantial infrastructure for industrialization (as for instance was the case with India) or in achieving greater welfare through the provision of social minima in food, health and education (as for instance was the case with Sri Lanka), also suggested that the State meant to play a positive role in the interests of clearly laid out policies which were, in turn, based on a forward-looking social and economic philosophy.

During the same period, the opening up of political space, either through exercise of adult franchise in the liberal polities, or through involvement in party structures and at production sites in socialist polities, or through a combination of competitive politics, local self-government and co-operatives in the rural areas in mixed-economies, all these also meant that leaders of those States were keen on involving the masses and seeking legitimacy from them. In fact, large segments of the masses accepted this new benevolent form of a paternalistic State, and hoped to use it to improve both their life chances and their status in society and, in the course of time, to challenge the hegemony of the dominant classes in society. In short, though not always stated in that manner, built into the positive thrust and progressivist creed of the post-colonial State was an eventual encounter between the "classes" and the "masses" with the State providing a frame for mediation through which a confrontation of contending interests was translated into a series of transformative policies.

Such a promise of the liberal polity based on a mixture of faith in "development", a high degree of zeal in "doing good" to the people and the availability of a credible and exemplary leadership that was on the whole not a prisoner of a particular class or estate was not without failings. It also had its serious critics. Inevitably, many compromises were effected along the way, as for instance in the implementation of land reforms or in establishing truly effective public distribution systems. Concessions were made when entrenched groups and interests put up tough resistance to intended changes. There was too much dependence on the bureaucracy which was, in most of these States, a direct continuation of the colonial civil service. And finally, there was a considerable degree of corruption and nepotism in high office. These were the inevitable compulsions of the middle class origins of the leadership and the social milieu in which ministers, their secretaries and the technocrats moved. The people knew this and were all along told about it. They had also been warned by some that the State was an instrument of a class or of a colonial power or simply of bureaucrats and policemen and soldiers. And yet whether it was Lenin or Mao, Nehru or Nkrumah, Nyerere or Nasser, they all pinned their visions of transformation on State power. Only Gandhi did not. But he was, even before India became independent, rendered impotent and irrelevant. Leaving the Gandhian stream aside—it is necessary to remember that most Gandhians also opted for a model of voluntarism and "constructive work" which depended heavily on State patronage—there was consensus across the board, from the industrialists to "left-of-centre" politicians to the radicals including the Marxists, on a positive and interventionist role for the State on behalf of the masses.

It is now clear that the expectation of such a role, and of the presumed alliance between the State and the masses in such an expectation, has been belied. Today the State is seen as having betrayed the masses; it has become the prisoner of the dominant classes and their transnational patrons and has increasingly turned anti-people. The State has failed to provide the means for a radical bourgeois transformation from the dynamics of which a revolutionary alternative would emerge. The State in the Third World, despite some valiant efforts by dedicated leaders in a few countries, has degenerated into a technocratic machine serving a narrow power group that is kept in power at the top by hordes of security men and a regime of repression and terror at the bottom. It is kept going by millions of hard-working people who must go on producing goods and services for the "system", for if they do not, everything would collapse. The truth is that without landless labourers and sharecroppers and without the unrelieved drudgery of women and children, the rural economy would collapse; without slum and pavement dwellers the urban economy would collapse. But there is no chance that any of these people can ever rise above their levels of penury and destitution; neither the landless will acquire land nor the homeless urbanites get their homes. The chances, on the contrary, are the opposite: they will sink below the existing levels in the wake of still greater increases in unemployment arising from still further modernization. Further, given the growing sentiment against migrant labourers, without whom the cities could not be built, but whose dwellings are becoming eyesores for the affluent middle classes, their settlements are being bulldozed away whenever they are put up.

The transformation during the post-colonial period in the role of the State *vis-à-vis* the masses, from being an instrument of liberation to being a source of so much oppression for the masses, is the result of a number of factors. Some of these were foreseen in theoretical models of historical change but many others have turned out to be a result of developments that were not foreseen then, at least not adequately.

One set of factors has to do with the very model of development that was adopted in most ex-colonial countries. Based on the urge to emulate and catch up with the countries that had once colonized them and from where the intellectuals continued to derive their main stimulus and sustenance after independence, "development" produced a structure of opportunities that was inherently inequitable and weighted against the masses. The emphasis on capital accumulation for rapid industrialization and the understanding of industrialization and the associated patterns of urbanization and modernization which were outward-oriented (from the villages to the metropolitan cities), inevitably distributed resources unevenly. The distribution was invariably against the poor. And it was not just the resources that were created by planned economic development but also the resources that originally belonged to the people or to which they had free and easy access. Initially it was thought that these inequalities and disparities—between classes or regions—were transitory and technological; they were thought to arise largely from the inevitable lag between accumulation and distribution. They were expected not only to disappear with further development but would be reversed in favour of the poor and towards a more egalitarian society. In fact, despite a degree of welfare measures and despite a mixed technological package that included development schemes for the rural areas which were meant to benefit the poor and the unemployed, the pattern of inequalities and increases in inequality have acquired a structure that has more or less become permanent. What is more, a great many vested interests have been created in the process.

The reasons for this are many. There is the greed of the classes that controlled or had access to State power and administration at different levels. They were unwilling to make the so-called "sacrifices", which in fact meant allowing the poorer classes access to a part of the surplus which the poor themselves had created in the first place. It was assumed that such access would allow the whole society to move forward and develop even more rapidly, benefiting all classes. This was the typical liberal bourgeois "democratic" assumption that has not worked in those highly divided societies where the classes and the masses constitute two worlds apart.

It was not simply a matter of greed and selfishness, nor of just the lack of empathy for the poor, nor even of a perspective on how better distribution can lead to even greater enlargement of the cake instead of the narrow view that there is not enough to distribute and therefore one must first enlarge the cake. It was none of this by itself. The lack of empathy on the one hand and the absence of perspective on the other, were caused by other pressures. At the level of individuals and groups of the properties classes, there was the snare of an imported package of consumption, amenities and lifestyles, a highly seductive "consumerism" that has had a powerful pull through the global outreach of a particular culture of consumption, namely the American mass culture. In the case of our societies, it has become the culture of the élites that has kept the masses out; indeed, it must keep out the masses.

In terms of the role of the State in this, what has happened is that, having created an adequate industrial infrastructure or enough exportable surpluses to satisfy the consumer needs of the owning clases and their middle class cohorts through the instrumentality of the State, these classes lost interest in continuing the operation of an interventionist state. That would have meant responding to the demands for redistribution, welfare and a more participative framework of economic management. The result has been an emphasis simultaneously on liberalization of the economy and lowering of taxes for the rich, presumably to increase incentives and to replace the role of the State by that of the market, and on modernization and computerization of the technological base, in which process, of course, the State is expected to play a big role. The "classes" (by which I mean the upper and the middle classes) are to wallow in the imported mass culture of consumption and comforts and the masses are to be left to the playground of the market and that, too, largely in the unorganized sector. The organized sector of the economy is to be modernized for effective competition in the export-led model of development to which all developing countries have of late subscribed, again because of a global mind-set fostered by international financial institutions and international academic and policy élites that are at once clients and consultants to these world bodies. It is all part of the "catching up" syndrome—in consumption patterns, in technology, in the ruling doctrine as regards the best path to economic affluence.

This is one set of factors. The other, and to my mind more powerful set, has to do with a still bigger process of "catching up" that is at work. This is the very strong drive at building an efficient, strong, "hard" State, heavily industrialized after the high-tech model on the one hand and with sufficient militarization on the other for which, too, the latest, sophisticated, state-of-the-art armaments are acquired. Once such thinking has become established, the transnational salesmen and experts in the latest civilian technologies, the merchants of violence and war and of repressive technologies, and intelligence systems come in and exhibit both their hardware as well as software. The mirage of greatness chased by Third World States in a world actually dominated by the superpowers and the multinationals only serves to drain away resources from the countryside to the urban areas, and from there to overseas markets in return for both civilian and military high-tech. It increases areas of tension as the phenomenon of regional overlordship begins to take shape as part of the global management structure. All this hardens the arteries of the State which finds it necessary to suppress local challenges in the name of dealing with external ones. State oppression lies in the very logic of a global order based on technocratic and militarizing States. As far as the masses of these States are concerned, high-tech and militarization only draw away economic resources that would have been available for their well-being. In fact, it is worse. Natural resources to which the masses hitherto had access are not only drained away, the new technologies which are adopted to exploit them even destroy them locally.

As a consequence of these factors—the greed of the classes, particularly under the impact of modern consumerism, the "catching up" syndrome, the drive towards a hard, efficient and militarized state, and above all the growing faith in market economics—we are witness to another important development that is still underway but is bound to grow: the collapse of the Welfare State and of those components of development that were directed to the amelioration and welfare of the underprivileged. We need to remember that one of the more progressive streams in modern economic thought, still within the broad bourgeois-liberal framework, has been the effort to soften the harshness of modern capitalism and technology through the mediation of the Welfare State. It has been said that the Welfare State has proved to be a major defence of the capitalist order against radical and revolutionary forces. When the post-colonial States designed their models of development from the experience of the West, they also incorporated the welfare components of western countries. Now with the Welfare State under attack everywhere (including in the West), those components have been the first to suffer in the Third World as well. The belief in the market and in technological solutions to social and political problems has taken the place of welfare. In highly urban societies that were industrialized over a long period, the growth of strong class consciousness permitted the demands for equity and justice to emanate from the social space in the form of pressures on the State. But, in predominantly rural and tribal societies, the State has become a direct, unmediated presence. Whether it treats its citizenry in a humane way or becomes oppressive depends largely on the model of development as well as on the balance of socio-political considerations that informs the model. The choice depends to a large extent on the ruling élite. When such an élite makes a direct jump to high-tech without having gone through the dynamics of capitalist growth, and when it allows the military, the tourist, the television and the computer full play, welfare obviously goes out of the window.

Once this happens both capitalism and the State get hardened; the latter becomes an instrument of the former instead of reining in its excesses. Thus, it surrenders to the compulsions of the latest, computerized phase of capitalism, namely automation, in the organized sector and permits a new division of labour in the unorganized sector in which migrant and bonded labour and women and children become the targets of exploitation. In both cases the "working class" and its organizations are destabilized. Their capacity to combat poverty, marginalization and destitution—slow death—declines as these conditions, in fact, become integral parts of the advance of the system, of science, and of modern civilization. They are inherent in a dual economy which, in turn, is inherent in the wholly technocratic vision of capitalism.

A new ideological crystallization has emerged of late which is taking hold of the minds of leaders and intellectuals in all parts of the world (including, to some extent, in the socialist world). The crux of the new ideology is breathtakingly simple: replacement of the State by the market. Building mainly on the right-wing critique of the positive and interventionist State and the phenomenon of bureaucracy, but also drawing indirect support from the critique of the State from the left and from liberals (though of course distorting it), the new thought that is emerging is to give full play to the market (euphemistically called a "free market"), to competition, to modernization, to technology and to the great catalyst of all this, namely, the transnational corporation. Paradoxically, in large part this is a doctrine promulgated by the State itself, or by the new bearers of power in it (the post-Fabian generation). But here too it is important to catch the nuance. The idea is to dismantle the State apparatus in regard mainly to the distribution of national product. In short, while dismantling the apparatus in the social sphere, the idea is to fully and systematically use the State for promoting high technologies and the dual economy that goes with them. Such a new State manages to don a human face, uses "liberal" symbols and invites everyone to come in, especially voluntary organizations and the NGOs, opposition groups and the liberal intelligentsia. As India's new Prime Minister puts it, his government wants to reduce the role of the bureaucracy, depoliticize government and the administration and he invites motivated and highly educated people to join India's great march into the twentyfirst century. In this vision the State still remains central, for it is the State that will drive us all like a homogeneous mass into the future. It is a grand strategy of co-optation of the classes away from the masses which are also, of course, being asked to look after themselves. That behind the State lurks the structure of corporate capitalism is true. But we are also witness to the rise of a new model of the

State, the corporate capitalist State. All over the ASEAN, and elsewhere too where the so-called newly industrialized countries (NICs) are to be found, there is a direct alliance of the State and corporate capitalism; it is not a marriage between the local bourgeoisie and foreign capital as was the case earlier. In fact, under the corporate capitalist State local business enterprises are being wiped out.

There is one final, and perhaps the most dangerous, element in this growing crystallization of the ruling class. Being aware of the fact that the dual economy and its likely consequences may lead to unrest and revolt at the bottom and lower-middle tiers of society as well as among the politicized elements of the middle classes, the new State has spread a completely novel canard about threats to the unity of the country. This is meant to distract attention away from the socio-economic sphere to the highly volatile "communal" and ethnic sphere. It has, thereby, released strong religious, linguistic and cultural sentiments, pitting people against people, utilizing the mafias and hordes of lumpens and criminals, and unleashing a reign of terror on vulnerable castes, communities and regions in the process. Obscurantist sentiments and fundamentalist ideologies are mobilized to counter the mythical threat. Simultaneously, the State acquires still more fire power, this time legitimized in the name of consolidating national unity, undermining in the process all the politics of struggle as well as the social movements themselves that had earlier challenged the hegemony of the upper castes. Draconian laws against "terrorism" are enacted; they are then used to deal with popular unrest and to suppress social movements. It is an extremely serious development that directly stems from the ruling élite wanting to somehow hang on to power and, to this end, introducing into the political process a strong dose of violence and civil strife. As it succeeds in undermining the caste (in India) and class basis (elsewhere) of social interactions, the State threatens to tear the social fabric apart, particularly the social fabric below the technocratic superstructure.

We are, thus, witness to the rise of not one but two new ideologies, technologism and fundamentalism, and the two coalesce as the exercise of power becomes increasingly cynical. The result is civil wars, ethnicization of civil society, and collapse of secularism as a mode of organizing plural societies. The conception of pluralism was of a unit that not only respected diversity but drew its resilience and strength from it. This has been totally undermined. In countries where a majority is able to, and wants to, steam-roll the whole society into a monolithic whole, it makes an alliance with the homogenizing drive of the modern corporate capitalist State. For the masses, it becomes a steam-roller in tandem.

Let us now turn to the masses, having considered at some length thus far the classes and the State the former have come to control, camouflage and commandeer. The question is: how did the masses allow the classes and the State to stampede them into what looks like abject surrender? How has this come about especially in this supposed age of the masses? After all, major observers of the human condition have pronounced the final arrival on the scene of the masses, the "revolt of the masses" as Ortega y Gasset announced some decades ago. The actual situation we face is "fascinating" as many

Americans would say and excruciating as we would put it. There is a flurry of mass action, in various social settings, at a variety of sites, and at many levels. There is also a spurt in State repression, usually at local and para-local levels but often escalating upwards to the urban metropolitan areas, including the capitals of countries. There is at the same time an increase in exploitation in the economic sense, not just in the wage-capital relationship but also in terms of the new production relations that have given rise to new structures of exploitation. Finally, there is wanton distortion and under-mining of whatever laws and allocations there are for the poor, the backward and the destitute.

It is against the matching of opposite forces, the deadlock, the tension, the peculiar state of stagnation and exhaustion arising precisely from so much action from so many opposing segments and sites that we have to evaluate the actual condition in which the mass of the people are placed. There is, first, the continuing drudgery of so-called "work" that must go on, for the system demands it even under deteriorating conditions of which everyone including those who drudge along are aware, though perhaps not always quite consciously aware. Secondly, there is the capacity of the ruling class to divide and split the labouring classes and the people generally, to break their strikes, to bring in "outsiders" and count on "black sheep" to make certain that when one set of people walk out or protect, another set will walk in or in any case incapacitate the protesting lot. The rulers know that scarcity and poverty are the best conditions for demobilization, not for mobilization as radical theory would have it. In rural areas and tribal belts even this is not necessary; the feudal order there, in league with the centralized bourgeois State, ensures full success for the chain of exploitation—all the way up and all the way down. The rural poor and the tribals "survive" precisely by surrendering. Thirdly, there is, beyond the drudgery, the divisions and the chain of exploitation, a deep and pervasive conditioning of the mind of the masses by the powerful impact of modern communications media on the one hand, and the deep schism and fear caused by fundamentalist drives, on the other. The unfortunate fact is that the masses are more duped than are the middle classes and the professionals by the media and the fundamentalist rhetoric; they have little information on which to base a more discerning and discrete structure of appraisal and choice. The moot point, of course, is that such conditioning perpetuates the situation of continuing drudgery and systemic exploitation.

Yet, we know that the masses are on the march, despite drudgery, exploitation, and conditioning. There is a great spurt in their consciousness and willingness to challenge hegemonies and unearned privilege. They are now prepared to protest against injustices and to mobilize horizontally to deal with oppressions of a vertical kind. There is no doubt that such awareness and willingness exists and is growing. What is it then that prevents it from crystallizing into an effective counter-force against back-breaking drudgery, inhuman exploitation and involuntary degradation?

This the crux of the problem. The masses in the post-colonial world are unorganized, they lack politicization, and they are unable to resist co-optation and conditioning despite constant struggle and growing consciousness. The poor, the minorities, those outside the stream of the main civil society—the tribals, the forest people, large segments of women—all suffer from this state of deep incohesion. This happens largely because the typical avenues of mass mobilization and redress of disabilities and deprivation have given way to larger forces that are seductive and corrupting. Political parties and trade unions were the two most important conventional channels and modes of mobilization and struggle. Unfortunately—and this observation applies almost across the board—political parties (not just ruling parties) have been so captivated by the compulsions of the electoral process that they have lost any capacity to serve the masses, in particular the more destitute and backward among them. As regards the trade unions, they have nearly collapsed as catalysts of working class consciousness and the working class movement. Even the press and the judiciary have failed in their appointed tasks; they too have been corrupted by the crumbs of "development" on the one hand and the miasma of a "national security State" and corrosive fundamentalism on the other. The masses are indeed on the rise but the institutional channels through which they ought to have found expression and which should have provided a springboard for radical action are grossly inadequate. They have been co-opted and corrupted to boot.

There is, thus, a state of vacuum in the traditional superstructure of the liberal polity that was supposed to render it humane despite powerful negative trends. But it is precisely in this vacuum that the real counter-trends are to be found. There is none in the party system, in the arena of electoral politics and of State power, and none in the typical confrontation between the so-called haves and the have-nots within the conventional economistic space dominated by trade unions. In this vacuum, there is emerging a new arena of counteraction, countervailing tendencies, counter-cultural movements and more generally a counter-challenge to the existing paradigms of thought and action.

It is necessary to understand the nature of this challenge. It is, in many ways, new and even unintended in the sense of a well thought-out grand design. It is composed of a series of obvious and inevitable strands, of struggles against existing hegemonies, organized resistance, mainstream protest, and of civil liberties and democratic rights. But the challenge is much more than all this. It is an effort to redefine the scope and the range of politics. It is an effort to open up new spaces in both the arena of the State and in several other spheres of civil society outside that arena. And it is based on new spurts in consciousness—beyond economism, beyond restraining definitions of the political process, beyond the facile (and false) dichotomy of the State versus the Market, beyond both dehumanizing religiosity and dehumanizing modernity. It is discovering new indigenous roots and sustenance and strength, based not so much on either the fractured Old or a mediocre and insipid New as on genuine possibilities of alternatives that can actually work. In this process of "conscientization" and actual struggle as well as of the search for new alternatives there has emerged a whole new class of people known as activists. They have essentially come from the conscious, enlightened and troubled streams of the middle class, and are engaged in a wide range of activities, from "Sarvodaya" style "constructive work" and NGO-type development projects to more struggle-oriented political work; but they essentially settle in the latter mode of intervention. From this convergence of a conscious and restless people and a conscientious and equally restless class of volunteer politicians (to be distinguished from professional party politicians), the new grass-roots movements are taking shape. It is a convergence that is making it possible to *conceive* the knitting of the thousands of micro struggles and experiments into some kind of a macro perspective.

The convergence of new grass-roots *politics* and new grass-roots *thinking* is leading to new definitions of the scope and range of politics. Around these redefinitions new social movements are emerging. The environment, the rights and the role of women, health, food and nutrition, education, shelter and housing, dispensation of justice, communications and dissemination of information, culture, and lifestyles, the achievement of peace and disarmament—none of these was considered the subject matter of politics, at any rate not for domestic politics or for mass politics in which ordinary people were involved. All this has now changed. Ecology cannot any longer be left to experts in ecology or in economic development, not even to departments of environment though the establishment of such departments is itself a new development; it is a concession to popular political pressure. Nor can ecological considerations be left to be sorted out in the future on the presumption that if technology-based development erodes the environment in the short run, this can be remedied by more technology in the long run. Ecology, the people say, must be preserved here and now; it cannot be left to the good intentions and pious declarations of governments. It must become part of the people's own concern, an organized concern at that, including agitations and movements to restrain the State and corporate interests from running amok and ruining the life chances of both the present, and even more so of future generations, and indeed of non-human species and plants as well. Concern for nature and reversing the rapacious approach of modern science to favour nature is becoming part of a political movement, both world-wide and within individual societies.

The same is the case with health, food and nutrition. These are matters that were hitherto left to specialists and experts and to the Ministries manned by them. Not any longer. It is increasingly being realized that the new hazards to health, the new epidemics that are breaking out, the iatrogenic diseases created by modern drugs are in good part a product precisely of the experts, the doctors, the medical scientists and the multi-billion dollar global drug industry which spends millions on research and development. They are also products of the kind of development that has been let loose on trusting people, of technology and the environmental hazards created by it. Modern civilization has created a whole new spectrum of diseases known as civilizational diseases which, in turn, have produced a whole phalanx of specialists who are nowhere near curing either cancer or hypertension or mental disorders; nor will they ever be. All these developments are being confronted by various strands in the alternative movements.

The availability of and access and entitlement to food, minimum nutrition, shelter and housing are among the most serious problems in distributive politics. The serious proportions which these problems have assumed is the clearest refutation of the logic of development based on accumulation and production where distribution was to be taken care of at a later stage. Implied in this logic was also a view that treated people as passive beneficiaries of the p:ocess of development, not direct participants in it; thus, they had no real control over how things would go. And things have indeed gone awry. This is now being realized. The faith in "green" and "white" revolutions, in the revolution in materials technology and in the so-called "cheap housing" has been shattered with the realization of growing hunger and malnutrition and the sight of millions living in slums and on pavements. The truth that these are matters of empowerment and rights for which people will themselves have to fight is beginning to surface. The realization is not just at the level of securing more of the same goods; it looks for alternative ways of attending to these needs, more often than not by the people themselves. The same is the case with education, so clearly related to being privileged or underprivileged. What was once supposed to be an instrument of liberation has turned out to be one of subjugation. So, education just cannot be left to the mercy of the so-called educationists. This whole perspective, applicable to so many areas, about de-expertizing and de-bureaucratizing the provision of basic needs is seeping into the grass roots political process and generating a new agenda of concerns for it.

Even such presumably learned and technical matters as the dispensation of justice on the one hand and the communication of information, on the other, are being subjected to not just greater public scrutiny but a large degree of direct involvement of activists. The rise of public interest, litigation and the growth of investigative journalism, in both of which human rights activists are getting deeply involved and which are together generating a substantial movement for civil liberties and democratic rights, provide ample testimony to the politicization of issue areas that were hitherto considered beyond the pale of politics, especially of mass politics.

Nowhere is the enlargement and redefinition of the scope of politics brought out as vividly and dramatically as in what is called the women's movement. I prefer to think of it as a feminist input into our whole thinking on politics. It is not just that the scope of politics has been enlarged by bringing into its ambit what was until recently considered a personal and private world. From a position that the personal and the political are polar opposites, to the one which holds that personal is the political, and onward to the position that the political is the personal is a massive shift not just in the position of women in politics but in our whole understanding of politics itself. But, in the process, new approaches and methods to deal with basic problems like the environment, health, drunkenness, sanitation and the choice of technology are gradually evolving, not just among women, but among men too, for there is no necessary exclusive overlap between feminism and being a woman. Above all, an unprecedented convergence is taking place between the environment and feminist movements, between these two and the human rights movement (the latter is becoming wholly redefined), and between all of them and the peace movement. This has already happened in Europe with the spectacular spread of the peace movement, with the affirmation that peace and disarmament are too important to be left to governments who, left to themselves, will in all likelihood blow up the world; and in this movement women have played a major role. This has yet to happen in the Third World because of the powerful hold of theories of threat from within and without. But it will happen there too; the Third World peoples just cannot afford to be prisoners of the arms race, and women will have to play a major role in changing this. But the more important point is one about the interrelationship of dimensions and movements, of a holistic approach to life, which goes against the grain of the modern scientific culture with its emphasis on specialization and fragmentation. As women come out of their presently narrow approach of catching up with men, and as the feminist values become more generalized, a holistic approach will develop. It will be an approach that is also plural and based on complementarities. This is more likely to happen in the non-Western world than in the West because of the former's traditions of plurality and androgyny.

This all too brief analysis of the grass-roots orientation of mass politics, a vast terrain that is just opening up and still being shaped, suggests one thing: the universe mass politics seeks to build would be much more worth living in than the universe the dominant tendencies seem to be building. The basic question is: can all this activity, all these "movements" produce a macro challenge, a general transformation (whether one calls it a revolution or not)? The analysis and prognosis presented in this essay says that the transformation cannot be achieved through the conventional channels of political parties, trade unions, peasant organizations or by the capture of State power through electoral mobilization. We need new building blocks, created partly through the non-party political process, partly through counter-cultural and alternative movements that are global in scope, and partly through "nationality" type movements for regional autonomy and within the caste and community framework for texturing a pluralist social order supported by a decentralized political order. It will be a convergence of class, culture, gender and nature. These are possibilities that have not yet acquired high probability but they alone can enable us to transcend the dual economy based on a technocratic and militarized vision. And all this, of course, must take place in close alliance with the more economic forms of struggle for fair wages and dignity in the treatment of the so-called lower rungs, the backward castes, the untouchables and the bonded labourers, or in the ranks of the social peripheries, the tribals, the forest people and the aboriginals.

I do not conceive of the non-party political process as being in any way hostile to the party political process. On the contrary. It is partly to revitalize the party political space, partly to correct its inadequacies but most of all to provide a constant grass-roots infrastructural process, not just to act as the watchdog but also to intervene whenever necessary and, moreover, to permit direct involvement of the people in both the non-party and the party political spaces that the whole conception of an autonomous grass-roots politics (instead of one which is a derivative of élite politics) has taken place. It is not in any way opposed to or even deflected from the party political process as is sometimes alleged by party leaders who want to occupy the whole political space and are particularly suspicious of autonomous formulations operating in it.

Where this conception of politics does differ from party politics is that for the former, State power is not the only or even predominant object of politics. It sees an equal, and perhaps even greater, necessity to keep struggling against injustices which are bound to occur no matter which party or coalition of parties is in power. It believes in experimenting with new modes of organizing social, economic and technological spaces and in insisting on norms in politics. And it wants to keep the intellectual ferment alive so that State-based politics does not become an orthodoxy. The new conception holds that it is not enough to provide participation in the system, even if this can be made less formal and more substantial; the aim is also to create a just society. Participation is necessary but not sufficient for this to happen. What is needed is self-government, a decentralized order through which the masses are empowered. This would not be decentralization in the sense of territorial devolution of functions and resources to lower levels but decentralization in which the people are the centre. It is towards this end that the various social movements of the type discussed above have a role to play, alongside of course the typical working class and peasant movements. It will, in short, be a coalition of social movements and mass struggle. One without the other cannot bring about the necessary transformation.

There is, moreover, a socio-demographic reason why such a direct and dynamic role of mass politics of the grass-roots variety becomes necessary as well as desirable. In a predominantly rural society with great diversity, party formations like the various social democratic parties or labour parties that emerged in Western Europe and heralded the dawn of a mass age are not likely to emerge. We also know that without such formations and the pressures they generated, the phenomenon of the modern welfare state would not have arisen. So, on both these counts—the role of parties on the one hand and of the State on the other—we need to think wholly afresh, for ourselves in the Third World, transcending all that we have imported to begin with. And as we do this, we will see that there is no alternative from moving towards a pluralist, decentralized polity with a humane technology and a relatively self-reliant economy, self-reliant for the people and not just for the State as has been the thinking on self-reliance till recently. The point is, in a Third World context, a just society cannot be built except by the people coming into their own and assuming responsibilities for shaping their lives. We certainly cannot afford to hand over things to experts. That may be possible in centralized and homogeneous societies like the Western ones. To follow the same model in the Third World is, of necessity, to create a dual society with large masses left out of citizenship; it is to banish them out of civilization!

Fundamentally, the vision that informs the grass-roots model of mass politics (as against the parliamentary or party model of mass politics) is one in which the people are more important than the State. This is crucial but it is not as simple as it sounds. In fact, in the times we are living in, it is a revolutionary idea. The dominant tendency and mode of thought today is to place the State above the people, the security of the nation-state above people's security, the removal of real or imaginary threats to the State more pertinent than those to the people. On the other hand, to restore to the people their sovereignty is not to undermine the role of the State but to transform it.

This can be achieved in four simple ways. The transformation of the State must be achieved through the transformation of the civil society, not the other way around. In past thinking, the State was to be the author of social transformation; *that* was the real misjudgement about the processes and pitfalls of secular power. Second, the role of the centralized State must decline. The State will continue to exist, some functions will have to be carried out by a central apparatus, but it must basically operate in concert with other centres as well as other institutional spaces in the civil society. Third, the State must be enabled to regain its autonomy from dominant interests and classes; it should be gradually made to wither away as an instrument of class and ethnic oppression but enabled to survive, and survive effectively, as a mediator in conflicts that will continue to take place in the civil society. And, fourth, we will need to move beyond the nation-state syndrome of statehood, in particular move beyond the national security state syndrome which has been the source of both authoritarianism and hegemonism in our time. In any case, so long as the national security state rules the roost, the masses cannot, and will not, come into their own.

In conclusion, it is necessary to clarify that I disclaim any vision of an idyllic Utopia. Even a polity in which the masses will come into their own and in which both the classes and the State will be held in restraint, cannot achieve a classless society, or a society where there will be no conflicts in the civil society, no strife or violence or war. I also disclaim a romantic faith in the masses as such. They are just as open to conditioning and corruption and consumerism. Indeed, in our age, they are as amenable to obscurantist notions of a State with a capital "S" and a Leader with a "L" as any others, say, the middle classes. All I look forward to, both politically and intellectually, is the achievement of minimum conditions of civilized living *for all beings*, in which exploitation does not disappear but is contained, where civil strife is waged within recognizable and predictable limits. I look forward to a society in which expansionist drives in both men and women and the socio-political apparatus are controlled, and where pluralism, including complementarity between genders and generations, is cherished and a society which, above all, allows individual creativity to flower and thereby to contribute to the creativity of the collective. If this sounds Utopian, so be it.